BARBRI MPRE Review

...odeled after the nation's #1 bar review

...RBRI MPRE Review covers more than the basic rules of professional responsibility. Our free, 24/7 online course is ...erred by most 2L and 3L students for its high level of detail, current and timely materials, and overall organization that ...Jels BARBRI Bar Review. Plus using BARBRI MPRE Review caan actually help you succeed in your law school legal ...cs and professional responsibility class.

FREE

BARBRI MPRE Review provides comprehensive preparation organized in modules based on the scope oaf topics covered on the exam.

Learn from our national PR expert through four hours of online, on-demand lectures segmented by topic module.

The BARBRI MPRE book (digital or printed copy) and lecture handout correspond with the lecture content and topic modules. Order online or pick up at your law school's BARBRI table.

Practice questions, simulated exams and the exclusive MPRE Maximizer quick-study "cram packet" all work together to help you efficiently pinpoint and remediate areas you are struggling to understand.

BARBRI advises dedicating at least 25 hours to MPRE Review — covering lectures, reading substantive outlines, studying lecture notes, answering practice questions and completing practice exams.

Enroll at
barbri.com/mpre-review

Test dates	Registration deadline (Fee $150)
August 9 or 10, 2023	June 8, 2023
November 2 or 3, 2023	September 12, 2023

The MPRE (Multistate Professional Responsibility Exam) is a two-hour, 60-question multiple choice exam developed by the NCBE (National Conference of Bar Examiners). A passing MPRE score is required for bar admission in all but three U.S. states*.

...MPRE is administered three times per year in March, August and November. The free, online BARBRI MPRE Review ...rse is available prior to each exam to help you prepare.

...RE passing scores

...L \ 75	*CT \ 80	ID \ 85	LA \ 80	MS \ 75	*NJ \ 75	OK \ 75	TN \ 82	**WI \ —.
...K \ 80	DE \ 85	IL \ 80	ME \ 80	MO \ 80	NM \ 80	OR \ 85	TX \ 85	WV \ 80
...Z \ 85	DC \ 75	IN \ 80	MA \ 85	MT \ 80	NY \ 85	PA \ 75	UT \ 86	WY \ 85
...R \ 85	FL \ 80	IA \ 80	MD \ 85	NE \ 85	NC \ 80	RI \ 80	VT \ 80	
...A \ 86	GA \ 75	KS \ 80	MI \ 85	NV \ 85	ND \ 85	SC \ 77	VA \ 85	
...O \ 85	HI \ 85	KY \ 80	MN \ 85	NH \ 79	OH \ 85	SD \ 85	WA \ 85	

...e: Connecticut and New Jersey will accept successful completion of a law school course on Professional Responsibility in lieu of a passing MPRE score.

...consin does not require an MPRE score for admission

We're here for you from day one

PROFESSIONAL
RESPONSIBILITY

2023 | 2024

TABLE OF CONTENTS

PR

TABLE OF CONTENTS

INTRODUCTION

ABOUT THE MPRE

On the Multistate Professional Responsibility Examination (MPRE), you will be required to answer 60 multiple-choice questions in a two-hour period. Fifty of those questions will be scored, and 10 will be unscored pretest questions. The pretest questions are indistinguishable from the scored questions, so be sure to answer all of the questions. You should choose the best answer from the four answer choices in each question. Scores are based on the number of questions answered correctly. Points are not subtracted for incorrect answers.

The MPRE is administered on computers at Pearson VUE testing centers. You will be provided with an erasable note board and marker to use during the test session. The test session will terminate automatically at the end of the two-hour period.

HOW TO USE THIS BOOK

As you start to prepare for the MPRE, be aware that the exam is designed to test your ability to apply a set of detailed legal rules—similar to the legal rules you have learned in other courses in law school. You cannot pass the exam simply by having good morals and good manners. You must know the rules, and you must know how to apply them.

The best way to prepare for the exam is to complete all of your course assignments. This will include reading the outline, watching the lecture, and answering black letter law questions and practice questions in the online learning platform.

Here's what you'll find in this book:

Comprehensive Outline of the Law: This outline not only summarizes all the essential law, but it also contains many examples to illustrate less obvious points.

Optional Review Questions: These are short-answer questions that test your basic understanding of the concepts discussed in the outline. Check your answers against the answers we have provided, referring back to the pertinent section of the outline if you need more review of a particular topic.

Practice Sets: You should complete the practice questions in the online learning platform as assigned so you can get immediate feedback after each question. These questions are also available in this book if you prefer to practice offline.

Practice Exam: There is a full practice exam online, but these questions are also available in this book if you would prefer to practice offline.

Simulated MPRE: We strongly recommend that you take this exam online under timed conditions—even if you don't feel fully prepared. There is no substitute for experiencing the time pressures imposed by a pace of approximately two minutes per question.

Conviser Mini Review: This is a condensed version of the comprehensive outline, and you should use it as a final refresher before you take the exam.

COMPREHENSIVE OUTLINE

PROFESSIONAL RESPONSIBILITY

TABLE OF CONTENTS

PROFESSIONAL RESPONSIBILITY

I. REGULATION OF THE LEGAL PROFESSION

A. SOURCES OF REGULATION

1. The State
The practice of law, like other professions and businesses, affects the public interest and is, therefore, subject to regulation by the states in the exercise of their police powers.

a. Courts
Because the practice of law is intimately connected with the administration of justice, the courts have the *inherent* power to regulate the legal profession in and out of court. The ultimate power thus rests with the *highest court* in the state, not with the state legislature. The highest court generally promulgates the ethics rules and oversees the discipline of lawyers.

1) Ethics Rules—The American Bar Association ("ABA") Model Rules and Judicial Code
Every state has professional ethics rules that govern the conduct of lawyers, and nearly every state has adopted some version of the ABA Model Rules of Professional Conduct. Likewise, most states have adopted some version of the ABA Model Code of Judicial Conduct.

2) Case Law
Every state has a body of judge-made case law concerning the rights and duties of lawyers. For example, the case law of a state may limit a lawyer's ability to enforce a fee contract after being fired by the client.

3) Rules of Court
State courts typically have rules of court with which lawyers must comply. For example, a rule of court may govern the lawyer's obligation to represent an indigent client at the court's request.

b. Bar Associations
Each state has an association of lawyers, commonly called the state bar association. A majority of states have an "integrated" bar system, meaning that every lawyer who is admitted to practice in the state must be a member of the state bar association. Common functions of a state bar association are to administer the state's bar examination, to provide continuing education programs for practicing lawyers, and to assist the state courts in regulating and imposing professional discipline on lawyers.

c. **Congress and State Legislatures**
Congress and the states have enacted statutes that govern some aspects of the practice of law. For example, the Sarbanes-Oxley Act imposes a mandatory reporting duty when a securities lawyer becomes aware of credible evidence that a client is materially violating a federal or state securities law. Also, a state evidence statute may define the scope of the attorney-client privilege.

2. **The Federal System**

a. **Courts**
A lawyer who practices in a federal court or agency is also constrained by federal statutes, federal case law, and the rules of that particular court or agency. Each federal court has its own bar, and a lawyer cannot practice before a particular court without first becoming a member of its bar.

b. **Government Attorneys**
An attorney for the federal government is subject to state laws and rules (as well as local federal court rules) governing attorneys in each state in which the attorney engages in her duties. [28 U.S.C. §530B(a)] Note that federal regulations interpret this statute as pertaining only to rules that prescribe ethical conduct for attorneys and that would subject an attorney to professional discipline (e.g., it does not apply to state rules of evidence or procedure, or state substantive law). [28 C.F.R. §§77.2, .3]

3. **Regulation by Multiple States**
A lawyer is subject to regulation by **each** state in which the lawyer is **admitted** to practice, regardless of where the lawyer actually practices law or where the lawyer's conduct occurred. [ABA Model Rule 8.5] If the rules of the states in which the lawyer is admitted are in conflict, choice of law rules apply (*see* C.4., *infra*).

B. **ADMISSION TO THE PRACTICE OF LAW**
In most states, to be admitted to the practice of law, a person must have success-fully completed college and law school, passed a bar examination, and submitted to a bar admission committee an application for admission, which generally includes proof of good moral character. If the committee approves the application, the candidate is sworn in to practice before the highest court of the state. Note that each state has its own "bar" (roster of lawyers who are admitted to practice), and admission to the bar of one state does not, without more, entitle a person to practice law in any other state.

1. **The Application**
An applicant for admission to the bar must respond truthfully and completely

to inquiries made on the application or otherwise by the admissions committee.

a.   False Statements

An applicant for admission to the bar, or a lawyer in connection with a bar admission application, must not **knowingly** make a false statement of material fact. [ABA Model Rule 8.1(a)]

EXAMPLE

When A applied for admission to the bar, he was required to fill out a personal information form that asked whether he had ever been convicted of a crime, received less than an honorable discharge from the military service, or been disciplined for dishonesty by any school. A knowingly failed to reveal that he had been suspended from college for a semester for cheating on an examination. A's failure to reveal the suspension is grounds for denying his bar application. If A's failure to reveal is discovered after A is admitted to the bar, A is subject to discipline. [See Carter v. Charos, 536 A.2d 527 (R.I. 1988)]

---

b.   Failure to Disclose Information

Likewise, an applicant (or a lawyer in connection with an applicant's application for admission to the bar) must not: (1) **fail to disclose** a fact necessary to correct a misapprehension **known** by the person to have arisen in the matter, or (2) **knowingly fail to respond** to a lawful demand for information from an admissions authority. [ABA Model Rule 8.1(b)] This rule does not, however, require disclosure of information otherwise protected by the confidentiality provisions of the Rules of Professional Conduct. (See III., infra.)

EXAMPLE

Bar applicant B applied for admission using a forged certificate of graduation from the State University School of Law. Attorney A knew about B's forgery, and she knew that the forgery had not been detected by the bar admission officials. A must voluntarily tell the bar admission officials about the forgery.

---

2.   Character and Fitness—"Good Moral Character"

The state has an interest in insuring that lawyers admitted to practice possess high moral standards and are mentally and emotionally stable.

a.   Investigative Procedure

A bar applicant is usually required to fill out a detailed questionnaire and list a number of references as part of his application. (Some states also

require the applicant to submit fingerprints and photographs.) This information is then checked either by letter or personal investigation. If there is a question concerning the applicant's moral fitness, the applicant may be asked to appear at a hearing before the committee.

1) Burden of Proof and Duties of Applicant

The burden of coming forward and establishing good moral character is on the applicant. In addition, the applicant owes a duty to cooperate in reasonable investigations by the state bar and to make disclosures relevant to his fitness to practice law. [*In re Anastaplo*, 366 U.S. 82 (1961)]

2) Procedural Rights

A bar applicant has a right to due process in committee proceedings. Thus, he has the right to know the charges filed against him, to explain away derogatory information, and to confront critics. [*Willner v. Committee*, 373 U.S. 96 (1963)] An applicant who is denied admission on the basis of bad moral character is entitled to judicial review, usually by the state's highest court.

b. Conduct Relevant to Moral Character

All aspects of an applicant's past conduct that reflect on his honesty and integrity are relevant to an evaluation of moral character. The committee may consider any conduct or charges against the applicant—including those charges of which the applicant was acquitted—and any litigation to which the applicant was a party.

EXAMPLE

In one case, an applicant was denied admission because of personality traits that were deemed to make him unfit to practice. It was shown that the applicant was overly sensitive, rigid, and suspicious; was excessively self-important; and had a tendency to make false accusations against others and ascribe evil motives to them. [Application of Ronwin, 555 P.2d 315 (Ariz. 1976)]

---

1) Criminal Conduct

Mere conviction of any crime is not sufficient to deny the admission of an applicant to practice law. To cause disqualification of an applicant, the crime in question must involve **moral turpitude**, such as a crime involving intentional dishonesty for the purpose of personal gain (e.g., forgery, bribery, theft, perjury, robbery, extortion) or a crime involving violence (e.g., murder, rape, mayhem). The nature of the offense and the motivation of the violator are also factors in determining whether moral turpitude exists.

a)   **"Adolescent Misbehavior" and Civil Disobedience**
Examples of criminal behavior that do not rise to the level of moral turpitude include an applicant's arrest when he was a youth for a fistfight (adolescent behavior that does not necessarily bear on the applicant's current fitness to practice law) and an applicant's arrest for nonviolent civil disobedience. [*See* Hallinan v. Committee of Bar Examiners, 65 Cal. 2d 447 (1966)]

2)   **Rehabilitation**
An applicant may still gain admission to the legal profession despite past conduct involving moral turpitude if he can demonstrate sufficient rehabilitation of his character and a present fitness to practice law. [*See, e.g.,* March v. Committee of Bar Examiners, 67 Cal. 2d 718 (1967)]

3)   **Concealment of Past Conduct Constitutes Moral Turpitude**
False statements or concealment of facts in response to an inquiry by the admissions committee is itself evidence of sufficient lack of moral character to deny admission—even if the underlying conduct does not involve moral turpitude. [ABA Model Rule 8.1; *and see* Geoffrey C. Hazard, Jr. and W. William Hodes, The Law of Lawyering (hereafter "Hazard & Hodes") §66.04 (4th ed. 2015)]

4)   **Political Activity**
An applicant who refuses to take the oath to uphold the state and federal Constitutions may be denied admission because there is a rational connection between this requirement and the practice of law. [Law Students Research Council v. Wadmond, 401 U.S. 154 (1971)] However, an applicant's mere membership in the Communist Party (when there is no showing that the applicant engaged in or advocated actions to overthrow the government by force or violence) is not sufficient to show a lack of moral character and deny the applicant admission to practice law. [Schware v. Board of Bar Examiners, 353 U.S. 232 (1957)]

3.   **Citizenship and Residency Are Not Valid Requirements**
A state cannot require that a person be a United States citizen to be admitted to the practice of law; such a requirement violates the Equal Protection Clause of the United States Constitution. [*In re* Griffiths, 413 U.S. 717 (1973)] Similarly, a requirement that a bar applicant be a resident of the state in which he is seeking admission to practice law violates the Privileges and Immunities Clause of the Constitution and is, therefore, invalid. [Supreme Court of New Hampshire v. Piper, 470 U.S. 274 (1985)]

C. REGULATION AFTER ADMISSION

Upon admission to the bar, a person becomes a lawyer and is thus subject to the applicable law governing such matters as professional discipline, procedure and evidence, civil remedies, and criminal sanctions.

1. What Constitutes Professional Misconduct

a. Violation of the Rules of Professional Conduct

It is professional misconduct for a lawyer to: (1) violate or **attempt** to violate any of the Rules of Professional Conduct, (2) knowingly **assist or induce another** person to violate the Rules, or (3) **use the acts of another person** to commit a violation. [ABA Model Rule 8.4(a)]

EXAMPLE

Attorney A knows that it is a violation of the Rules to approach an accident victim at the scene of the accident and offer his legal services. A asks his brother-in-law T, a tow truck driver, to give A's business cards to people involved in the accidents that T is called to tow. A is guilty of professional misconduct for using the acts of another to violate a rule.

---

b. Certain Criminal Acts

A lawyer is subject to discipline for committing a criminal act that reflects adversely on his honesty, trustworthiness, or fitness as a lawyer in other respects. [ABA Model Rule 8.4(b)] To constitute professional misconduct, the crime must involve some characteristic that is relevant to the practice of law. For example, crimes involving dishonesty, breach of trust, substantial interference with the administration of justice, and most crimes involving violence reflect on the lawyer's fitness to practice law. Other crimes (e.g., solicitation of prostitution, single offense of drunk driving, possession of a marijuana cigarette), while punishable by law, do not necessarily trigger professional discipline.

EXAMPLES

1) Attorney A willfully failed to file a personal federal income tax return, knowing that she owed a substantial amount of tax. Even though A's conduct was not connected with her practice of law, A is subject to discipline.

2) Lawyer L is arrested for soliciting sexual acts from an undercover police officer whom L believed to be a prostitute. L is not subject to discipline because his criminal conduct does not show dishonesty, untrustworthiness, or unfitness to practice law.

---

c. Dishonesty, Fraud, Deceit, or Misrepresentation

Any conduct involving dishonesty, fraud, deceit, or misrepresentation

constitutes professional misconduct. [ABA Model Rule 8.4(c)] Examples of this type of misconduct, which need not rise to the level of a crime, include cheating on a bar examination [*see In re* Lamb, 49 Cal. 3d 239 (1989)—lawyer who impersonated her husband for exam was disbarred], plagiarism [*see In re* Lamberis, 443 N.E.2d 549 (Ill. 1982)—plagiarism in preparation of LL.M. thesis resulted in discipline], and defrauding one's own law firm by misusing expense accounts [*see In re* Siegel, 627 A.2d 156 (N.J. 1993); *and see* Hazard & Hodes, §69.05].

d. Conduct Prejudicial to the Administration of Justice

A lawyer is subject to discipline for engaging in conduct that is prejudicial to the administration of justice. [ABA Model Rule 8.4(d)] This rule is rarely invoked because nearly all of the offenses that would arise under it (e.g., falsifying evidence, improper delaying tactics, frivolous claims) are dealt with more specifically in the rules relating to litigation (*see* VI., *infra*).

e. Stating or Implying Ability to Improperly Influence Officials

A lawyer must never state or imply that he has the ability to improperly influence a government agency or official or to achieve results by means that violate the law or legal ethics rules. [ABA Model Rule 8.4(e)]

f. Assisting a Judge in Violation of Judicial Code

A lawyer is subject to discipline for **knowingly** assisting a judge or judicial officer in conduct that violates the Code of Judicial Conduct or other law. [ABA Model Rule 8.4(f)]

g. Harassment or Discrimination in Law Practice

A lawyer must not, **in conduct related to the practice of law** (e.g., representing clients, interacting with witnesses, operating and managing a law practice), engage in conduct that the lawyer knows or reasonably should know is harassment or discrimination on the basis of race, sex, religion, national origin, ethnicity, disability, age, sexual orientation, gender identity, marital status, or socioeconomic status. *Note:* A trial judge's finding that a lawyer exercised peremptory challenges on a discriminatory basis does not, on its own, establish a violation of this rule. [ABA Model Rule 8.4(g)]

1) Permitted Actions

This rule does not limit a lawyer's ability to:

    a) Accept, decline, or withdraw from a representation in accordance with ABA Model Rule 1.16 (*see* II.G., *infra*), or limit her practice to members of underserved populations in accordance with the Rules of Professional Conduct;

b) Provide legitimate advice or advocacy that is otherwise consistent with the Rules of Professional Conduct; or

c) Promote diversity or inclusion (e.g., efforts aimed at recruiting, hiring, retaining, and advancing diverse employees).

2. **Duty to Report Professional Misconduct**

The legal profession prides itself on being self-policing. One element of a self-policing group is that each member of the group must be obligated to report misconduct by the other members. Therefore, a lawyer who **knows** that another lawyer has violated the Rules of Professional Conduct in such a way that it raises a **substantial** question as to that lawyer's honesty, trust-worthiness, or fitness as a lawyer must report the violation to the appropriate professional authority. Similarly, a lawyer who knows that a judge has violated the Code of Judicial Conduct in a way that raises a substantial question as to the judge's fitness for office must report the violation to the appropriate authority. [ABA Model Rule 8.3]

EXAMPLES

1) Attorney A learned that attorney B and accountant T had formed a tax service partnership in which T would do solely accounting work and B would do solely legal work. B has thus violated the disciplinary rule against partnerships with nonlawyers. (*See* H.2., *infra*.) A may report the violation, but she will not be subject to discipline if she fails to do so. A may decline to report B's violation because it concerns an arcane guild rule and does not indicate that B is dishonest, untrustworthy, or unfit to practice law. Other examples of violations that may not raise a substantial question as to a lawyer's fitness to practice include some types of improper solicitation and the improper use of nonlawyer assistants.

2) Lawyer M and lawyer N are good friends and golfing buddies. One day, they were golfing and mutually complaining about the tax laws; N mentioned that he does not worry about tax increases because he just underreports his income when the taxes go up. M must report N to the disciplinary authorities. Despite the fact that N was discussing his conduct in his personal affairs, it is illegal conduct involving dishonesty and must be reported. [*See* Hazard & Hodes, §68.04]

---

a. **Key Definitions**

"Knowledge" means actual knowledge, but it may be inferred from the circumstances. It has been held to mean more than mere suspicion. Thus, while a lawyer **may** report **suspected** misconduct, she **must** report **known** misconduct. "Substantial" means "a material matter of clear and weighty importance." [ABA Model Rules, Terminology]

b. Sanctions for Failure to Report Misconduct

A lawyer who fails to report this type of misconduct is herself subject to discipline for violating the rule requiring disclosure. [ABA Model Rule 8.3]

c. Exceptions—Confidential Information and Lawyers' Assistance Programs

This rule does not require disclosure of information protected by the confidentiality rules (*see* III., *infra*). Thus, if a lawyer learns about another lawyer's misconduct while representing the other lawyer or some other client, the lawyer has no duty to report the misconduct. Indeed, the lawyer would be subject to discipline for violating the confidentiality rules if he did report it. Moreover, there is no duty to disclose information gained by a lawyer or judge while serving as a member of an approved lawyers' assistance program that helps lawyers and judges with substance abuse problems. [ABA Model Rule 8.3(c) and comment 5]

EXAMPLES

1) Lawyer L sought legal advice from his mentor, lawyer M, as to what L should do about offering a certain piece of evidence in court. L made it plain that he was seeking advice from M in M's role as a lawyer. L told M that he knew the evidence was false. M, of course, advised L not to offer the evidence. A few months later, M learned that L had ignored her advice and had offered the evidence. Because M's knowledge of the matter is protected by the ethical duty of confidentiality, M must not report L's disciplinary violation.

2) Attorney X had long been aware that attorney Y, another partner in his firm, had a very serious drinking problem, but X did not have any proof that it was affecting Y's job performance. One day, X ran into Y as Y was on his way into court. Y was clearly drunk and could barely follow their conversation. X cautioned Y not to appear before the judge, but Y responded that he had tried cases when he was in worse shape than this. X must report Y to the disciplinary authorities. X did not learn of Y's substance abuse in the context of an approved lawyers' assistance program or an attorney-client relationship.

---

3. Disciplinary Process

"Professional discipline" means punishment imposed on a lawyer for breaking a rule of professional ethics.

a. Complaint

Disciplinary proceedings against a lawyer begin when a complaint

is made to the state disciplinary authority (usually the state bar). Complaints are often brought by aggrieved clients, but may also be brought by anyone with knowledge of the misconduct. Filing a complaint against a lawyer is considered privileged, and thus cannot be the basis of an action (e.g., defamation) by the lawyer against the complainant.

b.   Screening

If the complaint is without merit, it might be dismissed by the grievance committee without ever involving the lawyer. If the complaint appears to have merit, the lawyer will be asked to respond to the charges. After further investigation, the committee will either dismiss the complaint or schedule a hearing. If the committee dismisses the complaint, the complainant does not have any right to appeal; the decision is final.

c.   Hearing

1)   Due Process Required

If there is a hearing on the complaint, the accused lawyer is entitled to procedural due process, which means that she has the right to counsel, to proper notice, to be heard and introduce evidence, and to cross-examine adverse witnesses. In addition, the hearing must be limited to the charges made in the complaint. [*In re* Ruffalo, 390 U.S. 544 (1968)]

2)   Application of Other Rights

The exclusionary rules of criminal law do not apply to disciplinary proceedings. Thus, evidence obtained through an illegal search, for example, is admissible in a disciplinary proceeding. A lawyer may, however, invoke his Fifth Amendment privilege and refuse to answer questions at the hearing, and **no disciplinary action can be taken** against the lawyer if it is based solely on the claim of Fifth Amendment privilege. [Spevack v. Klein, 385 U.S. 511 (1967)]

3)   Burden of Proof

The burden of proof is on the party prosecuting the charge, and most states require proof of the charge beyond a preponderance of the evidence (but less than beyond a reasonable doubt). Most states also require that only evidence admissible under the rules of evidence be considered; thus, inadmissible hearsay would be excluded.

4)   Decision and Review

After the hearing, the grievance committee will either dismiss the charges or recommend sanctions. If sanctions are recommended or disciplinary action is actually taken, the lawyer is entitled to

review of the decision by the state's highest court. The burden is then on the lawyer to show that the committee's action or recommendation is not supported by the record or is otherwise unlawful.

d. Sanctions

The most common sanctions imposed on a lawyer found to have committed professional misconduct are:

1) ***Private or public reprimand or censure***, which is an acknowledgment of misconduct that goes on the lawyer's record with the disciplinary authorities;

2) ***Suspension*** of the lawyer's license to practice for a definite period of time, at the end of which the right to practice is automatically reinstated; and

3) ***Disbarment***, which is the ***permanent*** revocation of the lawyer's license to practice. A disbarred lawyer may, however, apply for readmission upon proof of rehabilitation.

Other sanctions available include probation, restitution, costs of the disciplinary proceedings, and limitations on the lawyer's practice. Which sanction is imposed generally depends on the severity of the misconduct and the presence or absence of mitigating or aggravating circumstances.

4. Choice of Law in Disciplinary Proceedings

If the conduct in question occurred in connection with a proceeding that is pending before a tribunal, the ethics rules of the jurisdiction in which the tribunal sits will be applied, unless the tribunal's rules provide otherwise. For any other conduct, the rules of the jurisdiction in which the conduct occurred will apply, but if the predominant effect of the conduct is in some other jurisdiction, that jurisdiction's rules will apply. A lawyer will ***not*** be subject to discipline if her conduct is proper in the jurisdiction in which she reasonably believes the predominant effect of her conduct will occur. [ABA Model Rule 8.5]

EXAMPLE

The legal ethics rules of East Dakota prohibit a lawyer from paying a "referral fee" to another lawyer as compensation for the referral of a legal matter. The legal ethics rules of West Dakota permit such referral fees if they are reasonable in amount and if the referred client consents. East Dakota lawyer Ed referred an estate planning client to West Dakota lawyer Wes. The client lives in West Dakota and most of her property is located there. With the client's consent, Wes sent Ed a reasonable referral fee. Wes is not subject to discipline in either state.

a. Conflicts of Interest—Choice of Law Agreements Permitted

As stated above, there is a safe harbor for a lawyer whose conduct conforms to the rules of a jurisdiction in which she "reasonably believes" the predominant effect will occur. Regarding conflicts of interest only, a lawyer and client may enter into an advance written agreement specifying the predominant effect jurisdiction, i.e., which jurisdiction's conflicts rules will apply to the matter. If the agreement is entered into with the client's informed consent and the client later tries to disqualify the lawyer from another matter or files a disciplinary complaint, the agreement may be considered by the court or disciplinary authority in determining whether the lawyer reasonably believed the jurisdiction's rules would apply. [ABA Model Rule 8.5, comment 5]

5. Effect of Sanctions in Other Jurisdictions

A suspension or disbarment in one jurisdiction does not automatically affect a lawyer's ability to practice in another jurisdiction.

a. Other States

Professional discipline imposed by one state is not necessarily binding on another. Most states recognize the determinations of lawyer misconduct by sister states, but they do not agree on the reasons for recognition. The preferred view is that sister states accept disciplinary action by one state as conclusive proof of the misconduct, but not of the sanctions imposed. [*See* Kentucky Bar Association v. Signer, 558 S.W.2d 582 (Ky. 1977); Florida Bar v. Wilkes, 179 So. 2d 193 (Fla. 1965); ABA Model Rule for Lawyer Disciplinary Enforcement 22E] Under this view, sister states are free to impose their own sanctions for the misconduct.

b. Federal Courts

Each federal court in which a lawyer is admitted to practice must make an independent evaluation of the lawyer's conduct. [Theard v. United States, 354 U.S. 278 (1957)] The fact that a lawyer has been disciplined by a state, however, is competent evidence in a federal proceeding and may in itself be sufficient to convince a federal court to impose a similar sanction. [*See In re* Rhodes, 370 F.2d 411 (8th Cir. 1967)]

6. Disability Proceedings

A lawyer who is incapacitated by an impairment such as substance abuse poses a particular risk of harm to clients, the public, and legal institutions. Most jurisdictions have disability proceedings, which result in the disabled lawyer's suspension from practice until she can show that rehabilitation has occurred. The procedures followed are generally the same as those of disciplinary proceedings, but provision may be made for psychiatric evaluation and diversion into a rehabilitation program. [Restatement of the Law (Third)

Governing Lawyers (hereinafter "Restatement") ch. 1, topic 2, tit. C, introductory note]

D. UNAUTHORIZED PRACTICE AND MULTI-JURISDICTIONAL PRACTICE

The rule against unauthorized practice of law has two prongs: (1) a lawyer is subject to discipline for practicing in a jurisdiction where she is not admitted to practice, and (2) a lawyer is subject to discipline for assisting another person in the unlicensed practice of law. [ABA Model Rule 5.5(a)]

1. Unauthorized Practice by Lawyer

A lawyer who is admitted to practice law in one jurisdiction is not, without more, authorized to practice in any other jurisdiction. A lawyer is subject to discipline for practicing in a jurisdiction where she is not admitted to practice. [ABA Model Rule 5.5(a)] Except as allowed by that jurisdiction's laws or ethics rules, the unadmitted lawyer must not: (1) represent that she is admitted to practice in that jurisdiction, or (2) establish an office or other systematic or continuous presence for the practice of law in that jurisdiction. [ABA Model Rule 5.5(b)]

2. Permissible Types of Temporary Multi-Jurisdictional Practice

The nature of modern law and commerce requires many lawyers to practice across state lines. ABA Model Rule 5.5(c) recognizes this fact and provides that if a lawyer is admitted to practice in one state, and is not disbarred or suspended from practice in any state, then she may provide legal services in a second state *on a temporary basis* in four situations:

a. Association with Local Lawyer

A lawyer may practice on a temporary basis in a state in which she is not admitted if she associates a local lawyer who *actively participates* in the matter. [ABA Model Rule 5.5(c)(1)]

> **EXAMPLE**
> Attorney A is admitted to practice in State One only, and she works for a law firm that regularly represents a nationwide labor union. The union is trying to organize workers in State Two, and A is sent there to give legal advice to the union's organizers. With the union's consent, A associates local labor lawyer L and rents a temporary office near L's office. L works actively with A in handling legal problems arising from the union's organizing efforts. A's temporary practice in State Two is proper.

b. Special Permission to Practice in Local Tribunal

An out-of-state lawyer may request special permission from a local court, administrative agency, or other tribunal to handle a matter in that tribunal. [ABA Model Rule 5.5(c)(2)] In a court, such permission is commonly called admission "pro hac vice," which means admission for purposes of this

matter only. (The rules of many states require the out-of-state lawyer to associate local counsel as a condition of pro hac vice admission.) An out-of-state lawyer who reasonably expects to be admitted pro hac vice may engage in preliminary activities in the state, such as meeting with clients, reviewing documents, and interviewing witnesses.

EXAMPLE

Toxic tort lawyer L is admitted to practice in Oklahoma only. He has been retained by three Oklahoma clients to bring a class action on behalf of persons injured by a herbicide manufactured by a California defendant. L plans to file the class action in a California state court, and he reasonably expects to be admitted pro hac vice to handle the case in that court. It would be proper for L to take a two-week trip to California to interview other potential class representatives, even though he has not yet filed the case in California or been admitted pro hac vice.

---

c. **Mediation or Arbitration Arising Out of Practice in Home State**

A lawyer may mediate, arbitrate, or engage in another form of alternative dispute resolution in a state in which she is not admitted to practice if her services arise out of, or are reasonably related to, her practice in the state in which she is admitted. [ABA Model Rule 5.5(c)(3)]

EXAMPLE

Attorney A is admitted to practice in State One only. She represents a State One client in a contract dispute, and the contract states that all such disputes will be submitted to arbitration in State Two. It is proper for A to represent her client in the State Two arbitration, and the same would be true of a mediation or other form of alternative dispute resolution.

---

d. **Other Temporary Practice Arising Out of Practice in Home State**

ABA Model Rule 5.5(c)(4) is a catch-all category that permits a lawyer to temporarily practice out of state if the lawyer's out-of-state practice is reasonably related to the lawyer's home state practice.

EXAMPLE

Lawyer L is admitted to practice in State One only. He represents a State One client that buys up and revitalizes run-down shopping centers. That client asks L to travel to State Two to negotiate with the owner of a State Two shopping center, and to draft a purchase agreement that will satisfy the owner and that will be valid under the law of State Two. It would be proper for L to render those services in State Two.

---

e. **Temporary Practice by Foreign Lawyers**
A lawyer who is licensed and in good standing in a foreign jurisdiction may engage in temporary practice in the United States under circumstances similar to those described in a. - d., above. Furthermore, a foreign lawyer may provide legal services temporarily in the United States if the services are governed primarily by international law or the law of a foreign jurisdiction. [ABA Model Rule for Temporary Practice by Foreign Lawyers] Foreign lawyers who seek pro hac vice admission are subjected to greater scrutiny than United States lawyers. Even if a lawyer is so admitted, the judge has the discretion to limit the foreign lawyer's participation in the matter. [ABA Model Rule on Pro Hac Vice Admission]

3. **Permissible Types of Permanent Multi-Jurisdictional Practice**
A lawyer who is admitted in one United States or foreign jurisdiction, and who is not disbarred or suspended from practice in any jurisdiction, may open a law office and establish a systematic and continuous practice in a different jurisdiction in two narrowly limited situations:

a. **Lawyers Employed by Their Only Client**
Some lawyers are salaried employees of their only client, e.g., in-house corporate lawyers and lawyers employed by the government. They may set up a permanent office to render legal services to their employer in a state in which they are not admitted to practice, but if they want to *litigate* a matter in that state, they must seek admission pro hac vice. [ABA Model Rule 5.5(d)(1)]

EXAMPLE
Attorney A is admitted to practice in Maryland and Virginia. She is employed by General Motors ("GM"), which assigns her to be the legal advisor in the GM office in Idaho. A need not be admitted to practice in Idaho, but if she wants to represent GM in a suit pending in an Idaho court, she must seek admission pro hac vice.

---

1) **Foreign Lawyers Advising on United States Law**
A foreign lawyer practicing under this rule (e.g., serving as in-house counsel for a corporation) *may not directly advise* her client on the law of a United States jurisdiction. Rather, she must consult with a lawyer who is licensed by the relevant jurisdiction and base any advice to her client on advice she obtains from the local lawyer.

b. **Legal Services Authorized by Federal or Local Law**
In rare instances, federal or local law authorizes a lawyer to practice a restricted branch of law in a state in which he is not otherwise admitted to practice. [ABA Model Rule 5.5(d)(2)]

> **EXAMPLE**
> Lawyer L is admitted to practice law in New York, and he is admitted to prosecute patents in the United States Patent and Trademark Office, which is located in Washington, D.C. When L "retired" and moved to Florida, he did not become a member of the Florida bar; rather, he set up a Florida practice that is limited to patent prosecution in the Patent and Trademark Office. L does not handle other patent matters, such as patent licensing or patent infringement, and he does not practice any other kind of law. L's restricted practice in Florida is proper. [*See* Sperry v. Florida, 373 U.S. 379 (1963)]

4. **Consequences of Multi-Jurisdictional Practice**
   A lawyer who is admitted to practice in only one jurisdiction but practices in another jurisdiction pursuant to 2. or 3., above, is subject to the disciplinary rules of both jurisdictions. [ABA Model Rule 8.5(a); comment 19 to ABA Model Rule 5.5] Furthermore, an in-house or government lawyer who practices under 3.a., above, may be subject to the second jurisdiction's client security assessments and continuing legal education requirements. [ABA Model Rule 5.5, comment 17]

5. **Unauthorized Practice by Nonlawyers**
   A person not admitted to practice as a lawyer must not engage in the unauthorized practice of law, and a lawyer must not assist such a person to do so. [ABA Model Rule 5.5(a); Restatement §4]

   a. **General Considerations in Defining "Practice of Law"**
      Important considerations in determining whether the practice of law is involved include: (1) whether the activity involves legal ***knowledge and skill*** beyond that which the average layperson possesses; (2) whether the activity constitutes advice or services concerning ***binding legal rights*** or remedies; and (3) whether the activity is one ***traditionally*** performed by lawyers. [ABA, Annotated Model Rule of Professional Conduct 5.5 (9th ed. 2019)]

      1) **Activities Constituting Law Practice**
         Examples of activities that courts have found constitute law practice when done on behalf of another include: appearing in judicial proceedings; engaging in settlement negotiations; and drafting documents that affect substantial legal rights or obligations (e.g., contracts, wills, trusts). Preparing an estate plan is generally considered the province of lawyers, and some courts have also held that nonlawyer clinics on how to obtain a low-cost divorce constitute unauthorized practice.

2) **Activities Not Constituting Law Practice**
   There are some activities that a nonlawyer may undertake that do not constitute the practice of law. For example, state and federal agencies often permit nonlawyers, such as accountants, to appear before them representing clients. Also, while nonlawyers may not draft legal documents, they can act as scriveners, filling in the blanks on standard forms. Thus, real estate brokers, title insurance companies, and escrow companies are usually permitted to fill in the blanks on standard documents related to the sale of real property. Nonlawyers can also publish books or pamphlets offering general advice, including most do-it-yourself books and kits.

3) **Tax Advice**
   Giving advice on tax *law* would probably constitute the unauthorized practice of law, but an accountant or other layperson may prepare tax returns and answer questions incidental to the preparation of the returns.

b. **Consequences of Unauthorized Practice**
   A nonlawyer who engages in the unauthorized practice of law is subject to several sanctions, including injunction, contempt, and criminal conviction. [Restatement §4, comment a] A lawyer who assists in such an endeavor is subject to professional discipline.

c. **Delegating Work to Nonlawyer Assistants**
   The rule stated above does not, of course, prohibit a lawyer from delegating tasks to a paralegal, law clerk, student intern, or other such person. But the lawyer must *supervise* the delegated work carefully and must be *ultimately responsible* for the results. [ABA Model Rule 5.5, comment 2]

   EXAMPLE
   Paralegal P is working under attorney A's supervision on a complex real estate transaction. P may write and sign letters on the law firm letterhead to make routine requests for information from banks, mortgage companies, and governmental agencies, provided that P indicates that she is a paralegal, not a lawyer. But P should not sign letters to clients, adversaries, opposing counsel, or tribunals; she may draft such letters, but they should be approved and signed by A. That helps assure that A is properly supervising P's work. [New Jersey Op. 611 (1988)]
   ---

d. **Training Nonlawyers for Law-Related Work**
   A lawyer may advise and instruct nonlawyers whose employment requires a knowledge of the law—e.g., claims adjusters, bank trust

officers, social workers, accountants, and government employees. [ABA Model Rule 5.5, comment 3]

e. Helping Persons Appear Pro Se

A lawyer may advise persons who wish to appear on their own behalf in a legal matter. [*Id.*]

EXAMPLE

Client C asked attorney A to represent her in a dispute with her landlord concerning the stopped-up plumbing in her apartment. After hearing C's explanation, A advised C that she would be able to handle the matter herself in small claims court at far less expense. A instructed C on how to obtain the proper forms for small claims court and gave her general advice on what facts to gather and how to prove her case. A's conduct is proper.

---

f. Assisting a Suspended or Disbarred Lawyer

A lawyer violates ABA Model Rule 5.5(a) if he assists a lawyer whose license has been suspended or revoked in practicing law. It is proper to hire a suspended or disbarred lawyer to do work that a layperson is permitted to do, but the suspended or disbarred lawyer must not be permitted to do any work that constitutes the practice of law.

E. RESPONSIBILITIES OF PARTNERS, MANAGERS, AND SUPERVISORY LAWYERS

1. Partners' Duty to Educate and Guide in Ethics Matters

The partners or managing lawyers of a law firm (and the supervisory lawyers in a governmental agency, business, or other group of lawyers) must make reasonable efforts to assure that the other lawyers adhere to the Rules of Professional Conduct. [ABA Model Rule 5.1(a); Restatement §11]

2. Duties of Direct Supervisor

A lawyer who directly supervises the work of another lawyer must make reasonable efforts to assure that the other lawyer adheres to the Rules of Professional Conduct. [ABA Model Rule 5.1(b)]

3. How Duties Are Fulfilled

The steps necessary to fulfill these two duties depend on the kind and size of the firm or other group. In a small private law firm, informal supervision and occasional admonition may be sufficient. In a larger organization, more elaborate steps may be necessary. Some firms provide continuing legal education programs in professional ethics, and some firms have designated a partner or committee to whom a junior lawyer may turn in confidence for assistance on an ethics issue. [ABA Model Rule 5.1, comment 3]

4. **Ethical Responsibility for Another Lawyer's Misconduct**
A lawyer is subject to discipline for a disciplinary violation committed by a second lawyer if:

a. The first lawyer *ordered* the second lawyer's misconduct or *knew about it and ratified it*; or

b. The first lawyer is a partner or manager or has direct supervisory responsibility over the second lawyer, *and* she knows about the misconduct at a time when its consequences can be avoided or mitigated and *fails to take reasonable remedial action*.

[ABA Model Rule 5.1(c)]

EXAMPLES

1) Attorney A is not a partner in the M, N & O firm, but she is a senior associate and has been assigned direct supervisory responsibility for the work of junior associate J in the case of *Cox v. Fox*. A told J to interview Ms. Cox and to prepare her to have her deposition taken. In a fit of misdirected zeal, J advised Ms. Cox to testify to a patent falsehood. After the Cox deposition was taken, but while Ms. Cox was still available as a witness, A discovered what had happened. A made no effort to reopen the Cox deposition or otherwise remedy J's misconduct. A is subject to discipline.

2) In the *Cox v. Fox* example, above, suppose that M, a partner in the firm, is not J's supervisor and has no connection whatever with the *Cox v. Fox* case. In a casual lunchtime conversation with J, M learned that J had advised Ms. Cox to testify falsely at her deposition. M made no effort to rectify the consequences of J's misconduct. M is subject to discipline.

F. **RESPONSIBILITIES CONCERNING NONLAWYER ASSISTANCE**

1. **Duty to Educate and Guide in Ethics Matters**
Law firms, governmental and business law departments, and other groups of lawyers employ many kinds of nonlawyers—secretaries, investigators, paralegals, law clerks, messengers, and law student interns. Lawyers who work with such employees—whether those nonlawyers are within or outside the firm—must instruct them concerning the ethics of the profession and should be ultimately responsible for their work. [ABA Model Rule 5.3, comment 1]

2. **Duty of Partners Respecting Nonlawyer Employees**
The partners and managers in a law firm (and the supervisory lawyers in a governmental agency, business, or other group of lawyers) must make

reasonable efforts to assure that the conduct of the nonlawyers is compatible with the obligations of the profession. [ABA Model Rule 5.3(a)]

EXAMPLE

Lawyer L hired secretary S without carefully checking her background. L put S in charge of his client trust fund account, but did not carefully supervise her bookkeeping procedures. S stole a substantial sum from the account. L failed to fire S even after he discovered her theft. L is subject to discipline for gross negligence. [*See In re* Scanlan, 697 P.2d 1084 (Ariz. 1985)]

---

3. **Duties of Direct Supervisor Respecting Nonlawyer Employees**
    A lawyer who directly supervises the work of a nonlawyer employee must make reasonable efforts to assure that the conduct of the nonlawyer is compatible with the obligations of the profession. [ABA Model Rule 5.3(b); Restatement §11(4)]

EXAMPLE

Deputy Public Defender D directly supervises the work of her secretary, S, and her investigator, I. D must instruct S and I about the need to keep clients' information in confidence, and D must make reasonable efforts to assure that they do so.

---

4. **Ethical Responsibility for Nonlawyer's Misconduct**
    A lawyer is subject to discipline in two situations when a nonlawyer does something that, if done by a lawyer, would violate a disciplinary rule. The lawyer is subject to discipline if:

    a. The lawyer **ordered** the conduct **or knew** about it and ratified it; or

    b. The lawyer is a partner or manager or has direct supervisory responsibility over the nonlawyer, **and** the lawyer knows about the misconduct at a time when its consequences can be avoided or mitigated and fails to take reasonable remedial action.

    [ABA Model Rule 5.3(c)]

G. **RESPONSIBILITIES OF A SUBORDINATE LAWYER**

    1. **Duties Concerning Clear Ethics Violation**
        Orders from a supervisory lawyer are **no excuse** for clearly unethical conduct—a lawyer must follow the ethics rules even when acting under the directions of another person. [ABA Model Rule 5.2; Restatement §12] However, the fact that a subordinate lawyer was acting on directions from a

supervisor may be relevant in determining whether the subordinate had the **knowledge** that is required for some ethics violations. [ABA Model Rule 5.2, comment 1]

EXAMPLE
Partner P gave associate A a memorandum of fact and asked A to draft a complaint for fraud based on the information in the memorandum. A had no way to know whether the information in the memorandum was complete and truthful. A's lack of opportunity to gather the facts personally is relevant in deciding whether to discipline A for participating in the filing of a frivolous complaint.

---

2. **Duties Concerning Debatable Ethics Questions**
   A subordinate lawyer does **not** violate the rules of professional conduct by acting in accordance with a supervisor's reasonable resolution of an **arguable question** of professional duty. When a debatable ethics question arises, someone must decide on a course of action, and that responsibility must rest with the supervisory lawyer. If the supervisor's judgment turns out to have been wrong, the subordinate lawyer should not be disciplined for doing what the supervisor directed. [ABA Model Rule 5.2 and comment 2]

EXAMPLE
Subordinate lawyer L was assisting supervisor S on a summary judgment motion in a products disparagement case. When drafting the reply memorandum on the motion, L stumbled across a new appellate decision in the controlling jurisdiction concerning libel and slander of persons. The new decision had not been cited by S and L's adversary. S and L's duty to call the new decision to the attention of the trial judge depends on whether it is "directly adverse" to their position. L argues that the law of products disparagement and the law of personal libel and slander are so closely related that the new decision must be considered "directly adverse." S, on the other hand, argues that the two bodies of law are similar only by crude analogy. On this debatable point of ethics, the responsibility for making the final decision rests with S, and L should not be disciplined for following S's instructions not to mention the new decision in the reply memorandum.

H. **PROFESSIONAL INDEPENDENCE OF A LAWYER**

1. **Fee Splitting with Nonlawyers and Temporary Lawyers**
   Except as provided below, a lawyer must not share her legal fee with a nonlawyer. [ABA Model Rule 5.4(a); Restatement §10] The purpose of this rule is ill-defined, but it is said to help "protect the lawyer's professional independence of judgment." [ABA Model Rule 5.4, comment 1] Obviously, the salaries of nonlawyer employees of a firm are paid with money earned as

legal fees, but that is not regarded as "sharing" a fee. Furthermore, a firm can employ temporary lawyers through a placement agency without violating the fee-splitting rule.

EXAMPLE

Lawyer L wants to practice law part-time, doing work for law firms that need extra temporary help. L gives copies of her resume to LawTemp, Inc., a placement agency that is owned by nonlawyers. When law firms need extra help, they call LawTemp, which sends them resumes of several available lawyers. By this route, L obtains temporary work at a firm that agrees to pay her $100 per hour for her work and to pay LawTemp a "placement fee" equal to 5% of the total amount it pays to L. The law firm's bill to its client includes the amount the firm pays to L and the "placement fee" paid to LawTemp. This arrangement is **_proper._** [ABA Formal Op. 88-356 (1988)]

---

a.   **Death Benefits Permitted**

The lawyers in a firm may agree that, when one of them dies, the others will pay a death benefit over a reasonable period of time to the dead lawyer's estate or to designated persons. [ABA Model Rule 5.4(a); Restatement §10]

EXAMPLE

The R, S & T firm set up a death benefit program. After a partner or associate dies, the firm will make monthly payments to her estate for three years after the death, each payment to equal 40% of her average monthly income during the year before death. The death benefit program is proper.

---

b.   **Compensation and Retirement Plans for Nonlawyer Employees**

The nonlawyer employees of a firm may be included in a compensation or retirement plan even though the plan is based on a profit-sharing arrangement. [*Id.*]

EXAMPLE

The U, R & S firm sets aside 10% of all legal fees in a fund to be used for year-end bonuses to the partners, associates, and nonlawyer employees. The year-end bonus program is proper, even though it is a profit-sharing arrangement with nonlawyers.

---

c.   **Sale of a Law Practice**

One lawyer's practice can be sold to another lawyer pursuant to rules that are discussed in J., *infra*. One who buys the practice of a

dead, disabled, or disappeared lawyer may pay the purchase price to the estate or representatives of the lawyer. [ABA Model Rule 5.4(a); Restatement §10]

d. **Sharing Court-Awarded Fee with Nonprofit Organization**
When a court awards attorneys' fees to the winning lawyer in a case, the lawyer may share the fee with a nonprofit organization that hired or recommended him as counsel. [*Id.*]

EXAMPLE

Justice International, a nonprofit organization, hired lawyer L to represent a class of persons who were imprisoned after 9/11 in violation of their civil rights. L won the case, and the court awarded her attorney fees to be paid by the defendants. L may share the fees with Justice International.

---

2. **Partnership with Nonlawyer to Practice Law Prohibited**
A lawyer must not form a partnership with a nonlawyer if **any** part of the partnership activities will constitute the practice of law. [ABA Model Rule 5.4(b)] Distinguish this from ancillary services provided by a separate entity (*see* K., *infra*).

EXAMPLE

Family lawyer F formed a partnership with marital psychologist P; their purpose was to offer a full range of counseling and legal services to family clients. All of the legal work was done by F, and all of the other counseling was done by P—neither transgressed into the domain of the other. Nevertheless, F is subject to discipline because part of the partnership activity constitutes the practice of law.

---

3. **Nonlawyer Involvement in Incorporated Firm or Other Association**
A lawyer must not practice in an incorporated law firm or association authorized to practice law for profit if:

a. A nonlawyer owns any interest in the firm or association (but, when a lawyer dies, her estate may hold an interest during the administration of the estate);

b. A nonlawyer is a corporate director or officer or the equivalent thereof; or

c. A nonlawyer has the right to direct or control the professional judgment of a lawyer.

[ABA Model Rule 5.4(d)]

EXAMPLE

M is a nonlawyer. She is the business manager of W, Y & U Ltd., an incorporated law firm. As business manager, she keeps the firm's calendar, does the firm's accounting, hires, fires, and supervises all of the firm's nonlawyer employees, procures all of the firm's supplies and equipment, and runs the firm's library. Despite M's central role in the firm's operations, M cannot become a stockholder in the firm.

---

4. **Interference with Lawyer's Professional Judgment**

A lawyer must not allow a person who recommends, employs, or pays her for serving a client to direct or regulate the lawyer's professional judgment. [ABA Model Rule 5.4(c)]

EXAMPLE

Federated Life Insurance Company employs lawyer L to prepare estate plans for potential life insurance customers. The potential customer pays nothing for the estate planning service; L works on a flat salary paid by Federated. L, realizing who provides his daily bread, makes sure that every estate plan includes a careful explanation of the "benefits of balanced protection through Federated's term and whole life policies." L is subject to discipline.

I. **RESTRICTIONS ON RIGHT TO PRACTICE**

1. **Restrictive Partnership and Employment Agreements**

A lawyer must neither make nor offer a partnership or employment or similar agreement that restricts a lawyer's right to practice after termination of the relationship, except for an agreement concerning benefits upon retirement. [ABA Model Rule 5.6(a); Restatement §13] Such agreements not only limit a lawyer's autonomy but also limit the freedom of clients to choose a lawyer.

EXAMPLES

1) Oakville practitioner A employed young lawyer L by an agreement that purported to prohibit L from practicing in Oakville after leaving A's employment. Both A and L are subject to discipline.

2) Sixty-four-year-old solo practitioner S took young lawyer Y in as a partner. Their partnership agreement provided that after S retired, the firm would pay S a retirement benefit of $5,000 per month so long as S did not re-enter the practice of law. The agreement is proper.

---

2. **Restrictive Settlement Agreements for Clients**

A lawyer must neither make nor offer an agreement in which a restriction on the lawyer's right to practice is part of the settlement of a client controversy. [ABA Model Rule 5.6(b); *and see* ABA Formal Op. 93-371 (1993)]

EXAMPLE
Over a period of several years, attorney A represented a series of federal employees in personal injury suits against the federal government concerning cancers allegedly caused by working in the Dos Arboles Radiation Laboratory. The government settled each suit as it came along, but the more suits the government settled, the more new plaintiffs A was able to find. Ultimately, the government offered to settle all then-pending suits for generous sums, provided that A would never again represent a claimant in a Dos Arboles Radiation case. If A agrees to settle on those terms, A will be subject to discipline. [*See* ABA Formal Op. 95-394 (1995)]

J. SALE OF A LAW PRACTICE

1. When Sale Permitted

ABA Model Rule 1.17 permits the sale of a law practice or a field of law practice, including goodwill, under certain circumstances. Pursuant to this rule: (1) the seller must **cease to engage in the private practice of law**, or in the sold field of practice, in the area where the practice has been conducted; (2) the entire practice, or the entire field of practice, must be sold to one or more lawyers or firms; and (3) **written notice** must be given to the seller's clients regarding the sale, the clients' right to retain other counsel or to take possession of their files, and the fact that consent to the transfer of the clients' files will be presumed if a client takes no action within 90 days of receipt of the notice. If notice cannot be given to a client, a court order is required to authorize the transfer of the representation of that client to the purchaser. [ABA Model Rule 1.17(c)] Also, the seller must "exercise competence in identifying a purchaser qualified to assume the practice." [ABA Model Rule 1.17, comment 11]

a. Selling Lawyer May Practice in Limited Circumstances

After the sale of his practice, a lawyer may still be employed as a lawyer on the staff of a public agency or legal services entity that provides legal services to the poor, or as in-house counsel to a business. [ABA Model Rule 1.17, comment 3] Additionally, a lawyer's return to private practice because of an unanticipated change in circumstances does not necessarily violate the Rules. [ABA Model Rule 1.17, comment 1]

2. Protection of Seller's Clients After Sale

The purchaser must undertake **all** client matters **in the practice**, and not just those that generate substantial fees (subject of course to client consent and conflict of interest rules). [*See* ABA Model Rule 1.17, comment 6] This

requirement prevents the sale of only fee-generating matters, which could leave clients whose matters are not very lucrative in a situation where they might find it difficult to find other representation. Also, clients' fees must not be increased because of the sale. [ABA Model Rule 1.17(d)] The purchaser must honor existing fee agreements made by the seller. [ABA Model Rule 1.17, comment 10]

K. LAW-RELATED (ANCILLARY) SERVICES

Lawyers are permitted to provide law-related services. Law-related services (often referred to as ancillary services) are services that might reasonably be performed in conjunction with (and are related to) the provision of legal services and that are not prohibited as unauthorized practice of law when provided by a nonlawyer. Examples of law-related services include financial planning, accounting, lobbying, trust services, real estate counseling, providing title insurance, and preparing tax returns. Even though law-related services are not legal services, a lawyer who provides such services is subject to the Rules of Professional Conduct in two situations:

1. Nonlegal Services and Legal Services Provided Together

If a lawyer provides nonlegal services in circumstances that are not distinct from her provision of legal services, then the Rules of Professional Conduct apply to both the legal and nonlegal services. [ABA Model Rule 5.7(a)(1)]

EXAMPLE

Attorney A is an expert in setting up new business ventures. He also knows many wealthy people who invest money in untried business ventures—so-called venture capitalists. When A draws up the articles of incorporation for client C's new business venture and also finds some willing investors for C, A is subject to the Rules of Professional Conduct in both activities.

---

2. Nonlegal Services Provided by Entity that Is Controlled by the Lawyer

If a lawyer provides nonlegal services through an entity that is not her law office but that she controls (either alone or with other lawyers), that lawyer must take reasonable steps to assure that people who receive the nonlegal services understand that those services are not legal services and that the Rules of Professional Conduct do not cover those services. For instance, the attorney-client privilege does not apply to the nonlegal services. If the lawyer does not take those reasonable steps, then the lawyer is subject to the Rules of Professional Conduct with respect to the nonlegal services.

EXAMPLE

Lawyer L is a certified specialist in family law. Many of her clients are women who want to divorce their husbands and also want to find work outside the

home. L and one of her nonlawyer friends own and manage Jobs-4-U, a job placement service. When one of her law clients needs a job, L usually refers the client to Jobs-4-U. L is always careful to tell the client that she has a personal financial stake in Jobs-4-U, but L does not explain that the Rules of Professional Conduct do not apply to services rendered by Jobs-4-U. L is therefore bound by the Rules of Professional Conduct in her job placement work.

3. **Providing Nonlegal Services to Clients**
    When a ***client-lawyer relationship*** exists between the lawyer and the individual receiving the law-related services, the lawyer must comply with Rule 1.8(a), which specifies the conditions a lawyer must satisfy when she enters into a business transaction with her own client. [ABA Model Rule 5.7, comment 5] Specifically, the transaction must meet the following requirements: the terms of the transaction must be fair to the client; the terms must be fully disclosed to the client in writing, and such disclosure must cover the essential terms of the transaction and the lawyer's role in the transaction; the client must be advised in writing that he should seek advice from an independent lawyer regarding the arrangement; and the client must give informed consent in a writing signed by the client. (*See also* IV.C.2.a., *supra.*)

II. THE CLIENT-LAWYER RELATIONSHIP

A. **NATURE OF THE RELATIONSHIP**
    The relationship between a lawyer and client is contractual. The terms of that contract are generally implied by custom, but for the most part can be varied by mutual agreement. The lawyer operates as both the client's fiduciary and agent, with the duties and limitations of those designations. For example, because the lawyer is considered a fiduciary, the contract between the lawyer and client will be construed against the lawyer and closely scrutinized for fairness. Similarly, the lawyer is subject to the limitations imposed by the laws of agency.

B. **CREATING THE LAWYER-CLIENT RELATIONSHIP**

1. **How Relationship Is Formed**
    In lore, although perhaps not in fact, an English barrister has an ethical duty to take any case offered upon tender of a proper fee. [Wolfram, Modern Legal Ethics §10.2.2 (1986)] In contrast, lawyers in the United States are generally free to refuse service to any person for any reason. A lawyer-client relationship arises when:

    (i)   A person manifests an intent that the lawyer provide legal services and the lawyer ***agrees***;

(ii) A person manifests an intent to have the lawyer represent him, the lawyer fails to make clear that he does not want to undertake the representation, and the lawyer knows or should know that the prospective client is **reasonably relying** on the lawyer to provide the services; or

(iii) A tribunal **appoints** a lawyer to represent a client.

[Restatement §14]

a. Implied Assent and Reasonable Reliance

The lawyer's assent is implied when he fails to clearly decline representation and the prospective client reasonably relies on the representation. The reasonableness of the reliance is a question of fact.

EXAMPLES

1) Client Carla writes a letter to attorney Aida, asking Aida to represent her in a personal injury case. Aida never responds to the letter. One year later, the statute of limitations expires on Carla's claim, and she sues Aida for malpractice for failing to file the suit. Here, there was no attorney-client relationship. Although Aida did not expressly decline the representation, it was unreasonable for Carla to rely on Aida's representation based on an unanswered letter. [See Restatement §14, illus. 3]

2) Client Casey calls lawyer Lisa's office asking that Lisa represent him in a court proceeding relating to his arrest for driving under the influence ("DUI"). Lisa is out of the office. Casey tells Lisa's secretary that he understands that Lisa handles many DUI cases and hopes that she will take the case even though the court date is only 10 days away. The secretary tells Casey to send over all papers relevant to the proceeding. She does not tell him that Lisa will decide whether to take the case only after reviewing the papers. One day before Casey's court date, Lisa phones Casey and declines to represent him. Here, it would likely be found that an attorney-client relationship existed because Casey's reliance was reasonable. Lisa regularly handled DUI cases, her agent responded to his request for help by asking him to send the papers, and the imminence of the hearing made it appropriate for Lisa to decline while there was still time for Casey to get another lawyer. [Restatement §14, illus. 4]

---

2. Duty to Reject Certain Cases

A lawyer must refuse employment in the following situations, as taking on a representation in these circumstances would violate the Rules of Professional Conduct.

a. Client's Motive Is Harassment

A lawyer is subject to discipline for bringing an action, conducting a

defense, asserting a position, or taking other steps if the client's motive is to embarrass, delay, or burden a third person. [ABA Model Rule 4.4(a)] Thus, a lawyer must reject any case where he believes this is the prospective client's motive.

b. Unsupportable Factual or Legal Position

A lawyer who is serving as an advocate in a legal proceeding must not take a position that is either factually or legally frivolous. [ABA Model Rule 3.1] A position is not frivolous if the lawyer can make a good faith argument that the facts are as claimed or that the present law should be changed. A position also is not frivolous merely because the lawyer does not have all the facts at hand at the outset, but expects to develop them during discovery. Note that in a criminal case, the defense lawyer may defend his client to the extent allowed by constitutional law even if the defense would otherwise violate this rule. [ABA Model Rule 3.1, comments 1 - 3; *and see* VI.A., *infra*]

c. Lawyer Not Competent

A lawyer must reject a case if he is too busy or too inexperienced to handle the matter competently. [ABA Model Rule 1.1]

d. Strong Personal Feelings

If a lawyer's personal feelings about a case are so strong that they would impair his ability to effectively represent the client, he must refuse the case. [ABA Model Rules 1.16(a)(1), 1.7(a)(2)]

e. Impaired Mental or Physical Condition

A lawyer must decline a case if his mental or physical condition would materially impair his ability to represent the client. [ABA Model Rule 1.16(a)(2)]

3. **Duties Owed to Prospective Client**

When a person consults with a lawyer about the possibility of forming a lawyer-client relationship, and no such relationship ensues, the lawyer has a duty to: (1) protect the prospective client's confidential information, which includes declining to represent other clients in the same or a related matter if the confidential information would be harmful to the prospective client; (2) protect any property the prospective client has given to the lawyer; and (3) use reasonable care in giving the person any legal advice, such as whether the claim has merit, whether conflicts of interest exist, and when the action must be commenced. [Restatement §15]

4. **Ethical Obligation to Accept Unpopular Cases**

Lawyers have an ethical obligation to help make legal service available to all who need it. A lawyer can fulfill this obligation by accepting a ***fair share***

of unpopular matters or indigent or unpopular clients. [ABA Model Rule 6.2, comment 1]

C. ATTORNEYS' FEES

The nature and amount of an attorney's fee are subjects for contractual agreement between the attorney and the client (except when the fee is set by statute or court order). In theory, the attorney and client bargain at arm's length over the fee, but in practice many clients are inexperienced with attorneys' fees. Thus, in fee disputes, courts strain to give the benefit of the doubt to the client. [*See, e.g.,* Terzis v. Estate of Whalen, 489 A.2d 608 (N.H. 1985); with respect to fee setting in general, *see* Restatement §§34 - 43]

1. Must Communicate Fee Arrangement to Client

A lawyer must, before or within a reasonable time after commencing a representation, communicate the basis or rate of the fee and the expenses for which the client will be responsible. Although a writing is preferable, it is generally **not** required (except in contingent fee agreements, *infra*). The lawyer also has an ongoing duty to communicate any changes regarding the fee arrangement. [ABA Model Rule 1.5(b)]

a. Exception—Regularly Represented Client

If the lawyer regularly represents the client and will be charging the same basis or rate as in other matters, the lawyer need not communicate the fee arrangement each time.

EXAMPLES

1) At the close of her first appointment with a new client, attorney A gave the client a simple written memorandum. The memorandum explained that her fee would be calculated at $175 per hour, and that the number of hours could not be predicted with certainty but would probably be about 100. Later, when the matter proved more difficult than A had anticipated, A gave the client a supplemental memorandum that doubled the estimated number of hours. A handled the fee issue properly under the ABA Model Rules.

2) At the end of his third appointment with lawyer L, a new client asked how L planned to charge him for the work. L responded: "In a matter of this nature, it's simply impossible to tell you in advance what the fee will be. But you have my assurance that it will be a fair fee." L's conduct is a disciplinary violation under ABA Model Rule 1.5(b).

---

2. Discipline for Unreasonable Fee

A court will not enforce a contract for an unreasonably high attorney's fee or an unreasonably high amount for expenses, and the attorney is subject to discipline for trying to exact such a fee or expenses. [ABA Model Rule 1.5(a)]

a. **Factors**

The factors considered in determining the reasonableness of a fee are:

1) The *time and labor* required;

2) The *novelty and difficulty* of the questions involved;

3) The *skill* needed to perform the legal services properly;

4) The likelihood, if apparent to the client, that *the work for this client will preclude the lawyer from doing fee-paying work for others*;

5) The *fee customarily charged* in the locality for similar legal work;

6) The *amount at stake and the results obtained* for the client;

7) The *time limitations* imposed by the client or the circumstances;

8) The *nature and length of the relationship* between the lawyer and the client;

9) The *experience, reputation, and ability of the lawyer* performing the services; and

10) Whether the fee is *fixed or contingent* (a contingent fee can be higher because it requires the lawyer to take a gamble).

[ABA Model Rule 1.5(a)]

b. **Items that May and May Not Be Billed**

The attorney must disclose the basis on which a client will be charged for legal services and expenses, and the attorney's bill should clearly show how the amount due has been computed. The attorney must not charge the client for ordinary overhead expenses associated with staffing, equipping, and running the attorney's office, but the attorney may charge the client for the *actual cost to the attorney* of special services such as photocopying, long distance calls, computer research, special deliveries, secretarial overtime, and the like. [Restatement §38(3)(a)] Alternatively, the attorney may charge a reasonable amount to which the client has agreed in advance. [ABA Model Rule 1.5, comment 1] The attorney must not charge the client more than her actual cost for services provided by third parties, such as court reporters, travel agents, and expert witnesses. Furthermore, the attorney must not "double bill" her time. [*See* ABA Formal Op. 93-379 (1993)]

EXAMPLE

Attorney spends three hours working on client A's case while flying on an airplane to take depositions in client B's case. Attorney must not bill B for three hours of travel time if she elects to bill A for three hours of work time. She may charge either one or the other for the full three hours, or she may apportion the time between the two clients.

---

3. **Collecting and Financing Attorneys' Fees**

   a. **Payment in Advance**

   A lawyer may require her fee to be paid in advance, but she must refund any unearned part of the advance if she is fired or withdraws. [ABA Model Rule 1.16(d); comment 4 to ABA Model Rule 1.5; *and see* G.5., *infra*] Be careful to **distinguish a true retainer fee** from a payment of a fee in advance. A true retainer fee is money that is paid solely to ensure the availability of the lawyer, and the lawyer who is fired or withdraws generally need not refund the retainer fee.

EXAMPLES

1) XYZ Oil Company pays the A & B environmental defense firm a monthly retainer fee of $1,000 simply to be available to represent XYZ in the case of an oil spill. The retainer fee agreement provides that the $1,000 per month will not be credited against hours spent on XYZ's legal work. This is a true retainer fee. If the A & B firm withdraws or is fired from a particular case, it may keep the retainer payments provided: (1) the retainer amount was reasonable, and (2) it has not violated the retainer agreement.

2) Lawyer L agreed to represent client C in a divorce case for $100 per hour. L's written fee contract with C provided that C would pay L a $2,500 "nonrefundable retainer" and that the retainer would be "credited against C's charges." C fired L after L did $1,000 worth of work on the case, but L refused to refund any part of the retainer. L must refund $1,500 to C; the fee contract does not clearly explain the meaning of "nonrefundable retainer," and it ought to be construed against L, who drafted it. [*See* Jacobson v. Sassower, 66 N.Y.2d 991 (1985)]

---

   b. **Property for Services**

   A lawyer may accept property in return for services (e.g., an ownership interest in a business), provided that this does not involve a proprietary interest in the cause of action or subject of litigation contrary to ABA Model Rule 1.8(i) (*see* IV.C.3., *infra*). Such an arrangement is also subject to scrutiny as a conflict of interest because it may be a business transaction between the lawyer and the client (*see* IV.C.2., *infra*). [ABA Model Rule 1.5, comment 4]

c.   **Cutting Off Services**
A lawyer must not make a fee agreement that could curtail services in the middle of the relationship and thus put the client at a bargaining disadvantage. [ABA Model Rule 1.5, comment 5]

EXAMPLE
Attorney A agreed to defend client D in a drug smuggling case. A clause buried in the middle of A's wordy fee agreement provides that all work must be paid for in advance. D paid A $2,000 in advance. In the middle of preparation for trial, A told D that the original advance was used up and that if D did not advance more money, the work would stop. A's conduct is not proper. [*Id.*; *and see* State v. Mayes, 531 P.2d 102 (Kan. 1975)]

---

d.   **Credit Arrangements and Security**
A lawyer may permit the client to pay a legal fee by credit card [ABA Formal Op. 00-419 (2000)], and a lawyer may participate in a bar association program that enables clients to finance fees through bank loans. A lawyer may also take an interest-bearing promissory note from a client to secure the payment of fees. [*See* Hulland v. State Bar, 8 Cal. 3d 440 (1972)] When permitted by local law, a lawyer may use a statutory, common law, or contractual attorney's lien to secure the payment of a fee. [ABA Model Rule 1.8(i)(1)]

4.   **Contingent Fees**
Under a contingent fee agreement, the lawyer collects a fee only if the matter is resolved in the client's favor. Often, the fee is expressed as a percentage of the client's eventual recovery in the case. However, a contingent fee need not be a percentage of the amount recovered; an otherwise proper contingent fee may still be proper even if there is no *res*, or pool of money, from which the fee can be paid. Contingent fees are regarded as unethical in some common law countries, but they are tolerated in the United States. Critics contend that they stir up litigation, encourage excessive fees, and give the lawyer an unprofessional stake in the outcome of the case. Proponents reply that only through a contingent fee arrangement can a client of modest means afford to litigate a claim. Some states have set statutory limits on the contingent fee percentages a lawyer can exact in personal injury, medical malpractice, and similar types of cases.

a.   **When Contingent Fee Prohibited**

1)   **Criminal Cases**
A lawyer is subject to discipline for using a contingent fee

arrangement when defending a person in a criminal case. [ABA Model Rule 1.5(d)(2)]

2) Domestic Relations Cases

A lawyer is also subject to discipline for using a contingent fee in a domestic relations case when the contingency is based on the securing of a divorce, the amount of alimony or support, or the amount of a property settlement. However, a lawyer may use a contingent fee in a suit to recover money that is *past due* under an alimony or support decree. [ABA Model Rule 1.5 and comment 6]

EXAMPLE

Lawyer L agreed to represent W in a marital dissolution case in exchange for 10% of the amount to be received by W as a property settlement. The arrangement would subject L to discipline.

---

b. Contingent Fee Must Be Reasonable

A contingent fee must be reasonable in amount; moreover, a lawyer must not use a contingent fee when the facts of the case make it unreasonable to do so. [ABA Model Rule 1.5, comment 3]

EXAMPLE

Client C asked lawyer L to represent her as plaintiff in a medical malpractice case. Liability was clear, the damages were large, and the defendants were affluent. The case was a clear winner, and L knew that he could settle it with only a few hours of work. Nonetheless, L signed C up to a 33% contingent fee agreement. After two hours of work, L arranged a lucrative settlement that C accepted. It was unreasonable for L to use a contingent fee agreement in the first place, and it would be unreasonable for L to collect one-third of the settlement proceeds. [See ABA Model Rule 1.5, comment 3]

---

c. Writing Requirement for Contingent Fee Agreements

A contingent fee agreement must be in a writing *signed by the client*, and the writing must state:

1) How the fee is to be *calculated*, including the percentage that the lawyer will get if the case is settled before trial, won after trial, or won after appeal;

2) What *litigation and other expenses* are to be *deducted* from the recovery;

3) Whether **deductions for expenses** will be made **before or after** the contingent fee is calculated; and

4) What **expenses the client must pay**, whether or not she wins the case.

At the **end** of a contingent fee case, the lawyer must give the client a written statement showing the outcome of the case, the remittance to the client, and how the remittance was calculated. [ABA Model Rule 1.5(c)]

5. **Fee Disputes**

   a. **In General**
   In seeking compensation from a client, a lawyer may not employ collection methods forbidden by law, improperly use confidential information, or harass a client. [Restatement §41]

   b. **Remedies**

   1) **Liens**
   In addition to filing a lawsuit to recover their fees, lawyers have several remedies if a client refuses to pay all or a portion of a fee. Most states recognize a common law or statutory charging lien, under which any recovery obtained for the client serves as security for the lawyer's fees. Even states that do not recognize a charging lien usually recognize such a lien if created by the lawyer and client's express agreement. [3 A.L.R.2d 148 (1949)] Many states also permit the lawyer to exercise a retaining lien, under which he can retain documents, funds, and property of the client until his fee is paid, but there is a strong minority view contra.

   2) **Retention of Funds in Trust Account**
   If a lawyer receives funds on behalf of a client from which his fee is to be paid (e.g., a settlement check), and the client disputes the amount of his fee, the lawyer must retain the **disputed** amount in a client trust account (IX.C.2.b., *infra*) until the dispute is resolved. [ABA Model Rule 1.15(e) and comment 3]

   3) **Arbitration or Mediation**
   Bar associations in many jurisdictions have established arbitration or mediation services to help lawyers resolve fee disputes with their clients. Comment 9 to ABA Model Rule 1.5 urges lawyers to use these services when they are available.

EXAMPLE
Lawyer L's standard retainer agreement includes a provision that

requires arbitration of both fee disputes and legal malpractice claims. The agreement is proper, provided that it is clear and that L's clients truly understand its ramifications. [District of Columbia Bar Op. 190 (1988)]

6. **Fee Splitting with Other Lawyers**

As a general rule, a lawyer must not split a legal fee with another lawyer. The rule is designed to prevent lawyers from becoming "client brokers" and to discourage excessive fees. The general rule is subject to three exceptions.

a. **Lawyers Within a Firm**

The partners and associates within a law firm may, of course, pool and split legal fees—that is the essence of practice in a law firm.

b. **Separation and Retirement Agreements**

A law firm may make payments to a former partner or associate under a separation or retirement agreement.

> **EXAMPLE**
> The partnership agreement of the P, D & Q law firm provides that when partner Q retires, the firm will pay her monthly benefits equal to 30% of Q's average monthly billings during the year prior to her retirement. The arrangement is proper.

c. **Certain Splits with Lawyers Outside Firm**

Sometimes two or more lawyers from different firms work together on a case. ABA Model Rule 1.5(e) permits them to submit a single bill to the client, and then to split the fee, *if* the following conditions are met:

1) The total fee is *reasonable*;

2) The split is *in proportion to the services performed by each lawyer*, or some different proportion if *each lawyer assumes joint responsibility* for the matter; and

3) The *client agrees to the split in a writing that discloses the share each lawyer will receive*.

> **EXAMPLE**
> In a complex corporate tender offer matter that involves both antitrust and securities law issues, lawyers from three firms join forces to represent Grundy, Inc. Lawyers from firm A will do whatever courtroom work needs to be done. Lawyers from firm B will do the out-of-court work on the antitrust issues, and lawyers from firm C will do the out-of-court work

on the securities law issues. The three firms do not agree to assume joint responsibility for the matter, but they agree to send Grundy, Inc. a single bill and to divide the proceeds in proportion to the work done by each firm. Grundy, Inc. is advised of the arrangement and consents to it in writing. Assuming that the total fee is reasonable, the arrangement is proper.

7. **True Referral Fees Are Unethical**

Referral of cases between lawyers is common, for instance, when the referring lawyer is too busy to handle a case or does not feel competent to handle a case. However, ABA Model Rule 7.2(b) prohibits a lawyer from paying anyone—including another lawyer—for recommending him or referring a matter to him. Furthermore, ABA Model Rule 1.5(e) does not permit fee splitting with a referring lawyer who neither assumes responsibility for a matter nor does work on the matter (*see* 6c., above). A lawyer may, however, set up a "reciprocal referral" arrangement with another lawyer or with a nonlawyer professional in which each person agrees to refer clients or customers to the other. The arrangement must not be exclusive, and the lawyer's client must be informed of the existence and nature of the arrangement. [ABA Model Rule 7.2(b) and comment 8] These reciprocal referral arrangements are discussed further in X.B.1.c., *infra*.

D. **SCOPE AND BOUNDS OF REPRESENTATION**

Generally, a lawyer must abide by a client's decisions concerning the objectives of a representation, and must consult with the client as to the means by which those objectives are pursued. A lawyer also may take actions that are *impliedly authorized* to carry out the representation. [ABA Model Rule 1.2(a)]

1. **May Limit Scope of Representation**

A lawyer may limit the scope of the representation if: (1) the limitation is *reasonable* under the circumstances, and (2) the client gives *informed consent*. For example, a lawyer might agree to counsel her client about a dispute with the client's landlord, but stipulate that if the dispute has to be arbitrated or litigated, the client will hire another lawyer for that purpose. [ABA Model Rule 1.2(c) and comment 7]

2. **Must Not Assist Client in Crime or Fraud**

A lawyer must not advise a client to engage in conduct that the lawyer knows is criminal or fraudulent, or assist the client in such conduct. However, the lawyer *may discuss the legal consequences* of any proposed course of conduct. The lawyer may also counsel or assist a client to make a good faith effort to determine the validity, scope, meaning, or application of the law (e.g., violating a statute to test its validity or scope in an enforcement proceeding). [ABA Model Rule 1.2(d)]

a. **Telling the Client "No"**

When a lawyer discovers that her client expects assistance that violates a law or legal ethics rule, or if the lawyer intends to act contrary to the client's instructions, the lawyer must explain why she cannot do what the client expects. [ABA Model Rule 1.2(d), comment 13]

b. **Discussing Proposed Conduct**

A lawyer may discuss a proposed course of conduct with a client, and explain to the client that the conduct would be unlawful. If the client later uses the lawyer's advice to carry out a crime or fraud, that does not make the lawyer a party to the illegal conduct. However, the lawyer must not recommend the illegal conduct or instruct the client on how to break the law and get away with it. [ABA Model Rule 1.2(d) and comment 9] If a client insists on illegal or unethical assistance, the lawyer must withdraw from representation. [ABA Model Rule 1.16(a)]

c. **Discovering a Client's Illegal Conduct**

When a lawyer discovers that a client has begun an illegal course of action and the action is continuing, the lawyer must not assist in the wrongdoing, e.g., by drafting fraudulent documents or suggesting how the wrongdoing can be concealed. [ABA Model Rule 1.2(d) and comment 10] In this situation, the lawyer **must** withdraw because continued representation would violate the rules of professional conduct. [ABA Model Rule 1.16(a)(1); *and see* G.3.b., *infra*] Sometimes withdrawal alone is not enough—the lawyer may have to make a "noisy withdrawal" in which she gives outsiders notice of her withdrawal and disaffirms any of her prior opinions, documents, affirmations, or the like that the client is using to carry out the wrongdoing. [ABA Model Rule 1.2, comment 10] The lawyer's noisy withdrawal may put the client's victim on guard, but that is permissible (and probably praiseworthy). [*See also* ABA Model Rule 4.1(b) and comment 3—concerning disclosure of confidential information]

3. **Decisions to Be Made by Client**

When a client brings a legal problem to a lawyer, it is the client who must decide what shall be the objectives of the lawyer's work. Thus, it is the client who must make the key decisions that affect the client's substantial legal rights. A lawyer must therefore abide by the client's decision regarding the following matters:

a. Whether to accept a **settlement offer**;

b. What **plea** to enter in a criminal case;

c. Whether to **waive a jury trial** in a criminal case;

d.   Whether the client will **testify** in a criminal case; and

e.   Whether to **appeal**.

[ABA Model Rule 1.2(a); Restatement §22(1)]

EXAMPLES

1) Lawyer L agrees to represent C on a contingent fee basis in C's suit against D for slander. L's fee agreement provides that the suit cannot be settled before trial without L's consent. L is subject to discipline. The decision to settle a suit is made by the client, not the lawyer—even in a contingent fee case. [*See* ABA Model Rule 1.2(a)]

2) Attorney A is defending B in a burglary case. A has carefully advised B about the legal and practical consequences of pleading not guilty, waiving a jury trial, and testifying on his own behalf. Having done that, A must now allow B to make the final decision on those three vital issues. [*Id.*]

---

a.   **Disagreements Between Lawyer and Client**
Lawyers and clients sometimes disagree about the means to be used to reach the client's objectives. Clients normally defer to their lawyers about issues of law, tactics, and strategy. Conversely, lawyers normally defer to their clients about questions of expense and concern for third persons who might be affected by a legal tactic. A lawyer and client should try to resolve their disagreements, but if they cannot, the lawyer may withdraw or the client may fire the lawyer. [*See* ABA Model Rule 1.16(a)(3), (b)(4)]

4.   Lawyer's Authority to Bind Client
A lawyer is the client's agent. Under the law of agency, the lawyer's actions on behalf of a client will legally bind the client if the lawyer acted with actual or apparent authority.

a.   **Actual Authority—Lawyer's Belief**
A lawyer has actual authority if she reasonably believes she is authorized to act based on her dealings with the client. Actual authority can be **express or implied** (i.e., what the client has expressly told the lawyer to do, along with anything else impliedly authorized to carry out the representation). A lawyer also has actual authority to take actions that she reasonably believes are required by law or court order. [Restatement §26]

b.   **Apparent Authority—Third Party's Belief**
When dealing with the court and third parties, a lawyer has apparent authority when the **court or third party reasonably assumes** that the

lawyer has authority to act **based on some manifestation from the client** that the lawyer had authority. Even if the lawyer acted without actual authority, the client is still bound if the lawyer had apparent authority. However, the client can sue the lawyer for damages (and of course, the lawyer is still subject to discipline). [Restatement §27 and comment f]

1) How Client Creates Apparent Authority

Often, the client's mere act of retaining the lawyer is enough to give the lawyer apparent authority to act on the client's behalf. However, when it comes to **settlement** and other decisions that are ultimately left to the client (*see* 3., above), merely retaining the lawyer is **not enough** to give the lawyer apparent authority. [Restatement §27, comment d] Thus, if a lawyer settles a case for a client without actual authority, the client is not bound to the agreement unless the client somehow indicated to the opposing party that the lawyer was authorized to settle the case.

c. Ratification

Even if a lawyer acted without any authority, the client may subsequently ratify the act (e.g., by cashing a settlement check). The effect of ratification is the same as if the lawyer had originally acted with actual authority. [Restatement §26] Consequently, the client is bound and may not sue the lawyer for damages. Note, however, that the lawyer would still be subject to discipline.

d. When Lawyer's Authority Ends

A lawyer's actual authority to represent a client ends when: (1) the matter is complete or the lawyer is **fired or withdraws**; (2) the **client dies** (or dissolves, if the client is an organization); or (3) the **lawyer dies** or is otherwise unable to continue the representation (e.g., because of disbarment or disability). The lawyer's apparent authority ends when the third party knows or should know that any of these events occurred, or whenever it can reasonably be inferred that the lawyer lacks actual authority. [Restatement §31]

1) Must Notify Third Parties Relying on Authority

When a lawyer's actual authority ends, the lawyer must no longer purport to have authority and must notify third parties who are relying on the continued existence of the authority. [Restatement §31, comment i]

5. Client with Diminished Capacity

a. Lawyer's Duties

Normally, it is assumed that a client can make decisions about important matters, but if the client is a minor or has diminished mental capacity, that may not be true. Nevertheless, such a client may be able to make some kinds of decisions that affect her own well-being. For example, even very young children can have valuable opinions about who should have custody of them. Similarly, even very old clients can handle routine financial matters, although they may need legal protection concerning major transactions. The lawyer has a duty, so far as reasonably possible, to maintain a normal lawyer-client relationship with the client. [ABA Model Rule 1.14(a) and comment 1] The lawyer must treat the client with attention and respect. Even if the client has a guardian or other representative, the lawyer should, so far as possible, treat the client as a client, particularly in communicating with the client about significant developments. [ABA Model Rule 1.14, comment 2]

b.   **Protective Action and Appointment of Guardian**
When the client has diminished capacity and faces a risk of substantial physical, financial, or other harm, the lawyer may take reasonable actions to protect the client. These actions include consulting with people or entities that can protect the client, and, when appropriate, seeking the appointment of a guardian or similar surrogate. [ABA Model Rule 1.14(b)] When taking protective action, the lawyer has implied authority to reveal the client's confidential information, but only to the extent necessary to protect the client. [ABA Model Rule 1.14(c)]

EXAMPLE
For many years, lawyer L has represented widower W in personal and business matters. Now W's physical and mental condition make it unsafe for him to continue living alone in the old family home, and he has no close relatives or friends to assist him. L may search out suitable living quarters for W, where eating facilities and medical help are close at hand. To the extent possible, L should involve W in making the decision to move. If L reasonably believes that W needs a conservator, she may seek to have one appointed; in the appointment process, she may, if necessary, disclose confidential information about W's condition. After a conservator is appointed, L should still treat W as her client, consulting with him, keeping him advised of developments, and allowing him to make all decisions of which he is capable.

---

6.   **Emergency Legal Assistance to Nonclient with Seriously Diminished Capacity**
When a person with seriously diminished capacity faces ***imminent and irreparable harm*** to her health, safety, or financial interest, a lawyer may take

legal action on her behalf, despite her inability to establish a lawyer-client relationship or to make or express considered judgments about the matter. However, the lawyer cannot act until the person (or someone acting on her behalf) has consulted the lawyer, and the lawyer should not act unless he reasonably believes the person has no other representative available. Any action undertaken should be limited to that which is reasonably necessary to maintain the status quo or otherwise avoid imminent and irreparable harm. [ABA Model Rule 1.14, comment 9]

a. Lawyer's Duties

A lawyer who represents a person in such emergency circumstances has the same duties as he would with respect to a client. [*Id.*] In an emergency situation, confidences may be disclosed only to the extent necessary to accomplish the intended protective action. The lawyer should disclose the nature of his relationship with the person to any tribunal or counsel involved in the matter. Furthermore, steps should be taken to regularize the relationship as soon as possible. [ABA Model Rule 1.14, comment 10]

b. No Compensation for Lawyer

Normally, a lawyer would not seek compensation for emergency actions taken on behalf of a nonclient. [*Id.*]

E. COMMUNICATING WITH THE CLIENT

1. Matters that Require Informed Consent

The lawyer must promptly inform the client of any decision or circumstance that requires the client's **informed consent**. [ABA Model Rule 1.4(a)] "Informed consent" means that the client agrees to a proposed course of conduct after the lawyer has sufficiently explained the material risks and reasonable alternatives. [ABA Model Rule 1.0(e)]

EXAMPLES

1) ABA Model Rule 1.7(b) permits a lawyer, in defined circumstances, to represent two clients who have a concurrent conflict of interests. One prerequisite is that both clients give informed consent in writing. The lawyer must sufficiently explain the material risks and reasonably available alternatives to both clients before they can give valid consent.

2) If an adversary offers to settle a civil case, or offers a plea bargain in a criminal case, the lawyer must promptly convey the offer to her client unless the client has previously instructed the lawyer that an offer on those terms is acceptable or unacceptable or has authorized the lawyer to accept or reject such an offer. [ABA Model Rule 1.4, comment 2]

---

2. **Information About Status of the Matter and Means to Be Used**
    The lawyer must keep the client reasonably informed about the status of the
    matter and about the means by which the lawyer plans to accomplish the
    client's objectives. [ABA Model Rule 1.4(a)(2), (3)] If the lawyer must make an
    immediate decision (such as whether to object to a line of questioning during
    a trial), the lawyer need not consult with the client before acting. [ABA Model
    Rule 1.4, comment 3] However, in less urgent situations, the lawyer should
    consult with the client before acting.

EXAMPLE

Client C hired lawyer L to negotiate on C's behalf in a real estate dispute. C told
L: "You have complete authority—just get the best deal you can." Despite the
grant of broad authority, L should keep C advised of the progress of the negotiations. When there is time to do so, L should review the material issues with C
before taking final action.

---

a. **Admitting Mistakes**
    To comply with the duty of communication, a lawyer must inform a
    current client if the lawyer believes he has "materially erred" in any
    representation of the client. An error is considered material if a disinter-
    ested lawyer would conclude that: (1) it is reasonably likely to harm or
    prejudice the client; or (2) even in the absence of harm or prejudice, it
    is of such a nature that it would reasonably cause the client to consider
    discharging the lawyer. However, once an attorney-client relationship
    has ended, the lawyer has no obligation to inform the former client of
    material errors discovered after the fact. [ABA Formal Op. 481 (2018)]

3. **Request for Information**
    If the lawyer keeps the client properly informed of developments in the
    matter, the client will not often need to ask the lawyer for information. When
    a client does make a reasonable request for information, the lawyer must
    respond promptly. If that is impossible, then the lawyer or a member of her
    staff should acknowledge the client's request and tell the client when the
    information will be available. [ABA Model Rule 1.4(a)(4) and comment 4]

4. **Consultation About Illegal or Unethical Conduct**
    If the client expects the lawyer to do something that is either illegal or uneth-
    ical, the lawyer must consult with the client and explain why he cannot do
    what the client wants. [ABA Model Rule 1.4(a)(5)]

EXAMPLE

Attorney A is representing defendant D at a criminal trial. They expected to
use an alibi defense based on the testimony of witness W, but the prosecution's case-in-chief proves beyond doubt that W's proposed testimony would

be perjurious. In a recess before the defense's case-in-chief, D tells A to call W according to plan. A must explain to D why he cannot use W's testimony and must consult with D about an alternative defense strategy.

5.   **Special Circumstances**

The amount and kind of information and explanations the lawyer should give to the client depend on the client's situation. If the client is young or has diminished capacity, the lawyer may have to do more explaining and assisting than if the client is an ordinary adult. If the client is an organization or group, the lawyer should ordinarily communicate with the appropriate officer. If the client and the lawyer have a regular, established relationship concerning many routine matters, the two of them may agree on a convenient arrange-ment for only limited or occasional reporting. [ABA Model Rule 1.4, comment 6]

EXAMPLE

For many years, attorney A has done the routine collection work for a major bank. In a normal week, the bank sends A 20 to 30 new collection cases. Over the years, A and the bank have settled on a standard procedure for han-dling these cases. It would be proper for A and the bank to agree that A must report only major or unusual occurrences.

6.   **Withholding Information from Client**

A lawyer may delay the transmission of information to a client if the client would be likely to react imprudently to an immediate communication. The lawyer must not, however, withhold information to serve the lawyer's or a third person's interest or convenience. [ABA Model Rule 1.4, comment 7]

EXAMPLE

Defendants D and E were charged with the felony murder of X, and they were granted separate trials. In the depths of despondency, D vowed to take his own life if E was convicted. That same day, E was convicted. D's lawyer may withhold that information from D until D is able to react to it more rationally.

a.   **Court Rule or Order**

A court rule or order may forbid a lawyer from sharing certain informa-tion with a client, and the lawyer must comply with such a rule or order. [ABA Model Rule 3.4(c); ABA Model Rule 1.4, comment 7]

EXAMPLE

In a patent infringement case, the patentee's lawyer demanded produc-tion of all of the defendant's laboratory operating manuals. The defendant complied with the demand and gave the patentee's lawyer the manuals. Subsequently, however, the defendant convinced the judge that the manuals contained valuable trade secrets, and the judge therefore issued a protective order forbidding the patentee's lawyer from sharing the information in the manuals with her client. Patentee's lawyer must either obey the order or use appropriate legal means to challenge its validity.

F. CONTRACTS CONCERNING CLIENT-LAWYER RELATIONSHIP

Contracts that concern the relationship between a lawyer and client usually involve fees, but may involve other issues such as the extent of the lawyer's services, the identity of the lawyers who will work on the matter, etc. Such a contract is generally enforceable by either party if it is otherwise lawful (e.g., contains all the required disclosures and does not provide for an unreasonable fee). However, **the client may avoid the contract** in the following circumstances. [Restatement §14]

1. Contract Not Made at Outset

A contract between a lawyer and client, including a modification to an existing contract, is subject to scrutiny if made beyond a reasonable time after the representation begins (e.g., mid-way through the client's case). The rationale is that the client may feel pressured to accept the contract or modification because it is burdensome to change lawyers during a representation. Thus, in this situation, the client may avoid the contract **unless the lawyer shows** that the contract and the circumstances of its formation were **fair and reasonable to the client**.

2. Contract Made After Work Completed

If the contract or modification was made after the lawyer had finished providing services, the client may avoid it if the **client was not informed of facts** needed to evaluate the appropriateness of the lawyer's compensation or other benefits conferred on the lawyer by the contract.

G. TERMINATING THE LAWYER-CLIENT RELATIONSHIP

Once established, the lawyer-client relationship ordinarily continues until the completion of the work for which the lawyer was hired. However, the relationship can end prematurely in any of three ways: (1) the client can **fire** the lawyer; (2) in some situations, the lawyer **must** withdraw; and (3) in some situations, the lawyer **may** withdraw. [*See* Restatement §32]

1. Client Fires Attorney

The client's complete trust is an essential part of any attorney-client relationship. The law thus allows the client to fire the attorney at any time, with or without just cause. Even if the client fires the attorney for no good reason, the client will not be held liable for breach of contract; for policy reasons, courts

construe all attorney employment contracts as being terminable at will by the client. [*See, e.g.,* Fracasse v. Brent, 6 Cal. 3d 784 (1972)]

a. Client's Liability for Fees

When the client fires the attorney, the client is liable to the attorney in quantum meruit (an equitable action to avoid unjust enrichment) for the reasonable value of the work the attorney did before being fired. If the contract between the attorney and client provides for a flat fee or a maximum fee, that constitutes a ceiling on the quantum meruit recovery. [*See* Rosenberg v. Levin, 409 So. 2d 1016 (Fla. 1982)] That is, the attorney cannot recover **more** than was provided for by express contract.

b. Contingent Fee Cases

When a client hires a lawyer on a contingent fee basis, and then fires the lawyer before the case is over, the lawyer is still entitled to quantum meruit recovery for the reasonable value of the work done before the firing. However, the lawyer's claim does not arise until the contingency comes to pass. [*Id.*]

EXAMPLE

Lawyer L agreed to represent plaintiff P in a personal injury case. L agreed to do the work for 40% of P's recovery, but not more than $10,000. After L spent hundreds of hours preparing the case for trial, P fired L for no apparent reason. Then P settled the case for $40,000. Before the settlement, L had no claim against P because the contingency had not come to pass. After the settlement, L is entitled to the reasonable value of his services, but not more than $10,000 (the maximum set in the contract).

---

2. Court Permission to Substitute Attorneys

After a lawsuit has been filed, the rules of most courts require the court's permission for a substitution of attorneys. When a party wants to fire her attorney, courts almost always grant the necessary permission, but permission may be denied if a substitution of attorneys would cause undue delay or disruption. [*See, e.g.,* Ruskin v. Rodgers, 399 N.E.2d 623 (Ill. 1979)—permission denied when client tried to fire attorney without cause two days before date set for trial] On the other hand, when an attorney seeks to withdraw from a case, the court may deny the necessary permission; in that event, the attorney must continue the representation, even if there is good cause for withdrawal. [ABA Model Rule 1.16(c)]

3. Mandatory Withdrawal

a. Disability

An attorney **must** withdraw if the attorney's mental or physical condition materially impairs the attorney's ability to continue representing the client. [ABA Model Rule 1.16(a)(2)]

b.   **Illegality or Ethical Violation**

If to continue with the representation will require the attorney to violate a law or a disciplinary rule, the attorney *must* withdraw. [ABA Model Rule 1.16(a)(1)]

> EXAMPLE
>
> Attorney A agreed to represent client C in a slander suit against D. At the outset, A believed in good faith that C had a sound claim against D. Discovery later showed not a shred of evidence to support C's contentions. C finally confessed to A that she was maintaining the suit simply to harass and injure D. A must withdraw because to continue would require him to violate the disciplinary rule against frivolous litigation. [ABA Model Rule 3.1]

4.   **Permissive Withdrawal**

An attorney *may* withdraw from representing a client *for any reason* if it can be done without material adverse effect on the client's interests or if the client consents. [ABA Model Rule 1.16(b)(1)] In addition, the attorney may withdraw despite an adverse impact on the client's interests in the situations listed below, provided the circumstances are severe enough to justify harming the client's interests. [*See* Restatement §32]

a.   **Client Persists in Criminal or Fraudulent Conduct**

A lawyer *may* withdraw from representing a client if the client persists in a course of action that involves the lawyer's services and that the lawyer *reasonably believes* is criminal or fraudulent. [ABA Model Rule 1.16(b)(2)] Note that if the client's criminal or fraudulent conduct involves some assistance by the lawyer, then the lawyer *must* withdraw. [ABA Model Rules 1.16(a)(1), 1.2(d)]

b.   **Client Has Used Attorney's Services to Commit Past Crime or Fraud**

An attorney *may* withdraw from representing a client if the client has used the attorney's services to commit a past crime or fraud. [ABA Model Rule 1.16(b)(3)]

c.   **Client's Objective Is Repugnant or Against Lawyer's Beliefs**

An attorney *may* withdraw from representing a client if the client insists on taking action that the attorney considers to be repugnant or with which the lawyer has a fundamental disagreement. [ABA Model Rule 1.16(b)(4)]

d.   **Client Breaks Promise to Attorney**

An attorney *may* withdraw from representing a client if the client

substantially fails to fulfill an obligation to the attorney and has been warned that the attorney will withdraw unless it is fulfilled (for instance, client refuses to pay attorney's fee, or refuses to appear for scheduled hearings despite promises to attorney). [ABA Model Rule 1.16(b)(5)]

e. Financial Hardship for Attorney
An attorney *may* withdraw from representing a client if to continue the representation will impose an unreasonable financial burden on the attorney. [ABA Model Rule 1.16(b)(6)]

f. Client Will Not Cooperate
An attorney *may* withdraw from representing a client if the client has made the attorney's work unreasonably difficult (e.g., where the client refuses to cooperate with the attorney in discovery proceedings). [*Id.*]

g. Other Good Cause
An attorney *may* withdraw if there is other good cause for withdrawal. [ABA Model Rule 1.16(b)(7)]

5. Attorney's Duties Upon Termination of Representation
An attorney who withdraws from a matter must comply with local laws that require notice to or permission of the tribunal before withdrawal. [ABA Model Rule 1.16(c)] Moreover, upon termination of the representation, the attorney must take reasonable steps to protect the client's interests, including:

a. Providing the client with *reasonable notice* of the withdrawal;

b. Providing the client with *time* to obtain another attorney;

c. *Refunding attorneys' fees* paid in advance and not yet earned and expense advances not yet spent; and

d. *Returning all papers and property* to which the client is entitled.

[ABA Model Rule 1.16(d)]

EXAMPLES
1) Lawyer L decided to withdraw from representing client C in a workers' compensation case because C repeatedly failed to comply with the adversary's legitimate discovery requests, repeatedly failed to show up to have his deposition taken, and deliberately refused to make the monthly fee payments that he had promised to L. C asked L to turn the case files over to C's new lawyer, but L refused to do so until his past due fees had been paid. The law of L's state (following the better view) does not allow a lawyer to hold case files hostage to compel payment of legal fees. [*See* Academy of California Optometrists, Inc. v. Superior Court, 51 Cal. App. 3d 999 (1975)] L is subject to discipline.

2) Attorney A was retained to represent client C in a divorce case. With C's consent, C's parents paid A $1,000 as an advance on attorneys' fees not yet earned. The parents understood that they could not attempt to influence A's judgment about how to handle C's case. (*See* IV.C.8., *infra*.) C then departed for parts unknown, making it impossible for A to pursue the divorce case. The parents would now like to have their $1,000 back, and A would like to withdraw from the matter. In these circumstances, it is proper for A to withdraw and to refund the fee advance to C's parents. [New York City Bar Op. 83-62 (1983)]

III. CLIENT CONFIDENTIALITY

A. **GENERAL RULE**

As a general rule, a lawyer must not reveal any information relating to the representation of the client. A lawyer may, however, reveal such information if the client gives **informed consent**, or if the disclosure is **impliedly authorized** to carry out the representation. [ABA Model Rule 1.6] The ethical duty is subject to some additional exceptions, discussed in D., *infra*. The rationale of the ethical duty is that it encourages candor between the lawyer and the client, encourages the client to seek early legal advice, and helps the lawyer discover all of the information relevant to the client's legal problem. [*See* ABA Model Rule 1.6, comment 2; with respect to the ethical duty of confidentiality, *see generally* Restatement §§59 - 67]

B. **RELATIONSHIP BETWEEN ETHICAL DUTY OF CONFIDENTIALITY AND ATTORNEY-CLIENT PRIVILEGE**

The ethical duty of confidentiality is closely related to the attorney-client privilege, but the two doctrines differ in three important ways.

1. **Compulsion vs. Gossip**

The **attorney-client privilege** is an exclusionary rule of evidence law. It prevents a court, or other governmental tribunal, from using the twin powers of subpoena and contempt to compel the revelation of confidential communications between an attorney and a client. In contrast, the **ethical duty of confidentiality** prohibits an attorney from **voluntarily** revealing information relating to the representation of a client—it applies in every context where the attorney-client privilege does not apply. [*See* ABA Model Rule 1.6, comment 3]

EXAMPLES

1) During the course of a civil trial, lawyer L's adversary called her to the witness stand and posed questions about her confidential communications with her client. In this context, the rights and duties of L and her client are governed by the attorney-client privilege, not by the ethical duty of confidentiality.

2) When lawyer L was chatting with a friend at a cocktail party, the friend asked L for some information that L had gained in the course of representing one of her clients. In this context, the attorney-client privilege is irrelevant—the

privilege does not apply at cocktail parties. Here, L is governed by the ethical duty of confidentiality.

2. **Kinds of Information Covered**

The ethical duty of confidentiality covers *more* kinds of information than the attorney-client privilege. The attorney-client privilege protects only *confidential communications* between the attorney and client (or the agents of either of them). The ethical duty, in contrast, covers not only confidential communications, but also *any other information* that the attorney obtains relating to the representation of the client, no matter what the source of that information. The ethical duty thus applies to *all* information that relates to the representation of the client, regardless of whether it is privileged, whether the client asked for it to be kept in confidence, and whether revealing it might harm or embarrass the client. For purposes of this outline, the term "confidential information" means all information protected by the duty of confidentiality expressed in ABA Model Rule 1.6.

EXAMPLE

Attorney A is representing client C in proceedings to challenge the will left by C's mother. While conducting her own investigation of the facts of the case, A learns from a third party that C is the illegitimate son of an itinerant book salesman. This information is not protected by the attorney-client privilege because A did not gain it through a confidential communication with C. Nevertheless, under ABA Model Rule 1.6, the information is covered by the ethical duty of confidentiality.

3. **Disclosure vs. Use**

The attorney-client privilege concerns only the disclosure of information. In contrast, the ethical duty of confidentiality concerns both the disclosure and use of information. An attorney can be disciplined for *disclosing* a client's confidential information without the client's informed consent (unless one of the exceptions to the ethical duty is applicable) [ABA Model Rule 1.6(a)], or for *using* confidential information to the disadvantage of a client, former client, or prospective client, without the affected client's informed consent. [ABA Model Rules 1.8(b), 1.9(c), 1.18(b)]

C. **SUMMARY OF ATTORNEY-CLIENT PRIVILEGE**

Because the ethical duty of confidentiality is so closely related to the attorney-client privilege, the following is a brief summary of the main features of the privilege. [*See* Restatement §§68 - 86—restates the law of attorney-client privilege]

1. **Basic Rule**

The attorney-client privilege prohibits a court or other governmental tribunal from compelling the revelation of confidential communications between an

attorney (or an attorney's agent) and a client (or a client's agent) if the subject of the communication concerns the professional relationship between the attorney and the client.

2. **Client**

A "client" means a person or entity that seeks legal services from an attorney. The privilege covers preliminary communications leading up to an attorney-client relationship, even if no such relationship develops. [*See also* ABA Model Rule 1.18—duty of confidentiality to a prospective client]

EXAMPLE

H wants to hire a lawyer to obtain a dissolution of his marriage. After speaking in confidence with lawyer L about his marital problems, H decides not to hire L as his lawyer. Even though no attorney-client relationship ultimately develops between H and L, the attorney-client privilege protects what H told L in confidence.

---

a. **Corporate Clients**

When the client is a corporation, the privilege covers communications between the lawyer and a high-ranking corporate official. It also covers communications between the lawyer and another corporate employee if the following conditions are met:

1) The employee communicates with the lawyer **at the direction of the employee's superior**;

2) The employee knows that the **purpose of the communication is to obtain legal advice for the corporation**; and

3) The communication concerns a **subject within the scope of the employee's duties to act** for the corporation.

[*See* Upjohn Co. v. United States, 449 U.S. 383 (1981)]

3. **Attorney**

An "attorney" means a person who is authorized (or whom the client reasonably believes to be authorized) to practice law in any state or nation. However, for the privilege to apply, the attorney must be acting as an attorney—not in some other capacity, such as a friend, business advisor, or member of the family.

4. **Communication**

The term "communication" covers information passed from the client to the attorney and from the attorney to the client. It also covers information passed to or from the agents of either the attorney or the client.

> **EXAMPLE**
> Whitney Corp. hires attorney A to represent it in a dispute over the construction of a nuclear power plant. A hires structural engineer E to assist her on the technical aspects of the case. At A's direction, E talks with F, the chief engineer of Whitney Corp., to find out certain facts about the case. E's discussion with F is covered by the attorney-client privilege.

a. Mechanical Details of Relationship

Usually the attorney-client privilege does not cover the mechanical details of the attorney-client relationship, such as the identity of the client, the fee arrangement between the attorney and client, and the bare fact that the attorney is acting for the client. But these mechanical details can be protected by the privilege if revealing them is tantamount to revealing a privileged communication. [See Christopher Mueller & Laird Kirkpatrick, Evidence §5.19 (6d ed. 2018)]

> **EXAMPLE**
> X came to lawyer L's office and asked to employ L in a confidential matter. X then said that he was the hit and run driver in the car wreck reported on the front page of today's newspaper. X asked L to negotiate with the authorities for him, but not to reveal his identity without first getting X's specific permission. Later, the parents of the victim in the hit and run brought a wrongful death action against a John Doe defendant. They subpoenaed L and asked her to reveal the identity of the person who had consulted her about the hit and run. A court cannot compel L to disclose X's identity; the attorney-client privilege protects it because to reveal it would be tantamount to revealing X's statement that he was the hit and run driver. [See Baltes v. Doe I, 4 ABA/BNA Lawyer's Manual on Professional Conduct 356]

b. Preexisting Documents and Things

The attorney-client privilege covers both oral and written communications. However, the client cannot protect a preexisting document or thing from discovery simply by turning it over to the attorney. If the document or thing would be discoverable in the client's hands, it is equally discoverable in the attorney's hands.

> **EXAMPLES**
> 1) Client C hires attorney A to defend her in a breach of contract case. C turns over to A her entire file of records relating to the contract. If the records would be discoverable when in the possession of C, they are equally discoverable when in the possession of A.

2) D tells his lawyer, L: "I just shot X, and I threw the revolver in the trash-can behind my apartment." The revolver itself is not privileged, but D's communication with L about the revolver is privileged. [California v. Meredith, 29 Cal. 3d 682 (1981)] L's knowledge of the whereabouts of the revolver is privileged. If L simply looks in the trashcan to confirm D's story, D can invoke the privilege and prevent L from testifying about what he saw. [*Id.*] L has no legal or ethical duty to retrieve the revolver from the trash-can. Furthermore, absent D's informed consent, L must not tell anyone where the revolver is. [ABA Model Rule 1.6] If L retrieves the revolver from the trashcan, he may keep it long enough to obtain from it any information that may be useful in D's defense. Then L must turn it over to the proper authorities. [California v. Meredith, *supra;* State v. Olwell, 394 P.2d 681 (Wash. 1964)] By removing the revolver from the trashcan, L has destroyed a valuable piece of evidence—the incriminating **location** of the revolver. L's action requires a compromise between the need to protect privileged communications and the need for relevant evidence. The compromise reached in *Meredith* and *Olwell* is as follows: The trier of fact will be told where the revolver was found, but the trier of fact will not be told that L was the source of that information. For example, L and the prosecutor can simply stipulate that the jury at D's trial will be informed of the location of the revolver, without telling them the source of that information. However, if L retrieves the revolver from the trashcan and hides or destroys it, L may face criminal liability for tampering with evidence, and L is also subject to professional discipline. [*In re* Ryder, 263 F. Supp. 360 (E.D. Va. 1967)]

5. **"Confidential" Defined**

To be covered by the attorney-client privilege, a communication must be "confidential"; it must have been made by a means not intended to disclose the communicated information to outsiders, and the communicating person must reasonably believe that no outsider will hear the contents of the statement.

a. **Presence of Third Party**

The presence of a third party will not destroy the confidentiality *if* the third party was present to help further the attorney-client relationship. However, the third party need not play a direct role in the communication and may be present because of the client's psychological needs (e.g., a family member accompanying the client). [Restatement §70, comment f]

EXAMPLE

Five persons were present during an office conference between Client and Attorney. In addition to Client and Attorney, the persons present were Client's accountant (who was there to help explain Client's books of

account), Attorney's law clerk (who was there to assist Attorney in drafting some interrogatory answers), and Attorney's legal secretary (who was there to take dictation). The presence of the accountant, the law clerk, and the secretary does not destroy the confidentiality.

COMPARE

During a recess in trial, Attorney and Client discussed Client's intended testimony in a crowded courthouse corridor where bystanders could obviously overhear. This conversation is not confidential for purposes of the attorney-client privilege. Thus, the privilege does not bar examination of either Client or Attorney regarding the conversation.

b. Eavesdroppers

In days gone by, the presence of an unsuspected eavesdropper was sometimes held to destroy the confidentiality of a communication. Under modern evidence law, that is no longer true; an eavesdropper can be prohibited from testifying about a confidential communication.

6. Client Is Holder of Privilege

The attorney-client privilege exists for the benefit of the client, not for the benefit of the attorney. Therefore, the client is the "holder" of the privilege—i.e., the client is the one who can claim or waive the privilege.

a. Waiver of Privilege

A waiver consists of a failure to claim the privilege when there is an opportunity to do so, or the intentional revelation of a significant portion of the privileged communication.

EXAMPLE

Client C shows his next-door neighbor the first two pages of a three-page privileged letter. In a later civil case, C's adversary can compel production of the entire letter. C has waived the privilege.

1) Client Puts Legal Services at Issue

The client may also waive the privilege by asserting a claim or defense that puts the legal services at issue in the case. For example, where a defendant appeals a criminal conviction on the basis of ineffective assistance of counsel at trial, the communications between the defendant and the trial attorney are not privileged. [Restatement §80]

b. Lawyer's Duty to Invoke Privilege

If the client has not waived the privilege, and if someone tries to obtain privileged information when the client is not present, the lawyer must claim the privilege on the client's behalf.

EXAMPLE

Lawyer L represents client C in a civil case. On a day when C is not present in court, C's adversary calls L to the witness stand and poses questions about confidential communications between C and L. L must claim the privilege on C's behalf.

---

7. **Duration of Privilege**

    The attorney-client privilege continues indefinitely. Termination of the relationship, even for cause, does not terminate the privilege. The privilege even survives the death of the client. [Swidler & Berlin v. United States, 524 U.S. 399 (1998)] Thus, a lawyer has a continuing obligation to assert the privilege on behalf of a client who has died, subject to exceptions relating to the deceased's disposition of property. [Restatement §77, comment c]

8. **Exceptions to Privilege**

    Modern evidence law provides several **exceptions** to the attorney-client privilege.

    a. The privilege does not apply if the client seeks the attorney's services **to engage in or assist a future crime or fraud**. [See Restatement §82]

    b. The privilege does not apply to a communication that is **relevant to an issue of breach** (by either the attorney or the client) **of the duties arising out of the attorney-client relationship**. [Id. §83]

    c. The privilege does not apply **in civil litigation between two persons who were formerly the joint clients of the attorney**. [Id. §75(2)]

    d. The privilege does not apply in a variety of situations in which the attorney can furnish evidence about the **competency or intention of a client who has attempted to dispose of property by will or inter vivos transfer**.

9. **Related Doctrine of Work Product Immunity**

    Generally, material prepared by a lawyer for litigation or in anticipation of litigation is immune from discovery or other compelled disclosure unless the opposition shows a substantial need for the material and an inability to gather the material without undue hardship. A lawyer's mental impressions or opinions are immune from discovery or compelled disclosure regardless of the opposition's need unless the immunity has been waived. [See Restatement §§87 - 93]

D. ETHICAL DUTY OF CONFIDENTIALITY AND ITS EXCEPTIONS

As explained previously (*see* B.1., *supra*), the ethical duty of confidentiality applies in every context in which the attorney-client privilege does not apply. The ethical duty also covers a broader range of information than the privilege. Finally, the ethical duty concerns not only the disclosure of information, but also the use of information to the disadvantage of a client, a prospective client, or a former client.

1. Duty Not Destroyed by Presence of Third Party

Unlike the attorney-client privilege, the presence of a nonprivileged third person does not necessarily destroy an attorney's duty of confidentiality. Confidential information remains confidential even if it is known to others, **unless the information becomes generally known**. Whether information is generally known depends on all the surrounding circumstances, but information is **not generally known** when it can be obtained only by means of **special knowledge or substantial difficulty or expense**.

2. Exceptions to the Duty of Confidentiality

The **exceptions** to the ethical duty are discussed separately in the following paragraphs.

a. Client's Informed Consent

An attorney may reveal or use confidential information if the client gives informed consent. [ABA Model Rule 1.6(a)] Remember that "informed consent" means that the client agrees to a proposed course of action after the lawyer has adequately explained the risks and reasonable alternatives. [ABA Model Rule 1.0(e)]

EXAMPLE
Attorney A is representing defendant D in an armed robbery case. D reluctantly tells A that at the time of the alleged robbery, D was 10 miles away visiting a house of prostitution, and that at least five witnesses can vouch for his presence there. A may disclose and use this embarrassing information in the defense of the armed robbery case if D gives informed consent.

b. Implied Authority

An attorney has implied authority from the client to use or disclose confidential information when appropriate to carry out the representation—unless, of course, the client gives specific instructions to the contrary. [ABA Model Rule 1.6(a)]

EXAMPLES
1) Lawyer L represents client A in negotiating a construction contract.

Unless A instructs L to the contrary, L has implied authority to disclose confidential information about A's business if that will serve A's interests in the negotiation. [ABA Model Rule 1.6, comment 5]

2) Lawyer M represents client B in litigation. Unless B instructs M to the contrary, M has implied authority to disclose confidential information in a fact stipulation if that will serve B's interests in the litigation. [*Id.*]

3) Lawyer N is drawing up a will and a trust agreement for client C. Unless C instructs N to the contrary, N has implied authority to discuss C's confidential information with other lawyers in N's firm if that will serve C's interests. [*Id.*]

4) Lawyer O is representing client D in a bankruptcy case. Unless D instructs O to the contrary, O has implied authority to allow her paralegal, her law clerk, her legal secretary, and the law firm's copy-machine operator to have access to D's confidential business papers. However, O must take reasonable steps to assure that those employees preserve the confidentiality of the information. [ABA Model Rule 5.3; ABA Formal Op. 95-398 (1995)]

5) Lawyer Q is representing X Corp. in secret merger negotiations with Y Corp. Secrecy is vital because if word leaks out, the stock prices of the two companies will move apart, making the merger impossible. On one knotty issue, Q seeks the informal, uncompensated advice of his friend, lawyer R, a merger expert in a different law firm. Q poses the issue to R in the form of a hypothetical that does not identify either X Corp. or Y Corp. by name. Unfortunately, Q is careless in posing the hypothetical, which allows R to deduce the identities of X Corp. and Y Corp. Q is subject to discipline for breaching the duty of confidentiality. A lawyer may use a hypothetical to obtain advice from a fellow lawyer for the benefit of the client, but the hypothetical must be discreet enough to preclude any reasonable chance that the fellow lawyer will be able to deduce the identity of the client or the situation at hand. [ABA Model Rule 1.6, comment 4; ABA Formal Op. 98-411]

c. **Disclosure to Prevent Death or Substantial Bodily Harm**
ABA Model Rule 1.6(b)(1) permits a lawyer to reveal the client's confidential information to the extent that the lawyer reasonably believes necessary to prevent *reasonably certain death or substantial bodily harm*. Note that the exception applies to death or bodily harm whatever the cause; it need not be caused by the client, and the cause need not be a criminal act. Notice also that the death or bodily harm need not be imminent—it need only be reasonably certain. Finally, notice that the exception gives the lawyer *discretion* to disclose the confidential

information; it does **not require** disclosure. Some states, however, do require disclosure.

EXAMPLES

1) Kidnapper K is in custody pending trial, and he hires attorney A to defend him against a charge that he kidnapped and murdered victim V. K tells A in confidence where he buried V's body. This is a completed crime—disclosure of K's secret could not prevent death or substantial bodily harm to anyone. If A reveals K's secret, A will be subject to discipline.

2) Kidnapper J telephones attorney B and asks for B's legal advice. J tells B in confidence that he has kidnapped victim U, that he has her bound and gagged in the back of his van, and that he is on the road to Lonesome Pine, where he plans to hold U for ransom. The legal advice J seeks from B is whether the penalty for murder is more serious than the penalty for kidnapping for ransom. B promises to call J back in a few minutes. B then telephones the police, tells them the situation, and tells them that J is on the road to Lonesome Pine. B's conduct is proper in light of the reasonably certain risk of death or substantial bodily injury to U.

---

d. **Disclosure to Prevent or Mitigate Substantial Financial Harm**
A lawyer may reveal the client's confidential information to the extent necessary to prevent the client from committing a crime or fraud that is reasonably certain to result in **substantial financial harm** to someone, if the client is using or has used the lawyer's services in the matter. The same is true if the client has already acted, and the lawyer's disclosure can prevent or mitigate the consequent financial harm. [See Restatement §67; ABA Model Rule 1.6(b)(2), (3)]

e. **Dispute Concerning Attorney's Conduct**
An attorney may reveal a client's confidential information to the extent necessary to protect the attorney's interests in a dispute that involves the conduct of the attorney. [ABA Model Rule 1.6(b)(5)] In using this exception, the attorney should: (1) reveal only what is necessary, (2) attempt to limit the disclosure to those who need to know it, and (3) obtain protective orders or take other steps to minimize the risk of unnecessary harm to the client. [ABA Model Rule 1.6, comment 14]

EXAMPLES

1) Attorney A represented client C in a child custody case. C told A in confidence about C's emotional difficulties, alcoholism, and inability to hold steady employment. These confidential disclosures made the task of representing C vastly more difficult and time-consuming than A had

originally anticipated. C ultimately lost the child custody case. C then refused to pay A's legal fee, claiming that it was unreasonably high. If A is unable to settle the fee dispute amicably and has to sue C to collect the fee, A may reveal C's confidential disclosures to the extent necessary to prove why A's fee is reasonable under the circumstances. [ABA Model Rule 1.6(b)(5)]

2) Lawyer L defended client D in an arson case. D told L in confidence that he did burn the building, hoping to collect the fire insurance. After careful consideration, D followed L's advice and did not testify on his own behalf at the trial. Furthermore, L refused to call two alibi witnesses whose testimony L knew would be false. D was convicted. D then sued L for legal malpractice. In defending against D's malpractice claim, L may reveal as much of D's confidential disclosures as is necessary to prove why L did not present the testimony of D and the two alibi witnesses. [*Id.*]

3) In the arson example described above, instead of suing L for malpractice, D filed a complaint with the state bar, accusing L of incompetence in the conduct of the trial. At the disciplinary hearing, L may reveal as much of D's confidential disclosures as is necessary to prove why L did not present the testimony of D and the two alibi witnesses. [*Id.*]

4) Client T hired attorney Y to help him form a limited partnership venture for real estate investments. T furnished Y with confidential data for Y to use in preparing financial statements and other documents needed in connection with the sale of the partnership shares. Unbeknownst to Y, some of the confidential data was fraudulent, and T's partners lost their investments as a consequence. Two of the partners confronted Y and accused him of being knowingly involved in the fraud. Y *may* reveal enough of T's confidential information to convince the partners that Y did not know that the data was fraudulent, even though Y has not yet been formally charged with a criminal or civil wrong or a disciplinary violation. [*See* ABA Model Rule 1.6, comment 10] This illustrates the doctrine called "preemptive self-defense." [*See* Hazard & Hodes, §10.37]

f.   **Disclosure to Obtain Legal Ethics Advice**
A lawyer may disclose enough of the client's confidential information as is necessary to obtain legal ethics advice for the lawyer. [ABA Model Rule 1.6(b)(4)]

EXAMPLE
Client C came to attorney A's office carrying a mysterious package about the size of a shoebox. C explained that federal narcotics agents were looking for C in connection with the illegal importation of a significant quantity of uncut heroin; C told A that he had no connection with any

heroin or any other drug trade. A agreed to represent C, and he asked C for a $5,000 advance on attorneys' fees. C replied that he had no ready cash, but that he would entrust A with the mysterious package, assuring A that its contents were worth much more than $5,000. A was uncertain about his ethical obligations in this situation so he excused himself, went to another room, and telephoned T, his old legal ethics professor. After disclosing enough facts to give T the essence of the problem—but not enough to disclose C's identity or the precise circumstances—A asked T for legal ethics advice. A's disclosure was proper. [*Id.*]

g. **Disclosure to Detect and Resolve Conflicts of Interest**
    When a lawyer changes firms, when two firms merge, or when a law practice is being purchased, lawyers may disclose limited client information (e.g., client names and a brief summary of the general issues involved) in order to detect and resolve conflicts of interest, subject to four conditions: (1) the disclosure may be made only after substantive discussions regarding the new relationship have occurred; (2) the disclosure must be limited to the minimum necessary to detect any conflicts of interest; (3) the disclosed information must not compromise the attorney-client privilege or otherwise prejudice the clients; and (4) the disclosed information may be used only to the extent necessary to detect and resolve any conflicts of interest. [ABA Model Rule 1.6(b)(7) and comments 13 and 14]

h. **Disclosure Required by Law or Court Order**
    ABA Model Rule 1.6(b)(6) permits a lawyer to reveal her client's confidential information to the extent that she is required to do so by law or court order.

EXAMPLES

1) Suppose that a federal anti-terrorism statute arguably requires lawyer L to reveal the whereabouts of client C, who is suspected of illegal entry into the United States. If L knows of C's whereabouts only because of a confidential communication from C, the information is protected by both the attorney-client privilege and the ethical duty of confidentiality. L must first determine whether the anti-terrorism statute purports to supersede the privilege and ethical duty. [*See* ABA Model Rule 1.6, comment 12] If L concludes that it does, she must next disclose the situation to C because this is the kind of vital information that a lawyer must communicate to a client. [*See* ABA Model Rule 1.4(a)(3)] If L cannot find a nonfrivolous ground for challenging the validity or applicability of the statute, ABA Model Rule 1.6(b)(6) permits her to reveal the information about C's whereabouts. [*See* ABA Model Rule 1.6, comments 12 and 13]

2) In the situation described in 1), above, suppose that a federal district judge is considering whether to order L to disclose C's whereabouts. Absent C's informed consent to the disclosure, L should assert all nonfrivolous grounds for not disclosing the information. If the court orders disclosure, L should consult with C about an appeal. If no appeal is taken, or if the order is upheld on appeal, then ABA Model Rule 1.6(b)(6) permits L to reveal the information about C's whereabouts. [*Id.*]

3.   **Protecting Confidential Information**
     A lawyer must make reasonable efforts to protect a client's confidential information from inadvertent or unauthorized disclosure by the lawyer and those under the lawyer's supervision, and from unauthorized access by third parties. [ABA Model Rule 1.6(c)] The reasonableness of the lawyer's efforts is determined by considering such factors as the sensitivity of the client's information, the cost of additional safeguards, and the difficulty of implementing the safeguards. [ABA Model Rule 1.6, comment 18]

IV.   CONFLICTS OF INTEREST

A.   **THE GENERAL RULES CONCERNING CONFLICTS OF INTEREST**
     Loyalty is an essential element in the relationship between a lawyer and client. The lawyer's professional judgment must be exercised solely for the benefit of the client, free of compromising influences and loyalties. [*See* Restatement §§121 - 135—restates the law of conflicts of interest; *see also* ABA Model Rule 1.7, comment 1] Thus, **absent the necessary informed consent** (*see* B.2., *infra*), a lawyer must not represent a client if a conflict of interest exists.

1.   **Consequences of a Conflict of Interest**
     If a conflict of interest is apparent **before** a lawyer takes on a client's matter, then the lawyer must not take it on. [ABA Model Rule 1.7(a)] If a conflict becomes apparent only **after** the lawyer has taken on the client's matter, and if informed consent of the affected client(s) will not solve the problem, then the lawyer must withdraw. [ABA Model Rule 1.16(a)(1); ABA Model Rule 1.7, comment 4] A lawyer's failure to handle a conflict properly can have three unpleasant consequences: (1) disqualification as counsel in a litigated matter, (2) professional discipline, and (3) civil liability for legal malpractice.

2.   **Imputed Conflicts of Interest**
     Generally, lawyers who practice together in a "firm" are treated as a single unit for conflict of interest purposes. That is, when one of the lawyers cannot take on a matter because of a conflict of interest, the other lawyers in the "firm" are also barred from taking on that matter. [ABA Model Rule 1.10(a)] The conflict is said to be "imputed" from the first lawyer to the other lawyers.

a. Meaning of "Firm"

The term "firm" includes not only an ordinary private law firm, but also other groups of lawyers who practice closely together, such as lawyers in a corporate law department, legal aid office, or prosecutors' or public defenders' office. [*See* ABA Model Rule 1.0(c) and comments 2 - 4] Whether a group of lawyers should be regarded as a "firm" for conflict of interest purposes depends on many factors, including: (1) do the lawyers have a formal agreement among themselves, (2) do they hold themselves out in a way that would make the public think they practice together as a firm, (3) do they share their revenues and responsibilities, (4) do they have physical access to each other's client files, (5) do they routinely talk among themselves about the matters they are handling, and (6) would the purpose of the particular conflict rule be served by imputing one lawyer's conflict to other lawyers in the group?

b. Exceptions to Imputed Disqualification

1) Conflict Based on Uniquely Personal Interest of Lawyer

As will be seen in the paragraphs below, some kinds of conflicts are **not** imputed to other lawyers in the firm. Generally, these conflicts are uniquely personal to the lawyer in question, which makes it unlikely that other lawyers in the firm would have divided loyalties. [ABA Model Rule 1.10(a) and comment 3]

> **EXAMPLE**
> Client C hires attorney A to defend her in a copyright infringement action. After A takes on C's case, C commences a sexual relationship with lawyer L, who is one of A's law partners. ABA Model Rule 1.8(j) prohibits a lawyer from starting a sexual relationship with a client (*see* C.9., *infra*); therefore, L would be subject to discipline if he himself were defending C in the copyright case. However, L's conflict is uniquely personal to L and is not likely to affect the way L's partner A handles C's case. Thus, L's conflict is not imputed to partner A.

2) Specific Situations Involving Lawyer's Former Dealings— Screening and Notice

As discussed in more detail *infra*, in certain situations involving conflicts based on a lawyer's former employment, or former consultation with a prospective client, the imputation will be cured provided the disqualified lawyer is timely screened from participation in the matter (does not have access to files, etc.) and is apportioned no part of the fee from the matter (apart from their normal salary or partnership share). Written notice of the procedures must

promptly be given to the affected client or person. [ABA Model Rule 1.10(a)(2)]

B. CONFLICTS OF INTEREST—CURRENT CLIENTS

1. Concurrent Conflicts of Interest

Except on the conditions stated in 2., below, a lawyer must not represent a client if the representation creates a concurrent conflict of interest. A concurrent conflict exists in two situations:

a. The representation of one client will be **directly adverse** to another client; or

b. There is a **significant risk** that the representation of one client will be **materially limited** by the lawyer's own interest or by the lawyer's responsibilities to another client, a former client, or a third person.

[ABA Model Rule 1.7(a)]

EXAMPLE

Client C asked attorney A to defend her in a vehicular manslaughter case in which C is charged with killing victim V while driving drunk. Unbeknownst to C, V was A's college roommate, and they remained best friends until V's death. There is a significant risk that A's efforts on C's behalf would be materially limited by A's personal grief at the loss of his best friend. Therefore, A must not take on C's case.

---

2. Informed Consent Can Solve Some Conflicts

Despite a concurrent conflict of interest, a lawyer **may** represent a client if all four of the following conditions are satisfied: (1) the lawyer reasonably believes that he can competently and diligently represent each affected client, despite the conflict of interest; (2) the representation is not prohibited by law; (3) the representation does not involve asserting a claim by one client against another client represented by that lawyer in the same litigation (or other proceeding before a tribunal); and (4) each affected client gives informed consent, confirmed in writing. [ABA Model Rule 1.7(b)]

a. Consent Must Meet Reasonable Lawyer Standard

Notice that the consent rule creates a **reasonable lawyer standard**. That is, if a reasonable lawyer looking at the facts would conclude that the client's interests would not be adequately protected in light of the conflict, then the conflict is **unconsentable**, meaning that the client's consent will not solve the conflict. [*See* ABA Model Rule 1.7, comments 14 and 15; *and see* ABA Formal Op. 05-436]

EXAMPLE

General practitioner G represents husband H in legal matters arising out of the investment of H's inherited fortune. G has represented H for many years, and he knows all of H's innermost secrets, both financial and personal. Now wife W has asked G to represent her in obtaining a divorce from H. In light of all of the confidential information G has learned about H over the years, a reasonable lawyer would have to advise H **not** to consent to the conflict of interest. Thus, even if H did consent, the consent would not solve the conflict.

---

b. **Consent Must Be Informed**

Only *informed* consent will solve a conflict. That means that the affected client is aware of all of the relevant circumstances, reasonable alternatives, and foreseeable ways the conflict might harm her. [*See* ABA Model Rule 1.0(e); ABA Model Rule 1.7, comment 18] Sometimes a lawyer cannot obtain informed consent from one client without revealing a fact that she learned in confidence from another client; if the second client will not permit the lawyer to reveal that confidence, then the lawyer cannot represent the first client; consent will not solve the conflict.

c. **Consent Must Be Confirmed in Writing**

A consent that is merely oral will not solve a conflict. The consent must be "confirmed in writing." Usually that means either of two things: (1) there is a *tangible or electronic record* that is physically or electronically *signed* by the client; or (2) there is an *oral* consent that is *promptly memorialized* in a tangible or electronic record that is promptly sent to the client. [*See* ABA Model Rule 1.0(b), (n); ABA Model Rule 1.7, comment 20] *But note*: The client's consent to an aggregate settlement or a business transaction with the lawyer must be *signed by the client* (*see* C.2.a. and C.7., *infra*). [ABA Model Rule 1.8(a), (g)]

1) **Rationale**

The writing requirement has two purposes: (1) it helps impress on the client that consent to a conflict is a serious matter, and (2) it helps avoid later disputes that might arise if there were no writing.

d. **Must Not Be on Both Sides of Litigation**

Even if the clients consent, a lawyer must not assert a claim on behalf of one client against another client represented by that lawyer in the same litigation (or other proceeding before a tribunal). In other words, the lawyer cannot be on both sides of the same proceeding. However, in a transactional matter, the lawyer may be able to address the conflict and act for both parties.

e. Revocation of Consent

Just as a client can almost always fire a lawyer, the client can almost always revoke a previously given consent to a conflict. [ABA Model Rule 1.7, comment 21] The revocation may or may not mean that the lawyer can continue representing other clients in the matter, depending on the particular facts. [*Id.*]

f. Consent to Future Conflicts

A lawyer may properly ask a client to consent to conflicts that may arise in the future, but only if it is **reasonable** to do so, and only if the client truly understands the particular kinds of conflicts that may arise and the consequences of consenting. [ABA Model Rule 1.7, comment 22; *and see* ABA Formal Op. 05-436]

EXAMPLE

The standard contract that a firm of class action lawyers uses when signing up class representatives provides that: "Client hereby consents to and waives any and all conflicts of interest, both present and future." The contract does not explain the possible present or future conflicts, nor do the lawyers offer any explanation when they sign up the class representatives. The consent provision is invalid.

---

3. **Specific Conflict Situations Concerning "Direct Adversity" Between Clients' Interests**

ABA Model Rule 1.7(a) prohibits a lawyer from representing one client whose interests are **directly adverse** to those of another client, unless both of the affected clients give their informed consent, confirmed in writing. The following examples show the bounds of "direct adversity."

EXAMPLES

1) Lawyer L represents patent owner O in connection with the licensing of O's patent. Manufacturer M is one of O's licensees, but M does not realize that L represents O. M asks L's law partner P to sue O for a declaratory judgment that O's patent is invalid and that O's license agreements are void. Obviously, L herself could not represent M because M's interests are directly adverse to O's interests. L's conflict is imputed to her law partner P. A reasonable lawyer would advise O and M not to consent to this conflict. Moreover, consent will not solve the conflict when one client sues another client represented by the lawyer in the same litigation. [*See* ABA Model Rule 1.7(b)(3)] Therefore, P must not represent M.

2) Attorney A represents GenCorp, a genetic engineering company that is working on a cure for melanoma. A's law partner P represents BioTek, another

genetic engineering company that is working on an entirely different way to cure melanoma. BioTek and GenCorp are head-to-head adversaries in an economic sense, but their interests are not adverse in any legal sense. If A and her partner P can disclose the situation to their respective clients without revealing confidential information, they may do so for the sake of client good-will, but they would not be subject to discipline for failing to do so. [*See* ABA Model Rule 1.7, comment 6]

3) Lawyer L is defending D, who is accused of the armed robbery of a liquor store. L is stunned when he sees the prosecutor's witness list because it includes Z, a purported eyewitness to the armed robbery. L knows Z very well because he is defending Z in a drunk driving case. From confidential informa-tion L gathered in the drunk driving case, L knows that Z is an alcoholic who sometimes sees things that are not there and sometimes remembers things that did not happen. In defending D, L will have to cross-examine Z about his capacity to perceive, remember, and relate events accurately. If L cross-examines Z vigorously, he might seem to be using information about Z that he learned in confidence, or at least Z might think so. On the other hand, if L soft-pedals the cross-examination of Z, D might think he is not getting the effective assistance of counsel. A reasonable lawyer would have to advise D and Z not to consent to this conflict of interest. L must seek the court's permission to withdraw from one case or the other, preferably the case in which his with-drawal will be least harmful to the client. [*See* ABA Model Rule 1.7, comment 6]

4) Attorney A represents client C as plaintiff in an employment discrimination case against Mack's Grill. While that matter is pending, one of A's regular cli-ents, Grinch Rentals, Inc., asks A to represent it in unlawful detainer proceed-ings to have C thrown out of her apartment for failure to pay rent. Even if the two cases are completely unrelated, A faces a conflict of interest. If A agrees to represent Grinch, C could feel betrayed by her own lawyer, and that could destroy A's ability to represent C effectively in the employment discrimination case. [*See* ABA Model Rule 1.7, comment 6] Would the conflict be solved by getting informed consent, confirmed in writing, from both C and Grinch? Com-ment 6 suggests that it could. (Do you agree?)

5) Lawyer L represents buyer B in negotiations for the purchase of a run-down shopping center from seller S. While those negotiations are in progress, S seeks to hire L to represent it in negotiations with the Planning Commission of a different city concerning an urban renewal project S wants to pursue. The shopping center sale is totally unrelated to the urban renewal project. Never-theless, L must not represent S without first getting informed consent, con-firmed in writing, from both B and S. [*See* ABA Model Rule 1.7, comment 7]

a. **Unnamed Members of a Class Do Not Count as Clients**
In class action litigation, the unnamed members of a class ordinarily are

not regarded as clients for purposes of the "direct adversity" conflicts rule. [ABA Model Rule 1.7, comment 25]

EXAMPLE

Lawyer L is presently representing victim V in a medical malpractice case against Dr. D. Today, United Motors Corp. asked L to defend it in a class action case that is unrelated to the malpractice case. V is not a named plaintiff in the class action, but she will be a member of the class if the court eventually certifies the case as a class action. L does not need to obtain V's consent before agreeing to defend United Motors. [*Id.*]

---

4. **Specific Conflict Situations Concerning "Material Limitation"**
    The discussion in 3., above, concerned conflicts caused by "direct adversity" between the interests of two clients. ABA Model Rule 1.7 also covers a second kind of conflict—situations in which there is a **significant risk** that the lawyer's representation of a client will be **materially limited** by the lawyer's own personal interests or by the lawyer's responsibilities to: (1) a different client, (2) a former client, or (3) a third person. [ABA Model Rule 1.7(a)(2)] When there is such a risk, the lawyer must not take on the matter (or must withdraw), unless each affected client gives informed consent, confirmed in writing. Illustrations of these "material limitation" conflicts are discussed in a. through e., below.

    a. **Representing Multiple Clients in the Same Matter**

        1) **Co-Parties in Criminal Litigation**
            The Sixth Amendment guarantees every criminal defen-
            dant the right to effective assistance of counsel. Because the
            interests of criminal co-defendants are very likely to diverge,
            ordinarily a lawyer should not try to defend two people in a
            criminal case. [ABA Model Rule 1.7, comment 23] If a trial judge
            requires two criminal defendants with divergent interests to
            share a single lawyer, and if they are prejudiced as a result, their
            Sixth Amendment rights have been violated. [*See* Strickland v.
            Washington, 466 U.S. 668 (1984); Cuyler v. Sullivan, 446 U.S. 335
            (1980)] Here are four examples of divergent interests:

            a) One defendant seeks to put the blame on the other;

            b) The story told by one defendant is inconsistent with the story
                told by the other;

            c) One defendant has a strong defense that is compromised to
                protect the other; and

            d) The trial tactics that would help one would harm the other.

2) Co-Parties in Civil Litigation

In civil litigation, one lawyer *may* represent multiple plaintiffs or defendants whose interests are potentially in conflict. However, the conflict must be addressed in accordance with 4), below. [*See* ABA Model Rule 1.7, comment 23] The advantages of having a single lawyer are obvious: the cost will probably be lower than having two lawyers, and the single lawyer can present a united front for both clients. The disadvantages are also obvious: the interests of the clients may be mostly harmonious but partly or potentially in conflict (e.g., one personal injury plaintiff may need money badly and may therefore be anxious to accept a joint settlement offer that the other plaintiff thinks is too low).

3) Nonlitigation Matters

Lawyers are often asked to represent more than one client in nonlitigation matters. Whether that creates a conflict of interest depends on many factors, including the length and intimacy of the lawyer's relationship with one or more of the clients, the kind of work the lawyer is asked to do, the chances of disagreement between the clients, and the consequences to the clients if the joint representation breaks down. [*See* ABA Model Rule 1.7, comment 26] If there is a conflict, the lawyer must follow the steps in 4), below.

EXAMPLES

1) Clients X, Y, and Z ask lawyer L to represent the three of them in forming a new business venture. X will supply the capital, Y will supply a valuable trade secret, and Z will supply the managerial skill. Although their interests are mostly harmonious, there are potential conflicts. For instance, if the venture folds, who will own the trade secret? L *may* represent all three clients if she follows the four steps outlined in 4), below.

2) Estate planning attorney E is asked to prepare estate plans and wills for four members of a family—G (the wealthy grandmother), H and W (the irresponsible parents), and D (the talented daughter). All four have the same basic goals: to maximize the family's wealth and to allocate it rationally. However, their interests are potentially in conflict. For instance, H and W may want to get their hands on money that G wants to preserve for D. E *may* represent all of the family members if she follows the four steps outlined in 4), below.

---

4) Handling Multiple Representation Conflicts

In both litigation and nonlitigation matters, there is a four-step guide for handling this situation:

a)   First, the lawyer should **analyze the facts** of the case and the applicable law. If she concludes that she can **effectively represent both clients**, despite their potentially conflicting interests, then she can move to the second step. [*See* ABA Model Rule 1.7, comment 15]

b)   Second, the lawyer should **disclose the potential conflict** to each client and explain how it can harm each client, the reasonably available alternatives, and the disadvantages of having only one lawyer for the two of them (*see* 6), below). [*See* ABA Model Rule 1.7, comment 18]

c)   Third, when the clients fully understand the situation, the lawyer may invite their **informed consent** to the joint representation and **confirm** such consent **in writing**. [*Id.*]

d)   Fourth, **if the potential conflict eventually ripens into a present conflict**, the lawyer must repeat steps a), b), and c), above. The lawyer must withdraw from the joint representation if a reasonable lawyer would have to advise either of the two clients not to consent. [*See* ABA Model Rule 1.7, comments 4, 14, and 15] The lawyer may continue to represent one consenting client, but only if the client who is dropped gives informed consent to the continuation, confirmed in writing. [*See* ABA Model Rule 1.9(a)]

EXAMPLE

Attorney A agreed to defend Ace Corp. and Bay Corp. in a negligence case. At the outset, A believed that neither Ace nor Bay caused the harm to the plaintiff. A went through steps a), b), and c), above, and obtained Ace's and Bay's informed, written consent to the joint representation. Discovery revealed that Ace had a credible defense, but that Bay was very likely negligent, and that its negligence probably harmed the plaintiff. A repeated steps a), b), and c), at which point Ace insisted on obtaining a separate lawyer. A **may** continue representing Bay, but **only if** Ace gives informed consent, confirmed in writing (under ABA Model Rule 1.9(a)), and Bay gives informed consent, confirmed in writing (under ABA Model Rule 1.7(b)).

---

5)   **Special Problems of Representing More than One Client**
A lawyer must be impartial in dealing with the multiple clients. If the relationships among the clients are already antagonistic, or

if contentious negotiations or litigation is on the horizon, a single lawyer ordinarily should not try to represent all of the clients. [ABA Model Rule 1.7, comment 29]

a) Confidentiality and Privilege Problems

In litigation between two people who were formerly joint clients of a single lawyer, neither of them can claim the attorney-client privilege for their communications with that lawyer. [*See* Restatement §75] That is one disadvantage of having one lawyer for multiple clients, and the lawyer should warn the clients about it before undertaking multiple representation. Moreover, a multiple representation is unlikely to work if one client wants to disclose material to the lawyer in confidence and wants to keep it confidential from the other clients. [ABA Model Rule 1.7, comment 31] Therefore, the lawyer should ordinarily make clear to all clients at the outset that whatever one client discloses will be shared with all of the other clients. [*Id.*] In special situations, however, the clients may agree that one of them may disclose a given item of information to the lawyer but not to the other clients.

EXAMPLE

Clients X, Y, and Z hire attorney A to represent all of them in forming a new business venture. Z's contribution to the business will be a valuable invention. Z has applied for a patent, but until a patent issues, the specifics of the invention are protected as Z's trade secret. X, Y, and Z may agree that Z may disclose the specifics of the invention to A in confidence and that A will not share that information with X or Y.

---

b. Representing Two Clients with Inconsistent Legal Positions in Two Unrelated Cases

Suppose a lawyer represents two clients in different cases that are pending in different tribunals. On behalf of Client One, the lawyer needs to argue that a certain statute is unconstitutional. On behalf of Client Two, the lawyer needs to argue that the same statute is constitutional. Aside from that legal issue, the cases are unrelated. On those bare facts, there is no conflict of interest between Client One and Client Two. [ABA Model Rule 1.7, comment 24] Suppose, however, that Client One's case will be heard next week in the intermediate appellate court that hears cases from Judicial District Six. Client Two's case will be tried seven months from now in a trial court in Judicial District Six. Thus, the appellate court's decision in Client One's case is likely to become the controlling precedent in Client Two's case. That presents a substantial risk that the lawyer's representation of one client will be materially limited by her responsibilities to the other client. [*Id.*] Therefore, the lawyer must fully disclose the situation to both clients and seek their informed consent, confirmed in writing. If either or both clients will not consent, the lawyer must seek the court's permission to withdraw from one or both cases. [*Id.*]

c. **Conflicts Caused by Lawyer's Own Interests**
    If a lawyer's own interests are likely to materially limit her ability to represent a client effectively, then she must not take on the matter (or she must withdraw) unless she obtains the client's informed consent, confirmed in writing. [*See* ABA Model Rule 1.7(a)(2)] The following paragraphs illustrate some of the lawyer's interests that may create a conflict. Additionally, note that there is a specific conflicts rule regarding sexual relationships with clients (*see* C.9., *infra*).

    1) **Lawyer's Financial Interest**
        A conflict of interest may be created by a lawyer's own financial interest. Suppose that attorney A is representing client C in a gender discrimination action against Magnum Corp. After one of the pretrial hearings, the general counsel of Magnum spoke quietly to A in the courthouse hallway, saying: "Your courtroom skills are first-rate. When you want to start playing in the big leagues, please come to see me—our law department could really use a person like you, and we pay top money." If the employment overture creates a substantial risk that A will curry favor with Magnum at C's expense, A must fully disclose the situation to C and obtain C's informed consent, confirmed in writing, before continuing as C's counsel.

    2) **Lawyers Who Are Close Relatives**
        A conflict of interest also may be created by a lawyer's relationship to another lawyer. Suppose that lawyer L is a partner in the J, K, & L firm. L lives with her parents, and her mother M is the senior litigation partner of the M, N, & O firm. M regularly serves as trial counsel for the Kansas Central Railway Co. in railway accident cases. L's regular client C was badly injured when his car was struck at a crossing by one of Kansas Central's trains, and C asked L to represent him in a suit against Kansas Central. If L serves as C's lawyer, and M serves as Kansas Central's lawyer, there is a risk that client confidences may be compromised (e.g., if M takes a telephone message at home for L, M may inadvertently learn something confidential about C). [ABA Model Rule 1.7, comment 11] Moreover, the family relationship may interfere with the loyalty or independent judgment of the two lawyers. [*Id.*] Thus, L and M must each disclose the situation to their respective clients and must

not proceed without their respective client's informed consent, confirmed in writing. The same is true of other lawyers who are closely related by blood or marriage (e.g., parent, child, spouse, or sibling). This kind of conflict is personal in nature and is ordinarily **not** imputed to other lawyers in a firm. [*Id.*]

d. **Conflict Between Client's Interest and Third Person's Interest**
Sometimes the interest of a third person may create a substantial risk of materially limiting the lawyer's ability to represent the client effectively. [ABA Model Rule 1.7(a)(2)] When that is true, the lawyer may represent the client, provided that: (1) the lawyer reasonably believes that the third person's interest will not adversely affect the representation; and (2) the client gives informed consent, confirmed in writing. [ABA Model Rule 1.7(b)]

EXAMPLES

1) Carter Corp. and its executive vice president K were indicted for mail fraud in connection with the interstate sale of certain investment properties. The bylaws of Carter Corp. provide that the corporation will pay for separate legal representation of any officer accused of wrongdoing in the course of the corporation's business; however, there is no provision for indemnifying officers who are found guilty of wrongdoing. Carter Corp. asks lawyer L to provide the necessary separate representation for K. L's fee will be paid by Carter Corp. L may represent K if: (1) the arrangement between Carter Corp. and L assures L's independence, (2) L reasonably believes that he can represent K effectively, and (3) K gives informed consent, confirmed in writing.

2) The United Coastal Charities Fund offers to pay attorney A's fee for drafting the will of any person who leaves a bequest of $2,000 or more to the Fund. If A agrees to the arrangement, he will be subject to discipline. [New York City Bar Op. 81-69 (1981)]

3) Lawyer L is a staff attorney for the County Legal Aid Society. Her salary is set by the board of directors of the Society, but her clients are those who come to the Society for legal assistance and are assigned to L. The board of directors may set general operating policies, but L must not allow the board of directors to influence her independent legal judgment about how to handle a particular client's legal matter. [ABA Model Rule 5.4(c); ABA Formal Op. 334 (1974)]

---

e. **Conflicts Raised by Liability Insurance**

1) **Policyholder's Interests**
Liability insurance policies commonly provide that the insurance

company will select and pay for a lawyer to defend the policy-holder in suits arising out of events covered by the policy. The policyholder, in turn, promises to cooperate with the defense. Generally, the policyholder wants a claim handled in a way that minimizes his risk of paying money out of his own pocket (e.g., if the policy limit is $50,000, but the claimant wins a judgment for $60,000, the policyholder would have to pay the $10,000 differ-ence from his own pocket).

2) **Insurance Company's Interests**
The insurance company generally wants a claim handled in a way that minimizes what it must pay, whether in litigation costs or payments to a claimant. To minimize litigation costs (and thus to keep insurance premiums affordable), some insurance companies adopt spending limits and audit procedures that limit the defense lawyer's fees and expenses for various steps in the litigation process. Insurance defense lawyers have complained that these limits sometimes undercut their ability to represent policyholders effectively.

3) **Whom Does the Defense Lawyer Represent?**
Does an insurance defense lawyer represent the policyholder (a person he is likely to encounter only once) or the insurance company (which pays his fees and can send him repeat business)? Curiously, the law on this question varies from state to state. [See ABA Formal Op. 01-421, notes 6, 7 (2001)] Some states say that the client is the policyholder only, but others say that the policyholder and the insurance company are joint clients. [See Restatement §134, comments a and f—insurance law and contract law deter-mine who is the client] No matter whether the defense lawyer represents the policyholder only or both the policyholder and the insurance company, the defense lawyer's ethical obligations are governed by the Rules of Professional Conduct and not by the insurance contract. [ABA Formal Op. 01-421]

4) **Conflicts Between Insurance Company and Policyholder**
Most of the time, the insurance company's interests are in harmony with those of the policyholder. Both of them want to see the claim defeated or settled at the least possible expense. Their respec-tive interests can, however, come into conflict, as in the following examples.

a) **Is the Event Covered by the Policy?**
Suppose that G drove her car over her boyfriend B in circum-stances that make it unclear whether G acted intentionally or

only negligently. B sued G, alternatively alleging negligence and intentional conduct. G's auto liability policy covers negligence, but not intentional conduct. G's insurance company hired lawyer L to defend the case, but it sent G a "reservation of rights" letter, informing her that it might ultimately contend that G acted intentionally, thus freeing the company from liability. During pretrial preparation, G told L in confidence that she ran over B intentionally. L must not disclose that confidential information to the insurance company. [*See* Parsons v. Continental National American Group, 550 P.2d 94 (Ariz. 1976)] If G's confidential statement means that L cannot defend G effectively, L must withdraw. [Restatement §134, comment f]

b) **Settlement Within the Policy Limits**

Suppose that Insco Insurance Co. hires attorney A to defend policyholder D in a slip-and-fall case brought by P. The liability limit in D's policy is $100,000, and P offers to settle for $90,000. D wants to settle because that would free him from paying P anything from his own pocket. Insco, on the other hand, might rather go to trial because its exposure is only $10,000 more than the settlement offer. The settlement offer creates a conflict of interest that has the following consequences: (1) A and Insco must disclose the conflict to D and invite D to obtain independent counsel (at Insco's expense) to advise D on the settlement issue; (2) if A fails to do that and negligently or in bad faith advises D to reject the settlement offer, A is subject to discipline and perhaps civil liability to D for malpractice; and (3) if Insco negligently or in bad faith rejects the settlement offer, Insco will be liable for the entire judgment P obtains against D, even the amount over the policy limits. [Easley v. State Farm Mutual Insurance Co., 528 F.2d 558 (5th Cir. 1976)]

c) **Settlement Controlled by Insurance Company**

Although the policyholder is usually glad to have the insurance company settle a claim within the policy limits, that is not always true. For example, a physician might not want her malpractice insurance company to settle for fear that the settlement will tarnish her medical reputation. Some insurance policies authorize the insurance company to control the defense and to settle within the policy limits at the company's sole discretion. In that situation, a lawyer hired by the insurance company must inform the policyholder, as early in the case as possible, about the constraints on the representation.

Having done that, the lawyer may then follow the insurance company's instructions about settlement. If the lawyer knows that the policyholder objects to a settlement, the lawyer must not proceed without first giving the policyholder a chance to reject the insurance company's defense and to assume responsibility for her own defense at her own expense. [ABA Formal Op. 96-403]

d) Unreasonable Limits on Defense Fees and Expenses

Seeking to control litigation costs, some insurance companies insist on detailed audits of a defense lawyer's time records and litigation files. Some companies also limit the amount a defense lawyer can spend in preparing the case for trial. Some companies use "litigation managers" who look over the lawyer's shoulder and sometimes try to micromanage the defense. A defense lawyer must not disclose a policyholder's confidential information to an outside auditor without the policyholder's informed consent, but he may disclose bills and time records containing confidential information to the insurance company itself if doing so will aid, not harm, the policyholder. [ABA Formal Op. 01-421] Furthermore, a defense lawyer must refuse to follow insurance company litigation management guidelines that interfere with the lawyer's professional judgment or prevent the lawyer from representing the policyholder competently. If the insurance company will not relent, the lawyer must withdraw. [*Id.*]

C. CONFLICTS OF INTEREST—SPECIFIC RULES FOR CURRENT CLIENTS

The discussion in B., *supra*, covered the general principles concerning conflicts of interest that involve one or more current clients, which is the subject matter of ABA Model Rule 1.7. However, some kinds of conflicts arise time and time again in law practice. They are so common that the drafters of the ABA Model Rules devised specific rules to deal with them. These rules are the subject matter of ABA Model Rule 1.8, discussed below.

1. Misuse of Client's Confidential Information

As was discussed previously in III.A., *supra*, a lawyer has a duty not to disclose information relating to the representation of a client, except when an exception to the duty of confidentiality applies. In addition, a lawyer must not use such information to the ***client's disadvantage***, unless the client gives informed consent or some other exception to the duty of confidentiality applies. [*See* ABA Model Rule 1.8(b)] The same rule applies to misuse of a ***former or prospective*** client's confidential information. [*See* ABA Model Rules 1.9(c)(1), 1.18(b)]

EXAMPLE

Prospective client P came to patent attorney A's office, seeking to hire A to file a patent application on P's behalf. In the course of their preliminary discussions, P told A what chemical compound he uses to make his invention work. P ultimately decided not to hire A. A then told one of his other inventor clients about the chemical compound, and that client used the information in a way that prevented P from obtaining a patent. A is subject to discipline. [*See* ABA Model Rule 1.18(b)]

---

a. **Use to Benefit Lawyer or Someone Else**

The rule applies not only when the lawyer uses the information for the lawyer's own benefit, but also when the lawyer uses it to benefit someone else, such as another client or a third party.

EXAMPLE

While representing client Chez Nous Catering Co., lawyer L learned that Chez Nous was teetering on the edge of insolvency. L knew that his good friend F had contracted with Chez Nous to cater F's daughter's big wedding reception. L advised F to cancel the contract and hire a different caterer. L is subject to discipline for using the information to the disadvantage of Chez Nous.

---

b. **Possible Civil Liability Even When Client Is Not Disadvantaged**

Note that the rule applies only when the lawyer's misuse of confidential information disadvantages the client, former client, or prospective client. However, a lawyer who uses the confidential information for his own pecuniary gain (other than in the practice of law) may be subject to *civil liability*—i.e., he may have to account to the client, former client, or prospective client for his profits. [Restatement §60(2)]

EXAMPLE

Attorney A's client C told A in confidence that she was about to build a large new medical complex on the corner of 5th and Main Streets. Without telling C, A quietly bought land at 4th and Main and built a four-story parking garage to serve the new medical complex. The garage did not harm C; in fact it was a benefit to her. Nevertheless, A must disgorge the garage profits to C because A used C's confidential information to enrich himself other than in the practice of law.

---

2. **Business Transactions with Client and Money or Property Interests Adverse to Client**

a. **Statement of the Rule**

A lawyer's professional training, together with the bond of trust and confidence between a lawyer and client, create a risk that the lawyer can overreach the client in a business, property, or financial transaction. Therefore, a lawyer must not enter into a business transaction with a client or knowingly acquire an ownership, possessory, security, or money interest that is adverse to a client, unless all of the following conditions are satisfied:

1) The terms of the business transaction (or the terms on which the interest is acquired) are *fair to the client*;

2) The terms are *fully disclosed* to the client *in writing*, expressed in a manner that the client can reasonably understand (i.e., not in technical legal terminology). The lawyer's disclosure to the client must cover the *essential terms* of the transaction and the *lawyer's role* in the transaction (including whether the lawyer is acting as the client's lawyer in the transaction);

3) The client is advised *in writing* that he should get the *advice of an independent lawyer* about the arrangement before entering into it (and the client must be given a reasonable chance to obtain that advice); and

4) The client gives *informed consent, in a writing that the client signs*.

[ABA Model Rule 1.8(a)]

b. **Outer Limits of the Rule**

The lawyer need not advise the client to consult independent counsel if the client already has independent counsel in the matter. Moreover, if the client has independent counsel, the disclosure of conflict can be made by the independent counsel. Finally, the rule about business transactions and adverse interests does not apply to an ordinary fee agreement between a lawyer and client or to standard commercial transactions in which the lawyer buys goods or services that the client routinely markets to the public (e.g., the lawyer who buys a car from his car dealer client or the lawyer who uses a client as her stockbroker). [*See* ABA Model Rule 1.8, comments 1 - 4]

3. **Proprietary Interest in Subject of Litigation**

Except as permitted below, a lawyer must not acquire a proprietary interest in the cause of action or the subject matter of litigation that the lawyer is conducting for the client. [ABA Model Rule 1.8(i); Restatement §36(1)]

EXAMPLES

1) Lawyer L regularly does consumer loan collection work for American Consumer Finance Company. When one of American's debtors defaults, American assigns the debt and cause of action to L; in return, L immediately pays American 50% of the face value of the debt. If L ultimately collects more than the 50%, she pays half of the excess to American and keeps the other half. L is subject to discipline.

2) F owns a United States patent on a process for manufacturing fertilizer. R brings a declaratory judgment action against F, alleging that F's patent is invalid. Attorney A agrees to represent F in the declaratory judgment action in exchange for an assignment of a one-half ownership interest in F's patent. A is subject to discipline.

a. Contingent Fee Exception

Despite the rule stated above, a lawyer may enter into a contingent fee arrangement with a client in a civil case. A contingent fee arrangement gives the lawyer a personal stake in the outcome of the case and may thus affect the lawyer's objectivity. This arrangement is thus clearly at odds with the spirit of the rule. Nevertheless, because contingent fees have been so long tolerated in the United States, they are excepted from the rule. [See ABA Model Rule 1.8(i)(2)]

EXAMPLE

In both the American Consumer Finance example and the patent case example (above), the lawyers can escape the general rule by using a contingent fee arrangement rather than an assignment of the cause of action or assignment of one-half ownership of the patent. In both examples, a contingent fee arrangement would be proper.

b. Attorney's Lien Exception

In some states, an attorney is allowed to secure payment of her fee and repayment of advanced litigation expenses by taking a lien on the proceeds of a client's case. Some states authorize attorney's liens by statute or case law. In other states, they must be created by contract between the attorney and the client. [See generally Pennsylvania Bar Op. 94-35 (1994)] An attorney's lien gives the attorney a personal stake in the outcome of the client's case, but this situation is tolerated as an exception to the general rule. [ABA Model Rule 1.8(i)(1)]

EXAMPLE

The law of East Carolina permits an attorney to contract with a client for a lien to secure the attorney's fee and advanced litigation expenses.

> Attorney A's fee agreement with client C provides that A shall have a lien on whatever C recovers in her case against X to secure payment of A's fee and to secure repayment of litigation expenses that A advances on C's behalf. This provision of A's fee agreement is proper.

4.   **Gifts to Lawyer from Client Who Is Not a Relative**

The following rules limit a lawyer's freedom to solicit or accept a substantial gift from a client who is not the lawyer's relative. The same rules apply to a substantial gift from a client to the lawyer's relative. In this rule, "relative" includes a spouse, child, parent, grandparent, grandchild, and other persons with whom the lawyer maintains a close, familial relationship. [ABA Model Rule 1.8(c)] "Gift" includes a testamentary gift. [*Id.*]

a.   **Soliciting Substantial Gift**

A lawyer must not ***solicit*** a ***substantial*** gift from a client who is not the lawyer's relative. However, a lawyer may accept a small gift from a client, such as a token of appreciation or an appropriate holiday gift. [ABA Model Rule 1.8, comment 6] Indeed, the rule does not prohibit a lawyer from accepting even a substantial gift, although the gift may be voidable for undue influence.

EXAMPLE

Lawyer L is a loyal alumnus of the Port Arthur School of Law. The school asked L to serve as a pro bono legal advisor to a committee that was drafting a new affirmative action policy for the school. L gladly agreed and worked many hours on the project for no fee. When the work was done, L told the school's dean that his daughter would love to attend the school, but that she could not afford the high tuition. The dean then arranged for L's daughter to be admitted on a full scholarship. L is subject to discipline for soliciting a substantial gift from the school to his daughter.

---

b.   **Preparing Legal Instrument that Creates Substantial Gift**

ABA Model Rule 1.8(c) also prohibits a lawyer from preparing a legal instrument (such as a will or a deed of property) that creates a substantial gift to the lawyer (or the lawyer's relative), except when the donor is one of the lawyer's relatives.

EXAMPLE

Attorney A's aged father asks her to draft a new will for him. The father tells A that he wants to set up a testamentary trust that will provide college funds for A's children. A may draft the will and related documents, but only because the client is her father.

c. Lucrative Appointments

ABA Model Rule 1.8(c) does not prohibit a lawyer from seeking to have himself or his law partner or associate named as executor of an estate or counsel to the executor or to some other fee-paying position. However, the general conflict of interest principles expressed in ABA Model Rule 1.7 do prohibit such efforts if the lawyer's advice is tainted by the lawyer's self-interest. [ABA Model Rule 1.8, comment 8] Moreover, lawyers with long experience in probate and estate planning law know that clients tend to rebel when they discover the lawyer trying to feather his own nest in this manner.

5. Acquiring Literary or Media Rights Concerning Client's Case

A lawyer must not acquire literary or media rights to a story based in substantial part on information relating to the lawyer's representation of a client. However, a lawyer may acquire such rights **after** the client's legal matter is entirely completed, appeals and all. [ABA Model Rule 1.8(d)] The reason behind the rule is that the client's interest in effective representation may conflict with the lawyer's interest in maximizing the value of the literary or media rights. For instance, the lawyer might conduct the client's criminal trial in a sensational manner, simply to pump up public interest in the client's story. The rule does not apply to literary or media rights that are not substantially based on information relating to the representation. [ABA Model Rule 1.8, comment 9]

> **EXAMPLE**
> Legendary rock star Deep River wrote an autobiography that tells the story of his rise from a poverty-stricken childhood to life as a beloved musical icon. Attorney A agreed to represent River in negotiating a book contract and a motion picture contract. In lieu of money, A agreed to do the legal work in return for 5% of the book and movie royalties. The literary rights rule does not apply to this arrangement because River's manuscript is about his life and not about negotiation of the book and movie contracts. [*Id.*] However, the arrangement must comply with ABA Model Rule 1.5 (prohibits unreasonably high fee) and ABA Model Rule 1.8(a) (business transactions with a client).

6. Financial Assistance to Client in Litigation

Except as permitted below, ABA Model Rule 1.8(e) prohibits a lawyer from financially assisting a client in connection with pending or contemplated litigation. For instance, the lawyer must not make or guarantee a loan to the client. The prohibition harkens back to ancient English common law, which forbade lawyers from stirring up litigation or supporting it out of their own purse. More to the point, a lawyer who has too great a financial stake in a case may be unable to give the client objective legal advice.

a. **Advancing Litigation Expenses**

A lawyer may advance court costs and other litigation expenses on the client's behalf, and repayment may be contingent on the outcome of the case. [ABA Model Rule 1.8(e)(1)]

EXAMPLE

Lawyer L's fee agreement with personal injury victim V provides that L will advance the court costs and litigation expenses in V's suit against the person who injured him. The agreement also states that if V wins the case, L will be repaid out of the judgment or settlement proceeds, but that if V loses, L will not be repaid. The fee agreement is proper.

---

b. **Paying Costs and Expenses for Indigent Client**

A lawyer may simply pay the court costs and litigation expenses for an indigent client, without any provision for repayment. [ABA Model Rule 1.8(e)(2)]

Note: These exceptions apply even if the representation is eligible for fees under a fee-shifting statute. In other words, the lawyer can advance or pay litigation expenses as permitted by this rule even if the client's opponent might end up being responsible for the client's fees and costs.

c. **Modest Gifts When Representing Indigent Client Pro Bono**

A lawyer representing an indigent client pro bono (on their own, or through a nonprofit organization or a law school clinical or pro bono program) may provide modest gifts (not loans) to the client for food, rent, transportation, medicine, and other basic living expenses. However, the lawyer must not: (1) promise or imply the availability of such gifts prior to retention, or as an inducement to continue the client-lawyer relationship after retention; (2) seek or accept reimbursement from the client or anyone affiliated with the client; or (3) publicize or advertise a willingness to provide such gifts to prospective clients. [RPC 1.8(e)(3)]

d. **Other Financial Help Is Prohibited**

A lawyer is subject to discipline for giving a client other financial help in the context of pending or contemplated litigation. [ABA Model Rule 1.8(e)]

EXAMPLE

Chem Corp.'s chemical plant blew up, spreading toxic fumes across pasture land belonging to dozens of dairy farmers. The grass shriveled, the cows died, and the farmers became destitute. The law offices of E.Z. Bucks took out newspaper ads offering to represent the farmers on

contingency, to advance the costs and expenses of litigation, and to lend them money to restore their pastures and dairy herds. The last feature of that offer makes the lawyers subject to discipline.

7. **Aggregate Settlement Agreements**

When a lawyer represents several co-parties in a matter (e.g., several plaintiffs or several defendants), the adversary sometimes makes an "aggregate settlement offer," for example, an offer to settle all claims for a lump sum of $1 million. That creates a potential conflict of interest among the lawyer's several clients. Some of them may want to settle for that amount, but others may want to hold out for a better offer. Moreover, the several clients may disagree about how the lump sum is to be allocated—who pays how much or who receives how much. Because of the potential conflict, the lawyer must not participate in the making of an aggregate settlement agreement unless all of the following conditions are met:

(i)   The lawyer must assure that the **clients have come to an agreement** among themselves about how the aggregate sum will be shared (who will pay how much or receive how much);

(ii) The lawyer must **disclose to each client all of the terms** of the aggregate settlement, including: (a) the total amount that will be paid or received; (b) the existence and nature of all the claims, defenses, and pleas involved in the settlement; (c) the details of every other client's participation in the settlement, including how much each will contribute or receive and how each criminal charge will be resolved; and (d) how the lawyer's fees and costs will be paid and by whom. *Note:* These extensive disclosures may require the lawyer to share one client's confidential information with the others, so at the outset of the matter, the lawyer should get each client's informed consent to do that; and

(iii) Each client must give informed consent to the aggregate settlement agreement in a **writing signed by the client**.

[ABA Model Rule 1.8(g); ABA Formal Op. 06-438]

a. **Class Action Settlements**

In a class action, the lawyer who represents the class ordinarily does not have a complete lawyer-client relationship with the unnamed members of the class. Even so, at settlement time, the class's lawyer must follow all of the class action rules concerning notice and other procedural requirements that protect the unnamed class members. [ABA Model Rule 1.8, comment 16]

b. **Aggregate Settlement of Criminal Case**

The same rules that apply to an aggregate settlement in a civil case also apply to a joint plea bargain in a criminal case [ABA Model Rule 1.8(g)], although ordinarily one lawyer will not be representing more than one defendant in a criminal case [*see* Restatement §129(1)].

8. **Compensation from Third Person**

A lawyer must not accept compensation from a third person for representing a client, *unless* three conditions are met:

a. The client *gives informed consent*;

b. The third person *does not interfere with the lawyer's independence* or the representation of the client; and

c. The arrangement *does not compromise the client's confidential information*.

[ABA Model Rules 1.8(f), 1.7(b), 5.4(c)]

EXAMPLES

1) T, a pimp, seeks to employ attorney A to defend C, who is charged with prostitution. T demands to be present whenever A talks with C, and T directs C to plead not guilty, promising to pay the fine if C is found guilty after trial. If A agrees to represent C under these conditions, A is subject to discipline.

2) Midwest Highway Construction Corp. and its executive vice president C are both indicted for conspiring with other highway contractors to rig the bids on government highway contracts. Midwest seeks to employ lawyer L to serve as C's separate defense counsel. Midwest will pay L's fee, but will not interfere with L's handling of the case or with the confidentiality of the relationship between L and C. Under these conditions, L may agree to represent C.

3) Trimmers and Fitters Union Local #876 established a group legal service program for the benefit of its members. Using money from union dues, the Local hired the law firm of R, S, and T to provide the necessary legal services to members. Union member C asked the firm to represent her in a sexual harassment case against her fellow worker D, a loyal member of the union. When the president of the Local heard about C's case, he called the law firm, demanding to know what C said about D and demanding that the firm dismiss the case. The law firm must not allow the union or its officials to interfere with the handling of C's case.

---

9. **Sexual Relationship Between Lawyer and Client**

Because a sexual relationship between a lawyer and client is likely to distort the lawyer's professional judgment and endanger confidentiality and the attorney-client privilege, such a relationship makes the lawyer *subject to discipline*, whether or not the client consents and whether or not the client is harmed—***unless*** their consensual sexual relationship ***predated*** the lawyer-client relationship. When the client is an organization, this rule applies to any person who supervises, directs, or regularly consults with the lawyer concerning the organization's legal matters. [*See* ABA Model Rule 1.8(j); ABA Model Rule 1.7, comment 12; ABA Model Rule 1.8, comments 20, 21, and 22]

a. No Imputation

All of the other specific conflicts discussed in 1 - 8., above, are imputed to other lawyers in the disqualified lawyer's firm. However, a conflict created by a sexual relationship is ***personal*** in nature and unlike most conflicts, it is not imputed to the lawyer's colleagues. [ABA Model Rule 1.8(k)]

b. Pre-Existing Relationship May Still Cause Conflict

Even where the sexual relationship predated the lawyer-client relation-ship, the lawyer should stop to consider whether the sexual relationship will "materially limit" the lawyer-client relationship and implicate the general conflict of interest rule for current clients (*see* B., *supra*). [ABA Model Rule 1.8, comment 21]

D. CONFLICTS INVOLVING FORMER CLIENTS

1. Continuing Duty of Confidentiality

An attorney's duty to preserve a client's confidential information does not cease when the representation ends. The attorney has a continuing obliga-tion to preserve information gained in confidence during the representation. [ABA Model Rule 1.9(c)]

EXAMPLES

1) When A retired from his solo law practice, he sold his practice to another lawyer. The purchaser received not only books, furniture, and an office lease but also all of A's files relating to past and pending legal matters. Many of the files contained confidential information, and A made no effort to obtain the consent of his clients and former clients before transferring the files. A is sub-ject to discipline. [*See* ABA Model Rules 1.17(c), 1.6, 1.9(c)]

2) Lawyer L, a solo practitioner, left instructions for the winding up of his law practice in the event of his unexpected death. L directed his personal repre-sentative to contact each client to find out whether that client's files should be delivered directly to the client, to another lawyer of the client's choice, or to a young lawyer designated by L. L's instructions are proper.

---

2. Using Confidential Information to Former Client's Disadvantage

When a lawyer has obtained confidential information from a former client, the lawyer must not thereafter use the confidential information to the former client's disadvantage, unless the former client gives informed consent, confirmed in writing. This rule does not apply to information that has become generally known. Furthermore, it does not apply to any information that the lawyer would be allowed to reveal or use under an exception to the general ethical duty of confidentiality. [ABA Model Rule 1.9(c)]

EXAMPLE

Three years ago, attorney A represented C, the son of a movie star, in a drug possession case. In that connection, C told A in confidence that he had abused drugs for several years and had become a hard drug addict. Based on information from other sources, several tabloid newspapers and gossip magazines published stories about C's drug problems; within a few weeks, the public knew all there was to know about C. Now A represents C's ex-wife in a dispute with C over the custody of their infant daughter. In the custody dispute, A may use publicly known information about C's history of drug abuse.

---

3. **Opposing Former Client in Substantially Related Matter**

A lawyer must not represent one client whose interests are materially adverse to those of a former client in a matter that is "substantially related" to a matter in which the lawyer represented the former client (unless the former client gives informed consent, confirmed in writing). [ABA Model Rule 1.9(a)] One purpose of this rule is to protect confidential information that the lawyer may have received from the former client, but the rule applies even when the former client cannot demonstrate that the lawyer received any confidential information.

a. **Meaning of "Substantially Related" Matter**

Matters are "substantially related" if: (1) they involve the *same transaction or legal dispute*, or (2) there otherwise is a substantial risk that *confidential factual information as would normally have been obtained* in the prior representation would *materially advance* the new client's position. Note, however, that if a lawyer routinely handled a type of problem for a former client, the lawyer may later oppose that former client in a factually distinct problem of the same general type. [ABA Model Rule 1.9 and comments 2 and 3]

EXAMPLES

1) Summitville Hospital employed lawyer L to draft a consent form to be signed by all patients scheduled for elective surgery at the hospital. L drafted the form and thereafter did no further legal work for the hospital. Three years later, client C asked L to represent her in a suit against the hospital; in that suit, C will contend that the consent form violates public policy and is therefore void. L must not represent C unless the hospital gives informed consent, confirmed in writing.

2) For many years, lawyer L represented client H in matters relating to H's business and personal finances. Then L and H had a sharp disagreement and came to a parting of the ways. Later, X asked L to represent her in her divorce from H. The information that L obtained in confidence about H's business and personal finances would materially advance X's case against H. Thus, L must not represent X unless H gives informed consent, confirmed in writing.

3) When attorney A was an associate in the M, N, O & P firm, she regularly represented the Magnum Oil Company in suits to eject service station dealers for failure to comply with the terms of their service station leases. Two years ago, A left the firm to enter solo practice. Now S, a Magnum service station dealer, has asked her to defend him in an ejectment suit brought by Magnum. A may represent S without getting Magnum's consent.

4. **Clients of Former Firm**

A lawyer's duties may extend not only to the clients she represented personally, but also to clients of the lawyer's former firm. A lawyer whose firm formerly represented a client in a matter and who acquired protected confidential information [Rule 1.6] or information pertaining to the representation [Rule 1.9(c)] may not thereafter represent another person in the *same or a substantially related matter* if that person's interests are *materially adverse* to those of the former client, unless the former client gives *informed consent, confirmed in writing*. [ABA Model Rule 1.9(b)]

EXAMPLE

Lawyer L is an associate at Firm One, which represents client A in the case of *A v. B*. L works on the *A v. B* case, and he receives reams of confidential information about the case from A. L then quits Firm One and becomes an associate at Firm Two.

Absent informed consent from A, confirmed in writing, L may not now represent B in the *A v. B* case. Furthermore, L may not represent C in the case of *C v. A* if the *C v. A* case is substantially related to the *A v. B* case and if the confidential information L obtained from A is material to the *C v. A* case.

5. **Disqualification of Lawyer's New Firm**

If a lawyer who is disqualified from representing a client under the rules set out in 3. - 4., above, joins a new firm, the new firm may be disqualified as well *unless the lawyer is properly screened* (i.e., the disqualified lawyer does not work on the case, discuss it with those who do, or have access to case files) and does not share fees from the matter, and the former client is given notice.

EXAMPLE

Same facts as in example in 4., above. A lawyer at Firm Two may not represent B in the *A v. B* case or C in the *C v. A* case, unless L is screened from the case and shares no fees, and A is given notice.

Note: The prohibition against sharing fees does not prevent the lawyer from receiving a regular salary or partnership share set by prior independent agreement. It means only that the lawyer's compensation must not be "directly related to the matter in which the lawyer is disqualified." [*See* ABA Model Rule 1.10, comment 8]

a.   **Notice and Certifications to Former Client**

Prompt written notice must be given to any affected former client detailing: (1) a description of the screening procedures employed, (2) a statement of the firm's and the lawyer's compliance with these requirements, (3) a statement that review before a tribunal may be available, and (4) an agreement by the firm to respond promptly to written inquiries or objections by the former client concerning the screening procedures. The disqualified lawyer and a partner of the firm must provide the former client with certifications of compliance with the ABA Model Rules and with the screening procedures at reasonable intervals upon written request, and upon termination of the screening procedures. [ABA Model Rule 1.10(a)(2)]

6.   **Disqualification of Lawyer's Former Firm**

A lawyer's former firm is prohibited from representing a person with interests materially adverse to those of a client of the formerly associated lawyer if: (1) the matter is the same or substantially related to that in which the formerly associated lawyer represented the client; and (2) a lawyer remaining in the firm has information protected by Rules 1.6 and 1.9(c) that is material to the matter. [ABA Model Rule 1.10(b)]

EXAMPLE

Lawyer L is a partner at Firm One. L and three associates of Firm One represent client A in the *A v. B* case. L and the three associates obtain reams of confidential information from A about the case. Then L leaves Firm One to form Firm Two. The three associates stay at Firm One. Now L and Firm Two represent client A in the *A v. B* case.

No lawyer at Firm One may represent B in the *A v. B* case because the three associates who obtained confidential information from A are still at Firm One.

No lawyer at Firm One may represent C in the case of *C v. A* if that case is substantially related to the *A v. B* case, and if the confidential information the three associates obtained from A is material to the *C v. A* case.

If the three associates had also left Firm One, and if no other lawyer in Firm One had been privy to the confidential information received from A, then any lawyer at Firm One may represent B in the *A v. B* case or C in the *C v. A* case.

The disqualification can be waived if A gives informed consent, confirmed in writing. Thus, if A consents, the results of the foregoing hypotheticals would be the opposite.

E. CONFLICTS INVOLVING PROSPECTIVE CLIENTS

1. **Lawyer's Duty Concerning Confidential Information**
   A prospective client is someone who consults with a lawyer about the possibility of forming a lawyer-client relationship. [ABA Model Rule 1.18(a)] The attorney-client privilege protects confidential communications between a lawyer and a prospective client. The ethical duty of confidentiality also applies to information learned during a consultation between a lawyer and prospective client. Thus, the lawyer must not reveal or use information learned from a prospective client, unless an exception to the duty of confidentiality applies.

EXAMPLES

1) Prospective client PC came to lawyer L's office seeking L's legal advice about a plan to murder PC's sister-in-law without getting caught. The attorney-client privilege would not protect PC's communication because he was seeking L's aid to commit a future crime. Furthermore, the ethical duty of confidentiality would not prohibit L from warning the sister-in-law and telling the police if L reasonably believes that PC really will carry out the plan. [ABA Model Rules 1.18(b), 1.6(b)(1)]

2) Senator S telephoned attorney A, asking A to visit him in the county jail. When A arrived, S explained in confidence that he was picked up for felony drunk driving, that he was very drunk at the time, and that he wanted A to represent him. A was overburdened with other work and could not do so. Several weeks later, the entire story of Senator S's drunken escapade became common knowledge after S talked about it on a popular television show. Not long afterward, in an unrelated matter, A had occasion to cross-examine S, who had testified on behalf of A's adversary. A asked S: "Sir, shortly before witnessing the events about which you testified on direct, had you drunk any alcohol?" S was outraged and accused A of violating the duty of confidence owed to a potential client. A's conduct was proper. The question on cross-examination was designed to test S's ability to perceive correctly. Furthermore, the information about S's drinking, although originally confidential, lost its protection when S himself made it public on television. [*See* ABA Model Rules 1.18(b), 1.9(c)(1)]

---

2. **Lawyer's Duty Concerning Conflict of Interest**

Subject to the exceptions stated in 3., below, a lawyer who obtains confidential information during a consultation with a prospective client must not later represent a different person in the same or a substantially related matter if the confidential information could significantly harm the prospective client. [ABA Model Rule 1.18(c)] This conflict is imputed to others in the lawyer's firm, but the imputation can be overcome by screening, as stated in 3., below.

3. **How to Overcome a Prospective Client Conflict**

One way to overcome the conflict described in 2., above, is to obtain informed consent, confirmed in writing, from both the affected client and the prospective client. [ABA Model Rule 1.18(d)(1)] A second way to overcome the conflict is to satisfy all of the following conditions:

a. Demonstrate that the lawyer who held discussions with the prospective client took care to **avoid exposure to any more confidential information than was necessary** to determine whether to represent the prospective client;

b. Demonstrate that the disqualified lawyer is **timely screened from any participation in the matter** and will not share the fee (but he may take his ordinary salary or partnership share); and

c. Give **written notice** to the prospective client.

[ABA Model Rule 1.18(d)(2)]

F. **CONFLICT RULES FOR CURRENT AND FORMER GOVERNMENT OFFICERS AND EMPLOYEES**

When a lawyer serves as an officer or employee of the government for a period and then leaves to enter private law practice, the government has a right to expect that its confidential information will not be abused. Furthermore, private clients should not be allowed to gain an unfair advantage from information known to a lawyer only because of prior government service, and lawyers should not be in a position to benefit private clients because of prior government service. Finally, possible future benefit to private clients should not distort a lawyer's professional judgment while working for the government. [See ABA Model Rule 1.11, comments 3 and 4] All of the foregoing would suggest that there should be a broad, rigid rule of disqualification for lawyers who move from the government to private practice. However, such a rule would have a serious drawback—the government would be hindered in recruiting good lawyers for short-term government service. Thus, the ABA Model Rules establish disqualification rules that are relatively narrow and flexible. [See also Restatement §133]

1. **Federal and State Conflict of Interest Laws**

Lawyers who move between government and private jobs must comply not

only with the ethics rules but also with various state and federal statutes and regulations. [*See, e.g.,* Federal Ethics in Government Act, 18 U.S.C. §§207 - 208] Those are not covered in this outline, but they must be considered in solving an actual problem of successive government and private employment.

2. **Private Work Following Government Work on Same Matter**
Except when expressly permitted by law, a lawyer who leaves government service and enters private practice must not represent a private client in a *matter* in which the lawyer participated *personally and substantially* while in government service, unless the government agency gives informed consent, confirmed in writing. [ABA Model Rule 1.11(a)]

a. **Meaning of the Term "Matter"**
As used in this rule, "matter" has a narrow, technical meaning. It does *not* mean "general topic" or "broad subject area." It means a *specific set of facts involving some specific parties*. [ABA Formal Op. 342 (1975)] ABA Model Rule 1.11(e) defines it more fully as, "any judicial or other proceeding, application, request for a ruling or other determination, contract, claim, controversy, investigation, charge, accusation, arrest, or other particular matter involving a specific party or parties" (plus anything else that is covered under the conflict of interest rules of the government agency in question).

EXAMPLES

1) When lawyer L worked for the State Consumer Protection Agency, she was assigned to draft some regulations to govern the conduct of door-to-door salespeople. The regulations that she drafted were ultimately adopted, almost verbatim, by the agency. A year later, L left government service and entered private practice. She was asked to represent American Encyclopedia Company (a door-to-door sales company) in a dispute with the State Consumer Protection Agency. The essence of the dispute is the proper application of the regulations that L herself drafted. L may represent American because the drafting of regulations is not a "matter"; it does not involve specific facts and specific parties.

2) When serving as Oakville City Attorney, lawyer L drafted a city ordinance for the rezoning of a particular tract of land owned by developer R. The drafting of the ordinance is a "matter" because it involved one narrow, specific situation. Thus, when L later enters private law practice, she may not work on a case that involves that ordinance. [*See* Restatement §133]

---

b. **Meaning of "Personally and Substantially"**
The term "personally and substantially" means just what it says—the

disqualification rule applies only when the lawyer's work on a matter was both personal and substantial. The term does not include work that is trifling, and it does not include mere supervisory responsibility. [*See* ABA Formal Op. 342 (1975)]

EXAMPLE

Attorney A is the District Attorney of Colma County. She is in charge of 16 deputies working out of five different offices spread through the county. A's rubber-stamped signature appears on every paper that goes out of the five offices. In theory, she is personally responsible for every detail of every case; in fact, most of A's day is consumed in supervision and administration. The disqualification rule would cover only the few, exceptional cases in which A does become personally and substantially involved. [*Id.*]

---

c. **Imputed Disqualification**

If a lawyer is disqualified by the rule stated above, then everyone in that lawyer's firm is also disqualified **unless** the lawyer is **timely screened from the case**, the lawyer **does not share fees** from the matter, and **written notice is promptly given to the governmental agency** to enable it to make sure that the above conditions are being met.

EXAMPLE

When lawyer L worked for the State Environmental Safety Bureau, he participated personally and substantially in an investigation of Noxatox Corp. concerning the dumping of radioactive industrial waste in Evergreen Slough. Later, L quit the Bureau and became a partner in the T, S & U firm. One of L's law partners is now asked to defend Noxatox in private litigation arising out of the Evergreen Slough matter. L will not work on the case, will have no access to the case files, and will not discuss the case with others in the office. L will receive his ordinary share of the proceeds of the partnership, set by prior independent agreement. Finally, the Bureau will be promptly informed of the foregoing facts in writing. Under these conditions, the partner may represent Noxatox.

---

3. **Subsequent Use of Information Gained During Government Service**

ABA Model Rule 1.11(c) provides that (except when expressly permitted by law) a government lawyer who receives confidential government information about a person must not later represent a private client whose interests are adverse to that person, when the information could be used to the material disadvantage of that person. The rule covers only information **actually received** by the government lawyer, not information that could be fictionally

imputed to the lawyer. "Confidential government information" means information that is gained under government authority and which the government is prohibited from revealing, or has a privilege not to reveal, and which is not otherwise available to the public. [ABA Model Rule 1.11(c) and comment 8]

EXAMPLE

When attorney A worked on the legal staff of the State Parole Board, he received confidential information about the personal life, character, and criminal proclivities of X, a parolee. Later, A entered private practice as a criminal defense lawyer. He was assigned to defend D in a case in which it appeared quite likely that X, not D, was the perpetrator. The proper defense of D would require a thorough investigation of the very facts that A learned about X in confidence. A must request the court to relieve him of the assignment to defend D.

---

a. Imputed Disqualification

If a former government lawyer is disqualified by this rule, then everyone in that lawyer's firm is also disqualified unless:

1) The lawyer is timely screened from the matter; and

2) The lawyer is not apportioned any part of the fee earned in the matter.

[ABA Model Rule 1.11(c)]

EXAMPLE

In the State Parole Board example above, attorney A's law partner P may defend D if A is screened from the case and is not apportioned any part of the fee earned in the case.

---

4. Current Government Service After Private Practice

ABA Model Rule 1.11(d) states the rules that apply to a person who becomes a government officer or employee after private practice or other nongovernmental work.

a. Ordinary Conflict Rules Apply

The ordinary conflict rules stated in ABA Model Rules 1.7 (current clients) and 1.9 (former clients) apply to a lawyer who enters government service after private practice or other nongovernmental work. [ABA Model Rule 1.11(d)(1)]

EXAMPLE

For the past five years, lawyer L worked for the M & N law firm. In that job, L worked on a few matters for Cosmoplex, a diversified communications company, and he gained considerable confidential information about the company's finances. Now, L has quit M & N and has gone to work for the United States Department of Labor, which is about to sue Cosmoplex for fraud in connection with the purchase of overvalued company stock for its employee pension plan. ABA Model Rule 1.9 prohibits L from working on that suit (unless Cosmoplex gives informed consent, confirmed in writing). However, if L is timely screened from the suit, other labor department lawyers may work on it—L's conflict will not be imputed to them.

b. "Personal and Substantial" Rule Also Applies

If a lawyer worked "personally and substantially" on a "matter" in private practice or other nongovernmental employment, the lawyer must not work on that same matter when she later enters government service, whether or not the later work would be adverse to a former client. However, informed consent, confirmed in writing, can solve the conflict.

EXAMPLE

In private practice, attorney A represented Electro Corp. in trying to obtain a license from the State Energy Commission to build a geothermal electric generating plant. While Electro's application was still pending, A quit private practice to become a lawyer for the Commission. A must not work on the Electro application unless she obtains the informed consent, confirmed in writing, from both the Commission [ABA Model Rule 1.11(d)(2)(i)] and Electro [ABA Model Rule 1.9(a)].

c. Negotiating for Private Employment

When a person in government service is currently working personally and substantially on a matter, she must not negotiate for private employment with any party or lawyer who is involved in that matter. There is a special exception for judges' and adjudicative officers' law clerks who are seeking work after their clerkships end (see G.3., infra). [ABA Model Rule 1.11(d)(2)(ii)]

EXAMPLE

Lawyer L currently serves on the State Agriculture and Fisheries Commission. L's work for the Commission is strictly nonlegal; he does not function as a lawyer for the Commission. Currently, L and the other Commissioners are working personally and substantially on a matter involving the Shady Bay Salmon Farm. Now, Shady Bay approaches L, asking if he would like to become Shady Bay's in-house general

counsel. If L negotiates for employment with Shady Bay, he will be subject to discipline. Notice that the rule applies to L, even though his work for the Commission is nonlegal.

G. **CONFLICTS INVOLVING FORMER JUDGES, ARBITRATORS, AND THE LIKE**
The conflict of interest problems posed when a lawyer switches between government and private practice are also present when a judge leaves the bench and enters private practice. Thus, the rules discussed here are similar to those discussed above.

1. **Switching from Judicial Service to Private Law Practice**
A lawyer must not represent a private client in a matter in which the lawyer has earlier participated personally and substantially while serving as a judge or other adjudicative officer (e.g., a referee or special master) or as a law clerk to such person, or as an arbitrator, mediator, or other third-party neutral, unless all parties to the proceedings give informed consent, confirmed in writing. [ABA Model Rule 1.12(a)] However, an arbitrator who is selected as a partisan of a party in a multi-member arbitration panel may subsequently represent that party. [ABA Model Rule 1.12(d)]

EXAMPLES

1) Lawyer L was selected as the partisan of union U on a three-member arbitration panel. L may serve as U's lawyer in later proceedings relating to the dispute that was arbitrated.

2) Law clerk C worked on the case of *P v. D* and made recommendations to Judge J about some discovery motions and a motion for default judgment. When C completes her clerkship and enters private practice, she cannot work on the case of *P v. D*. [*See* Maryland State Bar Op. 85-23 (1985)]

3) J was one of 15 judges on the County Superior Court (a trial court) while the case of *State v. Able* was pending in that court. However, the *Able* case was assigned to a different judge, and Judge J never had anything to do with it. Later, Judge J resigned from the bench and entered private practice. Able asked J to represent her on the appeal of her case. J may represent Able because J did not personally work on the *Able* case. [*See* ABA Model Rule 1.12(a)]

4) S was the Senior Presiding Judge of the Circuit Court of Appeal (an intermediate appellate court). In that capacity, Judge S was responsible for all court administration and for assigning judges to hear various cases. During that period, the case of *Commonwealth v. Beale* was heard and decided by the court, but Judge S had nothing to do with that case except to assign it to three other judges. Later, Judge S left the bench and entered private practice. S may represent Beale in a subsequent stage of Beale's case. [*Id.*]

---

2. **Screening Can Avoid Imputed Disqualification**
If a lawyer is disqualified under Rule 1.12(a), everyone else in the lawyer's firm is also disqualified unless the following conditions are met:

    a. The lawyer is timely screened from the matter;

    b. The lawyer is not apportioned any part of the fee earned in the matter; and

    c. Written notice is given to the parties and the appropriate tribunal so that they can ensure that the foregoing conditions are met.

[ABA Model Rule 1.12(c); ABA Formal Op. 342 (1975)]

3. **Law Clerks Negotiating for Private Employment**
A law clerk to a judge or other adjudicative officer must ***notify*** that judge/officer before negotiating for private employment with a party (or the attorney for a party) in a matter in which the law clerk is participating personally and substantially. [ABA Model Rule 1.12(b)] Law clerks are specially treated because they are usually newly admitted lawyers for whom a clerkship is only a temporary first step in a legal career.

EXAMPLE
After graduating from law school, S became a law clerk for Judge J. In that capacity, S wrote the bench brief and drafted an opinion in the case of *Arner v. Bosch*. While that case was still pending before the court, the attorney for Bosch invited S to visit her law firm and interview for a job. S must notify Judge J before discussing future employment with the attorney.

---

4. **Other Adjudicative Officers Negotiating for Private Employment**
The lenient rule that applies to law clerks does not apply to judges, arbitrators, mediators, third-party neutrals, and other adjudicative officers. They are forbidden to negotiate for private employment with a party (or the attorney for a party) in a matter in which they are participating personally and substantially. [ABA Model Rule 1.12(b)]

V. COMPETENCE, MALPRACTICE, AND CIVIL LIABILITY

A. **COMPETENCE**
When representing a client, a lawyer must act competently, i.e., with the legal knowledge, skill, thoroughness, and preparation reasonably necessary for the representation. [ABA Model Rule 1.1]

1. **Legal Knowledge and Skill**

a. **Factors in Determining Requisite Skill**
In deciding whether a lawyer has the knowledge and skill required to handle a particular matter, the following factors should be considered:

1) The complexity and specialized nature of the matter;

2) The lawyer's general experience;

3) The lawyer's training and experience in the field in question;

4) The preparation and study the lawyer is able to give the matter; and

5) Whether it is feasible to refer the matter to, or associate or consult with, a lawyer of established competence in the field.

[ABA Model Rule 1.1, comment 1] Note that most matters do not require specialized skill and that every lawyer is capable of competence either through necessary study or association of another lawyer. Thus, a lack of legal knowledge or skill really means a failure to seek it. [Hazard & Hodes, §4.02]

b. **Becoming Competent Through Preparation**
It follows from the above that a lawyer may accept representation despite lacking competence in the field involved if the requisite competence can be achieved by reasonable preparation. This often comes into play when a lawyer is appointed as counsel for an unrepresented person. [ABA Model Rule 1.1, comment 4]

c. **Emergency Situations**
In an emergency, a lawyer may assist a client, even if the lawyer does not have the skill ordinarily required in the field in question, if referral to or consultation with another lawyer would be impractical. However, the assistance should not exceed what is reasonably necessary to meet the emergency. [ABA Model Rule 1.1, comment 3]

EXAMPLE

In the middle of the night, attorney A's neighbor calls him and asks what to do about her estranged husband who is drunkenly trying to get into her house, in violation of a court order. The neighbor's regular lawyer is unavailable, and A knows little or nothing about family law. In this emergency situation, A may advise the neighbor, but his advice should be limited to the emergency at hand.

---

2. **Thoroughness and Preparation**
To handle a matter competently, a lawyer must inquire into and analyze the

facts and legal elements of the problem, applying the methods and procedures used by competent practitioners. Competence, of course, requires
adequate preparation. [ABA Model Rule 1.1, comment 5]

3.   **Retaining Other Lawyers to Assist in the Matter**
Sometimes a lawyer may gain competence in a matter by consulting with
other lawyers. Before a lawyer retains or contracts with lawyers outside her
firm to assist in the provision of legal services to the client, the lawyer: (1) must
reasonably believe that the services of the outside lawyers will contribute
to the competent and ethical representation of the client, and (2) "should
ordinarily" obtain the client's informed consent. The reasonableness of the
lawyer's decision to retain lawyers outside her firm will depend on factors such
as the background of the nonfirm lawyers, the nature of the services assigned
to the nonfirm lawyers, and the professional conduct rules in the jurisdictions
in which the services will be performed. [ABA Model Rule 1.1, comment 6]

4.   **Maintaining Competence—Technology and Continuing Legal Education**
Lawyers should keep abreast of changes in the law and its practice. As such,
a lawyer should take steps to understand the benefits and risks associated
with relevant technology. The lawyer also should engage in continuing legal
education programs sponsored by the organized bar and must comply with
all applicable continuing legal education requirements. [ABA Model Rule 1.1,
comment 8]

B.   **DILIGENCE**
A lawyer must act with ***reasonable diligence and promptness*** in representing a
client. [ABA Model Rule 1.3]

1.   **Diligence Defined**
A lawyer should pursue a matter on the client's behalf despite opposition,
obstacles, and personal inconvenience, and may take whatever lawful and
ethical measures are required to vindicate the client's cause. The lawyer
should act with dedication and commitment to the client's interests and with
zeal in advocacy on the client's behalf. [ABA Model Rule 1.3, comment 1]

    a.   **Diligence Does Not Require Incivility**
A lawyer should use good judgment in determining the means by which
a matter is pursued, and the lawyer is not bound by Rule 1.3 to press
every conceivable advantage. Moreover, the duty of diligence does not
require the lawyer to be offensive or uncivil toward the adversary or
other persons. [*Id.*]

    b.   **Workload**
A lawyer must control his workload so that each matter can be
adequately handled. [ABA Model Rule 1.3, comment 2]

2. Promptness

Procrastination is perhaps the professional shortcoming most widely resented. Procrastination often has severe or devastating consequences to the client's interests, as when a court-ordered deadline is missed or the statute of limitations is permitted to run. Even when procrastination does not harm the client's substantive interests, it can cause the client needless anxiety and can undermine confidence in the lawyer's trustworthiness. A lawyer may, of course, agree to a reasonable postponement if it will not prejudice her client. [ABA Model Rule 1.3, comment 3]

3. Completion of the Matter

Once a lawyer agrees to handle a matter for a client, the lawyer must see the matter through to completion (unless, of course, the lawyer is fired or is required or permitted to withdraw). If there is doubt about whether the lawyer-client relationship has come to an end, the lawyer should clarify it, preferably in writing. [ABA Model Rule 1.3, comment 4]

EXAMPLES

1) Over the past 15 years, attorney A has served as trademark counsel for Webb Corp., but in recent months the relationship has become somewhat strained. A is uncertain whether Webb Corp. wishes to continue to use her services. Today A read in a trademark newsletter that one of Webb's competitors is attempting to register a trademark that will seriously interfere with Webb's business. A should promptly call the matter to Webb's attention and ask Webb whether it wishes her to act on its behalf in this matter.

2) Client C hired lawyer L to defend her in a drunk driving case. At trial, C was convicted, and her driver's license was suspended. L is uncertain whether C expects him to do anything about an appeal. L must consult with C about the possibility of an appeal before relinquishing responsibility for the matter.

---

4. Existence of Lawyer-Client Relationship

A lawyer's obligation under the duties stated above, as with most of the lawyer's ethical duties, depends on whether there is a lawyer-client relationship. If there is any doubt, however, as to whether the lawyer-client relationship was either formed or terminated, the lawyer must either take affirmative steps to terminate the relationship or act with the required diligence. [Hazard & Hodes, §2.05]

5. Solo Practitioner's Duty to Plan for Death or Disability

The untimely death or disability of a solo practitioner can create havoc for her clients. To prevent that, every solo practitioner should designate another competent lawyer who, upon the death or disability of the solo practitioner, would review the clients' files, notify the clients of the circumstances,

and determine whether protective action is needed. [ABA Model Rule 1.3, comment 5]

C. SINGLE VIOLATION SUFFICIENT TO IMPOSE DISCIPLINE

Neither Rule 1.1 (competence) nor Rule 1.3 (diligence) requires a pattern of misconduct; a single incident is sufficient to impose professional discipline. Special circumstances should be considered when imposing the sanction, but not when determining whether there has been a violation. Even when the lawyer is in the midst of a personal crisis, he must take reasonable steps to put his cases on temporary hold, until he can give them his full attention. [Hazard & Hodes, §7.06, illus. 7.10]

EXAMPLE

Client Cathy came to lawyer Larry with a medical malpractice claim, the statute of limitations on which was due to run out within the week. Larry agreed to take the case and began drafting the complaint. Two days later, Larry's son was hit by a car. For several days, during which time the doctors performed several surgeries, they did not know whether the child would live or die. Larry did not leave his son's side during this critical time, and thus did not file Cathy's case within the statutory period. Cathy filed both a malpractice case and a disciplinary complaint against Larry. Larry is subject to discipline for lack of diligence in handling Cathy's case. The disciplinary authority will likely consider the circumstances in assessing a sanction, but they are irrelevant to the question of whether Larry breached his duty to Cathy. [*See* Hazard & Hodes, §7.06, illus. 7.10]

D. MALPRACTICE AND OTHER CIVIL LIABILITY

1. **Relationship Between Disciplinary Matters and Malpractice Actions**

    Professional discipline is only one of the possible consequences of incompetent or neglected legal work. Another possible consequence is civil liability for legal malpractice. A malpractice action differs from a disciplinary matter in three ways: (1) in a malpractice action, the forum is a **civil court**, not a disciplinary tribunal; (2) in a malpractice action, the attorney's adversary is an **injured plaintiff**, not the state bar; and (3) the purpose of a malpractice action is to **compensate** the injured plaintiff, not to punish the attorney, and not to protect the public from future wrongs.

2. **Ethics Violation as Evidence of Legal Malpractice**

    If a lawyer violates a legal ethics rule, does that automatically mean that she has also committed legal malpractice? If not, does it create a presumption that she has committed malpractice? The "Scope" section of the ABA Model Rules answers "no" to both questions: the legal ethics rules are for disciplinary purposes. They are not designed to be a basis for civil liability, and a lawyer's breach of an ethics rule does not automatically or presumptively

mean that the lawyer has committed malpractice. Courts do, however, regard an ethics violation as **relevant evidence** that the lawyer's conduct was below the appropriate standard of care. [*See* Fishman v. Brooks, 487 N.E.2d 1377 (Mass. 1986); *and see generally* Hazard & Hodes, §5.01]

3.   Theories of Malpractice Liability
The plaintiff in a legal malpractice case can invoke a variety of legal theories. The choice of theories can be important because of differences in the statutes of limitation and measures of damages.

a.   **Intentional Tort**
One theory is intentional tort. An attorney is liable (just as any nonprofessional would be) for fraud, misrepresentation, malicious prosecution, abuse of process, or misuse of funds.

b.   **Breach of Fiduciary Duties**
A second theory is breach of fiduciary duties. An attorney acting as a fiduciary for the client owes the client all of the customary duties of a fiduciary, including loyalty, confidentiality, and honest dealing.

c.   **Breach of Contract**
A third theory is breach of contract. For instance, an attorney may have breached a term of an express oral agreement with the client. If there is no express contract, a court may be willing to find an implied promise by the attorney to use ordinary skill and care to protect the client's interests.

d.   **Negligence**
A fourth theory, by far the most common, is unintentional tort—i.e., simple negligence. [*See generally* Restatement §§48 - 54] Using this theory, the plaintiff must establish the routine elements of any negligence case: a duty of due care, a breach of that duty, legal causation, and damages. These elements are discussed separately in the paragraphs that follow.

1)   **Duty of Due Care**

a)   **To Clients**
An attorney owes a duty of due care to a client, but it is not always clear when a person becomes a client. [*Id.* §50] Courts are quick to find that an attorney-client relationship has been established if the attorney's neglect has misled the alleged client. [*See* Restatement §14]

EXAMPLE
C asked attorney A to represent him as plaintiff in a products

liability case. A said she would have to check with her partners to make sure the case posed no conflict of interest, and A said that she would "get back to C one way or the other." A never checked with her partners, and she totally forgot C's case. The statute of limitations ran. A court could conclude that an attorney-client relationship had been established between A and C.

b) **To Prospective Clients and Third Parties**

If an attorney provides legal services during a consultation with a prospective client, the attorney must use reasonable care. [*See* Restatement §§51, 15] An attorney also owes a duty of due care to other nonclients in certain circumstances, including where: (1) the third party was *intended to benefit* by the attorney's rendition of legal services, or (2) the attorney *invited the third person to rely* on her opinion or legal services. [*See* Restatement §51]

EXAMPLES

1) C hired attorney A to draft a trust agreement naming B as beneficiary. A drafted the trust agreement negligently, making it subject to an unnecessary tax; the tax reduced the amount that B could receive from the trust. Because B was intended to benefit from A's services, and because the potential for harm to B should have been obvious, B has a good malpractice claim against A.

2) M hired lawyer L to bring a civil suit against D. As it turned out, M's claim against D had no sound factual basis, and L would have recognized that from the outset had L not been negligent. D incurred trouble and expense in defending the suit. D has no negligence claim against L because D was not intended to benefit from L's services and D was not any other type of protected nonclient.

3) X hired lawyer L to negotiate the sale of personal property to Y. The sales contract required L to give Y an opinion letter confirming the absence of liens on the property. After X assured L that there were no liens on the property, L decided not to conduct a search of the lien records. L transmitted the opinion letter to Y and the sale closed. Y later discovered that there was a lien on the property. Y has a malpractice claim against L because L invited Y to rely on the opinion letter.

c) **Standard of Care**
    The standard of care for an attorney is the competence and diligence normally exercised by attorneys in similar circumstances. If an attorney represents to a client that he has greater competence (e.g., is a specialist) or will exercise greater diligence than that normally demonstrated by attorneys undertaking similar matters, he is held to that higher standard. [Restatement §52 and comment d]

2) **Breach of Duty of Due Care**

    a) **Errors of Judgment**
        An attorney is liable for negligence, but not everything that causes harm is negligence. An attorney is not liable for "mere errors in judgment" if the judgment was ***well-informed and reasonably made***.

        > **EXAMPLES**
        > 1) Attorney A decided not to take the pretrial deposition of witness X. A's motive was to save litigation expenses for her client; further, it appeared that X's testimony would be peripheral and unimportant. At trial, X turned out to be a critical witness for the adversary. Even if A's failure to take X's deposition caused A's client to lose the case, A has not committed malpractice if her judgment was well-informed and reasonably exercised.
        >
        > 2) In a surgical malpractice case, lawyer L failed to interview the operating room nurse, an obvious witness who might have knowledge of key facts. L's client lost the case because of the failure to prove a fact that the nurse's testimony could have supplied. When the client sued L for legal malpractice, L responded that he had made a "tactical judgment" not to interview the nurse. Holding L liable, the court noted that "there is nothing tactical about ignorance."

    b) **Knowledge of Law**
        An attorney is expected to know the ordinary, settled rules of law known to practitioners of ordinary competence and diligence. Furthermore, an attorney has a duty to go to the library to look up rules of law that he does not know. If the answer is there to be found through standard research techniques and sources, and if the attorney does not find it, he has breached the duty of due care. [*See, e.g.,* Aloy

v. Mash, 38 Cal. 3d 413 (1985)] Obviously, some issues of law are unsettled and debatable; if the attorney has done reasonable legal research, then he has fulfilled the duty of due care—even if he makes the wrong guess about how an unsettled issue will ultimately be resolved by the courts.

c) **Calling in a Specialist**

Some legal problems are uniquely within the competence of a legal specialist. It is a breach of the duty of due care for a general practitioner to attempt to handle such a problem if a reasonably prudent lawyer would have sent the client to a specialist.

EXAMPLE

Client C asked attorney A to help him obtain legal protection for a new manufacturing process that C had invented. A realized that he was totally ignorant about the law of patents and trade secrets, but he nevertheless tried to advise C. As a result, C lost his opportunity to apply for a United States patent on his invention. A breached the duty of due care by failing to send C to a patent attorney.

---

3) **Legal Causation**

As in any tort case, the plaintiff in a professional negligence case must prove that the defendant's conduct was the legal cause of the plaintiff's injury. That is, the injury would not have happened **but for** the defendant's negligence, and furthermore, that it is fair to hold the defendant liable for unexpected injuries or for expected injuries that happen in unexpected ways. [*See* Restatement §53]

EXAMPLES

1) P hired lawyer L to represent her in a suit against the federal government. L neglected P's case, and the statute of limitations ran. P then sued L for legal malpractice. In the malpractice case, P must prove that she had a good claim against the federal government. If P did not have a good claim in the first place, then L's negligence was not the legal cause of injury to P.

2) History professor H hired attorney A to defend her in a plagiarism case. H lost the case because of A's failure to prepare adequately. The loss broke H's mind and spirit; she became a hopeless alcoholic and was fired from her university position. If H files a legal malpractice suit against A, a court would probably conclude that H's loss of earning power was not legally caused by A's negligence.

4) Damages

The plaintiff in a professional negligence case must prove damages—e.g., the money paid out to discharge an adverse judgment, or the value of a lost cause of action. The plaintiff can recover for direct losses and also for losses that are indirect but foreseeable. [*Id.* §53]

EXAMPLE

Attorney A did the legal work for the acquiring corporation in a large merger transaction. A bungled the merger agreement; in consequence, the merger fell through, and A's client suffered large legal expenses in defending against suits brought by aggrieved shareholders. In a malpractice action, A's client can recover both the legal expenses and the profits lost due to the aborted merger, provided that it can prove its losses with reasonable certainty.

---

4. Civil Liability Other than Malpractice

In addition to malpractice liability, a lawyer may be liable to a client on other grounds, including breach of contract (e.g., by failing to comply with the fee agreement). A lawyer also may be liable to the client for breach of warranty if the lawyer promises a specific result, knowing that the result has material importance to the client. However, general predictions of success in the case will not result in liability because such results are clearly dependent on circumstances outside of the lawyer's control. [Restatement §55]

EXAMPLE

D is on trial for burglary and is represented by lawyer L. After closing arguments, L tells D, "The prosecution didn't prove a thing. I'm pretty sure you're going home with your family tonight." The jury convicts D and he is sentenced to prison. L is not liable for breach of warranty.

---

5. Liability for Negligence of Others

The ordinary principles of ***respondeat superior*** apply in suits for professional negligence. Thus, an attorney can be held liable for injuries caused by a negligent legal secretary, law clerk, paralegal, or employee associate when acting within the scope of employment. Furthermore, under general principles of partnership law, each partner in a general partnership is ***jointly and severally liable*** for the negligence of another partner committed in the ordinary course of the partnership business (i.e., any partner may be held personally liable for the entire judgment even if they had nothing to do with the negligent act). However, many law firms are set up as limited liability partnerships, limited liability companies, or similar entities. The law varies widely from state to state, but usually a partner of a limited liability entity will be shielded from personal liability for the misconduct of others in the firm.

6. **Malpractice Insurance**
    Because legal malpractice actions have become commonplace, prudent lawyers carry ample malpractice insurance. A small number of states require lawyers to have malpractice insurance, but a growing number of states require lawyers to disclose their insured or uninsured status to the state bar, or, in a few states, directly to potential clients. [*See* ABA Journal 63 (May 2006)]

7. **Settling Malpractice Claims**
    The law favors the amicable settlement of claims. Thus, a lawyer *may* settle a malpractice claim or potential claim made by an unrepresented client or a former client, but *only if* the lawyer first advises the client *in writing* to seek the advice of an independent lawyer about the settlement, and the lawyer gives the client a reasonable chance to obtain such advice. [ABA Model Rule 1.8(h)(2)]

    EXAMPLE
    Defendant D hired attorney A to defend him in a criminal case, and D gave A $5,000 as an advance against attorneys' fees yet to be earned. Shortly before trial, D became dissatisfied with A's work, fired her, and threatened to sue her for malpractice. A returned the unearned portion of the fee advance to D by a check that had an endorsement on the back purporting to release A from all liability for malpractice. A did not advise D to seek advice from an independent lawyer. A is subject to discipline. [*See, e.g.,* New York State Bar Op. 591 (1988)]
    ---

8. **Prospective Waiver or Limit of Malpractice Liability**
    A lawyer must not make an agreement with a client that prospectively waives or limits the lawyer's liability for legal malpractice, except in the unlikely event that the client is independently represented in making the agreement. [ABA Model Rule 1.8(h)(1)] Note that unlike with settlements (above), the client must *actually* be represented by independent counsel; advising the client to seek representation is not sufficient.

    EXAMPLE
    Lawyer L requires his clients to sign a standard, preprinted retainer agreement that provides, in part, that the client cannot sue L for malpractice. L's clients are not independently represented in signing his retainer agreement. L is subject to discipline.
    ---

    a. **May Practice in a Limited Liability Entity**
        A lawyer may practice in a limited liability entity, provided that the

lawyer remains personally liable to the client for her own malpractice, and the entity complies with legal requirements for notice, insurance coverage, and the like. [ABA Model Rule 1.8, comment 17]

b. May Reasonably Limit Scope of Representation
A lawyer may enter into an agreement with his client that reasonably limits the scope of the lawyer's representation in accordance with ABA Model Rule 1.2. [*Id.*]

EXAMPLE
Client C is thinking of purchasing the worldwide distribution rights to a strain of pest-resistant rice. C asks lawyer L to find out whether any nation imposes trade restrictions on that kind of rice. L tells C that to research the laws of every nation could take as much as 300 hours and cost $60,000, but C said he could not afford that much enlightenment. C and L agreed that L would research as many nations as he could in 100 hours, starting with C's most likely markets. The agreement is proper.

---

c. May Arbitrate Legal Malpractice Claims
A lawyer may agree prospectively with a client to arbitrate all legal malpractice claims, provided that such an agreement is proper under local law and the client understands the scope and effect of the agreement. [*Id.*]

9. Reimbursement of Client
A lawyer who has breached a duty to his client with monetary effect *cannot escape discipline* by reimbursing the client for any loss. Thus, even if the lawyer pays the client back for any damage he caused, he is still subject to discipline.

VI. LITIGATION AND OTHER FORMS OF ADVOCACY

A. MERITORIOUS CLAIMS AND CONTENTIONS ONLY

1. Discipline for Asserting Frivolous Position
A lawyer is subject to discipline for bringing a frivolous proceeding, or for asserting a frivolous position in the defense of a proceeding. Likewise, a lawyer is subject to discipline for taking a frivolous position on an *issue* in a proceeding. A "frivolous" position is one that cannot be supported by a good faith argument under existing law *and* that cannot be supported by a good faith argument for changing the existing law. [ABA Model Rule 3.1; Restatement §110; *and see* Fed. R. Civ. P. 11—litigation sanctions for frivolous pleadings and motions] Note the following:

   a.   It is **not** frivolous to assert a position without first fully substantiating all
        the facts. [ABA Model Rule 3.1, comment 2]

   b.   It is **not** frivolous to assert a position knowing that vital evidence can be
        uncovered only through discovery proceedings. [*Id.*]

   c.   It is **not** frivolous to assert a position even though the lawyer believes
        that the position will not ultimately prevail. [*Id.*]

EXAMPLES

1) C purchased land bordering a government forest, hoping to obtain the
necessary government approval to build a ski resort. When the government refused to grant the necessary approval, C hired lawyer L to sue the government
for taking C's property without just compensation. L advised C that her legal
position was contrary to the existing law, but L developed two tenable arguments for distinguishing C's case from the existing law. Even though L believed
that his arguments were sound, he did not believe that they would ultimately
prevail in the United States Supreme Court. L is not subject to discipline.

2) An attorney may advise a client to take a tax position if the attorney believes that the position has a "realistic possibility of success if the matter is
litigated." The attorney need not be convinced that the position will ultimately
prevail. But when advising a client about a debatable tax position, the attorney must warn the client about possible penalties and other adverse legal
consequences. [ABA Formal Op. 85-352 (1985)]

---

2.   **Defending in Criminal Proceedings**
     Despite the general rule against taking frivolous positions, the lawyer for
     the defendant in a criminal case (or for the respondent in a proceeding that
     could result in incarceration) may conduct the defense so that the prosecutor
     must prove every necessary element of the crime. [ABA Model Rule 3.1;
     Restatement §110(2)]

EXAMPLE

Attorney A agrees to defend D in a kidnapping case. From the facts related in
confidence by D, A concludes that D is clearly guilty as charged. If D nevertheless wishes to plead not guilty, A will not be subject to discipline for putting the prosecution to its proofs and requiring every element of the case to
be proven beyond a reasonable doubt.

B.   **DUTY TO EXPEDITE LITIGATION**

1.   **Reasonable Efforts to Expedite Litigation**
     A lawyer must make reasonable efforts to expedite litigation, consistent with

the interests of the client. [ABA Model Rule 3.2] A lawyer may occasionally ask for a postponement for personal reasons, but he should not make a habit of it. [*See* ABA Model Rule 3.2, comment 1]

2. **Interests of the Client**

The duty to expedite does not require the lawyer to take actions that would harm the client's legitimate interests. [*See* ABA Model Rule 3.2] However, realizing **financial or other benefit** from otherwise improper delay is **not** a legitimate interest. [ABA Model Rule 3.2, comment 1]

EXAMPLE

Client C lost her case at trial, and a judgment for $500,000 was entered against her. C's obligation to pay the judgment was stayed pending appeal. C instructed her lawyer to appeal the case and to drag out the appeal as long as possible, pointing out that she could earn an 11% return on the $500,000 while the appeal was pending. C's lawyer obtained every possible extension of time and delayed the appeal as long as he could. Ultimately, the appellate court affirmed the judgment below. C's lawyer is subject to discipline for causing delay.

C. DUTY OF CANDOR TO THE TRIBUNAL

1. **Candor About Applicable Law**

An attorney must be candid with the court about the **law** that applies to the case.

a. **False Statements of Law**

An attorney is subject to discipline for knowingly making a false statement of law to the court or for failing to correct a previously made false statement of material law. [ABA Model Rule 3.3(a)(1)]

EXAMPLES

1) During oral argument, attorney A cited the court to an intermediate appeals court opinion, knowing that the opinion had later been reversed by the state's highest court. A is subject to discipline.

2) In a memorandum of points and authorities, attorney B cited an obscure case for a proposition, knowing that the case held precisely the opposite. B is subject to discipline.

---

b. **Failing to Disclose Controlling Authority**

An attorney is subject to discipline for knowingly failing to disclose to the court a legal authority in the **controlling jurisdiction** that is **directly adverse** to the client's position and that has not been disclosed by the opposing counsel. [ABA Model Rule 3.3(a)(2); Restatement §111(2); *and see* Jorgenson v. Volusia County, 846 F.2d 1350 (11th Cir. 1988)—Rule 11 sanctions imposed for failure to cite adverse authority] The attorney is, of course, free to argue that the cited authority is not sound or should not be followed.

EXAMPLES

1) Lawyer L is representing client C in a diversity of citizenship case pending in the United States District Court for the District of Nevada. Under the *Erie* doctrine, Nevada law (including Nevada's choice of law rules) governs on issues of substance. In the case at hand, Nevada's choice of law rules make the controlling law that of the state of New York. L's adversary fails to call the court's attention to a New York Court of Appeals case that is directly contrary to the position taken by L's client. L must cite the case to the court.

2) Under the facts given in the example above, L would have no duty to cite the court to a directly adverse Utah case or to a directly adverse case decided by the United States Court of Appeals for the Fifth Circuit. Nor would L have a duty to cite the court to a New York Court of Appeals case that was against L's position only by analogy. (Note, however, that many lawyers would cite these cases to the court as a matter of sound tactics.)

---

2. **Candor About Facts of Case**
    An attorney is subject to discipline for knowingly making a false statement of fact to the court or for failing to correct a previously made false statement of material fact. [ABA Model Rule 3.3(a)(1)] Ordinarily, an attorney is not required to have personal knowledge of the facts stated in pleadings and other litigation documents—those contain assertions made by the client or by other persons, not by the attorney. But when an attorney does make an assertion of fact to the court (e.g., in an affidavit or when asserting facts in oral argument), the attorney is expected either to **know** that the assertion is true or to **believe** it to be true based on reasonably diligent inquiry. Furthermore, an attorney's **failure to speak out** is, in some contexts, the equivalent of an affirmative misrepresentation (e.g., when the attorney or the client has caused a mistake or misunderstanding). [ABA Model Rule 3.3, comment 3]

EXAMPLES

1) When the court was pondering whether to release attorney A's client on his own recognizance, the court asked A: "Does your client have a steady job here in the city, counsel?" A answered: "Oh, yes, Your Honor." If A knew that his client was unemployed, A is subject to discipline. Furthermore, if A had

never inquired about his client's employment status and had no reasonable basis for the assertion, A is subject to discipline.

2) When the court was deciding what sentence to impose on attorney B's client, the court said: "I assume that this is your client's first drunk driving offense, counsel, so I am ordering him to attend drunk driving school and to pay a fine of $100." B knew that his client had two prior drunk driving offenses and that the mandatory sentence for the third such offense is revocation of license and 90 days in the county jail. Because neither B nor his client caused the court's mistake, B may keep quiet. *But note:* If B or his client had caused the mistake, B would have to speak up and correct it.

3.   **No Obligation to Volunteer Harmful Facts**
An attorney generally has no obligation to volunteer a fact that is harmful to his client's case. The adversary system assumes that opposing sides can use discovery proceedings and their own investigations to find out the facts. [*See* ABA Model Rule 3.3, comment 14] If an attorney's adversary fails to uncover a harmful fact, an injustice may result, but that is simply the way the adversary system works.

EXAMPLE

Lawyer L is defending D at the trial of a private treble damages antitrust case. Plaintiff's case-in-chief is defective. L knows that the defect could be cured if plaintiff were aware of a certain meeting between D and D's competitors. Throughout the long discovery proceedings, plaintiff never inquired about this meeting, although he had ample opportunity to do so. L has no duty to volunteer information about the meeting; L's ethical obligation is to move for a directed verdict at the close of plaintiff's case-in-chief.

---

a.   **Exception—Ex Parte Proceedings**
In an ex parte proceeding, only one side is present. Because the other side has no opportunity to offer its version of the facts, the model of the adversary system does not apply in the ex parte context. Therefore, a lawyer in an ex parte proceeding **must inform** the tribunal of **all material facts** known to the lawyer that will help the tribunal make an informed decision. [ABA Model Rule 3.3(d); Restatement §112(2)]

EXAMPLE

The same day that W filed for divorce from H, W's lawyer petitioned for a temporary restraining order to prevent H from entering the family home and from bothering the children. Because H could not be found, the court agreed to hear the petition ex parte. At the hearing, W's lawyer must inform the court of **all the material facts**, both helpful and harmful, that bear on the issue before the court.

4. Using False Evidence

In a matter pending before a tribunal, a lawyer is subject to discipline for offering evidence that the lawyer **knows** is false. [ABA Model Rule 3.3(a)(3)] "Knows" means actual knowledge, but actual knowledge can be inferred from the circumstances. [ABA Model Rule 1.0(f)] A lawyer should resolve doubts about veracity in favor of her client, but a lawyer cannot ignore an obvious falsehood. [ABA Model Rule 3.3, comment 8] Furthermore, a lawyer **may** refuse to offer evidence that she **reasonably believes** is false, except for a criminal defendant's testimony on his own behalf. [ABA Model Rule 3.3(a)(3)] These principles apply, not just in court, but also in an ancillary proceeding, such as a deposition.

a. **Discovery of Falsity After Evidence Has Been Offered**

If a lawyer has offered a piece of evidence and later discovers that it is false, she must take reasonable remedial measures. First, the lawyer must speak confidentially with her client, urging the client's cooperation in withdrawing or correcting the false evidence. [ABA Model Rule 3.3, comment 10] Second, if the client will not cooperate, the lawyer should consider asking the court's permission to withdraw. Ordinarily, withdrawal is not mandatory, but it becomes mandatory if the lawyer's discovery of the false evidence creates such a rift between the lawyer and client that the lawyer can no longer represent the client effectively. [ABA Model Rule 3.3, comment 15] Withdrawal alone is not a sufficient remedial step if it leaves the false evidence before the tribunal. The lawyer should also move to strike the false evidence or take other steps to cancel out its effect. [*See* Restatement §120, comment h] Third, if withdrawal is not permitted or will not solve the problem, the lawyer **must** disclose the situation to the judge, even if that means disclosing the client's information that would otherwise be protected under the duty of confidentiality. [ABA Model Rule 3.3, comment 10]

Note that the duty to rectify false evidence continues until the end of the proceedings, which means when a final judgment has been affirmed on appeal or the time for appeal has expired. [ABA Model Rule 3.3, comment 13]

b. **False Testimony by Criminal Defendant**

When a lawyer in a **civil** matter learns that her client has testified falsely or is about to testify falsely, the lawyer's path is clear. If the client has not yet testified, the lawyer cannot call her client to the stand. If the client has testified and the lawyer learns that the testimony is false, the

lawyer must take the reasonable remedial measures explained in a., above. However, when the setting is a **criminal** rather than civil case, the situation becomes more complicated. Indeed, one of the thorniest problems in legal ethics arises when a criminal defense lawyer learns that her client has testified falsely, or is about to testify falsely, in his own defense. A criminal defendant has a Sixth Amendment right to the effective assistance of counsel. A criminal defendant also has a constitutional right to testify on his own behalf. [Rock v. Arkansas, 483 U.S. 44 (1987)] On the other hand, a criminal defense lawyer must not present evidence that he knows is false, and ordinarily he must not reveal the client's confidential information. What is the criminal defense lawyer to do when the client insists on testifying to something that the lawyer knows (because of the client's confidential disclosures) is false?

1) **ABA Model Rules and Restatement Solution**

When you take the MPRE, apply the solution adopted by the ABA Model Rules and the Restatement. [*See* ABA Model Rule 3.3(a)(3); Restatement §120, comment i] That is, the criminal defense lawyer should follow the same three steps stated in a., above. First, the lawyer must try to convince the defendant not to testify falsely. Second, if the defendant insists on testifying falsely, the lawyer should consider withdrawal, if that will solve the problem. Usually it will not solve the problem, either because the court will not permit withdrawal or because withdrawal will not erase or prevent the false testimony. Third, if all else fails, the lawyer must reveal the situation to the judge, even if that means disclosing the client's confidential information. The judge must then decide what to do, perhaps declare a mistrial, make some kind of statement to the jury, or perhaps nothing. The duty to rectify false evidence continues until the end of the proceedings, which means when a final judgment has been affirmed on appeal or the time for appeal has expired. [ABA Model Rule 3.3, comment 13] This solution to the problem does not violate a criminal defendant's constitutional right to effective assistance of counsel. [Nix v. Whiteside, 475 U.S. 157 (1986)]

2) **Minority View**

Several jurisdictions (including New York and California) handle the problem by allowing the criminal defendant to testify in "narrative fashion." That means that the defense lawyer questions the defendant in the ordinary way up to the point of the false testimony. At that point, the defense lawyer asks a question that calls for a narrative answer (such as "What else happened?"). The defendant then tells his story. The defense lawyer is not permitted to rely on the false parts of the story when arguing the case to the trier of fact. ABA Model Rule 3.3 defers to the local law in jurisdictions that follow the minority view. [ABA Model Rule 3.3, comment 7]

5. **Other Corruption of an Adjudicative Proceeding**
   A lawyer who represents a client in an adjudicative proceeding must take appropriate measures to prevent any person (a client or anyone else) from committing criminal or fraudulent conduct that will corrupt the proceedings. [*See* ABA Model Rule 3.3(b)] Examples of such conduct are: (1) hiding or destroying evidence, (2) bribing a witness, (3) intimidating a juror, (4) buying a judge, and (5) failing to obey a law or court order to disclose information. [ABA Model Rule 3.3, comment 12] Appropriate measures include disclosure to the court, if that becomes necessary.

EXAMPLE
Attorney A is defending surgeon S in a medical malpractice case. Student nurse N observed the operation in question, including the act that allegedly constitutes the malpractice. Two days before plaintiff took N's deposition, S's father told N: "If you testify at your deposition that you saw S do the act in question, I'll make sure you never get a nursing job in this state." At her deposition, N testified that she was not in the operating room at the time of the alleged act. Two days after the deposition, A learned what S's father did. A must set the record straight; if all else fails, A must tell the tribunal what happened.

D. **DUTY OF FAIRNESS TO OPPOSING PARTY AND COUNSEL**

1. **Opponent's Access to Evidence**
   A lawyer must not unlawfully obstruct another party's access to evidence. Furthermore, a lawyer must not unlawfully alter, destroy, or conceal a document or other item having evidentiary value. In addition, a lawyer must not counsel or assist another person to do any of these things. [ABA Model Rule 3.4(a); Restatement §118] Suppressing or tampering with evidence may also constitute a crime. [*See, e.g.,* Cal. Penal Code §135]

EXAMPLE
A special prosecutor was appointed to investigate certain allegations against a government official. The official told his lawyer about some highly incriminating documents in a file in his office. The lawyer suggested that the official "deep six" the file in the nearest river. The lawyer is subject to discipline.

---

2. **Falsifying Evidence and Assisting in Perjury**
   A lawyer must not falsify evidence. Furthermore, a lawyer must not counsel or assist a witness to testify falsely. [ABA Model Rule 3.4(b); Restatement §118] Well-prepared lawyers seldom pass up an opportunity to talk to a

witness before the witness testifies. The lawyer may probe the witness's memory, explore the basis of the witness's knowledge, point out holes and fallacies in the witness's story, and seek to refresh the witness's recollection by proper means. [Restatement §116] However, the lawyer must not try to "bend" the testimony or put words in the witness's mouth. New York's Judge Finch put the matter this way in an 1880 disciplinary case: "[The lawyer's] duty is to extract the facts from the witness, not to put them into him; to learn what the witness does know, not to teach him what he ought to know." [*In re* Eldridge, 82 N.Y. 161 (1880)]

3. **Abusing Discovery Procedures**
    A lawyer must not make a frivolous discovery request, or fail to make reasonable efforts to comply with a legally proper discovery request made by the adversary. [ABA Model Rule 3.4(d)] Abuse of discovery proceedings can also subject both the lawyer and the client to fines and other sanctions. [*See, e.g.,* Fed. R. Civ. P. 37(b); Roadway Express, Inc. v. Piper, 447 U.S. 752 (1980)—federal court has inherent authority to hold counsel personally responsible for expenses and attorneys' fees incurred because of counsel's bad faith in discovery]

    EXAMPLE
    Lawyer L intentionally failed to produce a certain set of handwritten notes that were clearly called for by a court order. L's conduct caused L's adversary to spend several hundred hours in developing alternative evidence of the facts stated in the notes. L is subject to discipline and is subject to such other sanctions as the court may see fit to impose.

    ---

4. **Paying Witnesses**
    A lawyer must not offer an inducement to a witness that is prohibited by law. [ABA Model Rule 3.4(b); Restatement §117] However, except when prohibited by local law, the following payments to witnesses are proper.

    a. **Travel, Meals, and Lodging**
        An attorney may pay expenses reasonably incurred by the witness in attending and testifying (e.g., travel, hotel, meals, and incidental expenses). [ABA Model Rule 3.4, comment 3]

    b. **Loss of Time**
        An attorney may pay reasonable compensation for the witness's loss of time in attending and testifying (e.g., the amount the witness would have earned at her job had she not had to come to testify). [Restatement §117, comment b]

    c. **Experts' Fees**
        An attorney may pay a reasonable fee to an ***expert*** witness for

preparing to testify and for testifying. The fee must not be contingent on either the content of the testimony or the outcome of the case. [ABA Model Rule 3.4, comment 3]

EXAMPLE

In a complex securities case, client C needed the testimony of an expert on securities brokerage. C's lawyer L agreed to advance the expenses for expert E and promised to pay E's travel, hotel, meal, and incidental expenses. L also promised E a witness fee of $1,000 or 2% of C's eventual recovery, whichever was greater. The arrangement for expenses was proper, but the witness fee arrangement makes L subject to discipline.

---

5. **Securing Absence or Noncooperation of Witness**

   A lawyer must not advise or cause a person to secrete himself or to flee the jurisdiction for the purpose of making him unavailable as a witness. [ABA Model Rule 3.4(a); Restatement §116] A lawyer may, however, advise a person not to voluntarily give information to an opponent or other party if the following conditions are met:

   a. The person is a client, or a relative, employee, or agent of a client; and

   b. The lawyer reasonably believes that the person's interests will not be harmed by not volunteering the information.

   [ABA Model Rule 3.4(f)]

EXAMPLE

Attorney A represents W in a child custody dispute with W's former husband, H. A believes that H's lawyer will probably try to interview W's sister to find out information about W's fitness as a parent. Absent some kind of harm to the sister, A may advise the sister that she need not speak voluntarily with H's lawyer about the matter. However, if A learns that H's lawyer is trying to serve a deposition subpoena on the sister, A must not advise the sister to leave town or hide from the process server.

---

6. **Violating Court Rules and Orders**

   A lawyer must not knowingly violate a rule of procedure, a rule of evidence, a rule of court, or an order made by the court—but a lawyer may openly refuse to obey such a rule or order for the purpose of making a good faith challenge to the validity of the rule or order. [ABA Model Rule 3.4(c); Restatement §105]

EXAMPLES

1) At the jury trial of D for automobile theft, the trial judge ordered prosecutor P to make no mention whatsoever of D's former misdemeanor convictions. In

cross-examining one of D's witnesses, P asked: "When you and D were cell-mates in the county jail back in 1998, did D invite you to join a car theft operation after your release?" If P was intentionally trying to evade the trial judge's order, P is subject to discipline.

2) In the civil suit of *P v. D*, P demanded production of some documents that D claimed were protected by the attorney-client privilege. The trial judge ordered the documents to be produced *in camera* so that he could determine whether the documents were privileged. D's lawyer asserted that the state law of attorney-client privilege did not authorize the judge to require an *in camera* examination. The trial judge refused to stay the order long enough to allow D to pursue an interlocutory appeal. D's lawyer may refuse to produce the documents while she seeks a writ of mandamus or prohibition to test the validity of the trial judge's order. [*See also In re* Tamblyn, 695 P.2d 902 (Or. 1985)—attorney may advise client not to obey void court order]

7. **Chicanery at Trial**
    A lawyer is subject to discipline for engaging in the following types of chicanery during the trial of a case.

    a. **Referring to Inadmissible Material**
        During the trial of a case, a lawyer must not refer to material that the lawyer does not reasonably believe is relevant or that will not be supported by admissible evidence. [ABA Model Rule 3.4(e); Restatement §107]

        EXAMPLES

        1) At the trial of a railway accident case, plaintiff's lawyer made repeated reference to the great size and wealth of the railway company. The comments were irrelevant to any issue in the case and were made solely to inflame the jury. The lawyer is subject to discipline. [*See also* Simmons v. Southern Pacific Transportation Co., 62 Cal. App. 3d 341 (1976)—verdict for plaintiff reversed because of counsel's misconduct]

        2) During her opening statement to the jury, the defense lawyer pointed out that plaintiff had offered to settle his claim for a small sum. The defense lawyer knew that evidence of the settlement offer would not be admissible. The lawyer is subject to discipline.

        ---

    b. **Asserting Personal Knowledge of Contested Facts**
        During the trial of a case, a lawyer must not assert personal knowledge of facts in issue (except when testifying as a witness). [ABA Model Rule 3.4(e)]

EXAMPLE

Lawyer L represented the plaintiff in a dog bite case. The defendant contended that he was not the owner of the offending dog. In his closing argument to the jury, L said: "The defendant has solemnly told you that he does not own the dog. As it happens, I live down the street from the defendant, and every night about 10, I see the defendant taking that very same dog for a walk." L is subject to discipline.

---

c. **Asserting Personal Opinions**

During the trial of a case, a lawyer must not state a personal opinion about:

1) The justness of a cause;

2) The credibility of a witness;

3) The culpability of a civil litigant; or

4) The guilt or innocence of an accused.

[ABA Model Rule 3.4(e); Restatement §107] A lawyer may, of course, make an argument based on the *evidence* concerning any of these matters.

EXAMPLES

1) During his closing argument in a routine traffic accident case, attorney A said: "D has told you that the light was green. I was appalled to hear the man say that from the witness stand, under oath! I don't believe him for a minute, and I ask you not to believe him either." A's argument is not proper.

2) In the example above, it would have been proper for A to make his point by referring to the evidence rather than expressing personal opinion. For instance: "D has told you that the light was green. D stands to lose a great deal of money in this case. Two eyewitnesses, who have nothing to lose, testified that the light was red. It is up to you jurors to decide whom to believe."

---

8. **Using Threats to Gain Advantage in Civil Case**

Under the ABA Model Rules, a lawyer may bring, or threaten to bring, criminal charges against her adversary in order to gain an advantage in a civil case, provided that the criminal and civil matters are closely related and that both the civil case and criminal charges are warranted by the law and the facts. [ABA Formal Op. 92-363 (1992)] However, a lawyer must not threaten to report adversary counsel for a disciplinary violation in order to gain an

advantage for her client in a civil case. If the adversary counsel's disciplinary violation is the kind that must be reported, the lawyer should simply report it—she should not use it as a bargaining chip in the civil case. [ABA Formal Op. 94-383 (1994)]

EXAMPLE

Lawyer L has personal knowledge that adversary counsel lied to the judge about a certain document that L had requested in discovery. Lying to a judge is the kind of conduct that raises a substantial question about a person's fitness to practice, and L therefore must report it. L told adversary counsel: "If you accept my client's settlement proposal, then I will not report you for lying to the judge about that document." L's conduct is improper; she should simply have reported adversary counsel, not used the misconduct as a bargaining chip in the civil case.

E. DUTY TO PRESERVE IMPARTIALITY AND DECORUM OF TRIBUNAL

1. Improper Influence

A lawyer must not seek to influence a judge, court official, juror, or prospective juror by improper means. [*See* ABA Model Rule 3.5(a)] For example, a lawyer must not offer a gift to a judge unless the judge would be allowed to accept it under the ABA Code of Judicial Conduct.

EXAMPLE

Attorneys A and B frequently appear as counsel in the Superior Court. C is the chief clerk of that court. All three of them are avid fishermen. A and B invite C to join them, at their expense, for a week of salmon fishing at B's lodge in Alaska. It would not be proper under ABA Code of Judicial Conduct Rules 2.12(A) and 3.13(A) for C to accept such a gift, and it is not proper for A and B to offer it to C.

---

2. Improper Ex Parte Communication

While a proceeding is pending in a tribunal, a lawyer must not have an ex parte communication with a judge, court official, juror, or prospective juror except when authorized by law or court order. [*See* ABA Model Rule 3.5(b)] An "ex parte communication" is a communication that concerns the matter at issue and occurs outside the presence and without the consent of the other parties to the litigation or their representatives. [Restatement §113, comment c]

a. Judges and Court Officials

As ABA Model Rule 3.5(b) recognizes, local law and court orders may vary concerning ex parte communications with judges and court officials. Generally, a ***written*** communication to a judicial officer is not ex parte if a copy of the communication is timely sent to the opposing parties. [Restatement §113, comment c] A lawyer must not, however, communicate **orally** on the **merits** of a matter with the judge or other official before whom the matter is pending without giving **adequate notice** to the adversary. If the local rules of court allow lawyers to appear ex parte, without notice to the adversary, to obtain extensions of time to plead or respond to discovery, a lawyer may do so—but the lawyer must not discuss the **merits** of the case when requesting the extension of time. [*See* Restatement §113(1)]

b. **Jurors and Prospective Jurors**

ABA Model Rule 3.5(b) recognizes that local law may vary concerning contact between lawyers and jurors or prospective jurors. In general, however, before and during the trial of a case, a lawyer **who is connected with the case** must not communicate (outside of official proceedings) with a juror or member of the panel from which the jurors will be chosen. This rule forbids communication on **any subject**—even the weather. It does not matter who initiates the communication. If a juror or prospective juror attempts to communicate with a lawyer, the lawyer must refuse. [Restatement §115] On the other hand, a lawyer who is **not** connected to the case may talk to a juror or prospective juror but not about the case (e.g., lawyer may talk to her friend the juror about the weather).

1) **Investigation of Prospective Jurors**

It is not improper for a lawyer to investigate members of a jury panel to determine their backgrounds and the existence of any factors that would be grounds for a challenge (e.g., bias, relationship to a party). Such an investigation must be done discreetly and must not involve contact with the prospective juror or, in most cases, her family.

a) **Juror's Internet Presence**

Unless limited by law or court order, a lawyer may review a juror's or potential juror's public Internet presence (e.g., postings on social media websites) in advance of and during a trial. However, a lawyer must not send the juror an access request (e.g., a "friend" request) either personally or through an agent. This constitutes a prohibited ex parte communication. [ABA Formal Op. 14-466 (2014)]

2) **Post-Trial Communications with Jurors**

After the trial is over and the jury is discharged, a lawyer must not communicate with a former jury member (or even a person who was a prospective juror) if any of the following conditions is met:

(1) local law or a court order prohibits such communication; (2) the juror has told the lawyer that he does not want to communicate; or (3) the communication involves misrepresentation, coercion, or harassment. [ABA Model Rule 3.5(c)]

3. **Disruptive Conduct**

    A lawyer must not engage in conduct intended to disrupt a tribunal. [ABA Model Rule 3.5(d)] This rule applies in depositions as well as in the courtroom. [ABA Model Rule 3.5, comment 5]

    > **EXAMPLE**
    >
    > Despite repeated warnings by the trial judge, attorney A persisted in banging on the counsel table, interrupting the judge in mid-sentence, making sour faces while witnesses were examined, and leaning over the jury rail in an intimidating manner. A is subject to discipline (and, at the court's discretion, to punishment for contempt of court).

F. **TRIAL PUBLICITY**

    The litigants in a trial have a Fifth Amendment right to have their dispute resolved on admissible evidence, by fair procedures, in a tribunal that is not influenced by public sentiment or outcry. Protection of that right requires some limits on the kinds of information that can be disseminated to the public before trial—particularly where the trial is to be by jury. On the other hand, the public and the press have countervailing rights under the First Amendment. The public has a right to know about threats to its safety, and it has an interest in knowing about the conduct of judicial proceedings. Moreover, the subjects of litigation are often significant in debate over questions of public policy.

    1. **General Rule**

        A lawyer who is connected with a case must not make a public statement outside the courtroom that the lawyer reasonably should know would have a "substantial likelihood of materially prejudicing" the case (e.g., discussing the character or credibility of a party or witness, performance or results of an examination, possibility of a guilty plea, or existence or contents of a confession). [ABA Model Rule 3.6(a); Restatement §109]

    2. **Right of Reply**

        A lawyer may, however, make a public statement that "a reasonable lawyer would believe is required to protect a client from the substantial undue prejudicial effect of recent publicity not initiated by the lawyer or the lawyer's client." [ABA Model Rule 3.6(c)]

        > **EXAMPLE**
        >
        > Professional tennis star Jacques LaMont was arrested for sexually assaulting

an employee in the hotel where he was staying. Dozens of media reporters descended on the inexperienced prosecutor assigned to LaMont's case. The reporters demanded to know what evidence there was against LaMont, who was reputed to be a clean-living family man. The prosecutor said he could not disclose any details, but that there was "some incriminating physical evidence," plus a "helpful signed statement that LaMont gave to the police voluntarily." The prosecutor's comments got wide coverage in the press and on television. LaMont's counsel feared that the prosecutor's characterization of LaMont's signed statement as "helpful" would make people think that LaMont had incriminated himself. Seeking to dispel that false impression, LaMont's counsel told reporters, quite accurately, that the most "incriminating" parts of LaMont's statement were that he was a paying guest of the hotel on the night in question and that at the time in question LaMont was asleep in his own hotel room, alone. The prosecutor is subject to discipline, but the defense lawyer's statement was proper. [*See* ABA Model Rule 3.6(c) and comment 5; *see also* ABA Model Rule 3.8(f)]

3. **Additional Constraint on Criminal Prosecutors**
   There is an additional constraint on the prosecutor in a criminal case. The prosecutor must not make extrajudicial comments that have a "substantial likelihood of heightening public condemnation of the accused." [ABA Model Rule 3.8(f)]

4. **Dry Facts About Case Permitted**
   Notwithstanding the general rule against prejudicial statements, a lawyer who is connected with the case may publicly state the following "dry facts" about the case:

   a. The claim, charge, or defense involved (provided there is an accompanying statement that the charge is only an accusation and that the party is deemed innocent until proven guilty);

   b. The names of persons involved (unless the law prohibits it);

   c. Any information that is already in the public record;

   d. The scheduling or result of any step in litigation;

   e. The fact that an investigation is ongoing, a request for help in getting information, and a warning of danger (if appropriate); and

   f. Routine booking information about a criminal defendant, such as his name, address, occupation, family status, the time and place of arrest, the names of arresting officers, and the names of investigating officers or agencies.

5. Rules Also Apply to Associated Lawyers

The rules stated above apply equally to other lawyers who are associated in a law firm or agency with the lawyers participating in the case. [ABA Model Rule 3.6(d)]

G. TRIAL COUNSEL AS WITNESS

1. Reasons to Avoid Dual Role

Several problems are posed when a client's trial counsel also testifies as a witness at the trial.

a. Conflict of Interest

The dual role may create a conflict of interest between the client and the trial counsel. For example, the trial counsel's testimony may contradict the client's testimony, or the trial counsel's obvious bias may make her an ineffective witness on behalf of the client. [ABA Model Rule 3.7, comment 6]

b. Differing Functions

The functions of trial counsel and witness are different. A witness must state facts objectively, but a trial counsel is supposed to present facts as a partisan advocate. When the two roles are combined, it may be unclear whether a particular statement is to be taken as evidence or as advocacy. The tribunal itself can object when the dual role may confuse or mislead the trier of fact. [ABA Model Rule 3.7, comment 2]

c. Effect on Adversary

The adversary may be handicapped in challenging the credibility of one who serves as both trial counsel and witness. Courtesy and sound tactics may force the adversary to tread softly on cross-examination. Furthermore, a favorable impression created as trial counsel may lend unjustified believability to the trial counsel's words as witness.

2. Ethical Limitations Imposed

For the foregoing reasons, the ABA Model Rules place limits on serving as both trial counsel and witness. [*See also* Restatement §108] Except in the situations discussed below, a lawyer must not act as an advocate at a trial in which the lawyer is likely to be a ***necessary*** witness. [ABA Model Rule 3.7(a)]

a. Uncontested Matter or Mere Formality

A lawyer may serve as trial counsel if her testimony as a witness will relate solely to an uncontested matter or to a mere formality. [*See* ABA Model Rule 3.7(a)(1)]

EXAMPLE

Attorney A's testimony will be limited to the authentication of a letter, and

there is no reason to doubt the letter's authenticity. Either A or another lawyer in her firm may serve as trial counsel.

b. **Testimony About Legal Services Rendered in the Case**
A lawyer may serve as trial counsel if his testimony will relate solely to the nature and value of legal services he has rendered in the case. [ABA Model Rule 3.7(a)(2)]

EXAMPLE
State law allows attorneys' fees to be awarded to the victor in environmental suits brought under the public trust doctrine. Attorney B's client won such a case. At the fee setting hearing, B may continue as trial counsel and may also testify about the number of hours he spent on the case, the nature of the services, and the amount of his ordinary hourly fee.

---

c. **Substantial Hardship on Client**
A lawyer may serve as trial counsel and also testify about any matter if withdrawal as trial counsel would cause "*substantial*" hardship. [ABA Model Rule 3.7(a)(3)] Courts tend to be narrow-minded in applying this exception. Mere duplication of legal fees or the loss of a long working relationship with counsel are sometimes held not to constitute substantial hardship.

EXAMPLE
For the past five years, attorney C has worked full-time on the discovery and pretrial preparation of a major tax fraud case. Just before trial, C discovered that she would have to testify on a contested issue concerning some entries in her client's books of account. If C withdraws as trial counsel, it will cost her client many thousands of dollars in extra legal fees, and it will delay the trial by 18 months. The substantial hardship exception *ought to* apply here, but there is some authority to the contrary.

---

d. **Other Lawyers in Firm May Be Witnesses**
A lawyer is permitted to act as an advocate at a trial in which another lawyer in the lawyer's firm is likely to be called as a witness unless precluded from doing so by the conflict of interest rules. [ABA Model Rule 3.7(b)]

3. **Conflict of Interest Rules Also Apply**
A lawyer who is asked to be both an advocate and a witness must comply not only with ABA Model Rule 3.7, but also with the general conflict of interest

principles stated in ABA Model Rules 1.7 (current clients) and 1.9 (former clients). For instance, the dual role can create a conflict between the current client's interest in winning the case and the lawyer's interest in earning a fee as trial counsel.

EXAMPLE

Rock climbers A, B, C, and L (a lawyer) went on a rock climbing venture guided by professional climber Bea Lai Long. C was badly injured on the climb, allegedly by Bea's foolhardy decision to take an exposed route when a storm was approaching. A, B, and L were the only people who saw what happened to C, and their testimony will be vital to C's claim against Bea. C has asked L to be her trial counsel. L would like to earn the fee, but he also knows that his testimony about the accident will be open to attack for bias; C might be better off having another trial counsel and using L only as an eyewitness. L must not represent C unless he fully explains the conflict to C and obtains her informed consent, confirmed in writing.

VII. TRANSACTIONS AND COMMUNICATIONS WITH PERSONS OTHER THAN CLIENTS

A. TRUTHFULNESS IN STATEMENTS TO THIRD PERSONS

1. **Must Not Make False Statements of Material Fact or Law**
   When dealing on behalf of a client with a third person, a lawyer must not knowingly make a false statement of law or material fact. [ABA Model Rule 4.1(a); Restatement §98] Generally, a lawyer has no duty to inform a third person of relevant facts. [ABA Model Rule 4.1, comment 1] However, a lawyer must not misrepresent the facts.

   a. **Types of Misrepresentation**
      A misrepresentation can occur when the lawyer makes a statement knowing that it is false, when the lawyer affirms or incorporates a statement knowing that it is false, when the lawyer states something that is partly true but misleading, or in some contexts when the lawyer fails to speak or act. [*Id.*]

EXAMPLES

1) Lawyer L represented seller S in negotiating a sale of S's farm to buyer B. L and S accompanied B on a walking tour of the farmlands, and it soon became apparent to them that B knew little or nothing about farming. When B looked over the north 40 acres, he said: "I assume that the soil and water here would be good for a nice walnut orchard." L and S both knew that the soil was far too wet and heavy to grow walnuts. S replied: "Oh, you'd be surprised what can grow here." L said nothing. L's failure

to speak out in this context is equivalent to an affirmative misrepresentation. L is subject to discipline.

2) Attorney A represented plaintiff P in a personal injury case. P died while settlement negotiation was going on with the defendant. A must not pursue the settlement negotiation without notifying the defense lawyer of P's death. [ABA Formal Op. 95-397 (1995)]

b.   Distinguish Conventional Puffery

Under generally accepted conventions in negotiation, certain types of statements ordinarily are not taken as statements of material fact. Estimates of price or value placed on the subject of a transaction are ordinarily regarded as mere puffery, and so is a statement of a party's intentions as to settlement of a claim. [ABA Model Rule 4.1, comment 2]

EXAMPLE

Attorney A was employed by Consolidated Liability Insurance Company to defend its insured, D, in an automobile accident case. After careful investigation, A concluded that D was clearly at fault. A advised Consolidated to settle, and Consolidated authorized A to settle the case for any sum under $10,000. A few days later, plaintiff's lawyer telephoned A and suggested that they meet to discuss a settlement. A responded: "I will be glad to listen to whatever you have to propose, but I sincerely doubt that Consolidated will be interested in settling—I think we can win this one at trial." Under generally accepted conventions, A's statements would be regarded as mere puffery, not as false statements of material fact.

---

2.   Failure to Disclose Material Facts—Client's Crime or Fraud

A lawyer must disclose material facts to a third person when necessary to avoid assisting the client in a crime or fraud—unless the lawyer is forbidden to do so by the ethical duty of confidentiality. [ABA Model Rule 4.1(b)] Under the ABA Model Rules view, where the duty of confidentiality prevents the lawyer from disclosing material facts, and where continued representation would require the lawyer to assist in the client's crime or fraud, the lawyer must withdraw. [See ABA Model Rules 1.16(a)(1), 1.2(d); ABA Formal Op. 92-366 (1992)] The lawyer may notify the affected third person of the withdrawal and may withdraw or disaffirm any opinion, document, or affirmation previously furnished in connection with the matter. [See ABA Model Rules 1.2, comment 10; 4.1, comment 3; and see ABA Formal Op. 92-366 (1992)]

EXAMPLE

Client C hired attorney A to obtain import licenses to sell C's chemical fertilizer in Australia and New Zealand. While the license applications were pending,

C and A negotiated a contract to sell C's entire fertilizer business to X. At C's request, A prepared a "Statement of Operations, Assets, and Liabilities" for X. In the statement, A represented that the Australian and New Zealand import licenses were pending and that in A's opinion they would be granted. Before the sale was closed, both Australia and New Zealand notified C that they would not issue the import licenses, and C conveyed this information to A in confidence. A advised C that X must be informed of this material fact, but C responded: "To hell with X—your job is to get the sale completed. Now get busy." Under the ABA Model Rules view, the duty of confidentiality forbids A from revealing the license denial to X, but if A continues with the representation, he will be assisting C in defrauding X. A must withdraw. A may advise X of his withdrawal, and he may disaffirm his prior opinion as to the Australian and New Zealand import licenses. The Restatement takes a simpler, more forthright position. The news of the license denial is not protected by the duty of confidentiality because the law of fraud requires A to disclose it to X. [*See* Restatement §§63, 98, comment d]

B.   **COMMUNICATION WITH PERSONS REPRESENTED BY COUNSEL**

1.   **When Communication Forbidden**
     A lawyer must not communicate about a matter with a person the lawyer knows is represented by counsel, unless that person's counsel consents, or unless the law or a court order authorizes the communication. This is true even if the represented person initiates or consents to the communication. [ABA Model Rule 4.2; Restatement §99]

     EXAMPLES
     1) In the case of *P v. D*, the lawyer for D had excellent reason to believe that P's lawyer had failed to convey D's settlement offer to P. D's lawyer therefore telephoned P and made the settlement offer directly. D's lawyer is subject to discipline for communicating with a represented person without consent of that person's counsel. [ABA Formal Op. 92-362 (1992)] P's lawyer is also subject to discipline if he failed to convey D's settlement offer to P.

     2) Defendant D was in jail awaiting trial for murder. D was represented by appointed counsel. Without the consent of the appointed counsel, the prosecutor visited D at the jail and discussed the possibility of a plea bargain with D. The prosecutor is subject to discipline. [ABA Model Rule 4.2, comment 5; ABA Formal Op. 95-396 (1995); Restatement §99, comment h]

2.   **Application to Organizations**
     Corporations and other organizations are "persons" for purposes of this rule. Thus, a lawyer must get the consent of the organization's counsel before communicating with the following constituents of the organization:

a.   A person who **supervises, directs, or regularly consults with the organization's lawyer** about the matter at hand;

b.   A person whose conduct may be **imputed** to the organization for purposes of criminal or civil liability; or

c.   A person who has **authority to obligate the organization** concerning the matter.

[ABA Model Rule 4.2, comment 7] Note that if the constituent is represented in the matter by her own counsel, then consent by that counsel (rather than the organization's counsel) is sufficient. Consent is **not** needed before talking to a **former** constituent of the organization. [*Id.*] However, when talking with either a present or former constituent, a lawyer must take care not to violate the organization's legal rights, such as the attorney-client privilege.

EXAMPLE

Lawyer L represents the plaintiff in a defamation action against the Herald Newspaper Corp. Without getting the permission of the Herald's counsel, L interviewed the newspaper's former editor-in-chief and convinced him to disclose some privileged communications he had with the newspaper's lawyer about the case. L acted improperly in prying into the privileged communications. [*Id.; and see* ABA Model Rule 4.4, comment 1]

---

3.   **Communications Allowed by the Rule**
The rule does not prohibit: (1) a lawyer from communicating with a represented person when the communication is authorized by law or court order or when the communication does not concern the subject of the representation; (2) represented persons from communicating directly with each other; and (3) a lawyer from interviewing an unrepresented person who will be called as a witness by some other party. [ABA Model Rule 4.2, comment 4; *and see* Lewis v. S.S. Baune, 534 F.2d 1115 (5th Cir. 1976)]

EXAMPLE

In a complex contract suit between P and D, both parties were represented by counsel. For several months, the respective sets of lawyers tried to work out a satisfactory settlement, but without success. P concluded that the lawyers had become befogged by petty detail and bickering. P therefore invited D out to lunch, and the two of them worked out a settlement within the space of an hour. Direct communication between represented persons is not prohibited by the rule.

---

a.   **Exception—Lawyers Acting Pro Se**
Even though parties may generally communicate directly with each

other, when a lawyer is representing themselves (acting pro se), they are considered to be representing a client and therefore subject to the prohibition on communicating with a represented person. [ABA Formal Ethics Op. 502 (2022)]

C. DEALING WITH UNREPRESENTED PERSONS

When dealing with an unrepresented person, a lawyer must not state or imply that the lawyer is disinterested. When the lawyer knows, or reasonably should know, that the unrepresented person misunderstands the lawyer's role in the matter, the lawyer must make reasonable efforts to correct the misunderstanding. Likewise, if the lawyer knows or should know that her client's interests are likely to be in conflict with those of the unrepresented person, she must not give legal advice to that person (other than to get a lawyer). [ABA Model Rule 4.3; Restatement §103] The rule does not, however, prevent a lawyer from negotiating a transaction or settling a client's dispute with an unrepresented person. [ABA Model Rule 4.3, comment 2]

EXAMPLE

Property owner O wants to lease his empty retail store to merchant M, who wants to use it for a shoe store. M does not have a lawyer, but O is represented by attorney A. In negotiating the terms of the lease, A may communicate directly with M, but A should make clear to M that A represents O and is not looking out for M's interests. During the lease negotiations, A may tell M what terms will be acceptable to O. A may also draft a proposed lease agreement and may explain to M what A believes the legal effect of the lease will be. [*Id.*]

D. RESPECT FOR RIGHTS OF THIRD PERSONS

1. Heavy-Handed Tactics

In representing a client, a lawyer must not use means that have no substantial purpose other than to embarrass, delay, or burden a third person. [ABA Model Rule 4.4(a)] Furthermore, a lawyer must not use methods of obtaining evidence that violate the legal rights of a third person.

EXAMPLES

1) When preparing to cross-examine witness W, attorney A discovered that W had six misdemeanor convictions for prostitution. A knew that under the applicable evidence law, he would not be allowed to use those misdemeanor convictions for impeachment, and A knew that they were not otherwise relevant to the proceeding. Nonetheless, on cross-examination, A asked: "How old were you when you decided to devote your life to prostitution, Miss W?" A is subject to discipline.

2) Lawyer L represented P in a complicated trade secrets case against D Corporation. During discovery, L used a subpoena duces tecum to require

E Corporation (a nonparty) to produce thousands of documents in connection with the depositions of some employees of E Corporation. The lawyer for E Corporation allowed L to personally go through E Corporation's files to pick out and photocopy documents responsive to the subpoena. While doing that, L made copies of many other documents that were not covered by the subpoena, and L did not tell the lawyer for E Corporation what he had done. L is subject to discipline.

3) Deputy District Attorney A was assigned to prosecute a bank robbery case against D. A suspected that heroin addict X could probably furnish valuable evidence against D but that X would doubtless refuse to do so. Therefore, A told the police: "Go pick up X on suspicion of drug peddling, and we'll find out what he knows about D and the bank robbery." A is subject to discipline.

2. **Documents Sent to Lawyer by Mistake**
Lawyers sometimes receive documents that were sent to them by mistake. That happens with e-mail, fax transmission, postal service, and even personal messenger service. It can also happen when documents—whether paper documents or electronically stored information—are produced pursuant to a discovery request. When a lawyer obtains such a document, and when she knows or reasonably should know that it was sent by mistake, she must promptly notify the sender so that the sender can take protective measures. [ABA Model Rule 4.4(b) and comment 2] The Model Rule does not address some related questions on which state law is split: e.g., whether the recipient must return the document to the sender, or delete electronically stored information, and whether the inadvertent disclosure of the document waives a privilege that would otherwise protect it.

VIII. DIFFERENT ROLES OF THE LAWYER

A. LAWYER AS ADVISOR TO THE CLIENT

1. **Duty to Render Candid Advice**
When acting as advisor to a client, a lawyer must exercise independent judgment and render candid advice. [ABA Model Rule 2.1] Candid advice is sometimes hard to take—the facts may be harsh and the choices unattractive. The lawyer should attempt to keep the client's morale up but should neither sugarcoat the advice nor delude the client. [See ABA Model Rule 2.1, comment 1]

2. **Giving Advice Beyond the Law**
A lawyer may give a client not only legal advice, but also moral, economic, social, or political advice when relevant to the client's situation. [ABA Model Rule 2.1] When appropriate, a lawyer may also urge a client to seek advice

from persons in related professions—e.g., advice from an accountant, psychiatrist, physician, or family counselor. [*See* ABA Model Rule 2.1, comment 4]

3.   **Volunteering Advice**
     A lawyer ordinarily has no duty to give advice until asked. However, if the lawyer knows that the client is planning a course of action that will have substantial adverse legal consequences for the client, the lawyer may volunteer advice without being asked. [*See* ABA Model Rule 2.1, comment 5]

EXAMPLE
Client C hired lawyer L to do some tax work. In the course of that work, L learned that C was regularly putting large amounts of money into a trust established for her grandchildren. If L reasonably believes that C is endangering her ability to provide for her own needs in old age, L may call that fact to C's attention, and L may assist C in working out a safer plan for investment and disposition of her assets.

B.   **EVALUATION FOR USE BY THIRD PERSONS**
     ABA Model Rule 2.3 concerns the lawyer who is asked, expressly or impliedly, to evaluate the affairs of a client and to supply the evaluation for use by third persons.

EXAMPLES
1) Client X asks her lawyer to evaluate her legal title to 40 acres of ranch land and to furnish the evaluation to a proposed purchaser of the land.

2) Client Y Corp. wants to borrow a large sum from a bank and asks its lawyer to evaluate its legal and business affairs and to furnish a report to the bank.

3) Client Z, a school district, proposes to issue some school bonds and asks its lawyer to examine its situation and its proposed bond issue and to render a legal opinion for use by election officials, voters, and potential investors.

Note that in each of the foregoing examples, the client is the person or entity whose affairs are to be evaluated by the lawyer. ABA Model Rule 2.3 does not apply when a client asks a lawyer to evaluate the affairs of a third party and then to make a report to the client.

EXAMPLE
Bank proposes to lend a large sum of money to Y. Bank therefore asks its own lawyer to evaluate Y's business and legal affairs and to report back to Bank. ABA Model Rule 2.3 does **not** apply to this situation. [ABA Model Rule 2.3, comment 2]

---

1. **Requirements of the Rule**
    A lawyer may evaluate a client's affairs for the use of a third person if the lawyer reasonably believes that making the evaluation is compatible with the lawyer's other responsibilities to the client. [ABA Model Rule 2.3(a)]

    EXAMPLE
    Lawyer L is defending client D Company in a suit for infringement of three United States patents. If D loses the infringement suit, its business will be virtually wiped out. D seeks to borrow a substantial sum of money from trust company T, and D asks L to evaluate its business and its pending litigation and to render a report to T. L should decline to perform the evaluation. L's responsibilities to D as an advocate in the patent infringement case are not compatible with rendering a candid evaluation for use by T. [*See* ABA Model Rule 2.3, comment 3]

2. **Harmful Evaluation**
    If the lawyer knows or should know that the evaluation will materially harm the client, the lawyer must obtain the client's informed consent before making the evaluation. [ABA Model Rule 2.3(b)]

3. **Confidentiality**
    Except as disclosure is authorized in connection with a report of an evaluation, the ordinary rules of confidentiality apply to information gained during the evaluation. [ABA Model Rule 2.3(c)] The client may limit the scope of the evaluation or the sources of information available to the lawyer, but the lawyer should describe any material limitations in the report furnished to the third person. [ABA Model Rule 2.3, comment 4] The lawyer may have other legal duties to the third person in connection with the report—that depends on the applicable law and is not covered in ABA Model Rule 2.3. [ABA Model Rule 2.3, comment 3]

4. **Lawyer's Liability to Third Person**
    A lawyer who is hired to evaluate a client's affairs for a third person may be liable to the third person for negligence in rendering the evaluation.

    EXAMPLE
    Client C hired attorney A to evaluate C's financial condition for bank B in the hope that B would lend money to C. A's opinion letter to B negligently misrepresented C's financial condition, as a direct result of which B suffered a large loss. A is liable to B for the negligent misrepresentation. [*See* Vereins-Und Westbank, AG v. Carter, 691 F. Supp. 704 (S.D.N.Y. 1988)]

5. **Cases in Which Opinion Is to Be Widely Disseminated**

When a lawyer agrees to certify facts to a large number of persons who can be expected to rely on the lawyer, the lawyer has a special obligation to be complete, accurate, and candid.

a. **Securities Cases**

This special obligation most often arises when a lawyer has prepared an opinion letter to be used in disclosure documents for securities investors. The lawyer may be held liable for both misstatements and omissions of material facts. [SEC v. National Student Marketing Corp., 457 F. Supp. 682 (D.D.C. 1978)]

1) **Due Diligence Required**

A lawyer is not a guarantor of every fact in the disclosure materials about the company or transaction. However, if the disclosures are inconsistent, or the lawyer has any reason to doubt their accuracy, the lawyer has a **duty to inquire** to determine the correct facts. [ABA Formal Op. 335 (1974)]

b. **Tax Shelter Opinions**

When a lawyer gives a widely disseminated legal opinion about the tax treatment likely to be afforded an investment, the lawyer must candidly disclose and estimate the degree of risk that the IRS will not allow the tax treatment being sought, even if such disclosure will be contrary to the interest of the client in selling the investment. [ABA Formal Op. 346 (1982)]

C. **LAWYER AS NEGOTIATOR**

Lawyers must negotiate in both litigation (e.g., settlement negotiations) and nonlitigation contexts (e.g., real estate transactions, business merger negotiations). Issues of honest and affirmative disclosure often arise in connection with such negotiations. Thus, the Rules prohibit a lawyer from making a false statement of **material fact**. [ABA Model Rule 4.1(a)] However, the lawyer is under no duty to do the other side's fact research or volunteer any facts that would undermine the client's position.

1. **Puffing and Subjective Statements**

Because it is the essence of negotiation that the lawyer attempt to magnify the strength of the client's position, there are some statements that the ABA Model Rules will allow even though they may constitute "puffing" of the client's position—i.e., they are not considered statements of material fact. The key factor to examine when determining if a statement contains a material fact is whether the opposing party would be reasonable in relying on the statement made. Certain types of subjective statements, such as those relating to the relative merits of the case, estimates of price and value, and a party's intentions as to an acceptable settlement are not considered statements of material fact in this context. [ABA Model Rule 4.1, comment 2]

2. **Misapprehension**

A lawyer who believes an opponent is underestimating the strength of his client's position has no duty to correct that misapprehension unless the lawyer or the client caused it. [Brown v. County of Genesee, 872 F.2d 169 (6th Cir. 1989)—opponent miscalculated amount of lost pay] However, in certain instances, the opponent's lack of knowledge of pertinent facts may be so important that disclosure is required.

EXAMPLES

1) Plaintiff's lawyer failed to disclose to the defendant that, during the settlement negotiations, the plaintiff, who was considered to be a strong witness, died. The settlement of the case was set aside. [Virzi v. Grand Trunk Warehouse, 571 F. Supp. 507 (E.D. Mich. 1983)]

2) Prosecutor had a duty to disclose to a criminal defendant that, prior to the acceptance of his guilty plea, physical evidence of the defendant's guilt was accidentally destroyed. [Fambo v. Smith, 433 F. Supp. 590 (W.D.N.Y. 1977)]

D. **LAWYER AS THIRD-PARTY NEUTRAL**

1. **General Principles**

A lawyer serves as a third-party neutral when she assists two or more nonclients in resolving a dispute or other matter that has arisen between them. [ABA Model Rule 2.4(a)] Examples of a third-party neutral are an arbitrator, mediator, conciliator, or evaluator. [ABA Model Rule 2.4, comment 1] Nonlawyers can serve as third-party neutrals, but some court rules require lawyers for some types of cases. When a lawyer serves as a third-party neutral, she is subject not only to the ordinary rules of legal ethics, but also to various codes of conduct devised by groups such as the American Arbitration Association. [ABA Model Rule 2.4, comment 2]

2. **Warning to Unrepresented Parties**

A lawyer who serves as a third-party neutral does not represent any of the parties. A party who is not familiar with arbitration, mediation, or the like, and who is not represented by counsel, may erroneously believe that the lawyer third-party neutral is protecting his interests, but that is not so. The lawyer must therefore clearly explain the situation to the unrepresented party; e.g., the lawyer should explain that the attorney-client privilege does not apply to communications between them. [ABA Model Rule 2.4, comment 3]

3. **Conflicts of Interest**

A lawyer who serves as a third-party neutral in a matter must not thereafter

become the lawyer for anyone involved in the matter, unless all of the parties give their informed consent, confirmed in writing. [ABA Model Rule 1.12(a)] This conflict is imputed to other lawyers in the lawyer's firm, but it can be solved by screening the lawyer from the matter, assuring that he does not share the fee, and notifying the parties in writing about the screening arrangement. [ABA Model Rule 1.12(c)] No conflict arises when a lawyer who served as a *partisan* arbitrator for a party is later asked to become that party's lawyer. [ABA Model Rule 1.12(d)]

E.   **SPECIAL RESPONSIBILITIES OF A PROSECUTOR**

The prosecutor in a criminal case is not simply an advocate but also a minister of justice; the prosecutor's primary goal is to *seek justice*, not to convict. Thus, the prosecutor must assure that the defendant is tried by fair procedures and that guilt is decided on proper and sufficient evidence. Local laws may impose additional duties on a prosecutor, and failure to comply with such laws is grounds for professional discipline. [ABA Model Rule 3.8, comment 1]

1.   **Prosecuting Without Probable Cause**

A prosecutor must not prosecute a charge that she knows is not supported by probable cause. [ABA Model Rule 3.8(a)]

2.   **Protecting Accused's Right to Counsel**

A prosecutor must make reasonable efforts to assure that the accused is:

a.   Advised of the right to counsel;

b.   Advised of the procedure for obtaining counsel; and

c.   Given a reasonable opportunity to obtain counsel.

[ABA Model Rule 3.8(b)]

> **EXAMPLE**
>
> Sheriff S is in charge of the county jail. S has established jail regulations that frequently result in an accused being held incommunicado for a long period before being given a chance to use the telephone. County District Attorney A must make reasonable efforts to have the jail regulations changed. [*See* ABA Model Rule 3.8(b)]

3.   **Securing Waiver of Pretrial Rights**

A prosecutor must not seek to obtain from an unrepresented accused a waiver of important pretrial rights, such as the right to a preliminary hearing. *Note:* An accused who is appearing pro se with the court's approval is not "unrepresented" for purposes of this rule. [ABA Model Rule 3.8(c) and comment 2]

EXAMPLE

Indigent accused A was advised of his right to remain silent and of his right to have counsel appointed to defend him. A asked for the services of a public defender, and A said that he did not want to make any statement. Before the public defender arrived, A was brought to a small room and allowed to relax over a cup of coffee. At that time, prosecutor P urged him to "assist us voluntarily in finding out what happened so we can clear this up and get you out of here without getting into legal technicalities." P is subject to discipline.

---

4.   **Disclosing Evidence that May Help Defense**

A prosecutor must timely disclose to the defense all evidence and information known to the prosecutor that tends to negate the guilt of the accused or mitigate the degree of the offense. [ABA Model Rule 3.8(d)] Failure to disclose material information may deprive the defendant of due process. [*See* Brady v. Maryland, 373 U.S. 83 (1963), *explained in* United States v. Bagley, 473 U.S. 667 (1985)]

EXAMPLE

D was accused of second degree murder. Prosecutor P asked the county coroner to pay special attention to the size, shape, and location of the stab wound that killed the victim. The coroner reported that the wound was probably inflicted by a person who was being held down on the ground by the victim. Since this information tends to suggest self-defense, P must promptly report it to D's lawyer.

---

5.   **Disclosing Information that May Mitigate Punishment**

When a convicted person is to be sentenced, the prosecutor must disclose to the defense and to the court all unprivileged mitigating information known to the prosecutor (except when a protective order of the court relieves the prosecutor of this obligation). [ABA Model Rule 3.8(d)]

6.   **Public Statements About Pending Matters**

Except for statements that are necessary to inform the public of the nature and extent of the prosecutor's action and that serve a legitimate law enforcement purpose, a prosecutor must not make extrajudicial statements that have a "substantial likelihood of heightening public condemnation of the accused." A prosecutor must take reasonable care to prevent investigators, police, employees, and other subordinates from making such statements. [ABA Model Rule 3.8(f)]

7.   **Disclosing Evidence to Remedy Conviction**

A prosecutor must promptly disclose new, credible, and material evidence that creates a reasonable likelihood that a defendant was wrongly convicted. [ABA

Model Rule 3.8(g)] Further, the prosecutor must seek to remedy the conviction of a defendant in his jurisdiction if he knows of clear and convincing evidence that the defendant was innocent. [ABA Model Rule 3.8(h)]

8. **Subpoenaing Other Lawyers**

    A prosecutor must not subpoena another lawyer to give evidence about a client or former client unless the evidence is not privileged, is essential, and cannot be obtained in another way. [ABA Model Rule 3.8(e)]

9. **Other Government Lawyers**

    Many of the above duties are incumbent on all government lawyers, not merely public prosecutors.

    a. **Terminating Actions**

        A government lawyer with discretionary power relative to civil litigation should not institute or continue actions that are obviously unfair. [Freeport-McMoRan Oil & Gas Co. v. F.E.R.C., 962 F.2d 45 (D.C. Cir. 1992)]

    b. **Developing Full Record**

        Even if litigation appears warranted, a government lawyer has a responsibility to develop a full and fair record. The lawyer must not use her position or the economic power of the government to harass parties or to force unjust settlements or results.

F. **ADVOCATE IN LEGISLATIVE AND ADMINISTRATIVE PROCEEDINGS**

1. **Appearances in a Representative Capacity**

    Lawyers sometimes appear before legislatures, city councils, executive agencies, regulatory boards, and other groups that act in a rule-making or policy-making capacity. When a lawyer appears on behalf of a client before a legislative body or administrative agency, the lawyer must disclose that she is acting in a representative capacity (not on her own behalf). [ABA Model Rule 3.9; Restatement §104]

EXAMPLE

The Columbia Association of Manufacturers and Retailers hired lawyer L to assist it in opposing a proposed new inventory tax. In that capacity, L testified in hearings before the Finance Committee of the Columbia Municipal Council. In her testimony, L presented both legal and economic arguments against the proposed tax. L must disclose to the Finance Committee that she is acting in a representative capacity.

---

2. **Duties of Candor and Respect**

    When a lawyer represents a client before a legislative body or administrative agency in an official hearing or meeting at which the lawyer or client presents

evidence or argument, the lawyer must, generally speaking, follow the same rules as though in court. [ABA Model Rule 3.9 and comment 2] For example, the lawyer must not make false statements of fact or law, offer evidence known to be false, obstruct access to evidence, knowingly violate the rules and orders of the legislative or administrative body, seek to use undue influence, or engage in disruptive conduct. [ABA Model Rules 3.9, 3.3(a) - (c), 3.4(a) - (c), 3.5] A lawyer should comply with these rules even though the rules do not bind nonlawyers who do similar work. [ABA Model Rule 3.9, comment 2]

3. **Limits of These Rules**

The rules stated in 1. and 2., above, do **not** apply: (1) when a lawyer represents a client in bilateral negotiations with the government, (2) in an application for a license or other privilege, (3) when the government is investigating the client's affairs, or (4) when the government is examining the client's compliance with a regular reporting requirement (such as the filing of tax returns).

G. ORGANIZATION AS CLIENT

1. **Duty of Loyalty to Organization**

A corporation, governmental agency, unincorporated association, or similar organization is a legal entity, but it must act through the people who make up the organization—the directors, officers, agency employees, shareholders, owners, or the like. A lawyer who represents an organization obviously must work through those people. However, when the organization is the lawyer's client, the lawyer owes the duty of loyalty to the *organization*—not to the people who are its constituents. [ABA Model Rule 1.13(a); Restatement §96]

2. **Conflicts Between the Organization and Its Constituents**

Ordinarily, there is no conflict between the interests of the organization and the interests of the people who make up the organization. Sometimes, however, their interests do come into conflict. When they do, the lawyer for the organization should caution the person in question that the attorney represents the organization, not the person. For instance, the lawyer should warn the person that communications between them may not be protected by the attorney-client privilege. Furthermore, when appropriate, the lawyer should advise the person to obtain independent legal counsel. [ABA Model Rule 1.13, comment 10]

EXAMPLE

The board of directors of Growers' Export Corp. instructed the corporation's general counsel to give classes for all management personnel concerning the laws and corporate rules against using bribery and kick-backs when negotiating business contracts in foreign nations. After such a class, one of the foreign office managers told the general counsel that he had frequently used bribes to secure business for the corporation. The general counsel should remind the manager that she represents the corporation, not the manager, that bribery is both illegal and against the rules of the corporation, and, if appropriate, that the manager should seek independent legal counsel. [*See* ABA Model Rule 1.13(f); ABA Model Rule 1.13, comment 10]

3. **Protecting the Organization's Interests**

If the lawyer for an organization learns that a person associated with the organization has acted, or is about to act, in a way that violates a duty to the organization or a law in a way that might be imputed to the organization, and if the violation is likely to cause substantial injury to the organization, the lawyer must proceed as is reasonably necessary to protect the interests of the organization. [ABA Model Rule 1.13(b)]

a. **Duty to Report to Higher Authority in Organization**

In the situation described above, the lawyer must ordinarily report the violation to a higher authority in the organization (e.g., to a corporation's president). If necessary, the lawyer must report it to the organization's highest authority (e.g., a corporation's outside directors). ABA Model Rule 1.13(b) does, however, give the lawyer a narrow range of discretion—she need not report the violation if she reasonably believes that the organization's best interests do not require the violation to be reported. [*Id.*]

b. **Duty to Report Outside the Organization**

If the lawyer reports the violation to the organization's highest authority, but the highest authority fails to take timely, appropriate action, the lawyer *may* report the relevant information to appropriate persons outside of the organization. This is true even if the information would otherwise be protected by the duty of confidentiality expressed in ABA Model Rule 1.6. [ABA Model Rule 1.13(c)] However, the lawyer's authority to report to outsiders applies only if, and to the extent that, the lawyer *reasonably believes* that reporting is necessary to *prevent substantial injury* to the organization. The authority to report to outsiders does not apply to a lawyer who is hired by the organization to investigate an alleged violation of law or to defend the organization or its constituents against a claimed violation of law. [ABA Model Rule 1.13(d)]

EXAMPLE

Attorney A's corporate client produces frozen chicken pies. C's production process creates large quantities of liquid waste, which C is supposed to pump into recycling tanks. C's manufacturing vice president sometimes orders his workers to dump the waste into a ditch that drains into some neighboring wetlands; the dumping is cheaper and quicker, but it gradually destroys the wetlands in violation of state and federal environmental laws. When A learns about the dumping, she reports it to C's president and warns him that C will be fined millions of dollars if it gets caught. C's president ignored A's warning, so A reported the matter to the highest authority in the company—the audit committee of the board of directors. The audit committee did nothing. If A reasonably believes that the company will be seriously injured if the dumping continues, A *may* report the relevant information to the appropriate environmental enforcement authority, even if some of that information would otherwise be protected by the duty of confidentiality.

c. Whistle Blower Protection

A lawyer who reasonably believes that she has been fired because she acted pursuant to Model Rule 1.13(b) or (c) (see a. and b. above), or who withdraws under circumstances that require or permit her to act pursuant to either of those paragraphs, must proceed as she reasonably believes necessary to assure that the organization's highest authority is informed of the firing or withdrawal. [ABA Model Rule 1.13(e)]

4. Representing Both the Organization and an Associated Person

The lawyer for an organization may represent both the organization and one or more of the directors, officers, employees, or other persons associated with the organization, provided that the ordinary conflict of interest rules are satisfied. [ABA Model Rule 1.13(g); Restatement §§96, comment h, 131, comment e] When dual representation requires the consent of the organization, the consent must be given by an appropriate person other than the person to be represented. [ABA Model Rule 1.13(g)]

EXAMPLE

The Anti-Nuclear Coalition sued Consolidated Light and Power Co. and the president of Consolidated under federal, state, and common law to prevent Consolidated from starting up a nuclear generating plant that it had constructed. The firm of W, X & Y was retained to represent both Consolidated and its president. After careful examination, the firm concluded that it could represent both clients effectively, even though their interests potentially conflict on one or two points. After the firm explained the potential conflicts, the president gave informed consent on his own behalf, confirmed in writing, and the chairman of the board of directors gave informed consent on behalf of the company, confirmed in writing. The dual representation is proper.

5. Serving as Both Director and Lawyer

The ABA Model Rules do not forbid a lawyer from serving as both a director of an organization and as a lawyer for the organization, but the Model Rules point out that the dual role can create conflicts of interest. For instance, when the lawyer participates in a meeting as a director (rather than as the organization's lawyer), the attorney-client privilege will not apply to communications at the meeting, but some of the other directors may not realize that. If there is a substantial risk that the dual role will compromise the lawyer's professional judgment, the lawyer should either resign as director or not act as the organization's lawyer when a conflict arises. [*See* ABA Model Rule 1.7, comment 35]

6. **Securities Lawyer's Duties Under Sarbanes-Oxley Act**

In response to the collapse of several high-flying corporations in 2002, Congress passed the Sarbanes-Oxley Act. Among other things, the Act instructs the Securities and Exchange Commission ("SEC") to make rules for securities lawyers who discover their clients violating the federal or state securities laws or similar laws. The SEC did make rules, which are now part of the "law of lawyering" that is covered on the MPRE. [*See* 17 C.F.R. §205] The following discussion includes highlights of the Sarbanes-Oxley rules.

a. **Application to "Securities Lawyers"**

The rules apply to lawyers who represent an issuer of securities and who practice before the SEC ("securities lawyers"). This includes not only lawyers who transact business with the SEC, communicate with it, or represent a securities issuer before it, but also lawyers who give advice about a document that will be filed with the SEC or advice about whether information must be filed with the SEC.

b. **Reporting Requirement**

If a securities lawyer becomes aware of credible evidence that her client is materially violating a federal or state securities law, she **must** report the evidence to her client's chief legal officer ("CLO") or chief executive officer. The same reporting duty applies to credible evidence that one of her client's personnel has breached a fiduciary duty under federal or state law or has committed a "similar material violation" of federal or state law.

c. **Investigation by CLO**

The CLO must investigate the situation to determine whether a violation occurred. Alternatively, the CLO can turn the matter over to a legal compliance committee, but for purposes of this discussion, that complication will be ignored.

d. **If Violation Found—"Appropriate Response" Required**

If the CLO concludes that no violation occurred, he must report that conclusion back to the securities lawyer. If the CLO concludes that a violation did occur, is occurring, or is about to occur, the CLO must take all reasonable steps to get the client to make an "appropriate response." Roughly stated, that means that the client must stop or remedy the violation and make sure that it does not happen again. The CLO must report those results to the securities lawyer.

e.   When Appropriate Response Not Taken
If the securities lawyer believes that the CLO did not achieve an appropriate response from the client, the securities lawyer **must** report the evidence to one of the following: (1) the client's whole board of directors, (2) the audit committee of the board, or (3) a committee made up of outside directors (directors who are not beholden to the client). Notice that the Sarbanes-Oxley reporting rule is **mandatory**, unlike ABA Model Rule 1.13(b), which gives the lawyer some discretion about how to proceed (*see* 3., *supra*).

f.   Revealing Confidential Information
The securities lawyer **may** reveal to the SEC, without the client's consent, any confidential information that is reasonably necessary to: (1) stop the client from committing a violation that will cause substantial financial injury to the client or its investors; (2) rectify such a financial injury if the lawyer's services were used to further the violation; or (3) prevent the client from committing or suborning perjury in an SEC matter or lying in any matter within the jurisdiction of any branch of the federal government.

g.   Compliance with Rules
A securities lawyer who violates the Sarbanes-Oxley rules can be disciplined by the SEC, but a securities lawyer who complies with the Sarbanes-Oxley rules cannot be held civilly liable for doing so and cannot be disciplined under any inconsistent state rule.

h.   Action When Securities Lawyer Is Fired
If a securities lawyer is fired for complying with the Sarbanes-Oxley rules, she may report the firing to the client's board of directors (thus setting up the client for an expensive wrongful termination suit).

IX. SAFEKEEPING FUNDS AND OTHER PROPERTY

A. GENERAL DUTY
When money or property belonging to a client comes into the lawyer's hands, the lawyer must not steal it, borrow it, or put it to the lawyer's own use. Furthermore, the lawyer must keep it separated from the lawyer's own money and property. A lawyer is subject to discipline for commingling the client's money or property with the lawyer's own personal or business funds or property. [ABA Model Rule 1.15; *and see* Restatement §44—lawyer safeguarding client's property acts as a fiduciary and is subject to civil liability for failure to safeguard such property]

B. **SAFEGUARDING PROPERTY**

When the lawyer comes into possession of property (other than money) to be held on a client's behalf, the lawyer must identify it as belonging to the client and must put it in a safe place. [ABA Model Rule 1.15(a)] For small items, most lawyers use a bank safe deposit box. Lawyers are required to hold the property of others with the *care required of a professional fiduciary*. [ABA Model Rule 1.15, comment 1] Accordingly, a lawyer cannot use the client's property for her own purposes, and must promptly take steps necessary to safeguard the client's property as are appropriate to the circumstances.

EXAMPLE

Lawyer L represented horse breeder B in negotiating a contract whereby B exchanged two valuable horses for a lakeside cottage. While the transfer was pending, B turned the two horses over to L for safekeeping. L arranged for them to be boarded at a certified and bonded stable. L's conduct was proper.

C. **CLIENT TRUST FUND ACCOUNT**

All money that a lawyer receives *in connection with a representation* (whether from the client or a third party) must promptly be placed in a client trust fund account, separate from the lawyer's own personal and business accounts. [ABA Model Rule 1.15(a)]

1. **Type of Account**

The client trust fund account must be located in the state where the lawyer practices, unless the client or third person consents to having it elsewhere. [ABA Model Rule 1.15(a)] Ordinarily, a lawyer must never put her own money or her firm's money into the client trust account, but she may put some of her own money into that account for the sole purpose of paying bank service charges. [ABA Model Rule 1.15(b)]

a. **Large Sum Held for Long Period**

If a lawyer is entrusted with a large sum to hold for a long period, the lawyer should put it into a separate, interest-bearing account, and the interest it earns will belong to the client. [*See* Restatement §44, comment d] A separate account is recommended when the lawyer is administering estate funds or the like. [ABA Model Rule 1.15, comment 1]

b. **Small Sums**

Usually, lawyers are entrusted with only relatively small sums to hold for relatively short periods of time. The lawyer should put these sums into a pooled client trust account; the account is pooled in the sense that it holds funds entrusted to the lawyer by a variety of different clients. The pooled client trust account is typically a checking account that earns interest. If each client's small sum were put in an individual account, the amount of interest it could earn would be less than the bank's service charge for maintaining the individual account. The 50 states devised Interest On Lawyer Trust Account ("IOLTA") programs. If a client entrusts a lawyer with a sum that is too small to earn any net interest, the lawyer must put it into a pooled checking account that earns interest. After the bank deducts its service charges from the interest, the bank sends the remaining interest to the state bar or to a legal foundation, which uses the interest to fund charitable legal programs. In short, an IOLTA program creates an asset that would otherwise not exist, and it then puts that asset to a public use. In *Brown v. Legal Foundation of Washington*, 538 U.S. 216 (2003), a sharply divided Supreme Court upheld the constitutionality of IOLTA programs, holding that the individual clients whose interest was "taken" for "public use" were not entitled to "just compensation" because they did not lose anything they would otherwise have had.

2. **Funds that Must Be Placed in Account**

   a. **Money Advanced by Client to Cover Costs and Expenses**
      When the client entrusts the lawyer with money to pay costs and expenses not yet incurred, the advance ***must*** be put into the lawyer's client trust fund account. [ABA Model Rule 1.15] The lawyer can then pay the expenses with checks drawn on the account.

   b. **Legal Fees Advanced by Client**
      Sometimes a client entrusts the lawyer with an advance against legal fees that the lawyer has not yet earned. Such an advance must be put into the client trust account. That is because a lawyer must refund to the client any unearned, prepaid legal fees at the close of the representation, and an irresponsible lawyer could harm a client by frittering away a fee advance. When a lawyer holds a fee advance in her client trust account, she may make withdrawals as fees are earned if there is no existing dispute about the lawyer's right to do so. To make sure there is no dispute, cautious lawyers send the client an itemized bill before withdrawing legal fees from the trust account. [*See* Restatement §44, comment f]

   c. **Disputed Funds**
      If there is a dispute over funds (between the lawyer and the client, or between the client and some third person), the lawyer must keep the disputed portion in the client trust account until the dispute is resolved. [ABA Model Rule 1.15(e)] This is further discussed in E., *infra*.

D. **DUTY TO NOTIFY, KEEP RECORDS, RENDER ACCOUNTINGS, AND PAY OVER PROMPTLY**
   A lawyer has the following additional duties respecting a client's money or property:

   1. The lawyer must ***notify the client promptly*** when a third party turns over money or property to the lawyer to hold on the client's behalf;

2. The lawyer must **keep complete, accurate, and up-to-date records** of all money and property held on behalf of the client. These records must be kept in accordance with generally accepted accounting practice, and they must be preserved for five years after the termination of the representation;

3. The lawyer must **render appropriate accountings** of all money and property held on behalf of the client; and

4. When the time comes to **pay over money or deliver property** to which the client or a third party is entitled, the lawyer must do so **promptly**.

[ABA Model Rule 1.15(a), (d)]

E. **DISPUTED PROPERTY**

When a lawyer is in possession of property in which two or more persons (one of whom may be the lawyer) claim interests, the **disputed portion of the property must be kept separate** by the lawyer until the dispute is resolved. The lawyer must promptly distribute all portions of the property as to which the interests are not in dispute. [ABA Model Rule 1.15(e)]

1. **Funds in Which Both Client and Lawyer Have an Interest**

A lawyer sometimes receives funds from a third party that are to be used, in part, to pay the lawyer's fee. The lawyer must place such funds in a client trust account until there is an accounting and severance of the respective interests of the client and the lawyer. If the client disputes the amount that is due to the lawyer, then the disputed portion must be kept in the client trust account until the dispute is resolved. [ABA Model Rule 1.15(e)]

EXAMPLE

Attorney A agreed to represent P as plaintiff in a products liability case. P agreed to pay A $75 per hour for her work, and P agreed that the fee could be deducted from the proceeds of the suit before remittance to P. After expending 100 hours on the case, A arranged a settlement of $50,000, and the defendant sent A a check in that amount. A deposited the check in her client trust fund account and notified P that it had arrived. The same day, A sent P a statement for services showing 100 hours of work and a total fee of $7,500. P protested the fee, saying that she would pay $5,000, but not a cent more. Furthermore, P demanded immediate payment of the entire $50,000. A then sent P $42,500, transferred $5,000 to her personal bank account, and kept the remaining $2,500 in her client trust fund account. P and A ultimately submitted their fee dispute to arbitration; when the arbitrator ruled in A's favor, she transferred the $2,500 to her personal bank account. A handled the matter properly. [*See* Restatement §44, comment f]

---

2. **Funds in Which a Third Party Has an Interest**

Sometimes a third party has an interest in funds that come into the lawyer's possession on behalf of a client. Statute, common law, or contract may require the lawyer to protect the third party's interest against interference by the client; accordingly, when the third party's claim is not frivolous, the lawyer must refuse to surrender the funds to the client until the third party has been paid. However, a lawyer should not unilaterally presume to arbitrate a dispute between the client and the third party. If there are substantial grounds for the dispute, the lawyer may file an interpleader action to have a court resolve the dispute. [ABA Model Rule 1.15, comment 4] The lawyer must promptly distribute any sums that are not in dispute. [ABA Model Rule 1.15(e)]

EXAMPLE

When attorney A agreed to represent client C in a personal injury case, A and C made a three-way agreement with C's physician that A would pay C's medical bills out of the proceeds of C's suit. When C won a $10,000 judgment, he demanded that the entire sum be immediately paid over to him because of a dispute between C and the physician over the medical bills. A's legal and ethical obligation is to hold the amount of money necessary to pay C's medical bills until the dispute between C and the physician is resolved.

X. COMMUNICATIONS ABOUT LEGAL SERVICES

A. **CONTENT-BASED RULES FOR ADVERTISING AND OTHER COMMUNICATIONS**

The ABA Model Rules include various guidelines and restrictions concerning communications about the lawyer and the lawyer's services.

1. **Basic Rule—Communications Must Be True and Not Misleading**

A lawyer is subject to discipline for **any type** of communication about the lawyer or the lawyer's services that is **false or misleading**. [ABA Model Rule 7.1] This rule applies to all kinds of communications, including advertisements, personal communications, office signs, professional cards, professional announcements, letterheads, brochures, letters sent by post or e-mail, and recorded telephone messages. [*See* ABA Model Rule 7.1, comment 1]

a. **Types of False or Misleading Communications**

1) **Outright Falsehoods**

Obviously, a lawyer must not use a communication that is simply false.

EXAMPLE

Attorney A's office letterhead lists him as "Trial Counsel—

ExxonMobil Corporation." Indeed, A used to do trial work in the in-house law department of ExxonMobil, but no member of that department carries the title "Trial Counsel"; moreover, A left ExxonMobil 18 months ago. The listing is an outright falsehood.

2) Omitted Facts

A communication can be true but misleading if it omits a fact that is necessary to make the communication as a whole not materially misleading. [ABA Model Rule 7.1, comment 2]

EXAMPLE

Lawyer L's display advertisement in the telephone book Yellow Pages includes the phrase "Yale Law School—1987." Indeed, L did attend a two-week summer program at Yale Law School in 1987, but he earned his law degree at a school of considerably less distinction. The statement is misleading.

3) Unfounded Conclusions

A truthful communication can be misleading if there is a substantial likelihood that it will lead a reasonable person to formulate a specific conclusion about the lawyer or the lawyer's services for which there is no reasonable factual foundation. [*Id.*]

EXAMPLE

Lawyer L, who has no medical training, specializes in defending lawyers against medical malpractice claims. His billboard advertisement describes him as the "The Juris DOCTOR," states that he has "decades of experience in health care," and includes a photo of him in scrubs, wearing a stethoscope. The commercial is misleading if it would lead a reasonable person to believe L is a physician.

4) Unjustified Expectations

A true communication about a lawyer's accomplishments in past cases is misleading if it could make a reasonable person think that the lawyer could do as well in a similar case, without regard to the facts and law in that case. [ABA Model Rule 7.1, comment 3]

EXAMPLE

Attorney A won jury verdicts in excess of $500,000 in the last three asbestos cases she took to trial. Her television advertisement includes that truthful statement without explaining that the recovery in asbestos cases varies dramatically, depending on the precise

facts surrounding the plaintiff's exposure to asbestos. A's statement is misleading.

5) Unsubstantiated Comparisons

An unsubstantiated comparison of a lawyer's services or fees with those of other lawyers is misleading if it could make a reasonable person think that it can be substantiated. [*Id.*]

EXAMPLE

Lawyer L advertises that her fees for estate planning services are "15% lower than the prevailing rate in Fairmont County." If L cannot substantiate that statement with hard data, she is subject to discipline.

---

b. Including a Disclaimer

Depending on the circumstances, the inclusion of an appropriate disclaimer or other qualifying language may preclude a finding that the advertisement or other communication is misleading to the public. [ABA Model Rule 7.1, comment 3]

2. Required and Permitted Information

ABA Model Rule 7.2(a) gives lawyers broad latitude in advertising or otherwise communicating about their services in a true and nonmisleading manner. They may communicate through any type of media.

a. Identification of Advertiser

Every advertisement or other communication about the lawyer's or firm's services must include the name and contact information (website address, telephone number, e-mail address, or physical office location) of at least one lawyer or law firm that is responsible for its content. [ABA Model Rule 7.2(d)]

b. Generally Permitted Information

The following are among the types of information that a lawyer may publicly disseminate: (1) information concerning the name of the lawyer or her firm, and the lawyer's or firm's address, e-mail address, website, and telephone number; (2) the kinds of services the lawyer will undertake; (3) the basis on which fees are determined, including prices for specific services and payment and credit arrangements; (4) the lawyer's foreign language ability; (5) the names of references; and (6) other information that might invite the attention of persons seeking legal assistance. [ABA Model Rule 7.2, comment 1]

1) Consent of Named Clients
If a lawyer wishes to identify some regular clients in an advertisement, the lawyer must first obtain the clients' consent. [*Id.*]

3. Firm Names, Letterheads, and Other Professional Designations
Like all communications concerning a lawyer's services, law firm names and other professional designations must not be false or misleading.

a. Current, Deceased, and Retired Partners
A private law partnership may be designated by the names of one or more of its current members. "Member" is generally interpreted to mean a partner or shareholder, because it is inferred that such persons carry the liabilities and responsibilities for the firm's obligations. When partners die or retire, their names may be carried over to successor partnerships. For example, a law partnership may properly continue to practice under the name "X, Y, & Z," even though lawyer X has died. [ABA Model Rule 7.1, comment 5; ABA Informal Op. 85-1511 (1985)]

1) Misleading—Non-Associated Lawyers and Nonlawyers
A law firm name is misleading if it includes the name of (or otherwise implies a connection with): (1) a deceased lawyer who was not a former member of the firm, (2) the name of any lawyer who is not associated with the firm or predecessor firm, or (3) the name of a nonlawyer. [ABA Model Rule 7.1, comment 5]

b. Using Names of Lawyers Who Have Entered Public Service
A private law firm must not use the name of a lawyer who holds public office (either as part of the firm name or in communications on the firm's behalf) during any *substantial* period in which the lawyer is not *regularly and actively practicing* with the firm. [ABA Model Rule 7.1, comment 8]

EXAMPLE

Attorney Tzao took an indefinite leave of absence from the Tzao, Dean & Goldberg firm to serve as a commissioner on the Federal Communications Commission. The firm must remove Tzao's name from the firm name until he returns to regular, active practice.

---

c. Must Not Imply Connection with Public or Charitable Organization
Trade names (e.g., "The Bulldog Law Firm")—even ones that do not include the names of one or more partners—are permitted, provided the name is not misleading and does not imply a connection with a governmental agency or with a public or charitable legal services organization. If a firm name uses a trade name that includes a *geographical* name

(e.g., Greater Chicago Legal Clinic), a disclaimer explaining that it is not a public legal aid organization may be required to avoid a misleading implication. [ABA Model Rule 7.1, comment 5]

d. False Indications of Partnership

Lawyers must not imply that they are partners or are practicing together as one law firm unless they really are. [ABA Model Rule 7.1, comment 7]

EXAMPLE

Attorneys A and B share office space, secretarial services, and a common law library. They frequently refer cases to one another, and they continually consult each other on difficult legal questions. The sign on their office door says: "Offices of A and B, Attorneys at Law." The sign is not proper; it implies that they are in partnership when they are not.

---

1) Associated and Affiliated Law Firms

Two law firms may hold themselves out to the public as being "associated" or "affiliated" if they have a close, regular, ongoing relationship and if the designation is not misleading. But using such a designation has a significant drawback—ordinarily the two firms would be treated as a single unit for conflict of interest purposes. [ABA Formal Op. 84-351 (1984)]

EXAMPLE

The ABC firm practices business law in Denver. For many years it has worked regularly and closely with the XYZ firm, which practices patent law in Washington, D.C. If the ABC firm letterhead lists the XYZ firm as its Washington, D.C., affiliate in patent matters, then any conflict of interest that would disqualify the XYZ firm will ordinarily also disqualify the ABC firm.

---

e. Multistate Firms

A law firm that has offices in more than one jurisdiction may use the same name, Internet address, or other professional designation in each jurisdiction. [ABA Model Rule 7.1, comment 6]

4. Identifying Fields of Practice

A lawyer may communicate that she does or does not practice in particular fields of law. Additionally, the lawyer is permitted to state that she "concentrates in," "specializes in," or is a "specialist" in particular fields based on the lawyer's experience, specialized training, or education, as long as such communications are not false or misleading. However, a lawyer must not

state or imply that she is **certified as a specialist** in a particular field of law, unless: (1) the lawyer has in fact been certified as a specialist by an organization that has been approved by the ABA or by an appropriate state authority; and (2) the name of the certifying organization is clearly identified in the communication. [ABA Model Rule 7.2(c) and comment 9]

a. Patent and Admiralty Lawyers

Patent and admiralty lawyers have traditionally been accorded special treatment. A lawyer who is admitted to practice before the United States Patent and Trademark Office may use the designation "Patent Attorney," or something similar. A lawyer who is engaged in admiralty practice may use the designation "Proctor in Admiralty," or something similar. A lawyer's communications about these practice areas are not prohibited by the rule above. [ABA Model Rule 7.2, comment 10]

B. RECOMMENDATIONS

A communication about a lawyer's services is a "recommendation" if it endorses or vouches for the lawyer's credentials, abilities, competence, character, or other professional qualities. Subject to the exceptions below, a lawyer **must not compensate, give anything of value, or promise** to give anything of value to a person for recommending the lawyer's services. *Note:* Directory listings or group advertisements listing lawyers by practice area, without any further information, do not constitute prohibited recommendations. [ABA Model Rule 7.2(b) and comment 2]

1. Exceptions to General Rule

a. Paying for Advertising and Other Services

A lawyer may pay the **reasonable costs of permitted advertisements** (e.g., broadcast airtime, directory listings, or newspaper ads). Additionally, a lawyer may pay the **usual charges** of: (1) a legal service plan (*see* D., *infra*), (2) a not-for-profit lawyer referral service, or (3) a qualified lawyer referral service. "Qualified" means that the service has been approved by an appropriate regulatory authority. A lawyer who accepts assignments or referrals from a legal services plan or lawyer referral service must ensure that the organization's communications comply with the lawyer's obligations (that is, are not false or misleading). [ABA Model Rule 7.2(b)(1), (2) and comment 7]

EXAMPLE

The A, B & C firm seeks to increase its client base. The firm may hire and pay a media consultant to design some newspaper advertisements, and it may pay the newspaper for the advertising space. The firm may also participate in a prepaid legal service plan that advertises to obtain new members. Furthermore, some of the lawyers in the firm are listed with the nonprofit lawyer referral service run by the local county bar association; when those lawyers obtain clients through the referral service, they may pay the referral fees charged by the service.

1) **Paying Others to Generate Client Leads**

   "Lead generators" provide consumers with matching, referral, and directory services (e.g., a consumer goes to a website, selects a type of legal problem, and is provided with a list of lawyers who provide that service and the ability to select and contact one of those lawyers). A lawyer may pay others to generate client leads as long as the lead generator **does not recommend** the lawyer and the lead generator's communications are not false or misleading. A communication by the lead generator is false or misleading if it creates a reasonable impression that: (1) it is recommending the lawyer; (2) it has analyzed the person's legal problems when determining whether to refer the person to the lawyer; or (3) it is making the referral without any payment from the lawyer. [ABA Model Rule 7.2, comment 5]

b. **Purchase of a Law Practice**

   Of course, the lawyer may purchase a law practice (*see* I.J., *supra*) even though the seller is, in a sense, recommending the purchasing lawyer to her clients. [ABA Model Rule 7.2(b)(3)]

c. **Reciprocal Referral Agreements**

   Under certain circumstances, a lawyer is permitted to set up a reciprocal referral agreement with **another lawyer or with a nonlawyer professional**—i.e., "I will refer potential clients, patients, or customers to you if you will do likewise for me." [ABA Model Rule 7.2(b)(4)] "Another lawyer" means a lawyer at a different firm (the rule does not restrict referrals among members of the same firm). The term "nonlawyer professional" is not defined, but is generally interpreted as a person who belongs to a professional body that requires a high level of proficiency and regulates its members (e.g., doctor, accountant, insurance agent). A reciprocal referral agreement is subject to the following restrictions and guidance [ABA Model Rule 7.2(b)(4) and comment 8]:

   1) The agreement must **not be exclusive** (i.e., the lawyer must not promise to refer **all** potential estate planning clients to his friend F and to no one else).

   2) The **referred client must be told** about the agreement. If the agreement creates a conflict of interest for either the referring or the receiving lawyer, then that lawyer must obtain the client's

informed consent, confirmed in writing, under ABA Model Rule 1.7. (Of course, one must wonder whether a reciprocal referral agreement invariably creates a conflict because it gives the referring lawyer a personal financial interest in sending the case to his referral counterpart rather than to some other lawyer.)

3) The reciprocal agreement must **not interfere with the lawyer's professional judgment as to making referrals** or providing substantive legal services.

4) The agreement **"should not" be of indefinite duration** and should **be reviewed periodically** to make sure it complies with the ABA Model Rules.

d. Nominal Gifts or Gratuities

A lawyer may give a nominal gift or gratuity as an expression of appreciation to a person who recommended the lawyer or the lawyer's firm, provided the gift or gratuity was **not intended or reasonably expected to be a form of compensation** for recommending the lawyer's services. Such gifts must not exceed a token item that would be given for a holiday or in the course of ordinary social hospitality. A gift is prohibited if offered or given in consideration of any understanding that such a gift would be forthcoming or that referrals would be made or encouraged in the future. [ABA Model Rule 7.2(b)(5)]

C. SOLICITATION

A solicitation is a communication **initiated by a lawyer or firm** that is directed to a specific person the lawyer knows or reasonably should know **needs legal services in a particular matter**, and that offers to provide, or can reasonably be understood as offering to provide, legal services for that matter. However, a communication is **not** a solicitation if it: (1) is directed to the general public (e.g., through a billboard, website, television commercial, or Internet banner advertisement); (2) responds to a request for information; or (3) is automatically generated in response to an Internet search. [ABA Model Rule 7.3(a) and comment 1]

1. **Live Person-to-Person Solicitation Generally Prohibited**

Subject to the exceptions below, a lawyer or firm must not, by live person-to-person contact, solicit professional employment when a significant motive for doing so is the lawyer's or firm's pecuniary gain (i.e., money). "Live person-to-person contact" means in-person, **face-to-face**, **live telephone**, or other **real-time visual or auditory person-to-person communications** (e.g., Skype or FaceTime) where the targeted person is subject to a direct personal encounter without time for reflection. [ABA Model Rule 7.3(b)]

a. Exception to Prohibition—Significant Motive Is Not Pecuniary Gain

Offers to provide free legal services are generally permissible.

Furthermore, certain political or ideological solicitation (e.g., solicitation on behalf of a civil rights organization or nonprofit organization) is constitutionally protected. [*See* ABA Model Rule 7.3(b) and comment 5]

b. **Exceptions to Prohibition—Certain Targets Are Considered Less Vulnerable**

Subject to the limitations in 3., below, a lawyer or firm is generally not prohibited from initiating live person-to-person contact with (1) other *lawyers*; (2) persons with whom the lawyer or firm has a *familial, close personal, or prior professional or business relationship* (including current and former clients); or (3) *routine business users of the type of legal services* offered by the lawyer or firm (e.g., entrepreneurs, small business owners, executives who hire outside counsel to represent an entity, and any other persons who regularly engage lawyers for business purposes).

EXAMPLE

Attorney A prepared an estate plan for client C. A did no further work for C. Two years later, the state repealed its inheritance tax, thus creating a much more advantageous way for C to dispose of her assets on death. A may telephone C, advising C to have her estate plan revised, and A may do the necessary work if C asks her to do so.

---

2. **Written, Recorded, or Electronic Solicitation Generally Permitted**

Generally, a lawyer is not prohibited from sending truthful, nondeceptive communications (via mail, e-mail, text message, chat room message, etc.) to persons known to face a specific legal problem. These types of communications can be easily disregarded by the recipient and do not constitute live person-to-person contact. [ABA Model Rule 7.3, comment 2]

3. **Circumstances Rendering All Contacts Impermissible**

A lawyer is prohibited from soliciting professional employment, *regardless of what method is used or who the target is*, if [ABA Model Rule 7.3(c)]:

a. The target of the solicitation has *made known to the lawyer that she does not want* to be solicited by the lawyer; or

b. The solicitation involves *coercion, duress, or harassment*.

EXAMPLE

Lawyer L obtained a mailing list of all persons who used a certain prescription drug that allegedly caused grave side effects. L sent personal letters to each person, offering to represent them for a fee in litigation against the drug manufacturer. C, one of the recipients of L's letters, telephoned L's office and told her that she did not want to sue anybody and did not want to hear further

from L. L failed to remove C from the mailing list, so C received a series of follow-up letters, each urging C to join in litigation against the drug manufacturer. L is subject to discipline.

4. **Communications Authorized by Law or Court Order**
These rules do not prohibit communications authorized by law or ordered by a court or other tribunal (e.g., in class action litigation, a notice to potential members of the class). [ABA Model Rule 7.3(d)]

5. **Use of Others to Solicit**
A lawyer's responsibility for prohibited solicitation extends to actions by those employed by, retained by, and in certain circumstances, associated with the lawyer. [*See* ABA Formal Ethics Op. 501 (2022)]

a. **Agents**
Recall that a lawyer is always prohibited from using an agent to do that which the lawyer must not do, e.g., violate a law or disciplinary rule. [ABA Modle Rule 8.4(a)] Thus, a lawyer must not use an agent (sometimes called a "runner" or "capper") to contact prospective clients in a manner that would violate the Rules of Professional Conduct.

b. **People Employed, Retained, or Associated with Lawyer**
Lawyer supervisors are required to make reasonable efforts to ensure that all persons (lawyers and nonlawyers) employed, retained, or associated with the lawyer are trained to comply with solicitation rules. Recall that a lawyer is responsible for the conduct of others if the lawyer orders the conduct, knows and approves the conduct, or when acting as a manager or supervisor fails to take remedial action when the consequences could have been avoided. [*See* ABA Model Rule 5.3(b), (c)]

c. **Other Third Parties**
Recommendations or referrals by third parties who are not employees of a lawyer and whose communications are not directed to make specific statements to particular potential clients on behalf of a lawyer do not constitute "solicitations." Thus, a lawyer's colleagues in other professions, satisfied clients, and family and friends may provide information about a lawyer's services to other people. [ABA Formal Ethics Op. 501 (2022)]

EXAMPLES

1) Lawyer L hired R to be a "claims investigator." R's work involved checking accident and crime reports at the local police station and then personally contacting those involved to "advise them of their legal rights." L furnishes R with copies of her standard form retainer agreement and instructs R to sign up clients when possible. L is subject to discipline.

2) Attorney A has a reciprocal referral arrangement with a "debt consolidation" company. Employees of the company initiate personal, face-to-face conversations with debtors and advise them about loans and ways to get out of debt. If it appears that a debtor needs legal assistance, the company employee refers the debtor to A. In return, when one of A's clients needs help getting a loan or managing debts, A refers the client to the company. A is subject to discipline because he is using the debt consolidation company to initiate personal, face-to-face communications with potential clients.

COMPARE
A lawyer asks a personal friend and colleague who is a banker to provide the lawyer's contact information to banking customers the banker thinks might need an estate plan. The conduct does not violate the solicitation rules because the lawyer did not target a specific person in need of legal services in a particular matter, nor communicate or direct communications with that person. The lawyer has no authority over the banker's conduct. The lawyer does not control the content of any communication the banker makes nor even whether any communication occurs at all. The communication, if one occurs at all, is a recommendation, the type of "word-of-mouth" referral that is permissible. Moreover, because the lawyer is not directing what the banker should say and the banker's customers are not speaking directly to the lawyer, the lawyer's request to the banker is permissible. [ABA Formal Ethics Op. 501 (2022)]

D. **GROUP AND PREPAID LEGAL SERVICE PLANS**
Group or prepaid legal service plans typically are part of an employee benefit plan and bear some resemblance to health insurance plans. Participants typically pay a monthly premium, in return for which they may consult a plan-authorized lawyer and obtain legal services for a low or no cost. Such plans vary widely as to the services provided, ranging from a brief consultation to full representation, and as to the areas covered, ranging from estate planning to divorce, to civil or (less commonly) criminal actions.

1. **Lawyer May Personally Contact Sponsoring Organizations**
    A lawyer or firm may personally contact representatives of groups that might wish to adopt a legal service plan for its members, beneficiaries, etc. This is more akin to advertising than solicitation because it is not directed at people seeking legal services for *themselves*; the representatives are acting in a fiduciary capacity and seeking legal services for their members (who will later choose whether to become a client of the lawyer or firm). [ABA Model Rule 7.3, comment 7]

2. **Plan May Personally Contact Potential Members**
    Lawyers are permitted to participate in a group or prepaid legal service plan, even though the plan uses live person-to-person contacts to enroll memberships or sell subscriptions, provided that: (1) the **personal contact**

is not undertaken by the lawyer themselves; and (2) the plan only contacts persons who are *not known to need specific legal services in a particular matter* covered by the plan (as this does not fall within the definition of solicitation). [ABA Model Rule 7.3(e) and comment 9]

EXAMPLE

The X, Y & Z law firm learns that the Lincoln Teachers' Association wants to form a group legal service program for schoolteachers. In such a program, the association would contract with a local law firm to provide a specified yearly amount of legal service to each teacher subscriber. The X, Y & Z firm may initiate live person-to-person contact with the association to present a proposed plan. Furthermore, if the association ends up hiring the X, Y & Z firm, it is proper for the association (but not the X, Y & Z law firm) to make live person-to-person contact with schoolteachers to urge them to subscribe to the plan.

---

    a.   **Participating Lawyer Must Not Be Owner or Director**
        A lawyer must not participate in the legal service plan if the lawyer *owns or directs* the organization that operates the plan.

  3. **Must Assure Compliance With Advertising and Solicitation Rules**
     A lawyer who participates in a legal service plan must "reasonably assure" that the plan sponsors are in compliance with the advertising and solicitation rules (e.g., must not advertise in a false or misleading manner). [ABA Model Rule 7.3, comment 9]

E. **GOVERNMENT REGULATION OF COMMUNICATIONS ABOUT LEGAL SERVICES**
    The Supreme Court has recognized lawyer advertising as commercial speech protected by the First and Fourteenth Amendments, holding that a state may adopt reasonable regulations to insure that lawyer advertising is not false or misleading, but may not flatly prohibit all lawyer advertising. [Bates v. State Bar of Arizona, 433 U.S. 350 (1977)]

  1. **False and Misleading Ads and In-Person Solicitation May Be Banned**
     A state may flatly prohibit lawyer advertising that is false or misleading. [*In re* RMJ, 455 U.S. 191 (1982)] Similarly, a state may adopt prophylactic rules to forbid in-person solicitation for profit in circumstances that are likely to result in overreaching or misleading a layperson. [Ohralik v. Ohio State Bar Association, 436 U.S. 447 (1978)] In practice, misleading communications and in-person solicitation are regulated rather than completely banned.

  2. **Disclosure Requirements for Misleading Communications—Rational Basis Test**
     To *prevent* commercial speech from misleading consumers, the government

may require commercial advertisers to make certain factual disclosures if such a requirement is: (1) not unduly burdensome, and (2) reasonably related to the state's interest in preventing deception. [Zauderer v. Office of Disciplinary Counsel of Supreme Court of Ohio, 471 U.S. 626 (1985)]

EXAMPLE

Attorneys who provide bankruptcy assistance to consumer debtors ("debt relief agencies") may be required to include in their advertisements certain information—e.g., statements identifying themselves as debt relief agencies and disclosing that the advertised services relate to bankruptcy relief and may result in the debtor's filing for bankruptcy. [Milavetz, Gallop & Milavetz, P.A. v. United States, 559 U.S. 229 (2010)]

---

3. **Other Regulation of Truthful, Nondeceptive Communications— Intermediate Scrutiny**

Because attorney advertising is commercial speech, regulation of it is subject to only intermediate, rather than strict, scrutiny. [Florida Bar v. Went For It, Inc., 515 U.S. 618 (1995)] Thus, this type of commercial speech may be regulated if the government satisfies a three-prong test:

a. The government must assert a **substantial interest** in support of its regulation;

b. The government must demonstrate that the restriction on commercial speech **directly and materially advances the interest**; and

c. The regulation must be **narrowly drawn**.

[Florida Bar v. Went For It, Inc., *supra—citing* Central Hudson Gas & Electric Corp. v. Public Service Commission of New York, 447 U.S. 557 (1980)]

EXAMPLE

After conducting a two-year study on the effect of lawyer advertising on public opinion, which included surveys and hearings, Florida adopted a rule prohibiting lawyers from sending **any** targeted direct-mail solicitations to victims and their relatives for 30 days following an accident or disaster. The United States Supreme Court upheld the regulation, finding that it met the three-prong test above. The Court found that: (1) the state has a substantial interest in protecting the privacy and tranquility of its citizens as well as in protecting the reputation of the legal profession; (2) the studies show that the public was offended by these solicitations and that the 30-day ban directly advances the state's interests; and (3) the regulation is narrowly tailored to achieve the desired results. [Florida Bar v. Went For It, Inc., *supra*]

XI. LAWYERS' DUTIES TO THE PUBLIC AND THE LEGAL SYSTEM

A. PRO BONO PUBLICO SERVICE

Every lawyer has a professional responsibility to provide legal service to people who cannot pay for it. [ABA Model Rule 6.1] Violating ABA Model Rule 6.1 is not grounds for professional discipline; Model Rule 6.1 recommends that every lawyer *should* spend 50 hours per year on pro bono work. A "substantial majority" of those hours should be spent doing unpaid legal service for poor people or organizations that address the needs of poor people.

B. COURT APPOINTMENTS

Trial and appellate courts often find it necessary to appoint lawyers to represent indigent clients and clients with unpopular causes. ABA Model Rule 6.2 provides that a lawyer must not seek to avoid such an appointment except for good cause. Examples of good cause are stated below.

1. Violation of Law or Disciplinary Rule

A lawyer must decline a court appointment if to accept it would require the lawyer to violate a law or disciplinary rule. [ABA Model Rule 6.2(a)]

EXAMPLE

When attorney A was a deputy public defender, he represented client Q in an aggravated assault case, and he learned a great deal of confidential information about Q's life and criminal background. Later, A entered private practice, and the local court appointed him to defend D, who was charged with the attempted murder of Q. The confidential information A obtained from Q is highly relevant to the defense of D. A must therefore decline the appointment to defend D.

---

2. Unreasonable Financial Burden

A lawyer may seek to be excused from an appointment if to accept it would impose an unreasonable financial burden on the lawyer. [ABA Model Rule 6.2(b)]

EXAMPLE

The Supreme Court of West Dakota appointed lawyer L to represent D in the appeal of D's conviction and death sentence for three murders. The trial of D's case lasted 13 months and resulted in a trial record in excess of 150,000 pages. To handle the appeal properly, L would be required to work at least 600 hours. The West Dakota legislature has set legal fees at a paltry $17 per hour for appellate counsel in death penalty cases. L is a struggling solo practitioner and will not be able to support his family if he is required to take that much time away from his regular clients. L may seek to be excused from the supreme court appointment.

3. **Personal Inability to Represent Client Effectively**

A lawyer may seek to be excused from a court appointment if the lawyer finds the client or the cause so repugnant that the lawyer-client relationship would be impaired or the lawyer could not represent the client effectively. [ABA Model Rule 6.2(c)]

EXAMPLE

The trial court appointed attorney A to defend accused child molester M. As a young boy, A himself was molested by a similar person, and A finds that he cannot even look comfortably at M, much less represent him zealously. A may seek to be excused from the court appointment.

C. **LIMITED LEGAL SERVICES PROGRAMS**

Some courts and nonprofit organizations have established limited legal services programs in which lawyers offer "quick advice" to people who can then handle their own legal problem without further assistance. Examples are programs that show people how to fill out their own EZ tax forms, legal-advice hotlines, advice-only legal clinics, and programs that show people how to represent themselves in small claims court. A lawyer-client relationship exists between the lawyer and the person who obtains the quick advice, but neither person expects the relationship to continue past the quick-advice stage. [ABA Model Rule 6.5, comment 1] A lawyer may participate in a quick-advice program sponsored by a court or nonprofit organization, subject to the following rules.

1. **Client Consents to Short-Term, Limited Legal Service**

The lawyer must obtain the client's informed consent to the limited scope of the relationship. If the lawyer's quick advice is not enough to set the client on the right track, the lawyer must advise the client to obtain further legal help. [ABA Model Rule 6.5, comment 2]

2. **Applicability of Ethics Rules**

In a quick-advice situation, the conflict of interest rules are relaxed somewhat, as explained in 3., below. However, the remainder of the Rules of Professional Conduct apply to a quick-advice situation.

EXAMPLE

When attorney A was answering telephone calls on the bar association hotline, she took a call from a farmer who explained that six months ago he hired a farmhand to help him. The farmhand insisted on being paid in cash and insisted that the farmer not withhold any income taxes or pay any Social Security contributions on his behalf. Based on the farmer's answers to A's questions, A concluded that the farmhand was an employee, not an independent contractor. A then advised the farmer about his potential tax liability. The farmer's statements to A are protected by the attorney-client privilege and the

ethical duty of confidentiality; therefore, A must not disclose the farmer's confidential information or use it to the farmer's disadvantage. [See ABA Model Rules 1.6, 1.9(c)]

3. **Conflict of Interest Rules Are Relaxed**
   A lawyer who participates in a quick-advice program ordinarily has no time to conduct an ordinary conflict of interest check. Therefore, the general conflicts principles expressed in Rule 1.7 (current clients) and 1.9 (former clients) do not apply unless the lawyer actually knows that giving the quick advice creates a conflict of interest. [ABA Model Rule 6.5(a)(1)] As in other contexts, actual knowledge can be inferred from the circumstances. [ABA Model Rule 1.0(f)]

4. **Imputed Conflict Rule Is Also Relaxed**
   The rule of imputed conflicts of interest [ABA Model Rule 1.10] is also relaxed in a quick-advice situation. Therefore, a lawyer may dispense advice in a quick-advice program unless the lawyer **_actually knows_** that he is disqualified from doing so because of a conflict imputed from another lawyer in his firm. [ABA Model Rule 6.5(a)(2)] Conversely, a conflict created by advice a lawyer dispenses in a quick-advice program will not be imputed to others in the lawyer's firm. [ABA Model Rule 6.5(b)]

   EXAMPLES
   1) Lawyer L and partner P are partners in the 300-lawyer firm of R & Q. L participates in a quick-advice program sponsored by a local court. In that context, L advised apartment tenant T that she could withhold rent from her landlord Z to pay for repairing a leaking roof that made the apartment uninhabitable. L did not realize that Z had recently hired L's partner P to deal with legal issues arising out of the apartment house in question.

   2) In the example above, if L advised T about withholding rent on May 1, and landlord Z did not hire partner P until July 30, L's conflict is not imputed to P.

5. **Conflicts Rules Apply Fully If Quick Advice Leads to Regular Representation**
   If a person who has received quick advice from a lawyer then wants to hire that lawyer to render further service in the matter, the ordinary conflict of interest rules apply to that further service. [ABA Model Rule 6.5, comment 5]

   EXAMPLE
   After attorney A dispensed advice to client C in a quick-advice program, C asked to hire A as his trial counsel in the matter. Before agreeing to render the further service to C, A should check for conflicts of interest to make sure that neither she nor other lawyers in her office have a conflict that would disqualify her.

D. MEMBERSHIP IN LEGAL SERVICES ORGANIZATIONS

1. Statement of the Problem

Lawyers are encouraged to support and participate in legal services organizations—e.g., local legal aid societies that provide free legal assistance to underprivileged persons in civil matters. An officer or member of such an organization does not have a lawyer-client relationship with persons served by the organization, but there can be potential conflicts between the interests of those persons and the interests of the lawyer's regular, paying clients. [*See* ABA Model Rule 6.3]

2. General Rule

A lawyer may serve as a director, officer, or member of a legal services organization (apart from the lawyer's regular employment) even though the organization serves persons whose interests are adverse to the lawyer's regular clients. [ABA Model Rule 6.3] This general rule is, however, subject to the limitations stated below.

a. The lawyer must not knowingly participate in a decision or action of the organization if doing so would be incompatible with the lawyer's obligations to a client under the general conflict of interest rules. [*See* ABA Model Rules 1.7, 6.3(a)]

b. The lawyer must not knowingly participate in a decision or action of the organization if doing so would adversely affect the representation of one of the organization's clients whose interests are adverse to those of a client of the lawyer. [*See* ABA Model Rule 6.3(b)]

EXAMPLE

Lawyer L is a member of the board of directors of the Cuttler County Legal Aid Society. The board sets guidelines for the kinds of cases the society will and will not handle. The society's budget has recently been cut, and the board is forced to revise the guidelines to eliminate some kinds of service. L is also a partner in the R, S & T firm, and that firm is outside general counsel to the Cuttler County Apartment Owners Association, a trade association for landlords. One proposal pending before the Legal Aid Society Board is to eliminate free legal service in landlord-tenant cases. L must not participate in this decision.

E. LAW REFORM ACTIVITIES AFFECTING CLIENT INTERESTS

1. Activities that May Harm Client

A lawyer may serve as a director, officer, or member of a law reform group, even though a reform advocated by the group may harm one of the lawyer's clients. [*See* ABA Model Rule 6.4]

> **EXAMPLE**
>
> Attorney A is a member of the West Carolina Law Revision Commission, a private organization that drafts and recommends new legislation to the West Carolina Legislature. The commission is now working on new statutes that will revise the West Carolina law respecting administration of trusts. One of A's clients is the First Carolina Bank. The bank's trust operations will become less profitable if the legislature passes the statutes recommended by the commission. A may work on the trust law project for the commission, unless doing so would violate the general conflict of interest rules. [*See* ABA Model Rule 1.7; ABA Model Rule 6.4, comment 1]

2. **Activities that May Benefit Client**

   When a lawyer is working on a law reform project and is asked to participate in a decision that could materially benefit one of the lawyer's clients, the lawyer must disclose that fact—but the lawyer need not identify the client. [ABA Model Rule 6.4]

   > **EXAMPLE**
   >
   > In the Law Revision Commission example above, suppose that one of the statutes proposed by the commission will substantially increase trustee fees paid to commercial banks. Before participating in a decision about that statute, A must disclose to the other commissioners that she represents a major commercial bank, but she need not identify which bank.

F. **ASSISTING IN JUDICIAL MISCONDUCT**

   A lawyer is subject to discipline for **_knowingly_** assisting a judge or judicial officer in conduct that violates the Code of Judicial Conduct or other law. [ABA Model Rule 8.4(f)]

   > **EXAMPLE**
   >
   > R graduated from law school and became a member of the bar, but he never practiced law. Instead, he entered politics and was ultimately elected to a high federal office. When a drug charge was brought against R's chief deputy, R met personally with the judge before whom the case was pending and attempted to convince the judge to dismiss the charge. [*See* CJC Rule 2.9—prohibits ex parte communications about a pending matter] R is subject to discipline.

G. **STATEMENTS ABOUT JUDICIAL AND PUBLIC LEGAL OFFICIALS**

   A lawyer must not make a statement that the lawyer knows is false about the **_qualifications or integrity_** of a judge, hearing officer, or public legal official, or about a candidate for a judicial or legal office. The same rule applies to statements made with **_reckless disregard_** as to truth or falsity. [ABA Model Rule 8.2(a); Restatement §114]

EXAMPLE

Lawyer K made unfounded accusations in two petitions, asserting that certain appellate judges were deliberately dishonest in failing to recuse themselves in a case K was handling. Such accusations in court papers constitute criminal contempt that can be summarily punished. The court fined K and referred her to the state bar disciplinary authorities. [*In re* Koven, 134 Cal. App. 4th 262 (2005)]

H. **LAWYER RUNNING FOR JUDICIAL OFFICE**

A lawyer who is running for judicial office must comply with the applicable provisions of the Code of Judicial Conduct. [ABA Model Rule 8.2(b)]

EXAMPLE

Attorney A was one of two candidates for a vacant superior court judgeship. She personally solicited and accepted campaign contributions from other members of her law firm, a violation of ABA Code of Judicial Conduct 4.1(A). A is subject to discipline.

I. **ABILITY TO INFLUENCE GOVERNMENT OFFICIALS**

A lawyer must never state or imply that he has the ability to improperly influence a government agency or official or to achieve results by means that violate the law or legal ethics rules. [ABA Model Rule 8.4(e)]

EXAMPLE

Lawyer L is a member of a very politically prominent family. Both his mother and brother are judges, and his father was once governor of the state. It would be improper for L to mention his prominent relatives in the course of procuring legal employment, as this implies he has some sort of improper influence with the courts or the government. If a client mentions L's relatives, L is obligated to explain that he has no special influence to wield on the client's behalf.

J. **POLITICAL CONTRIBUTIONS TO OBTAIN GOVERNMENT EMPLOYMENT**

A lawyer or firm must not accept a government legal engagement (i.e., employment that a public official has the power to award) or an appointment by a judge if the lawyer or firm makes or solicits a political contribution *for the purpose of obtaining such employment or appointment* ("pay to play" contributions). [ABA Model Rule 7.6 and comment 1]

1. **Prohibited Contributions**

This rule does not prohibit all political contributions by lawyers or firms—only those that would not have been made *but for the desire to be considered for the employment or appointment*. The circumstances of the contribution may indicate its purpose. Contributions that are substantial compared to contributions made by other lawyers or firms, are made for the benefit of an official

who can award such work, and are followed by an award to the lawyer or firm support an inference that the contributions were for the purpose of obtaining the work. Other factors, such as a family or professional relationship with the judge or a desire to further a political, social, or economic interest, weigh against inferring a prohibited purpose. [ABA Model Rule 7.6, comment 5]

2. **Excluded Employment**

Excluded from the ambit of the rule are: (1) uncompensated services; (2) engagements or appointments made on the basis of experience, expertise, qualifications, and cost, following a process that is free from influence based on political contributions; and (3) engagements or appointments made on a rotating basis from a list compiled without regard to political contributions. [ABA Model Rule 7.6, comment 3]

XII. JUDICIAL ETHICS

A. SELECTION, TENURE, AND DISCIPLINE OF JUDGES

1. **Federal Judges**

Justices of the United States Supreme Court and judges of other Article III federal courts are appointed by the President with the advice and consent of the Senate. They hold office for life during good behavior. [U.S. Const. art. III, §1] A federal judge can be removed from office by impeachment and can be disciplined in less drastic ways by a committee of federal judges. [U.S. Const. art. II, §4; 28 U.S.C. §§351 - 363] Federal judges generally are governed by the Code of Conduct for United States Judges, which is based largely on the ABA Model Code of Judicial Conduct. Justices of the United States Supreme Court, however, have asserted that they are not bound by the Code of Conduct for United States Judges or the ABA Model Code of Judicial Conduct. [*See* Cheney v. United States District Court, 541 U.S. 913 (2004)—Scalia, J.]

2. **State Judges**

The constitutions of most states specify how judges are to be selected. In some states, judges are appointed by the governor or the state legislature, while in others they are elected by the voters. In still other states, judges are initially appointed and later retained or rejected by the voters. State judges can be removed from office or otherwise disciplined in accordance with state constitutional and statutory provisions.

3. **Code of Judicial Conduct**

The ABA has provided standards for judicial conduct since 1924. These materials discuss the ABA's Model Code of Judicial Conduct ("CJC").

a. **Adoption of the CJC**

The CJC becomes binding on the judges in a jurisdiction when it is adopted (sometimes with significant amendments) by the appropriate authority in that jurisdiction. [*See, e.g.,* California Code of Judicial Ethics]

b. **Who Is Subject to the CJC?**
Where adopted, the CJC applies to all persons who perform judicial functions, including magistrates, court commissioners, referees, and special masters. [CJC, Application] Retired judges, part-time judges, and pro tempore part-time judges are exempted from some provisions of the CJC, as explained in F., below.

c. **Format of the CJC**
The CJC contains four Canons, each of which encompasses several numbered Rules. The Canons state overarching principles of judicial ethics that all judges must follow. Also, the Canons guide the interpretation of the Rules. The Rules are rules of reason, to be applied in a manner that is consistent with the law (statutory, constitutional, and decisional). Comments accompany the Rules. The Comments set forth aspirational goals for judges and also provide guidance regarding the meaning and application of the Rules.

B. **PROMOTION OF JUDICIAL INTEGRITY AND AVOIDANCE OF APPEARANCE OF IMPROPRIETY**
The CJC requires a judge to uphold and promote the independence, integrity, and impartiality of the judiciary and avoid both actual impropriety and the appearance of impropriety. [CJC Canon 1]

1. **Compliance with Law and Promotion of Public Confidence in the Judiciary**
A judge must comply with the law (including the CJC). [CJC Rule 1.1] A judge must avoid *even the appearance* of impropriety. *At all times* a judge must act so as to promote public confidence in the independence, integrity, and impartiality of the judiciary. [CJC Rule 1.2]

EXAMPLES
1) Judge R discovered his estranged wife in an automobile with another man. The judge broke the car window (causing the other man to be cut with broken glass) and slapped his estranged wife. Judge R is subject to discipline, even though his conduct was unconnected with his judicial duties. [*See In re* Roth, 645 P.2d 1064 (Or. 1982)]

2) While driving under the influence of alcohol, Judge L ran a traffic signal and violated other traffic laws. Judge L is subject to discipline. [*See* Matter of Lawson, 590 A.2d 1132 (N.J. 1991)]

2. **Test for Appearance of Impropriety**
   An "appearance of impropriety" arises when a judge's conduct would create a reasonable perception that she has violated the CJC or acted in some other manner that reflects adversely on her honesty, impartiality, temperament, or fitness as a judge. [CJC Rule 1.2, comment 5]

3. **Community Outreach**
   To promote public understanding of and confidence in the administration of justice, a judge should initiate and participate in community outreach activities. [CJC Rule 1.2, comment 6]

4. **Abuse of Judicial Prestige**
   A judge must not abuse, or permit others to abuse, the prestige of her office to advance her personal or economic interests or those of others. [CJC Rule 1.3]

   a. **References and Recommendations**
      Based on personal knowledge, a judge may act as a reference or provide a recommendation for someone. Such a communication may be on official letterhead if: (1) the judge indicates that the reference is personal; and (2) there is no likelihood that use of the letterhead would reasonably be perceived as an attempt to use the judicial office to exert pressure. [CJC Rule 1.3, comment 2]

      EXAMPLES

      1) When Judge B was stopped for a routine traffic violation, he imperiously informed the traffic officer: "I am a judge in this town, young man, and I don't take kindly to being stopped for petty reasons!" Judge B is subject to discipline.

      2) Judge C used her official court stationery when writing to a building contractor with whom she was having a personal contract dispute. Judge C is subject to discipline.

      3) When Judge D's teenage daughter was charged with shoplifting, Judge D called Judge E, to whom the daughter's case was assigned. D said: "E, as a fellow judge, I want to tell you that my little girl is a good kid who deserves a break." Judge D is subject to discipline.

      4) Judge F writes materials and gives lectures for a proprietary continuing legal education company. Judge F should retain control over the company's advertisements of his materials and lectures to avoid exploitation of his judicial office. [CJC Rule 1.3, comment 4]

C. **IMPARTIAL, COMPETENT, AND DILIGENT PERFORMANCE OF JUDICIAL DUTIES**
   The CJC requires a judge to perform the duties of judicial office impartially, competently, and diligently. [CJC Canon 2]

1. **Judicial Duties—In General**
   Judicial duties include all the duties of the judge's office that are prescribed by law. Judicial duties take precedence over all of the judge's other activities, including personal and nonjudicial activities. [CJC Rule 2.1]

   EXAMPLE
   Judge P's elderly, infirm sister needs a custodian to look after her personal and financial affairs. Judge P should not undertake this responsibility if it will interfere with the proper performance of her judicial duties.

2. **Hearing and Deciding Matters Assigned**
   A judge must hear and decide all matters assigned to her, except those in which disqualification is required. [CJC Rule 2.7] Disqualification should not be used as a tool to avoid cases that present difficult, controversial, or unpopular issues. [CJC Rule 2.7, comment 1]

3. **Impartiality and Fairness**
   A judge must uphold and apply the law, and must perform her duties fairly and impartially. [CJC Rule 2.2]

4. **External Influences on Judicial Conduct**
   Public clamor or fear of criticism must not sway a judge. Family, social, political, or financial interests must not influence a judge's conduct or judgment. A judge may not convey, or allow others to convey, the impression that anyone is in a position to influence the judge. [CJC Rule 2.4]

5. **Competence, Diligence, and Cooperation**
   A judge must perform her judicial and administrative duties competently and diligently. [CJC Rule 2.5(A)] "Competence" requires the legal knowledge, skill, thoroughness, and preparation reasonably necessary to perform the judge's responsibilities. [CJC Rule 2.5, comment 1] To accomplish prompt disposition of the court's business, a judge must: (1) devote adequate time to her duties; (2) be punctual in attending court and expeditious in determining matters submitted to her; and (3) take reasonable measures to ensure that court officials, litigants, and attorneys cooperate in this regard. [CJC Rule 2.5, comment 3] Also, a judge must cooperate with other judges and court officials in the administration of court business. [CJC Rule 2.5(B)]

6. **Ensuring Right to Be Heard**
   A judge must allow every person with a legal interest in a proceeding the right to be heard according to law. Although a judge may encourage settlements, he must not act so as to coerce a party into settlement. It is important to keep in mind the possible effects of a judge's participation in settlement talks, i.e., the effects on the judge's views of the case as well as on the

parties' perceptions if the judge retains the case following unsuccessful negotiations. [CJC Rule 2.6 and comment 2]

a.   **Factors for Determining Appropriate Settlement Practice**
When deciding on an appropriate settlement practice, the judge should consider the following factors: (1) whether the parties have requested or consented to a certain level of participation by the judge in settlement discussions; (2) whether the parties and their attorneys are relatively sophisticated in legal matters; (3) whether the case will be tried by the judge or a jury; (4) whether the parties participate with their lawyers in the discussions; (5) whether any parties are not represented by counsel; and (6) whether the case is civil or criminal. [CJC Rule 2.6, comment 2]

7.   **Avoidance of Bias, Prejudice, and Harassment**
A judge must avoid bias, prejudice, and harassment and must require others (including lawyers) who are under the judge's direction and control to do likewise. [CJC Rule 2.3] Prohibited bias, prejudice, or harassment includes that which is based on race, sex, gender, religion, national origin, ethnicity, disability, age, sexual orientation, marital status, socioeconomic status, or political affiliation. [CJC Rule 2.3] Harassment consists of verbal or physical conduct that denigrates or shows hostility or aversion toward a person on any of the bases above. [CJC Rule 2.3, comment 3] A judge's duty to control lawyers does not preclude legitimate advocacy by lawyers when issues of prejudice arise in a case. [CJC Rule 2.3(D)] A judge should be aware that facial expression and body language can convey prejudice as easily as words. [CJC Rule 2.3, comment 2]

EXAMPLE
Whenever an old person testifies in Judge S's court, Judge S speaks extra loudly and in a patronizing manner. Whenever Judge S conducts the voir dire of a jury panel member who is poor, Judge S scowls and adopts a tone of voice normally reserved for slow learners and errant pets. Judge S is subject to discipline.

---

8.   **Ex Parte Communications**
"Ex parte" means one side only. An ex parte communication means a communication between a judge and representative from one side of a matter when no representative from the other side is present. A judge must not initiate, permit, or consider ex parte communications except in these three situations:

a.   **Expressly Authorized by Law**
A judge may have ex parte communications when expressly authorized by law [CJC Rule 2.9(A)(5)], which is defined to include court rules and decisional law, as well as constitutional and statutory law. [CJC,

Terminology] Some communications authorized by law occur in conjunction with a judge's service on certain "specialized" courts, such as drug courts or mental health courts. Judges serving on such courts may have to assume a more interactive role with parties, treatment providers, probation officers, and social workers. [CJC Rule 2.9, comment 4]

b. Mediation or Settlement

With the consent of the parties, the judge may confer separately with the parties and their lawyers in an effort to settle or mediate a pending matter. [CJC Rule 2.9(A)(4)]

c. Emergencies or Administrative Matters

In other situations, the judge may have an ex parte communication only if **all four** of the following conditions are met:

1) The **circumstances** require the judge to communicate with one side only (if the other side cannot be reached);

2) The communication concerns an **emergency or a scheduling or administrative matter** as distinct from a substantive matter or matter affecting the merits;

3) The judge believes that **no party will gain a procedural, substantive, or tactical advantage** from the communication; and

4) The judge **notifies** the lawyers for the other parties of the essence of the communication and gives them an opportunity to respond.

[CJC Rule 2.9(A)(1)]

d. Inadvertent Receipt of Unauthorized Ex Parte Communication

If a judge inadvertently receives an unauthorized ex parte communication that relates to substantive matters, she must make provision promptly to notify the parties of the substance of the communication and give them an opportunity to respond. [CJC Rule 2.9(B)]

9. Communications from Others

A judge must not initiate, permit, or consider communications from others made to the judge outside the presence of the parties' lawyers concerning a pending or impending matter, except in these two situations:

a. Court Personnel

A judge may consult about a matter with other judges and with other court personnel whose function is to aid the judge in carrying out adjudicative responsibilities (e.g., the judge's law clerk). However, the judge: (1) must make reasonable efforts to avoid receiving factual

information that is not part of the record; and (2) must not abrogate his responsibility to decide the matter. [CJC Rule 2.9(A)(3)]

b.   Disinterested Legal Experts

A judge may obtain the written advice of a disinterested expert on the applicable law, provided that the judge gives advance notice to the parties of the expert's identity and the subject matter of the advice to be solicited, and gives the parties a reasonable opportunity to object and respond to the notice and the advice. [CJC Rule 2.9(A)(2)]

10.   Independent Investigation of Facts

A judge must not independently investigate the facts in a case and must consider only the evidence presented. This prohibition extends to information available in all mediums, including electronic research (e.g., Internet research). [CJC Rule 2.9(C) and comment 6]

EXAMPLE

Judge U took a case under submission. While reading the transcript and pondering her decision, she became puzzled about the testimony of witness W. To save time and effort, Judge U simply telephoned W and asked him to clarify the point that puzzled her. Judge U's conduct is improper.

---

11.   Public Comments on Cases

When a case is pending or impending in *any* court, a judge must not make any *public* comment that might reasonably be expected to affect its outcome or impair its fairness, or make any *nonpublic* comment that might substantially interfere with a fair trial. The judge must require like abstention from court personnel under her control. [CJC Rule 2.10]

a.   Official Duties Excepted

The duty to abstain from comment does not prohibit judges from making public statements in the course of their official duties, or from publicly explaining court procedures. [CJC Rule 2.10(D)]

b.   Judge as a Party

The duty to abstain from comment does not apply if the judge is a litigant in a personal capacity. [*Id.*] The duty does apply, however, if the judge is a litigant in an official capacity, as in writ of mandamus proceedings.

EXAMPLE

During the trial of a state criminal case, Judge V ordered the State Governor to appear as a witness and to bring certain documents that the Governor claimed were protected as government secrets. The State Attorney General sought a writ of prohibition from the appellate court to block Judge V's order. At that point, Judge V made a public statement that "the Governor apparently has a lot to hide." If Judge V's statement might reasonably be expected to impair the fairness of the proceedings, Judge V is subject to discipline.

12. **Promises with Respect to Cases Likely to Come Before Court**
With respect to cases or issues that are likely to come before the court, a judge must not make pledges, promises, or commitments that are inconsistent with the impartial performance of the adjudicative duties of the office. [CJC Rule 2.10(B)]

13. **Decorum, Demeanor, and Communication with Jurors**
A judge must require order and decorum in court proceedings. With regard to persons with whom the judge deals in an official capacity (e.g., litigants, jurors, witnesses, lawyers, court staff, and court officials), a judge must be patient, dignified, and courteous, and must require similar conduct of others subject to his control. A judge must not commend or criticize jurors for their verdict other than in a court order or opinion. [CJC Rule 2.8]

EXAMPLE
After the jury came in with a multimillion-dollar verdict for the plaintiff, Judge X told the jurors: "Apparently you people just didn't understand what was going on in this case." Judge X then issued a court order setting aside the jury verdict and ordering a new trial. Judge X's order was proper, but his comment to the jury was not.

14. **Administrative Appointments**
Administrative appointments (e.g., appointments of assigned counsel, referees, special masters, guardians, and court personnel) must be made impartially on the basis of merit, without nepotism or favoritism. A judge must refrain from making unnecessary appointments and must not approve compensation of appointees in excess of the fair value of services rendered. [CJC Rule 2.13]

a. **Appointments of Lawyers Contributing to Judge's Election Campaign**
A judge must not appoint a lawyer to a position if the judge knows (or learns through a timely motion) that the lawyer, the lawyer's spouse, or the lawyer's domestic partner has contributed to the judge's election campaign more than the jurisdiction's specified dollar amount within a designated number of years prior to the judge's campaign. However, this provision does not apply if the appointive position is substantially uncompensated; the lawyer is selected as part of a rotation of qualified lawyers chosen without regard to their political contributions; or

the judge finds that no other lawyer is willing, competent, and able to accept the position. [CJC Rule 2.13(B)]

15. **Responding to Judicial and Lawyer Misconduct**

If a judge has ***knowledge*** that another judge has violated the CJC in a manner that raises a substantial question as to the other judge's honesty, trustworthiness, or fitness as a judge, the judge must inform the appropriate authority. The same duty applies if the judge has knowledge that a lawyer has committed a similar violation of the Rules of Professional Conduct. A judge who receives information indicating a ***substantial likelihood*** that another judge has violated the CJC (or that a lawyer has violated the RPC) must take "appropriate action." What is "appropriate" may range from direct communication with the alleged violator to reporting the suspected violation to the appropriate authority. [CJC Rule 2.15 and comment 2]

16. **Disability and Impairment of Other Judges or Lawyers**

A judge having a reasonable belief that the performance of a lawyer or another judge is impaired by drugs or alcohol or by a mental, physical, or emotional condition must take appropriate action, which may include a confidential referral to a lawyer or judicial assistance program. [CJC Rule 2.14] If the conduct of the impaired person is sufficiently serious, the judge may be required to report the person to the appropriate disciplinary authority. [CJC Rule 2.14, comment 2]

17. **Cooperation with Disciplinary Authorities**

A judge must cooperate and be honest with judicial and lawyer disciplinary agencies. Retaliation against a person known or suspected to have cooperated with an investigation of a judge or lawyer is not permitted. [CJC Rule 2.16]

18. **Disqualification**

a. **General Rule—Whenever Impartiality Might Reasonably Be Questioned**

CJC Rule 2.11(A) states the broad, general rule on disqualification of a judge: A judge must disqualify himself in a proceeding in which the judge's impartiality might reasonably be questioned. (Disqualification of federal judges is governed by 28 U.S.C. section 455.) Note that the rule employs a reasonableness standard; a far-fetched argument or litigant's whim is not sufficient to disqualify a judge. [*See In re* Drexel Burnham Lambert Inc., 861 F.2d 1307 (2d Cir. 1988), *cert. denied,* 490 U.S. 1102 (1989); *see also* Caperton v. A.T. Massey Coal Co., 556 U.S. 868 (2009)—due process required recusal when state supreme court justice received campaign contributions in an extraordinary amount from, and through the efforts of, the board chairman and principal officer of the corporate party]

1) **Disclosure by Judge**

The judge should disclose on the record any information the judge believes that the parties or their lawyers might consider relevant to the question of disqualification, even if the judge believes there is no reasonable basis for disqualification. [CJC Rule 2.11, comment 5]

EXAMPLE

Judge Y plans to retire from the bench at the end of the year and return to private law practice. Judge Y has held tentative discussions with the private firm of A, B & C about joining that firm. Now Judge Y is assigned to hear a case in which the defendant is represented by the A, B & C law firm. Judge Y should disclose the facts and let the parties decide whether to waive disqualification.

---

2) **Rule of Necessity**

Case law has created a rule of necessity that overrides the rules of disqualification. For example, suppose that Judge Z is the only judge available to rule on an emergency motion for a temporary restraining order. Judge Z may rule on the motion even though he might be disqualified were it not an emergency. Even in such a situation, Judge Z should disclose the ground for disqualification on the record and should use reasonable efforts to transfer the matter to a different judge as soon as possible. [CJC Rule 2.11, comment 3]

EXAMPLE

State trial judge A is assigned to hear a case concerning the constitutionality of a statute that will raise the salary of all trial judges in the state. Judge A may hear the case because the reason for disqualification applies equally to all other judges to whom the case might be assigned.

---

b. **Bias or Personal Knowledge**

A judge must disqualify himself if there is reasonable ground to believe that the judge has: (1) a personal bias concerning a party or a party's lawyer; or (2) personal knowledge of relevant evidentiary facts. [CJC Rule 2.11(A)(1)] To be disqualifying, a bias must be personal and stem from an extrajudicial source; adverse attitudes toward a party formed on the basis of evidence presented in the case are not disqualifying. [*See, e.g., In re* Cooper, 821 F.2d 833 (1st Cir. 1987)]

c. **Prior Involvement**

A judge must disqualify himself if the judge previously:

1) Served as a *material witness* in the matter;

2) Served as a *lawyer* in the matter;

3) Was *associated in law practice* with a person who participated substantially as a lawyer in the matter at the time they practiced together;

4) *Presided as a judge* over the matter in another court; or

5) Served in *governmental employment*, and in such capacity participated personally and substantially as a lawyer or public official concerning the proceeding, or publicly expressed in such capacity an opinion concerning the merits of the particular matter in controversy.

[CJC Rule 2.11(A)(6)]

EXAMPLES

1) Before her appointment as a state supreme court justice, Justice C practiced law with lawyer L. At the time C and L were in practice together, L represented X in the trial of *X v. Y.* After the trial, L withdrew as X's lawyer. Now the case is on appeal to the state supreme court. Justice C is disqualified.

2) In the preceding example, suppose that L did not begin representing X until C had left the practice and become a supreme court justice. Justice C need not recuse herself unless her prior association with L creates a reasonable question about her impartiality under the general rule of disqualification (*see a., supra*).

---

d. **Economic Interest**

A judge must disqualify himself if the judge knows that he, either as an individual or as a fiduciary, has an *economic* interest in the matter or in one of the parties. Disqualification is also required if the interest is held by the judge's spouse, domestic partner, parent, or child (wherever residing) or by any other member of the judge's family who resides in the judge's household. [CJC Rule 2.11(A)(3)] A judge must keep informed about his economic interests and must make a reasonable effort to keep informed about the economic interests of the judge's spouse or domestic partner and minor children residing in the judge's household. [CJC Rule 2.11(B)]

1) **Definition of "Economic Interest"**

For the purpose of this rule, the term "economic interest" means that a person owns more than a de minimis legal or equitable interest. A "de minimis interest" is an insignificant interest that raises no reasonable question regarding the judge's impartiality. [CJC, Terminology]

2) **Exceptions to Definition**

The following are excepted from the definition of "economic interest":

a) **Mutual Funds**

Ownership of an interest in a mutual fund or common investment fund that holds securities is not an economic interest in those securities unless: (1) the judge participates in the management of the fund; or (2) the proceeding could substantially affect the value of the interest.

EXAMPLE

Judge D's son owns 100 shares of Universal Diversified Fund, a mutual fund that owns common stocks of many different companies, including Ohio Chemicals, Inc. Judge D is assigned to hear a case in which Ohio Chemicals is the defendant. The outcome of the case will not significantly affect the value of the mutual fund shares, and Judge D does not participate in the management of the fund. Judge D is not disqualified.

---

b) **Securities Held by Organization**

Suppose that a judge is an officer, director, advisor, or other active participant in an educational, religious, charitable, fraternal, or civic organization. Suppose, further, that the organization owns securities of the XYZ Corporation, which is a party to a case that the judge is assigned to hear. The judge's involvement with the organization does **not** give the judge an economic interest in the XYZ Corporation. The same is true if a judge's spouse, domestic partner, parent, or child is an officer, director, advisor, or other active participant in such an organization.

EXAMPLE

Judge E's wife is a vice president of P.E.O. International, a philanthropic organization that promotes educational opportunities for women. Among its many investments, P.E.O. owns 1,000 shares of common stock in Delta Coal & Steel Inc. Judge E is assigned to hear a case in which Delta is a party. Judge E is not disqualified.

c) **Bank Deposits, Mutual Insurance Policies, and the Like**
Suppose that a judge, or member of the judge's family, owns a deposit in the First Federal Bank. That does not disqualify the judge from hearing a case in which First Federal is a party, unless the proceedings could substantially affect the value of the deposit. The same rule applies to a deposit in a mutual savings association or credit union.

d) **Government Securities**
An interest in the issuer of government securities is not a disqualifying economic interest, unless the value of the securities could be substantially affected by the proceedings.

> **EXAMPLE**
> Judge G has invested a substantial part of her retirement nest egg in municipal bonds issued by the city of Springfield. Springfield is on the brink of fiscal collapse, and Judge G is assigned to hear a case in which the outcome could substantially affect the value of her bonds. Judge G is disqualified.

e. **Involvement in the Proceeding**
A judge must disqualify herself if the judge knows that she, her spouse or domestic partner, or a person within the third degree of relationship to either of them, or the spouse or domestic partner of such a person, is:

1) A *party*, or an officer, director, general partner, managing partner, or trustee of a party;

2) A *lawyer* in the proceeding;

3) A *person with more than a de minimis interest* that could be substantially affected by the proceeding; or

4) Likely to be a *material witness* in the proceeding.

[CJC Rule 2.11(A)(2)]

1) **Meaning of Third Degree of Relationship**
Persons within the third degree of relationship are: great-grandparents, grandparents, parents, uncles, aunts, brothers, sisters, children, grandchildren, great-grandchildren, nieces, and nephews—in short, anyone related more closely than cousin. [CJC, Terminology]

f. **Persons Making Contributions to Judge's Election Campaign**
A judge who is subject to public election must disqualify himself if he

knows, or learns through a timely motion, that a party, a party's lawyer, or the law firm of a party's lawyer has, within a designated number of prior years, made contributions to the judge's election campaign that exceed the jurisdiction's specified amount. [CJC Rule 2.11(A)(4)]

g. **Public Statements of Judicial Commitment**
A judge must disqualify himself if he, while a judge or a candidate for judicial office, has made a public statement other than in a court proceeding, judicial decision, or opinion, that commits or appears to commit the judge to reach a particular result or to rule in a particular way in the proceeding or controversy. [CJC Rule 2.11(A)(5)]

h. **Remittal of Disqualification**
The parties and their lawyers can remit (waive) all of the foregoing grounds of disqualification, except personal bias concerning a party or a party's lawyer. [CJC Rule 2.11(C)] The procedure for remittal is as follows:

1) The judge discloses on the record the ground for disqualification. The judge may then ask whether the parties and their lawyers wish to discuss waiver.

2) The lawyers consult privately with their respective clients.

3) All of the parties and their lawyers meet, outside the presence of the judge, and agree that the judge should not be disqualified. The agreement must be incorporated into the record.

4) If the judge is willing to do so, she may then proceed with the case.

D. **EXTRAJUDICIAL ACTIVITIES**
A judge must conduct his personal and extrajudicial activities to minimize the risk of conflict with the obligations of judicial office. [CJC Canon 3]

1. **In General**
Judges are encouraged to engage in appropriate extrajudicial activities. Nevertheless, when engaging in such activities, a judge must not:

a. Participate in activities that will interfere with the proper performance of the judge's duties; lead to frequent disqualification; or reasonably appear to undermine the judge's independence, integrity, or impartiality;

b. Engage in conduct that would reasonably appear to be coercive; or

c. Use court premises, staff, stationery, equipment, or other resources, except incidentally, for activities that concern the law, the legal system,

or the administration of justice, unless such additional use is legally permitted.

[CJC Rule 3.1]

2. **Governmental Hearings and Consultations**
A judge must not appear voluntarily at a public hearing before, or otherwise consult with, an executive or legislative body or official, except on matters concerning the law, the legal system, or the administration of justice. However, this duty does not apply when the judge is acting pro se in a matter that involves the judge or his interests, or when the judge is acting as a fiduciary. Also, the duty does not apply in connection with matters about which the judge acquired knowledge or expertise in the course of her judicial duties. [CJC Rule 3.2]

EXAMPLES

1) Judge M is invited to testify before the State Assembly Committee on Criminal Justice concerning a proposed revision of the state's mandatory sentencing statute. Judge M may testify.

2) Judge N met privately with the Mayor of the city of Glenview to protest the city's plan to open a city dump adjacent to Judge N's property. As long as Judge N did not refer to his judicial position or otherwise use the prestige of his office (*see* B.4., *supra*), the meeting was proper because it concerned Judge N's own interests.

---

3. **Testifying as Character Witness**
A judge must not testify as a character witness, except when duly summoned to do so, i.e., by subpoena. Ordinarily, a judge should discourage parties from requiring his testimony as a character witness. [CJC Rule 3.3 and comment 1]

4. **Governmental Committees and Commissions**
A judge must not accept an appointment to a governmental committee or commission or other governmental position that does not relate to the law, the legal system, or the administration of justice. Such appointments are likely to be very time-consuming, can involve the judge in controversial matters, and can interfere with the independence of the judiciary. A judge may, however, represent a governmental unit on a ceremonial occasion, or in connection with a historical, educational, or cultural activity. [CJC Rule 3.4 and comments 1 and 2]

5. **Participation in Educational, Religious, Charitable, Fraternal, or Civic Organizations and Activities**
Subject to the general restrictions on extrajudicial activities, a judge may take part in activities sponsored by organizations or governmental entities

concerned with the law, the legal system, or the administration of justice, and those sponsored by or on behalf of educational, religious, charitable, fraternal, or civic organizations not conducted for profit. [CJC Rule 3.7(A)] Included among such permissible activities are the following:

(i) Assistance in planning for fund-raising, and participation in management and investment of funds;

(ii) Solicitation of contributions for the organization, but **only** from members of the judge's family or from judges over whom the judge has no supervisory or appellate authority;

(iii) Membership solicitation, even though the dues or fees generated may be used to support the objectives of the organization, but only if the organization is concerned with the law, the legal system, or the administration of justice;

(iv) Appearing or speaking at, receiving an award at, being featured on the program of, and permitting her title to be used in connection with an organization's event (if the event is a fundraiser, such participation is permitted only if the event concerns the law, the legal system, or the administration of justice);

(v) Making recommendations to a fund-granting organization in connection with its programs and activities, but only if the organization is concerned with the law, the legal system, or the administration of justice; and

(vi) Service as an officer, director, trustee, or nonlegal advisor, unless it is likely that the organization will be engaged in proceedings that would ordinarily come before the judge, or will frequently be engaged in adversary proceedings in the court on which the judge sits or one under its appellate jurisdiction.

a. **Encouraging Pro Bono Service**
A judge may encourage lawyers to provide pro bono publico legal services. However, in providing such encouragement, a judge must not use coercion or abuse the prestige of her office. [CJC Rule 3.7(B), comment 5]

6. **Affiliation with Discriminatory Organizations**
A judge must not hold membership in an organization that practices **invidious discrimination** based on **race, sex, gender, religion, national origin, ethnicity, or sexual orientation.** [CJC Rule 3.6(A)] Even if the judge is not a member of such an organization, he must not use the organization's benefits or facilities if he knows or should know that it practices one of the prohibited forms of invidious discrimination. However, the judge may attend an event

in a facility of the organization if his attendance is an isolated event that could not reasonably be perceived as an endorsement of the organization's practices. [CJC Rule 3.6(B)]

EXAMPLE

The Ashmount Golf and Tennis Club limits its membership to Caucasian males. Judge M is not a member of the club, but three times a week he eats lunch at the club as a guest of a member. Judge M is in violation of Rule 3.6(B).

---

a. **Determination of "Invidious Discrimination"**

An organization discriminates invidiously if it arbitrarily excludes from membership, on any of the bases enumerated above, persons who would otherwise be eligible for admission. An examination of the organization's membership rolls is not solely dispositive of the issue. It is important to determine how the organization selects its members. Other relevant factors include whether the organization is dedicated to the preservation of religious, ethnic, or cultural values of legitimate common interest to its members, or whether it is an intimate, purely private organization whose membership limitations could not constitutionally be prohibited. [CJC Rule 3.6, comment 2]

EXAMPLE

Judge G belongs to the Slovenian League, which limits its membership to all descendants (regardless of sex or race) of persons from Slovenia. The object of the organization is to preserve the culture and traditions of the Slovenian people. Judge G's membership is permissible.

---

b. **Exercise of Religion Does Not Violate Rule**

Membership in a religious organization as a lawful exercise of freedom of religion does not violate Rule 3.6. [CJC Rule 3.6, comment 4]

c. **Immediate Resignation Required**

Upon learning that an organization to which he belongs engages in invidious discrimination, a judge must resign immediately from the organization. [CJC Rule 3.6, comment 3]

7. **Use of Nonpublic Information**

A judge must not intentionally disclose or use nonpublic information acquired in his judicial capacity for any purpose unrelated to his judicial duties. [CJC Rule 3.5]

8. **Financial, Business, or Remunerative Activities**

Generally, a judge may not serve as an officer, director, manager, general partner, advisor, or employee of a business. However, a judge may hold and

manage her own investments and those of her family and may manage or participate in a business closely held by the judge or a family member, or in a business primarily engaged in investing the financial resources of the judge or her family, unless such activity will:

(i)   Interfere with the proper performance of the judge's duties;

(ii)   Lead to frequent disqualification of the judge;

(iii)   Involve the judge in frequent transactions or continuing business relationships with lawyers or other persons likely to come before the court on which the judge serves; or

(iv)   Result in a violation of other provisions of the CJC.

[CJC Rule 3.11]

a.   Divesting Problematic Interests
As soon as practicable without serious financial detriment, a judge must divest herself of investments and other financial interests that might require frequent disqualification or otherwise violate Rule 3.11. [CJC Rule 3.11, comment 2]

b.   Minimizing Time Spent on Business Activities
It is improper for a judge to devote so much time to her business activities that it interferes with her judicial duties. [CJC Rule 3.11, comment 1]

9. **Acceptance and Reporting of Gifts, Loans, Bequests, Benefits, or Other Things of Value**
A judge must not accept gifts, loans, bequests, benefits, or other things of value if acceptance thereof is prohibited by law or would reasonably appear to undermine the judge's independence, integrity, or impartiality. [CJC Rule 3.13(A)]

a.   Gifts Acceptable Without Reporting
If not prohibited by the requirements of Rule 3.13(A), the following may be accepted without being publicly reported:

1)   Items of little intrinsic value (e.g., plaques or certificates);

2)   Things of value from individuals whose appearance or interest in a case would require the judge's disqualification in any event—e.g., friends, relatives, or persons with cases pending or impending before the judge under Rule 2.11 (see C.18., *supra*);

3)   Ordinary social hospitality;

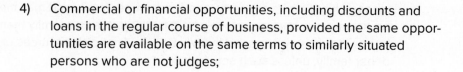

4) Commercial or financial opportunities, including discounts and loans in the regular course of business, provided the same opportunities are available on the same terms to similarly situated persons who are not judges;

5) Rewards and prizes given to participants in drawings and contests that are open to persons who are not judges;

6) Scholarships and fellowships, provided they are available to similarly situated persons who are not judges, based on identical criteria;

7) Books, magazines, journals, and other resource materials supplied by publishers on a complimentary basis for official use; and

8) Gifts, awards, or benefits associated with the business or separate activity of a spouse, domestic partner, or other family member residing in the judge's household, but that incidentally benefit the judge.

[CJC Rule 3.13(B)]

b. Gifts that Must Be Reported
If not prohibited by the requirements of Rule 3.13(A), the following may be accepted but must be publicly reported if so required by Rule 3.15:

1) Gifts incident to a public testimonial;

2) Invitations to the judge and her spouse, domestic partner, or guest to attend without charge an activity related to the law, the legal system, or the administration of justice, or an event associated with any of the judge's educational, religious, charitable, fraternal, or civic activities permitted by the CJC, if the same invitation is offered to nonjudges who are engaged in similar ways in the activity; and

3) Gifts, loans, bequests, or other things of value, if the source is a person who has come, or is likely to come, before the judge, or whose interests have come, or are likely to come, before the judge.

[CJC Rule 3.13(C)]

10. Fiduciary Activities
Generally, a judge must not serve as an executor, administrator, trustee, guardian, or other fiduciary. However, a judge may serve in such a capacity for a member of the judge's family, *if* the service will not:

(i)   Interfere with the judge's judicial duties;

(ii)   Involve the judge in proceedings that would ordinarily come before him; or

(iii)   Involve the judge in adversary proceedings in the court on which the judge sits or one under its appellate jurisdiction.

[CJC Rule 3.8]

a.   Financial Dealings as Fiduciary
The restrictions on financial dealings that apply to a judge personally also apply when the judge acts as a fiduciary. [CJC Rule 3.8(C)]

b.   Conflicting Duties
When the duties of a fiduciary conflict with the judge's duties under the Code of Judicial Conduct, the judge should resign as fiduciary. [CJC Rule 3.8, comment 1]

EXAMPLE
Judge V is appointed as trustee of a fund for the use and benefit of his invalid brother. The trust fund includes common stock of several companies that frequently appear as litigants before Judge V. The judge must manage her investments in a way that minimizes disqualifications. If the trust fund would be harmed by divestiture of those stocks, Judge V should not serve as trustee. [*Id.*]

---

c.   Fiduciary Who Becomes a Judge Must Comply with Rule
If a person serving as a fiduciary becomes a judge, she must comply with Rule 3.8 as soon as reasonably practicable, but no later than one year after becoming a judge. [CJC Rule 3.8(D)]

11. Service as Arbitrator or Mediator
A *full-time* judge must not act as an arbitrator, mediator, or private judge unless expressly authorized by law. This does not, of course, prevent the judge from participating in arbitration, mediation, or settlement conferences as part of her regular judicial duties. [CJC Rule 3.9 and comment 1]

12. Practice of Law
A *full-time* judge must not practice law. However, a judge may act pro se and may, without compensation, give legal advice to, and draft or review documents for, a member of her family. A judge must not, however, act as a family member's lawyer in any forum. [CJC Rule 3.10]

13. Compensation for Extrajudicial Activities
Reasonable compensation for a judge's extrajudicial activities (e.g.,

compensation for speaking, teaching, or writing) is permitted unless acceptance thereof would reasonably appear to undermine the judge's independence, integrity, or impartiality. Any such compensation must be reasonable and commensurate with the task performed. [CJC Rule 3.12 and comment 1]

14. **Reimbursement of Expenses and Waiver of Fees or Charges**
Unless otherwise prohibited by the CJC, a judge may accept reimbursement of necessary and reasonable expenses for travel, food, lodging, or other incidentals, or a waiver of fees or charges for registration or tuition, from sources other than the judge's employer, if such expenses are associated with the judge's participation in extrajudicial activities permitted by the CJC. Reimbursement for expenses may not exceed the actual costs reasonably incurred by the judge and, when appropriate, her spouse, domestic partner, or guest. A judge who accepts reimbursement of expenses or waivers of fees must comply with the public reporting requirements of Rule 3.15. [CJC Rule 3.14]

   a. **Factors Judge Should Consider in Determining Propriety of Reimbursement or Fee Waiver**
   A judge must assure herself that acceptance of reimbursement or a fee waiver would not appear to undermine her independence, integrity, or impartiality. In making this determination, a judge should consider the following:

   1) Whether the sponsor is an accredited educational institution or bar association rather than a trade association or a for-profit entity;

   2) Whether funding comes largely from numerous contributors rather than from a single entity and is earmarked for programs with specific content;

   3) Whether the content is related to the subject matter of litigation pending or impending before the judge, or to matters likely to come before the judge;

   4) Whether the activity is primarily educational rather than recreational, and whether the costs are reasonable and comparable to the costs of similar events sponsored by the judiciary or bar associations;

   5) Whether information related to the activity and its funding sources is available upon request;

   6) Whether the sponsor or source of funding is generally associated with parties or interests currently appearing or likely to appear in the judge's court, thus potentially requiring the judge's disqualification under Rule 2.11 (*see* C.18., *supra*);

7) Whether differing viewpoints are presented; and

8) Whether a broad range of judicial and nonjudicial participants are invited, whether a large number of participants are invited, and whether the program is designed specifically for judges.

[CJC Rule 3.14, comment 3]

15. **Reporting Requirements**
A judge must publicly report the amount or value of:

(i) Compensation received for extrajudicial activities as permitted by Rule 3.12 (*see* 13., *supra*);

(ii) Gifts and other things of value permitted by Rule 3.13 (*see* 9., *supra*), unless the value, alone or in aggregation with other items received from the same source during the same calendar year, does not exceed a dollar amount determined by other state law; and

(iii) Reimbursement of expenses and waiver of fees or charges permitted by Rule 3.14 (*see* 14., *supra*), unless the amount thereof, alone or in aggregation with other reimbursements or waivers received from the same source during the same calendar year, does not exceed a dollar amount determined by other state law.

[CJC Rule 3.15(A)]

a. **Contents of Public Report**
The public report must state the date, place, and nature of the activity for which the judge received compensation. Any gifts, loans, or other things of value must be described. The report must also state the source of reimbursement of expenses or waiver of fees or charges. [CJC Rule 3.15(B)]

b. **Time for Making Report**
Public reports must be made at least annually. However, reports of reimbursement of expenses and waiver of fees or charges must be made within 30 days after the conclusion of the event or program. [CJC Rule 3.15(C)]

c. **Location of Filing**
Public reports must be filed in the office of the clerk of the court on which the judge sits, or in some other office designated by law. If feasible, reports must also be filed on the court's website. [CJC Rule 3.15(D)]

E. JUDGES' POLITICAL AND CAMPAIGN ACTIVITIES

A judge or candidate for judicial office must not engage in political or campaign activity that is inconsistent with the independence, integrity, or impartiality of the judiciary. [CJC Canon 4] A person becomes a judicial candidate when she publicly announces her candidacy, declares or files with the election or appointment authority, authorizes or, where permitted, engages in solicitation or acceptance of contributions or support, or is nominated for election or appointment to office. [CJC Terminology]

1. **Political and Campaign Activities of Judges and Judicial Candidates in General**

   Except where permitted by law or by Rules 4.2, 4.3, or 4.4 of the CJC (discussed *infra*), a judge or a judicial candidate must not:

   (i) Lead or hold office in a political organization;

   (ii) Make speeches on behalf of a political organization;

   (iii) Publicly endorse or oppose a candidate for public office;

   (iv) Solicit funds for, pay an assessment to, or contribute to a political organization or a candidate for public office;

   (v) Attend or buy tickets for dinners or other events sponsored by a political organization or a candidate for public office;

   (vi) Publicly identify herself as a candidate of a political organization;

   (vii) Seek, accept, or use endorsements from a political organization;

   (viii) Personally solicit or accept campaign contributions other than through a campaign committee authorized by Rule 4.4;

   (ix) Use or permit the use of campaign contributions for private benefit;

   (x) Use court staff, facilities, or other court resources in her campaign;

   (xi) Knowingly, or with reckless disregard for the truth, make a statement that is false or misleading, or that omits facts necessary to make the communication considered as a whole not materially misleading;

   (xii) Make a statement that would reasonably be expected to affect the outcome or impair the fairness of a matter pending or impending in any court; or

   (xiii) In connection with cases, controversies, or issues that are likely to come before the court, make pledges, promises, or commitments that are inconsistent with the impartial performance of the adjudicative duties of judicial office.

[CJC Rule 4.1(A)]

a. **Activities of Other Persons**

A judge or candidate must take reasonable measures to ensure that other persons do not undertake on her behalf any of the prohibited activities set forth in 1., *supra*. [CJC Rule 4.1(B)]

b. **No "Family Exception" to Prohibition Against Candidate Endorsement**

A judge or candidate must avoid involvement in a family member's political activity or campaign for public office. Reasonable steps must be taken to avoid the implication that the judge or candidate endorses the family member. [CJC Rule 4.1, comment 5]

c. **Participation in Caucus-Type Elections Is Permitted**

Participation in a caucus-type election procedure does not constitute public support for or endorsement of a political organization or candidate. [CJC Rule 4.1, comment 6]

d. **Responding to Statements by Others**

A judicial candidate may make a factually accurate public response to false or misleading statements issued by her opponent, third parties, or the media, concerning, e.g., her integrity, experience, or fitness for office. [CJC Rule 4.1, comment 8] Although the candidate may respond directly, if the allegations to which she is responding relate to a pending case, it is preferable for someone else to respond. [CJC Rule 4.1, comment 9]

e. **Pledges or Promises**

To determine whether a candidate has made a pledge or promise, one must examine the totality of a statement. If a reasonable person would think that the candidate has ***specifically undertaken to reach a particular result***, then a pledge, promise, or commitment has been made. Note, however, that a statement of personal views on legal, political, or other issues is not prohibited. [CJC Rule 4.1, comment 13] The United States Supreme Court has held that such "announce clauses"—i.e., prohibitions on judicial candidates announcing their views on disputed legal or political issues—violate the First Amendment. [Republican Party of Minnesota v. White, 536 U.S. 765 (2002)]

1) **Promises Related to Judicial Organization Permitted**

A judicial candidate may make campaign promises related to judicial organization, administration, and court management, e.g.,

promises to dispose of case backlogs or to begin court sessions on time. It is also permissible to pledge to take certain actions outside the courtroom, such as working to improve the jury selection system or advocating more funds to improve the physical facilities of a courthouse. [CJC Rule 4.1, comment 14]

2) Responding to Media Questionnaires Requires Caution
Candidates often receive questionnaires or interview requests from the media or from issue advocacy groups, in an effort to discern their views on disputed or controversial issues. Responses to such questions might be viewed as impermissible promises or pledges. Thus, candidates who respond to such inquiries should give assurances that they will keep an open mind and will carry out their adjudicative duties faithfully and impartially if elected. If a candidate does not respond, she may state that a response might be perceived as undermining her independence or impartiality, or might lead to frequent disqualification. [CJC Rule 4.1, comment 15]

2. Political and Campaign Activities of Judicial Candidates in Public Elections
A judicial candidate in a partisan, nonpartisan, or retention public election must:

(i) Act in a manner consistent with the independence, integrity, and impartiality of the judiciary;

(ii) Comply with applicable election, election campaign, and campaign fund-raising laws and regulations of the jurisdiction;

(iii) Review and approve the content of campaign statements and materials produced by the candidate or her campaign committee before their dissemination; and

(iv) Take reasonable measures to ensure that other persons do not undertake on her behalf activities that the candidate is prohibited from doing by Rule 4.1.

[CJC Rule 4.2(A)]

a. Certain Activities Permitted
Unless prohibited by law, a candidate for elective judicial office may, no earlier than a minimum amount of time (to be determined by other state law) prior to the first applicable primary, caucus, or general or retention election, do the following:

(i) Establish a campaign committee pursuant to Rule 4.4 (*see* 4., *infra*);

(ii) Speak on behalf of her candidacy through any medium;

(iii) Publicly endorse or oppose candidates for the same judicial office for which she is running;

(iv) Attend or purchase tickets for dinners or other events sponsored by a political organization or a candidate for public office;

(v) Seek, accept, or use endorsements from any person or organization **other than a partisan political organization**; and

(vi) Contribute to a political organization or candidate for public office, but not more than a maximum dollar amount to be determined by each jurisdiction to any one organization or candidate.

[CJC Rule 4.2(B)]

1) Exception—Candidates in Partisan Elections May Be Identified with Political Organizations

Unless prohibited by law, a judicial candidate in a **partisan** election may, not earlier than a minimum amount of time designated by other state law prior to the first applicable primary, caucus, or general election:

a) Identify herself as a candidate of a political organization; and

b) Seek, accept, and use endorsements of a political organization.

[CJC Rule 4.2(C)]

3. Activities of Candidates for Appointive Judicial Office

A candidate for appointment to judicial office may communicate with the appointing or confirming authority, including any selection, screening, or nominating commission. Also, a candidate may seek the endorsement of a person or organization, other than a partisan political organization. [CJC Rule 4.3]

4. Campaign Committees

A judicial candidate running in a public election may establish a **campaign committee** to manage and conduct her campaign. The candidate is responsible for ensuring that the committee complies with applicable law and applicable parts of the CJC. [CJC Rule 4.4(A)]

a. Solicitation Time Limits

The candidate must direct the committee not to solicit or accept

contributions more than a certain amount of time (designated by other state law) prior to the applicable election, nor more than a designated number of days after the last election in which the candidate participated. [CJC Rule 4.4(B)(2)]

b. Campaign Contribution Limits

The candidate must direct the committee to solicit and accept only reasonable contributions, not to exceed the jurisdiction's specified limits. [CJC Rule 4.4(B)(1)]

c. Disclosure Requirements

The candidate must direct the committee to comply with any statutory requirements for disclosure and divestiture of campaign contributions, and to file with the appropriate authority a report that states the name, address, occupation, and employer of each person who has contributed an amount in excess of the applicable maximum. The report must be filed within a post-election time period designated by the jurisdiction. [CJC Rule 4.4(B)(3)]

5. **Activities of Judges Who Become Candidates for Nonjudicial Office**

When a judge becomes a candidate for a nonjudicial *elective* office, she must resign her judgeship unless applicable law permits her to retain her judicial office. If the judge becomes a candidate for a nonjudicial *appointive* office, she need not resign her judgeship, provided that she complies with all other provisions of the CJC. [CJC Rule 4.5]

F. APPLICATION OF THE CODE OF JUDICIAL CONDUCT

In jurisdictions that adopt the Code of Judicial Conduct, it applies to all persons who perform judicial functions, including magistrates, court commissioners, and special masters and referees. The Application section of the CJC contains a group of highly detailed exceptions that make various parts of the CJC inapplicable to several categories of retired and part-time judges. If your purpose in reading this book is to answer a specific question about the conduct of such a person, you should examine the Application section of the CJC with care. On the other hand, if your purpose is to prepare for the Multistate Professional Responsibility Examination, we suggest that mastering the detailed exceptions is not the best use of your time, and that you be content with the following broad generalizations:

1. A *retired judge* subject to recall is allowed to serve as an arbitrator or mediator (except while serving as a judge) and is allowed to serve as a fiduciary. [CJC Application II]

2. *Continuing part-time judges*, *periodic part-time judges*, and *pro tempore part-time judges* are exempt from many, but not all, of the CJC provisions that restrict outside activities and political activities. [*See* CJC Application III, IV, V]

REVIEW QUESTIONS

**FILL IN
ANSWER**

Answer each of the following review questions "Yes" or "No."

1. While lawyer Limpet was a law student, he took a job interview trip to a distant city. He requested and received reimbursement from two different law firms for the full expenses of his trip—thus receiving double what the trip cost him. Limpet's conduct came to light only ***after*** he was admitted to the bar of State A. State A has a statute that specifies under what circumstances a lawyer can be disciplined for misconduct, and the statute says nothing about discipline for conduct committed ***before*** being admitted to the bar. Is Limpet subject to discipline by the supreme court of State A for his dishonest conduct? _____

2. Lawyer Lupus is a member of the bar of State A, and one of his clients was sued in the United States District Court that sits in State A. Would it be proper for Lupus to serve as counsel of record in the case without being separately admitted to practice in that United States District Court? _____

3. Oster is a member of the bar of West Carolina, but he never practiced law in that state. After 27 years in politics, he was appointed to the United States Supreme Court. A few years later, he resigned from the Court under the threat of a bribery investigation. Would Oster be subject to discipline in West Carolina if there was an investigation? _____

4. Attorney Abydos is a member of the bar of State A, but not of State B. Some of Abydos's clients live across the river in State B. When one of her State B clients becomes a party to litigation pending in State B, may Abydos serve as counsel of record, without being admitted pro hac vice in State B and without associating with a State B lawyer? _____

5. To apply for admission to the state bar of East Dakota, one must fill out a long, complicated information form. One of the questions on the form asks for the address of every place the applicant has lived for longer than one month, from birth onward. Bar applicant Appleby had lived in a great many places and could not remember the addresses of most of them; furthermore, she concluded that the state bar had no business knowing such information in any event. Therefore, she listed only her current address and the address of the house in which she spent most of her childhood years. Was this proper? _____

6. Client Cronin asked lawyer Lavelle to take over as her counsel in a civil case. Cronin explained in confidence that she had fired Aspner, her former counsel, because he had used threats of violence to force her to have sexual relations with him. Cronin instructed Lavelle not to tell anyone what Aspner had done to her. Should Lavelle nevertheless report Aspner's conduct to the appropriate disciplinary authorities? _____

7. Mertin, a nonlawyer, worked as a messenger for lawyer Lefkowitch's law firm. Mertin asked Lefkowitch to refer him to a good form book so that Mertin could prepare the legal papers that his sister needed to adopt a baby. Should Lefkowitch comply with Mertin's request?

   _____

8. Shelby is employed by a cosmetics company, where she serves as in-house counsel. Shelby is licensed in the state of Oberon and has been working for the company in that state for 10 years; however, the company wants to relocate Shelby to the state of Tiberon. Shelby is not licensed in Tiberon. Would it be proper for Shelby to set up an office and conduct a continuous practice in Tiberon without being admitted to practice there?

   _____

9. Client Cardwell asked her neighbor's friend, lawyer Lubner, to represent her in a paternity suit against the suspected father of her first child. Without mentioning the matter of legal fees, Lubner did the work promptly and effectively. Then, when the matter was completed, Lubner sent Cardwell a bill for a reasonable fee. Was Lubner's conduct proper?

   _____

10. After a night of heavy drinking, Duphus and his friend Pugman got into a fight with each other. Pugman got the worst of it. The next day he sued Duphus for civil assault and battery. Duphus retained lawyer Laud, who agreed to defend Duphus for a $5,000 flat fee, payable in advance. Duphus paid Laud the fee. Two days later, Duphus and Pugman became friends again, and Pugman dismissed his suit. Duphus conveyed his good news to Laud and asked for his money back, but Laud would not return any of it. Was Laud's conduct proper?

    _____

11. Attorney Alarcon is one of the three best municipal bond attorneys in the state. He has done all of the bond work for the city of Denton for the past 28 years. Now, the city of Denton has asked him to write an opinion letter concerning a new paving and sewer bond issue. Alarcon consulted a similar letter he had written for Denton eight months earlier, checked to confirm the accuracy of the facts supplied to him, reread a recent appellate decision on municipal bonds, and completed the new opinion letter—all in less than six hours. For this work, Alarcon charged the city of Denton $10,000. Is Alarcon subject to discipline?

    _____

12. Is it true that a lawyer may allow clients to pay for legal fees by credit card?

    _____

13. Client Coro hired lawyer Low to defend him in a cocaine smuggling case. Coro agreed to pay Low $3,000 in advance and another $30,000 if Coro is acquitted. If $33,000 would be a reasonable fee in light of the nature of the case and the amount of work required, is Low's conduct proper?

    _____

14. One of the clauses in attorney Altman's standard employment contract provides that in the event that Altman and the client disagree over Altman's fee, the two of them will submit the matter to arbitration before a mutually agreeable arbitrator. Is Altman subject to discipline?

    _____

15. Client Culpa asked his neighbor, lawyer Ledbetter, for her advice about bringing suit against his employer for age discrimination. Ledbetter advised Culpa to retain attorney Arneson, an expert in employment discrimination matters. Culpa did so, and Arneson agreed to handle the case on a one-third contingent fee basis. When Culpa won a large judgment, Arneson sent Ledbetter 5% of the contingent fee. Was this proper? _____

16. Private criminal defense attorney Axelrodd was hired to defend Dervish in a mayhem case. After Dervish described the facts to Axelrodd in confidence, Axelrodd concluded that Dervish was guilty as charged. Dervish, however, insisted on pleading not guilty and going to trial. May Axelrodd continue as Dervish's counsel if Dervish persists in his desire to plead not guilty? _____

17. Lawyer Leonard represented the plaintiff in a products liability suit. The defense lawyer telephoned Leonard and made a settlement offer that was unreasonably low. Leonard rejected it instantly and said: "Don't call again unless you have something to say, meatball." Is Leonard subject to discipline? _____

18. Lawyer Lispley is defending Toxatec, Inc., in an air pollution case. At the close of discovery, Toxatec instructed Lispley to move for summary judgment. Lispley explained that there were a host of disputed fact issues and that a motion for summary judgment would be frivolous. Toxatec persisted in its instruction. Must Lispley do as his client has instructed? _____

19. Is it true that when representing a mentally disabled person, a lawyer should herself make the decisions that would ordinarily be made by the client? _____

20. Client Coleman obtained the services of legal aid attorney Adler in a dispute with the State Handicapped Assistance Commission over Coleman's eligibility for special medical assistance. The Commission Hearing Officer ruled that Coleman was not eligible for assistance. Such rulings can be appealed to the full Commission. Adler believed that an appeal would probably not be successful, and she therefore did not advise Coleman of the possibility of an appeal. Was Adler's conduct proper? _____

21. Client Croaque asked his friend and neighbor, lawyer Lugash, for legal advice about a problem that Croaque was having with attorney Ahman. Croaque had hired Ahman to do some legal work. One of the clauses in Ahman's standard form employment contract provided that Croaque could "terminate this contract at any time upon five days' notice and payment of a $10,000 severance fee." Before Ahman had spent any substantial amount of time on Croaque's matter, Croaque had lost confidence in Ahman's ability to do the work properly. Croaque asked Lugash whether he could fire Ahman without having to pay the so-called severance fee. Without telling Croaque that he and Ahman were good friends, Lugash advised Croaque that he would have to pay the severance fee if he fired Ahman. Is Lugash subject to discipline? _____

22. Is it true that a lawyer may withdraw from representing a client simply because the lawyer believes that the client's objectives are imprudent?

_____

23. Solo practitioner Plebert agreed to represent client Cisco in a real property dispute. The dispute became more and more complex as time wore on, and Cisco became unable to pay Plebert's fees. Ultimately, the matter became a serious threat to Plebert's financial well-being. May she withdraw from the matter?

_____

24. Lawyer Lerner was representing client Caufman in negotiations for the sale of Caufman's business. Despite Lerner's earnest admonitions, Caufman insisted that certain contingent liabilities not be disclosed to the prospective buyer. Finally, Lerner had no choice but to withdraw. In these circumstances, must Lerner give Caufman advance notice and time to get another lawyer?

_____

25. Lawyer Legree is the in-house general counsel of TransCoastal Corporation, a company that employs 500 people and sells its products in interstate commerce. As general counsel, Legree has overall responsibility for the company's legal affairs. Does Legree have any duty to keep abreast of current literature and current developments in the field of labor law?

_____

26. The state bar of State A brought disciplinary proceedings against attorney Admetus for incompetence in defending Dorner in a criminal case. Ultimately, the state bar decided not to impose discipline on Admetus. Thereafter, Dorner sued Admetus for legal malpractice; Dorner's claim was based on the same facts as the disciplinary proceedings. Can Admetus invoke the doctrine of res judicata and have Dorner's suit dismissed?

_____

27. Lawyer Lemur represented D in the civil case of *A v. D*. Later, Lemur represented B in a substantially related civil suit against D. D sued Lemur for legal malpractice. Lemur's state has adopted the ABA Model Rules of Professional Conduct. At the trial of the malpractice case, D offered evidence that Lemur's conduct was in violation of ABA Model Rules 1.7 and 1.9. Lemur objected that the evidence should be excluded as irrelevant. Should the trial judge sustain Lemur's objection?

_____

28. One of the terms of attorney Adoula's retainer agreement with client Cruz provided that Adoula would "exercise ordinary care in performing the aforementioned legal services." Two and a half years after Cruz learned that Adoula had been negligent in performing the legal services, Cruz sued Adoula for legal malpractice. Cruz's complaint alleged both tort and contract claims. The state law provides a two-year statute of limitations for negligence claims and a four-year statute of limitations for actions based on written contracts. Is Adoula entitled to have Cruz's entire complaint dismissed as untimely?

_____

29. Lawyer Lingam is a certified specialist in taxation law in State A. Lingam muddled a tax transaction for client Chang, and Chang sued Lingam for

legal malpractice. In that suit, Chang asserted that the relevant standard of care is that of certified specialists in taxation, not that of ordinary lawyers. Is Chang correct?

30. Attorney Aisha lost her client's case because she placed her total reliance on an appellate court case that had later been overruled. Had Aisha bothered to Shepardize the case, or to use WESTLAW or LEXIS, she would have discovered that the case had been overruled. If her client sues her, is Aisha subject to civil liability?

31. When the local newspaper printed a patently false story about Crullner, he hired Arnott (who is engaged in general civil and criminal practice) to sue the paper for libel. The newspaper won the case on summary judgment. Is Arnott subject to civil liability for failing to refer the case to a specialist in the law of libel and slander?

32. When young attorney Amax was training his new legal secretary, Stacey, he told her always to send a copy of litigation papers to opposing counsel. Amax was assigned to assist senior partner Pough in pretrial phases of a civil case. After careful study, Pough and Amax concluded that their client would probably lose if the case went to trial. Pough told Amax to write a confidential letter to their client to explain the weaknesses in the case and to recommend settling it for whatever sum the adversary would offer. Amax wrote the letter, and Stacey dutifully sent a copy of the letter to opposing counsel. If the client is able to prove that this blunder resulted in a lower settlement than he otherwise would have received, is senior partner Pough subject to civil liability?

33. Is it true that a lawyer must carry a "reasonably adequate" amount of malpractice insurance?

34. When lawyer Langur was fired by client Conorf, Langur declined to send Conorf's litigation files to Conorf's new lawyer until Conorf signed a release discharging Langur from liability for malpractice. Was Langur's conduct proper?

35. Deputy Public Defender Fox was assigned to defend Dix on a charge of selling heroin. In confidential communications with Fox, Dix insisted that he was not guilty and had been framed by the police. Fox then sought out and found an ex-convict whom she knew to be a heroin user; the ex-convict told her that Dix was widely known throughout the city as a steady source for heroin. Is the information that Fox got from the ex-convict protected by the attorney-client privilege?

36. Robul showed up unannounced in the offices of attorney Astorian, told Astorian that he had robbed a bank and was being pursued by the police, and asked Astorian to give him legal assistance. Astorian told Robul that he was an estate planning specialist, never practiced criminal law, and did not wish

to represent Robul. Robul thereupon left as quickly as he had come. The police arrested Robul a block down the street, and they then asked Astorian what Robul had said to him. May Astorian respond to the police inquiry?

37. The president of Dorsett Corporation suspected that some of the corporation's sales personnel were engaging in price-fixing with their counterparts from other corporations. She therefore hired an outside lawyer, Longfellow, to investigate the matter and to prepare a full report for her use. She instructed each of the corporation's regional sales representatives to cooperate completely with Longfellow's investigation. Longfellow interviewed each sales representative and wrote a report to the president in which he concluded that some of the sales representatives had indeed engaged in unlawful price-fixing. Longfellow was later subpoenaed to testify before a grand jury about the communications he previously had with the regional sales representatives. May he do so?

38. Angus and Bane jointly consulted an attorney on a problem that concerned both of them. The attorney was unable to help them resolve their problem amicably, and Angus ultimately sued Bane. Is it true that in this litigation neither Angus nor Bane can claim the attorney-client privilege regarding communications they had with the attorney?

39. Client Custer told attorney Ames in confidence that he had figured out a way to tap a local bank's computer records and to transfer funds from other accounts to his own. Custer asked for Ames's legal services in devising a money laundering operation for the funds thus transferred. Ames refused to assist Custer. Ames's state has adopted the ABA Model Rules. May Ames warn the bank of Custer's scheme?

40. Dornan and Demming were charged with acting jointly to defraud the United States Postal Service. They asked the firm of Apelt & Aluss to defend them at their joint trial. The testimony of witness Woeler will implicate Dornan but will exculpate Demming. Would it be proper for partner Apelt to defend Dornan and for partner Aluss to defend Demming?

41. Attorney Argus has her office in a small town where there are only two other lawyers. She represents Cox in a suit for partition of some real property. While that suit is pending, Cramer asks Argus to represent her in a personal injury suit against Cox. Is Argus subject to disqualification if she represents Cramer without obtaining Cox's consent?

42. Attorney Acosta represents Poponovich in a suit against Detroit Investors Corporation. While that suit is pending, another client offered Acosta a 10% ownership interest in Detroit Investors in lieu of a fee the other client owed Acosta. If Acosta accepts the 10% ownership interest without obtaining the signed written consent of Poponovich, will Acosta be subject to discipline?

43. Lawyer Lundstrum represented Dreggs at his trial for the murder of 10 schoolboys. After the trial and all possible appeals, Lundstrum acquired the right to publish a book about the case. Is Lundstrum's conduct proper? _____

44. Client Courbert was severely injured when he was struck by a golf ball while watching a celebrity golf tournament. Attorney Addison agreed to represent him in a personal injury suit, to do the work for a contingent fee, to pay Courbert's medical bills, and to advance the costs of the litigation. Is Addison subject to discipline? _____

45. Lawyer Lutza represented four physicians in a medical malpractice case. The plaintiff offered to settle the case for a lump sum of $1.1 million. Because the liability seemed clear and the injuries were very serious, the insurance carrier for the four defendants agreed to contribute $1 million toward settlement. Three of the physician defendants agreed to contribute the other $100,000. Lutza did not consult the fourth physician about the settlement until after it was accomplished because Lutza knew that the fourth physician would contribute nothing and would insist on taking the case to trial. Was Lutza's conduct proper? _____

46. The city of Pautuckette brought a lawsuit to close down and dismantle the Inglewood Rendering and Glue Works on the grounds that it was a public nuisance and a source of noxious odors. Practitioner Pugh agreed to defend the Inglewood corporation in the case in return for 12% of Inglewood's common stock. Assuming that the value of the stock is less than a reasonable fee would be, is Pugh's conduct proper? _____

47. Lawyer Lim was employed on the in-house legal staff of Marketway Stores, Inc., for five years. He was assigned to handle all of Marketway's labor law matters. Later Lim entered private practice in partnership with lawyer Lee. Lee was asked to represent the plaintiff in an employment discrimination action against Marketway. The alleged discriminatory acts took place while Lim was still working for Marketway. If Marketway provides informed consent, confirmed in writing, may Lee take the case? _____

48. Lawyer LaRosa was one of three attorneys who defended Pakilite Fabrics Corp. in a series of suits concerning flammable pajama fabric sold by Pakilite. Several years later, LaRosa left her former law firm and entered solo practice. She was asked to represent client Cantrell in a suit against Pakilite concerning flammable raincoat fabric. Pakilite used the same chemicals to treat both the pajama fabric and the raincoat fabric. May LaRosa represent Cantrell without Pakilite's consent? _____

49. For three years following her graduation from law school, attorney Alcock worked for the State Internal Revenue Department. One of the cases that occupied a substantial amount of her time was *State v. Devereaux Industries,* a complex inventory tax matter. Later, Alcock quit government service and

entered private practice with the Cerle & Meros firm. Devereaux Industries asked senior partner Meros to represent it in an appeal of the inventory tax case to the United States Supreme Court. May Meros represent Devereaux, provided that Alcock does not work on the appeal?

50. Attorney Aikawa was the in-house general counsel of MacroComp, Inc., and was gathering information to be included in an SEC disclosure statement. In doing so, Aikawa discovered that one of MacroComp's vital manufacturing steps was clearly infringing two patents held by one of the company's competitors. Aikawa informed MacroComp's president of this new development, and she advised the president that the securities laws require such information to be disclosed. After checking to make sure no one else knew of the infringement, the president told Aikawa: "For the good of the company, and for my sake, and for your own sake, I am instructing you simply to forget what you have learned. May I have your promise to do that?" Under the ABA Model Rules, must Aikawa do as the president has asked?

51. Is it true that a lawyer is subject to discipline for depositing clients' funds in an interest-bearing time-deposit account?

52. When lawyer Stillwater agreed to represent the Minnequa Tribe in a fishing rights dispute, the tribe gave him a $5,000 advance to cover future litigation expenses. Would it be proper for Stillwater to deposit the advance in his client trust fund account?

53. When attorney Ayala settled a personal injury case on behalf of his client, Cooper, the defendant sent Ayala a check for $12,000. At the outset, Ayala and Cooper had agreed that Ayala's fee would be one-third of the eventual recovery in the case. When Ayala received the check, he cashed it, deposited $4,000 in his personal checking account, and deposited the other $8,000 in his client trust fund account. Did Ayala handle the matter properly?

54. Solo practitioner Pendergast told her legal secretary, Brett, to manage her client trust account and to keep the appropriate records in an office ledger book. When Pendergast suddenly learned that the account was overdrawn, she found that, over a period of 18 months, Brett had been keeping the records by the "shoebox" method—a shoebox filled with a tangle of deposit receipts, cancelled checks, unverified bank statements, and mysterious notes written on scraps of waste paper. Is Pendergast subject to discipline?

55. Client Coddlemeyer asked lawyer Lutza to draft him a new will in which Coddlemeyer's daughter would receive nothing. Lutza was aware that Coddlemeyer, a truculent old scoundrel, had convinced the daughter to give up her job in the big city to return home to care for Coddlemeyer in his old age. Would it be proper for Lutza to point out the moral, as well as the legal, implications of disinheriting his daughter?

56. In the case described above, suppose that Lutza is unable to convince Coddlemeyer to change his mind. Would it be proper for Lutza to refuse to draft the new will for Coddlemeyer?

_____

57. In the case described above, suppose that Lutza is unable to convince Coddlemeyer to change his mind. Would it be proper for Lutza to tell the daughter of her father's plan in an effort to remedy whatever has come between the two of them?

_____

58. Professors Herch, Loomis, and Jantrell jointly wrote a treatise on the aboriginal cultures of North America. The three authors were unable to come to an agreement on who should receive primary credit for the work and on how the publication royalties should be divided among them. Therefore, the three asked attorney Abberman to help them work out a mutually acceptable compromise. May Abberman serve in this role?

_____

59. Client Cullen asked lawyer Langtree to represent her as plaintiff in a medical malpractice action against a physician and others who helped deliver her first child. Based solely on the physical condition of the mother and child immediately after the birth, it appeared that some malpractice had been committed—aside from that, Langtree could obtain no other information about what had happened in the delivery room. Would it be proper for Langtree to file a malpractice action?

_____

60. Attorney Atherton represents the plaintiff shareholders in a shareholder derivative action. After 18 months of intensive discovery, Atherton's clients instructed him to prepare and file a massive fifth set of interrogatories. When he protested that a fifth set of interrogatories would be a patent waste of time and money for everyone concerned, they responded: "Our adversaries can't hold out much longer; if we make it expensive enough, they will come begging to settle." Is Atherton subject to litigation sanction if he prepares and files a fifth set of interrogatories?

_____

61. Is it true that a lawyer is subject to discipline for citing a case to the court knowing that the case does not stand for the proposition for which it is cited?

_____

62. Under West Dakota law, a defendant cannot appeal from an adverse money judgment in a civil case without first posting an appeal bond in a sum equal to the judgment. Trial courts, however, routinely waive the appeal bond if it appears that the defendant is solvent and can pay the judgment if the appeal is unsuccessful. Lawyer Loutson requested such a waiver based on his client's affidavit. The affidavit incorporated a statement of net worth that materially understated the client's liabilities. Loutson knew of this inaccuracy and knew that his client was in a precarious financial condition. Is Loutson subject to discipline?

_____

63. Is it true under the ABA Model Rules that a lawyer must allow his criminal defendant client to testify even if the lawyer knows that the client will testify falsely?

_____

64.   Lawyer Lucinda represents defendant Dodgeville Motor Company in a products liability action brought by plaintiff Paul. Paul had purchased the new model Z manufactured by Dodgeville. Two weeks after his purchase, Paul was injured when his car crashed into a stoplight because the brakes had failed. Paul has requested all documents and reports pertaining to the design and manufacture of the model Z. Dodgeville's president, Dufus, gives Lucinda a report that indicates that the brakes on the model Z failed in half of the model Z's test drives (Dufus ignored the report and released the model Z for sale without redesigning the brakes). Lucinda tears up the report and tells Dufus: "Forget that this report ever existed or you won't stand a chance at trial!" Is Lucinda subject to criminal liability?

65.   Attorney Ahern was preparing a summary judgment motion on behalf of her client. She needed an affidavit of her client to establish certain facts, but the client had just left the state for a five-week vacation. Ahern, therefore, prepared the affidavit and signed her client's name to it. Ahern had her secretary notarize the affidavit, and Ahern filed it with the court along with the other summary judgment papers. Everything stated in the affidavit was true, and the client would happily have signed it had he been there to do so. Was Ahern's conduct proper?

66.   Lawyer Lew represents the plaintiff in an automobile case pending in Hawaii. Plaintiff's key witness is Werner. Werner lives in Iowa, and she saw the accident while vacationing in Hawaii. May Lew have his client pay Werner's airfare, hotel, meal, and other expenses incurred in coming back to Hawaii to testify at the trial?

67.   The State Air Quality Control Board has brought a civil action against Elmore Electric & Power Company for polluting the air with the discharge from its generating plant smokestacks. Attorney Ackroid is defending Elmore. Ackroid asks Elmore to advise all of its employees that they need not talk about the case with anyone representing the Air Quality Control Board, and that if any such person attempts to interview them, they should contact Ackroid. Is this proper?

68.   At the jury trial of a civil action against Donato Linen Supply Corp., one of the defense witnesses was old Mr. Donato, the founder and majority shareholder of the company. Everyone in town knows that 25 years ago, Mr. Donato served time in jail for tax fraud, and common gossip has it that he was also once connected with organized crime. At the final pretrial conference, the trial judge ordered plaintiff's lawyer, Lippert, not to refer to either of these matters at the trial, holding that they were too far distant in the past to be used fairly for impeachment. In his closing argument to the jury, Lippert said: "You jurors are probably all aware of Mr. Donato's unsavory background—but you should not consider that in deciding whether to believe what he told you on the witness stand. Who knows, he may have changed in his old age." Is Lippert subject to discipline?

69. Lawyer Langdon defended Dostert Manufacturing Company in a Robinson-Patman Act price discrimination case. The plaintiff requested production of Dostert's copies of the invoices for all of Dostert's sales over the relevant four-year period—more than 35,000 individual pieces of paper. Langdon agreed to furnish plaintiff's counsel with xerographic copies of the invoices (made at plaintiff's expense), and Langdon agreed further to keep the original invoices available at Dostert's offices, should plaintiff need to examine them. At Dostert's offices the invoices were filed in chronological order in labeled file drawers. Before Langdon turned the xerographic copies over to plaintiff, he instructed his assistant to thoroughly shuffle the copies so as to put them in a purely random order. Langdon's object was to make it difficult and expensive for plaintiff to find out anything useful from the invoices. Is Langdon subject to litigation sanction?   _____

70. Is it true that, in arguing a case to the jury, a lawyer may state personal opinions, as long as they are supported by evidence in the record?   _____

71. During the recess between the morning and afternoon sessions of a jury trial, lawyer Luban went to a local delicatessen for lunch. The delicatessen was crowded, and Luban found himself seated at a table with two jurors in the case he was trying. To avoid embarrassment, Luban greeted them in an ordinary way, and the three of them chatted over lunch about the local baseball team's chances of ending up in the World Series. Is Luban subject to discipline?   _____

72. Judge Jordach was assigned to preside at the trial of a notorious police brutality case that had received a vast amount of coverage in the national media. Prosecutor Prunella held a press conference at which she discussed the evidence that the prosecution would offer at the trial and expressed her personal opinion that the "defendants have lied about this matter repeatedly; they are guilty as sin, and the jury will soon find that out." Is Prunella subject to discipline?   _____

73. Lawyer Lindner is plaintiff Papman's trial counsel in a civil rights action where there is a fee-shifting statute that makes the loser pay the winner's attorneys' fees. The jury awarded Papman a large sum, and the judge then called for evidence on attorneys' fees. May Lindner take the witness stand and testify about the number of hours she spent on the case and the rates she ordinarily charges for similar work?   _____

74. Midway through the trial of a criminal case, defense lawyer Lucero overheard the prosecutor tell a witness: "Listen, buddy, if you don't stick to the story we rehearsed, you will spend the rest of this century in a prison cell." Lucero was the only person who overheard the prosecutor's threat. May Lucero testify about what he heard and still continue to serve as trial counsel for the defense?   _____

75.   Does a prosecutor have a duty to assure that criminal suspects are told how to secure legal representation?

_____

76.   When a member of the bar is acting as a lobbyist, and not as an attorney, is she subject to discipline for conduct that violates the rules of legal ethics?

_____

77.   Client Cejay hired attorney Arbor to represent her in connection with the sale of a controlling block of stock in Ceamus Corporation. Cejay authorized Arbor to sell the stock for $30 per share, or more if possible. When the lawyer for a prospective buyer telephoned Arbor and offered $28 per share, Arbor responded: "I'm sorry, but you are not even in the ballpark. This is a controlling block of stock, and it's worth at least $45 per share." Is Arbor subject to discipline for misrepresentation?

_____

78.   Carl and Cora hired separate counsel to represent their respective interests in their divorce proceedings. One Saturday afternoon, Carl was unable to reach his own lawyer, so he telephoned Cora's lawyer to ask a simple question about a proposed division of the marital assets. Cora's lawyer refused to discuss the matter with Carl and told him to call his own lawyer on Monday morning. Should Cora's lawyer have responded differently?

_____

79.   Lawyer Lutenberger agreed to represent Price for a one-third contingent fee in a personal injury action against Dolen. Lutenberger told Price that his claim against Dolen was worth at least $100,000 if settled before trial. The case dragged on for several years, despite several settlement efforts by the lawyers for the respective parties. Finally, Price became impatient, got in touch with Dolen directly, and agreed with Dolen to settle for $50,000. When Price told Lutenberger about the settlement and asked Lutenberger to prepare the settlement papers, Lutenberger was outraged. He refused to draw up the settlement papers, and he promptly sent Price a bill for $33,333. Was Lutenberger's conduct proper?

_____

80.   Attorney Arundale was representing two engineers, Enman and Erwin, in seeking venture capital for their new medical equipment company. Potential investor Ibbersole (who was not represented by a lawyer in the matter) asked Arundale what risks she would be taking if she invested in the company. Would it be proper for Arundale to advise Ibbersole in this matter?

_____

81.   Young lawyer Lacy was assisting senior partner Parner in a civil case. Parner assigned Lacy to take the deposition of a nonparty witness, Woeford. Because it was Lacy's first deposition, Parner accompanied her to provide advice and assistance. Counsel for the adversary party was present at the deposition, but witness Woeford was not represented by counsel. During a recess in the deposition, Parner instructed Lacy to ask Woeford to reveal what Woeford had told his wife about a certain matter. Lacy protested, pointing out that Woeford's communications with his wife are protected by the marital communications privilege and that they could not lead to relevant

evidence in any event. Parner responded: "Do as I say. Woeford probably doesn't know about the privilege. Even if he does, your questions will get him rattled and upset, and he may blurt out something that could be useful to us." Should Lacy follow Parner's instructions?   _____

82. With reference to private law firms, is it true that the term "member of the firm" usually means the same as "associate"?   _____

83. Is it true that a nonlawyer employee of an incorporated law firm may be a shareholder in the firm?   _____

84. Is it true that a lawyer is subject to discipline for failing to do 50 hours per year of pro bono work?   _____

85. Attorney Adelano opened her own law office in a neighborhood shopping center. She announced the opening of the office by distributing circulars door-to-door at every house in the neighborhood. The circulars invited everyone in the neighborhood to attend an "office warming party" to meet Adelano and to celebrate the opening of her office. Is Adelano's conduct proper?   _____

86. Shortly after attorney Andrews opened his solo law practice in Bakersburg, 1,250 students from Bakersburg City College were arrested during a demonstration to protest the use of United States military personnel in Central America. Andrews visited one of the demonstration leaders in the city jail and offered to defend all of them without charging any fee. Is Andrews subject to discipline?   _____

87. Lawyer partners Layton and Letonen have both been certified as specialists in criminal defense work by the American Institute of Criminal Defense Counsel, a private organization that has rigorous, carefully enforced standards for certifying specialists. The state in which Layton and Letonen practice has no program for approving private certification agents, and the organization has not been approved by the ABA. In their law firm advertising material, may Layton and Letonen state that they are "Certified Specialists in Criminal Defense"?   _____

88. Is it true that, because federal judges hold office for life during good behavior, the only way a federal judge can be disciplined for misconduct is through impeachment proceedings?   _____

89. Judge Jarmon's staff includes an attractive young woman, attorney Lightner. When Lightner is present in chambers during the judge's conferences with male attorneys, the judge invariably makes lecherous comments about her. He does not make such comments in open court or in other public places. May Lightner report Judge Jarmon to the appropriate authorities?   _____

90. Attorney Allright is a trustee of Welborne College. Allright frequently appears as counsel in Judge Jerginson's court. When Allright learned that

Judge Jerginson's daughter had applied to Welborne, he visited the judge in his chambers and offered to drive the judge and his daughter up to the campus for a weekend visit and to do all that he could to make sure that her application was accepted. May Judge Jerginson accept Allright's offer?

91. A judge should not comply with a subpoena to serve as a character witness, but a judge may appear voluntarily as a character witness. Is this a true statement?

92. Judge Jones regularly eats lunch at a local restaurant that refuses to alter its 100-year-old policy of reserving some of its space for men only. When the issue became a topic of heated public debate, Judge Jones publicly stated: "Why should the restaurant have to bow to political correctness? Women have plenty of other places they can eat." Is Judge Jones's comment proper?

93. Justice Juarez is a member of the board of directors of the American Institute for Mental Health, a nonprofit organization that funds scientific research in the field of mental health. The Institute's endowment fund holds 10,000 shares of the common stock of Carnegie Steel Corporation. Carnegie Steel is the appellant in a case now pending before Justice Juarez's court. The appellee in the case is represented by Justice Juarez's best friend, lawyer Lee. Should Justice Juarez hear the appeal?

94. When she was appointed to the bench, Judge Jimerson was an active member of the Cascades Club, a conservation group that is heavily involved in environmental protection litigation. The club is a party litigant in hundreds of cases pending around the state, but none of the cases is presently pending in Judge Jimerson's court. Would it be proper for Judge Jimerson to serve as treasurer of the organization and to engage in public fund-raising activities on its behalf?

95. Judge Joiner serves full-time as a United States District Court Judge. When his Aunt Agnes died, he discovered that she had designated him to serve as attorney for the executor of her estate. Would it be proper for Judge Joiner to serve in that capacity?

96. Justice Jessup and her husband were invited to attend the State Bar Convention in a distant state; Justice Jessup was scheduled to be the keynote speaker at the convention. May she accept an honorarium for giving the speech, and may she accept reimbursement of the expenses that she and her husband incur in attending the convention?

97. Lawyer Lenox would like to be appointed by the Governor to a municipal court judgeship. Would it be proper for Lenox to contact the Governor to make known his interest in the position?

ANSWERS TO REVIEW QUESTIONS

1. **YES** The highest court of a state, not the state legislature, has inherent final authority to regulate the legal profession. [Page 1, I.A.1.a.; Stratmore v. State Bar of California, 14 Cal. 3d 887 (1975); *and see In re* Nellelson, 390 N.E.2d 857 (Ill. 1979)]

2. **NO** Each federal court has its own bar, and a lawyer must become a member of that bar before appearing for a client in that court. [Page 2, I.A.2.a.]

3. **YES** West Carolina has jurisdiction to discipline Oster, even though his conduct may have taken place elsewhere. [Page 2, I.A.3.; Page 11, I.C.5.a.] If Oster did in fact take a bribe, then he is subject to discipline because bribery is a crime that involves dishonesty and demonstrates his unfitness to practice law. [Page 6, I.C.1.b.]

4. **NO** The right to practice in one state does not, without more, entitle an attorney to practice in another state. A lawyer may temporarily practice in a state in which she is not admitted if: (1) she associates with a local lawyer, (2) she is admitted pro hac vice, (3) she is mediating or arbitrating a dispute arising out of her home-state practice, or (4) her out-of-state practice is reasonably related to her home-state practice. [Page 2, I.B.; Pages 12-14, I.D.1.-2.] Here, Abydos is not associating with a State B lawyer or seeking admission pro hac vice. Moreover, her State B practice is not reasonably related to her State A practice; neither does it involve mediation or arbitration arising out of her State A practice. Thus, Abydos may not serve as counsel of record in State B.

5. **NO** A bar applicant must provide all of the information requested, to the best of her ability. [Page 2, I.B.1.] In most states, the state bar conducts a routine character investigation of some or all candidates; the purpose of asking for the addresses where the applicant has lived is to facilitate this investigation. If Appleby could not remember all of the addresses and could not obtain them from others in her family, she should simply have explained that on the application form.

6. **NO** Aspner's conduct is a disciplinary violation because it is criminal and demonstrates his unfitness to practice law. [Page 6, I.C.1.b.] Ordinarily, another lawyer who learns of such conduct must report it to the appropriate professional authority. [Page 7, I.C.2.] Here, however, Lavelle knows of Aspner's conduct only through a privileged communication from Cronin, and he must respect Cronin's instructions to keep the information in confidence. [Page 8, I.C.2.c.; Page 46, III.A.] (Common sense, however, suggests that Lavelle should explain to Cronin why it is important to have such information reported; that may cause her to change her instructions.)

7. **NO** A lawyer must not assist a nonlawyer in the unlicensed practice of law. [Page 12, I.D.; Page 15, I.D.5.]

8. **YES** A lawyer may open a law office and establish a systematic and continuous practice in a jurisdiction in which she is not admitted if the lawyer is a salaried employee of her only client. Note though that Shelby may not litigate a matter in Tiberon without being admitted pro hac vice. [Page 14, I.D.3.a.]

9. **NO** A lawyer must reach an early, clear agreement with the client about the lawyer's fee unless the lawyer has regularly represented the client in the past. [Page 28, II.C.1.]

10. **NO** A lawyer is subject to discipline for charging an unreasonable fee. [Page 29, II.C.2.] Five thousand dollars seems clearly unreasonable for little or no work in a common assault and battery case. [*See In re* Kutner, 399 N.E.2d 963 (Ill. 1979)—attorney censured for charging $5,000 in similar circumstances]

11. **NO** If the number of hours spent were the only relevant factor in setting a reasonable fee, then Alarcon's fee would seem exorbitant, but many other factors are relevant. [Page 29, II.C.2.a.] No doubt Alarcon's many years of experience enabled him to do the work in much less time than other lawyers would have taken. Furthermore, the issuer of municipal bonds commonly wants an opinion letter from a recognized expert. Alarcon's reputation, built over many years of work, justifies a higher fee than would be charged by an unknown novice.

12. **YES** A lawyer may permit a client to pay her fee by credit card. [ABA Formal Op. 00-419 (2000)] [Page 31, II.C.3.d.]

13. **NO** A lawyer is subject to discipline for using a contingent fee arrangement in a criminal case. [Page 32, II.C.4.a.1)]

14. **NO** One proper way to resolve a fee dispute with a client is to submit it to arbitration, and the client and lawyer may agree in advance to do that. [Page 33, II.C.5.b.3)]

15. **NO** A lawyer is subject to discipline for splitting fees with another lawyer unless: (1) the total fee is reasonable; (2) the split is in proportion to the services performed by each lawyer or some other proportion if each lawyer assumes joint responsibility for the matter; and (3) the client agrees to the split in a writing that discloses the share each lawyer will receive. The arrangement described here does not meet all of the above requirements and, thus, is an impermissible forwarding or referral fee. [Pages 34-35, II.C.6.c. and 7.]

16. **YES** The decision to plead either guilty or not guilty to a criminal charge is for the client, not the lawyer, to make. [Page 36, II.D.3.] Furthermore, Axelrodd may conduct the defense so as to require the prosecutor to prove every element of the crime, even though Axelrodd may personally believe that Dervish is guilty. [Page 101, VI.A.2.]

17. **YES**   Leonard is subject to discipline for failing to convey the settlement offer to his client before rejecting it—settlement is for the client, not the lawyer, to decide. [Page 36, II.D.3.; Page 40, II.E.1.]

18. **NO**   The decision to move for summary judgment is a tactical decision, and clients normally defer to their lawyers regarding tactical decisions. If there is a dispute between the lawyer and client regarding a tactical decision that cannot be resolved, the lawyer may withdraw as counsel or the client may fire the lawyer. [Page 37, II.D.3.a.] Moreover, if Lispley files a summary judgment motion that he knows is frivolous, he is subject to discipline. [Page 100, VI.A.1.]

19. **NO**   The lawyer's obligations depend on the particular facts and the extent of the client's disability. A client with diminished mental capacity may be able to make some kinds of decisions on her own behalf. In addition, the lawyer has a duty to maintain a normal lawyer-client relationship with the client so far as possible—treating the client as a client. Under some circumstances, the lawyer may be required to seek the appointment of a guardian for the client. [Pages 38-39, II.D.5.a. and b.]

20. **NO**   An attorney must promptly inform the client of any decision or circumstance that requires the client's informed consent. [Page 40, II.E.1.] Also, the attorney should act with zeal on the client's behalf; once the attorney has taken on a matter, she should see it through to completion. [Pages 91-92, V.B.1. and 3.] Adler should have advised Coleman of the possibility of an appeal, although she might also advise that an appeal would probably not succeed.

21. **YES**   The law allows a client to fire a lawyer at any time, with or without cause, subject only to liability for the fair value of the work the lawyer has already done. [Page 43, II.G.1. and a.] Lugash is subject to discipline for incompetence (if his erroneous advice resulted from ignorance of the law) or for disloyalty (if his erroneous advice resulted from a desire to protect his friend Ahman).

22. **YES**   An attorney may withdraw from representing a client if the attorney considers the client's objective to be repugnant or fundamentally against the attorney's beliefs. [Page 45, II.G.4.c.]

23. **YES**   ABA Model Rule 1.16(b)(6) permits an attorney to withdraw from representing a client when the continuation of the representation would impose an unreasonable financial burden on the attorney. [Page 45, II.G.4.e.]

24. **YES**   Even when the withdrawal results from the client's reprehensible conduct, the attorney must take reasonable steps to protect the client's interests. [Page 45, II.G.5.]

25. **YES** Labor law is of obvious importance to TransCoastal, and a lawyer should keep abreast of current literature and current developments in the fields of law in which the lawyer practices. [Page 91, V.A.4.]

26. **NO** The purposes and issues in a malpractice case are different from those in a disciplinary proceeding. [Page 93, V.D.1.] (In any event, Admetus could not invoke the collateral estoppel branch of the res judicata doctrine against Dorner because Dorner was not a party to the prior proceeding.)

27. **NO** According to the "Scope" section of the ABA Model Rules, a disciplinary violation does not itself give rise to civil liability and does not create a presumption that a legal duty has been breached. However, Lemur's violation of ABA Model Rules 1.7 and 1.9 is at least relevant to the issue of whether his conduct falls below the applicable standard of care. [Page 93, V.D.2.]

28. **NO** An action for legal malpractice can be based on many different theories, including negligence and breach of contract. Cruz's contract claim is timely, even though his negligence claim is barred by the two-year statute of limitations. [Page 94, V.D.3.c. and d.]

29. **YES** A lawyer who purports to be a specialist is held to a higher standard of care than ordinary lawyers—it is the degree of care, skill, and prudence possessed by other lawyers who specialize in the field in question. [Page 95, V.D.3.d.1)c)]

30. **YES** If Aisha's failure to do standard legal research is the legal and proximate cause of injury to her client, she has committed malpractice and is subject to civil liability. [Page 96, V.D.3.d.2)b)] Every first-year law student is taught never to rely on a case without checking its history through one of the standard research sources.

31. **NO** In some instances, an attorney's failure to refer a case to a specialist can constitute malpractice, thereby subjecting the attorney to civil liability. [Page 96, V.D.3.d.2)c)] Libel, however, is a routine part of tort law, well within the capacity of a general civil and criminal practitioner. As long as Arnott's work met the standard of care of general practitioners, he should not be held liable for malpractice. [Page 95, V.D.3.d.1)c)]

32. **YES** Under general partnership principles, as well as the doctrine of respondeat superior, partner Pough is civilly liable for the negligence of other lawyers in the firm and of nonlawyer employees. [Page 98, V.D.5.]

33. **NO** The ABA Model Rules and the vast majority of states do not impose such a duty, but prudent lawyers carry adequate malpractice insurance in their own self-interest. [Page 98, V.D.6.]

34. **NO**   Langur is subject to discipline for attempting to free himself from potential malpractice liability in this manner. [Pages 98-99, V.D.7. and 8.] A lawyer who is fired must promptly return all papers to which the client is entitled, and that includes litigation files. [Page 45, II.G.5.] (A lawyer may, however, make and retain *copies* of the files.)

35. **NO**   The information is not protected by the attorney-client privilege because it is not a confidential communication. Fox obtained the information from a third party, not from her client or an agent of her client. The information is, however, covered by Fox's ethical duty of confidentiality. [Page 47, III.B.2.]

36. **NO**   The attorney-client privilege and the ethical duty of confidentiality apply here, even though no attorney-client relationship ultimately developed. Robul was *seeking* legal assistance from Astorian, even though he did not get it. [Page 48, III.C.1. and 2.]

37. **NO**   Longfellow's communications with the regional sales representatives are covered by the attorney-client privilege. [Page 48, III.C.2.a.] In the grand jury proceeding, Longfellow must claim the attorney-client privilege on Dorsett's behalf. [Page 51, III.C.6.b.]

38. **YES**   The attorney-client privilege cannot be claimed by either of two joint clients in later litigation between them concerning the subject of the joint consultation. [Page 52, III.C.8.c.]

39. **NO**   Under the ABA Model Rules, a lawyer may reveal a client's confidential information to the extent necessary to prevent the client from committing a crime or fraud that is reasonably certain to result in substantial financial harm to someone, *if the client is using or has used the lawyer's services in the matter*. [Page 55, III.D.2.d.] Here, Custer did not use Ames's services in transferring the funds, and Ames refused to assist in the money laundering; thus, Ames may not warn the bank of Custer's scheme.

40. **NO**   A lawyer must not represent a client if the representation creates a concurrent conflict of interest. A concurrent conflict exists if there is a significant risk that the representation of one client will be materially limited by the lawyer's responsibility to another client. [Page 59, IV.B.1.] This conflict is imputed to other lawyers in the lawyer's firm. [Page 58, IV.A.2.]

41. **YES**   Even assuming that the two suits are totally unrelated, an attorney must not represent one client if the representation of that client will be directly adverse to another client, without the informed consent of each affected client, confirmed in writing. [Page 60, IV.B.2.]

42. **YES**   Acosta would be acquiring a pecuniary interest adverse to Poponovich. [Page 72, IV.C.2.a.]

43. **YES**   After a matter is entirely completed, a lawyer may acquire such publication rights. [Page 75, IV.C.5.]

44. **YES**   The contingent fee and advance of litigation costs are proper, but the agreement to pay the client's medical bills is not. [Pages 75-76, IV.C.6.a.-d.]

45. **NO**   An attorney representing co-parties in litigation may not agree to an aggregate settlement without informed consent in a signed writing from each client after disclosure of the settlement terms. Therefore, Lutza is subject to discipline for failing to consult the fourth physician about the settlement. [Page 77, IV.C.7.]

46. **NO**   If the suit is lost, Inglewood will be closed down and dismantled. By acquiring 12% of the stock, Pugh has, in essence, acquired an ownership interest in the subject of the litigation, which is impermissible under ABA Model Rule 1.8. [Page 73, IV.C.3.]

47. **YES**   Ordinarily, Lee could not handle a matter that was substantially related to work Lim did for Marketway, but he may do so with Marketway's informed consent, confirmed in writing. [Page 80, IV.D.3.]

48. **NO**   An attorney must not oppose a former client in a matter that is "substantially related" to a matter in which the attorney represented the former client without the former client's informed consent, confirmed in writing. Here, the two matters are "substantially related" because of the chemicals used to treat both types of fabric. [Page 80, IV.D.3. and a.] Thus, LaRosa cannot represent Cantrell without Pakilite's consent.

49. **NO**   Three other conditions must be met as well. Alcock must be screened off from the case, and she must not be apportioned any part of the fee in the case. Furthermore, the State Internal Revenue Department must be notified in writing so that it can make sure these conditions are met. [Page 85, IV.F.2.c.]

50. **NO**   Under the ABA Model Rules, when a lawyer for an organization learns that a person associated with the organization has acted in a way that violates a duty to the organization, the lawyer must ordinarily report the violation to a higher authority in the organization, or if necessary, to the highest authority in the organization. [Page 129, VIII.G.3. and a.] Aikawa's client is the company, not the president. She must not allow the president to interfere with her legal judgment about how best to protect the company's interests. If necessary, she should go over the president's head to the highest authority in the corporation, the board of directors. [Page 129, VIII.G.3.a.] Notice that under the Sarbanes-Oxley Act, Aikawa would be required to report the violation to the organization's board of directors, and she may reveal confidential information concerning the violation to the SEC. [Page 132, VIII.G.6.e. and f.]

51. **NO** Lawyers' client trust fund accounts are usually ordinary checking accounts, but if a lawyer is asked to hold a large sum of money for a long period, an interest-bearing time-deposit account would be appropriate. [Page 133, IX.C.1. and a.]

52. **YES** ABA Model Rule 1.15 *requires* such advances to be put into the client trust fund account. [Page 134, IX.C.2.a.]

53. **NO** The proper procedure would have been to deposit the entire $12,000 in the client trust fund account. Ayala was not entitled to withdraw his portion until he rendered an accounting to Cooper and obtained Cooper's agreement to the amount due. [Page 135, IX.E.1.]

54. **YES** Pendergast's failure to supervise her secretary's recordkeeping is grounds for discipline. [Page 135, IX.D.; Page 19, I.F.3.; *see* Gassman v. State Bar of California, 18 Cal. 3d 125 (1976)—attorney disciplined for failing to oversee secretary's records of client trust account]

55. **YES** A lawyer may dispense moral advice as well as legal advice. The client need not accept it, but the lawyer is entitled to offer it. [Page 121, VIII.A.2.]

56. **YES** Lutza is not required to render legal services to Coddlemeyer. [Page 26, II.B.] If Lutza has already entered into an attorney-client relationship with Coddlemeyer, he may withdraw if he finds Coddlemeyer's objectives repugnant. [Page 45, II.G.4.c.]

57. **NO** Lutza would be subject to discipline for breach of the ethical duty of confidentiality if he revealed the plan to the daughter without Coddlemeyer's consent. [Page 52, III.D.]

58. **YES** Abberman may serve as a third-party neutral. A third-party neutral assists two or more nonclients to resolve a dispute between them. Note that the third-party neutral must inform all unrepresented parties that he does not represent any of the parties and is not protecting their interests. [Page 125, VIII.D.1. and 2.]

59. **YES** As long as Langtree is acting in good faith, it is *not* frivolous for him to file a malpractice complaint, even though he knows that the evidence needed to back up the complaint can be obtained only through discovery proceedings. [Page 100, VI.A.1.]

60. **YES** To file a frivolous discovery request solely to harass the adversary is grounds for litigation sanction. [Page 100, VI.A.1.; Page 107, VI.D.3.]

61. **YES** Intentionally trying to mislead the court about the applicable law is grounds for discipline. [Page 102, VI.C.1.]

62. **YES** Loutson has knowingly used false evidence. [Page 104, VI.C.4.] Also, because an attorney is subject to discipline if he knowingly makes a false statement of fact to the court, Loutson is also subject to discipline for violating this duty of candor to the tribunal. [Page 103, VI.C.2.]

63. **NO** Under the ABA Model Rules, a lawyer must first try to persuade his client to testify truthfully. If that fails, the lawyer may seek to withdraw if that will remedy the situation, but if withdrawal will not remedy the situation, the lawyer must disclose the situation to the court. [Page 105, VI.C.4.b.1)]

64. **YES** It is a crime to suppress or tamper with evidence. Here, Lucinda knowingly destroyed a report requested by the plaintiff. Lucinda also would be subject to discipline for unlawfully destroying a document having evidentiary value. [Page 106, VI.D.1.]

65. **NO** Ahern is subject to discipline for using false evidence. [Page 107, VI.D.2.] An affidavit is supposed to be made under oath and signed by the affiant. Ahern has also corrupted her secretary, the notary public, by having her attest to the forged signature. [*See* Garlow v. State Bar of California, 30 Cal. 3d 912 (1982)—attorney disciplined for, among other things, signing client's name to declaration under oath]

66. **YES** Except when prohibited by local law, it is proper to pay such expenses incurred by a lay witness. [Page 107, VI.D.4.a.]

67. **YES** This is proper, as long as Ackroid reasonably believes that the employees' interests will not be harmed by declining to be interviewed. [Page 108, VI.D.5.; *and see* Page 119, VII.B.2.—concerning impropriety of interviewing employees of represented adversary]

68. **YES** Lippert is subject to discipline, both for violating the judge's order given at the final pretrial conference and for referring in closing argument to material not in the record. [Page 108, VI.D.6.; Page 109, VI.D.7.a.]

69. **YES** Even if Langdon has not technically obstructed plaintiff's access to evidence, he has abused the discovery process by destroying the meaningful order of the documents. [Page 107, VI.D.3.] Here, at the very least, the trial judge would be justified in ordering Langdon to furnish plaintiff with a new set of copies, properly arranged, at no cost to plaintiff. Landon also would be subject to discipline for abusing the discovery process.

70. **NO** A lawyer is subject to discipline for stating personal opinions when arguing a case to the jury. The proper technique is to point out the relevant evidence in the record and to let the jurors form their own opinions and conclusions. [Page 110, VI.D.7.c.]

71. **YES** During the trial of a case, a lawyer who is connected with the case must not communicate with a juror on **any** subject. [Page 111, VI.E.2.b.; *and see* Florida Bar v. Peterson, 418 So. 2d 246 (Fla. 1982)—lawyer disciplined in similar circumstances]

72. **YES** Prunella is subject to discipline for violating Rule 3.6, which states that a lawyer connected with a case must not make a public statement outside the courtroom that the lawyer reasonably should know would have a substantial likelihood of materially prejudicing a case. [Page 113, VI.F.1.] Furthermore, as a prosecutor, Prunella is subject to discipline for violating Rule 3.8, which provides that a prosecutor must not make extrajudicial statements that have a substantial likelihood of heightening public condemnation of the accused. [Page 113, VI.F.3.; Page 127, VIII.E.6.]

73. **YES** Trial counsel may testify as a witness if her testimony is limited to the nature and value of the services she rendered in the case. [Page 115, VI.G.2.b.]

74. **YES** On the facts given, it is fair to assume that the defendant would suffer substantial hardship if he were forced to obtain a new lawyer in the middle of the trial. Thus, it would be proper for Lucero to testify and to continue as trial counsel. [Page 115, VI.G.2.c.]

75. **YES** A prosecutor must make reasonable efforts to assure that the accused is advised of the procedure for obtaining counsel. [Page 126, VIII.E.2.]

76. **YES** Attorneys are subject to the rules of legal ethics in whatever capacity they act. Furthermore, when an attorney is acting for a client in the legislative arena, the attorney must follow the same rules of candor and forthrightness as though in court. [Page 128, VIII.F.2.]

77. **NO** A statement like this one is regarded as mere puffery, a conventional bargaining ploy. [Page 124, VIII.C.1.]

78. **NO** A lawyer must not communicate about a matter with a represented adversary, absent the consent of the adversary's counsel. [Page 118, VII.B.1.]

79. **NO** Whether to settle a case is a decision to be made by the client, not by the lawyer. [Page 36, II.D.3.] The rule that prohibits a lawyer from communicating directly with a represented adversary does not prohibit the parties themselves from communicating directly with each other. [Page 119, VII.B.3.] Thus, Lutenberger should have drawn up the settlement papers as Price requested because a lawyer is normally required to see a matter through to completion. [Page 92, V.B.3.] Furthermore, Lutenberger is entitled to only $16,666 (one-third of $50,000) as his fee. [Page 31, II.C.4.]

80. **NO** When dealing with an unrepresented person on behalf of a client, a lawyer must not give legal advice to the unrepresented person if the client's interests are likely to conflict with those of the unrepresented person. [Page 120, VII.C.]

81. **NO** Parner is asking Lacy to abuse the rights of an unrepresented third person. [Page 120, VII.D.1.] When an ethics question is ***reasonably debatable***, a junior lawyer may abide by a senior supervising lawyer's resolution, but query whether Parner's position is reasonably debatable. [Page 20, I.G.2.] As a practical matter, Lacy would be prudent to ask Parner to explain his position more fully before she decides whether to ignore his instructions.

82. **NO** "Member of the firm" usually means the same as "partner" in a law partnership or "shareholder" in an incorporated law firm. [*See* page 139, X.A.3.a.]

83. **NO** A nonlawyer must not own any interest in an incorporated law firm. [Page 22, I.H.3.]

84. **NO** A lawyer should do such work, but the ABA Model Rules do not impose discipline for failing to do so. [Page 147, XI.A.]

85. **YES** If the information in the circulars is true and not misleading, her conduct is proper. [Page 136, X.A.1.]

86. **NO** ABA Model Rule 7.3 prohibits solicitation only when a "significant motive" is the "lawyer's pecuniary gain." [Page 143, X.C.1.] (One might argue that Andrews volunteered his free legal services in this case with the ulterior motive of seeking publicity and thus luring fee-paying clients in other cases. Query whether such conduct could constitutionally be prohibited.)

87. **NO** An attorney may state to the public that he is a certified specialist only if the certifying body has been approved by the state or the ABA. [Page 140, X.A.4.] Here, the state has no program for approving private certification, and the ABA has not approved the certifying body; thus, Layton and Letonen may not state in their firm advertising material that they are certified specialists in criminal defense.

88. **NO** Federal law authorizes federal judges to be disciplined (by sanctions less drastic than removal from office) upon recommendation by a specially constituted group of other federal judges. [Page 153, XII.A.1.]

89. **YES** A judge must maintain high standards of personal conduct, both in and out of the courtroom. [Page 155, XII.B.1.; *and see* Geiler v. Commission on Judicial Qualifications, 10 Cal. 3d 270 (1973)—judge removed from the bench for similar conduct] If the judge's conduct raises a substantial question about his fitness for office, a lawyer who learns of the conduct must report it to the appropriate authorities. [Page 7, I.C.2.]

90.   **NO**   A judge must not allow family or social relationships to interfere with the judge's conduct or judgments. [Page 156, XII.C.4.] Furthermore, a judge generally should not accept favors from someone who is likely to appear before the judge. Accepting such a favor could reasonably appear to undermine the judge's integrity or impartiality. [Page 170, XII.D.9.]

91.   **NO**   The statement is backwards. A judge must not appear voluntarily as a character witness, but may comply with a subpoena to serve as a character witness. [Page 167, XII.D.3.]

92.   **NO**   Assuming the restaurant has engaged in invidious discrimination, Judge Jones is subject to discipline for publicly manifesting his approval of it. [Page 168, XII.D.6.]

93.   **NO**   The Institute's ownership of the Carnegie stock does not disqualify Justice Juarez because a judge may be a director of a nonprofit organization and that organization may own securities of a party appearing in a case before the judge. [Page 164, XII.C.18.d.2)b)] However, a judge must disqualify himself in a case in which his impartiality might reasonably be questioned. A judge should disclose any information the judge believes the parties or their lawyers might consider relevant to the question of disqualification, even if the judge believes there is no reasonable basis for disqualification. [Page 162, XII.C.18.a.1)] In this case, the judge's impartiality can reasonably be questioned by Carnegie, the appellant, because the appellee's lawyer, Lee, is the judge's best friend. Thus, the judge should disclose his friendship with Lee, and if the parties believe that the judge can be impartial, they can always waive the judge's disqualification. [Pages 166, XII.C.18.h.]

94.   **NO**   A judge shall not serve as an officer of an organization that frequently is engaged in adversary proceedings in the court on which the judge sits. Assuming that the Cascades Club's cases often are brought in Judge Jimerson's court, she should not serve as treasurer. [Page 168, XII.D.5.(vi)] Also, a judge must not personally participate in fund-raising activities for an organization, except for soliciting funds from members of the judge's family or from other judges who are not under her supervisory or appellate authority. [Page 168, XII.D.5.(ii)]

95.   **NO**   A full-time judge must not practice law. [Page 172, XII.D.12.] Acting as attorney for the executor of Aunt Agnes's estate probably does not fall within the limited exception that allows a full-time judge to render some kinds of uncompensated legal service for family members.

96.   **YES**   She may accept the honorarium if it is reasonable and commensurate with the task performed, and she may accept reimbursement of reasonable expenses incurred by herself and her husband. (The honorarium and reasonable expense reimbursement here do not create an appearance of impropriety or of influencing the judge's performance of her judicial duties.) [Page 172, XII.D.13., 14.]

97. **YES** Because Lenox is a candidate for appointive judicial office, he may communicate with the appointing authority (the Governor). [Page 177, XII.E.3.]

PRACTICE SET 1

Question 1

A full-time judge lives in State A. Her father lives in a retirement home in State B. The judge's father told her that several of his friends in the retirement home had employed an attorney to write wills for them, and that in each will the attorney had included a bequest to himself. Each bequest was approximately 50% of the estimated total value of the person's probable estate. The friends told the judge's father that they did not really want to leave the attorney anything, but they had assumed it was merely a matter of routine, a part of the attorney's compensation for drafting the will. The attorney is admitted to practice in State B, but not in State A. The judge did not talk personally with any of her father's friends, but she believes that her father's rendition of the story is entirely accurate.

Would it be proper for the judge to communicate directly with the attorney about the matter, and if that does not satisfy her, to communicate with the attorney disciplinary authority in State B about the matter?

(A) Yes, because she has received information indicating a substantial likelihood that the attorney has violated a legal ethics rule.

(B) Yes, because she has personal knowledge that the attorney has violated a legal ethics rule.

(C) No, because legal ethics violations that take place outside State A are not her concern.

(D) No, because she is not allowed to communicate directly with the attorney about the supposed legal ethics violation.

Question 2

A young attorney, three years out of law school, had never set foot in a courtroom. The attorney was on the board of directors of a nonprofit preschool. One of the preschool's teachers was charged with felony child abuse for allegedly molesting three pupils. After conducting its own careful investigation, the preschool's board of directors concluded that the criminal charge was totally unfounded, and the board resolved to provide defense counsel for the teacher. The young attorney volunteered to do the work without a fee. A few days before the trial was to begin, the attorney became convinced that he was not competent to serve as the teacher's trial counsel. He asked the trial judge for permission to withdraw. After thoroughly questioning the attorney about his preparation for trial, the judge said that while he understood the attorney's anxiety, he believed that the attorney was perfectly competent to handle the case. The judge denied the attorney's motion to withdraw but postponed the trial for seven days to allow him to complete his preparation.

Instead of doing what the judge ordered, the attorney advised the teacher that he would not defend her. He handed her all of the files in the case and advised her to retain another attorney.

Is the attorney subject to discipline?

(A) Yes, because he abandoned his client in direct violation of the trial judge's order.

(B) Yes, because he undertook a case that he was not competent to handle.

(C) No, because he believed that he was not competent to represent his client at trial.

(D) No, because he was working pro bono, not for a fee.

GO ON TO THE NEXT PAGE

Question 3

An attorney represented a defendant in a criminal trial. After the jury returned a guilty verdict, the defendant was taken to jail and the jury was discharged. While walking to his car, the disappointed attorney spotted one of the courtroom spectators in the parking lot. The attorney recalled that the spectator had been a member of the jury pool, but he had exercised a peremptory challenge against her because he instinctively felt that she would vote against the defendant. Despite not being selected as a juror, the spectator developed an interest in the case and had attended the entire trial.

In an attempt to determine whether his instinct during jury selection was correct, the attorney approached the spectator and asked her whether she would have voted to convict the defendant. The spectator said, "I'd rather not talk about it." When the attorney explained that he was simply looking for constructive feedback, the spectator changed her mind and agreed to a brief interview. The attorney and spectator spoke for a few minutes, and the communication did not involve misrepresentation, coercion, duress, or harassment.

Is the attorney subject to discipline?

(A) Yes, because the spectator initially declined to speak with the attorney.

(B) Yes, because post-trial contact with prospective jurors is prohibited.

(C) No, because the communication did not involve misrepresentation, coercion, duress, or harassment.

(D) No, because the spectator was not chosen for the jury.

Question 4

An attorney assigned his secretary to manage his client trust account. The attorney gave the secretary extensive, detailed instructions about the kinds of records to keep, the kinds of funds that she must deposit, and the kinds of permissible withdrawals that she could make. The attorney had complete faith in the secretary's ability and honesty, and therefore did not supervise the secretary's management of the account. Three years later, during an audit, it was discovered that on 18 different occasions during that period, the account balance fell below the amount that should have been there. The attorney was unaware of these occasions until he received a copy of the audit.

Is the attorney subject to discipline?

(A) Yes, because he did not adequately supervise the secretary.

(B) Yes, because a lawyer must manage his client trust account himself.

(C) No, because he took reasonable steps to train the secretary and did not realize that the account balance had fallen below the proper level.

(D) No, because he did not have actual knowledge that the secretary was not performing the account management function properly.

GO ON TO THE NEXT PAGE

Question 5

A potential client consulted an attorney, hoping to hire her to represent him as plaintiff in a medical malpractice action against his doctor. Without mentioning the doctor's name, the client described the alleged acts of malpractice and said that they happened more than two years ago. Only at that point did the potential client mention his doctor's name. The attorney immediately stopped the potential client and said she could not represent him because she was already representing the doctor in an unrelated matter, and she urged him to consult another lawyer. That was the end of the conversation. The potential client did nothing further for 15 months, at which point he consulted another lawyer. By that time, the statute of limitations had run on the potential client's claim against the doctor. The potential client then sued the first attorney for legal malpractice, alleging that the attorney was negligent in not warning him about the statute of limitations.

Is the attorney subject to civil liability in the potential client's malpractice case?

(A) No, because the attorney did what a reasonably prudent lawyer would do in the circumstances—decline to represent the potential client and suggest that he consult other counsel.

(B) No, because the potential client never became the attorney's client and is therefore not a proper plaintiff in a malpractice action against the attorney.

(C) Yes, because the attorney had no legal or ethical reason to reject the potential client as a client and therefore had a duty to warn him about the statute of limitations.

(D) Yes, because a reasonably prudent lawyer would have foreseen that the potential client might delay in consulting another lawyer.

Question 6

A client hired an attorney to do the legal work in connection with a complex public securities offering. The attorney agreed to do the work for a set hourly fee. The attorney did a great deal of legal research, prepared numerous memoranda of fact and law, and drafted most of the documents needed for the public offering. At that point, the client became angry with the attorney for no apparent reason and fired him. The client paid the attorney at the agreed rate for the work the attorney had done and demanded that the attorney turn over to him the papers that the attorney had prepared, including the legal and fact memoranda and the document drafts.

What papers must the attorney turn over to the client?

(A) Only the document drafts, but not the legal and fact memoranda.

(B) Only the legal and fact memoranda, but not the document drafts.

(C) None of the papers, because the client fired the attorney.

(D) All of the papers, even though the client fired the attorney.

GO ON TO THE NEXT PAGE

Question 7

A judge serves on a state trial court that has nine other judges. Her husband is a life insurance salesman for a large life insurance company. The life insurance company is occasionally a litigant in the court on which the judge sits. Every year the life insurance company runs a national sales contest in which the person who sells the most life insurance during the year receives a valuable prize. The judge's husband won this year and took the judge on an all-expenses-paid vacation in Europe. She did not make a public report of the prize.

Was it proper for the judge to allow her husband to accept the prize and take her on the European vacation?

(A) Yes, because acceptance of the prize cannot reasonably be perceived as undermining the judge's integrity or impartiality.

(B) Yes, because the prize was won by her husband, not by the judge.

(C) No, because the judge did not make a public report of the prize.

(D) No, because the life insurance company may later appear as a litigant in the court on which the judge sits.

Question 8

A law student is applying for admission to the State A Bar. When the law student was in high school, he and his parents lived in State B. His next door neighbor was an attorney admitted to practice in State B, but not in State A. The attorney knew that during the law student's senior year in high school, he was convicted of burglarizing a liquor store. After serving his sentence, the law student went to college and later to law school. The attorney has had no contact with the law student since his high school years, and as far as she knows, the law student has not done anything since high school that would reflect badly on his character. The Bar of State A sent the attorney a routine questionnaire, asking a series of questions about the law student's character. The attorney does not know whether the law student disclosed the burglary conviction on his bar application, and she does not know where to contact him to find out.

Which of the following would be a proper response to the questionnaire?

(A) She should not respond at all because she has no relevant information to provide.

(B) She should not respond at all because as a State B lawyer she is not obligated to provide information to the Bar of State A.

(C) She should not mention the law student's burglary conviction in her response unless she first contacts him and obtains his permission to do so.

(D) She should state what she knows about the law student, including mention of his burglary conviction.

GO ON TO THE NEXT PAGE

Question 9

An attorney received her law degree two years ago from a small local college of law and technical sciences. Last summer she attended a three-day trial practice seminar at the Harvard Law School. During her brief career, she has tried five cases—two jury trials and three bench trials. She won both of the jury trials and two of the three bench trials.

The attorney placed an ad under the subject heading "Trial Lawyers" in the classified pages of the local phone book. Her ad states in relevant part:

Trial Attorney

Harvard Trained

Never Lost a Jury Trial

Which of the following is correct?

(A)   To make the ad proper, the references to "Harvard Trained" and "Never Lost a Jury Trial" must be deleted.

(B)   To make the ad proper, the references to "Trial Attorney" and "Harvard Trained" must be deleted.

(C)   To make the ad proper, the references to "Trial Attorney" and "Never Lost a Jury Trial" must be deleted.

(D)   The ad is proper as written.

Question 10

Two years ago, when a couple divorced in State A, the court awarded the wife custody of the three children and ordered the husband to pay the wife $3,000 per month in child support and alimony payments. The husband failed to make the $3,000 payments for 17 months in a row. In desperation, the wife hired a new attorney to represent her in a proceeding to collect the past due payments from the husband. State A has no law or court rule that requires the loser to pay the winner's attorneys' fees in domestic relations matters. Because the wife had no money to pay her new attorney a regular fee, the new attorney agreed to do the work on a contingent fee basis for 10% of whatever amount the wife was ultimately able to recover. The new attorney won an award for the wife of the entire amount due ($51,000), and by tracking down and attaching the husband's secret bank account, he got the full amount paid to the wife. He then sent the wife a bill for his share, $5,100.

Is the wife's new attorney subject to discipline?

(A)   No, as long as $5,100 is a reasonable fee for the work he did.

(B)   No, because the wife had no money to pay a regular fee.

(C)   Yes, because the new attorney used a contingent fee in a domestic relations matter.

(D)   Yes, because the new attorney took a portion of the money that was intended for support of the wife and the children.

GO ON TO THE NEXT PAGE

Question 11

An attorney regularly represented an older client in matters relating to the investment of the client's considerable wealth. The client told the attorney that he wanted to put $500,000 into a sound, income-producing investment. The attorney suggested that the two of them pool their money and talent and buy an apartment house. The attorney would put up $75,000 and do the legal work, and the client would put up $500,000 and serve as the live-in manager of the apartment house. The client enthusiastically agreed to the arrangement and told the attorney to draw up the papers.

The attorney drafted an agreement between himself and the client, negotiated the purchase of the apartment house, and drafted a deed from the seller to himself and the client as joint tenants with right of survivorship. The attorney gave the client a carefully written explanation of the terms of the transaction, but he forgot to explain the significance of the joint tenancy, i.e., that upon the death of one joint tenant, the property would pass automatically to the other joint tenant. The attorney advised the client, in the writing explaining the terms of the transaction, to have an outside lawyer look over the transaction, and he also urged him orally to do so. However, the client said that he trusted the attorney and signed all of the papers without further ado. The attorney and the client operated the apartment house successfully for several years, until the client died. The executor of the client's estate sued the attorney to have the apartment house declared part of the client's estate, but the court concluded that the joint tenancy created a gift to the attorney, effective on the client's death.

Were the attorney's actions proper?

(A) Yes, because the court concluded that the joint tenancy created a gift from the client to the attorney.

(B) Yes, because the attorney might have died first, thus bestowing a gift on the client.

(C) No, because the attorney entered into a business transaction with the client.

(D) No, because the attorney drafted the deed that bestowed a substantial gift on himself.

GO ON TO THE NEXT PAGE

Question 12

For the past five years, an attorney has represented an art dealer in the sale of many valuable paintings. One of the major transactions occurred three years ago, when the art dealer sold a landscape purportedly painted by Vincent van Gogh to an art museum for $23 million. The museum subsequently resold the painting for $35 million.

Now the art dealer has asked the attorney to do the legal work in connection with the sale of another landscape, also a purported van Gogh. The proposed purchase price is $12 million, and the prospective purchaser is a wealthy television personality who knows nothing about art. During a confidential conversation in the attorney's office, the attorney asked the art dealer if he had appraisal letters certifying the painting as a genuine van Gogh. The art dealer replied that he indeed had letters—letters he had forged himself—and that he had also forged the letters for the purported van Gogh sold to the art museum. When the attorney inquired further, the art dealer told him in confidence that both of the purported van Gogh paintings were in fact counterfeits created by a clever art student.

Which of the following must the attorney do at this point?

(A)   Report the art dealer to the law enforcement authorities.

(B)   Warn the prospective purchaser about the proposed sale.

(C)   Inform the art museum of the truth about the first painting.

(D)   Refuse to represent the art dealer in the present transaction.

Question 13

Two years ago, an attorney represented his client when he sold his property. Unbeknownst to the attorney, the client made some fraudulent statements to the buyer about the value of some mineral deposits on the property. The buyer recently discovered the fraud and is now in the attorney's office threatening to immediately file a civil fraud suit against both the client and the attorney. The buyer accuses the attorney of engineering the fraud and helping his client carry it out. The only way that the attorney can convince the buyer that he had no part in the fraud is to tell the buyer a fact that the client disclosed to him in the deepest confidence when he was working on the property transaction.

May the attorney disclose the fact without the consent of the client?

(A)   No, if doing so will harm the client.

(B)   No, because doing so would breach his duty of confidentiality to the client.

(C)   Yes, but only after the buyer files the civil fraud suit against him.

(D)   Yes, even if doing so will subject his client to civil or criminal liability.

GO ON TO THE NEXT PAGE

Question 14

An attorney is representing a defendant on trial for armed robbery of a liquor store. The defendant tells the attorney in confidence that at the time in question, he was sitting at home watching television with his aged mother, and that his mother can confirm his alibi. The attorney interviews the mother, who solemnly confirms the defendant's story. After talking with her, the attorney strongly suspects that she is lying to protect the defendant. The attorney does not know for sure that the defendant and his mother are lying, but every instinct tells him that they are. The attorney has warned both of them about the dangers of perjury, but both have insisted that they want to testify to the alibi at trial.

May the attorney call the defendant, or his mother, or both, as trial witnesses?

(A) Yes, as to both the defendant and his mother.

(B) Yes, as to the defendant, but no, as to his mother.

(C) No, as to both the defendant and his mother.

(D) No, as to the defendant, but yes, as to his mother.

Question 15

The State A Bar has established an Interest on Lawyers' Trust Accounts ("IOLTA") program, whereby lawyers deposit client trust funds into special client trust accounts that pay interest to the State A Bar, which then uses the money to help fund legal services for poor people. The program requires lawyers to deposit a particular client's funds in an IOLTA account unless the funds would earn more than $50 in interest during the time they are entrusted to the lawyer. If the client's funds would earn more than $50 in interest during

that time, the lawyer must deposit them in a separate interest-bearing trust account and pay the interest to the client.

An attorney settled a personal injury case brought by her client. The defendant sent the attorney a check for $9,000. Because she was leaving that day for a one-month vacation, the attorney instructed her assistant to deposit the check in the attorney's IOLTA account. The assistant is authorized to make deposits to and withdrawals from the account. The attorney did not tell her assistant to notify the client that the check had arrived. When the attorney returned a month later, she notified the client that the check had been received, and the client came to the attorney's office that same day to collect the $9,000. At the prevailing rate of interest, the $9,000 would have earned $40 during the month that the attorney was gone.

Was the attorney's handling of the matter proper?

(A) No, because she should have instructed her assistant to deposit the check in a separate trust account that would earn interest for the client.

(B) No, because she should have instructed her assistant to notify the client promptly that the check had arrived.

(C) Yes, because she handled the matter in accordance with the State A IOLTA program.

(D) Yes, because the client was not harmed.

GO ON TO THE NEXT PAGE

Question 16

A new associate at a law firm was asked to help a partner advise a state university on how to comply with a federal statute that requires colleges and universities to make many changes in their facilities to accommodate students with disabilities. After graduating from law school, the associate had worked on the congressional staff of a United States senator. In that role, she personally drafted a bill that was ultimately enacted as the federal statute.

In light of the associate's earlier role as the drafter of the federal statute, which of the two lawyers may work on the matter?

(A)   Neither the partner nor the associate.

(B)   The partner only, and only if the associate is properly screened off from the matter.

(C)   Both the partner and the associate.

(D)   The partner only, and only if the state university consents after full disclosure.

Question 17

An insurance company offers a legal services insurance policy. In return for a yearly premium, an insured will be reimbursed by the insurance company for a specified amount for legal services during the year. The insured selects a lawyer from a list of "authorized providers" supplied by the insurance company. Any lawyer who agrees to follow a maximum fee schedule set by the insurance company can become an "authorized provider." The insurance company solicits insurance sales by in-person and live telephone contact with potential insurance buyers, working systematically through local telephone directories.

Will an attorney be subject to discipline if he becomes an "authorized provider" and receives clients through the insurance company's insurance plan?

(A)   No, because the insurance company does not specifically target persons whom it knows are in need of legal services in a particular matter covered by its insurance plan.

(B)   No, because the insurance company's insureds are allowed to select whatever lawyer they wish from among the "authorized providers."

(C)   Yes, because the insurance company uses a specified maximum fee schedule.

(D)   Yes, because the insurance company uses in-person and live telephone solicitation to get business.

GO ON TO THE NEXT PAGE

Question 18

An attorney represented a landlord in a dispute with her longtime tenant, who had recently decided not to renew his lease. The landlord wanted to retain the security deposit to pay for extensive damage to the carpeting, while the tenant insisted that the damage was normal wear and tear. The attorney and the tenant's lawyer negotiated for days, but neither party would settle for less than two-thirds of the security deposit. Finally, the landlord telephoned the attorney and said: "The tenant asked if I want to talk about the security deposit. We've known each other for years, and I think we might have better luck if we work things out ourselves." The attorney encouraged the landlord to talk with the tenant if she thought it would help, but advised her not to finalize any agreement until both parties could consult with their respective counsel. The landlord and tenant had a productive discussion. The following day, the tenant's lawyer called the attorney and said the tenant would accept one-half of the security deposit. The attorney communicated the offer to the landlord, who agreed and returned the funds to the tenant.

Is the attorney subject to discipline?

(A) Yes, because the attorney encouraged the landlord to speak to the tenant without obtaining the consent of the tenant's lawyer.

(B) Yes, because the attorney encouraged the landlord to speak to the tenant without notifying the tenant's lawyer.

(C) No, because the tenant initiated the conversation with the landlord.

(D) No, because the landlord and tenant spoke to each other directly.

GO ON TO THE NEXT PAGE

Question 19

A building contractor and his attorney met with a landowner to negotiate a contract for construction of an office building on the landowner's property. The contractor, the attorney, and the landowner were the only persons present at the meeting. Ultimately, the three of them worked out a written agreement, and the contractor commenced work. However, it soon became apparent that the building site required far more preparation work than the contractor had contemplated when he agreed to the contract price. The contractor and the landowner argued about who had to pay for the additional site preparation. One important issue is whether the landowner made certain oral representations to the contractor during the contract negotiating session that the attorney attended. The contractor contends that the landowner did make the representations, while the landowner contends that he did not. The attorney was present during the entire negotiating session, and she is virtually certain that the landowner did not make the representations.

The contractor refused to proceed with construction until the landowner paid for the extra site preparation. The landowner then sued the contractor for specific performance of the construction contract. The contractor asked the attorney to represent him as trial counsel.

The attorney should:

(A) Agree to serve as trial counsel for the contractor because the contractor is entitled to the counsel of his choice.

(B) Agree to serve as trial counsel for the contractor because she can refuse to testify if she is called as a witness by the landowner.

(C) Decline to serve as trial counsel for the contractor because a lawyer is not allowed to testify in a manner that is prejudicial to her client.

(D) Decline to serve as trial counsel for the contractor because she can foresee that she will be called as a witness.

GO ON TO THE NEXT PAGE

Question 20

An author wrote a best-selling novel based on the life and crimes of John Dillinger, the famous bank robber. The author sold the movie rights to a film producer, who promised to pay the author a lump-sum royalty of $5 million upon the release of the movie. After the producer hired an actor to play the lead role and made other expensive preparations for filming, the author repudiated the contract. The producer hired an attorney to sue the author for a declaratory judgment that the contract was valid and enforceable. At the producer's request, the attorney agreed to do the legal work on a contingent fee basis: If the producer wins, the attorney will be paid 1.75% of the gross receipts from the movie, but if the producer loses, the attorney will be paid nothing. The producer and the attorney entered into a written fee agreement that contains all the details required by the rules of legal ethics.

Which of the following statements is true?

(A)　The attorney is subject to discipline for entering into a publication rights contract with his client.

(B)　The attorney is subject to discipline for acquiring a personal interest in the subject of the litigation.

(C)　The attorney's fee agreement is proper, but only if the author gives informed consent.

(D)　The attorney's fee agreement is proper, even though it gives the attorney a personal interest in the subject of the litigation.

Question 21

For many years an attorney has done business transactions work for a wealthy client. The client was recently injured in an automobile crash, and she has asked the attorney to represent her as plaintiff in an action against the driver who injured her. The attorney has taken some business cases to trial, but he has never handled a personal injury case.

The attorney would like to help his client and also generate some income. Which of the following would be an improper way for him to do so?

(A)　Take the case and, with the client's consent, associate a co-counsel who is competent in the field of personal injury law.

(B)　Refer the client to a competent personal injury lawyer and charge that lawyer a $1,000 forwarding fee.

(C)　Refer the client to a competent personal injury lawyer and charge the client a reasonable sum for the time spent in making the referral.

(D)　Take the case and, with the client's consent, undertake additional research to bring himself up to speed in the field of personal injury law.

GO ON TO THE NEXT PAGE

Question 22

An attorney is a voting member of the legislation committee of a consumer-based law reform group that drafts and advocates the passage of proposed statutes on food safety. The law reform group is currently debating a draft statute that sets quality and safety standards for growth hormones administered to chickens, turkeys, and other poultry. The attorney is also engaged in the private practice of patent law. She regularly represents a biotechnology firm. Using the techniques of genetic engineering, the biotechnology firm invents, develops, and sells a variety of patented growth hormones. The attorney herself has obtained patents on some of these hormones for the biotechnology firm. If enacted into law, the law reform group's proposed statute on poultry hormones could materially increase the biotechnology firm's hormone sales because it is the only firm whose hormones would meet the statute's quality and safety requirements.

Would it be proper for the attorney, as a member of the law reform group's legislation committee, to participate in the debate on, and to cast her vote on, the proposed statute?

(A) No, because the statute could materially benefit the biotechnology firm.

(B) No, because the attorney may not serve as a member of the law reform group while representing the biotechnology firm.

(C) Yes, provided that she informs the legislation committee that she represents an unnamed client whose interests could be materially benefited by the statute.

(D) Yes, provided that she informs the legislation committee that she represents the biotechnology firm, whose interests could be materially benefited by the statute.

Question 23

A judge sits on a federal appellate court. He and two other federal judges heard a diversity of citizenship case in which they were required to interpret a state statute concerning the marital communications privilege. The judge's two colleagues wrote the majority opinion, in which they concluded that the statute gives only the witness-spouse the right to claim the privilege. The judge wrote a vigorous and scholarly dissent, arguing that the statute gives both spouses the right to claim the privilege.

Later, a state senator introduced a bill to amend the statute to reflect the judge's position. The state senate invited the judge to testify about the public policy reasons for giving both spouses the right to claim the privilege.

May the judge testify?

(A) Yes, but only if the two judges who wrote the majority opinion are also allowed to testify.

(B) Yes, because a judge may engage in activities designed to improve the law.

(C) No, because a judge must not become involved in politics, subject to certain exceptions that do not apply here.

(D) No, because a judge is not allowed to make public statements about disputed propositions of law, except when acting in his judicial capacity.

GO ON TO THE NEXT PAGE

Question 24

An attorney has organized his law practice as a professional corporation. The attorney is the sole shareholder. The sign on the office door states:

> *Professional Corporation—*
> *Attorney at Law*
>
> *Corporate and Business Law,*
>
> *Torts and Domestic Relations*

The attorney has one lawyer-employee, who was admitted to practice two years ago. The attorney pays his employee a modest monthly salary plus 60% of the fees collected in cases that the employee handles by herself. The attorney has a general business practice and is not a certified specialist in any practice area. When a client needs representation in a tort or domestic relations matter, the attorney turns the case over to his lawyer-employee. When the attorney turns a case over to the employee, he provides general guidance and is available to answer any questions she may have, but he does not supervise every step she takes.

Is the attorney subject to discipline?

(A) Yes, because he splits fees with his employee in matters she handles by herself.

(B) Yes, because he does not closely supervise the work done by his employee.

(C) No, but he should change his sign to show the fields of practice that he personally handles.

(D) No, because the employee is a lawyer-employee of the attorney.

Question 25

An attorney was representing the plaintiff at a bench trial of a civil action pending before a judge. Midway through the plaintiff's case-in-chief, the judge called the attorney into his chambers. The judge told the attorney that he thought the attorney's case was very weak, but that he could be mistaken because he was distracted by money troubles. The judge went on to say that if he could get a $50,000 loan, he would feel much better. The attorney responded that he would be happy to loan the judge $50,000 to help him out as a friend. Later that afternoon, a messenger delivered an envelope containing $50,000 in cash to the judge's chambers. No mention was made of a promissory note, a repayment date, or an interest rate. Two days later, the plaintiff settled his lawsuit so the judge never had to decide the case. Three months later, the judge repaid the $50,000 to the attorney, together with interest at the market rate.

Is the attorney subject to criminal liability for lending the money to the judge?

(A) Yes, if it is proven that the judge intended to induce the attorney to make the loan in return for a decision in favor of the plaintiff.

(B) Yes, if it is proven that, in making the loan, the attorney intended to induce the judge to decide the case in favor of the plaintiff.

(C) No, because as the matter turned out, the judge never had to decide the plaintiff's case.

(D) No, because the judge repaid the loan with interest.

GO ON TO THE NEXT PAGE

Question 26

A steel company merged with an iron corporation. The state attorney general sued the steel company and the iron corporation in federal court to enjoin the merger, alleging that it was in violation of the federal antitrust laws. The federal district judge enjoined the merger, and the steel company appealed the judge's decision.

The steel company's attorney, doing the legal research for the appeal, found a recent merger decision rendered by the Federal Trade Commission ("FTC") that is directly adverse to the steel company's position. FTC decisions do not control in the United States Courts of Appeal, but they are persuasive. The attorney general failed to cite the FTC decision.

Must the steel company's attorney disclose it to the court?

(A) Yes, because it is persuasive authority.

(B) Yes, because the FTC decision is directly adverse to the steel company's position.

(C) No, because a lawyer has no obligation to volunteer facts harmful to his client's case.

(D) No, because the court of appeals is not obliged to follow the FTC ruling.

Question 27

A solo practitioner is one of only three lawyers in a small town. The solo practitioner is presently defending a client in a criminal action for assault and battery. This morning one of the solo practitioner's regular clients, a gas and grocery store, asked the solo practitioner to sue the same client to recover a past due amount on a gasoline and grocery charge account.

Would it be proper for the solo practitioner to represent the gas and grocery store in the charge account case?

(A) No, because it is presumed that a lawyer obtains confidential information in the course of representing a client.

(B) No, unless the other two lawyers in town are disqualified from representing the gas and grocery store.

(C) Yes, because there is no substantial relationship between the charge account case and the assault and battery case.

(D) Yes, if both the client and the gas and grocery store consent after full disclosure of the conflict, and such consent is confirmed in writing.

GO ON TO THE NEXT PAGE

Question 28

An attorney agreed to represent a wife on an hourly fee basis in securing a divorce from her husband. The husband is also represented by an attorney. Despite repeated warnings by her attorney, the wife kept pestering her attorney with telephone calls and office visits concerning inconsequential details and trifling personal complaints. When the wife was unable to contact her own attorney on the phone or in person, she would telephone her husband's attorney, and try to put her questions and complaints to him. The husband's attorney always refused to talk to his client's wife. The wife's attorney repeatedly told her not to contact her husband's attorney, but to no avail. Finally, the wife's attorney told the wife that she would withdraw unless the wife changed her ways, but the wife did not do so. The wife's attorney withdrew and sent the wife a fee bill for the total number of hours she had spent on the case. The wife refused to pay the bill, and after futile efforts to settle the matter, the wife's attorney sued her to collect the fee, and stated that she would be holding the file until her bill was paid.

Which of the following propositions is not true?

(A) It was proper for the wife's attorney to withdraw.

(B) It was proper for the husband's attorney to refuse to talk with the wife on the phone.

(C) It was proper for the wife's attorney to bill the wife for the total amount of time she spent on the case.

(D) It was proper for the wife's attorney to hold the wife's file until paid.

Question 29

An attorney in solo practice published a brochure regarding what one should do when injured. The brochure contains accurate, helpful information about obtaining proper medical treatment, recording details of the accident, notifying insurance companies, not making harmful statements, and the like. The attorney's name, address, and telephone number are printed on the brochure's cover. One afternoon, the attorney saw a pedestrian knocked down in a crosswalk by a hit-and-run driver. He and another bystander called 911 and gave the pedestrian emergency first aid until an ambulance arrived. The next day, the attorney visited the pedestrian in the hospital and gave the pedestrian a copy of his brochure.

Which of the following is correct?

(A) The attorney is subject to discipline, both for publishing the brochure and for giving the brochure to the pedestrian in the hospital.

(B) The attorney is subject to discipline for publishing the brochure.

(C) The attorney is subject to discipline for giving the pedestrian a copy of the brochure at the hospital.

(D) The attorney's conduct was proper because the brochure's contents are neither false nor misleading.

GO ON TO THE NEXT PAGE

Question 30

The state bar association has established a peer counseling program whereby lawyers who are addicted to alcohol or other drugs can receive confidential counseling from other lawyers. The bar association's ethics rule on confidential information provides that communications between the counselor lawyer and the counseled lawyer are to be treated just like confidential communications between an attorney and client.

A lawyer is addicted to alcohol and is receiving peer counseling under the program from another lawyer. The lawyer is a large, strong man, and his addiction has made him subject to periodic fits of physical violence. This afternoon, during their peer counseling session, the lawyer told his peer counselor that his client had refused to pay the fees he owes, and that he intended to punch out the client the next time he got roaring drunk. From working with the lawyer over an extended period, the peer counselor believes that he may really do it.

May the peer counselor disclose the lawyer's statement to the client and the police?

(A)   No, unless the lawyer consents.

(B)   No, unless the peer counselor is certain that the lawyer will carry out his threat.

(C)   Yes, even if the lawyer objects.

(D)   Yes, because he is serving as a peer counselor, not a lawyer.

Question 31

An elderly widower has one living child, a daughter. The widower's main asset is a 51% partnership interest in a wealthy real estate syndicate that owns and operates mobile home parks throughout the state. The daughter's husband is an attorney. One of the husband's regular clients asks the husband to represent him in negotiating the sale of 3,000 acres of roadside property to the real estate syndicate. The real estate syndicate is represented by its own lawyer in the matter.

May the husband represent his regular client in a sale with the real estate syndicate?

(A)   No, even if the client gives informed consent, confirmed in writing.

(B)   No, because to do so would create an appearance of impropriety.

(C)   Yes, because the husband has no significant personal interest in the real estate syndicate.

(D)   Yes, but only if the client gives informed consent, confirmed in writing.

GO ON TO THE NEXT PAGE

Question 32

A swimming coach was charged with assault of another coach. The swimming coach hired a criminal attorney to defend him. Subsequently, the swimming coach pleaded not guilty and was released on his own recognizance. At his first trial, a jury was empanelled, and the prosecutor was almost finished presenting the testimony of her first witness when a signal from her electronic pager interrupted her. The trial judge granted her request for a short recess, at the end of which the prosecutor told the judge that her office had instructed her not to proceed with this case at this time. The judge responded that if the prosecutor stopped now, the defendant would go free. When the prosecutor indicated that she understood, the judge entered a judgment of acquittal and set the swimming coach free.

Twenty days later, the prosecutor recharged the swimming coach with the same offense. The swimming coach hired his original criminal attorney to defend him. The same judge presided over the second trial. The swimming coach's attorney made no pretrial motions. This time the prosecutor did not falter, and in due course the jury at the second trial found the swimming coach guilty as charged. The judge sentenced him to prison for the period required by law, but she stayed the sentence and released him on his own recognizance pending appeal. The swimming coach reluctantly paid the criminal attorney's bill for the second trial—$5,000. However, the swimming coach hired a new lawyer for the appeal, and in due course the appellate court reversed the conviction and set aside the prison sentence. The appellate court's opinion stated it had never seen a clearer double jeopardy violation.

Will the swimming coach's original criminal attorney be subject to civil liability in a legal malpractice action brought by the swimming coach for having missed the double jeopardy issue?

(A) No, because the swimming coach never served jail time as a result of the original attorney's error.

(B) No, even if the swimming coach proves by a preponderance of evidence that he did not commit the assault on the opposing coach.

(C) Yes, provided that the swimming coach proves by a preponderance of evidence that he did not commit the assault on the opposing coach.

(D) Yes, but the swimming coach can recover only nominal damages.

GO ON TO THE NEXT PAGE

Question 33

An attorney and a licensed real estate developer, a nonlawyer, created a partnership to serve people who want to invest in commercial real estate. The real estate developer finds promising commercial real estate projects, brings together groups of investors, and works with local planning authorities to gain approval for the projects. The attorney drafts the legal documents for the projects, assists the investors with the legal technicalities, advises the investors on their tax liabilities, and does whatever legal work the investors need in connection with management and operation of the projects. The attorney and the real estate developer charge the investors a single fee for their work, and they divide the partnership profits 50%-50%.

Is the attorney subject to discipline?

(A) No, provided the investors give informed consent to the potential conflicts of interest, and such consent is confirmed in writing.

(B) No, because the real estate developer does only development work, and the attorney does only legal work.

(C) Yes, because the attorney and the real estate developer are partners in the business.

(D) Yes, because she is aiding the real estate developer in the unauthorized practice of law.

Question 34

A bank and trust company maintains a list of approved estate and trust lawyers as a service to their customers who seek advice on estate planning matters. When a young attorney opened her trust and estate practice in town, she asked other lawyers how she could get on the bank's approved list. They explained that the bank lists lawyers who always name the bank in wills and trust agreements they draft for clients who need an institutional executor or trustee. The bank is one of the most stable and reputable banks in the state, and its fees for executor and trustee services are competitive with those of similar institutions.

In light of what she has been told by the other lawyers, may the young attorney seek to have her name included on the bank's list?

(A) No, because a tacit condition of being on the list is always to name the bank as executor or trustee.

(B) No, because a lawyer must not solicit business through an intermediary.

(C) Yes, because naming the bank causes no harm to clients who need an institutional executor or trustee.

(D) Yes, because those who use the bank's list are already bank customers.

GO ON TO THE NEXT PAGE

Question 35

A man alleges that a very wealthy actor punched him in the face. He contacted an attorney about representing him in a civil action against the actor. After several lengthy discussions with the attorney about the merits of the case, the man decided to employ another lawyer instead. The actor was later charged with criminal assault in connection with this incident, and the trial was televised. As the attorney was watching the trial, she was astonished when the man testified to facts that the attorney knew from their previous discussions to be false.

The attorney sent a letter with a messenger over to the court to notify the court that the man had perjured himself.

Were the attorney's actions proper?

(A) Yes, because her actions were necessary to prevent the man from perpetrating a fraud on the court.

(B) Yes, because the man committed a criminal act by testifying falsely.

(C) No, unless she sent copies of the letter to the prosecution and defense lawyers and they are given an opportunity to respond.

(D) No, because the attorney's information was gained during her discussions with the man.

Question 36

An attorney regularly represents a manufacturer of electric kitchen appliances. One morning the president of the manufacturing company called the attorney and asked if the attorney had seen the newspaper story about a woman who was electrocuted when she opened the door of her dishwasher. The company president stated that he believed the dishwasher was one that his company had manufactured. The company president also stated that he found some quality control records from that period which reflected that some dishwashers left the plant without proper testing. He continued that the records should have been shredded, but somehow had been overlooked, and said that he intended to send the records to the shredder immediately unless the attorney told him that he could not.

Must the attorney advise the president to keep the records?

(A) Yes, unless the company has a clearly established policy of shredding quality control records after two years.

(B) Yes, because the records have potential evidentiary value if the company gets sued.

(C) No, because at this point there is no litigation pending against the company respecting this matter.

(D) No, unless it was certain that the company was the manufacturer of the dishwasher in question.

Question 37

An attorney practices environmental law. He also happens to be one of the nation's leading experts on the environmental effects of filling wetlands. The state legislature has scheduled hearings on a bill to prohibit the filling of wetlands surrounding a bay. One of the attorney's regular clients is a development company, which owns development rights to some of the wetlands in question. The development company wants to fill its wetlands so that it can build low-cost housing for underprivileged families. The development company hired the attorney to appear as a witness at the legislative hearings and to testify in opposition to the ban on wetland filling. The attorney appeared as a witness, identified himself as an expert on wetlands, and testified vigorously against the proposed legislation.

Was the attorney's conduct proper?

(A)   Yes, unless his testimony was contrary to his own beliefs about the environmental effects of filling wetlands.

(B)   Yes, because he is a leading expert on the environmental effects of filling wetlands.

(C)   No, unless he informed the legislators that he was appearing in a representative capacity.

(D)   No, because a lawyer must not be a witness for his client on a contested matter.

GO ON TO THE NEXT PAGE

Question 38

An attorney represents the defendant in a criminal case. The defendant is charged with vehicular homicide, a felony. Under the criminal statute in question, a defendant is guilty if he caused the victim's death by driving a motor vehicle either intentionally or recklessly in disregard of the safety of others. In the defendant's case, the critical issue is whether the traffic light facing the defendant's traffic lane was green at a specified moment. If the light was green, then the defendant is not guilty, but if it was red, then the defendant is guilty.

The defendant himself has blocked the entire event from memory and has no idea whether the light was green or red. Five bystanders were in a position to see the light at the time in question. The attorney interviewed four of them. With varying degrees of uncertainty, all four of them told the attorney that they believe the light was red but that they are not positive. Based on their recollections, as well as certain physical evidence in the case, the attorney herself believes that the light was probably red, but of course she was not present at the scene and cannot be certain. Then the attorney interviewed the fifth bystander, who said that he simply could not remember what color the traffic light was. The attorney replied: "My client is facing 20 years in jail, and the whole case against him turns on the color of that light. My client and I would both be eternally grateful to you if you could testify that the light was green. Would you help us out?" After thinking it over, the fifth bystander said he would be glad to help by testifying that the light was green. At the trial, the attorney presented the fifth bystander's testimony that he saw the light, that he remembers what color it was, and that it was green. The jury believed the fifth bystander, and the defendant was acquitted.

Is the attorney subject to criminal liability for inducing the fifth bystander to testify falsely?

(A) Yes, because both the bystander and the attorney knew that the bystander did not remember what color the light was.

(B) Yes, because neither the bystander nor the attorney was certain that the light was green.

(C) No, because neither the bystander nor the attorney was certain what color the light was.

(D) No, because the defense lawyer in a criminal case must resolve all doubtful facts in her client's favor when she presents evidence on her client's behalf.

GO ON TO THE NEXT PAGE

Question 39

A law professor was selected as the neutral arbitrator of a boundary line dispute between an elderly couple and the couple's next-door neighbors. The law professor decided the matter in favor of the elderly couple. Shortly thereafter, the law professor quit his teaching position and entered private law practice. The elderly couple's next-door neighbors brought suit to have the arbitration award set aside. The elderly couple asked the law professor to represent them in the suit.

If the law professor takes the case, will he be subject to discipline?

(A)   No, because serving as the elderly couple's lawyer is consistent with his decision as arbitrator in their favor.

(B)   No, because by seeking to hire the law professor, the elderly couple is deemed to have consented to the conflict of interest.

(C)   Yes, because his earlier service as neutral arbitrator creates a conflict of interest.

(D)   Yes, because there is reasonable ground to doubt his impartiality in the case.

Question 40

A plaintiff brought a civil action to recover damages for personal injuries he suffered as the victim of alleged police brutality inflicted by three defendant police officers. The trial was widely reported by the media. The jury returned a verdict in favor of the plaintiff and against the three police officers for $500 million. When the trial judge received the verdict, he was shocked by the size of the award. Before dismissing the jurors, the judge told the jurors that when they were sworn in, they had promised that they would deliver a verdict based on the evidence and that they

would not be swayed by passion or prejudice. The judge further admonished the jurors that they had failed in those duties, that they had made a mockery of justice, and that they should be ashamed of themselves.

He then dismissed the jury, and the defense lawyers renewed their motion for judgment as a matter of law and, alternatively, moved for a new trial. The judge announced that he would rule on the motions the following Monday at 10 a.m. in open court. The press reports of the verdict and the judge's comments to the jury created a great public tumult in the city where the case was tried.

On the following Monday, the courtroom was jammed with reporters. Primarily for the purpose of educating the reporters, the judge first gave a detailed explanation of the legal requirements for granting a renewed motion for judgment as a matter of law and for granting a new trial motion. He then granted the renewed motion for judgment as a matter of law and, alternatively, the motion for a new trial.

Were the judge's actions proper?

(A)   Both the statements to the jury and the communication with the reporters were proper.

(B)   Neither the communication with the reporters nor the statements to the jury were proper.

(C)   The statements to the jury were proper, but the communication with the reporters was not.

(D)   The communication with the reporters was proper, but the statements to the jury were not.

GO ON TO THE NEXT PAGE

Question 41

A client lives in State A and is a regular client of an attorney who is admitted to practice only in State A. When the client was on vacation in distant State B, she was injured in a car accident caused by a resident of State B. The client hired the attorney to represent her in a civil action against the State B driver. For reasons of jurisdiction and venue, the case had to be filed and tried in State B. The written fee agreement between the client and the attorney provided that:

(1) The attorney would assume full responsibility for the case as lead lawyer;

(2) The client would pay the attorney 40% of the net recovery after deduction of litigation expenses;

(3) The attorney would associate a State B lawyer to serve as trial counsel in State B;

(4) The State B lawyer would assume responsibility only for his work as trial counsel; and

(5) The attorney would pay the State B lawyer an appropriate portion of the 40% contingent fee.

Would it be proper for the attorney to split his fee with the State B lawyer under the circumstances described above?

(A) No, because the attorney is not admitted in State B.

(B) No, because the share that each lawyer will receive was not disclosed in the written fee agreement.

(C) Yes, because the State B lawyer was assuming responsibility for his work as trial counsel.

(D) Yes, because there was a written fee agreement.

Question 42

An attorney is a partner in a private law firm. That firm regularly provides legal services to three major banks and two other important lending institutions in the community. The attorney has been invited to become a member of the board of directors of the local legal aid society, the group that sets overall governing policies for the local legal aid office. One of the major issues that will soon face the board of directors is whether to amend the case intake guidelines to allow the legal aid office to represent clients in disputes with banks and other lending agencies.

Which of the following statements is correct?

(A) The attorney may join the board of directors, but she must refrain from participating in the decision about the case intake guidelines.

(B) The attorney will be subject to discipline if she joins the board of directors because service on the board is in conflict with the interests of her firm's bank and lending institution clients.

(C) It would be proper for the attorney to join the board of directors, and it would be proper for her to participate in the decision about the case intake guidelines.

(D) The attorney may join the board of directors to help discharge her pro bono obligation, and she may vote in favor of amending the case intake guidelines in order to make it easier for low income persons to sue banks and other lending institutions.

GO ON TO THE NEXT PAGE

Question 43

A 12-year-old boy was badly injured when he was struck by a dump truck owned by a construction company and driven by the company's employee. The boy and his parents sued the construction company and the employee. The first count of their complaint alleges that the employee drove negligently while acting within the scope of his duties for the construction company, and that the construction company is therefore liable for the boy's injuries. The second count alleges that the employee drove negligently while on a frolic of his own, and that the employee is therefore liable for the boy's injuries.

The construction company hired an attorney to defend both the construction company and its employee. The attorney conducted a careful investigation of the facts and concluded that the employee was in no way negligent; he was driving slowly and carefully when the boy suddenly ran out into traffic from between two parked cars. The attorney further concluded that the employee was acting within the scope of his duties when the accident happened. The attorney concluded that he could win the case because of the lack of negligence, and that he could effectively represent both the employee and the construction company. He then carefully explained the potential conflicts of interest to both of them and obtained their informed consent, confirmed in writing, to the joint representation. After exhaustive discovery proceedings, the attorney remained convinced that the employee was not negligent, but he nonetheless explained the potential conflicts to the employee and the construc- tion company a second time and again obtained their informed consent, confirmed in writing, to the joint representation. Three weeks before the case was scheduled for trial, counsel for the plaintiffs moved to disqualify the attorney due to a conflict of interest between the employee and the construction company.

Must the trial judge disqualify the attorney?

(A) No, because there is no actual or poten- tial conflict between the employee and the construction company.

(B) No, because the employee and the construction company gave informed consent, confirmed in writing, to the joint representation.

(C) Yes, because the potential conflict creates an appearance of impropriety.

(D) Yes, even though the employee and the construction company gave informed consent, confirmed in writing, to the joint representation.

GO ON TO THE NEXT PAGE

Question 44

A client hired an attorney to put together a complex real estate syndicate. In connection with that work, the client disclosed to the attorney a great deal of confidential information about the client's financial affairs. When the task was about half completed, the attorney's wife was killed in a car accident and his family's house burned down, all in the same week. The attorney was so emotionally and physically drained that he felt he could not competently continue with the work for his client. The client refused to allow the attorney to withdraw. The attorney begged the client to allow him to turn the files over to his law partner, an excellent real estate lawyer who was completely trustworthy and perfectly competent to handle the matter. The client refused to allow his files to be turned over to any other lawyer and insisted that the attorney himself promptly complete the work.

What should the attorney do?

(A) Turn the files over to his partner, and remain available to assist his partner to the extent possible.

(B) Withdraw and turn the client's files over to the client.

(C) Set the client's work aside until he recovers from the ills that have befallen him.

(D) Continue with the matter and do the best that he can under the circumstances.

Question 45

An attorney is defending a marine supply company in a civil action brought by the state attorney general under a statute that makes it a civil offense for any person or business entity to bribe or give a kickback to a state official. The statute authorizes fines of up to $100,000 per transaction for any violation. The marine supply company has a strict corporate policy that prohibits its employees from bribing or giving kickbacks to anyone. Employees who violate the policy are subject to immediate discharge and are required to indemnify the marine supply company for any loss it suffers as a consequence of the violation.

The attorney general has noticed the depositions of dozens of the marine supply company's employees. One of these employees, prior to his recent retirement, was the sales manager of the marine supply company. The attorney met with this employee to prepare him for his deposition. At the outset of the interview, the attorney agreed to represent the employee without charge, and the attorney told the employee that anything said between them would be confidential. During the interview, the attorney asked the employee whether he had ever bribed any state officials. The employee confessed that he had, but said it had been necessary because all of the company's competitors were doing it, too.

What course of action may the attorney pursue at this point?

(A) Withdraw from the case and inform the attorney general what the employee said.

(B) Withdraw from the case and keep the employee's statement in confidence.

(C) Withdraw from representing the employee and inform the marine supply company what the employee said.

(D) Continue in the case, inform the marine supply company what the employee said, and advise the marine supply company to seek prompt settlement.

GO ON TO THE NEXT PAGE

Question 46

An attorney who limits his practice to bankruptcy law has signed up on the local court roster of lawyers who are willing to take court-appointed criminal defense matters on a pro bono basis. He has taken approximately one such pro bono criminal case each of the past 10 years, but he has won only two of them. The day after tomorrow, the attorney will start the jury trial of a criminal defendant charged with indecent exposure. This morning, the prosecutor held a press conference, at which he told reporters that this defendant had been accused of various sex offenses on six prior occasions. The prosecutor's statements are correct, but none of the prior incidents will be admissible in evidence at the upcoming trial. The defendant's attorney thinks that the prosecutor was simply trying to poison the jury pool by degrading the defendant. The attorney is planning to call his own press conference at which he will give the reporters the rest of the story. The attorney intends to explain that on all six prior occasions, the defendant was arrested but never charged, and all six arrests were made by the same police officer, who holds a personal grudge against the defendant.

Which of the following is correct?

(A) The attorney is subject to discipline for accepting this court appointment in light of his apparent lack of talent for criminal trial work.

(B) The attorney's proposed statements at the press conference are proper in light of the prosecutor's prior statements to the press.

(C) The attorney is subject to discipline for accepting court appointments in criminal matters when his active practice is limited to bankruptcy law.

(D) The attorney will be subject to discipline if he holds the press conference and makes the statements described above.

Question 47

A Hollywood movie producer was charged under a criminal statute for unfair trade practices, and now faces a civil claim under the same statute. The producer retains an attorney to represent him in both suits. The attorney is a nationally known defense attorney who has represented many famous people. Most recently, he defended a celebrity in a notorious murder case that held the country rapt for several weeks. The attorney explains to the producer that the representation is very complex and would take a majority of his time for several months. Given the attorney's steep hourly rate, the producer's legal fees would likely be around $1 million. The producer is short on cash and makes the following proposal: If the attorney will represent him in both the civil and criminal suits, the producer will produce a movie based on the attorney's most famous past cases, told from the attorney's viewpoint. The attorney would have complete creative control and would be entitled to all of the movie's profits, which could be anything from $0 to $100 million. The producer had his personal attorney draw up a proposal to this effect and submitted it to the attorney.

Assuming that the attorney receives any consent necessary from his former clients who might be portrayed in the movie, is this proposed arrangement proper?

(A) Yes, but only if the payment from the movie profits is for the civil suit only.

(B) Yes, but only if the ultimate amount paid to the attorney is not excessive in light of the work done.

(C) No, because any amount over $1 million is clearly excessive, and this arrangement could be worth $100 million.

(D) No, because a lawyer must not acquire media rights to a story concerning the lawyer's representation of a client.

GO ON TO THE NEXT PAGE

Question 48

A patent attorney focuses her practice on patents that involve genetically engineered medicines. Representatives of a bioengineering firm had a preliminary conversation with the attorney about representing the bioengineering firm in a patent infringement action against a pharmaceutical corporation. The attorney had never represented either company previously. The bioengineering firm's representatives talked to the attorney for more than an hour about the bioengineering firm's patent and about the pharmaceutical corporation's supposedly infringing product. This conversation covered only public information, nothing confidential. The bioengineering firm's representatives detected a distinct lack of enthusiasm from the attorney, and they ended the conversation cordially but without hiring her. In due course, the bioengineering firm hired a different patent attorney and sued the pharmaceutical corporation for patent infringement. The pharmaceutical corporation hired the attorney as defense counsel in the infringement case. The bioengineering firm's attorney promptly made a motion in the trial court to disqualify the attorney because of her earlier conversation with the bioengineering firm's representatives.

Is the attorney subject to disqualification?

(A) Yes, because the bioengineering firm had previously consulted the attorney on the same matter.

(B) Yes, because the infringement suit is substantially related to the earlier conversation between the attorney and the bioengineering firm's representatives.

(C) No, because the bioengineering firm was never the attorney's client.

(D) No, because the prior conversation between the attorney and the bioengineering firm's representatives did not involve confidential information.

GO ON TO THE NEXT PAGE

Question 49

A plaintiff, represented by his attorney, brought suit in federal district court against a pest control company and nine chemical companies for physical and emotional injuries the plaintiff suffered after accidentally inhaling cockroach spray emanating from an apartment that had recently been fumigated by the pest control company. The attorney's theory for suing the nine chemical companies was that the pest control company had probably purchased its cockroach spray from at least one of the nine chemical companies. A large law firm represented one of the nine chemical company defendants. By using depositions and document demands early in the discovery phase of the case, the law firm established that the chemical company it represented had never at any time sold any type of chemical to the pest control company. The law firm then moved for summary judgment as to its client. The plaintiff's attorney offered no substantive response to that motion, but rather filed a countermotion to disqualify the law firm on the ground that the firm was biased against the plaintiff.

The trial judge denied the motion to disqualify the law firm and granted the chemical company's summary judgment motion, whereupon the plaintiff's attorney immediately moved for a rehearing, moved to stay the trial judge's two orders, and moved to disqualify the trial judge for bias and prejudice against the plaintiff and in favor of the defendant chemical company, the nature of the bias and prejudice being unspecified. The disposition of these motions consumed an entire year, due to the attorney's obstreperousness and his repeated requests for postponements and extensions of time. Meanwhile, the law firm had to stay actively involved in the case to protect the chemical company's position. This year-long ordeal ended up costing the chemical company

$14,500 in attorneys' fees and $6,750 in litigation costs.

Is the plaintiff's attorney subject to litigation sanction in the form of an order against the attorney personally to pay the $14,500 in attorneys' fees and the $6,750 in litigation costs?

(A) No, because the attorney was representing his client zealously within the bounds of the law as he was required to do by the rules of legal ethics.

(B) No, because litigation sanctions can be imposed only on parties to the litigation, not on their lawyers personally.

(C) Yes, even if the attorney was acting in good faith, mistakenly but genuinely believing in the validity of the legal positions he took.

(D) Yes, provided that the chemical company can show that the attorney either intentionally or recklessly took frivolous legal positions in order to harass the chemical company.

GO ON TO THE NEXT PAGE

Question 50

A police officer was charged with murder. He is alleged to have savagely beaten and ultimately killed a teenage gang member in the course of an arrest. Neither the police department nor the officer's union was willing to provide legal counsel for his defense, and the officer himself lacked funds to hire private counsel. The public defender's office could not represent him due to a conflict of interest from a related case. The trial court therefore appointed an attorney to defend the officer. The attorney is only three years out of law school. The attorney practices criminal defense, but he has never handled a murder case before.

For which of the following reasons may the attorney decline the court appointment?

(A) Based on what he has read in the newspapers, he sincerely believes that the officer is guilty.

(B) He has no experience in the defense of a murder case.

(C) He is of the same race as the teenage victim, and he is in sympathy with the plight of young gang members.

(D) He recently was diagnosed with severe depression, which is affecting his ability to handle his existing caseload.

Question 51

Two sisters are partners in a bakery. Their partnership agreement says that they will share the work and the profits equally. They are very close, but they constantly bicker— each claims that the other is taking an unfair share of the profits and shirking on the work. Six months ago, they hired an attorney to act as a third-party neutral, to help them resolve their differences once and for all. At the outset, the attorney explained that he would

be strictly neutral between them; he would not be representing either one, and neither of them would be entitled to the protections afforded by an attorney-client relationship. After a long series of meetings with them (sometimes separately, sometimes jointly), the attorney proposed a solution. The sisters liked his solution, reduced it to writing, and signed it, vowing to end their bickering forever. Six months later, the feud erupted again, worse than ever. One of the sisters asked the attorney's law firm to represent her in a lawsuit against her partner-sister, seeking to declare the partnership at an end and to bar her partner-sister from entering the bakery premises.

Which of the following is correct?

(A) The attorney is subject to discipline for his failed effort to serve both sisters when their interests were patently in conflict.

(B) It would be proper for the attorney to represent the sister in the lawsuit as she requested, even without the informed consent of her partner-sister.

(C) The attorney's law firm partner may represent the sister in the lawsuit as she requested, but only if her partner-sister is notified in writing, and only if the attorney is timely screened and does not share in the fee earned in the lawsuit.

(D) The attorney's law firm partner would be subject to discipline for representing the sister in the lawsuit as she requested, even if the attorney is timely screened and does not share in the fee earned in the lawsuit.

GO ON TO THE NEXT PAGE

Question 52

After graduating from law school, an attorney was admitted to practice in one state and not in any other jurisdiction. She joined the United States Army Judge Advocate General's ("JAG") Corps—the corps of lawyer-soldiers who provide legal services to the Army throughout the world. After completing her officer training and her training in military law, she was assigned to the JAG office at a military base in a different state. Even though she was not admitted to practice in that state, she was assigned to the legal assistance desk. According to Army regulations, her job is to provide legal services to military personnel and their dependents concerning a wide range of personal legal problems, including civil, domestic, and financial matters. An officer and his wife ask the attorney for legal advice about financing a mobile home, which they plan to put in a mobile home park located in the town closest to the military base. The attorney knows absolutely nothing about the business and legal issues involved in financing a mobile home, but she is willing to undertake additional research to learn about these issues.

Would it be proper for the attorney to give the requested advice to the officer and his wife?

(A) Yes, because she is willing to do the research necessary to give competent advice on mobile home financing.

(B) No, because she is not knowledgeable about these business and legal issues.

(C) No, because she is not admitted to practice general civil law in the new state.

(D) No, because mobile home financing is not directly related to the Army's mission.

Question 53

A personal injury attorney and an orthopedic surgeon are good friends, and they have a high mutual regard for each other's professional abilities. One day on the golf course, they made a reciprocal referral agreement: whenever the attorney has a personal injury client with need for an orthopedic surgeon, the attorney promised to refer the client to the surgeon. Similarly, whenever the surgeon has an injured patient with a need for a personal injury attorney, the surgeon promised to refer the patient to the attorney. The agreement was oral, not written, and there was no mention of an expiration date; both women simply assumed that the agreement would continue indefinitely until one or the other wanted to end it. Likewise, they did not discuss whether the agreement would be exclusive; both women simply assumed that neither of them would refer someone to a competitor of the other.

Was it proper for the attorney to make this agreement with the surgeon?

(A) No, because the agreement was not reduced to writing.

(B) No, because the agreement was of an indefinite duration.

(C) No, because a lawyer must not give anything of value to a person for recommending her services.

(D) No, because a lawyer must not enter into a reciprocal referral agreement with a nonlawyer.

GO ON TO THE NEXT PAGE

Question 54

The attorney general's office does not include any lawyers who are skilled in the field of condemnation law (the law of eminent domain). Consequently, whenever the state wants to use its power of eminent domain to condemn some private property for a public use, the attorney general must hire a private law firm to represent the state in the condemnation proceedings. In contrast to the paltry fees that the state pays to appointed defense counsel in criminal cases, the attorney general pays quite handsomely for condemnation work. The attorney general is a partisan political position that is filled by a contested election every four years. A large state law firm limits its practice to condemnation law. The founding partner is an 87-year-old multimillionaire who remains active on the firm's management committee. When it is time to elect a new attorney general, the partner makes large donations from his personal wealth to each candidate who has any reasonable chance of becoming the next attorney general. The other members of the firm's management committee know about the partner's contributions, and they have formally and informally expressed the firm's thanks for helping the firm obtain future appointments by the attorney general.

May the firm accept an appointment from the new attorney general to represent the state in a condemnation case?

(A) Yes, because the partner makes his contributions from his personal wealth, and he has a constitutional right to participate personally in the political process.

(B) Yes, because the partner's personal political contributions cannot be imputed to the law firm.

(C) No, because a lawyer or law firm must not accept appointed legal work from a governmental official after making a political contribution for the purpose of obtaining such work.

(D) No, because to accept such an appointment would create an appearance of impropriety in light of the partner's political contributions.

Question 55

A retired attorney practiced admiralty and maritime law for 45 years in Maine. He stopped paying his bar dues in Maine when he retired, and he is no longer licensed to practice there. He and his wife moved to a retirement village in New Mexico, but he did not seek to become licensed to practice law in New Mexico. After a few months of playing golf and puttering in the garden, the retired attorney got bored and started missing the challenges of law practice. He therefore joined the unpaid staff of volunteer lawyers at the Rio Grande Walk-In Legal Advice Clinic, which is run by a nonprofit organization. The clinic's purpose is to offer free, quick, accurate, compassionate legal advice to walk-in clients who cannot afford ordinary legal service and who have legal problems that can be solved quickly, without litigation or other time-consuming procedures. Before they ever see one of the clinic's lawyers, all of the clients must give informed consent to the limited nature of the legal services they will receive. The retired attorney works at the clinic three days a week, and he dispenses legal advice on all sorts of matters—although he has yet to find a client who needed admiralty or maritime advice. The retired attorney enjoys the work because it makes him feel useful again, and because it gives him a cornucopia of interesting stories to tell his wife about his clients' various legal troubles.

Which of the following statements is correct?

(A)   The retired attorney is subject to discipline for practicing law without a license.

(B)   The retired attorney is subject to discipline for failing to pay his bar dues in Maine.

(C)   The retired attorney's volunteer work is proper because one does not need to be licensed to dispense legal advice at a quick-service clinic like this one.

(D)   The retired attorney's conversations with his wife are proper because no confidential lawyer-client relationship is formed at a quick-service clinic like this one.

GO ON TO THE NEXT PAGE

Question 56

An attorney practices real estate law in an old-fashioned jurisdiction in which almost every real estate transaction requires the services of one or more lawyers. The attorney is also licensed by the state as a real estate broker. The attorney conducts her law practice and her real estate brokerage business in a single office, using one secretary and one paralegal as her support staff. The attorney specializes in small, relatively old apartment buildings that are not in peak condition. They make good investments because they can be bought cheap, fixed up, and leased at favorable rates. When the attorney hears that an owner of a suitable building is looking to sell, she visits them in person and asks them to consider using her to find a buyer. After an owner signs her up as their real estate broker, the attorney lets them know that she can also do the necessary legal work—the title search, the financing documents, the land transfer documents, and the like.

Is the attorney subject to discipline?

(A) Yes, because a person who is engaged in full-time law practice must not conduct a related business from a single office.

(B) Yes, because a person who offers legal services along with real estate brokerage services must not engage in face-to-face solicitation of persons known to need real estate brokerage services.

(C) No, because the attorney's real estate brokerage services are ancillary to her law practice, and the two operations are conducted from a single office.

(D) No, so long as her face-to-face pitch to the owners of apartment buildings is truthful and not misleading.

Question 57

An attorney was a widely admired, highly compensated trial attorney in solo practice. He represented clients in all types of civil and criminal litigation, mostly in high-profile cases that drew a lot of media attention. The governor of the state where the attorney practiced had been harshly criticized for appointing appellate judges who lacked significant experience as trial counsel. Hoping to silence his critics, the governor appointed the attorney to serve out the remaining seven years of a recently deceased supreme court justice's 12-year term. After the seven years, the attorney can run for election to a new 12-year term. Before taking the oath as judge, the attorney sold his entire law practice— books, client files, office lease, furniture, and goodwill—to another lawyer. The attorney gave appropriate advance notice to the clients, and the purchasing lawyer covenanted that he would not raise their legal fees. A few years later, one of the cases that the attorney transferred to the purchasing lawyer came before the state supreme court on appeal.

Which of the following propositions is false?

(A) The attorney's sale of his law practice was proper.

(B) The purchaser's covenant not to increase the fees paid by the attorney's clients was proper.

(C) The attorney must disqualify himself from the case involving his former client.

(D) The attorney may participate in the decision of the case involving his former client, provided that all of the other supreme court justices give their informed consent.

GO ON TO THE NEXT PAGE

barbri

Question 58

A client hired an attorney to draft a will for him. The client willed his entire estate to a 43-year-old widow. The client told the attorney in confidence that he was neither a relative nor a friend of the widow. The client explained that he felt a moral obligation to the widow because he had killed her husband, and he had never become a suspect or confessed his sin to anyone. One day after signing the will, the client committed suicide. In due course, all of the client's assets were distributed to the widow, and the probate court closed his estate and discharged his executor. The attorney never told the widow or anyone else that the client had confessed to killing the widow's husband. Now, a few years later, an enthusiastic young prosecutor is charging an innocent man with murdering the widow's husband in the first degree with aggravating circumstances, and the prosecutor is seeking the death penalty.

May the attorney voluntarily tell the innocent man's defense counsel what his client told him in confidence about killing the widow's husband?

(A) Yes, the attorney not only may, but he must, tell the defense counsel what the client told him.

(B) Yes, the attorney may tell, but he would not be subject to discipline if he decides not to do so.

(C) No, the attorney would be subject to discipline if he told defense counsel because the attorney-client privilege survives the death of the client.

(D) No, because the client's confidential confession to the attorney would be inadmissible hearsay if offered against the prosecution in the murder trial.

GO ON TO THE NEXT PAGE

Question 59

A state university receives 45% of its annual budget from the state. The other 55% of the budget comes from private sources. The university is chartered by the state constitution, and it is regarded for all purposes as a unit of the state government. The governing body of the university is its board of overseers, a group of 17 citizens. The chief executive officer of the university is the chancellor, and the chief legal officer is the general counsel. The university has always strived for a student body and faculty that are diverse in age, politics, wealth, race, nationality, religion, sex, and sexual orientation. One year ago, the voters passed a ballot initiative that prohibits all units of the state government, including the university, from considering a person's race when offering employment or admission to school. The initiative prohibits giving any state funds to a governmental unit that violates the initiative. With reluctance, the university board of overseers adopted a new university-wide regulation that requires all admissions officers and hiring committees to obey the initiative. The state supreme court sustained the constitutionality of the initiative, and the United States Supreme Court denied certiorari. An attorney is one of 15 lawyers in the university general counsel's in-house law office. The general counsel assigned the attorney to work with the university's admissions office to develop new admissions criteria that will comply with the initiative. At the outset, the attorney reminded the admissions director that she was not his lawyer, but rather the university's lawyer. The admissions director told the attorney that despite any new admissions criteria, he would continue to consider race because he believed that was the right thing to do. Deep in her heart, the attorney agrees with the admissions director.

Which of the following may the attorney do in responding to this situation?

(A) Keep the admissions director's statement in confidence, even if she reasonably believes that the university is likely to lose its state funding as a consequence.

(B) Promptly disclose the admissions director's statement to the state attorney general, who is the official in charge of enforcing the voter initiative.

(C) Attempt to convince the admissions director to obey the voter initiative, and if he refuses, then disclose the situation to the university's general counsel.

(D) Anonymously leak the admissions director's statement to the university's board of overseers.

Question 60

A prospective client comes to a law office seeking a lawyer to defend him in a civil action for aggravated assault and battery. An attorney agrees to talk preliminarily with the client, just to obtain enough background information to decide whether she can defend him. The client explains that he has an alcohol problem; indeed, he gets roaring drunk about three nights a week. On the night in question, the client said that a loud-mouthed stranger in his neighborhood tavern made a derogatory comment about the client's favorite basketball team. The client responded by "tapping" the stranger over the head with a pool cue, not once but four times. At that point, the attorney suddenly realizes that the client must be the rotten husband in the hotly disputed divorce and child custody case in which her law partner is representing the aggrieved wife. The attorney stops the client and tells him that she cannot defend him in the assault and battery case because of her partner's work for the client's wife.

Which of the following is true?

(A) The partner must withdraw from representing the wife because the attorney has received confidential information from the client that would be harmful to the client if used in the divorce and child custody case.

(B) It would be proper for the partner to represent the wife and for the attorney to represent the client in the assault and battery case because the two matters are not substantially related.

(C) The partner may continue representing the wife, but only if the wife gives informed consent, confirmed in writing.

(D) The partner may continue representing the wife if the attorney is screened off from participation in the case and obtains no part of the fee in the case, and if the firm promptly sends the client written notice of the situation.

STOP

ANSWER SHEET

1 (A) (B) (C) (D)		31 (A) (B) (C) (D)	
2 (A) (B) (C) (D)		32 (A) (B) (C) (D)	
3 (A) (B) (C) (D)		33 (A) (B) (C) (D)	
4 (A) (B) (C) (D)		34 (A) (B) (C) (D)	
5 (A) (B) (C) (D)		35 (A) (B) (C) (D)	
6 (A) (B) (C) (D)		36 (A) (B) (C) (D)	
7 (A) (B) (C) (D)		37 (A) (B) (C) (D)	
8 (A) (B) (C) (D)		38 (A) (B) (C) (D)	
9 (A) (B) (C) (D)		39 (A) (B) (C) (D)	
10 (A) (B) (C) (D)		40 (A) (B) (C) (D)	
11 (A) (B) (C) (D)		41 (A) (B) (C) (D)	
12 (A) (B) (C) (D)		42 (A) (B) (C) (D)	
13 (A) (B) (C) (D)		43 (A) (B) (C) (D)	
14 (A) (B) (C) (D)		44 (A) (B) (C) (D)	
15 (A) (B) (C) (D)		45 (A) (B) (C) (D)	
16 (A) (B) (C) (D)		46 (A) (B) (C) (D)	
17 (A) (B) (C) (D)		47 (A) (B) (C) (D)	
18 (A) (B) (C) (D)		48 (A) (B) (C) (D)	
19 (A) (B) (C) (D)		49 (A) (B) (C) (D)	
20 (A) (B) (C) (D)		50 (A) (B) (C) (D)	
21 (A) (B) (C) (D)		51 (A) (B) (C) (D)	
22 (A) (B) (C) (D)		52 (A) (B) (C) (D)	
23 (A) (B) (C) (D)		53 (A) (B) (C) (D)	
24 (A) (B) (C) (D)		54 (A) (B) (C) (D)	
25 (A) (B) (C) (D)		55 (A) (B) (C) (D)	
26 (A) (B) (C) (D)		56 (A) (B) (C) (D)	
27 (A) (B) (C) (D)		57 (A) (B) (C) (D)	
28 (A) (B) (C) (D)		58 (A) (B) (C) (D)	
29 (A) (B) (C) (D)		59 (A) (B) (C) (D)	
30 (A) (B) (C) (D)		60 (A) (B) (C) (D)	

Answer to Question 1

(A)   Yes, it would be proper for the judge to take the steps mentioned because she has received information indicating a substantial likelihood that the attorney has violated a legal ethics rule. The attorney has apparently violated ABA Model Rule 1.8(c), which generally prohibits a lawyer from drafting a will under which he will receive a substantial gift. A judge who receives "information indicating a substantial likelihood" that a lawyer has violated a legal ethics rule *must* take "appropriate action," which may include direct communication with the lawyer, direct action, and reporting the violation to the appropriate authority. [CJC Rule 2.15(D)] (B) is wrong because it is factually incorrect—the judge does not have personal knowledge; rather she has received second-hand information about the attorney. [*See* CJC, Terminology] (C) is wrong because the duties imposed by CJC Rule 2.15 are not confined to lawyers in the judge's own jurisdiction. (D) is wrong because "appropriate action" may include direct communication with the lawyer who violated the legal ethics rule. [CJC Rule 2.15(D), comment 2]

Answer to Question 2

(A)   When ordered to do so by a tribunal, a lawyer must continue representation notwithstanding good cause for terminating the representation. [ABA Model Rule 1.16(c)] Even if the attorney was absolutely convinced of his own incompetence, he is subject to discipline for abandoning the teacher in violation of the trial judge's order. (C) is wrong for the reason stated above. (B) is wrong because a lawyer is not subject to discipline for taking on a case that he is not competent to handle if he puts in the time and study needed to make himself competent to handle it. [*See* comment 4 to ABA Model Rule 1.1] Having volunteered to take on the case, the attorney's duty was to put in the requisite time and study. (D) is wrong because a lawyer's duties of competence, diligence, and loyalty are no lower in a pro bono matter than in a fee-paying matter.

Answer to Question 3

(A)   The attorney is subject to discipline because the spectator initially declined the attorney's request for an interview. ABA Model Rule 3.5(c) provides that after the trial is over and the jury is discharged, a lawyer must not communicate with a former juror or prospective juror if *any* of the following conditions is met: (1) local law or a court order prohibits such communication; (2) the juror has told the lawyer that she does not want to communicate; or (3) the communication involves misrepresentation, coercion, duress, or harassment. Here, the attorney violated the second condition—he persisted with his interview request after the spectator said that she did not want to talk with him. (C) is incorrect. Even though the communication did not involve coercion, duress, or harassment, the attorney still spoke with the spectator after she declined his request, violating the rule. (D) is incorrect because ABA Model Rule 3.5(c) applies to all jurors and even prospective jurors. (B) is too broad. There is no blanket prohibition regarding post-trial contact with jurors and prospective jurors. Rather, such communications are subject to conditions, and the attorney violated one of these conditions.

Answer to Question 4

(A) ABA Model Rule 5.3(b) requires that "a lawyer having direct supervisory authority over the nonlawyer shall make reasonable efforts to ensure that the person's conduct is compatible with the professional obligations of the lawyer." Although the attorney provided "extensive, detailed instructions" regarding the client trust account, he subsequently did nothing to supervise the secretary's management of the account, thereby violating Rule 5.3(b). (B) is incorrect because a lawyer is not required to manage his client trust account himself. (C) and (D) are incorrect because the attorney's duty to supervise is not contingent on learning of a potential problem.

Answer to Question 5

(A) Generally speaking, a lawyer must not represent a client in a presently pending piece of litigation and simultaneously oppose that client in a different piece of litigation, without each client's informed consent, confirmed in writing. [See comment 6 to ABA Model Rule 1.7] Here, the attorney may have believed that the conflict of interest that would have been created by his undertaking representation of the prospective client was unconsentable. Thus, he acted properly in declining to represent the prospective client, even though the prospective client's case was unrelated to the one in which the attorney was representing the doctor. However, a lawyer does owe a duty of reasonable care to a prospective client, even though no attorney-client relationship ever comes about. [See Restatement of the Law Governing Lawyers (hereinafter "Restatement") §15] Ordinarily, that duty would include cautioning the prospective client about an impending statute of limitations deadline. [Id.] Here, however, a cautionary word to the prospective client would constitute disloyalty to the existing client, the doctor. [See, e.g., Flatt v. Superior Court, 9 Cal. 4th 275 (1994)—warning prospective client about statute of limitations was not required when it would be disloyal to present client] The attorney therefore acted properly in simply suggesting that the prospective client consult other counsel. (B) is incorrect because a lawyer does owe a duty of reasonable care to a prospective client. (C) is incorrect because the attorney did have a legal and ethical reason to reject the prospective client as a client: the simultaneous representation of the doctor in the unrelated matter. (D) is incorrect because the foreseeability of the harm is not the whole of the analysis. Even if the attorney could foresee that the prospective client would dawdle and let the statute of limitations run, the attorney's duty of loyalty to the doctor required him not to warn the prospective client about the statute of limitations.

Answer to Question 6

(D) The attorney must turn over all of the papers to the client. When a lawyer is fired, he must return all "papers and property to which the client is entitled." [ABA Model Rule 1.16(d)] In this case, the client is entitled to all the papers the attorney has prepared. Under the law of many states, a lawyer can assert a lien on client papers in her possession to secure the payment of her fee, but here the client has paid the attorney for all the work the attorney did. (A) is wrong because the attorney must turn over the memoranda as well as the other documents. (B) is wrong because the attorney must give the client the document drafts as well as the memoranda. (C) is wrong because the fact that the attorney was fired, even without cause, does not in any way change the attorney's duty to give the client all of the papers.

Answer to Question 7

(A) It was proper for the judge to allow her husband to accept the prize because acceptance thereof does not reasonably appear to undermine the judge's integrity or impartiality. A judge may accept benefits associated with her spouse's business activity that incidentally benefit the judge. [CJC Rule 3.13(B)(8)] (B) is wrong because it ignores the general rule on family members' accepting gifts and other benefits. (C) is wrong because such benefits of a spouse are not subject to the public reporting requirement. [CJC Rule 3.13(B)] (D) is wrong because if the prize is proper under CJC Rule 3.13(B)(8), it does not become improper simply because the insurance company may later appear as a litigant in the judge's court.

Answer to Question 8

(D) The attorney should state what she knows about the law student, including mentioning his burglary conviction. A lawyer who is properly asked for information about a bar applicant's character has a duty to respond and to do so accurately. [ABA Model Rule 8.1] (A) is wrong because the attorney does have relevant information—she knows about the law student's burglary conviction, and that is relevant to (but certainly not conclusive of) the inquiry about his character. (B) is wrong because a lawyer's duty to provide bar applicant

information is not confined to the state in which the lawyer practices. (C) is wrong because the burglary conviction is relevant to the character inquiry, and nothing indicates that the attorney learned about it in confidence.

Answer to Question 9

(A) The attorney would be subject to discipline for the last two statements in her advertisement. It is misleading for her to state that she is "Harvard Trained," because reasonable readers could interpret that to mean that she received her law degree from that school. [See ABA Model Rule 7.1 and comment 2] The statement "Never Lost a Jury Trial," although literally true, could create unjustified expectations and is therefore misleading. [See ABA Model Rule 7.1 and comment 3] The reference to "Trial Attorney" would not make the attorney subject to discipline. Given her brief time in law practice, she has had significant experience as a trial lawyer. A lawyer is allowed to state the fields of law in which she does or does not practice. [ABA Model Rule 7.2, comment 9] (B), (C), and (D) are all incorrect because they would permit "Harvard Trained" or "Never Lost a Jury Trial" (or both) to remain in the advertisement.

Answer to Question 10

(A) The new attorney is not subject to discipline for this fee arrangement if $5,100 is a reasonable fee. The ABA Model Rules flatly prohibit a lawyer from using a contingent fee arrangement when the payment of the fee is contingent on the securing of a divorce or an amount of alimony or support (or property settlement in lieu thereof). The Rules do not, however, prohibit a lawyer from

using a contingent fee to recover money that is past due under a child support order. [ABA Model Rule 1.5(d)(1) and comment 6] In the wife's case, she had already obtained her divorce, and the amount of alimony and child support payments had already been set. The only problem was extracting the money from the husband; thus, the new attorney's use of the contingent fee arrangement in this case was proper. The contingent fee arrangement is particularly appropriate in light of the wife's lack of money to pay a regular fee and State A's failure to provide for fee shifting in domestic relations matters. [*See* Restatement §35, comment b] (B) is wrong because it ignores the possibility that $5,100 may be unreasonably high for the work the new attorney did. Also, the new attorney would not necessarily be subject to discipline for using this fee arrangement even if the wife had money to pay a regular fee. (C) is wrong because the collection of past due amounts of child support on a contingency fee basis is not considered a prohibited contingent fee in a domestic relations case under the Rules. (D) is wrong because it invokes a nonexistent policy. Contingent fees are generally allowed, even though they typically involve taking a share of money awarded for the support or compensation of the client (as in the ordinary personal injury case).

Answer to Question 11

(D) The attorney's actions were not proper because a lawyer may not draft a legal instrument for a client that gives a substantial gift to the lawyer, unless the client is a relative of the lawyer. [ABA Model Rule 1.8(c)] The deed creating the joint tenancy bestows a substantial gift on the attorney, particularly

in light of the high likelihood that the client would die first. The transaction is also particularly suspect in light of the attorney's failure to explain the joint tenancy to the client. [*See* ABA Model Rule 1.8(a)—business transaction with client requires full disclosure of interest granted lawyer] (A) is wrong because the court's determination does not free the attorney from discipline for drafting the deed that bestowed the gift on him. (B) is wrong because the right of survivorship is a substantial gift regardless of who actually dies first; thus, it was not proper for the attorney to draft the document. (C) is wrong because it is overbroad. A lawyer may enter into a business transaction with a client, provided he follows certain safeguards. Here, for example, had the attorney met all of the requirements of ABA Model Rule 1.8(a), the transaction would have been a proper business transaction. However, the transaction still would have been improper because the attorney drafted the deed.

Answer to Question 12

(D) The attorney must refuse to represent the art dealer in the present transaction. Note that the call of the question asks what the attorney *must* do, not what he would be *allowed* to do. ABA Model Rule 1.2 states that a lawyer must not counsel or assist a client in conduct that the lawyer knows is criminal or fraudulent. Here, the attorney must refuse to represent the art dealer in the sale of the painting to the television personality because the sale would be fraudulent— the attorney knows that the painting is not a van Gogh as the art dealer represented to the television personality. ABA Model Rule 1.6(b) permits a lawyer to reveal a client's confidential information to the extent necessary to prevent the client from committing a crime or fraud that would result in substantial financial harm to a person, if the client is using or has used the lawyer's services to further the crime or fraud. A lawyer also may reveal confidential information if the client has already acted and the disclosure will mitigate the consequent financial harm. Thus, the attorney is permitted to disclose information to law enforcement authorities in order to prevent harm to the television personality and possibly mitigate subsequent financial harm caused by the first transaction to the art museum; however, the attorney is **not required** to do so. The same holds true regarding the attorney's warning the television personality about the proposed sale. Consequently, (A) and (B) are wrong. (C) is also wrong because even if it can be argued that the attorney's revealing information about the fraudulent sale to the museum would mitigate subsequent financial harm, the attorney is not required to reveal the art dealer's confidential information.

Answer to Question 13

(D)   The attorney may reveal the confidence even if doing so will subject his client to civil or criminal liability. A lawyer may disclose a client's confidence "to establish a defense to a criminal charge or civil claim against the lawyer based upon conduct in which the client was involved . . . ." [ABA Model Rule 1.6(b)(5)] Although the lawyer must wait until the assertion of misconduct arises, he need not await the filing of a formal charge or complaint. The lawyer may defend himself by responding directly to a third party who has made such an assertion. [*See* Restatement §64, comment c] (A) is wrong because

the lawyer may disclose the fact even if doing so harms the client. (C) is wrong because the lawyer need not wait for the complaint to be filed, as explained above. (B) is wrong because it ignores the self-protection exception to the general rule of confidentiality.

Answer to Question 14

(A)   A lawyer has a general duty of loyalty to the client and a general duty to represent the client with dedication and commitment to the client's interest and with zeal in advocacy on the client's behalf. When acting as an advocate for a client, as the attorney is doing here, a lawyer must resolve reasonable doubts in favor of his client. There are certain situations under which the lawyer must act in a way that is adverse to his client, but each of the situations requires that the lawyer have **actual knowledge** of adverse facts, not just doubt or suspicion. [*See* ABA Model Rule 3.3(a)] Here, the attorney does not have actual knowledge that the defendant and his mother are lying or even any knowledge of circumstantial facts that indicate that they are lying; at best, he has a strong suspicion based on his instincts. This falls well short of actual knowledge. Note that a lawyer **may refuse** to offer evidence if he **reasonably believes** that it is false, other than the testimony of a criminal defendant. [ABA Model Rule 3.3(a)(3)] This rule does not apply to the defendant's testimony because the defendant is a criminal defendant; it also does not apply to the defendant's mother's testimony for two reasons: First, the question asks whether the attorney **may offer** the testimony, not whether he may **refuse** to offer it. Second, there is nothing in the facts to indicate that the attorney's belief that the testimony is false is reasonable. Thus, the attorney may call the defendant and his mother as trial witnesses.

Answer to Question 15

(B) The attorney's handling of the matter was not proper because she should have made sure that the client was promptly notified that the check had arrived. When someone delivers money to a lawyer to hold for the lawyer's client, the lawyer must promptly notify the client that the money has arrived. [ABA Model Rule 1.15(d)] Had the client known that the money had arrived, she could have promptly collected it and put it to her own use. (A) is wrong because the IOLTA program required the funds to be deposited in an IOLTA account. (C) is wrong because although the attorney did comply with the IOLTA requirement, she failed to take appropriate steps to have the client promptly notified that the money had arrived. (D) is wrong because the client was harmed; she was deprived of the use of the money during the month that the attorney was on vacation.

Answer to Question 16

(C) Both the partner and the associate may work on the matter, assuming the associate complies with the applicable federal statutes and regulations concerning former government employees. Drafting a piece of legislation is not regarded as a "matter" for purposes of the legal ethics rules on former government employees. [ABA Model Rule 1.11(e); ABA Formal Op. 342 (1975)] Therefore, the associate may advise the state university. Because the associate is not disqualified, neither is her firm. Thus, the partner may also work on this project. (A) is wrong because, as discussed above, the associate's congressional work disqualifies

neither the associate nor the partner. (B) is wrong because it states one of the requirements for the partner's representation had the associate been disqualified. As discussed above, the associate is not disqualified and thus need not be screened off. (D) is wrong for the reasons stated above. Moreover, it is not the state university that would need protection if this were a "matter" for the purpose of disqualification under the conflict of interest rules. In that case, the associate would have been screened off, the associate would not be apportioned any part of the fee, and written notice would be promptly given to the *government agency*.

Answer to Question 17

(A) The attorney will not be subject to discipline if he becomes an authorized provider under the insurance company's plan. The insurance company has set up a prepaid legal services plan of the kind referred to in the ABA Model Rules. A lawyer may receive legal business through such a plan, unless the operator of the plan uses live person-to-person contact to solicit people who it knows are in need of legal services in a particular matter covered by the plan. [ABA Model Rule 7.3(e)] (B) is wrong because there is no rule concerning the selection of counsel in a legal services insurance plan. (C) is also wrong because it would be an antitrust violation (and also an ethics violation) for a group of lawyers to conspire to follow a minimum or maximum fee schedule [*see* Arizona v. Maricopa County Medical Society, 457 U.S. 332 (1982)], but it is neither illegal nor unethical for a lawyer to agree to follow an insurance company's maximum fee schedule for work done for that company's insured. (D) is wrong because it is too broad. ABA Model Rule 7.3(e) permits a lawyer to participate in a legal services plan that uses live person-to-person contact, as long as it does not contact persons who are known to need legal services in a particular matter covered by the plan.

Answer to Question 18

(D) A lawyer who represents a client in a matter must not communicate about the matter with a person the attorney knows is represented by counsel, unless that person's counsel consents or the communication is authorized by law or a court order. [ABA Model Rule 4.2] Here, however, the attorney did not communicate with the tenant. Rather, the attorney told the landlord to talk with the tenant if she thought it would be helpful, and even took care to make sure that the parties would not finalize any agreement without consulting their respective counsel. Although a lawyer must not use an agent to do what the lawyer is prohibited from doing [ABA Model Rule 8.4(a)], that was not the case here. Comment 4 to Rule 4.2 states that parties may communicate with each other directly, as the landlord and tenant did, and a lawyer is not prohibited from advising a client concerning a communication that the client is legally entitled to make. Because the attorney was not required to obtain the consent of the tenant's lawyer in this situation, (A) is incorrect. Similarly, (B) and (C) are incorrect because the no-contact rule does not apply to these facts. Even if it did apply, these choices do not accurately reflect Rule 4.2. The attorney must obtain consent from the represented person's lawyer before communicating with the person about the matter; notifying the lawyer is not sufficient.

Additionally, it is immaterial whether a represented person initiates or consents to a prohibited communication.

Answer to Question 19

(D) The attorney should decline to serve as trial counsel because she can foresee that she will be called as a witness. A lawyer must not act as an advocate at a trial at which the lawyer is likely to be a *necessary* witness. [ABA Model Rule 3.7(a)] The attorney was the only person other than the parties present at the negotiating session. The landowner will almost certainly call the attorney as a witness. Because the attorney can foresee at the outset that she will likely be called as a witness, she should decline to serve as trial lawyer for the contractor, even if the contractor is willing to consent to the conflict of interest. [ABA Model Rule 1.7(a); comment 6 to ABA Model Rule 3.7] (A) is wrong because a person's choice of counsel is limited by the restraints imposed by the ethics rules. The client may choose the attorney, but the attorney cannot ethically accept the employment. (B) is wrong because the attorney cannot refuse to testify if the landowner calls her to the witness stand. (C) is wrong because if a lawyer is called to the witness stand and sworn to tell the truth, she must do so, even if it is prejudicial to her client.

Answer to Question 20

(D) The attorney's fee agreement is proper even though it gives the attorney a personal interest in the subject of the litigation. The attorney has acquired a personal interest in the movie, which is in one sense the real subject of the litigation. However, the rule against acquiring a personal interest in the subject of litigation has an exception that allows a lawyer to represent a client for a contingent fee. [ABA Model Rule 1.8(i)(2)] (A) is wrong because the rule on literary rights contracts covers only literary works based in substantial part on information relating to the representation. Here, the movie concerns John Dillinger, not the producer. [*See* ABA Model Rule 1.8(d)] (B) is wrong because, as discussed above, a lawyer may acquire an interest in the subject matter of the litigation in the form of a contingent fee. (C) is wrong because the fee agreement between the producer and the attorney does not require the author's informed consent. The author is not a current or former client of the attorney, and the author has no apparent interest that would cause the attorney a conflict and force him to disclose and explain the material risks and available alternatives and obtain the author's consent.

Answer to Question 21

(B) A "forwarding fee" is another term for a "referral fee," and payments for referrals are prohibited. [ABA Model Rule 7.2(b)] (A) is proper because a lawyer may take on a case that he is not competent to handle if he obtains his client's consent to associate a lawyer who is competent to handle it. [Comment 2 to ABA Model Rule 1.1] (C) is proper because a lawyer may refer her client to another lawyer who is competent to handle the case. Making a sound referral can take a significant amount of time, especially if the referring lawyer needs to research the backgrounds of several lawyers with whom she is not personally familiar. It is appropriate for the referring lawyer to charge her client for the time spent making the referral, subject of course to the general rule on reasonableness.

[ABA Model Rule 1.5] (As a practical matter, however, many lawyers would not charge a regular client for making such a referral.) (D) is proper because a lawyer may take on a case that he is not competent to handle if he undertakes the study necessary to provide competent representation. [Comment 2 to ABA Model Rule 1.1]

Answer to Question 22

(C) It would be proper for the attorney to participate in the debate and cast her vote on the proposed legislation, provided that she informs the committee that she represents a client whose interests could be materially benefited by the statute. A lawyer may participate in a law reform activity that will affect the interests of the lawyer's client. [ABA Model Rule 6.4] When a lawyer knows that a client will be materially benefited by the activity, the lawyer must disclose that fact, but she need not name the client. (A) is wrong because a lawyer is not prohibited from engaging in a law reform activity that might benefit her client. (B) is wrong because a lawyer is not prohibited from participating in a law reform activity, unless the participation would create an impermissible conflict of interest. [ABA Model Rule 1.7(a)] That is not the case here. A client who hires a lawyer does not thereby purchase the right to control the lawyer's views and activities in all contexts. [*See* ABA Model Rule 1.2(b)] The attorney may even advocate new legislation that she thinks is sound that would harm the biotechnology firm's sales. [*See* ABA Model Rule 6.4] (D) is wrong because the attorney need not disclose the name of her client; simply disclosing the fact of representation will inform the legislation committee of her possible bias.

Answer to Question 23

(B) The judge may testify at a public hearing in connection with matters concerning the law. [CJC Rule 3.2(A)] (A) is wrong because there is no rule requiring "equal time." (C) is wrong because it is overbroad. The general rule against judicial involvement in politics limits only *some* types of political activities, not including legislative testimony. [CJC Canon 4] (D) is wrong because, with respect to issues that are likely to come before the court, a judge is prohibited from making pledges, promises, or commitments that are inconsistent with the impartial performance of his duties. [CJC Rule 4.1(A)(13)] That Rule does not apply here because the judge's testimony, which would be designed to improve the law, would not constitute a promise that is inconsistent with the performance of his adjudicative duties.

Answer to Question 24

(D) The attorney is not subject to discipline. Because the employee is a lawyer-employee of the attorney, she is regarded as being "in the same firm." She and the attorney are thus allowed to split fees without complying with the rules that govern fee splits between lawyers who are not in the same firm. [ABA Model Rule 1.5(e)] (A) is wrong for the reason just stated. (B) is wrong because no Rule requires the attorney to supervise the lawyer-employee at every turn, so long as he takes reasonable steps to assure that she performs her work competently and otherwise within the bounds of legal ethics. [*See* ABA Model Rule 5.1—supervisory duties of lawyers within a firm] (C) is wrong; a law firm may state particular fields of law that the firm's lawyers handle. [ABA Model Rule 7.2,

comment 9]

Answer to Question 25

(B) The attorney is subject to criminal liability if he intended to induce the judge to decide the case in the plaintiff's favor. The common law crime of bribery consists of the corrupt payment or receipt of anything of value in return for official action. The $50,000 loan was obviously a thing of value. Thus, if the attorney intended the loan as an inducement to the judge to decide the case in favor of the plaintiff, then the attorney is guilty of bribery. (A) is wrong because in deciding whether the attorney is subject to criminal liability, it is the attorney's intent that counts, not the judge's intent. (C) is wrong because the attorney's crime was complete when he gave the loan, even though the judge never had to decide the case. (D) is wrong because bribery does not require an outright gift; a $50,000 loan is a thing of value, especially a loan with no repayment date, no promissory note, and no interest specified.

Answer to Question 26

(D) The steel company's attorney need not disclose the FTC ruling because the court need not follow the decision. A lawyer can be disciplined for failing to cite the court to legal authority that is "directly adverse" to the client's position and is from the "controlling jurisdiction." [ABA Model Rule 3.3(a)(2)] Although the decision is directly adverse to the steel company's position, the facts state that FTC decisions do not control in the United States Courts of Appeal. Thus, the decision is not from the "controlling jurisdiction." (A) is wrong because in order to invoke the disclosure rule, the decision must be from a controlling jurisdiction, not merely persuasive. (B) is wrong because it states only one portion of the test that triggers the disclosure rule. While true that the decision is adverse, it is not from a controlling jurisdiction, and thus need not be revealed. (C) is wrong because although the Rule as stated is true, in this case we are not concerned with harmful *facts*. The issue is whether the steel company's attorney must reveal harmful *law*.

Answer to Question 27

(D)   It would not be proper for the solo practitioner to represent the grocery store unless both the client and the grocery store give informed consent, confirmed in writing, to the representation. A lawyer who is presently representing a client in one litigation matter should not simultaneously oppose that client in a different litigation matter, even if the two matters are unrelated. [ABA Model Rule 1.7(a) and comment 6] The purpose of the rule is to avoid putting the client into the difficult position of treating the lawyer simultaneously as friend and foe. The conflict can be solved only by informed consent, confirmed in writing, from both the client and the grocery store. (A) is wrong because the rule prohibiting the representation applies regardless of whether the solo practitioner has obtained relevant confidential information. (B) is wrong because the conflict is not obviated by the shortage of legal talent in the small town. (C) is wrong because the Rule applies even if the two cases are unrelated.

Answer to Question 28

(D)   It was improper for the lawyer to hold the client's file. (A) is true because one of the grounds for permissible withdrawal is that the client has made

the lawyer's task unreasonably difficult (e.g., the client will not cooperate with the lawyer). [ABA Model Rule 1.16(b)(6)] (B) is true because a lawyer must not communicate about a matter with a person who is represented by another lawyer in the matter, unless that other lawyer consents. [ABA Model Rule 4.2] (C) is true because there is no reason in this case for the wife's attorney to charge the wife less than the full amount (assuming, of course, that the fee is reasonable in the circumstances). However, a lawyer has a duty to turn over the papers to the client. [*See* ABA Model Rule 1.16(d)]

Answer to Question 29

(C)   A potential problem arises when the content of a brochure is improper or when the printed material is used as part of an act of solicitation. Here, the content was proper, but when the attorney gave the brochure to the hospitalized pedestrian, he crossed the line into impermissible in-person solicitation. [*See* ABA Model Rule 7.3; *see also* Ohralik v. Ohio State Bar Association, 436 U.S. 447 (1978)—noting the particular potential for undue influence and overreaching in the hospital context, where individuals are often especially vulnerable] (A) and (B) are incorrect because publishing the brochure, in and of itself, is not problematic, just as the act of printing business cards is fully permissible. (D) is incorrect because the truthfulness of the brochure's contents does not counteract the attorney's impropriety in providing his contact information during a hospital visit.

Answer to Question 30

(C)   The peer counselor may disclose the statement even if the lawyer objects.

barbri

The state ethics rule on confidentiality treats communications between a lawyer and his peer counselor just like communications between an attorney and a client. If the counselor had heard one of her clients make this threat, she could have warned the police and the intended victim. An attorney may reveal confidential information to the extent she reasonably believes necessary to prevent reasonably certain death or substantial bodily harm. [ABA Model Rule 1.6(b)(1)] Thus, the peer counselor may warn the client and the police. (A) is wrong because the peer counselor may act to prevent the lawyer from causing substantial bodily harm. The lawyer's consent is not necessary. [ABA Model Rule 1.6(b)(1)] (B) is wrong because if an attorney reasonably believes that her client (or anyone else) is about to inflict substantial bodily harm on someone, she may take steps to prevent it, even if she is not certain that the client (or other person) will do it. (D) is wrong because the state ethics rule on confidentiality equates the peer counselor relationship with the relationship between an attorney and client; thus, the ability to disclose is the same.

Answer to Question 31

(D) The husband may represent his regular client if the client gives informed consent, confirmed in writing, to the representation. His wife is likely to inherit her father's interest in the real estate syndicate. That gives the husband a personal interest in the real estate syndicate, albeit an attenuated interest. If the husband is to represent his regular client in selling land to the real estate syndicate, he must first disclose his personal interest to the client. If the client gives informed consent, confirmed

in writing, then the husband may represent the client. [ABA Model Rule 1.7(b)] (A) is wrong because informed, written consent will solve the potential conflict of interest. (B) is wrong because informed consent, confirmed in writing, will solve the conflict problem. Furthermore, the "appearance of impropriety" is not a basis for discipline or disqualification under the ABA Model Rules. This is an outdated concept from the old ABA Model Code. (C) is wrong because the husband's personal interest is significant, even though it is remote.

Answer to Question 32

(C) The criminal attorney will be subject to civil liability in a legal malpractice action brought by the swimming coach for failing to object to the second trial on double jeopardy grounds. A reasonably competent criminal defense attorney would know that a defendant is put in jeopardy when a jury is empanelled and sworn, not to mention that the prosecutor started presenting her case-in-chief. The swimming coach was obviously a proper plaintiff, and he was injured by the criminal attorney's error; he should be able to recover at least part of the $5,000 attorneys' fee, plus damages for his anguish and for the reputational injury caused by the conviction at the second trial. Note that (C) provides that in the malpractice action the swimming coach must prove by a preponderance of the evidence that he was innocent of the underlying criminal offense. That is required by the law of most states that have ruled on the issue. [*See* Restatement §53, comment d] Observe that in this particular case, a good argument can be made for allowing the swimming coach to recover even without proof of innocence. Here, the malpractice was the criminal attorney's failure to object to the second trial. If the attorney had acted competently, the second trial would never have taken place, and the swimming coach would have lawfully gone free, even if he were unquestionably guilty of the assault. [*See* Levine v. Kling, 123 F.3d 580 (7th Cir. 1997)— Judge Posner's dictum] (A) and (D) are incorrect because they overlook the $5,000 fee and other less tangible injuries the swimming coach suffered. (B) is incorrect for the reasons stated above with respect to (C).

Answer to Question 33

(C)   The attorney is subject to discipline because she and the real estate developer are partners in the business described in the question. A lawyer is prohibited from entering into a partnership with a nonlawyer if any of the partnership activities constitutes the practice of law. [ABA Model Rule 5.4(b)] The rationale and social policy behind this Rule have been sharply questioned, but the ABA has not abandoned its traditional distrust of partnerships with nonlawyers. [*See* Hazard & Hodes, §45.7] (A) is wrong because although there are potential conflicts here in that the attorney appears to work partly for the investors and partly for the developer and herself in putting the real estate projects together, informed consent, confirmed in writing, by the investors will solve these conflict issues. In any event, the attorney is still subject to discipline for entering into the partnership with a nonlawyer. (B) is wrong because the division of responsibility does not solve the partnership with a nonlawyer problem. (D) is wrong because the developer is not engaging in activities that could be construed as practicing law. All of the legal work (i.e., work calling for the

professional judgment of a lawyer) is done by the attorney.

Answer to Question 34

(A)   The young attorney may not seek to have her name included on the list because naming the bank as executor or trustee in wills and trusts is a tacit condition of being on the list. A lawyer generally may not give anything of value to a person for recommending the lawyer's services. [ABA Model Rule 7.2(b)] When a lawyer names a bank as institutional executor or trustee for a client, the lawyer confers a monetary benefit on the bank in the form of the fees the bank will earn from the client's trust or estate. Here, the bank apparently lists only those lawyers who are willing to compensate it in this manner. That makes the arrangement "exclusive" and prevents the arrangement from being a reciprocal referral agreement of the kind permitted by ABA Model Rule 7.2(b)(4). Moreover, the bank's scheme creates a conflict of interest between the attorney and the client who needs an institutional executor or trustee. The attorney has a personal interest in staying on the bank's referral list, and that interest may skew the attorney's judgment in advising a client whether to name the bank or a different institution. [*See* ABA Model Rule 1.7(a)] (B) is wrong because it is overbroad and does not hit on the specific problem with the bank's scheme. In proper circumstances, a lawyer may solicit business through an intermediary, e.g., through a prepaid legal service program or an approved lawyer referral service. (C) is wrong because a client is entitled to the unbiased advice of a lawyer in deciding what institutional trustee or executor to name. Even if the bank is just as good and its fees are as reasonable as other institutional fiduciaries, the bank's scheme deprives clients of unbiased advice. (D) is wrong because clients who use the bank for their routine banking needs might nevertheless desire to name some other institution as their executor or trustee; in any event, they are entitled to unbiased legal advice on that subject.

Answer to Question 35

(D)   The attorney's actions were not proper because her information was gained from a confidential lawyer-client communication. [*See* ABA Model Rule 1.6] It was both privileged and confidential, and could be disclosed only if one of the exceptions to the duty of confidentiality applies. None of the exceptions applies here. The fact that the man did not hire the attorney to represent him does not affect her duty of confidentiality; he was seeking legal advice and representation when he spoke to her. [*See* ABA Model Rule 1.18(b)] (A) is wrong because there is no exception to the duty of confidentiality to prevent a fraud on the court when the lawyer is not appearing before the court. (B) is wrong because this too does not fit within any exception to the duty of nondisclosure. A lawyer may reveal confidential information to the extent she reasonably believes necessary to prevent, mitigate, or rectify substantial injury to the financial interests of another that is reasonably certain to result or has resulted from the client's commission of a crime or fraud, if the client has used the lawyer's services in furtherance of such crime or fraud. [ABA Model Rule 1.6(b)(3)] Here, the facts do not indicate that the man used the attorney's services in furtherance of his perjurious testimony. Thus, although the perjury could result in substantial injury to the actor's financial interests, the attorney is not permitted to reveal the confidential information. (C) is wrong because it states the rule for an ex parte communication to the judge by one of the parties. Here, the attorney does not represent one of the parties. Furthermore, the information is confidential and cannot be disclosed to the disadvantage of the client regardless of whether the attorney sends copies to all parties.

Answer to Question 36

(B)   The attorney must advise the president to keep the records because the records have potential evidentiary value if the company is sued. A lawyer must not counsel or assist a person to destroy material that has "potential evidentiary value." [ABA Model Rule 3.4(a)] Although it is not certain that the company manufactured the dishwasher in question, the president said he was "pretty sure that it was one of ours." Furthermore, it is not certain that the company will be sued if it was one of their washers, but the chances are good that it will be. If commencement of proceedings can be foreseen, the documents have potential evidentiary value and cannot be destroyed. [Comment 2 to ABA Model Rule 3.4] (A) is wrong because even if the company's records retention program called for the routine shredding of these records long ago, they were not shredded then, and they have potential evidentiary value now. (C) is wrong because commencement of proceedings is foreseeable. (D) is wrong because the standard is backward. The records should be preserved until the company is certain that the dishwasher in question was *not* manufactured by the company.

Answer to Question 37

(C)   The attorney's conduct was not proper unless he informed the legislators that he was appearing in a representative capacity. When a lawyer appears before a nonadjudicative body on behalf of a client, he must disclose that he is acting in a representative capacity. [ABA Model Rule 3.9] One important purpose of the Rule is to enable the members of the nonadjudicative body to assess the biases that may influence the lawyer's testimony. In this case, the legislators might well think that the attorney was speaking in his capacity as a wetlands expert, rather than as a developer's spokesman. (A) is wrong because the attorney should have told the legislators that he was acting in a representative capacity, whether or not his testimony was consistent with his own views. (B) is wrong; indeed, the fact that he is an expert in his own right makes his appearance particularly misleading. (D) is wrong because it invokes a nonexistent rule. There are limits on when a client's trial counsel may testify in a court proceeding, but no such limits apply in nonadjudicatory proceedings.

Answer to Question 38

(A)   The attorney is subject to criminal liability because she knew that the fifth bystander did not remember the color of the light. The crime of subornation of perjury is the corrupt procurement of perjured testimony. [*See* R. Perkins & R. Boyce, Criminal Law (hereinafter "Perkins & Boyce") 524-26 (3d ed. 1982)] Perjured testimony means a false oath in a judicial proceeding in regard to a material matter. [*Id.*] A false oath means a willful and corrupt sworn statement made without sincere belief

in its truthfulness. [*Id.*] In this case, the falsehood was not about the color of the traffic light, but rather about the fifth bystander's **memory** of the color of the traffic light. The fifth bystander testified that he saw the light and remembered what color it was—but in truth, he did not remember. The attorney knew that the bystander did not remember, and the attorney knew that the bystander knew that he did not remember. Therefore, the attorney is guilty of subornation of perjury. (B) and (C) are both incorrect because they focus on the wrong thing—the color of the light, rather than the witness's memory. (D) is generally correct statement, but it does not apply here. A criminal defense lawyer must indeed resolve doubtful facts in her client's favor, but the state of the bystander's memory was not a doubtful fact—the bystander told the attorney at the outset that he "simply could not remember what color the traffic light was."

Answer to Question 39

(C)   The law professor would be subject to discipline for representing the elderly couple because his earlier service as neutral arbitrator creates a conflict of interest. A lawyer must not represent a private client in a matter in which the lawyer has earlier participated personally and substantially while serving as an arbitrator. [ABA Model Rule 1.12(a)] (A) is wrong because the consistency of his position does not solve the conflict of interest. (B) is wrong because it does not go far enough. Informed consent, confirmed in writing, by both landowners would solve the conflict, but consent by the elderly couple alone will not suffice (and their consent was not confirmed in writing). (D) is wrong because it invokes a nonexistent rule;

unlike judges, lawyers are not expected
to be impartial. Here, the law professor
would be acting as an advocate, not as
a judge or arbitrator; thus, he should be
partial to his client. The issue here is not
partiality but conflict of interest.

Answer to Question 40

(D)   The communication with the reporters
was proper, but the statements made to
the jury were not. A judge should not
"commend or criticize jurors for their
verdict other than in a court order or
opinion in a proceeding." A judge's
commendation or criticism may impair
a juror's ability to be impartial in a
subsequent case. [CJC Rule 2.8(C)] The
judge's statements to the jury clearly
violate this Rule; thus, (A) and (C) are
incorrect. Although judges should not
comment on pending cases in a manner
that might interfere with fairness, judges
are not prohibited from making public
statements in the course of their official
duties or from explaining for public
information the procedures of the court.
[CJC Rule 2.10(D)] The judge's explanation of the motions to the reporters
was an appropriate way to inform the
public of the meaning and significance
of the judge's decision to reject the $500
million verdict; thus, (B) and (C) are
incorrect.

Answer to Question 41

(B)   It would not be proper for the attorney
to split his fee with the State B lawyer
because the written fee agreement with
the client does not comply with the ABA
Model Rules. ABA Model Rule 1.5(e)
allows a lawyer to split a fee with a
lawyer who is not in his firm if: (1) the
total fee is reasonable; (2) the split is in
proportion to the services rendered by
each lawyer, or in some other proportion

if each lawyer assumes joint responsibility for the matter; and (3) the client
agrees to the split in a writing that
discloses the share that each lawyer will
receive. Here, the written fee agreement did not specify the share that each
lawyer will receive; thus, a fee split
between the attorney and the State B
lawyer would be improper. (A) is wrong
because there is no requirement that a
lawyer be licensed in the same state as
the lawyer with whom he is splitting a
fee. (C) is wrong because the written
fee agreement with the client did not
indicate the share that each lawyer will
receive, and thus the agreement was
improper regardless of whether the State
B lawyer was assuming responsibility
for his work. (D) is wrong because even
though there was a fee agreement, it did
not comply with the ABA Model Rules.

Answer to Question 42

(A)   The attorney may join the board of
directors, but she must refrain from
participating in the decision about the
case intake guidelines. A lawyer may
not participate in a legal service board
decision that may adversely affect one
of the lawyer's clients. [ABA Model
Rule 6.3(b)] (B) is wrong because ABA
Model Rule 6.3 encourages work with
a legal services organization, even if
the organization serves people whose
interests conflict with the interests of
the lawyer's clients. (C) and (D) are
wrong because ABA Model Rule 6.3(b)
prohibits a lawyer from taking part in a
legal services organization decision if
the decision will adversely affect one of
the lawyer's clients.

Answer to Question 43

(B)   The judge must not disqualify the
attorney because the employee and the

construction company gave informed consent, confirmed in writing, to the joint representation. The interests of the employee and the construction company are in potential conflict with respect to the agency issue: If the employee were on a frolic of his own, the construction company will not be liable, but if he were acting within the scope of his duties, the construction company will be liable. A lawyer may represent two clients in civil litigation if their interests are potentially in conflict, provided that the lawyer: (1) reasonably believes he can represent both clients effectively; (2) discloses the potential conflict and explains how it can harm each client; and (3) obtains informed consent, confirmed in writing, from each client. Because it appears that the employee was not negligent, the conflict between the employee and the construction company is only potential. The attorney apparently believes that he can represent both parties effectively and took all of the right steps to deal with this potential conflict. Because the employee and the construction company gave informed consent in writing, the trial judge should refuse to disqualify the attorney. [ABA Model Rule 1.7(b); Restatement §122] The judge should also consider that it is the plaintiffs who seek the disqualification; one may reasonably conclude that they were trying to harass the defendants rather than serve the interests of justice. (A) is wrong because, as discussed above, there is a potential conflict between the employee and the construction company. (C) is wrong because the potential conflict has been handled properly and does not create an appearance of impropriety. Furthermore, avoiding the "appearance of impropriety" is an outdated concept from the old ABA Model Code. The term does

not appear in the ABA Model Rules because its meaning is too uncertain to be useful in a professional code of conduct. (D) is wrong because informed consent, confirmed in writing, is sufficient in this situation. A client cannot be asked to consent when a disinterested lawyer would conclude that the client's interests would not be adequately protected in light of the conflict. Here, the conflict is merely *potential*; thus, a disinterested lawyer could conclude that the clients can agree to the representation. Consequently, the employee's and the construction company's informed consent, confirmed in writing, are sufficient to solve the potential conflict of interest.

Answer to Question 44

(B) A lawyer must withdraw if the lawyer's physical or mental condition will materially impair his ability to represent the client. [ABA Model Rule 1.16(a)(2)] The client may be right in thinking that hard work will be good for the attorney, but the attorney has to be the ultimate judge of his own physical and mental capacity to carry on. If the attorney believes that his condition prevents him from serving the client competently, he must withdraw regardless of what the client wants. (A) is wrong because the files include confidential information about the client's financial affairs, and the attorney cannot turn them over to his law partner against the client's express wishes. [ABA Model Rule 1.6] (C) is wrong because the client has asked the attorney to complete the work promptly. The attorney's recovery may take months or years. The attorney must not continue representing the client unless he can complete the work with reasonable diligence and promptness. [ABA Model Rule 1.3] (D) is wrong because, as discussed above, if the attorney believes his mental and physical conditions prevent him from serving the client competently, he must withdraw.

Answer to Question 45

(B) The attorney may withdraw from the case and keep the employee's statement in confidence. When an organization is the lawyer's client, the lawyer owes a duty of loyalty to the organization. When the interests of the organization and its constituents conflict, the lawyer should remind the person that the lawyer represents the organization and not the person. It would be appropriate for the lawyer to remind the person that communications between them may not be protected by the attorney-client privilege, and that the person may want to obtain independent counsel. [ABA Model Rule 1.13] Here, the attorney should not have asked the question unless he was prepared for an affirmative answer. He should have known before asking that if the answer was yes, the employee's interests and the marine supply company's interests would conflict; thus, the attorney should not have offered to represent the employee, and certainly should not have promised to keep the employee's statements in confidence. (Note that the attorney could be subject to discipline for this conduct.) The issue here, however, is what course of action the attorney may now take. Now that the attorney has agreed to represent the employee, and the employee has confessed in confidence, the only thing the attorney can do is withdraw from the matter entirely and keep the employee's confession in confidence. [*See* ABA Model Rule 1.9] (A) is wrong because he would violate the employee's confidence by disclosing

the confession to the Attorney General. (C) and (D) are wrong because revealing the employee's confession to the marine supply company would also violate the employee's confidence.

Answer to Question 46

(B) A lawyer is permitted to "make a statement that a reasonable lawyer would believe is required to protect a client from the substantial undue prejudicial effect of recent publicity not initiated by the lawyer or the lawyer's client." [ABA Model Rule 3.6(c)] The attorney is permitted to make these clarifying statements in response to the true, but incomplete, statements made by the prosecutor at a press conference. Thus, (D) is incorrect. (A) and (C) are incorrect because the attorney has 10 years of experience handling pro bono criminal defense cases, and his win-loss ratio may be reflecting the underlying merits of the cases rather than the attorney's trial ability.

Answer to Question 47

(B) This arrangement is proper if the fee is reasonable under the circumstances. As long as the fee paid does not turn out to be excessive, taking into account the attorney's risk of not being paid, the delay in payment, etc., this arrangement is acceptable. A lawyer may enter into a business relationship with a client, provided certain safeguards, such as an opportunity to consult with independent counsel, are used. [ABA Model Rule 1.8(a)] (A) is wrong because although it is improper to use a contingent fee in a criminal case, this fee is not a contingent fee. Whether the attorney gets paid does not depend on the outcome of the case; it depends on how well the movie does. (C) is wrong because it is not clear that any amount over $1 million is excessive, given that the attorney is risking that he will be paid nothing and is delaying payment by a substantial period of time. (D) is wrong because it misstates or incompletely states the Rule. The Rule is that *prior to the conclusion of the representation of the client*, a lawyer cannot acquire media rights to a story based substantially on information relating to the representation. In this case, the movie does not relate to the current representation, rather it involves past representations in the attorney's career. While the attorney could not disclose any information related to those representations without the clients' consents, the acquisition of such media rights is not improper.

Answer to Question 48

(D)   ABA Model Rule 1.18 provides that a lawyer must not use or reveal confidential information of a prospective client. [*See also* ABA Model Rule 1.6] Here, the information communicated to the patent attorney was not confidential; thus, the patent attorney's undertaking representation of the pharmaceutical corporation did not create a concurrent conflict of interest—there is no significant risk that the representation of the pharmaceutical corporation would be materially limited by the patent attorney's responsibilities to the bioengineering firm. Consequently, the patent attorney may continue to represent the pharmaceutical corporation. (A) is wrong because it does not matter that the bioengineering firm previously consulted the patent attorney on the same matter if the patent attorney did not obtain any confidential information that would limit her representation of the pharmaceutical corporation, and she does not breach

any duty owed to the bioengineering firm. (B) is wrong for the same reason as (A)—even if the infringement suit is substantially related to the patent attorney's conversation with the bioengineering firm's representatives, unless the patent attorney obtained confidential information from the bioengineering firm, she may represent the pharmaceutical corporation. (C) is not as good as (D) because (C) is general, while (D) is specifically on point. Here, the patent attorney did not get any material confidential information from the bioengineering firm's representatives during the preliminary conversation, but if she had, she would be subject to disqualification as defense counsel, even though the bioengineering firm never became the patent attorney's actual client.

Answer to Question 49

(D)   The attorney is subject to litigation sanction because Federal Rule of Civil Procedure 11 provides that sanctions can be imposed on a lawyer, firm, or party for filing a pleading, motion, or other paper merely to harass, delay, or multiply expenses for the opponent. [*See also* Hudson Motors Partnership v. Crest Leasing Enterprises, Inc., 845 F. Supp. 969 (E.D.N.Y. 1994)—federal courts have inherent power to sanction lawyers for frivolous legal positions to harass or delay; *and see* 28 U.S.C. §1927—court can impose sanctions on lawyers who knowingly or recklessly multiply proceedings unreasonably and vexatiously] (A) is incorrect because it is beyond the bounds of the law to harass an opponent with a legal position that the proponent knows is frivolous. (B) is incorrect because Rule 11 allows the court to sanction both the lawyers and the parties they represent. (C) is incorrect because lawyers are not subject to litigation sanction for taking legal positions that they, in good faith, believe to be meritorious.

Answer to Question 50

(D)   A lawyer is subject to discipline for trying to avoid a court appointment without good cause. [ABA Model Rule 6.2] (D) is good cause because the attorney's severe depression is preventing him from handling his existing caseload competently. [*See* comment 2 to ABA Model Rule 6.2—good cause exists if the lawyer could not handle the matter competently; *and see* ABA Model Rule 1.16(a)(2)—requiring withdrawal when the lawyer's physical or mental condition materially impairs the lawyer's ability to represent the client] (A) is not good cause because a lawyer's belief that the defendant is guilty is not a sufficient reason to turn down a court appointment. Competent defense of a murder case certainly does not require a defense lawyer to believe in the client's innocence. (B) is not good cause because the facts state that the attorney is three years out of law school and practices criminal defense law. That indicates that his training in criminal law and procedure is recent, and that he knows how to defend a criminal case, even though he has not handled a murder case before. Thus, the attorney cannot claim lack of competence as an excuse for turning down the appointment. [*See* Hazard & Hodes, §51.3] ABA Model Rule 6.2(c) recognizes that a lawyer may turn down an appointment if the client or cause is so repugnant to him as to interfere in the lawyer-client relationship. Neither the attorney's race nor his sympathy for young people who get involved with gangs should be regarded,

without more, as likely to interfere with the attorney's ability to represent the police officer competently. Thus, (C) is not good cause.

Answer to Question 51

(C)   The attorney was not representing either sister; rather, he was acting as a third-party neutral to help them resolve their differences. ABA Model Rule 2.4 permits a lawyer to serve in that role. ABA Model Rule 1.12(c) permits screening to avoid a conflict in this situation. Therefore, (A) and (D) are incorrect. (B) is incorrect because, when a lawyer has served as a third-party neutral between two conflicted parties, he cannot later represent one of the parties in that matter, unless both parties give informed consent, confirmed in writing. [ABA Model Rule 1.12(a)]

Answer to Question 52

(A)   The attorney does not need to be admitted to practice in the new state because the JAG Corps is an organ of the federal government, and Army regulations authorize JAG officers to provide legal services to Army personnel and their dependents on a wide range of personal legal problems. [*See* ABA Model Rule 5.5(d)(2)] But before she advises the officer and his wife, the attorney must do enough research to become competent on the legal aspects of mobile home financing. [*See* comment 2 to ABA Model Rule 1.1] (B) is wrong because she is willing to undertake the additional study necessary to become competent in these matters, and therefore her current lack of knowledge is not dispositive. [*See* comment 2 to ABA Model Rule 1.1] (C) is wrong for the reason stated in the explanation of (A), above. (D) is wrong because the problem specifies that Army regulations authorize a legal assistance officer to give legal advice on a wide range of personal legal problems that affect military personnel and their dependents. These regulations reflect the Army's strong interest in keeping its people out of legal troubles no matter what the source.

Answer to Question 53

(B)   ABA Model Rule 7.2(b)(4) permits a lawyer to make a reciprocal referral agreement with another lawyer, or with a nonlawyer professional, if the agreement is not exclusive and the referred person is told about the agreement. However, comment 8 to ABA Model Rule 7.2 cautions lawyers that such an agreement should not be indefinite in duration. (A) is wrong because ABA Model Rule 7.2(b)(4) does not require a reciprocal referral agreement to be in writing. (C) is wrong because reciprocal referral agreements are one of four exceptions to the general rule that a lawyer must not give something of value for a referral. [*See* ABA Model Rule 7.2(b)] (D) is wrong because ABA Model Rule 7.2(b)(4) expressly permits reciprocal referral agreements with nonlawyer professionals.

Answer to Question 54

(C)   ABA Model Rule 7.6 prohibits "a lawyer or law firm" from accepting an appointed legal engagement if "the lawyer or law firm" makes a political contribution "for the purpose of obtaining or being considered for" that kind of legal engagement. The tricky part of this question is whether a political contribution by one of the firm's lawyers ought to bar the entire firm from taking subsequent appointments. Neither the Rule nor its comments speak

directly to that point, but the purpose of the Rule would be served by imputing one lawyer's contribution to the entire firm, just as a conflict of interest would be imputed under ABA Model Rule 1.10(a). To adopt the opposite position would make ABA Model Rule 7.6 too easy to evade—the firm could simply ask its lawyers to make "pay-to-play" contributions from their own pockets. Using a different theory, at least the founding partner's colleagues on the management committee should be barred from accepting appointments from the attorney general because they knew about the partner's political contributions and thanked him rather than stopped him. [*See* ABA Model Rule 5.1(c)—ratification or acquiescence by managing lawyers] (B) is wrong for the reasons stated above. (A) is wrong because the partner's practice of contributing generously to all candidates who have a reasonable chance to win the attorney generalship demonstrates that his purpose is to secure business for the firm, not to participate legitimately in the political process. (D) is not as good as (C) because (D) relies on the outdated "appearance of impropriety" rubric of the old ABA Model Code, Canon 9. That rubric was cast aside in the ABA Model Rules—seeking to avoid even the "appearance of impropriety" is useful in a person's own moral creed, but it is too amorphous to be useful in a professional code of conduct.

Answer to Question 55

(A)   (A) is correct because the retired attorney's dispensation of legal advice constitutes the "practice of law," and he is doing it in a jurisdiction where he is not licensed. [*See* ABA Model Rule 5.5(a)] (B) is incorrect because the retired attorney is under no obligation to pay bar dues in a state where he no longer lives or practices. (C) is incorrect because one does need to be licensed in order to dispense legal advice at a walk-in legal clinic. [*See* ABA Model Rule 6.5, which loosens the conflict of interest rules for clinic lawyers but does not authorize them to practice without a license] A law student or similar unlicensed person can work at such a clinic under the close supervision of a lawyer, but the question makes no mention of the retired attorney's work being supervised. [*See* comment 1 to ABA Model Rule 5.3] (D) is incorrect because there is a lawyer-client relationship between the retired attorney and his walk-in clients. [Comment 1 to ABA Model Rule 6.5] One element of that relationship is the lawyer's duty of confidentiality [ABA Model Rule 1.6], and the retired attorney breaches that duty when he tells his wife about his clients' legal troubles.

Answer to Question 56

(B) The attorney's real estate brokerage business is a "law-related service" within the meaning of ABA Model Rule 5.7, and the attorney offers her real estate brokerage services "in circumstances that are not distinct from" her provision of legal services. [*See* ABA Model Rule 5.7(a)(1)] That means that she must follow the rules of legal ethics in her real estate brokerage work as well as her law work. [*Id.*] One of the legal ethics rules forbids a lawyer from initiating live person-to-person contact with a person known to need legal services in a particular matter when a significant motive for doing so is the lawyer's pecuniary gain. [*See* ABA Model Rule 7.3(b)] Therefore, the attorney must not

initiate face-to-face contact with potential real estate clients to interest them in using her brokerage services. (A) is wrong because it overstates the rule expressed in ABA Model Rule 5.7. (C) is wrong because it turns ABA Model Rule 5.7 on its head—because the attorney is offering her ancillary service in circumstances that are not distinct from her legal service, she must follow the legal ethics rule for both kinds of service. (D) is wrong because the attorney's face-to-face pitches violate the no-solicitation rule even if her statements are truthful and not misleading. [*Compare* ABA Model Rule 7.1 *with* ABA Model Rule 7.3(b)]

Answer to Question 57

(D) (D) is false. CJC Rule 2.11(C) explains remittal of a judge's disqualification, and remittal requires the agreement of all of the parties and their lawyers, not the other justices. (A) is true. ABA Model Rule 1.17 permits the sale of an entire law practice, or an area of practice, subject to some conditions, all of which are met here. (B) is true. ABA Model Rule 1.17(d) provides that when a practice is sold, the fees charged to the clients cannot be increased by reason of the sale. (C) is true. CJC Rule 2.11(A)(6)(a) says that a judge must disqualify himself if he previously served as a lawyer in the matter.

Answer to Question 58

(B) The controlling doctrine in this case is the lawyer's ethical duty of confidentiality, not the attorney-client privilege. The attorney needs to know whether he can *voluntarily* reveal the client's confession, not whether he would be forced to do so if he were put on the witness stand in a court. ABA Model

Rule 1.6(b)(1) states the applicable exception to the ethical duty of confidentiality: A lawyer *may* reveal confidential information if the lawyer reasonably believes that doing so is necessary to prevent reasonably certain death or substantial bodily harm. One might quibble whether the innocent man's death is "reasonably certain" when his trial has not even started, but surely the ethics rule should not be read to require the innocent man to order his last meal before being loosed from the executioner's grip. (A) is wrong because ABA Model Rule 1.6(b)(1) gives the lawyer *discretion* to reveal the client's confession; the Rule does not force him to do so. [*See* comment 15 to ABA Model Rule 1.6] (A few states go farther and *require* disclosure to prevent death or substantial bodily harm, but they are a small minority.) (C) is wrong for two reasons. First, the applicable doctrine is the ethical duty of confidentiality, not the attorney-client privilege. Second, even if the privilege were the applicable doctrine, who could claim it in this situation? The client cannot because he is dead. The client's executor cannot because the client's estate was closed and the executor was discharged. The attorney cannot claim it because a lawyer's right to claim the privilege is only derivative from the client. (D) is wrong for two reasons. First, the admissibility of this hearsay is irrelevant to the ethics issue. Second, the client's confession would likely be admissible if offered by the innocent man against the prosecution because it is a declaration against penal interest by an unavailable declarant, and the client's will and suicide are independent evidence of the confession's trustworthiness. [*See* Fed. R. Evid. 804(b)(3); *see also* Chambers v. Mississippi, 410 U.S. 284 (1973)—due process violation where another man's confession was excluded in a murder trial]

Answer to Question 59

(C)   ABA Model Rule 1.13 governs this question. The attorney has been informed about the stated intent of a university admissions director to violate the voter initiative in a manner that imperils 45% of the university's funding. The attorney began her conversation with the admissions director in a proper manner by reminding him that she is the university's lawyer, not his lawyer. However, the attorney may not allow her personal views about the use of race in university admissions to affect how she responds to the director's stated intent. Here, the voters have spoken by passing the initiative, the university's board of overseers has acquiesced in the initiative, and the constitutional challenge to the initiative has failed. If the attorney feels strongly enough about the issue to resign her position, she may do so [*see* ABA Model Rule 1.16(b)(4)], but she cannot remain in the general counsel's office while subverting the voter initiative. Thus, (A) is wrong. (C) is correct; if the attorney cannot convince the admissions director to obey the voter initiative, she *must* "refer the matter to higher authority in the organization." [ABA Model Rule 1.13(b) and comment 4] In this instance, the attorney's immediate boss, the general counsel, is the obvious first choice. ABA Model Rule 1.13 requires the attorney to report up the chain of command, not leap immediately to the top rung. [*Id.*] Only if her report to the general counsel proves futile should she take the matter to the board of overseers, and if she needs to report it to the board of overseers, she should do so forthrightly, not by an "anonymous leak" that the board would be likely to ignore. Therefore, (D) is wrong. (B) is wrong because it appears to allow the attorney to report first to the state attorney general, who should be regarded as outside the structure of the university for this purpose. [*See* ABA Model Rule 1.13(c)] True, the university is part of the state, and the attorney general is the state's highest law enforcement official, but ABA Model Rule 1.13 seeks to have legal issues resolved at the lowest possible command level, not the highest possible level. [*Compare* Rule 1.13(b) *with* 1.13(c) and comment 6]

Answer to Question 60

(D) This question is governed by ABA Model Rule 1.18, which concerns duties to a prospective client. The information that the attorney obtained about the prospective client's alcohol abuse and his violent response to the stranger's comment could be harmful to the prospective client if the wife uses it to help prove that the couple should be divorced and that the prospective client should not be given custody of their children. Therefore, the attorney herself could not represent the wife in the divorce and child custody case. [*See* ABA Model Rule 1.18(c)] The attorney's disqualification is imputed to her law partner. [*Id.*] However, if the conditions mentioned in (D) are satisfied, then her law partner may continue representing the wife. [*See* ABA Model Rule 1.18(d)(2)] (C) is wrong because it calls for informed consent by the wife only. ABA Model Rule 1.18(d)(1) would require informed consent, confirmed in writing, from both the prospective client and the wife. (B) is wrong because the two matters are "substantially related"

[ABA Model Rule 1.18(c)] in that use of the information that the prospective client disclosed to the attorney could be harmful to the prospective client if used in the divorce and child custody case. (A) is wrong because it ignores the two possible ways that would allow the law partner to continue representing the wife. [ABA Model Rule 1.18(d)(1), (2)]

PRACTICE SET 2

Question 1

A corporation is named as the defendant in an employment discrimination suit. The corporation's attorney has scheduled the taking of a deposition of one of the corporation's employees who is in poor health, as a precaution in case the employee should die before trial. The employee is not an officer or shareholder in the corporation, and he is not a party to the lawsuit. He is in charge of the corporation's personnel department, and he is responsible for ensuring that the corporation's hiring practices comply with the laws against employment discrimination. Without seeking the consent of the corporation's attorney, or even telling him, the plaintiffs' attorney had lunch with this employee several days before the deposition, and on that occasion the plaintiffs' attorney pumped the employee for information relevant to the lawsuit. When the corporation's attorney learned what had happened, he telephoned the plaintiffs' attorney and called him a slimy, mud-sucking sneak.

Which of the following is correct?

(A) The corporation's attorney's conduct was proper.

(B) The plaintiffs' attorney's conduct was proper.

(C) The plaintiffs' attorney is subject to discipline because he should not have talked with the employee about the case without the consent of the corporation's attorney.

(D) The plaintiffs' attorney is subject to discipline because he talked with a deposition witness about the subject of the litigation before the deposition was taken.

Question 2

A juvenile charged with auto theft, which is a felony, hires an attorney to represent him. Before the case comes to trial, his attorney confers with the prosecutor who has been assigned to prosecute the case. The prosecutor suggests to the juvenile's attorney that, because her client is a juvenile, the charge might be reduced to "joyriding," a misdemeanor. The juvenile's attorney flatly refuses without explanation, unreasonably, in the prosecutor's opinion.

It would be improper conduct for the prosecutor to:

(A) Ask the court to dismiss the auto theft charge and prosecute the juvenile for joyriding.

(B) Prosecute the auto theft charge.

(C) Send an investigator to talk to the juvenile about the offer to lower charges.

(D) Remind the juvenile's attorney of the duty to communicate settlement offers to the client.

GO ON TO THE NEXT PAGE

Question 3

A man who has been arrested and charged with aggravated battery hires an attorney recommended to him by his brother. Neither the accused nor his brother knows that the attorney plans to run for public office and is always interested in getting as much publicity as possible. She is often referred to in the press as a "hotshot" criminal defense attorney, and almost all of her victories over the state are publicized. Before the accused's trial begins, the assistant district attorney ("ADA") who has been assigned by the district attorney's office to prosecute the case suggests to the accused's attorney that, because her client is a first-time offender and an otherwise model citizen, and there were certain extenuating circumstances that would cause a jury to be sympathetic to him, the charge might be reduced to simple battery, a misdemeanor. The attorney refuses, telling the ADA that she is not about to cop a misdemeanor plea for her client because her client is socially prominent, and trying the case will bring both a great deal of publicity and greater vindication for her client. The attorney did not discuss the misdemeanor plea with her client, and the case proceeded to trial. During trial, the attorney held daily press conferences, which kept both the attorney and her client in the public eye. Ultimately, the accused was found not guilty of the felony charge.

Is the attorney subject to discipline?

(A) Yes, because the attorney stated that one of her motives was to gain publicity.

(B) Yes, because the attorney did not convey the offer of a lesser charge to her client.

(C) No, because the attorney competently represented her client.

(D) No, because the client's complete exoneration at trial was a better outcome than agreeing to plead guilty to a lesser charge.

Question 4

During his second year in law school, a law student's wife divorced him, as a result of which he suffered serious emotional imbalance. Ultimately, he managed to graduate, and the state bar sent a routine form letter to one of his professors, asking her to comment on the law student's fitness to practice law. The professor is a member of the bar of that state. In response, she gave her candid opinion—that the law student was prone to extreme and irrational tirades against women, and that he was not yet recovered from his emotional trauma. Based partly on this information, the state bar denied the law student's petition for admission. Now, three years later, the law student has asked the professor to support his re-petition for admission. After carefully checking the facts, the professor concludes that the law student has regained his emotional balance.

Which of the following is correct?

(A) Three years ago, it would have been proper for the professor to keep her opinion to herself because emotional imbalance is not a valid ground for denying admission to the bar.

(B) Three years ago, it would have been proper for the professor to keep her opinion to herself because she is untrained in psychology or the science of emotional illness.

(C) Now, the professor may support the law student's re-petition because she believes that he has regained his emotional balance.

(D) Now, the professor may remain neutral because she is untrained in psychology or the science of emotional illness.

GO ON TO THE NEXT PAGE

Question 5

An attorney has a high-profile divorce law practice in the town in which he resides. Because of his heavy caseload, the attorney often appears before the four chancery judges of the county court. One of the chancery judges is getting married, and he sends a wedding invitation to the attorney. The attorney wishes to send the judge, as a wedding gift, an imported Italian machine that makes espresso and cappuccino coffee because he knows that the judge loves fine coffee. The coffee machine sells for $200 at the town's best cooking equipment store. The attorney sent the coffee machine to the judge, and the judge duly made a public report of the gift.

Was it proper for the attorney to send the coffee machine to the judge?

(A) Yes, because the judge would not be unduly influenced by a $200 gift.

(B) Yes, because the judge made a public report of the gift.

(C) No, because the gift was not a campaign contribution, and lawyers should not give other types of gifts to judges.

(D) No, because the value of the gift exceeded $150.

Question 6

The state in which a tax attorney practices levies an annual tax on trusts for the benefit of minors. Tax returns must be filed, and the taxes must be paid, by March 15; late filing results in an automatic penalty of 15%. In mid-January, the trustee of such a trust retained the attorney to prepare and file a tax return. The trustee heard nothing from the attorney during February, and he became seriously alarmed when the first week of March passed with no apparent action from the attorney. He called the attorney repeatedly during late February and early March, but each time the attorney was in a conference, in court, or in a deposition. The attorney never returned any of the trustee's phone calls. On March 10, the trustee fired the attorney and hired a certified public accountant to do the necessary work. She was able to complete the tax return and get it filed on time.

Is the attorney subject to discipline?

(A) Yes, even though the March 15 deadline had not yet passed.

(B) No, because the attorney had legitimate excuses for not taking the client's calls.

(C) No, because the March 15 deadline had not passed.

(D) No, because neither the trustee nor the trust suffered any loss.

GO ON TO THE NEXT PAGE

Question 7

A district court judge heard through the "courthouse grapevine" that the district attorney was investigating corrupt practices in the courts and that the investigation focused on some as yet unascertained time in the past. The "rumor mill" also indicated that several judges and former judges were likely to be indicted for taking bribes to "fix" cases and to generate business for certain lawyers. The judge was alarmed at this news, and he telephoned a retired attorney, arranging to meet him for cocktails and dinner. At the restaurant, the judge slipped the maitre d' a 10-dollar bill to secure seating at a secluded corner booth. Over dinner, the judge told the retired attorney that he had accepted bribes in the past and that he did not know what he should do in light of the district attorney's investigation. The retired attorney advised the judge to do nothing. The judge picked up the $120 dinner tab, and the retired attorney thanked him for the fine meal.

A month later, indictments were handed down against two sitting judges and three former judges. The judge was not among them, and it turned out that the period covered by the district attorney's investigation was prior to the judge's election to the bench. Six months after the indictments were announced, a member of the state appellate court died, and the governor announced that he was appointing the judge to serve the remaining three years of the justice's unexpired term.

Must the retired attorney report his knowledge of corruption in office by the judge?

(A) Yes, because the retired attorney never entered into an attorney-client relationship with the judge.

(B) Yes, because the retired attorney's knowledge bears upon maintaining the integrity of the courts, which takes precedence over other ethical considerations.

(C) No, because the retired attorney is retired from practice.

(D) No, because the judge's disclosures to the retired attorney dealt with past crimes.

GO ON TO THE NEXT PAGE

Question 8

In a trade secret action against a corporation pending in a United States district court, the plaintiff's lawyer gave timely notice that on July 22 at 9 a.m., he would take the deposition of the corporation's vice president for manufacturing and marketing. From earlier discovery in the case, the plaintiff's lawyer had good reason to believe that the vice president's testimony would prove that the corporation had stolen and was using the plaintiff's trade secrets. On the appointed day, the defense attorney showed up with no witness; she explained that the vice president was a very busy man and had been unavoidably detained on a trip to one of the corporation's factories in Asia. The plaintiff's lawyer rescheduled the deposition for August 3, and the defense attorney promised to have the witness available that day.

On August 3, the defense attorney again showed up with no witness, explaining that he had to take his aged mother to the doctor that day. The plaintiff's lawyer rescheduled the deposition for August 14. On August 14, the defense attorney showed up for the deposition in the company of a nine-year-old boy, whom she introduced as the vice president. Upon questioning by the plaintiff's lawyer, the defense attorney laughingly explained that the young boy was the vice president's son, that he knew nothing about the case, and that the vice president was unable to attend. At that point, the plaintiff's lawyer invited the defense attorney to accompany him to see the judge to whom the case was assigned.

After hearing the story, the judge asked the defense attorney what day and time the witness would assuredly be available, and the defense attorney said that August 16 would be good. The judge then entered a formal order that the deposition would be taken that day. The judge also warned that the defense

attorney would be sanctioned if she did not present the witness on August 16, and that the issues of trade secret misappropriation and use would be deemed proven in plaintiff's favor. Alas, on August 16, the defense attorney again showed up alone, explaining that the vice president had to make an unexpected trip out of state. After appropriate notice and hearing, the judge ordered that the issues of trade secret misappropriation and use would be deemed proven in plaintiff's favor. She also ordered the vice president to pay 60% of the plaintiff's expenses and attorneys' fees incurred because of the failed deposition attempts, and she ordered the defense attorney to pay the other 40% of plaintiff's expenses and attorneys' fees.

Was the judge correct in holding the defense attorney subject to litigation sanction?

(A) Yes, because the defense attorney violated the court's discovery order by showing up on August 16 without the witness.

(B) Yes, because the facts show that the defense attorney acted obstinately and disrespectfully in defiance of the judge's direct order.

(C) No, because the facts show that the defense attorney could not control the witness, and that she was therefore not at fault when he failed to show up on August 16.

(D) No, because when a party or a managing agent of a party violates a discovery order, the sanction must be imposed on the party or managing agent, not on the lawyer.

GO ON TO THE NEXT PAGE

Question 9

While she was attending law school at night, a law student served as a clerk for a judge of the county court. During the course of her employment, a public interest case came before the judge. The case was very complicated, and the law student did a lot of research on the case for the judge, submitting a number of memoranda on issues in the case. The judge always carefully supervised his clerks, and this case was no exception. He was exceptionally pleased with the care and high quality of the law student's work. Shortly after the judge handed down his final judgment, the law student graduated, was admitted to the bar, and accepted employment with a prominent local law firm. A few days later, the defendant from that case, who lost, appeared at the offices of the law firm. He told the interviewing attorney that his trial attorney was terrible. He wants the firm to handle his appeal.

If the law firm accepts the client, and the former law student's supervising attorney asks her to handle the appeal, would it be proper for the former law student to do so?

(A) Yes, because no confidential information was revealed to the former law student during her work on the case for the judge.

(B) Yes, because the former law student was not licensed to practice law when she worked on the case for the judge.

(C) No, because the judge must consent.

(D) No, because the former law student was previously personally and substantially involved in work on the case.

Question 10

The State Bar and the State University are joint sponsors of the State Continuing Legal Education Foundation. The purpose of the foundation is to provide continuing legal education to lawyers and judges in the state. Its board of directors is composed one-half of members of the legal profession and one-half of university personnel. A prominent judge has been invited to serve on the board of directors, and is offered the same modest salary paid to the other board members.

Which of the following is correct?

(A) The judge may serve on the board of directors if it does not interfere with her judicial duties.

(B) It would not be proper for the judge to serve on the board of directors because to do so would involve her in the teaching of law.

(C) It would not be proper for the judge to serve on the board of directors because she would necessarily be fraternizing with lawyers who had occasion to practice in her courtroom.

(D) The judge may serve on the board of directors, but it would not be proper for the judge to accept the modest salary that is paid to other directors.

GO ON TO THE NEXT PAGE

Question 11

An assistant district attorney ("ADA") has been assigned to prosecute a vagrant for petty theft and attempted sale of stolen property. The vagrant's arrest was the result of information provided by a local pawnbroker. The pawnbroker has himself been in trouble with the law on prior occasions, but he is not suspected of any present crime. The vagrant is represented by a public defender. The ADA wants to interview the pawnbroker for possible use as a prosecution witness.

Which of the following is correct?

(A) The ADA may interview the pawnbroker without the public defender's consent.

(B) The ADA may interview the pawnbroker without the public defender's consent, but he would be subject to discipline for inquiring about the pawnbroker's prior criminal record.

(C) The ADA would be subject to discipline if he interviewed the pawnbroker without the public defender's consent.

(D) The ADA may interview the pawnbroker, but only with the public defender's consent, and the ADA would be subject to discipline for inquiring about the pawnbroker's prior criminal record.

Question 12

Two cities are located right across the river from one another, in States A and B, respectively. Many people who live in one city work and shop in the other and vice versa. An attorney is admitted to practice in State A, but not State B, and has his law office in State A. When he is asked to represent a criminal defendant in the Superior Court of State B, he usually (but not always) refers the case to a crony who is admitted to practice in State B, but not State A, and has his law office in State B. Likewise, when the crony is asked to represent a client in the Superior Court of State A, he usually (but not always) refers the case to the attorney. The two attorneys have evolved their mutual arrangement in order to provide better service to their respective clients, and they always tell referred clients about the arrangement.

Is the arrangement proper?

(A) Yes, because the attorney is not licensed in State B, and his crony is not licensed in State A.

(B) Yes, because the arrangement between the two attorneys is nonexclusive and is always disclosed to referred clients.

(C) No, because, on the facts given, the referral fee could not be proportionate to the services rendered by the referring attorney, and there is no indication of joint representation.

(D) No, because a lawyer is not allowed to participate in a reciprocal referral arrangement with another lawyer.

GO ON TO THE NEXT PAGE

Question 13

An attorney was engaged in a partnership law practice for almost 10 years with his sister, who then decided to run for judge. She was successful in her efforts and was duly sworn in as one of the 15 sitting judges on the district court. According to state venue rules, at least 90% of the cases that the attorney usually handles must be filed with the district court. When opposing counsel in one of the attorney's cases learned that the attorney's sister was a judge, he objected. The attorney responded that it was his sister's duty to uphold the law and no one would receive special favors.

Is it proper for the attorney to handle such cases and appear before the district court?

(A) No, because an opposing party objected.

(B) No, because it creates an appearance of impropriety.

(C) No, because a lawyer should not appear in a district court where a close relative serves as one of the judges.

(D) Yes, because the attorney did not suggest that his clients will receive unfair advantages because his sister is a judge.

Question 14

A consumer who bought a defective product that injured him hired an attorney to represent him in a personal injury action against the large corporation that made the product. As the consumer and the attorney discussed the case, the consumer stated that he probably would not agree to a settlement under $500,000. The attorney agreed that the claim was worth at least that, but felt they would receive a much higher award if the case went to a jury. Shortly before the trial started, the lawyer for the corporation contacted the consumer's attorney with a settlement offer of $150,000. The consumer's attorney tried to call his client, but could not reach him. After two hours of trying to reach his client, the attorney called opposing counsel and rejected the offer. At trial, the jury awarded the consumer $1 million.

Is the consumer's attorney subject to malpractice liability for his actions?

(A) Yes, because a lawyer has a duty to keep his client informed of all settlement offers.

(B) Yes, because decisions to accept or reject settlement offers are to be made by the client.

(C) No, because the consumer impliedly authorized the attorney to reject any offer under $500,000.

(D) No, because the jury award was much greater than the settlement offer.

GO ON TO THE NEXT PAGE

Question 15

During the course of researching a reply brief, an attorney discovered a case in the controlling jurisdiction that seemed to be right on point on one of the key issues involved in the case on which she was working. Although much of the dicta in the case seemed to favor the attorney's client, one critical sentence in the holding clearly put the court behind the position asserted by opposing counsel. However, the opposing counsel had done a slipshod job of researching the issues and had failed to find the case and to cite it in his brief. The attorney decided to cite the case in her reply brief, but she cited the case as favoring her client by quoting much of the dicta and deliberately omitting the key sentence in the holding. The attorney filed the reply brief with the court and sent a copy to the opposing counsel, who she knew often bragged about not having read a case since law school. The attorney was also aware that this judge's clerks tended to be overworked and so did not always read all the cases cited by lawyers in their briefs. Therefore, she hoped that the negative aspects of the case might slip by unnoticed by the judge and opposing counsel.

Is the attorney subject to discipline?

(A)   Yes, because a lawyer has a duty to cite all opposing cases accurately and objectively.

(B)   Yes, because the attorney is attempting to mislead the tribunal.

(C)   No, because a lawyer has a duty to present cases in the light most favorable to her client.

(D)   No, because a lawyer has no duty to educate, and the attorney fulfilled her duties to the court and the opposing party by citing the case.

Question 16

An attorney had an office in a small town located on the extreme western border of the state in which he was licensed to practice. The attorney received a retainer from a client, with the agreement that the attorney would use funds from the retainer for such things as filing fees when they came due. There was no federally insured bank or savings institution in the small town in which the attorney's office was located. The nearest such institution in the state was located in the county seat, which was over 60 miles away from the attorney's office and where the attorney and the client resided. Therefore, the attorney decided, with the client's consent, to put the client's money in his client trust account in a bank in a medium-sized city located just across the state line in a neighboring state. The account was fully insured by the federal government, but was not an interest-bearing account. The attorney is not licensed to practice law in that state.

Was it proper for the attorney to place the client's money in an account in the neighboring state?

(A)   Yes, because retainer fees belong to the attorney and not to the client.

(B)   Yes, because the client consented to the deposit in the neighboring state.

(C)   No, because the attorney is not licensed to practice in the neighboring state.

(D)   No, because the funds were not placed in an interest-bearing account.

GO ON TO THE NEXT PAGE

Question 17

A man was charged with first degree murder. It is claimed that he captured his victim, dragged her into dense woods, and stabbed her with a knife. The accused has pleaded not guilty. During the prosecution's case-in-chief, one of the prosecutor's witnesses testified that he had seen the accused's car near the scene of the crime shortly before the murder. This courthouse has no private room set aside for conferences between defendants and their counsel. Thus, at the next recess, the accused and his attorney held a hurried, whispered conference in the hallway, during which the attorney asked the accused why he had not told him about driving around that area. The accused replied that he had not realized that anyone had seen him.

Unbeknownst to the accused and his attorney, the prosecutor was standing nearby and overheard their whispers.

Which of the following statements is correct?

(A) The prosecutor must seek the court's permission to withdraw as trial counsel and testify to what she heard.

(B) The prosecutor must ignore what she heard and proceed with the case in the normal manner.

(C) The defense attorney must seek the court's permission to withdraw as trial counsel and inform the trial judge in chambers what the accused said.

(D) The defense attorney must seek the court's permission to withdraw as trial counsel, but not inform the trial judge as to what the accused said.

Question 18

The plaintiff in a personal injury suit arising out of an automobile collision asserted that he had the right-of-way to enter the intersection where the accident occurred. The defendant claimed otherwise, but the plaintiff told his attorney that there was a witness present who would be able to verify his version of the accident. The plaintiff's attorney obtained a copy of the police report on the accident, but the name of the witness was not contained in the report. The plaintiff's attorney contemplated running an ad in the newspaper or hiring an investigator to find the witness, but she reasonably concluded that her client's testimony ought to be strong enough to win the case. The case went to trial, and the jury found for the defendant.

Is the plaintiff's attorney subject to discipline for failure to try to find the witness?

(A) Yes, because she failed to properly prepare the case.

(B) Yes, because her client lost.

(C) No, because she reasonably believed that her client's testimony would be sufficient.

(D) No, because the name of the witness was not in the police report.

Question 19

A newspaper reporter writes a semi-humorous gossip column in which she reports on the vices and victories in the private lives of prominent citizens. Among her favorite targets are judges and lawyers. Over the years, the reporter and a local attorney have worked out a tacit arrangement. Every now and then in her column, the reporter gives glowing praise to the attorney's legal talents and recommends him to her readers. In return, the attorney calls the reporter whenever he learns a truthful, juicy tidbit about another lawyer or judge.

Is the attorney's conduct proper?

(A) Yes, because the information that he gives the reporter is truthful.

(B) Yes, because the information that he gives the reporter is not the subject of a confidential relationship with a client.

(C) No, because a lawyer is subject to discipline for demeaning members of the legal profession.

(D) No, because a lawyer should not give something of value in return for a recommendation.

Question 20

After a major airplane crash in the vicinity of an affluent island town, in which 122 passengers and crew were killed, the town's lawyers swarmed like locusts to get a "piece of the action" and the potentially huge contingent fees that were likely to arise from the case. Interested in fees himself, but also rather disgusted at the performance of some of his colleagues of the bar, one attorney placed an ad in the town's weekly legal newspaper, whose readership was almost entirely lawyers. The ad suggested that any lawyers representing plaintiffs in the airline crash matter contact him in order to consolidate lawsuits against the airline, and that legal fees would be divided in proportion to the work performed. The ad was signed by the attorney and indicated his office address and telephone number.

Was it proper for the attorney to place such an advertisement?

(A) Yes, because the ad was not misleading.

(B) Yes, because the lawyers will split the fees in proportion to work done.

(C) No, because the attorney is soliciting business.

(D) No, because the ad is in bad taste.

GO ON TO THE NEXT PAGE

Question 21

A sales manager testified before a federal grand jury that was investigating price-fixing in the automobile tire industry. Ultimately, the grand jury indicted the sales manager for price-fixing, a felony under the Sherman Act. After his indictment, the sales manager sought to hire a prominent attorney to represent him at his criminal trial. The sales manager is a middle class business executive with enough savings to pay for private counsel. He told his attorney in confidence that he had lied to the grand jury about several meetings he had had with competitors. Furthermore, he told her that he wanted to plead not guilty to the criminal charge and that he intended to testify at trial as he did before the grand jury.

Which of the following would be proper for the attorney to do in this situation?

(A) Decline to represent the sales manager.

(B) Agree to represent the sales manager and tell no one what he told her.

(C) Inform the sales manager that unless he pleads guilty to the criminal charge, she will tell the prosecutor about his false testimony before the grand jury.

(D) Decline to represent the sales manager and inform the prosecutor about his false testimony before the grand jury.

Question 22

An attorney limits her law practice to the representation of plaintiffs in actions for medical malpractice. She has developed a standard employment contract to use with all clients who desire a contingent fee arrangement. The contract requires the client to pay in advance the first $500 of litigation expenses (which is a reasonable sum in the ordinary medical malpractice case), and states that the attorney's fee shall be 20% of any amount recovered without going to trial, 30% of any amount recovered if the case goes to trial, and 35% of any amount recovered if the case is appealed. A client signed the attorney's standard form contract, and after putting in only 10 hours' work on the client's case, the attorney was able to work out a settlement agreement in which the client received $10,000 from the defendant's malpractice insurance carrier. The client was delighted with the settlement, but he is unhappy with having to pay 20% of it ($2,000) to the attorney for so few hours' work.

With respect to the clause of the attorney's standard form contract that requires the client to pay in advance the first $500 of litigation expenses, which of the following is correct?

(A) The clause is proper.

(B) The attorney must delete the clause because it is an effort to impose a uniform provision on all clients, irrespective of their particular needs and situations.

(C) The attorney is subject to discipline for using the clause because a lawyer is required to advance reasonable litigation expenses to contingent fee clients.

(D) The attorney is subject to discipline for using the clause because clients are required to pay litigation expenses as they are incurred.

GO ON TO THE NEXT PAGE

Question 23

An airline passenger was involved in an aviation mishap. The airline company has admitted liability and has settled with 10 other persons involved in the mishap for amounts ranging between $120,000 and $150,000. The passenger's injuries are very similar to those suffered by the persons with whom the airline has settled. The passenger received a settlement offer of $135,000 from the airline company. Upon receiving the offer, the passenger decided to employ counsel to determine if the offer was a fair amount, and generally to read over the settlement papers and the release that the airline asked the passenger to sign to get the $135,000. The passenger went to the offices of a local attorney, bringing the settlement papers and release with her. She asked the attorney what his hourly fee for reading the papers would be. The attorney told the passenger that she had a personal injury case and that his standard fee for personal injury cases was 30% of any settlement or judgment received by the plaintiff.

Is the attorney subject to discipline?

(A) Yes, because the attorney's fee bears no rational relationship to the time and effort required to perform the work requested by the client.

(B) Yes, because 30% is an unreasonable contingent fee percentage.

(C) No, because contingent fees are appropriate in personal injury cases.

(D) No, because the passenger was free to obtain counsel other than the attorney.

Question 24

Before a judge was elected to the bench, she and her law partner purchased a piece of property to be held in co-tenancy by the judge and her law partner. After the judge was elected to the bench, she agreed to pay her law partner an annual fee to manage the property because her own time would be severely limited by her judicial duties. The judge and her law partner meet every three months to discuss the status of the property. The law partner sometimes appears as an attorney in the judge's courtroom.

Was it proper for the judge to make this arrangement with her law partner?

(A) Yes, because the judge acquired the property before she became a judge.

(B) Yes, because the judge made arrangements to ensure that her judicial duties would not suffer.

(C) No, because judges should not engage in remunerative outside enterprises.

(D) No, because the law partner appears in cases before the judge's court.

GO ON TO THE NEXT PAGE

Question 25

An attorney represented a defendant in a felony case that charged him with intentional evasion of over $9 million in state income tax. The accused allegedly earned the unreported income from selling child pornography. The state's criminal procedure law requires a unanimous jury verdict to convict in a felony case. Midway through the prosecutor's case-in-chief, the defense attorney instructed one of the accused's employees to attend the trial daily, to sit in the spectator section as close as possible to the defense counsel table, and to put the "evil eye" on a particular juror to intimidate him. The employee, a wicked-looking man with a jagged scar down the side of his face, attended every court session and stared constantly with cold, squinting eyes at the juror. One day, when no one but that juror was looking, the employee pointed his hand like a pistol directly at the juror's head and pretended to shoot by moving his thumb downward. Then the employee smiled an evil smile and continued to stare. The juror was too frightened to tell anyone, but he endured the torment day after day. Finally, the case was submitted to the jury, and the juror joined the rest of the jurors in returning a prompt, unanimous verdict of guilty.

Is the defense attorney subject to criminal liability for what the employee did?

(A) No, the attorney may be subject to sanction by the court or discipline by the bar, but not criminal liability.

(B) No, because the juror was not intimidated; he voted to convict along with the rest of the jury.

(C) No, because the facts do not state that the attorney gave the employee money, or something else of value, to stare and gesture at the juror.

(D) Yes, because the attorney induced the employee to intimidate the juror for the purpose of influencing the jury verdict.

Question 26

An attorney placed an advertisement in a newspaper of general circulation published in the city in which she practiced. The ad contained the attorney's name, office address, telephone number, and the following additional, truthful information: (1) "Attorney is a graduate of State University Law School"; (2) "Attorney has an M.B.A. from the Graduate School of Business of State University"; and (3) "Attorney is the only lawyer in town who speaks fluent Spanish."

Is the advertisement proper?

(A) Yes, the ad is proper.

(B) Yes, because the ad was published in a newspaper in the city in which the attorney practiced.

(C) No, because the ad is self-laudatory.

(D) No, because an M.B.A. is not law-related.

Question 27

An attorney was employed to represent a man at his trial for treason; the man was charged with smuggling top secret military information to a foreign government. The attorney had reason to suspect that some of the prosecution's witnesses were paid liars. Therefore, with his client's consent, the attorney hired to assist him in the defense a psychologist whose specialty is the behavior of liars. The client consented to the attorney's advancing the psychologist's fee as a part of the expenses of litigation. At the trial, the psychologist sat with the attorney at the counsel table. She watched the witnesses testify, and she advised the attorney when she believed that a witness was lying and ought to be pursued on cross-examination. Most of the time, the attorney followed the psychologist's advice, but sometimes he did not. Ultimately, the client was convicted and sent to prison for 20 years.

Which of the following propositions is correct?

(A)   The attorney is subject to discipline for allowing a third party to interject herself into the relationship between him and his client.

(B)   The attorney is subject to discipline for advancing the psychologist's fee as a part of the expenses of litigation.

(C)   The attorney is subject to discipline for allowing a nonlawyer to sit at the counsel table and to participate in his legal representation of a criminal defendant.

(D)   The attorney is not subject to discipline because he did not give up his discretion to the psychologist, as shown by the fact that he did not always follow her advice.

Question 28

A married couple experienced continuing marital difficulties and, being unable to resolve their problems, decided to divorce. The wife retained an attorney, who filed papers on the husband. Shortly after he was served, the husband telephoned his wife's attorney and suggested that the matter could be resolved amicably. The wife's attorney asked the husband if he was represented by counsel. The husband replied that he was not. The wife's attorney strongly urged the husband to retain a lawyer to represent him and to safeguard his interests, but the husband insisted that he did not need a lawyer. A few weeks later, after ascertaining that the husband still had not retained counsel, the wife's attorney sent the husband a proposed settlement dividing the marital property. There were spaces at the bottom for both the husband and the wife to sign, but the copy sent to the husband was unsigned by the wife. In his cover letter to the husband, the wife's attorney indicated that the husband could sign the settlement agreement, which the attorney characterized as being fair and equitable. However, the attorney's letter also stated that he could not advise the husband as to whether he should sign, and strongly urged the husband to obtain independent counsel to review the papers before signing them.

Were the attorney's actions in handling the divorce proper?

(A)   Yes, because the attorney did not give the husband legal advice.

(B)   Yes, because the attorney urged the husband to obtain representation.

(C)   No, because the attorney did not have the wife sign the settlement papers before sending them to the husband.

(D)   No, because the attorney should have required that the husband have the papers reviewed by a lawyer.

GO ON TO THE NEXT PAGE

Question 29

A car owner is insured under an auto liability policy issued by a nationally known insurance company. The policy requires the insurance company to provide a lawyer to defend the car owner, and it requires the car owner to cooperate in the defense. The car owner had an accident and was sued. In a sworn statement to the insurance company's investigator, the car owner told a story that showed he was clearly not at fault. Based on that story, the insurance company rejected plaintiff's offer to settle the case for a modest sum. The insurance company hired an attorney to represent the car owner at the trial of the case. Shortly before trial, the car owner told the attorney in confidence that he had lied to the investigator, and he recounted facts that showed he was clearly at fault in the accident. The attorney realized that under the applicable state law, the car owner's falsehood was a breach of the "cooperate in the defense" clause, and that it relieved the insurance company of any further duties to the car owner.

At this juncture, what must the attorney do?

(A) Promptly advise the insurance company of the situation and carry out its instructions as to how to dispose of the matter.

(B) Promptly advise the car owner that his best interests will be served by reverting to the story he told originally to the insurance investigator.

(C) Promptly seek the court's permission to withdraw from the matter, without revealing the car owner's confidential statement to anyone.

(D) Promptly advise the car owner of the legal consequences of his false statement, and continue representing him and the insurance company in the matter as best he is able in the circumstances.

Question 30

Three months from now, a local judge will be up for reelection. His opponent is a bright and ambitious young attorney in the prosecutor's office. Due to the press of his judicial duties, the judge has not paid much attention to the upcoming election. One afternoon an old law school friend visits him in his chambers. She convinces him that he must get busy if he hopes to defeat his opponent. The friend frequently represents clients in the judge's court, and he trusts her judgment and ability; thus, he agrees to have her serve as chairperson of his reelection campaign committee. In her capacity as the chairperson of the judge's reelection campaign committee, the friend contributed $200 of her own money to the campaign fund. She also urged other lawyers who appeared in the judge's court to make contributions to his campaign fund, and further urged those lawyers to allow their names to be listed in a half-page newspaper advertisement in favor of the judge's reelection. Finally, the friend arranged for the taping of a television advertisement in which the judge pledged never to believe the sworn testimony of a criminal defendant when there was conflicting sworn testimony from a law enforcement officer.

Which of the following was improper in the context of the judge's campaign for reelection?

(A) Contributing $200 to the judge's campaign fund.

(B) Urging other lawyers who appear in the judge's court to make contributions to the judge's campaign fund.

(C) Urging other lawyers who appear in the judge's court to allow their names to be listed in a half-page newspaper advertisement in favor of the judge's reelection.

(D) Creating the television advertisement.

GO ON TO THE NEXT PAGE

Question 31

An attorney represented a married couple for many years, handling such matters as wills, real estate closings, and the occasional lawsuit. The wife died suddenly, and shortly after her funeral the attorney paid a visit to the husband, wishing to pay her respects as a friend as well as his attorney. The attorney found the husband in an obviously drunken state. He told the attorney that he just could not go on without his wife and that he planned to commit suicide that evening. He told the attorney not to do anything to try to stop him. Using a ruse to distract the intoxicated husband, the attorney called the police, who promptly took the husband to the psychological emergency receiving area of the local hospital.

Was the attorney's conduct proper?

(A) Yes, because her client was drunk.

(B) Yes, because her client proposed to commit suicide, which act would result in his death or substantial bodily harm.

(C) No, because she revealed a client's confidences to the police.

(D) No, because she disobeyed a clear directive of her client.

Question 32

Two attorneys, a brother and sister, were licensed to practice in a province in Canada. The sister moved to the United States and passed a state bar examination. She opened a law office in that state and had letterhead stationery printed which contained the names of both the sister and brother, followed by the words "Partners, Attorneys at Law."

Is it proper for the sister to use such letterhead?

(A) Yes, because United States courts have no jurisdiction over Canadian lawyers.

(B) Yes, because both the sister and the brother are licensed to practice law.

(C) No, because the letterhead indicates that the sister is aiding the unauthorized practice of law.

(D) No, because Canadian lawyers must swear an unconstitutional oath of loyalty to a foreign monarch.

GO ON TO THE NEXT PAGE

298. PRACTICE SET 2

Question 33

An attorney was formerly employed by a branch office of the Environmental Protection Agency ("EPA") as government counsel. In this capacity, he acted as chief counsel in several suits brought by the EPA involving chemical dumping into public waterways. Two years after leaving the employ of the EPA, the attorney was retained to represent a large corporation in a suit brought by the EPA alleging violations of certain EPA regulations regarding the dumping of chemical wastes. While with the EPA, the attorney was never directly involved in a case concerning this particular corporation. A different EPA branch office had exclusive responsibility for the drafting, promulgation, and enforcement of the regulations in question.

Which of the following statements is correct?

(A)   The attorney may represent the corporation, but only with the consent of the EPA.

(B)   The attorney may represent the corporation, whether or not the EPA consents.

(C)   If the attorney represents the corporation without the consent of the EPA, he will be subject to discipline.

(D)   If the attorney represents the corporation, he will be subject to discipline, even if the EPA consents to the representation.

Question 34

A criminal defendant is facing trial for the unlawful possession of a large quantity of a controlled substance—specifically, 400 kilograms of cocaine. The accused originally asserted that he could not afford to pay a lawyer, and the court arranged for him to be represented by a public defender. Later,

the accused was visited in jail by a man who identified himself as a skilled criminal defense lawyer who had been hired by the accused's "friends" to defend him. The man said that the accused would not have to pay anything for the legal defense if he "played the game straight" and did not implicate the "friends" in the cocaine caper. The accused consented to the conditions and to the third party payment of his legal fees. In due course, the man was substituted in as defense counsel. Shortly before trial, the prosecutor offered the accused an attractive plea bargain—a mere six months in jail in exchange for a guilty plea, an identification of the persons for whom the accused was transporting the cocaine, and testimony against those persons. The man solemnly advised the accused to reject the plea bargain, saying there would be dire consequences. The accused did reject the plea bargain. Thereupon the prosecutor moved to disqualify the man as defense counsel on the ground that he was being paid by an unidentified third party and that the third party was unduly interfering with the accused's constitutional right to effective assistance of counsel.

Is the man subject to disqualification?

(A)   Yes, because in a criminal case it is unlawful for a private criminal defense lawyer to accept compensation from an outsider for his legal services.

(B)   Yes, because both the prosecutor and the judge have a duty to protect the defendant's constitutional right to the effective assistance of legal counsel.

(C)   No, because the accused consented to the fee arrangement after having been informed of the conditions on which it was offered.

(D)   No, because the prosecutor has no right to interfere with a criminal defendant's choice of counsel.

GO ON TO THE NEXT PAGE

Question 35

An amateur inventor comes to an attorney with an invention he wants to patent. The inventor explains that he and a competitor have been racing one another to come up with the ideal cleaning solution. If the inventor's competitor were to find out that the inventor was at the patent stage, and worse, if he found out the inventor's formula, the inventor would be ruined. The attorney, a trained and certified patent attorney, agrees to represent the inventor in the patent process. The invention involves complex chemical formulae, and the attorney's particular area of expertise is electronic devices. However, having worked with inventions of all types, she has no doubt that she can properly shepherd the solution through the patent process. In putting together the necessary paperwork, the attorney asks two associates in her firm who hold chemistry degrees to help her out on the project. In due time, the inventor's product receives a patent. The total bill for legal fees was $60,000, which was reasonable for the work done. When the attorney received the inventor's final payment, she decided to give the two associates each a $10,000 bonus from the fee.

Are the attorney's actions proper?

(A) Yes, because with the aid of her associates, she was competent to handle the matter.

(B) Yes, because the division of the fee was in proportion to the work performed by the two associates.

(C) No, because the attorney shared information about the case with the two associates.

(D) No, because the inventor did not consent to the splitting of the fee with the two associates.

Question 36

Two attorneys who are law partners are contemplating incorporation of their law practice. The attorneys believe that by incorporating their law practice, they will be able to convey an interest in the corporation to their children; may avoid liability to clients for malpractice; and will achieve some desirable benefits when they die—specifically, that a fiduciary representative of their estates may hold stock in the corporation for a reasonable time during administration, and ultimately that their corporate stock can pass to their children.

With respect to the proposed incorporation, which of the following statements best describes what the two attorneys may properly do?

(A) They may incorporate their law practice and convey an interest in the corporation to their children.

(B) They may incorporate their law practice and thus avoid liability to clients for malpractice.

(C) They may incorporate their law practice and when they die, a fiduciary representative of their estates may hold the stock in the corporation for a reasonable time during administration.

(D) They may incorporate their law practice and when they die, their corporate stock can pass to their children.

GO ON TO THE NEXT PAGE

Question 37

The driver of a car and his passenger were injured as the result of a collision with a bus. They believe the bus driver was entirely at fault, and they want to bring a negligence action against the bus company. They engage in an initial consultation with a local attorney. In the course of the consultation, the attorney realizes that the bus at issue belongs to a bus company that the attorney's firm is representing in an unrelated matter. The attorney interrupts the conversation, explains this potential conflict of interest, and obtains the written consent of both the driver and passenger to represent them.

Which of the following is not true?

(A) The attorney may not represent the car's driver and passenger because he has not obtained the written consent of the bus company.

(B) The attorney may not represent the car's driver and passenger because he did not inform the passenger that he may have a cause of action against the car driver.

(C) The attorney may represent the car's driver and passenger.

(D) The attorney may appear on the bus company's behalf at a court hearing that afternoon.

Question 38

An attorney attended a local law school under an honors program, whereby accepted students who had an undergraduate grade point average of 3.8 or higher receive a full tuition-paid scholarship. While in law school, the attorney completed the requirements for a taxation concentration, for which she received a certificate at graduation. She passed her state's bar examination, and she currently limits her practice to tax law. She is drafting an advertisement for her legal services. Her current draft states that: she is an honors graduate of the local law school; she is a certified tax specialist; she practices only tax law; and she likely can save clients money on their federal and state income taxes.

The current draft of the advertisement is improper for which of the following reasons?

(A) A lawyer may specialize, but may not claim to be a certified specialist in a particular field of law.

(B) The ad is undignified and may cause readers to lose respect for the legal profession.

(C) The reference to tax savings is likely to create unjustified expectations about the results the attorney can achieve.

(D) The ad contains false and misleading information.

GO ON TO THE NEXT PAGE

Question 39

The Department of Children's Services ("DCS"), a state agency, has removed a woman's children from her home and is attempting to terminate her parental rights. The woman retains an attorney to fight DCS's actions. Prior to the first hearing on the matter, a lawyer from DCS contacted the woman's brother to set up an interview. The lawyer told the brother that he wanted to talk to him about his sister, and that the interview would last for about one hour. The brother, who is childless, had never had any contact with DCS before, and did not know what his duties were. He told the lawyer he would get back to him. The brother then called his sister's attorney. He told her that he does not want to talk to DCS because he is afraid he might inadvertently say something that will hurt his sister's case. He asked his sister's attorney how he should proceed. She advised him simply to refuse the interview, because he was not required to talk to them and his sister would be better off if he did not.

Is the attorney subject to discipline?

(A) Yes, because she is attempting to secure the noncooperation of a witness.

(B) Yes, because she gave advice to an unrepresented party.

(C) Yes, because she did not advise the brother to seek the advice of independent counsel.

(D) No, because the brother is her client's brother and he did not want to hurt her case.

Question 40

An attorney is representing a client. Judgment at the trial court is against the client. The client wants to appeal the case. The appellate court rules provide a 60-day deadline for the filing of appeals, and no exception is ever granted. During the first 30 days of the period, the attorney was frantically busy in his office on other matters, and he had no chance to file the appeal. Then, during the second 30 days, he went on vacation and simply forgot to file the appeal. The trial court's error was so obvious that the appellate court would undoubtedly have reversed the case and entered judgment in the client's favor.

Which of the following is correct?

(A) The attorney is both subject to discipline and liable for malpractice.

(B) The attorney is neither subject to discipline nor liable for malpractice.

(C) The attorney is subject to discipline, but he is not liable for malpractice.

(D) The attorney is liable for malpractice, but he is not subject to discipline.

GO ON TO THE NEXT PAGE

Question 41

A basic tenet of the professional responsibility of lawyers is that every person in our society should have ready access to the independent professional services of a lawyer of integrity and competence. One way of fulfilling this responsibility is by accepting court appointments.

In this regard, which of the following statements is correct?

(A)   A lawyer may decline representation because a client or a cause is unpopular.

(B)   A lawyer may decline representation when there is adverse community reaction.

(C)   A lawyer may decline representation if the intensity of his personal feelings will impair his effective representation of a prospective client.

(D)   A lawyer may decline representation in favor of accepting the representation of a paying client.

Question 42

An attorney represents a man who has pleaded guilty to a burglary charge. The accused told the attorney during one of their confidential conversations that this is the fourth time he has been busted for burglary—one other time in this state and two times in the neighboring state. The accused could be facing a mandatory 5-10 years in prison as a repeat offender, but he and the attorney are hoping that his pleading guilty will result in a shorter sentence. Unknown to the attorney or the accused, a glitch in the state computer files resulted in a pre-sentencing report that did not pick up either the accused's in-state or out-of-state prior convictions. At sentencing, the judge states, "Normally, I throw the book at young men like you who have no respect for the property of others. However, because I see you have no prior criminal record, I think you deserve another chance. I sentence you to two years' probation and 300 hours of community service." Both the attorney and the accused remain silent.

Is the attorney subject to discipline?

(A)   Yes, because failure to speak out when one knows that the court is operating on false information is the equivalent of affirmative misrepresentation.

(B)   Yes, because this is a sentencing hearing rather than a trial.

(C)   No, because the mistake did not originate with the attorney or the accused.

(D)   No, because the attorney could not reveal the confidential information even if he had been asked directly.

GO ON TO THE NEXT PAGE

Question 43

An attorney represents a client who is a writer and producer of Broadway stage plays. This morning the client telephoned the attorney with great news—a famous actor has agreed to star in his new stage play. The client stated that with this famous actor in the lead, the play is certain to be a long-running blockbuster. The client instructed the attorney to tell no one, because the information was not public yet, and asked the attorney to draft the necessary papers. After drafting the legal papers as the client requested, the attorney telephoned her friend, who owns one of the best theaters on Broadway. The attorney told her friend that she had a tip, but it would cost her $5,000. The friend agreed to pay the attorney $5,000 for the tip, and the attorney then told her friend to make a deal with her client to run his new play. The attorney stated that she could not explain how she knew this, but to trust her when she said that even at a low rent her friend would make millions on the play because it is going to be a long-running blockbuster. The friend promptly made the deal with the client, and paid the attorney the $5,000.

Is the attorney subject to civil liability to her client for selling the tip to her friend?

(A) No, because the attorney did not reveal her client's confidential information to her friend; indeed, the attorney told her friend that she could not disclose how she knew that her client's play would be a long-running blockbuster.

(B) No, because the client was not harmed by what his attorney told her friend; in fact, the client benefited by getting one of the best theaters at a low rent.

(C) Yes, because the attorney profited by $5,000 from trading on her client's confidential information. She can be ordered to disgorge her profit to her client.

(D) Yes, but only if the client was harmed by his attorney's unauthorized disclosure to her friend.

Question 44

An attorney seeks new group and prepaid legal service organizations (such as businesses, unions, student organizations, churches, fraternal organizations, and the like) as clients. For that purpose, the attorney hired an advertising agency to design and place radio, television, and print media advertisements that will lure such clients. The attorney agreed to compensate the advertising agency for its services by paying it 3% of the legal fees that he earns during the first two years of representing new clients who come to him because of the agency's advertisements. The advertising agency does a great job, creating high profile, memorable advertisements that are truthful, not misleading, and identify the attorney as the person responsible for the content. The ads generated a tremendous amount of new business for the attorney.

Is this arrangement proper?

(A) No, because it is an improper fee split with nonlawyers.

(B) No, because it is essentially a payment for luring clients.

(C) Yes, because the advertisements are truthful and not misleading.

(D) Yes, because the attorney was identified in the advertisements as the person responsible for their content.

GO ON TO THE NEXT PAGE

Question 45

An attorney who is a member of the state bar and a judge who sits on the district court set up a probate workshop. The announced purpose of the workshop was to educate laypersons as to probate procedures, and thereby enable them to file their own papers and avoid the expense of obtaining counsel for the probate process. The tuition was a modest $50 per student, which barely covered the expenses of books and forms provided to the students. The attorney and the judge donated their time and received no remuneration. Each student was required to sign a paper stating that the $50 tuition fee established an attorney-client relationship between the lawyer conducting the workshop and the students. The paper further stated that all lawyers connected in any way with the workshop were not liable for any damages that might be incurred by students as a result of pro se filings made in accordance with, or at variance from, the instructions provided during the workshop. The paper was signed by the attorney and the judge.

Is the attorney subject to discipline?

(A) Yes, because she has participated in the forcing of an attorney-client relationship upon the students.

(B) Yes, because a lawyer may not limit her malpractice liability by contract.

(C) No, because the attorney is helping the public to avoid excessive legal fees through her participation in the workshop.

(D) No, because the clients agreed to the contract as a precondition for obtaining the benefits offered by the workshop.

Question 46

An attorney is a fully licensed member of the state bar, but she is a rather junior associate with a prominent law firm that handles many securities law matters. The attorney interviewed a client who brought an exceedingly complex securities matter to the firm. Although the attorney was highly competent, a couple of points in the client's complex case were beyond her range of experience. Therefore, she consulted one of the firm's senior partners regarding these complicated issues. The attorney did not obtain her client's consent before consulting with the senior partner, and in the course of the consultation, the attorney revealed a client confidence. However, the attorney did not reveal her client's identity. The senior partner gave her excellent advice on how to handle the matters based upon his 30 years of experience in securities law. The attorney continued to handle the client's case and brought it to a successful conclusion.

Was the attorney's conduct proper?

(A) Yes, because she kept the identity of her client secret when she consulted the senior partner.

(B) Yes, because she consulted with a lawyer in her own firm who had no reason to be screened from the case.

(C) No, because she did not obtain her client's consent.

(D) No, because she revealed a client confidence to the senior partner.

GO ON TO THE NEXT PAGE

Question 47

A title insurance agent, in serving his customers, routinely fills in the blanks in standard form documents that are prepared by lawyers. These documents include warranty deeds, quitclaim deeds, mortgages, releases of mortgages, affidavits as to debts and liens, lien waivers, and the like. On occasion, when his customers specifically ask, he advises them about the meaning and legal effect of the technical language used in the forms.

Which of the following constitutes the unauthorized practice of law by the title insurance agent?

(A)   Filling in the blanks on warranty deeds and quitclaim deeds.

(B)   Filling in the blanks on affidavits as to debts and liens and lien waivers.

(C)   Advising customers, at their request, about the meaning and legal effect of the technical language used in the forms.

(D)   Filling in the blanks on mortgages and releases of mortgages.

Question 48

An attorney knows that the statute of limitations on her client's claim has run. However, the statute of limitations is an affirmative defense that the defendant in the case would waive if she failed to plead it. The attorney's client is willing to incur the legal fees and court costs of filing the lawsuit, and understands the risks.

What may the attorney do?

(A)   File the suit because her client is willing to incur the legal fees and court costs.

(B)   File the suit but inform the court that the statute of limitations has run.

(C)   Not file the suit unless her client consents to disclose to the court the fact that the statute of limitations has run.

(D)   Not file the suit as it is now a frivolous claim.

GO ON TO THE NEXT PAGE

Question 49

An attorney and a real estate broker are friends. The real estate broker is of the opinion that the attorney is one of the best real estate lawyers in the community, and she recommends him to those persons seeking a lawyer to close real estate transactions. The attorney needs the business and appreciates the real estate broker's recommendations. The attorney has given the real estate broker some of his business cards to give to individuals seeking a real estate lawyer. Currently, the attorney does not pay the real estate broker a referral fee. However, the attorney feels guilty for accepting the much-needed business and giving nothing in return. He has been considering a more formal arrangement whereby he would pay the real estate broker a modest $100 referral fee. In addition, he has been considering taking the real estate broker and her husband on a European vacation with him as a way of expressing his appreciation for her past referrals.

Which of the following is correct?

(A) The attorney may represent clients referred by the real estate broker only if he continues his current practice of not paying the real estate broker a referral fee.

(B) The attorney properly gave the real estate broker some of his professional business cards to give to individuals seeking a real estate lawyer.

(C) The attorney may take the real estate broker and her husband on the European vacation as a way of expressing his appreciation for her referrals.

(D) The attorney may pay the real estate broker the modest $100 referral fee.

Question 50

Over the past year, a local judge was paid for teaching a course in advanced trial practice at a seminar for practicing lawyers. The judge also wrote an article about fly fishing for a national magazine, served as the weekend manager at a local antiques store, and drafted a will for her aged father.

Which of the judge's activities was improper?

(A) Teaching the course in advanced trial practice.

(B) Writing the article about fly fishing.

(C) Serving as the weekend manager at a local antiques store.

(D) Drafting the will.

GO ON TO THE NEXT PAGE

Question 51

For many years, an attorney has represented a wealthy building contractor in a wide variety of legal matters, including disputes with suppliers and customers. The contractor is a contentious man; indeed, he is the attorney's most lucrative client. The contractor built a single-family home for a married couple. When the contractor finished, the couple confronted him with a list of 289 items that they claimed were either construction defects or uncompleted tasks. The couple refused to pay the contractor the final 25% installment under their construction contract until all 289 items were remedied. The contractor contested all 289 items and demanded immediate payment. The couple refused to pay and refused to talk further with the contractor. At that point, the contractor called in the attorney, who met with the couple and offered to represent both them and the contractor in trying to find an amicable solution to their dispute. The attorney said that if his efforts failed, he would charge no fee; if his efforts produced an amicable solution, then his total fee would be $2,500, half to be paid by the couple and half by the contractor.

May the attorney represent both the couple and the contractor on those terms?

(A) No, because the attorney has proposed a contingent fee arrangement, and there is no res from which the fee can be paid.

(B) No, because the attorney cannot reasonably believe that he can represent the couple competently and diligently in light of his relationship with the contractor.

(C) Yes, but only if both the couple and the contractor give informed consent, confirmed in writing, to the arrangement.

(D) Yes, because the attorney would, in essence, be serving as a third-party neutral between the couple and the contractor.

Question 52

An attorney works full-time for the United States Department of Agriculture's Forest Service. She is assigned to a particular region within State A, and both her office and home are in State A. She went to law school and is admitted to practice in State B; she is not a member of the bar in any other state. Her work for the Forest Service does not require her to litigate, mediate, or arbitrate claims before any tribunal. She is strictly an office lawyer, and most of her workday is spent advising Forest Service managers on environmental law issues that arise under federal law or under the law of State A. To earn some extra money, the attorney moonlights as an estate planner, drafting wills and trust agreements for other Forest Service employees who live and work in State A. She does not advertise her estate planning services, and she serves only Forest Service employees, not the general public.

Is the attorney subject to discipline by State A for the unlicensed practice of law?

(A) No, because State A has no jurisdiction to discipline her, but she could be disciplined by State B for practicing without a license in State A.

(B) No, because her work for the Forest Service is done under federal authority, and her moonlighting is done only for other federal employees, not members of the general public.

(C) Yes, with respect to her moonlighting as an estate planner, but not with respect to her environmental law work for the Forest Service.

(D) Yes, with respect to both her moonlighting as an estate planner and her environmental law work for the Forest Service.

GO ON TO THE NEXT PAGE

Question 53

A bondsman is licensed by the state to act as a surety on bail bonds, subject to extensive state regulations. When he acts as surety on a bail bond, the bondsman pledges to pay the court a specified sum if a person who has been released on bail fails to show up for court proceedings on a given date. Often a family member or friend of an accused person comes to the bondsman's office to arrange for a bail bond. On these occasions, the family member or friend sometimes asks the bondsman to recommend a good criminal defense lawyer. The bondsman always refers the person to one attorney whom the bondsman believes to be the best criminal defense lawyer in the county, a lawyer who limits his practice to the defense of people accused of felonies. The bondsman and the attorney have worked out a reciprocal referral agreement. In return for the referrals he gets from the bondsman, the attorney always sends people to him for bail bonds. The attorney would do that even without the reciprocal agreement because he regards the bondsman as the most honest and dependable bondsman in the county. The attorney does not disclose the reciprocal referral agreement to the people he refers because they are invariably under great stress and not interested in arcane technicalities.

Is the attorney's participation in the reciprocal referral agreement proper?

(A) No, because the attorney does not disclose the agreement to the people he refers to the bondsman.

(B) No, because lawyers must not encourage nonlawyers to refer legal work to them.

(C) Yes, because the agreement simply reflects what the attorney would do even without the agreement.

(D) Yes, because the attorney has a right of free speech under the First and Fourteenth Amendments to refer people to whomever he wishes.

Question 54

An attorney limits his practice to criminal defense. About 40% of his workload comes from court appointments. When a conflict of interest prevents the public defender from representing an indigent defendant, the presiding judge appoints defense counsel from a list of volunteer lawyers. The state pays appointed defense counsel at a modest hourly rate. The attorney observed with envy that his lawyer friend was appointed about twice as often as he was. The attorney asked his friend how one goes about getting more appointments, and the friend responded that although lawyers were to be selected randomly from the list, the lawyers who contributed to the political campaigns of local incumbent judges running for re-election were being selected more often. The attorney took this advice to heart and started making significant contributions to the campaign committees of incumbent judges running for re-election; he would not have made such contributions but for his friend's advice. As predicted, the attorney started getting significantly more appointments than before.

Are the attorney's political contributions proper?

(A) No, but only because his contributions constitute common law bribery.

(B) No, because his motive in making the contributions is to obtain more appointments.

(C) Yes, because lawyers are permitted to participate freely in the political process.

(D) Yes, even though his motive in making the contributions is to obtain more appointments.

GO ON TO THE NEXT PAGE

Question 55

An attorney is a partner in a 300-member law firm that serves as outside general counsel to one of the world's largest manufacturers of tactical-guided missiles. The manufacturer employs many engineers, mechanics, and assembly line workers who have immigrated to the United States from various parts of the world. The United States Department of Homeland Security "strongly advised" the company to fire 42 of these employees, whose names appear on the federal government's terrorist watch list. The manufacturer regards all 42 people as valuable, dependable employees, so it consulted the attorney in the strictest of confidence, asking for legal advice about what to do. Other lawyers at the attorney's law firm were not told about the manufacturer's request, nor about the advice that the attorney gave the manufacturer. The manufacturer ended up firing two engineers and one assembly line worker, but it kept the other 39 people. The fired assembly line worker went to a storefront legal clinic to obtain some advice about his legal rights. The clinic is run by a nonprofit religious organization; the clinic's mission is to offer free, fast legal advice to anyone who cannot afford to obtain it elsewhere. The clinic receptionist sent the worker to the desk of a volunteer lawyer who is a brand new associate in the attorney's law firm, and she did not know that the manufacturer is one of the firm's clients. She also knew nothing about the advice the attorney gave the manufacturer. The volunteer lawyer dutifully advised the worker of his rights under state and federal employment law and under the collective bargaining agreement between his union and the manufacturer. Based on that advice, the worker sued the manufacturer for discriminatory termination; the attorney represented the manufacturer in that litigation.

Which of the following is correct?

(A) Both the volunteer lawyer and the law firm will be subject to civil liability in a legal malpractice action brought by the manufacturer because the volunteer lawyer's advice causes the worker to sue the manufacturer for discriminatory termination.

(B) The volunteer lawyer is subject to discipline for failing to do a conflict-of-interest check before giving legal advice to the fired worker.

(C) The volunteer lawyer's conduct was proper because she did not know that the manufacturer was her law firm's client or that the attorney had advised the manufacturer on the issue at hand.

(D) The attorney is subject to discipline for representing the manufacturer in the litigation because the volunteer lawyer gave legal advice to the worker at the clinic.

GO ON TO THE NEXT PAGE

Question 56

An attorney limits her practice to corporate securities law. A small start-up company wholly owned and operated by two brilliant young computer geeks has hired the attorney to guide them through an initial public offering of shares in their company. One of the attorney's first recommendations was to fire their current lazy, in-house accountant and hire a skilled outside accounting firm to keep the company's books and prepare the financial documents required for an initial public offering. The attorney recommended a small, local accounting firm, but in doing so the attorney orally cautioned the company owners that she was a certified public accountant as well as a lawyer, and that she owned one of the three partnership shares in the accounting firm that she recommended to them, so she had a significant financial interest in the firm. The attorney explained that she no longer practiced accounting, but that she kept her partnership share as an investment. The attorney further explained that if they decided to hire the accounting firm, their dealings with the accounting firm would not be governed by the rules of legal ethics and anything told to the accounting firm in confidence would not be protected by the attorney-client privilege.

The company owners orally indicated that they understood, and they subsequently hired the accounting firm.

Was the attorney's conduct proper?

(A)   Yes, because the attorney was not offering the accounting service ancillary to her legal service; the accounting service was offered by the accounting firm, an independent entity.

(B)   Yes, because the attorney fully disclosed the situation to the company's owners and obtained their informed consent.

(C)   No, because the attorney was essentially entering into a business transaction with her client.

(D)   No, because the attorney did not put her cautionary words in writing, she did not give the company owners a chance to consult an outside lawyer, and she did not obtain their consent in writing.

GO ON TO THE NEXT PAGE

Question 57

The law of a particular state prohibits agreements not to compete, except for agreements that are ancillary to the sale of a business or professional practice and are reasonable in both duration and geographic scope. For 20 years, an attorney practiced patent, copyright, and trademark law in an area within the state. Seeking a new challenge, the attorney entered the political race for a trial court judgeship. He won a four-year term. Before taking the oath of judicial office, the attorney sold his entire law practice to a young lawyer for $150,000. In the sale contract, the attorney promised the younger lawyer not to re-enter the practice of patent, copyright, or trademark law in the area for five years. At the end of his four-year term, the attorney ran for re-election to his judgeship; to everyone's great surprise, he lost the election to a much less qualified opponent. Because he needed to earn a living, the attorney immediately re-entered the practice of patent, copyright, and trademark law in the area in which he formerly had practiced.

Is the attorney subject to discipline?

(A)   Yes, because the attorney re-entered law practice in the area after the sale to the younger lawyer.

(B)   Yes, because the attorney made an agreement that restricts his right to practice law and it was not incident to a retirement benefits plan.

(C)   No, but the attorney could be subject to civil liability to the younger lawyer in a suit to enforce the agreement not to compete, assuming that the agreement was reasonable in duration and geographic scope.

(D)   No, because the sale of the attorney's law practice was proper, but the agreement not to compete is void, even if it is reasonable in duration and geographic scope.

GO ON TO THE NEXT PAGE

Question 58

In the most recent election, an attorney who practices election law represented a candidate who, several days before the election, told the attorney in confidence that he had hired some gangs of thugs to frighten voters away from the polls in neighborhoods where most people would vote for his opponent. The attorney was shocked and immediately advised the candidate to call off the thugs or withdraw from the race. The candidate refused to do either, whereupon the attorney withdrew as the candidate's lawyer. The attorney did not, however, tell anyone about the candidate's evil plan. On election day, the candidate's thugs did what the candidate paid them to do, and the candidate defeated his opponent by a narrow margin. A few days later, the opponent learned what the thugs had done. The opponent was furious and called a press conference at which he accused the candidate and the attorney of conspiring to intimidate his supporters and keep them away from the polls. The local newspaper printed his allegations in a front-page story, accompanied by a large photograph of the candidate and the attorney smiling at each other.

Which of the following propositions is false?

(A) It was proper for the attorney to withdraw after the candidate refused to call off the thugs or drop out.

(B) It was proper for the attorney not to tell anyone before the election about the candidate's evil plan.

(C) After the opponent's press conference and the newspaper story, but before any kind of formal proceeding, it would be proper for the attorney to disclose what the candidate told him in confidence about the thug plan and about his own response.

(D) After the opponent's press conference and the newspaper story, but before any kind of formal proceeding, it would be improper for the attorney to disclose what the candidate told him in confidence about the thug plan and about his own response.

GO ON TO THE NEXT PAGE

Question 59

An attorney practices in State A. State A's rules of legal ethics depart from the ABA Model Rules in one significant respect: State A has no "financial injury" exception to the lawyer's duty of confidentiality. Thus, when a State A lawyer learns in confidence that her client is about to use her legal services to inflict serious financial injury on someone, the lawyer may withdraw, but she must not reveal what she learned in confidence. The attorney limits her practice to federal securities law, and she regularly appears before the Securities and Exchange Commission ("SEC"). One of her major clients is a company that makes and sells cotton textiles. The company's shares are traded on the New York Stock Exchange and in securities matters the company is regulated by the SEC. While working on an SEC registration statement for the company, the attorney learned in confidence that three of the company's top executives were cooperating in a scheme to loot the company of millions of dollars. If their scheme continues, it could drive the company into insolvency. The attorney alerted the chief legal officer of the company to the situation, but he did nothing. She then alerted the chief executive officer, who also did nothing. Finally, she alerted the six outside members of the board of directors, but they too failed to act. In disgust, the attorney withdrew from the matter and vowed never again to represent the company.

Must the attorney now tell the SEC about the scheme?

(A)   Yes, the SEC's regulations under the Sarbanes-Oxley Act require her to alert the SEC if her other efforts have proven fruitless.

(B)   No, the SEC's regulations give her discretion to either reveal or not reveal the matter to the SEC.

(C)   Yes, because the shareholders could be seriously financially injured if the scheme continues.

(D)   No, because State A's legal ethics rules do not allow her to reveal confidential information in this situation.

GO ON TO THE NEXT PAGE

barbri

Question 60

When a farmer sold the family farm many years ago, he told his lawyer that he wanted to reserve all of the subsurface rights—i.e., the rights to mine or drill for oil, gas, minerals, geothermal energy, and the like. The lawyer drafted a deed that was supposed to accomplish that goal. Ten years later, the farmer died and the subsurface rights passed by his will to his beloved granddaughter. Thirty years after that, the granddaughter received a letter from a petroleum exploration and drilling company offering to lease the subsurface drilling rights from her in return for $10,000 plus 15% of the wellhead selling price of all gas and oil obtained from the property. All the granddaughter had to do was sign the lease and supply the company with a letter from a qualified oil and gas attorney, certifying that the granddaughter was indeed the owner of the subsurface rights. The granddaughter hired an oil and gas attorney to research her title, write the letter, and send it to the company. After doing a little research, the oil and gas attorney concluded that the farmer's lawyer had bungled the deed. Instead of reserving the subsurface rights, the lawyer had inadvertently sold them to the man who bought the farm. With a heavy heart, the oil and gas attorney put her findings in an opinion letter and mailed duplicate originals to the company and the farmer's granddaughter.

Was it proper to do so?

(A) No, because the oil and gas attorney should have obtained the granddaughter's informed consent before sending the letter to the company.

(B) No, because the interests of the company and the granddaughter were concurrently conflicting.

(C) Yes, because the granddaughter had previously authorized the oil and gas attorney to send the letter to the company.

(D) Yes, because to withhold the information from the company would amount to a misrepresentation of a material fact.

barbri

ANSWER SHEET

1 (A)(B)(C)(D)	31 (A)(B)(C)(D)	
2 (A)(B)(C)(D)	32 (A)(B)(C)(D)	
3 (A)(B)(C)(D)	33 (A)(B)(C)(D)	
4 (A)(B)(C)(D)	34 (A)(B)(C)(D)	
5 (A)(B)(C)(D)	35 (A)(B)(C)(D)	
6 (A)(B)(C)(D)	36 (A)(B)(C)(D)	
7 (A)(B)(C)(D)	37 (A)(B)(C)(D)	
8 (A)(B)(C)(D)	38 (A)(B)(C)(D)	
9 (A)(B)(C)(D)	39 (A)(B)(C)(D)	
10 (A)(B)(C)(D)	40 (A)(B)(C)(D)	
11 (A)(B)(C)(D)	41 (A)(B)(C)(D)	
12 (A)(B)(C)(D)	42 (A)(B)(C)(D)	
13 (A)(B)(C)(D)	43 (A)(B)(C)(D)	
14 (A)(B)(C)(D)	44 (A)(B)(C)(D)	
15 (A)(B)(C)(D)	45 (A)(B)(C)(D)	
16 (A)(B)(C)(D)	46 (A)(B)(C)(D)	
17 (A)(B)(C)(D)	47 (A)(B)(C)(D)	
18 (A)(B)(C)(D)	48 (A)(B)(C)(D)	
19 (A)(B)(C)(D)	49 (A)(B)(C)(D)	
20 (A)(B)(C)(D)	50 (A)(B)(C)(D)	
21 (A)(B)(C)(D)	51 (A)(B)(C)(D)	
22 (A)(B)(C)(D)	52 (A)(B)(C)(D)	
23 (A)(B)(C)(D)	53 (A)(B)(C)(D)	
24 (A)(B)(C)(D)	54 (A)(B)(C)(D)	
25 (A)(B)(C)(D)	55 (A)(B)(C)(D)	
26 (A)(B)(C)(D)	56 (A)(B)(C)(D)	
27 (A)(B)(C)(D)	57 (A)(B)(C)(D)	
28 (A)(B)(C)(D)	58 (A)(B)(C)(D)	
29 (A)(B)(C)(D)	59 (A)(B)(C)(D)	
30 (A)(B)(C)(D)	60 (A)(B)(C)(D)	

Answer to Question 1

(C) (A) is incorrect because lawyers should treat all participants in a proceeding with courtesy, respect, and cooperation. [*See* Restatement §106] (D) is incorrect because there is nothing that prohibits a lawyer from talking with a deposition witness about the case before a deposition. However, a lawyer must not communicate about a case with a person he knows to be represented by a lawyer, without first getting the lawyer's consent. [ABA Model Rule 4.2] Thus, (C) is correct and (D) is incorrect. Also, Comment 7 to ABA Model Rule 4.2 states that, in the case of a represented organization, a lawyer for one party may not communicate concerning the matter with persons whose acts or omissions in connection with the matter may be imputed to the organization for purposes of civil or criminal liability. Here, the corporation's employee fits the description of such a person. Thus, (B) is incorrect.

Answer to Question 2

(C) A lawyer must not communicate about a matter with a person the lawyer knows is represented by counsel, unless that person's counsel consents or the law authorizes the communication. [ABA Model Rule 4.2] Thus, (C) is clearly improper. Because it is within a prosecutor's discretion to request that the court prosecute on a lesser offense, (A) is proper. (B) is proper because there is no indication that the juvenile could not legitimately have been prosecuted for auto theft. (D) is proper because the communication is between counsel, and defense counsel must promptly inform her client of a proffered plea bargain "unless the client has previously indicated that the proposal will be acceptable or unacceptable or has authorized the lawyer to accept or to reject the offer." [*See* Comment 2 to ABA Model Rule 1.4]

Answer to Question 3

(B) In a criminal case, it is for the client to decide what plea to enter. [ABA Model Rule 1.2(a)] Also, the attorney's apparent lack of concern for the accused's interests raises a serious question about her fitness to practice law. [*See* ABA Model Rule 1.3] Therefore, the ADA must report the incident to the disciplinary authorities. [ABA Model Rule 8.3(a)] (A) is incorrect because as long as the attorney properly represented her client and did not violate the Rules, her desire to gain publicity is irrelevant. (C) and (D) are incorrect because neither the attorney's competent representation of the accused at trial nor winning the case undo the violation of attorney ethics resulting from the attorney's failure to convey the offer to the accused.

Answer to Question 4

(C) An applicant for admission to the bar may be unqualified due to mental or emotional instability. The professor here had an obligation three years ago to report her candid opinion to the state bar, even though she lacks training in the field of mental health. Likewise, she is now obliged to support the law student's re-petition for admission to practice. ABA Model Rule 8.1 prohibits a lawyer in connection with a bar admission application from knowingly making a false statement of material fact. Thus, the professor must now disclose her current feelings regarding the law student's fitness to practice law. Thus, (C) is correct, and (A), (B), and (D) are incorrect.

Answer to Question 5

(B)   ABA Model Rule 3.5(a) forbids a lawyer from seeking to influence a judge by means prohibited by law. CJC Rule 3.13(C)(3) permits a judge to accept a gift from someone who has come or is likely to come before the judge if the judge files a public report of the gift. (A) is wrong because there is no specific value that is tied to undue influence. (C) is wrong because campaign contributions are not the only types of gifts lawyers may make to judges. (D) is wrong because the value of the gift triggers only a reporting requirement. The gift is not improper as such.

Answer to Question 6

(A)   A lawyer must not neglect a legal matter that has been entrusted to him; i.e., a lawyer must act with reasonable diligence and promptness in representing a client. [ABA Model Rule 1.3] Furthermore, a lawyer has a duty to keep the client reasonably informed about the status of a matter and to promptly comply with reasonable requests for information. [ABA Model Rule 1.4(a)(3), (4)] The attorney's failure to begin the work before March 10, coupled with his failure to return his client's telephone calls or otherwise assure the client that the work would be completed on time, constitutes client neglect and is grounds for discipline. Thus, (A) is correct, and (B) and (C) are incorrect. (D) is incorrect because, as stated above, the attorney neglected his client and is subject to discipline even though the client and the trust ultimately suffered no loss.

Answer to Question 7

(D)   Although the retired attorney has retired from active practice, it is clear from the facts that the judge consulted him *as a lawyer*, rather than as a friend; thus, the retired attorney may not reveal the judge's disclosures of past crimes. [*See* ABA Model Rule 1.6] Therefore, (D) is correct and (C) is incorrect. (A) is incorrect because an ongoing lawyer-client relationship need not be established for the rules of confidentiality to apply. (B) is an incorrect statement of a lawyer's ethical obligations, as no present fraud upon the tribunal or system of justice is contemplated, and ABA Model Rule 8.3 specifically states that matters considered confidential under Rule 1.6 are not included in the obligation to reveal judicial misconduct.

Answer to Question 8

(A)   There are several legal theories on which sanctions could be imposed here, but the most obvious is Rule 37 of the Federal Rules of Civil Procedure, which is specifically designed for discovery abuse. When a party's managing agent fails to show up for a properly scheduled deposition, Rule 37 gives the judge a wide choice of sanctions, including such things as: an order that the issues in question be deemed proven in favor of the innocent party; an order forbidding the offender from offering proof on the issues in question; an order striking the offender's pleadings; an order finding the offender guilty of contempt of court; and an order that the offending party, its lawyer, or both must pay the innocent party's expenses and attorney fees incurred because of the violation. (A) is better than (B) because (B) implies an incorrect legal standard; a lawyer can be sanctioned under Rule 37 even if she did not act obstinately or disrespectfully. (C) and (D) are not as good as (A) because they imply that a lawyer cannot be sanctioned for discovery abuses by her client or her client's managing agent. That is not correct. A lawyer has to walk a thin line between bullying her client and being bullied by her client. The defense attorney was not blame-free here. She was on notice that the deponent was an uncooperative witness. He had failed to show up three times previously, and the judge had specifically warned the defense attorney that she would be sanctioned if she showed up without the deponent on August 16. The defense attorney could have informed the deponent's corporate superior about the situation, seeking to have the superior force the deponent to behave. She could also have reminded her client that she *may* withdraw as counsel if the deponent does not cooperate [ABA Model Rule 1.16(b)], and that she *must* withdraw if the deponent's mulishness forces her to violate a court order [ABA Model Rule 1.16(a)]. The defense attorney's failure to take these or similar steps to assure the deponent's presence makes the sanctions order appropriate.

Answer to Question 9

(D) Under ABA Model Rule 1.12(a), the former law student should be barred from representing the client because she was personally and substantially involved in his case while a law clerk. (Note that ABA Model Rule 1.12(a) would permit the representation if both parties gave informed consent, confirmed in writing, to the representation, but there is no mention of both parties giving informed consent in these facts.) (A) is incorrect because the former law student's previous personal and substantial involvement in the case

will prohibit her from representing the client regardless of whether she learned any confidential information. (B) is incorrect because the former law student is presently licensed, and Model Rule 1.12 clearly applies to former law clerks. (C) is incorrect because Model Rule 1.12 allows such representation only if *all parties* consent after full disclosure.

Answer to Question 10

(A) Under CJC Rules 3.1(A) and 3.7(A)(6), it would be proper for the judge to serve on the board of this foundation that provides legal education for lawyers and judges. CJC Rule 3.12 would permit her to accept the modest salary that is paid to other directors. Accordingly, (A) is the correct answer and (B), (C), and (D) are incorrect.

Answer to Question 11

(A) A lawyer does not need the consent of adversary counsel to interview a nonparty witness. Furthermore, nothing in the Rules would prevent the ADA from asking the pawnbroker about his prior criminal record, and he would have good reason for doing so because the pawnbroker's criminal record can be used to impeach his testimony. Thus, (A) is correct, and (B), (C), and (D) are incorrect.

Answer to Question 12

(B) ABA Model Rule 7.2(b)(4) permits reciprocal referral arrangements among lawyers if the arrangement is nonexclusive and disclosed to referred clients. (A) is wrong because the parties to a reciprocal referral arrangement need not be licensed in different states. (C) is wrong because the facts do not involve the division of a legal fee. (D) is wrong

because it ignores ABA Model Rule 7.2(b)(4).

Answer to Question 13

(D) A lawyer must not imply that he can improperly influence a government official. [ABA Model Rule 8.4] Here, the attorney is not actually appearing before his sister, and so (B) and (C) are incorrect. Without more, the mere objection of an opposing party should not keep the attorney from appearing in district court; thus, (A) is incorrect. (D) is therefore the best answer.

Answer to Question 14

(D) The consumer's attorney is not subject to *malpractice* liability because his client (the consumer) has no damages. Damages are part of the cause of action for legal malpractice. The attorney may be subject to discipline, but not malpractice liability. (A) is incorrect because, although it correctly states the attorney's duty, there is no malpractice claim because of the lack of damages. (B) is incorrect for the same reason. (C) is incorrect because the consumer's statement that he probably would not accept an offer under $500,000 does not constitute authorization of the attorney to accept or reject offers without consulting him. Furthermore, to avoid problems such as this, authorization to accept or reject settlement offers without consulting the client should be in writing.

Answer to Question 15

(B) A lawyer is subject to discipline for making a false statement of law to the court. [ABA Model Rule 3.3(a)(1)] (A) is overbroad because a lawyer need not cite opposing cases from noncontrolling jurisdictions, and a lawyer may argue the case from an advocate's viewpoint, which may not necessarily be "objective." (C) and (D) are incorrect because they do not take into account the stricture against making a false statement of law. The attorney here has gone beyond the bounds of zealous representation.

Answer to Question 16

(B) A client's funds are ordinarily deposited in an account where the lawyer's office is located, but they can be deposited elsewhere with the client's consent. [ABA Model Rule 1.15(a)] (A) is wrong because the client's funds appear to be an expense advance, not a "true retainer fee." (C) and (D) are wrong because there are no such requirements.

Answer to Question 17

(B) The old common law rule regarding attorney-client privilege allowed an eavesdropper to testify to an otherwise privileged communication, but the modern law is to the contrary. [*See, e.g.,* Cal. Evid. Code §§952, 954] Because the prosecutor can reasonably anticipate that the accused will claim the attorney-client privilege, she has no obligation to try to testify to what she heard. In addition, ABA Model Rule 3.8(b) mandates the prosecutor to protect the defendant's right to counsel. Accordingly, (B) is correct and (A) is incorrect. As to the defense attorney's obligations, the facts given in the question do not justify an assumption that the accused has asked his attorney to present false evidence on his behalf, or that he is planning to take the witness stand and perjure himself. Accordingly, we are not faced with any questions under ABA Model Rule 3.3. Thus, the defense attorney should preserve what the accused said in confidence and proceed with the case in the normal manner. [*See* ABA Model Rule 1.6(a)] This makes (C) and (D) incorrect.

Answer to Question 18

(C)   A lawyer must provide competent representation to a client. [ABA Model Rule 1.1] This includes use of methods and procedures meeting the standards of competent practitioners. It also includes adequate preparation. In the case at bar, the plaintiff's attorney's decision on whether to further search for the unknown witness was a matter of judgment. If she was reasonable in believing that the plaintiff's testimony would be sufficient, then her preparation will not be deemed inadequate. Thus, (C) is the correct answer, and (A) is incorrect. (B) is incorrect because even though the plaintiff lost, his attorney may have provided him with competent representation. (D) is irrelevant.

Answer to Question 19

(D)   ABA Model Rule 7.2(b) prohibits a lawyer from giving anything of value to a person in return for a recommendation of the lawyer's services. (A) and (B) are incorrect because the truth of the information or lack of confidentiality is beside the point. (C) is incorrect because there is no prohibition, as such, against demeaning members of the profession.

Answer to Question 20

(A)   This is the best answer here because nothing in this advertisement violates the ABA Model Rules. The fact that the ad is not misleading is important because neither the ABA Model Rules nor the First Amendment protects misleading or deceptive advertising.

(B) is incorrect because fee splitting is a separate issue; it does not affect the propriety of the ad. (C) is incorrect because the attorney here is *not* soliciting business, and also because the traditional ban on all solicitation is no longer constitutional. (D) is incorrect in that the ad is *not* patently in bad taste, and even if it were, it would probably be protected by the First Amendment unless it was misleading or overreaching.

Answer to Question 21

(A)   The attorney has no duty to represent the sales manager, so (A) is proper. (B) is improper because the attorney may only represent the sales manager if he does not insist on testifying falsely. [*See* ABA Model Rule 3.3(a)(3)] (C) is improper because it is a form of extortion. (D) is improper because the sales manager's confession to past perjury is protected by the duty of confidentiality. [*See* ABA Model Rule 1.6]

Answer to Question 22

(A)   There is nothing in the ABA Model Rules that prohibits a lawyer from requiring a client to pay in advance the first $500 of litigation expenses, so long as the $500 payment is reasonable. [ABA Model Rule 1.5(a)] (B) is incorrect because the ABA Model Rules do not suggest that every clause of a standard form employment contract must be individually tailored to each client. (C) is incorrect because ABA Model Rule 1.8(e) *permits* lawyers to advance litigation expenses, but does not *require* them to do so. (D) is incorrect because nothing in the Rules requires the client to pay litigation expenses as they are incurred.

Answer to Question 23

(A) The usual rationale supporting relatively high contingent fees is that the lawyer is taking a gamble in handling the case. Here, no gamble is involved, and the attorney is subject to discipline under ABA Model Rule 1.5(a) for attempting to exact an unreasonable fee. The criteria of (A) more clearly establish excessiveness than those in (B). (C) is incorrect because even though contingent fees may be thought generally appropriate for personal injury cases, an excessive fee, whether contingent or hourly, is never appropriate. (D) is incorrect because even though the client could have gone to another attorney, the attorney tried to exact an unreasonable fee from her.

Answer to Question 24

(D) A judge should refrain from financial and business dealings that involve her in frequent transactions with lawyers or persons likely to come before the court on which she sits. [CJC Rule 3.11(C)(3)] Here, the judge's close business relationship with a lawyer who appears in her courtroom violates CJC Rule 3.11(C)(3). It makes no difference that the judge acquired the property before she became a judge. Thus, (A) is incorrect. (B) is incorrect because even if the judge's dealings with the property do not take up too much of her time, there will still be an adverse reflection on her impartiality. (C) is incorrect because CJC Rule 3.11(A) permits a judge to hold investments, including real estate, and to engage in other remunerative activity.

Answer to Question 25

(D) All jurisdictions in the United States have obstruction of justice statutes that prohibit threatening jurors, witnesses, and judges and also prohibit similar misconduct. For example, 18 U.S.C. section 1503 makes it a felony to "endeavor . . . to influence, intimidate, or impede any . . . juror." The term "endeavor" is broader than "attempt," and one can be guilty of endeavoring to intimidate a juror even though the juror is not intimidated. [*See also* United States v. Atkin, 107 F.3d 1213 (6th Cir. 1997)—attorney violated section 1503 by obtaining money from defendant to bribe judge, even though attorney ultimately did not offer the bribe] (A) is incorrect because it overlooks obstruction of justice statutes such as section 1503. (B) is incorrect because the effort need not be successful, as in the *Atkin* case, above. (C) is incorrect because the defense attorney can be punished as an accomplice, even if he did not give the defendant's employee anything of value. The employee did the intimidating, but it was the defense attorney who instructed or induced him to do it.

Answer to Question 26

(A) This is the best answer here because it complies with the ABA Model Rules' view that advertising must not be "false or misleading." [*See* ABA Model Rule 7.1] It also takes into account First Amendment freedoms. (B) is incorrect because the geographic scope of lawyer advertising is not limited to the city in which the lawyer practices. (C) is incorrect because there is no prohibition on "self-laudatory" advertising in the ABA Model Rules. The attorney's statement regarding proficiency in Spanish compared with other local lawyers is factually verifiable and thus does not run afoul of ABA Model Rule 7.1. (D) is incorrect because the listing of academic degrees is clearly proper.

Answer to Question 27

(D) (A) reflects a misconception of ABA Model Rule 1.8(f), which prohibits a lawyer from allowing the interests of a third party to interfere with the relationship between the lawyer and the client. That is not the case where an alleged expert like the psychologist is hired to assist the lawyer in representing the client. (C) reflects a similar misconception. Lawyers frequently use a variety of experts to advise them during trial. The attorney did not give up his discretion to the psychologist, as evidenced by the fact that he sometimes did not follow her advice. Furthermore, such experts frequently sit at the counsel table so they can be close to the lawyer during trial. (B) is incorrect because a lawyer is allowed to advance litigation expenses. [See ABA Model Rule 1.8(e)(1)] Although some lawyers might question the wisdom of spending money on a purported expert on liars, that would seem to be a matter best left to the discretion of the individual lawyer, and the Model Rules do not suggest otherwise. Thus, (D) is correct, and (A), (B), and (C) are incorrect.

Answer to Question 28

(A) ABA Model Rule 4.3 forbids a lawyer to give advice to an unrepresented person if the lawyer knows that the person's interests conflict with those of the client. Thus, (A) is correct. The attorney is *allowed* to advise the unrepresented person to obtain a lawyer, but the critical issue is giving advice. Thus, (A) is a better answer than (B). (C) is irrelevant to any ethical issue. (D) is incorrect because there is no way a lawyer can compel a third party to obtain counsel.

Answer to Question 29

(C) Ordinarily, a lawyer can act for both the insured and the insurance company because their interests are only potentially in conflict. But here they have come into present, actual conflict. The insurance company's attorney cannot adequately represent the car owner without harming the insurance company, and he cannot protect the insurance company's interests without harming the car owner. Therefore, he must seek the court's permission to withdraw from the case entirely, and he must not reveal the car owner's confidential statement. [See ABA Model Rules 1.6, 1.7, 1.16(a)(1)] In a case very much like this one, the Seventh Circuit held that the attorney "should have refused to participate further in view of the conflict of interest" between the insured person and the insurance company. [State Farm Mutual Automobile Insurance Co. v. Walker, 382 F.2d 548 (7th Cir. 1967); *and see* ABA Informal Op. 1476 (1981)] Thus, (C) is correct, and (A) and (D) are incorrect. (B) is incorrect because of the conflict of interest and because the attorney may be advocating perjury.

Answer to Question 30

(D) CJC Rule 4.4 allows a candidate for an elected judicial office to have a campaign committee to solicit campaign funds and publicly stated support for the candidate. No provision of either the CJC or the ABA Model Rules prohibits a lawyer who frequently appears before a judge from contributing to or publicly endorsing the campaign. Thus, (A), (B), and (C) are all proper here. However, (D) was improper because judges and judicial candidates are not permitted to "make pledges, promises or commitments that are inconsistent with

the impartial performance of the adjudicative duties of judicial office." [CJC Rule 4.1(A)(13)]

Answer to Question 31

(B) ABA Model Rule 1.6(b)(1) allows a lawyer to disclose a client's confidential information to prevent reasonably certain death or substantial bodily harm. Here, the husband planned to commit suicide, which clearly falls within this rubric. Thus, (B) is correct, and it logically follows that (C) and (D) are incorrect. (A) does not go directly to the ethical question involved.

Answer to Question 32

(C) A lawyer who is licensed to practice in one state (or in a foreign country or province) is not, without more, entitled to practice in any other state. A lawyer is subject to discipline for practicing in a jurisdiction without being licensed to do so. Because there is no indication on the letterhead regarding limitation of the brother's practice to a province in Canada, the sister is abetting the unauthorized practice of law. [See ABA Model Rule 5.5(a)] Thus, (C) is correct and (B) is incorrect. (A) is a true statement but irrelevant. (D) is nonsensical.

Answer to Question 33

(B) ABA Model Rule 1.11(a) prohibits a lawyer from representing a private client in a matter in which the lawyer participated personally and substantially as a public employee, unless the government agency in question gives its informed consent, confirmed in writing. The attorney here was neither personally nor substantially involved with any matter concerning the corporation, so he may now represent the corporation without obtaining the EPA's consent. Thus, (B) is correct, and (A), (C), and (D) are incorrect.

Answer to Question 34

(B) ABA Model Rule 1.8(f) prohibits a lawyer from accepting compensation for representing a client from anyone other than that client, unless two conditions are satisfied: (1) the client gives informed consent, and (2) the person who pays the compensation does not interfere with the representation of the client or with the lawyer's independence. [See also Restatement §134, comment d] In this case, the "friends" are interfering with the lawyer's representation of the client and with his independence by conditioning their financial aid on the accused's not implicating them in the cocaine caper. The results of their interference become obvious when the accused is coerced into turning down the attractive plea bargain. [See Quintero v. United States, 33 F.3d 1133 (9th Cir. 1994)—similar facts] (A) and (C) are both incorrect because they misstate the principles expressed in ABA Model Rule 1.8(f)—(A) is too broad, and (C) does not take into account the interference by the "friends." (D) is incorrect because the prosecutor has an ethical obligation to help assure a criminal defendant's right to counsel. [See ABA Model Rule 3.8(b)]

Answer to Question 35

(A) The attorney's actions are proper. With the aid of her associates, the attorney, an experienced patent lawyer, was clearly competent to handle the case. (B) is wrong because it states one of the limitations on fee splitting between lawyers in different firms. It does not apply to lawyers in the same firm. (C) is wrong because this is the type of disclosure that is impliedly authorized to carry out the representation. It does not abrogate the protections of privilege or confidentiality, and no formal consent by the client is required. [*See* ABA Model Rule 1.6(a)] (D) is wrong because it too states a limitation concerning fee splits between lawyers in different firms. No client consent is required to split a fee in any manner among lawyers in the same firm. [ABA Model Rule 1.5]

Answer to Question 36

(C) Under ABA Model Rule 5.4(d)(1), a nonlawyer may not own an interest in a professional legal corporation. Thus, (A) and (D) are incorrect. (B) is incorrect because incorporation will limit the malpractice liability of the lawyers only to the extent permitted by the law of the state in question. [Restatement §58, comment c] (C) is correct because ABA Model Rule 5.4(d)(1) permits this exception to the general rule that a nonlawyer may not hold stock in a professional legal corporation.

Answer to Question 37

(C) The attorney may not represent both the passenger and the driver when there is a *potential* conflict of interest between them unless: (1) the attorney reasonably believes that he can represent both clients effectively; and (2) the passenger and the driver give informed consent, confirmed in writing. The attorney must withdraw from the joint representation, however, if later discovery shows that the passenger has an actual claim against the driver. Here, there is no indication that the driver, the passenger, and the bus company all gave informed consent, confirmed in writing, and thus (C) is not a true statement. [*See* ABA Model Rule 1.7] (A) is a true statement

for the same reason. (B) is true because a lawyer must not represent a client if the representation of that client will be directly adverse to the representation of another client, unless both clients give informed consent, confirmed in writing. [*See* ABA Model Rule 1.7] (D) is true because the attorney already represents the bus company in the unrelated matter.

Answer to Question 38

(D) ABA Model Rules 7.1 and 7.2 provide that communications about legal services must not be false or misleading. Attending a law school under an "honors program" is not the same as being an "honors graduate" of the law school; one could receive high grades as a college undergraduate but graduate at the bottom of her law school class. In addition, a law school concentration certificate is not the same as being a "certified specialist." Accordingly, the attorney's current draft does not comport with ABA Model Rules 7.1 and 7.2. Thus, (D) is correct. (A) is incorrect because a lawyer may claim to be a certified specialist under the circumstances specified in ABA Model Rule 7.2(c). (B) is incorrect because the facts do not suggest that the ad was undignified, and the greater problem with the ad is the reason stated in (D). (C) is incorrect due to the modifier "likely" and the lack of specificity regarding the amount of the potential tax savings. [*See* Comment 3 to ABA Model Rule 7.1—"The inclusion of . . . qualifying language may preclude a finding that a statement is likely to create unjustified expectations or otherwise mislead the public."]

Answer to Question 39

(D) The attorney is not subject to discipline because of the brother-sister relationship. A lawyer may advise a person not to voluntarily give information to an opponent or other party if the person is a relative of the client and that person's interests will not be harmed by not volunteering the information. [ABA Model Rule 3.4(f)] Here, there is nothing in the facts to suggest the brother's interests would be harmed by not volunteering the information about his sister. (A) is wrong because of the exception stated above. (B) is wrong because this type of advice is not prohibited. If the facts indicated that the brother's interests might be harmed by not granting the interview (e.g., if he had a matter pending with DCS that might be negatively influenced by his noncoopera-tion), the attorney could not have advised him as she did and should then have advised him to seek independent counsel. (C) is wrong for the reason just stated.

Answer to Question 40

(A)   A lawyer must act with reasonable diligence and promptness in repre-senting a client. [ABA Model Rule 1.3] Thus, a lawyer must not neglect a matter entrusted to him. An example of neglect is failure to file necessary papers, as in this case. It seems clear that the attorney has violated this standard. He is, of course, also liable to his client for the client's loss due to his own neglect. Thus, the attorney is guilty of malprac-tice and violating an ethics rule. There-fore, (A) is correct, and (B), (C), and (D) are incorrect.

Answer to Question 41

(C)   According to ABA Model Rule 6.2(c), a lawyer may decline employment if the intensity of his personal feelings, as distinguished from a community attitude, will impair his effective representation of

a prospective client. Thus, (C) is correct. (A) and (B) are incorrect because regard-less of his personal feelings, a lawyer may not decline representation because a client or a cause is unpopular or commu-nity reaction is adverse. [*See* Comment 1 to ABA Model Rule 6.2] (D) is incor-rect because the standard is causing an "unreasonable" burden, such as "when it would impose a financial sacrifice so great as to be unjust." [*See* Comment 2 to ABA Model Rule 6.2]

Answer to Question 42

(C)   The attorney is not subject to disci-pline for failure to correct the court's mistake because the mistake did not originate with the attorney or his client. In this setting, the attorney would have a duty to speak out if something he or his client had done had given the court a false impression, but otherwise, he cannot breach his duty of confidentiality to the disadvantage of his client. [*See* ABA Model Rules 1.6(a), 3.3] Thus, (A) is incorrect. The fact that this is a sentencing hearing does not affect the attorney's duties in any way. This is not an ex parte proceeding (which would be a much thornier issue). Thus, (B) is incorrect. (D) is incorrect because had the judge asked the attorney directly whether this was his client's first offense, the attorney would have had to respond truthfully or have asked to withdraw (which would also have given the judge his answer). To answer otherwise would be perpetrating a fraud on the court.

Answer to Question 43

(C)   Restatement section 60(2) states that a lawyer who self-deals in a client's confidential information can be forced to disgorge any profit she makes, even if the client is not harmed by the self-

dealing. Here, the attorney was self-dealing, even though she did not tell her friend the precise reason why she was certain her client's play would be a hit. For that reason, (A) is incorrect. (B) and (D) are incorrect because harm to the client is not required.

Answer to Question 44

(A)   The advertising agency is not a lawyer or law firm, and a lawyer is prohibited from sharing legal fees with a nonlawyer except under specified limited circumstances, none of which applies here. [*See* ABA Model Rule 5.4(a)] (B) is incorrect because lawyer advertising is permitted subject to the provisions of ABA Model Rules 7.1 and 7.2. (C) and (D) are incorrect because they do not act to undo the impropriety of the fee split.

Answer to Question 45

(B)   ABA Model Rule 1.8(h) makes it clear that a lawyer is subject to discipline for attempting to prospectively limit malpractice liability by contract with a client. The ABA Model Rules provide an exception if the client secures independent counsel in making the agreement. That exception does not apply here. (A) is incorrect because the "clients" are free to go elsewhere for representation and no relationship is "forced" on them. (C) is incorrect because high-sounding rhetoric and purpose do not change the impropriety of attempts to limit malpractice liability by contract. (D) is incorrect because the clients were not independently represented in making agreements to the contract.

Answer to Question 46

(B)   A lawyer has implied authority to consult other members of her firm

regarding a case unless there is a specific instruction from the client to the contrary or some other compelling reason. [*See* ABA Model Rule 1.6(a) and Comment 5] It logically follows that (A), (C), and (D) are incorrect.

Answer to Question 47

(C)   Generally, title insurance agents and others whose businesses border on the practice of law are allowed to fill in the blanks on standard form documents that have been prepared by lawyers. Therefore, (A), (B), and (D) do not constitute the unauthorized practice of law. But in *State Bar v. Guardian Abstract & Title Insurance Co.,* 587 P.2d 1338 (N.M. 1978), it was held that a title insurance company could not advise its customers about "the legal effect of the language contained in" such standard form documents. Thus, (C) is an example of unauthorized practice. (C) is therefore correct, and (A), (B), and (D) are incorrect.

Answer to Question 48

(A)   (D) is incorrect; the claim is not frivolous under ABA Model Rule 3.1. The statute of limitations merely destroys the remedy and not the right. Unless the defendant pleads the statute of limitations, the claim is valid. Thus, (A) is correct. (B) and (C) are incorrect; there is no duty to inform the court that the statute of limitations has run.

Answer to Question 49

(A)   ABA Model Rule 7.2(b) provides that, subject to certain exceptions, a lawyer must not give anything of value to a person for recommending the lawyer's services. Thus, (A) is correct, and (D) is incorrect. (C) is incorrect. Although there is an exception that allows a lawyer to give a person a nominal gift as an expression of appreciation for recommending the lawyer's services, such gifts must not exceed what would be given at a holiday or in the course of ordinary social hospitality. A European vacation is not a nominal gift. (B) is incorrect because a lawyer generally must not, personally or through a representative, initiate live person-to-person contact with an individual known to need legal services in a particular matter, for the purpose of offering legal services in that matter. [ABA Model Rule 7.3(b)]

Answer to Question 50

(C) CJC Rule 3.11(B) states that generally a judge must not serve as a manager or employee of a business. Thus, the activity in (C) is an improper activity for a judge. On the other hand, judges are encouraged to engage in appropriate extrajudicial activities, such as teaching. [CJC Rule 3.1, comment 1] Thus, (A) is proper. (B) is proper because the CJC does not forbid extrajudicial activities that do not interfere with a judge's official duties. [See CJC Rule 3.1(A)] (D) is proper because although a judge is not permitted to practice law, a judge may "give legal advice to and draft or review documents for a member of the judge's family." [See CJC Rule 3.10]

Answer to Question 51

(B) (A) is wrong because a contingent fee can be proper even if there is no res—no pool of money—from which the fee can be paid. [See ABA Model Rule 1.5(c), (d)] (D) is wrong because the attorney is not neutral; he was called into the matter by the contractor, his most lucrative client. ABA Model Rule 2.4(a) says that a lawyer can serve as a third-party neutral when he "assists two or more persons **who are not clients** of the lawyer to reach a resolution of a dispute or other matter that has arisen between them." (B) and (C) draw upon comments 26 - 33 to ABA Model Rule 1.7, concerning concurrent conflicts of interest between two clients in a non-litigation matter. Here, the attorney cannot **reasonably believe** that he can represent the couple competently and diligently in negotiating with the contractor, his longtime and most lucrative client. [See ABA Model Rule 1.7(b)(1)] Moreover, the interests of the contractor and the couple are so "fundamentally antagonistic" that the conflict is "unconsentable." [Comment 28 to ABA Model Rule 1.7]

Answer to Question 52

(C) ABA Model Rule 8.5(a) permits State A to discipline an out-of-state lawyer "if the lawyer provides or offers to provide any legal services" in State A. Here, the attorney's environmental law work for the Forest Service is proper under ABA Model Rule 5.5(d)(1) because she is providing that work only to her employer-client, and the work does not require pro hac vice admission in State A. However, State A could discipline her for moonlighting as an estate planner; she is not providing that work to her employer-client, even though her estate planning clients are Forest Service employees. [Comment 16 to ABA Model Rule 5.5] Thus, (C) is correct, and (A) is wrong. (B) is wrong for the same reason. The attorney's day job for the Forest Service "does not authorize the provision of personal legal services to the employer's officers or employees." [Id.] (D) is wrong. The moonlighting part of it is correct, but the remainder is not. As indicated above, the attorney's environmental law work is proper under ABA Model Rule 5.5(d)(1) because she is providing it only to her employer-client.

Answer to Question 53

(A) The general rule is that a lawyer must not give anything of value to a person for recommending the lawyer's services. [ABA Model Rule 7.2(b)] Referral of business is certainly something of value, so the attorney's agreement with the bondsman would violate the general rule unless an exception applies. The attorney might try to invoke the exception stated in ABA Model Rule 7.2(b)(4), which permits a lawyer to have a reciprocal referral agreement with another lawyer, or with a nonlawyer professional, if two conditions are satisfied. Before examining the two conditions, one must first decide whether a bail bondsman is a "professional." Black's Law Dictionary defines "profession" as a vocation that requires an advanced education and training. [Black's Law Dictionary (11th ed. 2019), profession] ABA Model Rule 7.2(b) would be served by including a state-licensed and regulated bail bondsman as a "professional." That brings us to the two conditions. First, a reciprocal referral agreement must be nonexclusive—i.e., each party must be free to refer a person to a competitor of the other party. Second, the referral agreement must be disclosed to the person who is referred. The agreement between the attorney and the bondsman fails to satisfy the second condition, and perhaps the first as well. (B) is wrong because it overstates the general rule expressed in ABA Model Rule 7.2(b). (C) is wrong because the agreement must be disclosed, whether or not it changes what the attorney would do absent the agreement. (D) is wrong because the attorney's free speech rights are trumped by the legal ethics rule, and the same is true for many other legal ethics rules.

Answer to Question 54

(B) ABA Model Rule 7.6 says that a lawyer must not accept an appointment made by a judge if the lawyer makes a political contribution "for the purpose of obtaining or being considered for" that type of appointment. The question states that the attorney would not have made the contributions but for the advice he obtained from his friend; that is sufficient proof of his improper motive. [See comment 5 to ABA Model Rule 7.6] (D) is wrong for the reason stated above. (A) is wrong. Common law bribery is the giving of money, or something else of value, in return for a specified act by a judge or other public official; the person on the receiving end also commits common law bribery. The attorney's contributions are improper under ABA Model Rule 7.6, whether or not they rise to the level of common law bribery. [See comment 6 to ABA Model Rule 7.6] (C) is wrong because ABA Model Rule 7.6 limits one specific kind of participation in the political process—so-called pay-to-play political contributions.

Answer to Question 55

(C) This question is governed by ABA Model Rule 6.5, which relaxes the ordinary conflict of interest rules for legal service programs that offer quick legal advice to a client without expectation that the lawyer will continue representing the client. ABA Model Rule 6.5(a)(2) states that the ordinary rule of imputed disqualification will apply only if the lawyer who offers the quick legal advice **knows** that a different lawyer in her firm would be disqualified by a conflict, and "knows" means **actually** knows. Here, the volunteer lawyer did not know that the attorney had advised the manufacturer on the matter; indeed, she was a new associate and did not even realize that the manufacturer was one of the firm's clients. Therefore, the volunteer lawyer acted properly in advising the fired worker. (A) is wrong because the question does not supply any facts that would support a valid legal malpractice claim or other civil claim against either the volunteer lawyer or the law firm. (B) is wrong because ABA Model Rule 6.5 recognizes that quick-service providers cannot realistically perform the thorough conflicts checks that private firms perform. (D) is wrong because the volunteer lawyer's legal advice to the fired worker will not disqualify the attorney from representing the manufacturer in later litigation. [*See* comment 4 to ABA Model Rule 6.5]

Answer to Question 56

(D)   Comment 5 to ABA Model Rule 5.7 states: "When a client-lawyer relationship exists with a person who is referred by a lawyer to a separate law-related service entity controlled by the lawyer, individually or with others, the lawyer must comply with Rule 1.8(a)." ABA Model Rule 1.8(a), in turn, says that when a lawyer enters into a business transaction with her own client, she must (1) disclose the terms to the client *in an understandable writing*, (2) give the client a chance to *consult independent counsel*, and (3) obtain the client's *consent in writing*. The attorney did not do those things, so her conduct was not proper. (B) is wrong for the same reason.

(C) is not as good as (D) because (C) overlooks the circumstances that would make it proper to enter into a business transaction with one's own client. (A) is wrong because it misses the point. Accounting service is a "law-related" service, and the attorney and the other two partnership owners control the accounting firm. Thus, if the attorney recommends the accounting firm, she must take the precautionary steps outlined in ABA Model Rule 1.8(a).

Answer to Question 57

(C)   ABA Model Rule 1.17 permits a practicing lawyer to sell his entire law practice or an area of his law practice to one or more lawyers or law firms. That is what the attorney did here shortly before becoming a judge. One of the conditions specified in ABA Model Rule 1.17 is that the seller must cease "to engage in the private practice of law . . . in the [jurisdiction or geographic area] in which the practice has been conducted." [ABA Model Rule 1.17(a)] The attorney satisfied that condition by becoming a judge—engaging in judicial duties does not constitute the private practice of law, nor does working as a government lawyer, lawyer for the poor, or an in-house lawyer for a business. [*See* comments 2 and 3 to ABA Model Rule 1.17] The attorney's re-entry into private practice does not violate ABA Model Rule 1.17 because it was caused by an "unanticipated change in circumstances"—i.e., his failure to win re-election. [*See* comment 2 to ABA Model Rule 1.17, which uses re-election defeat as an example of "unanticipated change"] (A) is wrong for the reason just stated. (B) is wrong because ABA Model Rule 5.6 (the rule that prohibits agreements that restrict a lawyer's right to practice) does not apply to agreements that are ancillary to the sale of a law practice. [Comment 3 to ABA Model Rule 5.6] (D) is wrong because the law of the state makes the attorney's agreement not to compete *valid* if it is reasonable in duration and geographic scope.

Answer to Question 58

(D)   (A), (B), and (C) are true. (A) is true because ABA Model Rule 1.16(b)(4) permits a lawyer to withdraw if the client insists upon taking action that the lawyer considers repugnant or with which the lawyer has a fundamental disagreement. (B) is true because of the attorney's ethical duty of confidentiality. The duty has some exceptions, but none of them quite fits this situation. One might argue that ABA Model Rule 1.6(b)(2) fits because the attorney could reveal the candidate's evil plan in order to prevent "substantial injury to the financial interests or property of another." Perhaps the candidate's opponent has a financial interest in being elected to the post. However, there is nothing in the attorney's services to form or carry out the evil plan, and that is an important requirement of ABA Model Rule 1.6(b)(2). Even if ABA Model Rule 1.6(b)(2) would *permit* the attorney to reveal the confidential information, it does not *require* him to do so—it gives the attorney discretion as to whether to reveal. [*See* comment 15 to ABA Model Rule 1.6] (C) is true because ABA Model Rule 1.6(b)(5) allows a lawyer to reveal confidential information "to establish a defense to a criminal charge or civil claim against the lawyer based upon conduct in which the client was involved, or to respond to allegations in any proceeding concerning

the lawyer's representation of the client." The lawyer's right to disclose in self-protection does not require that a criminal charge, civil complaint, disciplinary case, or other formal proceeding has already started. "The lawyer's right to respond arises when an assertion of complicity has been made." [Comment 10 to ABA Model Rule 1.6] The opponent's press conference and the newspaper story amply satisfy that requirement. For the same reasons, (D) is false.

Answer to Question 59

(B)   The SEC's regulations under the Sarbanes-Oxley Act *permit*, but do not require, a securities lawyer to reveal a client's confidential information to the SEC when the lawyer reasonably thinks that doing so is necessary to prevent or rectify a securities act violation (or similar law violation) that is likely to cause substantial financial injury to the client or its shareholders. (A) and (C) are wrong because the regulation permits, but does not require, the attorney to alert the SEC. (D) is wrong because the SEC regulations purport to preempt any inconsistent state ethics rules. [*See* 17 C.F.R. §§205.1, 205.6(c)] (It remains to be seen whether courts will uphold the SEC's effort to preempt the field and override inconsistent state ethics rules.)

Answer to Question 60

(A)   The granddaughter hired the oil and gas attorney to evaluate her title for the use of a third party, the petroleum exploration and drilling company. ABA Model Rule 2.3 governs this kind of representation. ABA Model Rule 2.3(b) states that when the lawyer knows (or should know) that the representation will harm the client, the lawyer should not provide the evaluation without first obtaining the client's informed consent. The granddaughter apparently told her attorney at the outset to send the evaluation to the company, but the granddaughter did not know at that point what the evaluation would show. One purpose for the attorney to obtain her client's informed consent before sending the letter to the company is to give her a chance to obtain a second opinion from a better oil and gas lawyer; perhaps it is the attorney who fouled up rather than the grandfather's lawyer. (B) is wrong because ABA Model Rule 2.3 permits a lawyer to undertake an evaluation for a third party, and the third party's interests are quite commonly in concurrent conflict with those of the client. (C) is wrong because the granddaughter's prior authorization is not enough; her attorney should have obtained informed consent after she discovered that the letter would harm her. [*See* ABA Model Rule 2.3(b) and comment 5] (D) is wrong because, if the attorney never sent the opinion letter to the company, she would have no duty to disclose anything to the company.

INSTRUCTIONS FOR PRACTICE AND SIMULATED EXAMS

Although *we suggest doing practice questions online* to simulate the exam experience and get detailed score information, you may wish to practice offline. A full practice exam and a simulated exam follow. You have *two hours* to answer the questions in an exam. An answer sheet is provided after the questions portion of the exams.

The exams each contain 60 questions, as does the actual MPRE. On the actual exam, 50 questions are scored and 10 are nonscored "pretest" questions. Because *you will not know which are the nonscored questions,* you must answer all questions.

Your score will be based on the number of questions you answer correctly. It is therefore to your advantage to answer as many questions as you can. Use your time effectively. If a question seems too difficult, go on to the next one. Nevertheless, you should try to answer *all* questions because wrong answers are not deducted from the right answers.

As on the actual MPRE, a few questions in each practice exam will measure aspects of the ABA Code of Judicial Conduct. The remaining questions are designed so that disciplinary questions can be answered solely under the ABA Model Rules of Professional Conduct, and questions outside the disciplinary context should be answered under the general law governing lawyering, including statutory and common law.

Each question may include, among others, one of the following key words or phrases:

1. *Attorney* usually refers to the particular lawyer whose conduct is at issue. *Lawyer* in the same question usually refers to a different lawyer whose conduct is not at issue. Specific functional names for a lawyer, e.g., *litigator, judge, managing partner, associate, prosecutor*, etc., may also be used if those names do not create ambiguity.

2. *Subject to discipline* asks whether the conduct described in the question would subject the lawyer to discipline under the provisions of the ABA Model Rules of Professional Conduct. In the case of a judge, the test question asks whether the judge would be subject to discipline under the ABA Model Code of Judicial Conduct.

3. *May* or *proper* asks whether the conduct referred to or described in the question is professionally appropriate in that it: (1) would not subject the lawyer or judge to discipline; (2) is not inconsistent with the Preamble, Comments, or text of the ABA Model Rules of Professional Conduct or the ABA Model Code of Judicial Conduct; and (3) is not inconsistent with generally accepted principles of the law of lawyering.

4. *Subject to litigation sanction* asks whether the conduct described in the question would subject the lawyer or the lawyer's law firm to sanction by a tribunal, such as punishment for contempt, fine, fee forfeiture, disqualification, or other sanction.

5. **Subject to disqualification** asks whether the conduct described in the question would subject the lawyer or the lawyer's law firm to disqualification as counsel in a civil or criminal matter.

6. **Subject to civil liability** asks whether the conduct described in the question would subject the lawyer or the lawyer's law firm to civil liability, such as claims arising from malpractice, misrepresentation, and breach of fiduciary duty.

7. **Subject to criminal liability** asks whether the conduct described in the question would subject the lawyer to criminal liability for participation in or aiding and abetting criminal acts, such as prosecution for insurance and tax fraud, destruction of evidence, or obstruction of justice.

8. When a question refers to discipline by the **bar, state bar,** or **disciplinary authority,** it refers to the appropriate entity in the jurisdiction with authority to enforce the rules of professional conduct.

9. The phrases **client-lawyer relationship** and **lawyer-client relationship** have the same meaning.

PRACTICE EXAM

Question 1

A solo practitioner who does municipal bond work in a single state is nearing retirement age and takes on a young attorney as a partner. Their partnership agreement provides that the solo practitioner will train the young attorney and will receive 75% of the partnership's net earnings during the first three years, and that the young attorney will receive the remaining 25%. The agreement also provides that if the young attorney leaves the partnership before the end of the first three years, he will remit to the solo practitioner 75% of all fees he earns thereafter from municipal bond work in the state. Finally, the agreement provides that if the solo practitioner and the young attorney are still partners when the solo practitioner retires, the young attorney will pay the solo practitioner retirement benefits of $3,000 per month until the solo practitioner's death; in return, upon his retirement, the solo practitioner will turn over to the young attorney all of the partnership assets (including goodwill) and will not there-after practice municipal bond law in the state.

Are the solo practitioner and the young attorney subject to discipline for entering into this partnership agreement?

(A) No, because the agreement gives the solo practitioner retirement payments in return for the restriction on his right to practice.

(B) No, because the agreement enables the solo practitioner to sell the partnership assets in return for the restriction on his right to practice.

(C) Yes, because of the restriction on both the solo practitioner's and the young attorney's right to practice.

(D) Yes, because of the restriction on the young attorney's right to practice if he leaves the partnership within the first three years.

Question 2

A justice was on the state supreme court. The state's supreme court rules provide that in capital punishment cases, any one justice of the supreme court is empowered to grant a stay of execution pending appeal to the supreme court. The justice granted such a stay in a recent criminal case, on the ground that the defendant had been denied the effective assistance of counsel at his trial. A few months later, the justice retired from the supreme court and went back to private law practice.

In due course, the supreme court heard the appeal in the case, rejected the defendant's effective assistance of counsel contention, and affirmed the death penalty. The defendant then commenced a federal habeas corpus proceeding in an appropriate federal district court and asked that court to appoint a private lawyer to represent him. The district court appointed the retired justice to represent the defendant. A key issue in the habeas corpus proceeding is whether the defendant was deprived of the effective assistance of counsel at his trial.

May the retired justice represent the defendant without getting informed consent, confirmed in writing, from all parties to the habeas corpus proceeding?

(A) No, because there is reasonable ground to doubt the justice's impartiality in the matter.

(B) No, because when the retired justice was a supreme court justice he granted a stay of execution to the defendant.

(C) Yes, because the retired justice was appointed by the district court, and his prior involvement in the matter is not suffi-cient grounds for refusing the appointment.

(D) Yes, because the respondent in the habeas corpus case is the prison warden, not the state.

GO ON TO THE NEXT PAGE

Question 3

A farmer asked an attorney to represent him in an eminent domain proceeding in which the state sought to obtain a right-of-way across the farmer's land. The attorney had not handled an eminent domain case before, but she planned to make herself competent through diligent research and study. As it turned out, the attorney did not have enough time to do what she had planned, so she associated an eminent domain specialist as her co-counsel in the case. The attorney did not consult the farmer about associating the specialist. The specialist did about 90% of the work in the case, and the attorney did the other 10%. Together they secured a very favorable result for the farmer, and the attorney sent the farmer a fee bill for a reasonable amount. The farmer paid the bill, and the attorney remitted 90% of the proceeds to the specialist.

Is the attorney subject to discipline?

(A) Yes, because she took on a case that she was not competent to handle.

(B) Yes, because she did not consult the farmer about associating the specialist.

(C) No, because the fee split was in proportion to the work done by the two lawyers.

(D) No, because she associated a co-counsel who was competent to handle the case.

Question 4

An attorney is defending her client in a civil fraud case in which it is relevant to know what advice the client received in confidence from an independent certified public accountant. The jurisdiction has no evidentiary privilege for confidential communications between accountants and their clients. The accountant telephoned the attorney and asked how he should respond to the plaintiff's lawyer's request to speak with him privately about the case. Reasonably believing that the accountant would not be harmed by refusing to talk informally with the plaintiff's lawyer, the attorney responded that if the plaintiff's lawyer subpoenaed him to testify, then he must do so, but encouraged him not to talk to the plaintiff's lawyer about the case unless under subpoena.

Was the attorney's advice to the accountant proper?

(A) No, because the advice the accountant gave the client was not protected by an evidentiary privilege.

(B) No, because the attorney interfered with the plaintiff's access to evidence.

(C) Yes, because the accountant acted as the client's agent in rendering accounting advice to the client.

(D) Yes, because it was improper for the plaintiff's lawyer to seek a private discussion with the accountant about the case.

GO ON TO THE NEXT PAGE

Question 5

Solo practitioners Alpha and Beta share office space. Each of them has organized her practice as a professional corporation. The sign on their office door reads:

Attorney Alpha, P.C.

Personal Injury Law

————————

Attorney Beta, P.C.

General Practice

Alpha and Beta frequently consult each other about their respective cases, and they often refer clients to one another. Sometimes they work on cases together under a fee-sharing arrangement. When one of them is out of the office, the other responds to client inquiries to the extent that she is able, and to facilitate that practice, each attorney has physical access to the other's client files. A plaintiff hired Alpha to sue a bakery for personal injuries he sustained when he bit into a piece of glass in a dinner roll baked by the bakery. The bakery's liability insurance carrier asked Beta to serve as defense counsel in the case. Alpha and Beta each disclosed her relationship with the other to their clients, and the plaintiff, the bakery, and the insurance company each gave written consent to Beta's serving as defense counsel.

May Beta take the case?

(A) Yes, because Alpha and Beta believe that they can effectively represent their respective clients.

(B) Yes, because the rule of imputed disqualification does not apply to Alpha and Beta.

(C) No, even though Alpha and Beta believe that they can effectively represent their respective clients.

(D) No, because Alpha and Beta sometimes share fees.

Question 6

A client made a preliminary contact with an attorney to see if she wanted to hire the attorney to defend her in a tort case that had been assigned to a judge. The attorney told the client that the initial consultation was free of charge. After listening to the client's brief outline of the case, the attorney told her that she knew how to get a favorable decision from that judge. She said that he would be running for re-election 18 months from now, and he would need money for his campaign. She advised the client to send him a $2,000 campaign contribution now, with a nice note wishing him well in his bid for re-election. She explained that the judge's opponent in the election would be a local lawyer, and that although the local lawyer was an honest fellow, his two brothers were associated with organized crime. The attorney offered to write a guest editorial for the local paper, praising the judge's judicial record and implying that the local lawyer was a crook. With the contribution and the letter, the attorney said she thought they could count on the judge to reach a wise decision in the client's case.

The client hired the attorney and sent the judge the $2,000. The attorney wrote the guest editorial, and it was published in the local paper.

For which of the following is the attorney not subject to discipline?

(A) Saying that she knew how to get a favorable ruling from the judge.

(B) Advising the client to send the judge a campaign contribution.

(C) Writing the guest editorial.

(D) Accepting the case after giving free legal advice.

GO ON TO THE NEXT PAGE

Question 7

After a series of brutal muggings, the police captured a person whom they charged with the crimes and the person was eventually ordered to stand trial. Two days before jury selection for the case began, a local newspaper reporter cornered the prosecutor, a district attorney, in a cafe. The district attorney said she was certain the defendant was the right man because, among other things, they had discovered that he was previously convicted three times for brutal muggings in other states.

Is the district attorney subject to discipline for making the statement to the reporter?

(A) No, because prior criminal convictions are a matter of public record.

(B) No, because a lawyer has a First Amendment right to inform the public about pending cases.

(C) Yes, because the district attorney should have known that the statement would be quite likely to prejudice the trial.

(D) Yes, because a prosecutor must not make public comment on a pending case.

Question 8

An attorney was assigned by the court to defend an indigent teacher at her murder trial. The jury convicted the teacher, and she was sentenced to 40 years in prison. The attorney's court appointment expired at the end of the trial, but he promised the teacher that he would represent her without cost in taking an appeal from her conviction. The attorney advanced $350 on the teacher's behalf to cover the expenses of the appeal, knowing that the teacher would probably not be able to pay him back. While the appeal was pending, the teacher wrote the manuscript for a book about life in prison. She hired the attorney to negotiate a contract with a publisher to have the book published, and in return for the contract work, she promised to pay the attorney 30% of the royalties from her book.

Is the attorney subject to discipline?

(A) Yes, because he entered into a literary rights contract with his client while her appeal was still pending.

(B) Yes, because he advanced appeal expenses for his client, knowing that she probably could not pay him back.

(C) No, unless 30% of the book royalties is unreasonably high for the contract negotiation work.

(D) Yes, because he agreed to represent his client pursuant to a court appointment and therefore is not entitled to book royalties.

GO ON TO THE NEXT PAGE

Question 9

A probate attorney obtained a decedent's coin collection in order to inventory it. The attorney put the coin collection into a heavy brown envelope, labeled it as part of the decedent's estate, put the brown envelope and the decedent's other belongings into the file drawer of his desk, and left for lunch without locking the file drawer. The attorney's secretary saw the coins and saw what the probate attorney did with them. While the attorney was at lunch, the secretary took the envelope of coins and disappeared, never to be seen again.

Is the probate attorney subject to discipline?

(A) Yes, because the attorney did not put the coins in a safe place.

(B) Yes, because the attorney is responsible for his employee's dishonest act.

(C) No, because the loss was proximately caused by the secretary's dishonesty, not by the attorney's conduct.

(D) No, because the attorney took reasonable precautions to safeguard the coins in the circumstances.

Question 10

A paralegal works for the law firm of Alpha & Beta. Her direct supervisor is partner Alpha, whose practice is limited to international trade law. Partner Beta is the firm's leading trial lawyer, both in commercial and personal injury cases. On her way to work one morning, the paralegal saw a pedestrian run down in a crosswalk by a speeding car. The paralegal rendered first aid, and while she was waiting with the pedestrian for the ambulance, the paralegal provided the pedestrian with a business card and urged him to call the firm to obtain legal representation in connection with his injuries. When she got to work, she told partner Alpha what she had done. Alpha admonished the paralegal not to hand out the firm's cards in such situations, but he did not discuss the matter with partner Beta.

Is Alpha subject to discipline?

(A) Yes, because he failed to warn Beta not to take the pedestrian's case.

(B) Yes, because as the paralegal's supervisor, he is responsible for any unethical act she commits.

(C) No, because as a nonlawyer, the paralegal is free to recommend a lawyer to someone if she wishes.

(D) No, because the paralegal may not have been aware at the time that she did anything wrong.

GO ON TO THE NEXT PAGE

Question 11

An attorney worked at the United States Department of Labor and was responsible for compiling certain corporate safety records into an annual report containing the accident statistics. The report is used internally and in discussions with companies, but it is not distributed to the general public. However, a person may obtain a copy of the report by filing a formal request under the Freedom of Information Act. During the last three years, Company A has had more accidents than any of the other reporting companies. Six months ago, the attorney left the Labor Department and took a job with a private law firm. Recently, a person came to the attorney seeking representation in a suit against Company A for injuries he sustained while working at Company A's factory. The attorney agreed to represent the client.

Is the attorney subject to discipline?

(A) Yes, because he obtained relevant information about Company A while working as a government attorney.

(B) Yes, because the attorney did not obtain the consent of the Department of Labor.

(C) No, because the information is available by formal request under the Freedom of Information Act.

(D) No, if the attorney does not use the information obtained while employed as a government attorney to the material disadvantage of Company A.

Question 12

An attorney and her client endured a stormy attorney-client relationship until the attorney finally withdrew due to the client's repeated refusals to pay the attorney's fee bills. At the end of the relationship, the client owed the attorney more than $10,000. The client said he would not pay because the attorney's legal services were "defective." In a final effort to avoid having to sue the client for the unpaid fees, the attorney proposed a settlement agreement to the client. Under the proposed agreement, the attorney would accept $4,000 as full payment, reserving the right to sue the client for the other $6,000 if the client filed a State Bar disciplinary complaint against the attorney or filed a legal malpractice action against the attorney. The client signed the settlement agreement without consulting outside counsel, and the attorney did not suggest that he should consult outside counsel before signing it.

Is the attorney subject to discipline for entering into the settlement agreement with the client?

(A) No, because the attorney brought about an amicable settlement of the fee dispute with the client.

(B) No, because there was a good faith dispute between the attorney and the client about the quality of the attorney's services and the amount of fees due.

(C) Yes, because the attorney did not advise the client to seek outside counsel before entering into the settlement agreement.

(D) Yes, because the attorney compromised a potential malpractice claim by the contract with her client.

GO ON TO THE NEXT PAGE

Question 13

A worker sued his employer, claiming that he was permanently and totally disabled due to a back injury he suffered on the job. The employer's attorney strongly suspected, but had no proof, that the worker continued his hobby of skydiving after the alleged back injury. In due course, the employer's attorney met with the worker's lawyer for a settlement discussion. The employer's attorney told the worker's lawyer that they had movies of the worker jumping out of an airplane two weeks after his purported injury. The worker's lawyer excused herself to make a telephone call to the worker. When she asked the worker whether he had been skydiving after the accident, he admitted that he had. With the consent of their respective clients, the two lawyers then settled the case for $400.

Is the employer's attorney subject to discipline?

(A) No, because bluffing is an accepted tactic in settlement negotiations between lawyers.

(B) No, because the employer's attorney's bluff successfully unmasked a fraudulent claim.

(C) Yes, because it was improper to pay $400 to settle a fraudulent claim.

(D) Yes, because the employer's attorney lied about having movies.

Question 14

A law student is applying to become a member of the state bar. The bar application questionnaire asks whether the applicant has ever used any illegal drug in violation of state law. When the law student was in high school, she occasionally smoked marijuana, which is a misdemeanor under state law. However, the statute of limitations has run on these incidents, and the law student believes that she could not validly be kept out of the state bar for those offenses. She therefore believes that the question is irrelevant and an invasion of her privacy in violation of the state constitution. She fears, however, that challenging the question could brand her as a troublemaker and delay her admission to the bar.

Which of the following would be proper?

(A) Answer the question in the negative, without saying more.

(B) Answer the question in the negative, citing the state constitution's privacy provision.

(C) Decline to answer the question, citing the state constitution's privacy provision.

(D) Decline to answer the question, citing the federal constitutional privilege against self-incrimination.

GO ON TO THE NEXT PAGE

Question 15

A judge presides over a state trial court. Every six years, trial judges in the state must stand as candidates in a partisan public election to determine whether they will retain their positions. The judge will be a retention candidate in the election to be held nine months from now. In that same election, the judge's husband, an attorney, will be a candidate for lieutenant governor of the state.

The state allows judicial candidates to form campaign committees up to a year before the election.

Which of the following may the judge do?

(A) Establish a campaign committee that will solicit reasonable contributions for the judge's campaign.

(B) Publicly endorse her husband as a candidate for lieutenant governor.

(C) Attend political gatherings in the company of her husband, and speak on behalf of both herself and him.

(D) Personally solicit contributions to her own campaign.

Question 16

Continuously since 1910, the law firm of Alpha & Beta has practiced under that name. The founders of the firm are long dead. No partner named Beta now practices with the firm. Two partners named Alpha were practicing with the firm, but one recently left because she was appointed to the state supreme court.

May the firm continue to use the name Alpha & Beta?

(A) No, because no partner named Beta now practices with the firm.

(B) No, because one partner named Alpha left the firm to enter public service.

(C) Yes, unless the firm name would be misleading.

(D) Yes, even if the firm name will mislead some prospective clients.

Question 17

For three years, an attorney was a partner in a law firm. During that period, the attorney represented a client, Alpha, in obtaining a business loan from a bank. Alpha disclosed to the attorney a great deal of confidential information about his business and his personal assets. No other attorney in the law firm gained access to that confidential information. Recently, the attorney died. Shortly thereafter, Beta asked the senior partner of the law firm to represent him in a civil suit for serious personal injuries Beta suffered when he was run over by a delivery truck driven by one of Alpha's employees.

Would it be proper for the senior partner to represent Beta?

(A) Yes, because the information obtained by the deceased attorney about Alpha's assets has no effect on liability in a personal injury suit.

(B) Yes, because neither the senior partner nor any other attorney in the law firm gained access to Alpha's confidential information.

(C) No, because the conflict created by the deceased attorney's work for Alpha is imputed to the senior partner.

(D) No, because the senior partner did not obtain Alpha's informed consent, confirmed in writing.

GO ON TO THE NEXT PAGE

Question 18

A young associate was assisting a senior partner in writing the reply brief in an appeal for one of the partner's clients. In doing the legal research, the associate discovered a recent case from the controlling jurisdiction that had not been cited in the adversary's brief. In the associate's opinion, the case was directly opposed to the position of the partner's client. The associate asked the partner about citing it in the reply brief, but the partner explained that, in his view, the case was not directly on point and did not have to be cited. The associate and the partner argued back and forth at some length and finally decided to submit the question to one of the other senior partners in the firm for a fresh view. That partner sided with the other partner, and the reply brief was filed without mentioning the case.

May the associate write a short letter to the appellate court and the adversary lawyer, explaining his position and enclosing a copy of the case?

(A) Yes, because the associate had a duty to call the case to the court's attention.

(B) Yes, because the associate must not allow another person to interfere with his professional judgment.

(C) No, because the associate must not communicate with a court ex parte about the merits of a pending case.

(D) No, because the associate should abide by the partner's resolution of the matter.

Question 19

Alpha Corporation ("Alpha") is incorporated in State A and its principal place of business is located there. It manufactures and sells clothing under the trademark *Alpha* ® and licenses its trademark to garment makers in other states. Beta Clothing Co. ("Beta") is incorporated in State B and has its sole place of business there. Beta hired an attorney licensed to practice only in State B to accompany Beta's chief buyer on a trip to State A to negotiate a license to use Alpha's trademark. Beta's attorney will be negotiating with Alpha's lawyer, who is licensed to practice only in State A. Neither lawyer is licensed to practice before the United States Patent and Trademark Office.

If Beta's attorney travels to State A to negotiate the contract, is she subject to discipline?

(A) No, because admission to practice in State A was not necessary to negotiate the trademark license there.

(B) No, because Alpha's lawyer is licensed to practice in State A.

(C) Yes, because the attorney was not admitted to practice in State A.

(D) Yes, because the attorney was not admitted to practice before the United States Patent and Trademark Office.

GO ON TO THE NEXT PAGE

Question 20

An attorney recently opened his solo law practice in a small town. His practice is fairly evenly divided between civil litigation and criminal defense. The Superior Court has just appointed the attorney to represent two defendants, who will be tried jointly for their alleged kidnapping and brutal murder of nine local schoolchildren.

Which of the following is not a valid reason for the attorney to decline the appointment?

(A) He believes that to represent the two defendants will take so much time away from his newly opened practice as to impose an unreasonable financial burden on him.

(B) He believes that one defendant coerced the other defendant into helping kidnap and kill the children.

(C) He believes many of his potential clients will be outraged if he represents the two defendants.

(D) He believes that confidential information he received when representing one of the prosecution's key witnesses will be useful in impeaching that witness's credibility.

Question 21

A federal prosecutor is stationed in State A and is gathering evidence to support federal racketeering charges against a swindler. The prosecutor believes in good faith that a wealthy banker in State B has personal knowledge about three federal felonies committed by the swindler, but the banker will not disclose what he knows. The prosecutor discovers from a secret informant that the banker illegally drained off $4.7 million from a failing State B bank—a state felony punishable by 10 years in prison. The prosecutor therefore mails a letter from his office to the banker, stating in relevant part: "I am coming to State B next week. If you don't give me what I need concerning the swindler, I am going to tell the State B prosecutors what you did to that bank."

Is the federal prosecutor subject to criminal liability because of his evidence-gathering technique?

(A) No, because the federal prosecutor had a legal right to tell the State B prosecutors about the banker, and he simply warned the banker what he intended to do if the banker did not cooperate.

(B) No, because the federal prosecutor was acting in good faith, believing that the banker had relevant, unprivileged information that was material to an ongoing federal criminal investigation.

(C) Yes, because the federal prosecutor made an interstate threat to accuse the banker of a crime for the purpose of extracting valuable information that he could use against the swindler.

(D) Yes, because the federal prosecutor acted under color of law to deprive the banker of his federally protected civil rights.

GO ON TO THE NEXT PAGE

Question 22

An attorney is the head of the in-house law department of a children's clothing company, which has its principal place of business within the state. Under state law, it is a felony to manufacture or sell children's sleepwear that is not fire retardant. The president of the company informed the attorney in confidence that the company is stuck with a whole warehouse full of children's pajama fabric that does not meet the state's fire standards, and that to avoid financial disaster, the company will use the fabric to make children's sleepwear and take its chances on legal liability. The attorney was unable to convince the president to change his mind; she then raised the issue with the company's board of directors, which ratified the president's decision.

Will the attorney be subject to discipline if she resigns as house counsel and reports the matter to the appropriate state law enforcement authorities?

(A) Yes, because the attorney is required to preserve the corporation's confidential information even after she resigns.

(B) Yes, because there is no adequate reason for permissive withdrawal on these facts.

(C) No, because the attorney is entitled to reveal this type of confidential information.

(D) No, because the attorney's duty to preserve confidential information ceases with her resignation as house counsel.

Question 23

An attorney is a partner in a four-partner law firm. A client entrusted $40,000 to the attorney, instructing the attorney to hold it in safekeeping for a few days and then to use it as the down payment on a piece of lakefront property. The attorney promptly deposited the money in his law firm's law office account, a special bank account that the firm uses to pay the office rent, pay staff salaries, advance litigation expenses on behalf of clients, and the like. A few days later, when it was time to make the down payment, the attorney discovered that one of his law partners had made two large withdrawals from the law office account, reducing the account balance far below the $40,000 needed for the client's down payment. The client's attorney was unable to come up with other money to make up the difference, and the client thus lost the chance to buy the lakefront property.

Is the attorney subject to civil liability to the client for mishandling the money?

(A) No, because it was the attorney's law partner, not the attorney, who made the two large withdrawals that made it impossible to come up with the down payment.

(B) No, because the legal ethics rule governing safekeeping of clients' funds is for professional disciplinary purposes only; it is not intended as a standard for civil liability purposes.

(C) Yes, because the attorney mishandled the money and is therefore civilly liable to the client for breach of his fiduciary duty.

(D) Yes, because a lawyer is strictly liable to a client for harm incident to the disappearance of money that the client has entrusted to the lawyer.

GO ON TO THE NEXT PAGE

Question 24

A law firm represented an oil company in a merger transaction in which the oil company acquired all of the assets of a smaller petroleum company in exchange for a specified amount of capital stock of the oil company. The law firm's work for the oil company was limited to the antitrust and securities law issues raised by the merger, and the firm lawyers who worked on the matter did not become privy to any confidential information concerning the routine operations of the oil company's business. The merger work was completed two years ago, and the law firm has not subsequently represented the oil company in any other matter.

Recently, the law firm took in a new partner who had previously practiced as a solo practitioner. One of the cases that the new partner brought the firm from his solo practice was an employment discrimination case in which the new partner's client claims that the oil company fired him solely because of his age. When the new partner joined the law firm as a partner, the oil company promptly made a motion in the trial court to disqualify the new partner and the law firm as counsel for the plaintiff due to the law firm's earlier representation of the oil company in the merger matter.

Are the new partner and the law firm subject to disqualification?

(A) No, because the merger matter and the discrimination case are unrelated matters and because the law firm did not gain confidential information from the oil company that would be material in the discrimination case.

(B) No, because whatever material confidential information the oil company might have picked up in the merger matter is not imputed to the new partner.

(C) Yes, because the law firm owes continuing duties of loyalty and confidentiality to its former client, the oil company.

(D) Yes, even though the merger matter and the discrimination case are unrelated and even though the law firm did not gain confidential information from the oil company that would be material in the discrimination case.

Question 25

A lawyer in a partnership died, leaving his daughter, a doctor, as his sole heir. Under the partnership agreement, the firm plans to make the following payments to the deceased lawyer's daughter: $100,000, which represents the decedent's share of the firm's assets, as measured by his capital contribution; $45,000, which represents the decedent's share of fees that had been earned but not collected from clients at his death; and a $125,000 death benefit, representing a percentage of the decedent's earnings the year prior to his death, and payable in 12 monthly installments.

Under the Model Rules, which of the following represents the most that the firm may properly pay to the decedent's daughter?

(A) $100,000 for the decedent's share of the firm's assets.

(B) $145,000 for the decedent's share of the firm's assets and his share of uncollected fees.

(C) $170,000, which represents the death benefit and the decedent's share of uncollected fees.

(D) $270,000, which includes the decedent's share of the firm's assets, his share of uncollected fees, and the death benefit.

GO ON TO THE NEXT PAGE

Question 26

A concerned environmentalist hired an attorney to obtain preliminary and permanent injunctions against a highway construction project that would require draining and filling certain wetlands inhabited by migratory waterfowl. The attorney is the nation's leading expert in wetland preservation law, and he charges $400 per hour for his services. The environmentalist agreed to pay him at that rate. She gave him a $40,000 advance on attorneys' fees and a $5,000 advance to cover future litigation expenses. The attorney deposited the entire $45,000 in his client trust account.

The attorney then spent 80 hours preparing and filing a complaint and preparing and arguing a motion for a preliminary injunction. He paid a court filing fee of $50, plus $1,950 in witness fees to wetlands experts who testified at the hearing on the preliminary injunction motion. The judge denied the preliminary injunction motion. The attorney sent the environmentalist a bill for $32,000 in attorneys' fees and $2,000 in litigation expenses, and he told her he would deduct those sums from the advances she had given him unless he heard from her to the contrary within 15 days. In light of the loss of the preliminary injunction motion, the environmentalist was outraged at the size of the attorney's fee; she immediately fired him and demanded the prompt refund of her entire $45,000.

Which of the following amounts must the attorney promptly refund to his former client, the environmentalist?

(A) $0

(B) $11,000

(C) $13,000

(D) $43,000

Question 27

An attorney is admitted to practice only in State A, where he specializes in securities and real estate finance law. In that role, the attorney advised his client that the law of State B did not require the client to include information about certain mineral rights in a disclosure statement that the client had to file in State B in order to sell some real estate limited partnership interests to State B citizens. Acting on the attorney's advice, the client did not disclose the information and did sell partnership interests to State B citizens.

Later, the attorney became a full-time trial court judge in State A. Later still, State B brought a criminal action against the client for failing to disclose the mineral rights information in his State B disclosure statement. One of the client's defenses is that he lacked the necessary criminal intent because he was acting in good faith based on the advice of his counsel, the attorney who is now a judge. The client needs the judge's testimony to prove that the judge did indeed advise him that he was not required to disclose the mineral rights information. The judge, in State A, is beyond the subpoena power of the State B court.

May the judge voluntarily testify on behalf of the client?

(A) No, because judges are disqualified from serving as witnesses in criminal cases.

(B) No, because he is not admitted to practice in State B, and his testimony about State B law would be inadmissible.

(C) Yes, because a judge may testify as a witness, except in his own court or one under its appellate jurisdiction.

(D) Yes, because his testimony would concern the giving of the advice, not his client's character.

GO ON TO THE NEXT PAGE

Question 28

A client sought the advice of an attorney on a difficult and sensitive family problem. The client suspected that her husband had been molesting the client's 12-year-old daughter by a prior marriage. The client asked the attorney what she should do. The attorney advised the client that all three members of the family should consult a licensed family counselor who specializes in precisely this sort of problem. Fearing that if the client were aware of the law she would not seek counseling, the attorney purposely failed to tell the client that a new state statute requires family counselors to report to the district attorney all instances of suspected child abuse.

The client and her family consulted the family counselor, and the family counselor reported the matter to the district attorney, as she was required to do by law. The district attorney commenced criminal proceedings against the client's husband, much against the wishes of both the client and her daughter.

Were the attorney's actions proper?

(A) Yes, because the attorney feared that the client would not seek counseling if she knew about the statute.

(B) Yes, because it is the policy of the state that all instances of child abuse be reported to the appropriate authorities.

(C) No, because a lawyer should fully advise a client of relevant information.

(D) No, because as an officer of the court, the attorney had a duty to protect the minor.

Question 29

When an attorney was an associate at a law firm, she did the legal work for one of the firm's clients on a land sale transaction that earned the client millions of dollars. In gratitude, the client asked the attorney whether she had any unfulfilled wishes. The attorney told the client that she wished she had enough money to start her own solo law practice. The client then told her that he would lend her $100,000 to set up her new practice. In return, she would thereafter do all of his legal work at a 5% discount from her normal hourly fee, and she would pay off the $100,000 loan by monthly payments equal to 10% of her net income for the prior month. The attorney was delighted. She drafted a complete, detailed agreement between herself and the client, and she advised the client in writing to obtain outside legal advice before signing the agreement. The client obtained the outside advice and signed the agreement, and the attorney set up her solo practice accordingly.

Is the attorney subject to discipline?

(A) No, unless she allows the client to interfere with her professional judgment in handling work for other clients.

(B) No, unless the attorney fails to give the law firm timely notice of the transaction.

(C) Yes, unless the law firm consented to the loss of the client as a firm client.

(D) Yes, unless the client is a lawyer.

GO ON TO THE NEXT PAGE

Question 30

An attorney represented a woman in a court proceeding to raise the alimony and child support payments set in the woman's divorce decree. The woman's ex-husband refused to get a lawyer in the matter. The evening before the court hearing, the ex-husband telephoned the attorney at home and asked the attorney to explain the legal standard the judge would apply to his wife's request for increased payments. The attorney responded that she was not his lawyer, and could not give him legal advice. She urged him to get a lawyer.

The ex-husband said he did not want a lawyer, and then asked the attorney whether his wife and the children really needed more money to live on. The attorney responded that she had no personal interest to serve here— that she was simply trying to do what was best for everyone involved, and that he should pay the extra money because they did need it to live on.

The ex-husband thanked the attorney and hung up.

Was the attorney's handling of the matter proper?

(A) No, because as the wife's lawyer, the attorney should not have communicated directly with the ex-husband at all.

(B) No, because the attorney pretended to be disinterested and advised the ex-husband to pay the extra money.

(C) Yes, because the attorney advised the ex-husband that she was not his lawyer, that the ex-husband should retain one, and that the attorney could not give him legal advice.

(D) Yes, because the attorney only stated her opinion and did not purport to give the ex-husband advice.

Question 31

An attorney represents a defendant in a drug smuggling case. The defendant is in pretrial custody in a distant city and cannot be reached by telephone. One key issue in the defendant's case is on the cutting edge of search and seizure law, and the attorney believes that he needs help to deal with the issue competently. The attorney's former law professor is a nationally known expert on search and seizure law, but is not licensed to practice law in that state. The attorney calls his former professor to ask for help and also asks that the professor keep their conversation confidential. To frame the issue accurately, the attorney tells the law professor some information that the defendant revealed to the attorney in confidence. The attorney does not tell the professor the name of his client.

Is the attorney subject to discipline for disclosing the defendant's confidential information to the professor?

(A) Yes, because the professor was not licensed to practice in that jurisdiction.

(B) Yes, because the defendant did not specifically authorize the attorney to make the disclosure.

(C) No, because the disclosure was necessary to effectively carry out the representation.

(D) No, because the attorney did not reveal his client's name.

GO ON TO THE NEXT PAGE

Question 32

For many years, a tax attorney has handled all of the tax work for his client, a sculptor. One evening, the sculptor invited the attorney to his studio to discuss some tax returns that had to be filed the next day. In the studio, the attorney saw a small sculpture that would be perfect for his office. At the close of their tax discussion, the attorney offered to buy the sculpture for $10,000, its approximate fair market value. The sculptor told the attorney that it was not for sale. In due course, the attorney sent the sculptor a bill for a $750 fee for the tax work. A few days later, the small sculpture was delivered to the attorney's office with a note from the sculptor, saying that he hoped the sculpture would satisfy the recent bill, and he wanted the attorney to have the sculpture as a token of his gratitude for the excellent tax advice.

Would the attorney be subject to discipline for accepting the small sculpture from the sculptor?

(A)   Yes, because the gift is of significant monetary value.

(B)   Yes, because the value of the sculpture is far out of proportion to the $750 worth of work the attorney did for the sculptor.

(C)   No, because the attorney did not solicit the gift.

(D)   No, because the $10,000 is only an approximation of market value.

Question 33

A public defender was assigned to represent a defendant at the defendant's preliminary hearing on a charge of kidnapping for ransom. Against the public defender's advice, the defendant testified on his own behalf at the preliminary hearing. The defendant was bound over for trial. At that point, the defendant's brother provided money to hire a private lawyer to represent the defendant, and the public defender was discharged. The defendant testified on his own behalf at the trial, and the matter concluded after the jury acquitted him. Later, in connection with his work on another matter, the public defender read the transcript of the defendant's trial. Based on information the public defender learned while representing the defendant, the public defender concluded that the defendant had committed perjury, both at the preliminary hearing and at the trial. However, the public defender does not believe that the defendant poses a danger to the community.

May the public defender reveal the defendant's perjury?

(A)   Yes, the public defender may reveal the perjury committed at the defendant's preliminary hearing.

(B)   Yes, the public defender may reveal both instances of perjury.

(C)   No, because the public defender does not believe that the defendant poses a danger to the community.

(D)   No, because disclosure would violate the public defender's duty of confidentiality.

GO ON TO THE NEXT PAGE

Question 34

A bank operates a professional referral hotline for its depositors. Any bank depositor who needs to find a physician, lawyer, accountant, dentist, or the like can telephone the hotline and obtain a free referral from lists of professionals compiled by the bank. The lists are limited to professionals who maintain an average balance of at least $10,000 in an account at the bank, but the professional does not pay a fee to the bank for receiving a particular referral. An attorney keeps $10,000 on deposit with the bank for the express purpose of being included on its lawyer referral list.

Is this arrangement proper?

(A) Yes, because the bank is functioning in the role of a lawyer referral service.

(B) Yes, because neither the bank's depositors nor the professionals pay a fee for referrals.

(C) No, because the attorney is required to keep $10,000 on deposit to be included on the list.

(D) No, because this arrangement constitutes an association with a nonlawyer for the practice of law.

Question 35

An inventor asked a patent attorney to represent him in obtaining a patent on a new computer technique for predicting the growth patterns of tumors in the human body. The attorney informed the inventor that he had never worked on that kind of patent application before, and that he would have to do extensive background research on the patentability of computer techniques. The attorney will be able to use the knowledge that he gains through the research to serve other clients who wish to obtain patents for all manner of other computer techniques. The attorney offered to do the work for the inventor for his standard hourly rate, but the inventor proposed instead to assign the attorney a 10% interest in the patent, if and when it was issued. The attorney agreed to do the work on that basis, and he and the inventor entered into an appropriate written fee agreement.

The attorney did the work; the patent was ultimately issued and proved so valuable that the attorney was able to sell his 10% interest for $9.7 million (which was a reasonable fee for the work performed).

Is the attorney subject to discipline?

(A) Yes, because he acquired a proprietary interest in the subject of the representation.

(B) Yes, because it is unreasonable to charge one client for background research that will be used to earn fees from other clients.

(C) No, because the inventor agreed to the fee arrangement.

(D) No, because $9.7 million is not an unreasonably high fee for the work that the attorney did.

GO ON TO THE NEXT PAGE

Question 36

An attorney is admitted to practice only in one state. One of her regular clients is a corporation incorporated in the same state and has its principal place of business there. The president of the corporation went to another country to negotiate a contract that would be governed by foreign law. He telephoned the attorney to ask whether a particular provision that he proposed would be lawful under foreign law, and he needed a quick answer because he had to resume negotiations in a few minutes. The attorney had studied that country's law in school, but warned the president about the danger of relying on off-the-cuff, unresearched legal advice. The president asked the attorney to do the best she could. She then advised the president that the contract provision would be lawful. The president signed a contract that included the questioned provision. As it turned out, the provision violated that country's law and rendered the contract unenforceable.

Is the attorney subject to discipline?

(A) No, because she did the best she could in an emergency situation.

(B) No, because a lawyer in the United States is not expected to be competent in foreign law.

(C) Yes, because she is not licensed to practice in another country.

(D) Yes, because she gave legal advice without adequate research.

Question 37

An entertainment attorney has for many years represented a country music star. One evening, the attorney and the music star were having a quiet business dinner together at a restaurant. Another diner approached their table and in a loud voice began a vulgar and defamatory tirade against the music star. Everyone in the restaurant heard the entire exchange. While all of the defamatory comments about the music star involved her personal life, about which the attorney had no real knowledge, he felt that they could not possibly be true. At the music star's request, the attorney commenced a slander suit against the diner, after spending considerable time reacquainting himself with slander law. In his answer to the complaint, the diner admitted making the allegedly slanderous statements, and as an affirmative defense, he alleged that the statements were entirely truthful.

When the case comes to trial, would it be proper for the attorney to act as the music star's trial counsel?

(A) Yes, if the star gives informed consent, confirmed in writing.

(B) Yes, because the attorney is not a necessary witness.

(C) No, because there is a possibility that the attorney may be called as a witness.

(D) No, because he was not competent to take a slander case.

GO ON TO THE NEXT PAGE

Question 38

An attorney is on the in-house legal staff of a large corporation. In that capacity, she works daily with the corporation's top executive officers. She was assigned to defend the corporation in a lawsuit brought by a bank to collect a $750,000 promissory note. The note was signed on behalf of the corporation by its treasurer and chief financial officer. The corporation's defense is that the treasurer had no authority to sign the note and that the bank knew it. The corporation has advised the treasurer that it may seek indemnification from him if it is held liable to the bank. The treasurer is not represented by counsel. Shortly before the treasurer was to have his deposition taken by the bank, he called the attorney and asked her what to expect at the deposition and how to respond to the bank's questions.

What should the attorney do?

(A) Advise the treasurer to hire a lawyer to represent him at the deposition.

(B) Tell the treasurer that she cannot discuss the matter with him unless he wants her to represent him at the deposition.

(C) Advise the treasurer to tell the truth, to answer fully all questions that are asked, and to pause before each answer to give her time to object to the bank's questions.

(D) Advise the treasurer that his own interests will be best served by answering truthfully and demonstrating, if he can, that he had authority to sign the note.

Question 39

An attorney is licensed to practice law in State A, but he is not engaged in the active practice of law. The attorney and his non-attorney partner operate a temporary placement service for legal secretaries in State B. The attorney performs most of his work for the agency in State A and is not licensed to practice law in State B. Neither does he hold himself out to be so licensed. An investigation by State B authorities results in the discovery that the attorney and his partner have intentionally filed improper state business tax returns.

Is the attorney subject to discipline in State A?

(A) Yes, because his actions in State B constitute fraud.

(B) Yes, because he supervises the temporary service business from State A.

(C) No, because the attorney is not licensed to practice law in State B.

(D) No, because this situation does not involve the practice of law.

GO ON TO THE NEXT PAGE

Question 40

An attorney takes on a client who was hit by a car and was unable to work for 18 months. At the client's request, the attorney agreed to represent the client on a contingent fee basis. The client requested that the attorney provide him with certain financial assistance during the pendency of the lawsuit. The attorney agrees to provide a $20,000 loan, in an agreement reviewed by independent counsel. The $20,000 would cover $5,000 to support the client's family, $5,000 for the client's medical treatment, $5,000 to retain an expert witness, and $5,000 for job training.

Which of the following was proper?

(A) The $5,000 to support the client's family during the pendency of the suit.

(B) The $5,000 for the client's medical treatment.

(C) The $5,000 to pay the expert witness fee.

(D) The $5,000 for job training.

Question 41

In an effort to prevent gay persons from moving to their small town, a city council passed a zoning ordinance prohibiting the use of any dwelling house as a residence for two or more adults of the same sex unless they are related to each other. Violation of the ordinance is a misdemeanor and carries a fine of $10,000. A landlord who owns several rental houses in the city and does not want his potential renter pool limited hired an attorney to advise him. The attorney advised the landlord that the ordinance could probably be overturned under the state constitution, but that one would have to obtain legal standing to challenge the ordinance. The attorney advised that one way to obtain legal standing would be for a landlord to bring an appropriate action for declaratory judgment, and another way would be to simply violate the ordinance and raise the constitutional challenge as a defense to its enforcement.

After receiving this advice, the landlord promptly rented one of his houses to two gay men. The landlord was cited for violation of the ordinance. The landlord subsequently brought an action to challenge the ordinance, and the ordinance was held unconstitutional.

Was the attorney's conduct proper?

(A) Yes, because violating the ordinance was one of the few ways to gain legal standing to challenge the constitutionality of the law.

(B) Yes, because the ordinance was ultimately held unconstitutional.

(C) No, because the attorney counseled and assisted the landlord in conduct the attorney knew was illegal.

(D) No, because the attorney did not advise against renting houses to unrelated adults of the same sex.

GO ON TO THE NEXT PAGE

Question 42

An attorney has just opened an office in a town where he does not know many people and has few contacts. The attorney has just heard that a group of townspeople, including a former client, have been arrested and are being held at the county jail for conducting a noisy demonstration outside the local high school to protest an impending strike by the teachers. The attorney strongly believes that the arrests were politically motivated and that the demonstrators have been deprived of their freedom of expression in violation of the First Amendment. He also realizes that he might gain some favorable public exposure if he were to help the arrestees. He therefore goes down to the county jail and offers his legal services, free of charge, to any of the arrested demonstrators who want legal assistance.

Are the attorney's actions proper?

(A)   Yes, because one of the arrested demon-strators was a former client.

(B)   Yes, because the attorney was offering his services free of charge.

(C)   No, because to do so would involve in-person solicitation of legal business.

(D)   No, because he was motivated at least in part by a desire to obtain publicity for his law practice.

Question 43

A full-time trial judge, in addition to her judicial work, is the chief executive officer of a corporation that is closely held by the judge and her three brothers. The corporation owns and operates a nursing home. Because of strong anti-gay religious beliefs on the part of residents, the nursing home does not employ gay people. The judge's responsibilities for the corporation do not interfere with her judicial duties.

Is it proper for the judge to continue as chief executive officer of the corporation?

(A)   Yes, because a judge is only prohibited from associating with an organization that practices invidious discrimination on the basis of race, sex, religion, or national origin.

(B)   Yes, because the management of the family-owned business does not take so much time that it interferes with the judge's judicial duties.

(C)   No, because a judge is not allowed to serve as an officer, director, manager, general partner, advisor, or employee of a business entity.

(D)   No, because the nursing home practices employment discrimination against gay people.

GO ON TO THE NEXT PAGE

Question 44

An attorney was appointed by the court to defend a client at his criminal trial for second degree murder. The attorney started interviewing potential witnesses. When she interviewed the client's landlord, the landlord said that on the night of the murder, the client came home very late and was wearing a shirt covered with blood. The landlord died before trial without speaking to state authorities.

Which of the following best states what the attorney should do with respect to the information she has learned from the landlord?

(A) The attorney should voluntarily reveal the information to the prosecutor prior to trial because the death of the landlord has made it impossible for the prosecutor to obtain the information in any other way.

(B) The attorney should urge the client to allow her to reveal the information to the prosecutor, and if the client refuses, the attorney should withdraw.

(C) The attorney should keep the information in confidence unless the client authorizes her to reveal it, even though the death of the landlord has made it impossible for the prosecutor to obtain the information in any way other than from the attorney.

(D) The attorney should use her own best judgment about how to treat the information; it is neither privileged nor confidential because it was not given to her by her client or by an agent of her client.

Question 45

The mother of a full-time trial judge owns a small business that she wishes to sell. After she and a prospective buyer come to terms on the sale, the buyer has his lawyer draw up a sales contract and presents it to the judge's mother, who asks her son, the judge, to review it for her. The judge agrees, marks up the contract, and returns it to his mother to present to the buyer's attorney. The judge's mother did not tell the buyer that her son reviewed the contract. The buyer has no known reason for being likely to appear in the judge's court.

Were the judge's actions proper?

(A) Yes, because the buyer is not likely to appear in the judge's court in the future.

(B) Yes, because he did not charge his mother a fee.

(C) No, because a full-time judge is not permitted to practice law.

(D) No, because the judge's identity was not disclosed to the buyer or the buyer's attorney.

GO ON TO THE NEXT PAGE

Question 46

A private adoption agency handles over 65% of all private adoptions in the state in which the agency is located. The agency provides each set of prospective adoptive parents with a list of lawyers whom the agency recommends and tells them that it is in their best interest to obtain a lawyer experienced in adoptions. The agency has investigated each lawyer on its list to ensure the lawyer's experience and reputation for honesty and ethical behavior. To further protect prospective adoptive parents, the agency also requires each lawyer on the list to agree not to withdraw from any case where he has been retained by parents adopting through the agency.

An attorney who has handled many private adoptions and is highly regarded as an honest and competent lawyer would like to be placed on the agency's list.

Would it be proper for the attorney to sign the agreement and have himself included in the list?

(A) Yes, because the list is a valuable service, and people often do not know where to find a lawyer qualified to handle a matter such as a private adoption.

(B) Yes, because the attorney does not give anything of value to the agency in exchange for being placed on the list.

(C) No, because the agency is acting as the attorney's agent, and a lawyer may not use an agent to contact persons in a manner that would be unethical solicitation if done by the lawyer.

(D) No, because the agreement allows a third party to exercise influence over the lawyer-client relationship.

Question 47

Attorneys Alpha and Beta have been law partners for six years. Beta was suspended from practice for one year based on an intentional tax law violation. Alpha took over Beta's clients when his suspension went into effect. Shortly before his suspension, Beta had negotiated a $30,000 personal injury settlement with an insurance company on behalf of his client. Two weeks after the settlement was reached, the insurance company sent a $30,000 check to the law offices. By this time Beta's suspension had gone into effect. Alpha placed the check in the proper firm account and confirmed the amount of the fee with Beta's client. Alpha then promptly forwarded a $20,000 check to the client and a $10,000 check to Beta, the latter check representing Beta's one-third contingent fee.

Is Alpha subject to discipline?

(A) Yes, because she should have held the $10,000 in the client trust account until Beta's suspension had ended.

(B) Yes, because a lawyer is prohibited from sharing legal fees with a nonlawyer.

(C) No, because Beta earned the fee prior to his suspension.

(D) No, because the $10,000 belonged to Alpha's firm, and she could do anything she wished with it, including sending it to Beta as a gift.

GO ON TO THE NEXT PAGE

Question 48

A judge is a loyal member of the alumni association of the women's college from which she was graduated. The 25th reunion of her graduating class is coming up, and she has been asked to participate in some activities designed to raise money for a gift from the class to the college scholarship fund.

Which of the following activities would be improper for the judge to do?

(A)   Make a substantial personal donation to the class gift fund.

(B)   Telephone other members of her graduating class and urge them to make a donation to the class gift fund.

(C)   Serve on the scholarship fund committee, which devises the various fund-raising strategies.

(D)   Attend a fund-raising dinner for the class gift.

Question 49

A defendant asked an attorney to defend him in a criminal case in which the defendant was charged with running a gambling operation. The defendant was known in the community as a wealthy person, but one who seldom kept his word and seldom paid his bills. The attorney agreed to do the necessary work for a flat fee of $5,000, which was reasonable in light of the difficulty of the case and the number of hours required. However, the attorney required that the defendant pay $3,000 in advance. When the defendant protested that he did not have that amount available in ready cash, the attorney accepted the defendant's full-length fur coat in lieu of the cash advance. The fair market value of the coat is $3,000, and the attorney agreed to return it upon payment of his fee. Their agreement was reduced to writing and signed by both parties.

After the attorney had put in considerable time in preparing the case for trial, the defendant fired the attorney for no good reason and refused to pay him anything for the work already done. Assuming the reasonable value of the attorney's services to date is $4,000, which of the following statements is correct?

(A)   The attorney is subject to discipline for demanding that the defendant pay $3,000 in advance, before any legal services had been rendered.

(B)   The attorney is subject to discipline for taking the coat in lieu of cash as an advance on legal fees.

(C)   The attorney is not subject to discipline because the client had a reputation for not paying his bills.

(D)   The attorney is not subject to discipline because all of his described conduct was proper.

GO ON TO THE NEXT PAGE

Question 50

An attorney is interested in obtaining legal business from a mineworkers' union that has many members in the state in which the attorney practices. As a result of a recent mine fire and explosion in which several union members were killed, the union has succeeded in persuading the appropriate state agency to bring an administrative action against the company that owns the mine for failing to install smoke detectors, which might have saved some lives in the disaster.

Although the attorney is in no way involved in the case, he sees this as an opportunity to obtain future business from the union by showing the union that he is strongly on its side in the mine disaster case. The attorney telephones a popular call-in radio show, and says that he is shocked and appalled at the callousness of the mining company that caused the recent disaster in which so many miners were killed. He further opines that the mining company was willful and wanton in its failure to install smoke detectors, and expresses hope that the company will not be allowed to escape the consequences of its despicable conduct.

Without the attorney's knowledge or consent, his statement was later printed in several newspapers in the state.

Is the attorney subject to discipline for his conduct?

(A) Yes, because he was substantially moti-vated by his desire to attract fee-paying business.

(B) Yes, because lawyers must not make public comments concerning pending litigation.

(C) No, because he did not make any false or misleading claims about himself or his services.

(D) No, because the statement was printed in the newspapers without his knowledge or consent.

GO ON TO THE NEXT PAGE

Question 51

An attorney limits her practice to family law. A married couple came to her, hoping to save their marriage. After hearing their story, the attorney explained that she could act as a third-party neutral between them—not representing either one of them, but facilitating their efforts to work through their difficulties. The attorney explained that neither of them would have the protections afforded by an ordinary attorney-client relationship, such as the attorney-client privilege, and both said that they understood. The attorney held a series of meetings with the couple (sometimes with both, and other times with just one). The attorney began each meeting with a reminder that, in the event of later litigation between the husband and wife, the attorney-client privilege would not protect what was said at the meeting. At one of the attorney's individual meetings with the husband, he disclosed that he occasionally used drugs and sometimes used the family's savings to purchase them. Ultimately, the husband and wife were unable to resolve their differences, and the wife sued the husband for a divorce and for custody of their three children. At the custody hearing, the wife's lawyer called the attorney to the witness stand and asked what the husband told her about his drug use. The attorney refused to answer, citing the attorney-client privilege.

Which of the following is correct?

(A) The privilege claim should be overruled; if the attorney refuses to answer, she would be subject to litigation sanction.

(B) The privilege claim should be sustained; if the attorney reveals what the husband said, she would be subject to discipline.

(C) The attorney is subject to discipline for attempting to serve as a third-party neutral in a family law matter.

(D) The attorney is subject to civil liability for attempting to serve as a third-party neutral in a family law matter.

GO ON TO THE NEXT PAGE

Question 52

A technology company makes computer chips. It is incorporated in State A and it has a chip manufacturing plant in State B. Recently, the chip manufacturing plant has been afflicted with a rash of employment discrimination claims. The company's general counsel instructs one of the company's attorneys, who is admitted to practice only in State A, to move temporarily to State B, settle all existing meritorious claims, prepare all nonmeritorious claims for trial, and train the managers of the State B plant to comply with federal and state employment discrimination laws. The general counsel knows that the attorney is not admitted to practice in State B. State B requires out-of-state lawyers to seek pro hac vice admission before undertaking pretrial preparation.

May the attorney do as the general counsel has instructed?

(A) Yes, because the attorney's right to practice temporarily in State B is a debatable issue of legal ethics, and it is appropriate for such an issue to be decided by a lawyer's supervisor.

(B) Yes, but because State B requires out-of-state lawyers to be admitted pro hac vice in order to engage in pretrial preparations, the attorney must seek such admission.

(C) No, because the attorney must take and pass State B's bar exam.

(D) No, because the attorney must associate a State B lawyer who will actively participate with the attorney in settling the meritorious claims and preparing the nonmeritorious claims for trial.

Question 53

The state bar certifies specialists in nine fields of law, one of which is tax law. An attorney has not yet earned her certificate of specialization in tax law, but she is working toward that goal. The attorney's ad states that she is a specialist in tax law, and that tax law is a field in which the state bar grants certificates of specialization.

The attorney limits her practice to tax matters; she refers all other kinds of legal matters to a solo practitioner in general practice. The solo practitioner, in turn, refers all tax matters to the attorney. Without exception, the solo practitioner and the attorney have followed that pattern of referrals for five or six years; they have no formal reciprocal referral agreement, but each invariably follows the pattern, expecting the other to reciprocate.

Which of the following most correctly describes the attorney's situation?

(A) The attorney is subject to discipline for her ad, but not for maintaining the referral relationship with the solo practitioner.

(B) The attorney's ad is proper, and so is her referral relationship with the solo practitioner.

(C) The attorney is subject to discipline for her ad, and her referral relationship with the solo practitioner is improper because it would need to be nonexclusive, and the two lawyers would need to disclose it to referred clients.

(D) The attorney's ad is proper, but she is subject to discipline for maintaining the referral relationship with the solo practitioner.

GO ON TO THE NEXT PAGE

Question 54

An attorney is one of only nine lawyers who practice probate law in a particular county. In that county, all probate matters go before a single judge—the probate judge. The probate judge's duties include appointing counsel for the administrators of intestate estates. Serving as an administrator's counsel can be very lucrative. The incumbent probate judge recently retired. Her custom was to appoint out-of-county lawyers to serve as administrators' counsel, believing that such lawyers are less subject to local political and social pressures than county lawyers. The probate judgeship will be filled in six months in a partisan, contested election, and the attorney is one of the candidates.

The attorney met jointly with the county's eight other probate lawyers and said he was seeking the probate judgeship, and would be making some important changes, such as appointing only local lawyers as counsel for administrators of intestate estates. He also said that if they'd like to contribute money or time, to please get in touch with his campaign committee via his website. Five of the eight lawyers sent generous monetary donations to the attorney's campaign committee for the self-confessed purpose of securing legal appointments if the attorney wins. The other three lawyers volunteered generous amounts of their time in the attorney's campaign, but their motives for doing so were unexpressed and unclear.

Which of the following is correct?

(A) The attorney is subject to discipline for personally soliciting money and publicly stated support from the eight lawyers. The five lawyers who contributed money will be subject to discipline if the attorney wins and if they accept appointments from him.

(B) The attorney's conduct was proper because he was a candidate for a judicial office in a contested election. All eight lawyers, however, are subject to discipline because a practicing lawyer must not contribute either money or time to the political campaign of a judge before whom the lawyer expects to appear.

(C) The attorney is subject to discipline for promising to appoint only local lawyers as counsel for administrators, in the hope of securing the publicly stated support of the eight lawyers. The conduct of all eight lawyers, however, was proper because lawyers are permitted to support or oppose candidates in contested elections for judgeships.

(D) The attorney's conduct was proper because he was a lawyer-candidate, not a judge, at the time he met with the eight lawyers. The conduct of the five lawyers who contributed money was proper because a person's motive for making a political contribution is a private matter that is protected by the First and Fourteenth Amendments.

GO ON TO THE NEXT PAGE

Question 55

An attorney volunteers her legal services one night each week at a county legal advice hotline. The hotline is run under the auspices of the superior court, and it supplies free legal advice by telephone to callers who could not otherwise obtain legal services. Every caller assents to a "Statement of Understanding" at the outset of the call, informing the caller of the limited nature of the legal services that the hotline provides. Eighty-five lawyers volunteer their services as the attorney does. They come to the hotline office at various times on various days, and the volunteers hardly ever see or talk with each other. The nature of the hotline's work makes it impossible for the lawyers to conduct the kind of conflict-of-interest checks that an ordinary law firm would conduct before taking on a new client. One Tuesday night, the attorney counseled a distraught mother about her husband's physical and mental abuse of their school-age children. The attorney told the mother how to seek help from Child Protective Services. On the following Friday evening, a different hotline lawyer volunteer counseled the mother's husband about how to prevent Child Protective Services from scooping up his children and putting them in a foster home. Because the hotline does not do conflict-of-interest checks, the lawyer who counseled the husband had no way to know that the first attorney had counseled the mother a few nights before.

Which of the following is correct?

(A) The judges of the superior court are subject to discipline for permitting the hotline to operate under their auspices without making a conflict-of-interest check before dispensing legal advice to a new client.

(B) Both lawyers and the judges of the superior court all acted properly

because the hotline cannot do the kind of conflict-of-interest checking that a private law firm would do.

(C) The first attorney acted properly in advising the mother, but the second lawyer is subject to discipline for giving legal advice to the father on the same subject.

(D) Neither the mother nor the father was a "client" of the respective lawyers who advised them. Therefore, there was no conflict of interest, and both lawyers acted properly.

Question 56

An attorney practices sports law, primarily representing professional women's basketball players in contract negotiations and other kinds of civil matters. The attorney also serves as a sports agent for a number of clients, taking steps to advance their careers in every way possible, such as team placement, public relations, product sponsorship, and the like. The attorney uses a single office for her law work and her sports agent work, but she charges her clients separately for the two types of work. For her sports agent work, she charges a flat annual fee that she negotiates with the client once a year. For her law work, she charges the client by the hour at a reasonable hourly rate. The attorney is lawyer and sports agent for two players on the local basketball team, Alpha and Beta. Both women are excellent players, and both are well-educated, well-spoken, photogenic, and popular with fans. A local bank approached the attorney, expressing interest in signing up Alpha to serve as the bank's spokeswoman. The attorney responded that Alpha would fit the bank's needs well, but that Beta would be an equally good fit and would do the work "for substantially less money." In due course, the attorney served as Beta's lawyer in negotiating an 18-month exclusive sponsorship contract with the bank.

Is the attorney subject to discipline?

(A) No, because when the attorney acts on behalf of a client as sports agent, she need not follow the lawyer conflict of interest rules.

(B) No, because the attorney charged her clients separately for her sports agent work and her law work, and therefore she need not follow the legal ethics rules when doing sports agent work.

(C) Yes, because the attorney was in essence charging twice for the same work when

she attempted to serve as sports agent for Alpha and Beta.

(D) Yes, because the attorney does not keep her sports agent work clearly distinct from her lawyer work, and therefore she must follow the lawyer conflict of interest rules in both kinds of work.

Question 57

A solo practitioner limits her law practice to two kinds of cases: medical malpractice and products liability. When the solo practitioner turned 67, she began looking for someone to buy her law practice. Ultimately, she sold the medical malpractice part of her practice to lawyer Alpha for $400,000, and she sold the products liability part of her practice to attorney Beta for $250,000. The solo practitioner then retired. Within 30 days after the sales to Alpha and Beta, approximately 40% of the solo practitioner's former clients decided to collect their case files and take their business to different lawyers.

Were the sale from the solo practitioner to Alpha and the sale from the solo practitioner to Beta proper?

(A) Yes, even though the solo practitioner sold pieces of her practice to two different buyers, and even though 40% of the solo practitioner's clients left the buyers within 30 days.

(B) Yes, but the solo practitioner is subject to civil liability to the two buyers for unjust enrichment because 40% of the solo practitioner's clients left the buyers within 30 days.

(C) No, because the solo practitioner sold pieces of her practice to two different buyers.

(D) No, because 60% of the solo practitioner's clients stayed with the buyers for more than 30 days.

GO ON TO THE NEXT PAGE

Question 58

A man walked into an attorney's office and explained that he is a dealer of illegal drugs, that one of his sales associates has just been arrested, and that he would like the attorney to defend the sales associate. The drug dealer offered to leave a $10,000 retainer comprised of a shoebox of $100 bills. The attorney was uncertain about getting involved with the drug dealer and especially about accepting a large sum in cash from the dealer. The attorney told the dealer that he would think about his request and would let him know later that day. When the drug dealer left the office, the attorney telephoned his friend and mentor, a retired judge. The attorney told the judge the entire story, including the dealer's name, and asked the judge whether it would be ethical to defend the sales associate and accept the dealer's cash.

Is the attorney subject to discipline for telling the judge the whole story?

(A) Yes, because the attorney-client privilege forbids the attorney from revealing what the drug dealer told him in confidence.

(B) Yes, because the solo practitioner revealed the drug dealer's name.

(C) No, because the attorney's prospective client was the accused sales associate, not the drug dealer.

(D) No, because the ethical duty of confidentiality has an exception that allows a lawyer to reveal confidential information to obtain legal ethics advice.

Question 59

A family-owned chemical company receives information that some of its sales associates may have entered into price fixing agreements in violation of federal antitrust laws. The shares of the chemical company are not publicly traded and the company is not subject to the jurisdiction of the Securities and Exchange Commission. The general counsel of the corporation hires an outside antitrust attorney to investigate the matter. The antitrust attorney and her associate investigated the matter and discovered that some of the sales associates had indeed entered into agreements that could make the corporation civilly and criminally liable under the antitrust laws. The antitrust attorney reported these findings and her antitrust advice in a confidential letter addressed jointly to the company's chief executive officer and the general counsel. The general counsel wrote back, asking the antitrust attorney to stand by to defend the company if needed. Months went by, and the antitrust attorney heard nothing more. Her associate grew restless, and without telling the antitrust attorney, he told a friend in the Justice Department what the company's salespeople had done. The Justice Department began a price fixing investigation of the company and its competitors.

Which of the following is correct?

(A) The antitrust attorney is subject to discipline for failing to report the company's situation to the antitrust enforcement authorities in the Justice Department, but her associate's conduct was proper.

(B) The conduct of both the antitrust attorney and the associate was proper, and neither of them will be subject to civil liability if the company sues them for legal malpractice.

(C) The associate is subject to discipline for tipping off the Justice Department, but the antitrust attorney's conduct was proper.

(D) Neither the antitrust attorney nor the associate is subject to discipline, but both of them may be subject to civil liability if the company sues them for legal malpractice.

GO ON TO THE NEXT PAGE

Question 60

An attorney represented a plaintiff in a personal injury case. While on his way home after the first day of the trial, the attorney stopped for dinner at the pub down the street from the courthouse. A juror walked in, sat at the barstool next to the attorney, and complimented the attorney on his opening statement. In an effort to be polite and without any intention of influencing the juror, the attorney replied, "Thanks. I did my best to explain the scope of my client's injuries—she's had a really hard time since the accident." The attorney then excused himself and moved to a table. The jury eventually returned a verdict in favor of the plaintiff.

Is the attorney subject to discipline?

(A) Yes, because the attorney spoke with the juror outside of the official proceedings.

(B) Yes, because the jury returned a verdict for the plaintiff.

(C) No, because the attorney did not intend to influence the juror.

(D) No, because the juror initiated the conversation.

STOP

barbri

ANSWER SHEET

1 (A) (B) (C) (D)	31 (A) (B) (C) (D)	
2 (A) (B) (C) (D)	32 (A) (B) (C) (D)	
3 (A) (B) (C) (D)	33 (A) (B) (C) (D)	
4 (A) (B) (C) (D)	34 (A) (B) (C) (D)	
5 (A) (B) (C) (D)	35 (A) (B) (C) (D)	
6 (A) (B) (C) (D)	36 (A) (B) (C) (D)	
7 (A) (B) (C) (D)	37 (A) (B) (C) (D)	
8 (A) (B) (C) (D)	38 (A) (B) (C) (D)	
9 (A) (B) (C) (D)	39 (A) (B) (C) (D)	
10 (A) (B) (C) (D)	40 (A) (B) (C) (D)	
11 (A) (B) (C) (D)	41 (A) (B) (C) (D)	
12 (A) (B) (C) (D)	42 (A) (B) (C) (D)	
13 (A) (B) (C) (D)	43 (A) (B) (C) (D)	
14 (A) (B) (C) (D)	44 (A) (B) (C) (D)	
15 (A) (B) (C) (D)	45 (A) (B) (C) (D)	
16 (A) (B) (C) (D)	46 (A) (B) (C) (D)	
17 (A) (B) (C) (D)	47 (A) (B) (C) (D)	
18 (A) (B) (C) (D)	48 (A) (B) (C) (D)	
19 (A) (B) (C) (D)	49 (A) (B) (C) (D)	
20 (A) (B) (C) (D)	50 (A) (B) (C) (D)	
21 (A) (B) (C) (D)	51 (A) (B) (C) (D)	
22 (A) (B) (C) (D)	52 (A) (B) (C) (D)	
23 (A) (B) (C) (D)	53 (A) (B) (C) (D)	
24 (A) (B) (C) (D)	54 (A) (B) (C) (D)	
25 (A) (B) (C) (D)	55 (A) (B) (C) (D)	
26 (A) (B) (C) (D)	56 (A) (B) (C) (D)	
27 (A) (B) (C) (D)	57 (A) (B) (C) (D)	
28 (A) (B) (C) (D)	58 (A) (B) (C) (D)	
29 (A) (B) (C) (D)	59 (A) (B) (C) (D)	
30 (A) (B) (C) (D)	60 (A) (B) (C) (D)	

Answer to Question 1

(D) The solo practitioner and the young attorney are subject to discipline for entering into the partnership agreement because of the restriction on the young attorney's right to practice. A lawyer must neither make nor offer a partnership agreement that restricts a lawyer's right to practice after termination of the relationship, except for an agreement concerning benefits upon retirement. [ABA Model Rule 5.6(a)] Under the agreement here, if the young attorney leaves the partnership within the first three years, he must pay the solo practitioner 75% of the fees he earns thereafter from municipal bond work he does in the state. This provision unduly restricts the young attorney's right to practice. (A) is wrong because it overlooks the improper restriction on the young attorney's right to practice. (B) is wrong because it overlooks the restriction on the young attorney. Furthermore, it implies that the sale of assets in exchange for the restriction on the solo practitioner is necessary to restrict the solo practitioner's right to practice; it is not. (C) is wrong because the restriction on the solo practitioner's right to practice is properly incident to the retirement benefits he will receive from the young attorney.

Answer to Question 2

(B) The justice may not represent the defendant in the habeas proceeding because, while serving as a supreme court justice, the retired justice granted the defendant a stay of execution. A lawyer must not represent a client in a "matter" in which the lawyer earlier participated "personally and substantially" as a judge. [ABA Model Rule 1.12(a)] The habeas corpus proceeding and the earlier appeal should be regarded as the same matter because the habeas corpus proceeding will doubtless raise many of the same issues that were decided on the earlier appeal. (The effective assistance of counsel issue is one example.) The stay of execution should be regarded as personal, substantial participation. (A) is wrong because it confuses the roles of judge and lawyer; a judge is expected to be impartial, but a lawyer is expected to be a partisan. (C) is wrong because one of the proper reasons for turning down a court appointment is that it would require the lawyer to violate a disciplinary rule. [ABA Model Rule 6.2(a)] (D) is wrong because it elevates form over substance; the similarity of legal issues, not the case caption, should be determinative here.

Answer to Question 3

(B) The attorney is subject to discipline because she did not consult the farmer about associating the specialist. A lawyer may split her fee with a lawyer outside her firm if the total fee is reasonable, the split is either in proportion to the work done (or in some other proportion if the splitting lawyers assume joint responsibility), and the client agrees to the split in a writing that discloses the share that each lawyer will receive. [ABA Model Rule 1.5(e)] Because the attorney did not tell the farmer about the arrangement, she is subject to discipline. (A) is wrong because a lawyer may take on a case she knows she is not competent to handle if she prepares as needed to become competent, or if she associates a lawyer who is competent to handle it. [Comment 1 to ABA Model Rule 1.1] (C) and (D) are wrong because they ignore the need to inform the farmer.

Answer to Question 4

(C) The attorney's advice to the accountant was proper because the accountant acted as the client's agent in rendering accounting advice. A lawyer may request that someone other than a client refrain from voluntarily giving relevant information to another party if the person is a relative or agent of the client and the lawyer reasonably believes that the person's interests will not be adversely affected by refraining from giving the information. [ABA Model Rule 3.4(f)] Here, the attorney reasonably believed that refusing to talk informally with the plaintiff's counsel would not harm the accountant, and the accountant was the client's agent in rendering the accounting advice. (A) is wrong because it is the accountant's agency, not privilege, that affects the propriety of the attorney's advice. The lack of an evidentiary privilege does not give the plaintiff's counsel a right to talk to the accountant informally if the accountant chooses not to. (B) is wrong because the attorney did not interfere with the plaintiff's access to evidence; if the plaintiff wants to know what the accountant has to say, he can simply take the accountant's deposition. (D) is wrong because it was not improper for the plaintiff's counsel to attempt to talk informally with a third-party witness such as the accountant.

Answer to Question 5

(C) Beta may not take the case even if Alpha and Beta believe that they can effectively represent their respective clients, and even if all parties give informed consent, confirmed in writing. The key issue is whether Alpha and Beta are considered a "firm" for purposes of the imputed disqualification rule with respect to conflicts of interest. Because lawyers in a firm are usually treated as a single unit for conflict of interest purposes, different lawyers in the same firm must not represent opposing parties in a civil case. [ABA Model Rule 1.10(a)] Relevant factors in determining whether lawyers who share office space are deemed a firm include whether they: hold themselves out to the public as a single unit, frequently consult and assist each other, refer cases to each other, work jointly on cases, and have access to each other's files. All of these factors are present in this case. Thus, Alpha and Beta are deemed a firm, and Beta is disqualified from accepting the employment because Alpha's disqualification is imputed to her. (A) is wrong because a client must not be asked to consent if a disinterested lawyer would conclude that the client should not agree to the representation. Representing both sides in litigation is such a circumstance. [ABA Model Rule 1.7, comment 23] Moreover, ABA Model Rule 1.7(b)(3) does not permit client consent to solve a conflict of interest when one client sues another client represented by the lawyer in the same proceeding. (B) is wrong because, as discussed above, the rule of imputed disqualification does apply to Alpha and Beta even though they are not partners. (D) is wrong because, as discussed above, the key issue is whether the lawyers here would be considered a firm. The mere fact that the lawyers sometimes share fees does not make them a firm.

Answer to Question 6

(D) The attorney is not subject to discipline for (D) because she was not offering *unsolicited* free legal advice, then accepting employment arising from it. [*See* ABA Model Rule 7.3] The client initiated the contact, asked for the advice, and was in the midst of negotiating the attorney's employment when the advice was given. On the other hand, a lawyer must not state or imply that she has the ability to improperly influence a government official or that she can achieve results by means that violate the Rules of Professional Conduct or other law. [ABA Model Rule 8.4(e)] Thus, the attorney is subject to discipline for (A), saying that she knows how to get a favorable ruling from the judge, which implies that she can influence the judge. Advising the client to make the campaign contribution can be viewed in two ways, both of which subject the attorney to discipline. If the $2,000 is viewed harshly as a bald bribe, then the attorney is subject to discipline for counseling a client to commit a crime. [ABA Model Rule 1.2(d)] If the $2,000 is viewed benignly as a campaign contribution, the attorney is subject to discipline for assisting a judge to violate a judicial ethics rule. [ABA Model Rule 8.4(f)] The Code of Judicial Conduct prohibits the judge from personally accepting campaign contributions. Contributions must be given to a campaign committee. [CJC Rule 4.1(A)(8)] Thus, (B) subjects the attorney to discipline. The attorney is subject to discipline for (C) because the attorney apparently believes that the local lawyer running against the judge is an "honest fellow," yet her editorial implies that the local lawyer is a crook. A lawyer is prohibited from making a statement about a judicial candidate, either knowing that the statement is false or with reckless disregard as to its truth or falsity. [ABA Model Rule 8.2(a)]

Answer to Question 7

(C) The district attorney is subject to discipline because she should have known that the statement was likely to prejudice the trial. A lawyer who is connected with a case must not make a public statement outside the courtroom that the lawyer reasonably should know would have a substantial likelihood of materially prejudicing the case. [ABA Model Rule 3.6(a)] The district attorney's comment to the reporter falls in that category because it revealed very damaging material that had not been, and probably would not be, admitted into evidence. A defendant's prior convictions generally are inadmissible as evidence of his conduct on the occasion in question. [*See* Fed. R. Evid. 404] Even if the defendant elected to waive his privilege against self-incrimination and testified on his own behalf, the prior convictions would probably not be admissible to impeach him. [*See* Fed. R. Evid. 609(a)—mugging does not involve dishonesty or false statement, and a judge would probably exclude felony mugging convictions because of the high risk of prejudice] Note that there is an additional constraint on the prosecutor in a criminal case. A prosecutor must not make extrajudicial comments that have a substantial likelihood of heightening public condemnation of the accused. [ABA Model Rule 3.8(f)] The district attorney's statement also runs afoul of this rule by revealing prior crimes that would heighten public condemnation of the defendant. (A) is wrong because even if the prior convictions are a matter of public record, that does not absolve the district attorney for making a statement she knew would substantially prejudice the case. Furthermore, while in a technical sense the defendant's prior convictions in other states are matters of public record (if one knew where to go and what to look for, one could dredge them out of the court records of the other states), the prior convictions were doubtless not part of the public record in the defendant's present prosecution. (B) is wrong because it is too broad; lawyers do have First Amendment rights to express themselves about pending cases, but those rights are limited by the due process rights of litigants to fair court proceedings. (D) is wrong because it is also too broad; a prosecutor may make some kinds of public comment about pending cases, but not comments that are likely to cause prejudice.

Answer to Question 8

(C) The attorney is not subject to discipline unless 30% of the book royalties is unreasonably high for the contract negotiation work. Here, the attorney has, in essence, agreed to negotiate the publication contract in return for a contingent fee. Like all other fees, a contingent fee is subject to the general requirement of reasonableness. [ABA Model Rule 1.5] (A) is wrong because this is not the kind of literary rights contract that is prohibited. A lawyer must not acquire literary or media rights to a story concerning the lawyer's representation of a client until after the legal matter is entirely concluded. [ABA Model Rule 1.8(d)] Here, the client is the author, and the book is about her life in prison, not about her case or her attorney's representation of her. A lawyer may represent a client in a transaction concerning literary property in which the lawyer's fee consists of a share of the ownership of the property, provided that the arrangement complies with the general rules about attorneys' fees and does not give

the lawyer a proprietary interest in the subject of litigation. [Comment 9 to ABA Model Rule 1.8] (B) is wrong because a lawyer may advance litigation expenses for a client, even though he is aware that she probably cannot pay him back. ABA Model Rule 1.8(e)(2) permits the lawyer simply to pay the litigation expenses for an indigent client, even without the pretense of calling it an advance. (D) is wrong because the literary rights contract was a separate representation from, and did not concern the story of, the murder trial.

Answer to Question 9

(A) The probate attorney is subject to discipline because he did not put the coins in a safe place. When a lawyer comes into possession of property to be held on a client's behalf, the lawyer must identify it as belonging to the client and must put it in a safe place. [ABA Model Rule 1.15(a)] Although the Rules do not define "safe," common sense suggests that allowing a valuable coin collection to be viewed by employees, placing it into an unlocked desk file, and then leaving the office is not safe. A lawyer should use the same level of care required of professional fiduciaries. The probate attorney's actions fall well short of that. (B) is wrong. The attorney may be liable to the estate in civil damages for his secretary's dishonest act, but the question here is professional discipline, not civil liability. The attorney could be disciplined if he did not take reasonable steps to train his secretary properly [ABA Model Rule 5.3], but if he took such steps, he should not be disciplined for her criminal act. (C) is wrong. The issue here is the attorney's failure to safeguard the coins; the proximate cause of the loss is beside the point.

Technically, a lawyer could be subject to discipline for failure to safeguard the property even if no loss occurred. (D) is wrong. Placing the coins in an unlocked desk file and leaving the office was not a reasonable way to safeguard them.

Answer to Question 10

(A) Alpha is subject to discipline for failing to warn Beta not to take the case. If the paralegal were a lawyer, her conduct would violate ABA Model Rule 7.3(b), which prohibits in-person solicitation. The partners in a firm are responsible for educating their nonlawyer employees about ethics issues and making reasonable efforts to assure that those employees comply with ethics rules. [ABA Model Rule 5.3(a)] Moreover, a partner is subject to discipline if he learns about the violation of an ethics rule by a nonlawyer employee "when its consequences can be avoided or mitigated," but the partner "fails to take reasonable remedial action." In this case, the consequences of the paralegal's solicitation could have been avoided by warning Beta not to take the pedestrian's case. Because he failed to warn Beta, Alpha is subject to discipline. (B) is wrong because it is too broad. A lawyer's responsibility for a nonlawyer employee's ethics violation is limited to situations in which the lawyer orders it, ratifies it, or learns about it in time to remedy it and does not do so. [ABA Model Rule 5.3(c)] (C) is wrong because even though people are generally free to recommend a lawyer to someone else, that does not allow the paralegal to solicit business for the firm that employs her. [ABA Model Rule 8.4(a)] (D) is wrong because Alpha and the other partners in the firm had a duty to educate the paralegal about ethics rules.

[ABA Model Rule 5.3(a)] Furthermore, even if the paralegal acted innocently, that does not excuse Alpha's failure to warn Beta not to take the case.

Answer to Question 11

(C) The attorney is not subject to discipline for taking the case because the relevant information he obtained while working as a government attorney is not confidential. The general rule is that a government lawyer who receives confidential government information about a person must not later represent a private client whose interests are adverse to that person, if the information could be used to the material disadvantage of that person. [ABA Model Rule 1.11(c)] The rule covers only "confidential" information, which means information that the government is prohibited from revealing or has a privilege not to reveal, and which is not otherwise available to the public. Here, because the information is available under the Freedom of Information Act, it is not confidential. In fact, any attorney representing the client could obtain the information; thus, the attorney is free to use it. (A) is wrong because a lawyer is not barred from ever working on a case where he gained any relevant information while working for the government. To bar representation, the information must be confidential. (B) is wrong because this type of consent is required when the attorney takes on a representation in private practice in a matter in which the lawyer participated personally and substantially while in government service. A "matter" is a set of specific facts involving specific parties. Here, the attorney was not involved in any matter while in government service that concerned the client's claim against the chemical company.

(D) is wrong because the information is not confidential and thus can be used against the chemical company. Furthermore, even if the information were confidential, mere nonuse would not be sufficient; the attorney would not be permitted to represent the client.

Answer to Question 12

(C) The attorney is subject to discipline because she did not advise the client to seek outside counsel. A lawyer may not settle a legal malpractice claim or potential claim with an unrepresented client or former client without first advising that person in writing to seek outside legal advice about the settlement and giving the person a reasonable chance to obtain such advice. [ABA Model Rule 1.8(h)(2)] Although the client has apparently not made a formal claim of malpractice here, he has asserted that the attorney's services were "defective," and that is regarded as sufficient to bring Rule 1.8(h)(2) into play. The settlement agreement in this question also gives the client an incentive not to report a lawyer's misconduct to the bar. Some state bars have found similar settlement agreements improper because they frustrated the bar's efforts at self-regulation and could be prejudicial to the administration of justice. [*See* Arizona State Bar Op. 91-23 (1991)] (A) is wrong because although lawyers are urged to settle fee disputes amicably [comment 9 to ABA Model Rule 1.5], this particular settlement agreement involves both a fee dispute and a malpractice claim. (B) is wrong because the dispute about the quality of the attorney's services is what causes the problem here, as explained above. (D) is wrong because it is too broad. A lawyer may settle a malpractice claim if the claimant is independently

represented or if the lawyer advises the claimant in writing that he should seek independent legal advice before entering into the settlement. [ABA Model Rule 1.8(h)(2)]

Answer to Question 13

(D) The employer's attorney is subject to discipline because he lied about having movies. When dealing on behalf of a client with a third person, a lawyer must not knowingly make a false statement of law or material fact. [ABA Model Rule 4.1(a)] The employer's attorney knew that he had no movies; his statement to the worker's lawyer was a bald lie. (A) is wrong because the employer's attorney's statement was a knowing misrepresentation of material fact, not the kind of puffery that is tolerated in settlement negotiations. [*See* comment 2 to ABA Model Rule 4.1] (B) is wrong because the ends do not justify the means. (C) is wrong because the employer consented to the $400 settlement. Given the employer's risk of going to trial in a case where the plaintiff is claiming total and permanent disability due to a back injury, the small settlement was not unreasonable.

Answer to Question 14

(C) While a bar applicant must cooperate in reasonable investigations by the state bar and make disclosures relevant to her fitness to practice, she may challenge the validity of a question on legally tenable grounds. [*See* ABA Model Rule 3.4(c)] That a question violates the state constitution would be a legally tenable argument. Moreover, by declining to answer, the law student has not made an untrue statement. (A) and (B) would not be proper because a bar applicant must not make untrue statements on a bar application. [ABA Model Rule 8.1(a)] If the law student answers in the negative, she will have made an untrue statement. (D) would not be proper because the self-incrimination privilege is inapplicable here. Even if the privilege against self-incrimination applies to questions on bar applications (a debatable proposition), it does not apply when criminal punishment is barred by the statute of limitations. [*See* Hazard & Hodes, §62.6]

Answer to Question 15

(A)   A judge may establish a campaign committee no earlier than an amount of time prior to the election set by the jurisdiction. [CJC Rule 4.2(B)(1)] Because the state allows campaign committees to be formed up to one year before the election, and it is nine months before the election under the facts given, (A) is proper. (B) is improper; a judge may not publicly endorse a candidate for another public office. [CJC Rule 4.1(A)(3)] (C) is improper; the judge may attend a political gathering in the company of her husband, and she may speak on her own behalf, but she must not speak on his behalf. [CJC Rules 4.1(A)(3), 4.2(B)] (D) is improper; a judge is prohibited from personally soliciting contributions for her own campaign. [CJC Rule 4.1(A)(8)]

Answer to Question 16

(C)   The firm may continue to use the name Alpha & Beta if it is not misleading. A firm may practice under a trade name, provided that the trade name is not misleading. [Comment 5 to ABA Model Rule 7.1] (A) is wrong because a firm may continue using the name of a deceased partner. [*Id.*] (B) is wrong because the person who left was not a name partner. Generally, when a name

partner enters public service and is not in private practice for a substantial period, the firm must cease using that person's name. [Comment 8 to ABA Model Rule 7.1] Here, the Alpha surname refers to the deceased founder and not the partner who was appointed to the state supreme court. If, however, the use of the Alpha name in the firm name would mislead potential clients (e.g., by making them think they could gain an advantage in the state supreme court by hiring that firm), then continued use of the name would violate the ethics rules. [*See* ABA Model Rule 7.1] (D) is wrong because the rules on firm names are subject to the more general provisions on misleading communications.

Answer to Question 17

(B)   It would be proper for the senior partner to represent Beta because neither the partner nor any other lawyer in the firm gained access to Alpha's confidential information. Even though Alpha's bank loan is not substantially related to Beta's personal injury suit, the confidential information that the deceased attorney got from Alpha may well become important in Beta's suit. Knowing the extent and nature of Alpha's assets could be of great value to counsel for Beta in advising Beta whether to settle or in collecting on a judgment against Alpha. Here, however, the deceased attorney was the only attorney who gained access to Alpha's financial information, and the attorney is now dead. Under ABA Model Rule 1.10(b), the senior partner may represent Beta, because neither he nor any other attorney remaining in the firm had access to Alpha's confidential information. (A) is wrong because it ignores the issue presented by the confidential

information. (C) is wrong because ABA Model Rule 1.10(b) creates an exception to the ordinary rule that confidential information gained by one lawyer in a firm is deemed to be known by all lawyers in the firm. (D) is wrong because ABA Model Rule 1.10(b) allows the senior partner to serve even without the consent of Alpha.

Answer to Question 18

(D) The associate should abide by the partner's resolution of the matter. A subordinate lawyer does not violate the Rules of Professional Conduct by acting in accordance with a supervisor's reasonable resolution of an *arguable question* of professional duty. [ABA Model Rule 5.2(b)] Here, it seems clear that the question was arguable because the third attorney called in to determine the relevance of the case also felt it was not on point. (A) is wrong because the associate only has a duty to call the case to the court's attention if the case is directly on point. That is a debatable question, and the associate's supervisors have determined the case is not directly on point. Thus, the associate need not reveal the case. (B) is wrong because this is not the situation intended to be addressed by the rule against allowing a third party to influence the lawyer's judgment, which usually arises when a third party pays the lawyer's fees to represent another. Of course, a subordinate lawyer should be influenced by his supervisor. That is not an excuse for clearly unethical conduct, but on a debatable issue, such as the one presented here, the subordinate lawyer is free to defer to the supervisor's judgment. (C) is wrong because in most jurisdictions a lawyer may communicate in writing with the court about the

merits of a pending case if he sends a copy to opposing counsel. This communication is not considered ex parte. [*See* Restatement §113, comment c]

Answer to Question 19

(A) Beta's attorney is not subject to discipline because admission to practice in State A is not required to negotiate a license there. A lawyer must not practice law in a state where she is not admitted to practice. [ABA Model Rule 5.5(a)] No state, however, would regard the lawyer's conduct as unauthorized practice. The attorney was admitted in State B, she was representing a State B client, and the trademark license has an important nexus to State B because Beta's manufacturing operations will take place in State B. [*See* Hazard & Hodes, §46.6] Moreover, ABA Model Rule 5.5(c)(4) permits a lawyer to temporarily practice out of state if that practice is reasonably related to the lawyer's home state practice. Here, the attorney's going to State A to negotiate a license to use Alpha's trademark is reasonably related to her State B practice of representing Beta. (B) is wrong because it is irrelevant. As discussed above, Beta's attorney's conduct would not be considered to be unauthorized practice. If it were, the fact that the license was drafted by Alpha's lawyer would not protect Beta's attorney. (C) is wrong because the attorney need not be admitted in State A to negotiate with a company located there. (D) is wrong because a lawyer need not be admitted to practice before the United States Patent and Trademark Office in order to negotiate a trademark license. One must be admitted to practice before that agency to prosecute an application for a United States patent, but the attorney is obviously not doing that here.

Answer to Question 20

(C)   A lawyer can be disciplined for trying to avoid a court appointment without good cause. [ABA Model Rule 6.2] The reason stated in (C) is not an acceptable reason for declining the appointment; a lawyer has a duty to represent his fair share of indigent or unpopular clients. [Comment 1 to ABA Model Rule 6.2] (A) is a legitimate reason for declining an appointment. A lawyer is permitted to turn down a court appointment if it "is likely to result in an unreasonable financial burden." [ABA Model Rule 6.2(b)] (B) is also a legitimate basis for declining appointment because a lawyer may turn down a court appointment if it is likely to cause the lawyer to violate a rule of professional conduct. [ABA Model Rule 6.2(a)] If the two defendants are to be tried jointly, and if one defendant did coerce the other defendant into helping with the kidnapping and killing, there is a sharp conflict of interest between the two defendants. [*See* ABA Model Rule 1.7(a)] It would be an ethical violation to represent co-defendants with conflicting interests (consent will not solve the conflict); thus, the attorney can decline the appointment on this ground. (D) raises another conflict of interest that would justify the attorney in declining the appointment. Had he not gained confidential information from the prosecution's witness, he might have discovered that information independently and been able to use it to impeach the witness. As it stands, however, his ability to impeach is constrained by his duty not to use the confidential information to the disadvantage of the witness, his former client. [ABA Model Rule 1.9(c)(1)]

Answer to Question 21

(C)   The federal prosecutor is subject to criminal liability because his evidence-gathering technique amounted to extortion, an interstate threat against the banker for the purpose of extracting information to use against the swindler. Under modern statutory law, the crime of extortion covers obtaining anything of value, tangible or intangible, by making various kinds of threats, including a threat to accuse a person of a crime. [*See, e.g.*, 18 U.S.C. §875(d)—felony to obtain something of value by transmitting in interstate commerce a threat to accuse a person of a crime; *see also* Perkins & Boyce, 442-52] The information that the federal prosecutor wanted from the banker was something of value in the swindler investigation, and the prosecutor clearly threatened to accuse the banker of a crime if the banker did not cooperate. Furthermore, the threat was transmitted interstate, thus bringing it within the scope of the federal statute cited above. (A) is incorrect because the federal prosecutor did have a legal right to tell the State B prosecutors about the banker and the savings and loan, but the federal prosecutor did not have a right to threaten to do so (i.e., to commit extortion) in order to coerce the banker to cooperate. (B) is incorrect because it ignores the law of extortion. Just as it would have been illegal for the federal prosecutor to extract the information by physical torture, it was illegal to extract it by extortion. (D) is not as good as (C) because it is vague and because the right to be free from extortion, though important, is not a federally protected civil right.

Answer to Question 22

(C) The attorney will not be subject to discipline for reporting the matter to the appropriate authorities because she is entitled to reveal this type of confidential information. The attorney may resign her in-house counsel position because the company's board insists on following a course of action that is both repugnant and criminal. [ABA Model Rule 1.16(b)(2), (4)] The children's sleepwear is likely to cause substantial bodily harm or even death. Because a lawyer is entitled to reveal confidential information to the extent she reasonably believes necessary to prevent reasonably certain death or substantial bodily harm, the attorney may report this matter to the appropriate authorities. [ABA Model Rule 1.6(b)(1)] In addition, if the highest authority for an organization fails to take appropriate action regarding a violation of law, then a lawyer for the organization may report the relevant information to an appropriate person outside of the organization, if the lawyer reasonably believes that reporting is necessary to prevent substantial injury to the organization. This is true even if the information would otherwise be protected by the duty of confidentiality (which is not the case here because the sale of the fabric is likely to cause substantial bodily harm). [ABA Model Rule 1.13(c)] Here, the sale of the fabric is a violation of law, and selling the fabric could result in substantial injury to the organization if the fabric catches fire. (A) is wrong because the attorney is entitled to reveal confidential information to prevent reasonably certain death or substantial bodily harm or to prevent substantial injury to the organization. (B) is wrong because the repugnance and criminality of the proposed conduct are both sufficient grounds for permissive

withdrawal. [ABA Model Rule 1.16(2), (4)] (D) is wrong because the duty of confidentiality continues even after the termination of the attorney-client relationship. [*See* comment 18 to ABA Model Rule 1.6]

Answer to Question 23

(C) The attorney is subject to civil liability for mishandling the client's money because he breached his fiduciary duty to the client. When the attorney received the $40,000 from the client, he should have deposited it in a client trust account, not in the account that the law firm uses for office expenses. The attorney's failure to put the money in the correct account was a breach of fiduciary duty that can result in both professional discipline under ABA Model Rule 1.15(a) and in civil liability under the principles expressed in the Restatement. [*See* Restatement §49; *see also* Lurz v. Panek, 527 N.E.2d 663 (Ill. App. Ct. 1988)—lawyer civilly liable for loss client suffers from lawyer's delay in paying money over to client] (A) is incorrect because the attorney remains liable even though it was the attorney's law partner who withdrew the money from the law firm account. [*See, e.g.,* Blackmon v. Hale, 1 Cal. 3d 548 (1970)—lawyer civilly liable when former law partner converted client's funds] (B) is incorrect because a lawyer's breach of fiduciary duty can result in both professional discipline and civil liability to a client who suffered loss as a result. (D) is incorrect because the legal standard is breach of fiduciary duty, not strict liability.

Answer to Question 24

(A) The new partner and the law firm are not subject to disqualification because from the facts given in the question, it appears that the merger matter and the age discrimination case are not substantially related to one another, and that the firm lawyers did not gain confidential information in the merger matter that would be material to the discrimination case. [*See* ABA Model Rule 1.9] Therefore (C) and (D) are incorrect. (B) is incorrect because if the firm lawyers who worked on the merger matter had obtained confidential information that would be material in the discrimination case, their knowledge would be imputed to the new partner, even though he was not a member of the firm when the knowledge was obtained. [*See* ABA Model Rules 1.9, 1.10]

Answer to Question 25

(D) The firm may pay all of the money as planned. Even though the decedent's daughter is a nonlawyer, the firm may make certain kinds of payments to her from money originally earned as legal fees. [ABA Model Rule 5.4(a)(1)] The $100,000 is a proper payment because it reflects the decedent's share of the capital assets of the firm. The $45,000 is a proper payment because the fees it represents had been earned, albeit not collected, at the time the decedent died. The $125,000 is a proper payment because it is a reasonably computed death benefit payable over a reasonable period of time.

Answer to Question 26

(B) The attorney must promptly refund $11,000 because that amount is not in dispute. The attorney claimed $32,000 in fees (80 hours at $400 per hour) from the $40,000 fee advance (leaving an excess of $8,000). The attorney further claimed $2,000 from the $5,000

advance for expenses (leaving an excess of $3,000). Adding $8,000 and $3,000 produces an $11,000 refund due immediately from the attorney to the environmentalist. [ABA Model Rule 1.16(d)] The environmentalist apparently disputes the attorney's right to $32,000 in fees; thus, that disputed amount must remain in the attorney's client trust account until the fee dispute is settled. [ABA Model Rule 1.15(e)] (A) is wrong because when a lawyer is fired or withdraws, he must immediately refund the unspent portion of the expense advance and the portion of the fee advance that he does not claim to have earned. [ABA Model Rule 1.16(d)] (C) is wrong because the attorney may retain the disputed portion of the expense advance, as explained above. (D) is wrong because the attorney is entitled to retain the disputed $32,000 in his client trust account until the fee dispute is settled.

Answer to Question 27

(D) The judge may testify because he is testifying to facts, not the defendant's character. CJC Rule 3.3 prohibits a judge from testifying voluntarily as a character witness, but it says nothing about serving as an ordinary fact witness. (A) is wrong because there is no such rule. Judges are not disqualified from testifying in criminal cases. (B) is wrong because a lawyer need not be admitted to practice in State B in order to advise a client about State B law. Even if that were untrue, the judge's testimony would still be admissible as evidence of the client's lack of criminal intent. (C) is wrong because it states a nonexistent rule. While a judge is not competent to be a witness at a trial over which he himself is presiding [*see* Fed. R.

Evid. 605], no rule forbids a judge from serving as an ordinary fact witness in a case that is pending before a different judge in his own court or a court that is under his court's appellate jurisdiction.

Answer to Question 28

(C)   The attorney's actions were not proper because a lawyer should fully advise a client of all relevant information, particularly when the lawyer has reason to believe that the information would be regarded as important by the client. The lawyer should furnish the client with all the information that is necessary to allow the client to participate intelligently in making decisions about the matter. [ABA Model Rule 1.4] Here, the existence of the statute was a fact necessary for the client to know to make an intelligent decision about how to proceed. (A) is wrong because it is not the attorney's place to withhold information because she believes she knows what is best for the client. The client is entitled to all relevant information. (B) is wrong because the state policy does not absolve the attorney from her ethical duty to keep her client informed. (D) is wrong because the attorney does not owe a duty to the minor from the mere fact that she is a minor.

Answer to Question 29

(A)   The attorney is not subject to discipline unless she allows the client to interfere with her judgment in handling other clients' matters. [See ABA Model Rule 5.4] (B) is wrong because there is no law or disciplinary rule that requires the attorney to notify the law firm regarding the transaction. (C) is wrong because no law or disciplinary rule requires the law firm's consent to the client's leaving the firm and giving his business to the

attorney as a solo practitioner. (D) is wrong because the loan payback clause does not violate the rule against splitting a legal fee with a nonlawyer. [ABA Model Rule 5.4(a)] True, the clause does measure the monthly payments as a percentage of the attorney's net income in the prior month and most of her net income will probably come from legal fees. However, it makes sense to tailor her loan payments to her income, and the arrangement does not invite the evil that the no-splitting rule was designed to prevent—interference with the attorney's professional judgment.

Answer to Question 30

(B)   The attorney's conduct was not proper because she pretended to be disinterested and advised the ex-husband to pay the extra money. When dealing on behalf of a client with a person who is not represented by counsel, a lawyer must not state or imply that the lawyer is disinterested, and the lawyer must not give that person advice (other than advice to secure counsel) if the lawyer knows that the person's interests may conflict with those of the client. Clearly, the ex-husband's interests do conflict with the wife's interests. [ABA Model Rule 4.3] Here, the attorney advised the ex-husband that he ought to pay increased alimony and child support. She compounded the problem by pretending to be disinterested, a direct violation of Rule 4.3. (A) is wrong because it is overbroad; it was proper, for example, for the attorney to advise the ex-husband to get a lawyer and to offer to postpone the hearing. Moreover, if an adversary refuses to retain counsel, a lawyer must communicate directly with that person. (C) is wrong because making those statements does not exempt the attorney from those provisions that prohibit implying disinterest and giving advice. (D) is wrong because the attorney did give advice to the ex-husband—the advice to pay the extra money that the wife was asking for.

Answer to Question 31

(C) The attorney is not subject to discipline for disclosing the defendant's confidential information to the professor because the disclosure was necessary to effectively carry out the representation. Unless a client has specifically instructed the lawyer to the contrary, a lawyer can reasonably assume that he has implied authority from the client to disclose confidential information when necessary to carry out the representation. That is particularly true in cases such as this one—where the lawyer cannot easily communicate with his client. [ABA Model Rule 1.6(a)] (A) is wrong because a lawyer may seek advice from an expert without the expert being licensed in the jurisdiction; and in any case, it does not affect the confidentiality rules. (B) is wrong because specific authorization is not required; it may be implied. (D) is wrong because refraining from revealing the client's name is not sufficient to permit revelation of confidential information. There must be an exception to the confidentiality rules or authorization by the client.

Answer to Question 32

(C) The attorney would not be subject to discipline for accepting the sculpture because he did not solicit the gift. Although ABA Model Rule 1.8(c) prohibits a lawyer from soliciting a substantial gift from a client when the lawyer is not related to the client, it does not prohibit a lawyer from *accepting an*

unsolicited gift from a client, even if the gift is substantial (although the gift may be voidable for undue influence). Moreover, comment 6 to ABA Model Rule 1.8 states that a lawyer may accept a gift from a client if the transaction meets general standards of fairness. Here, the attorney did not solicit the gift, and there are no facts to suggest undue influence or unfairness. Thus, the gift is proper. (A) is wrong because it is too broad. A lawyer may accept a gift of substantial value from a client if the conditions stated above are satisfied. (B) and (D) are wrong because the value of the attorney's recent work and the value of the sculpture are irrelevant. The attorney did not charge more than the $750. In addition to discharging the $750 fee bill, the sculptor obviously intended to make a gift to the attorney in gratitude for years of work in the past.

Answer to Question 33

(D) The public defender may not reveal the defendant's perjury because to do so would violate the public defender's duty of confidentiality. No exceptions to the confidentiality requirement apply to these facts. There is no indication that revealing the perjury is necessary to prevent reasonably certain death or substantial bodily harm. Also, there is no indication that the defendant's perjury is a crime that is reasonably certain to result in substantial injury to the financial interests of another, in furtherance of which the defendant has used the public defender's services. The obligation to reveal perjury under the Model Rules does not apply because that obligation ceases at the end of the proceedings, and both proceedings here have concluded. (A) is wrong because the proceeding has ended and, therefore, the public defender is obligated to keep the information in confidence. (B) is wrong for the same reason. Furthermore, even if the trial was ongoing, the public defender would not be obligated to reveal the perjury because he was not representing the defendant at trial. The public defender represented the defendant in the preliminary hearing, which has concluded, ending his obligation to disclose. (C) is wrong because what the public defender believes about the defendant's dangerousness is not relevant. There is no exception to the duty of confidentiality based on the client's violent propensities.

Answer to Question 34

(C)   The arrangement is not proper because the attorney is required to keep $10,000 on deposit to be included on the list. A lawyer may not give "anything of value" to a person for recommending the lawyer's services. [ABA Model Rule 7.2(b)] The bank benefits in many ways by increasing the amount of its deposits; for example, its deposits determine how much it can lend to borrowers. Thus, obtaining deposits from lawyers is of value to the bank, and that is one reason it has devised the referral scheme. (A) is wrong because although a lawyer may pay the usual charges of a *not-for-profit* or qualified lawyer referral service [ABA Model Rule 7.2(b)], banks operate for profit, and there is no indication that the bank has been approved by the appropriate regulatory authority as a qualified lawyer referral service. (B) is wrong because the attorney is giving something of value for the referrals, as explained above, even though there is no fee for individual referrals. (D) is wrong because this arrangement does not constitute an improper partner-

ship or association with a nonlawyer for the purpose of practicing law. A lawyer's professional association with a nonlawyer is improper if the nonlawyer: (1) owns an interest in the practice; (2) is an officer or director of a business involving law practice; or (3) has the right to control the lawyer's professional judgment. [ABA Model Rule 5.4(d)] None of these is the case here; the bank is acting solely as a referral agent, and has nothing to do with the operation of the attorney's practice.

Answer to Question 35

(D)   The attorney is not subject to discipline because $9.7 million is within the bounds of reason as a fee for the work the attorney did. [*See* ABA Model Rule 1.5(a)] Among the various factors that point to the reasonableness of the attorney's fee are: the novelty and difficulty of the patentability issue, the fact that the inventor was the one who suggested the fee arrangement after having been offered a standard hourly fee, the value of the result that the attorney obtained for the inventor, and the contingent nature of the arrangement, which imposed a high risk on the attorney. (A) is wrong because a lawyer is prohibited from acquiring a proprietary interest in the subject of *litigation* he is conducting [ABA Model Rule 1.8(i)], and obtaining a patent is not litigation. Even if this were a litigation case, the contingent fee exception to the rule would apply. [ABA Model Rule 1.8(i)(2)] (B) is wrong because a fee that is otherwise reasonable does not become unreasonable simply because the lawyer can use the knowledge gained to earn fees from other clients. (C) is wrong because the mere fact that the client agreed to the fee arrangement does not by itself make the fee reasonable. Many factors, including the time, labor, and skill required to do the job, are considered in determining whether the fee is reasonable. [ABA Model Rule 1.5(a)]

Answer to Question 36

(A) The attorney is not subject to discipline because she did the best she could in an emergency situation. In an emergency situation, a lawyer may give legal advice on a matter that she would not be competent to handle in an ordinary situation. [Comment 3 to ABA Model Rule 1.1] Here, the attorney's advice was limited to the narrow question the client posed. She is not subject to discipline because she did the best she could in the heat of the moment, and she warned the client about the dangers of relying on unresearched legal advice. (B) is wrong because a lawyer who renders advice about the law of another jurisdiction in an ordinary, nonemergency situation is expected to be competent to render such advice. [ABA Model Rule 1.1] (C) is wrong because the attorney was not engaged in unauthorized practice when she advised her client about foreign law. She need not be admitted in another country in order to advise her local client about foreign law. (D) is wrong because the attorney is not subject to discipline for rendering legal advice that turns out to be mistaken if she acted competently in light of the time-constrained circumstances in which she found herself.

Answer to Question 37

(B) The attorney may act as the music star's trial counsel because he is not a *necessary* witness. [ABA Model Rule 3.7(a)] A roomful of witnesses heard the diner's

comments and could testify to them. Moreover, the diner has made a judicial admission that he made the statements; thus, no testimony is required on that point. The attorney has no knowledge as to the truth of the statements, as he knows nothing of the star's personal life; thus, he would have no relevant testimony on that issue. Therefore, the attorney is neither a "necessary" witness, nor a witness who "ought" to be called. (A) is wrong because there is no need for informed consent in this situation. (C) is wrong because even if there is a remote possibility that the attorney might be called, he is not a necessary witness, and it is unlikely that he would be called by the diner's lawyer because he could not have anything favorable or relevant to add. A mere remote possibility that a lawyer will be called as a witness is not sufficient to disqualify the lawyer from representing a client. (D) is wrong because every lawyer generally is considered competent to take any case as long as the lawyer sufficiently prepares. Here, the attorney spent considerable time preparing before he filed the complaint.

Answer to Question 38

(A) The attorney should not discuss the matter with the treasurer, and should advise him to hire his own lawyer. When an organization is the lawyer's client, the lawyer owes the duty of loyalty to the organization—not to the people who are its constituents. If there is a conflict between the interests of the organization and the interests of one of its constituents, the lawyer should advise the constituent to obtain independent legal counsel. [Comment 10 to ABA Model Rule 1.13] The attorney's client is the corporation, and the corporation's interests are in conflict with the interests of the treasurer. If the corporation proves that the treasurer had no authority to sign the note, the bank may sue the treasurer himself. If the corporation is held liable to the bank, it may sue the treasurer for indemnification. In these circumstances, the treasurer needs his own lawyer, and the attorney must not try to represent both him and the corporation. Furthermore, because the treasurer is presently unrepresented in the matter and his interests conflict with those of the corporation, the attorney must not try to give him legal advice, except to get a lawyer. [*See* ABA Model Rule 4.3] (B) is wrong because the attorney must not try to represent the treasurer at the deposition due to the conflict of interest explained above. (C) is wrong because the attorney must not try to give the treasurer legal advice, except to get a lawyer. (D) is wrong for the reason just stated. Furthermore, as the corporation's lawyer, the attorney must not give legal advice to a person with conflicting interests (particularly advice to testify in such a way as to damage her client's position).

Answer to Question 39

(A) The attorney is subject to discipline because his actions in State B constitute fraud. A lawyer is subject to discipline not only for violating a disciplinary rule, but also for committing a criminal act that reflects adversely on his honesty, trustworthiness, or fitness as a lawyer in other respects, or for engaging in conduct involving dishonesty, fraud, deceit, or misrepresentation. [ABA Model Rule 8.4] The type of fraud described clearly falls within this rule. (B) is wrong because a lawyer is subject to discipline in a state where he is licensed to practice even if the misconduct occurred in another jurisdiction. [ABA Model Rule 8.5(a)] (C) is wrong because the fact that the attorney was not licensed in State B is irrelevant. He was not practicing law in State B, so he is not subject to discipline on the ground of unauthorized practice. He is subject to discipline, however, for filing improper tax returns. As discussed above, the attorney cannot escape discipline for his fraudulent conduct because it occurred in another jurisdiction. (D) is wrong because, as discussed above, a lawyer may be disciplined for dishonest conduct regardless of whether it is related to the practice of law.

Answer to Question 40

(C) A lawyer must not provide financial assistance to a client in the context of contemplated or pending litigation, with the following exceptions: (1) the lawyer may advance court costs and litigation expenses on the client's behalf; (2) where the client is indigent, the lawyer may pay the court costs and litigation expenses outright; and (3) where the lawyer is representing an indigent client pro bono, the lawyer may provide modest gifts to the client for basic living expenses. [ABA Model Rule 1.8(e)] The attorney is not representing the client pro bono in this lawsuit, so the attorney is allowed to advance court costs and litigation expenses only, and must not provide any other financial assistance. (C) represents court costs and litigation expenses, which are permissible. Family support is not an expense of litigation; thus (A) is improper. Similarly, treatment of the client's injuries and job retraining are not expenses of litigation, therefore (B) and (D) also are improper.

Answer to Question 41

(A) The attorney's conduct was proper because violating the ordinance was one of the ways to gain legal standing to challenge the constitutionality of the ordinance. A lawyer must not counsel or assist a client in conduct that the lawyer knows is criminal or fraudulent. However, a lawyer may counsel or assist a client to make a good faith effort to determine the validity, scope, meaning, or application of a law even if it requires the client to disobey the law. [ABA Model Rule 1.2(d)] This situation usually arises when a lawyer is asked how a particular law may be challenged, and the lawyer advises the client on ways to obtain legal standing, which include disobedience of the law. Here, the attorney was merely advising the landlord on methods of obtaining legal standing, including renting houses in violation of the ordinance. (B) is wrong because the ultimate outcome of the challenge is irrelevant. It is important that the attorney believed there was a good faith basis for challenging the validity of the ordinance, but whether the challenge succeeds does not determine the propriety of his conduct. (C) is wrong because, as discussed above, there is an exception to this rule for a good faith effort to determine the validity of a law. (D) is wrong because there is no affirmative duty to counsel the client in this way. In fact, as discussed above, there is an exception for a good faith challenge to the law that would permit the attorney to do just the opposite.

Answer to Question 42

(B) The attorney's actions are proper because he offered his services free of charge. Generally, a lawyer is prohibited from seeking employment by initiating live person-to-person contact with a person known to need legal services in a particular matter. However, this prohibition applies only when "a significant motive" for the solicitation is the lawyer's pecuniary gain. [ABA Model Rule 7.3(b)] Thus, a lawyer who volunteers to represent someone free of charge is not subject to discipline for solicitation. (A) is incorrect because, as discussed above, it is not necessary for the attorney to have previously represented any of the demonstrators in order for his actions to have been proper. (C) is incorrect because, as discussed above, this situation falls within an exception to the ban on live person-to-person solicitation. (D) is incorrect because the attorney's actions are proper even if he is motivated by a desire to obtain publicity, provided that this is not a *substantial* motive for his offer.

Answer to Question 43

(D) A judge may not be affiliated with an organization that practices invidious discrimination on the basis of race, sex, gender, religion, national origin, ethnicity, or sexual orientation. [CJC Rule 3.6] The corporation excludes gay people who are otherwise qualified, making it improper for the judge to continue as chief executive officer. (A) is incorrect because it fails to include sexual orientation discrimination. (B) is incorrect because, as discussed above, the judge's remaining an officer in the corporation would be improper even if the time it took did not interfere with her judicial duties. (C) is incorrect because it is too broad; CJC Rule 3.11(B) allows a judge to be involved with a business that is closely held by the judge or her family.

Answer to Question 44

(C)   The attorney should keep the information in confidence unless the client authorizes her to reveal it, even though the death of the landlord has made it impossible for the prosecutor to obtain the information other than from the attorney. The attorney obtained this information from the landlord in the course of representing her client; therefore, it is subject to the attorney's duty of confidentiality. Absent the consent of the client, a lawyer must not reveal *any* information relating to the representation of the client. [ABA Model Rule 1.6] (A) is incorrect because a lawyer has no ethical obligation to reveal harmful facts, and, in fact, may be disciplined for doing so. (B) is incorrect because, as noted above, there is no duty to reveal this information; thus, there is no obligation to urge the client to reveal the information or withdraw. (D) is incorrect because this information is confidential. The ethical duty of confidentiality covers more kinds of information than the attorney-client privilege, which covers only confidential communications between the lawyer and client. The ethical duty of confidentiality covers any information the lawyer obtains relating to the representation of the client, no matter what the source of the information.

Answer to Question 45

(B)   The judge's actions were proper because he did not charge his mother a fee. Although a full-time judge may not practice law, there is an exception for this type of transaction. A judge may, without compensation, give legal advice to, and draft and review documents for, a member of the judge's family. [CJC Rule 3.10] (A) is wrong because whether the buyer might appear in the judge's court does not affect the judge's ability to prepare documents for his mother. If the buyer does appear in his court, the judge's participation in that proceeding will be evaluated at that time in light of the facts. (C) is wrong because, as stated above, there is an exception for reviewing documents for relatives without compensation. (D) is wrong because, although the judge cannot act as a negotiator, there is no requirement that his identity as the person who made the revisions be kept a secret.

Answer to Question 46

(D)   It would not be proper for the attorney to have his name included on the agency's list because the agreement allows a third party to exercise influence over the lawyer-client relationship. A lawyer must not allow a person who recommends, employs, or pays her for serving a client to direct or regulate the lawyer's professional judgment. [ABA Model Rule 5.4(c)] The agency is, in effect, recommending the attorney, and the restriction on withdrawal in the form agreement clearly interferes with the attorney's professional judgment. (A) is wrong because the good intentions behind the list do not remove the interference with the attorney's professional judgment. Likewise, (B) is wrong because, even if the attorney does not give the agency anything of value, the arrangement is still improper because of the restriction on withdrawal. (C) is wrong because the list does not amount to improper solicitation.

Answer to Question 47

(C)   Alpha is not subject to discipline because Beta earned the fee prior to his suspension. Despite his suspension, Beta is entitled to the fees he earned while he was still lawfully practicing law. It is true that a lawyer is prohibited from aiding a nonlawyer in the unauthorized practice of law, but here Beta is not practicing law, and Alpha is merely forwarding his previously earned fee. (A) is wrong because Beta need not wait until he is reinstated to collect a fee he earned prior to his suspension. (B) is wrong because Beta is not a nonlawyer, and Alpha is not splitting legal fees with him in any case. Alpha is merely transmitting Beta's own money to him. (D) is wrong because the money does not belong to Alpha, and even if it did, she cannot do anything she wishes with it. For example, there are rules prohibiting the sharing of legal fees with nonlawyers.

Answer to Question 48

(B) A judge may not personally solicit contributions for an organization other than from her family or certain other judges. [CJC Rule 3.7(A)(2)] Thus, (B) is improper. (A) is proper because Judge Jones, like anyone else, may contribute to any cause she likes. (C) is proper because a judge may assist an organization in planning fund-raising, although the judge may not actually participate in the fund-raising activity. [CJC Rule 3.7(A)(1)] A judge must not be a speaker or guest of honor at an organization's fund-raising event, but mere attendance at such an event is permissible. [CJC Rule 3.7(A)(4), comment 3] Thus, (D) is proper.

Answer to Question 49

(D) A lawyer may require his fee to be paid in advance and may accept property in return for services, provided it does not involve a proprietary interest in the subject of litigation. [Comment 4 to ABA Model Rule 1.5] Thus, the attorney here has done nothing wrong. (A) is incorrect because, as discussed above, a lawyer may take an advance. (B) is incorrect because the coat is not the subject of litigation; thus, accepting the coat as payment was proper. (C) states the correct conclusion but is based on a faulty rationale—the propriety of the attorney's conduct does not depend on the client's reputation for paying bills.

Answer to Question 50

(C) The attorney is not subject to discipline because he did not make any false or misleading claims about himself or his services. Lawyers, like other citizens, have the right to express their views in the media on newsworthy issues. Even if a lawyer's sole purpose in seeking media publicity is to lure clients, the state may not impose professional discipline on the lawyer absent a compelling state interest. A lawyer who uses the media to lure clients may, however, be disciplined for making statements or claims that are false or misleading about the lawyer or his services. [ABA Model Rule 7.1] Here, the attorney made no statements about himself or his services other than the fact that he is a lawyer and his opinion about the incident. There is nothing false or misleading in his communication. (A) is wrong because, as discussed above, the fact that the attorney was motivated by the desire to attract fee-paying business is irrelevant. This is not a case of live person-to-person solicitation, which is the only circumstance in which this consideration is relevant. (B) is wrong because it is overbroad. Lawyers can and do make public statements about pending litigation all the time. Lawyers who are

involved in a proceeding cannot make statements that they know will have a substantial likelihood of materially prejudicing an adjudicative proceeding. [ABA Model Rule 3.6(a)] That is not the case here; the attorney has no reason to believe his opinion will materially prejudice the state agency bringing the action. (D) is wrong because the fact that the statement was printed in the newspapers is of absolutely no consequence; it does not affect the propriety of the attorney's behavior regardless of whether he gave consent.

Answer to Question 51

(A)   (C) is incorrect because there is no disciplinary rule against a lawyer acting as a third-party neutral in a family law matter, and it was proper for the attorney to undertake the neutral's role in helping the husband and wife try to resolve their marital problems. [*See* Restatement §130, comment d] (D) is incorrect because the facts contain nothing to support a civil claim against the attorney for the work she did as a third-party neutral. (B) is incorrect because when two parties jointly consult a lawyer on a matter of common interest, neither of them can claim the attorney-client privilege in subsequent civil litigation between them. [See Restatement §75] (A) is correct because the husband cannot claim the privilege for the reason stated above. If the judge overrules the privilege claim and the attorney nevertheless refuses to answer the question, she can be sanctioned for contempt of court.

Answer to Question 52

(B)   ABA Model Rule 5.5(c) concerns temporary practice in a state where the lawyer is not admitted. Rule 5.5(c)(4)

permits the attorney to practice temporarily in State B to the extent that his work in that state is reasonably related to the work he does for the company in State A. However, because State B requires out-of-state lawyers to seek pro hac vice admission before engaging in pretrial preparation, ABA Model Rule 5.5(c)(2) and (3) require the attorney to seek such admission. (A) is wrong because the application of ABA Model Rule 5.5(c) to the attorney's situation is clear, not debatable. (C) is wrong because ABA Model Rule 5.5(c) allows the attorney to perform the assigned tasks without taking a bar exam in State B. (D) is wrong because associating a local lawyer is only one of four different ways to satisfy ABA Model Rule 5.5(c).

Answer to Question 53

(C)   ABA Model Rule 7.2(c) prohibits a lawyer from stating or implying that she is a certified specialist unless she has been certified by an appropriate organization that is clearly identified in the lawyer's communication. The attorney's ad appears to have been artfully crafted to make unsophisticated readers think that the attorney has been certified by the state bar. Thus, the ad violates both ABA Model Rule 7.2(c) and ABA Model Rule 7.1, which prohibits misleading advertising. As for the attorney's reciprocal referral relationship with the solo practitioner, the applicable rule is ABA Model Rule 7.2(b)(4), which permits a reciprocal referral agreement between lawyers, provided that the agreement is nonexclusive and the referred clients are told about the existence and nature of the agreement. ABA Model Rule 7.2(b)(4) has not yet been prominently interpreted, leaving one to wonder whether the relationship between the attorney and the solo practitioner should be regarded as an "agreement." On the one hand, the question states that they have no "formal reciprocal referral agreement." On the other hand, in some legal contexts, a consciously reciprocal course of dealing can be the equivalent of an agreement. [*See, e.g.*, United States v. Container Corp. of America, 393 U.S. 333 (1969)—competitors' reciprocal exchange of price data was held to be an agreement under section 1 of the Sherman Antitrust Act] However, for purposes of this question, the relationship between the attorney and the solo practitioner will be deemed an agreement under ABA Model Rule 7.2(b)(4) because it is bound to influence their judgment about referrals to some degree. Here, the relationship violates the nonexclusive requirement because the two lawyers follow the pattern "without exception." Furthermore, the relationship would be proper only if the attorney tells referred clients about the relationship so that they can decide for themselves how to value the referral. One can reach the same conclusion by applying ABA Model Rule 1.7(a)(2)—the attorney's reciprocal relationship with the solo practitioner gives the attorney a personal interest (obtaining future referrals) that is in conflict with the interest of her client (obtaining an unbiased referral). The conflict could be solved only by full disclosure and informed consent of the affected client, confirmed in writing. [ABA Model Rule 1.7(b)]

Answer to Question 54

(A)   The attorney is subject to discipline under CJC Rule 4.1(A)(8), which prohibits a judicial candidate from personally soliciting campaign contributions or publicly stated support. The five lawyers who contributed money will be subject to discipline if the attorney

wins and if they accept appointments from him. [*See* ABA Model Rule 7.6] (B) is wrong because the attorney is subject to discipline under CJC Rule 4.1(A)(8), as noted above. The second sentence of (B) is wrong because it overstates the constraints on a lawyer's participation in a judicial campaign. (C) is wrong because the five lawyers who contributed money violated ABA Model Rule 7.6, as noted above. The first sentence of (C) is a misapplication of CJC Rule 4.1(A)(13), which prohibits a judge from making pledges or promises that are inconsistent with the impartial performance of the judge's adjudicative duties "*in connection with cases, controversies, or issues that are likely to come before the court.*" Here, the policy regarding whom the probate judge will appoint as administrators' counsel is not the kind of litigation issue to which the highlighted language of CJC Rule 4.1(A)(13), above, refers. The second sentence of (C) is wrong because the motive of the five money contributors was to obtain appointments if the attorney won. [*See* ABA Model Rule 7.6] (D) is wrong because a lawyer who runs for a judicial post must follow the CJC. [*See* CJC Rule 4.1, comment 2] The second sentence of (D) is wrong because ABA Model Rule 7.6 trumps whatever privacy rights one can find in the peripheral glow of the First and Fourteenth Amendments.

Answer to Question 55

(B)   The county legal advice hotline is the kind of operation envisioned in ABA Model Rule 6.5. Under ABA Model Rule 6.5, walk-in legal clinics, advice-only clinics, legal advice hotlines, and the like are not held to the high conflict-of-interest standards that govern ordinary law offices. Legal hotlines, walk-in clinics, and similar providers of quick legal service typically operate under conditions that make it difficult or impossible to conduct ordinary conflict-of-interest checks. Under ABA Model Rule 6.5(b), the second lawyer would be subject to discipline only if he *actually knew* that the first attorney had previously counseled the mother of the abused children. A lawyer's actual knowledge can be inferred from the circumstances [ABA Model Rule 1.0(f)], but the question does not mention any circumstances from which an inference could be made that the second lawyer had actual knowledge. (A) is wrong because it fails to account for ABA Model Rule 6.5. (C) is wrong because, absent *actual knowledge* of a conflict, the rule of imputed disqualification does not apply between two lawyers in a quick-legal-service program. [*See* comment 4 to ABA Model Rule 6.5] (D) is wrong because both the mother and father were "clients" of the respective lawyers who advised them. [Comment 1 to ABA Model Rule 6.5] This is important because ABA Model Rule 6.5 loosens only the conflict-of-interest rules, not other aspects of the lawyer-client relationship, such as the duty of competence, the duty of diligence, and the duty of confidentiality.

Answer to Question 56

(D) ABA Model Rule 5.7 provides that when a lawyer offers another kind of service ancillary to her practice of law, and the ancillary service is provided "in circumstances that are not distinct from the lawyer's provision of legal services," the lawyer must follow the legal ethics rules in the ancillary service as well

as the legal service. Here, the attorney does bill separately for her two kinds of service, but she offers both out of the same office, and the tasks she does as sports agent shade imperceptibly into the tasks she does as lawyer, as is illustrated by the exclusive sponsorship contract with the bank. Thus, the attorney must follow the lawyer conflict of interest rules when she acts as sports agent. [*See* comment 10 to ABA Model Rule 5.7] When the attorney diverted the bank ad campaign from Alpha to Beta, she violated ABA Model Rule 1.7(a)(1) (concurrent conflict when the representation of one client will be directly adverse to another client), or at least ABA Model Rule 1.7(a)(2) (significant risk that the representation of one client will be limited by the lawyer's responsibility to another client). Incidentally, the attorney may also be *subject to civil liability* in a suit by Alpha for breaching the duty of loyalty an agent owes to a principal. [*See* Restatement of the Law of Agency 2d §§391, 394] (A) is wrong for the reasons stated above. (B) is wrong because the separate charging arrangement is not sufficient by itself to clearly segregate the attorney's sports agent work from her lawyer work. (C) is wrong because the attorney is not doing the "same work" when she acts as sports agent for two different players.

Answer to Question 57

(A) ABA Model Rule 1.17 permits a lawyer to sell her entire law practice, or an area of her law practice, to one or more lawyers or law firms. Here, the solo practitioner sold her entire law practice to two different lawyers, and ABA Model Rule 1.17 permits that. The departure of 40% of the solo practitioner's clients does not cause the sales to violate ABA Model Rule 1.17. Indeed ABA Model Rule 1.17(c)(2) requires the selling lawyer to notify her clients that they have a right to pick up their files from the buyer and take them to a different lawyer. [*See also* comment 2 to ABA Model Rule 1.17] (B) and (D) are wrong because clients are not like sheep that can be bought and sold, willy-nilly. To hold the solo practitioner either subject to discipline or civilly liable in unjust enrichment would be inconsistent with the clients' right to pick up their files and take them to a different lawyer. The solo practitioner, Alpha, and Beta made their sales contracts in the context of ABA Model Rule 1.17 so Alpha and Beta cannot claim that they were surprised when clients departed. (C) is wrong because ABA Model Rule 1.17(b) permits a lawyer to sell her entire practice to *one or more* lawyers or law firms. One might also argue that the solo practitioner's medical malpractice cases are in a different "area of practice" (professional malpractice) from her products liability cases. But that argument is not necessary here because the solo practitioner sold her entire law practice.

Answer to Question 58

(D)   ABA Model Rule 1.6(b)(4) and comment 9 explain that a lawyer may reveal information that would otherwise be confidential if the lawyer's purpose is to obtain legal advice about complying with the legal ethics rules. (A) is wrong because the applicable doctrine here is the ethical duty of confidentiality, not the attorney-client privilege, and the ethical duty contains the exception described above. (B) is wrong because the exception to the ethical duty would apply in this situation, whether or not the

attorney identified the dealer by name. As a practical matter, however, a lawyer who discloses confidential information to obtain legal ethics advice may wish to couch the information hypothetically, in order to minimize the chance of harm to the client. [*See* comment 4 to ABA Model Rule 1.6] (C) is wrong because the exception to the ethical duty would apply in this situation whether the drug dealer or the sales associate is regarded as the client.

Answer to Question 59

(C)   This question is governed by ABA Model Rule 1.13, not by the SEC's regulations under the Sarbanes-Oxley Act, because the company is not publicly owned and is not subject to the jurisdiction of the SEC. The associate is *subject to discipline* for tipping off the Justice Department because he violated the duty of confidentiality imposed by ABA Model Rule 1.6(a). When the antitrust attorney and the associate investigated the price fixing rumor at the request of the company's general counsel, they were operating under ABA Model Rule 1.13(d), which applies to lawyers who are hired "to investigate an alleged violation of law" or to "defend an organization" or its people against a claim arising out of an alleged violation of law. That means that ABA Model Rule 1.13(c) does *not* apply, and they *must not* report to outsiders about what they find. Both parts of (A) are wrong—the antitrust attorney acted properly, and the associate is subject to discipline, as explained above. (B) is wrong because the associate's conduct was not proper. Moreover, the associate probably committed legal malpractice when he tipped off the Justice Department, and the antitrust attorney might be vicariously liable for his malpractice because she was his supervisor. (D) is wrong because the associate is subject to discipline for violating ABA Model Rule 1.6(a).

Answer to Question 60

(A)   A lawyer must not communicate ex parte with a juror unless authorized by law or court order. [ABA Model Rule 3.5(b)] Communicating with a juror is generally improper even if the subject matter is unrelated to the case. [*See* Restatement §115] Here, the attorney's remark about his client's injuries was a clear violation. (D) is incorrect because the prohibition applies even if the juror initiated the conversation. (C) is incorrect. Although ABA Model Rule 3.5(a) forbids a lawyer from attempting to influence a juror, the prohibition on ex parte communications is separate and applies regardless of the lawyer's intentions. (B) is incorrect because it is immaterial whether the jury returned a verdict for the plaintiff—the communication was improper regardless of whether it ultimately benefited the attorney's client.

SIMULATED MPRE

YOU HAVE 120 MINUTES TO COMPLETE THE EXAM.

SIMULATED MPRE

Question 1

An attorney is prosecuting a complex tax case. After two government witnesses testified, the defendant took the stand in his own defense. He asserted that he always complied with all tax rules and regulations. He also testified that the two government witnesses had deliberately falsified his Internal Revenue Service records because the witnesses belonged to a Satanic cult which bore a long-standing grudge against him.

Which of the following statements about the defendant's testimony, if made by the attorney in her closing argument, would make the attorney subject to discipline?

(A) "The defendant's testimony is clearly in conflict with the testimony of two government witnesses."

(B) "Of the persons who have given testimony, who has the better reason to lie, the defendant or the government's witnesses?"

(C) "If you believe the testimony of the defendant, you will also believe that the moon is made of green cheese!"

(D) "I know you will consider the evidence carefully and reach a reasonable conclusion."

Question 2

A judge ruled in favor of a plaintiff in a civil action where the defendant was ordered to pay the plaintiff $50,000 in damages. The judge has since resigned from the bench. The defendant has refused to pay the $50,000, asserting that the verdict was obtained through improper means. The defendant asks the judge, now in private practice, if she will represent him.

Would the judge be subject to discipline if she represents the defendant?

(A) No, because the judge is no longer on the bench.

(B) No, because the judge was not a party to fraud when the original verdict was handed down.

(C) Yes, because the judge ruled on this case when she was a judge.

(D) Yes, because former judges may not engage in private practice.

GO ON TO THE NEXT PAGE

Question 3

An attorney has hired a third-year law student to assist him as his clerk. The law student is not licensed under any state law or court rule that allows third-year law students to engage in practice under the supervision of a licensed attorney. The attorney has permitted the law student to perform a variety of tasks.

For which of the following tasks that the attorney has the law student perform would the attorney be subject to discipline?

(A) Drafting a release form for personal injury plaintiffs to sign after their cases have been settled. (The attorney himself has the plaintiffs sign the forms.)

(B) Interviewing witnesses to accidents, and having them sign the law student's written version of the interview.

(C) Reaching settlement agreements with insurance company representatives before suit has been filed.

(D) Undertaking legal research and drafting research memoranda.

Question 4

The mayor of a small city is also a licensed attorney who has a law partnership with a fellow attorney in the city. Under the city's charter, the mayor has the authority to determine what issues are to be placed upon the agenda of the city council. Several council members have told the mayor that they would like to see a particular zoning measure placed upon the agenda. This proposed ordinance would ban commercial development of a certain area within the city limits.

The mayor's law partner has been retained as attorney for a development company that has acquired land in the proposed noncommercial zoning area and has plans to construct a large shopping center there. The mayor has agreed to take no direct role in the representation, not to share any fees from the case, and not to attend any city council meetings at which the matter will be discussed.

May the mayor's law partner represent the development company in this matter?

(A) Yes, because the development company is not a client of the mayor.

(B) Yes, because the mayor will not be present at any city council meetings at which the matter is discussed.

(C) No, because of the mayor's position as mayor.

(D) No, because the mayor will have no direct role in the representation and will not share in any fees from the case.

GO ON TO THE NEXT PAGE

Question 5

An attorney represented a fired employee, a "service station field representative," of a petroleum corporation in a wrongful discharge action against the corporation. Such representatives are responsible for visiting and inspecting the corporation's service stations to ensure that the station operators are obeying the terms of their leases; following the corporation's rules about retail gasoline pricing; keeping full stocks of the corporation's brand of tires, batteries, and accessories; not carrying competitors' tires, batteries, and accessories; and maintaining the stations in a clean and attractive condition. The corporation claimed that it fired the employee for poor job performance, but he claimed that he was fired because he refused to enforce certain corporate policies that he believed were violations of federal and state antitrust laws. In the course of preparing the case for trial, the attorney and the employee talked in confidence at great length about how the corporation expects its field representatives to enforce its allegedly anticompetitive rules against service station operators. Shortly before trial, the corporation settled with the employee for a generous sum. He did not, however, return to his job at the corporation, nor has he communicated with his attorney since the case ended.

Now, three years later, a service station operator of the same corporation has hired the attorney to represent him in a federal antitrust action to collect treble damages from the corporation for subjecting him to the very same anticompetitive policies that cost her former client his job. The attorney is handling her new client's case on a contingent fee basis. In preparing his case for trial, the attorney was able to save many hundreds of hours of discovery and research work because of the information she learned in confidence from her former client about the way the corporation treats its service station operators. Thanks to what he taught her about the corporation's business practices, the attorney was ready for her new client's trial in record time—which panicked the lawyers for the corporation and ultimately resulted in an extraordinarily generous settlement for her new client. The attorney, of course, took her share of the settlement under the contingent fee arrangement and thus profited personally from her former client's information.

Is the attorney subject to civil liability to her former client for using his confidential information for her own monetary benefit?

(A) No, because the attorney's recycling of the information did not harm her former client; she simply took advantage in her law practice of her earlier experience and accumulated knowledge.

(B) No, because her former client ceased being the attorney's client at the time he settled his case with the corporation, and the attorney's duty of confidentiality ended when the lawyer-client relationship ended.

(C) Yes, because the attorney did not obtain informed consent, confirmed in writing, from her former client before using his information to hasten her preparation of her new client's case.

(D) Yes, because the contingent fee arrangement allowed the attorney to profit personally from material disclosed to her in confidence by her former client.

GO ON TO THE NEXT PAGE

Question 6

An attorney is representing a defendant in a civil case that arose out of a business deal gone sour. One evening after court was out of session, but with the trial set to resume the next day, the attorney attended a $5,000 per person charity fundraising dinner. When he found his assigned seat, he was shocked to find that he was seated next to the plaintiff in the suit. The attorney asked the hostess if she could change his seat, but she said it would be impossible. Determined to make the best of it, the attorney and the plaintiff did not discuss the case but made small talk about the charity, the weather, etc. They soon found that they had much in common, including a love of sports. After a long, enjoyable evening of discussing their favorite teams, the plaintiff gets up to leave. He turns to the attorney, and says he has enjoyed talking with him, and says that he intends to call his attorney first thing in the morning to talk about reaching an agreeable settlement in the case. The next day, the plaintiff calls his lawyer and tells her that after talking to the defendant's attorney the evening before at a fundraiser, he has decided to settle the case for the amount proposed in the last negotiating session. The plaintiff then instructs his lawyer to draw up the appropriate papers. Furious, the plaintiff's lawyer does as her client asks, but reports the defendant's attorney to the proper disciplinary authorities.

Is the defendant's attorney subject to discipline?

(A) Yes, because he communicated with a represented party without the consent of that party's attorney.

(B) Yes, because this is an improper ex parte communication while the matter is still pending.

(C) No, because they discussed the charity, the weather, and sports.

(D) No, because the attorney did not know he would be seated next to the plaintiff and asked to have the seating assignment changed as soon as he discovered it.

Question 7

An attorney represents the plaintiff in a personal injury case. The plaintiff has authorized her attorney to settle the case for $2,000. She further tells him that if he receives $2,000 from the defendant, he may keep $750 of it as his fee, and that he should pay the physician who examined her $250 for his examination and treatment of her injuries. The attorney reaches a $2,000 settlement with the defendant. Upon receipt of a $2,000 check from the defendant, the attorney immediately places $750 in his personal account, sends the plaintiff's physician a check for $250, and places $1,000 in his clients' trust account at the local bank. Sixty days after the attorney received the $2,000 check, his client calls him to inquire about any progress made on a settlement of her case. The attorney tells her that he has settled the case and paid her physician. Immediately after he hangs up the phone, he writes out a check to his client in the amount of $1,000 and mails the check on his lunch hour.

Is the attorney subject to discipline?

(A) Yes, because he paid himself his fee without informing his client.

(B) Yes, because he did not promptly pay his client the money due her.

(C) No, because he placed the funds due his client in the trust account.

(D) No, because he was negligent but did not violate a disciplinary rule.

GO ON TO THE NEXT PAGE

Question 8

An attorney represents a plaintiff in a personal injury suit arising out of a tour bus accident in Hawaii. Nearly all of the eyewitnesses were tourists who have now returned home to the mainland. Without notifying the defense attorney, the plaintiff's attorney has interviewed most of the witnesses by phone. By far the most compelling witness, and the one most favorable to the plaintiff, is a librarian who lives in North Dakota and had spent the bulk of her life savings on a vacation to Hawaii. It was on this vacation that she witnessed the tour bus accident. She is a very appealing witness, and the attorney is confident that if a jury saw her testify personally, the plaintiff would win his suit. The attorney tells the witness that if she is willing to come to Hawaii for one week to testify, he will pay for her plane tickets, an oceanfront hotel room at a first class hotel, all meals, and one week's salary for her lost time. This is the same offer that the attorney makes to all witnesses traveling to testify in any of his cases. The witness, who cannot believe her good fortune, readily agrees.

Is the attorney subject to discipline?

(A) Yes, because a lawyer may not offer an inducement to a witness to testify.

(B) Yes, because he interviewed the witnesses without notifying the defense attorney.

(C) No, because a lawyer may pay a witness's reasonable expenses and lost wages.

(D) No, because the trip and accommodations are substantially more expensive than the witness could afford.

Question 9

A wife whose husband was hard-drinking and abusive went to see an attorney about getting a divorce. However, because the wife did not work outside the home, she told the attorney that she could not afford to pay a big legal fee. The attorney was sure that the wife had adequate grounds for divorce in that her husband was adulterous, an alcoholic, and frequently beat her. Therefore, the attorney told the wife that if she could put up the $200 filing fee, he would do all the work for 10% of whatever he was able to obtain in alimony and child support on her behalf. The wife was elated and immediately agreed to the arrangement, thanking the attorney profusely. The attorney left his office that night with a warm feeling that he had helped a fellow human being, secure in the knowledge that at least one person in the community would have something nice to say about lawyers.

Personal satisfaction aside, was the attorney's conduct proper?

(A) Yes, because the fee is reasonable and is not excessive.

(B) Yes, because the attorney is providing legal services to a person who might not otherwise be able to afford them.

(C) No, because a contingent fee arrangement is prohibited when the fee is based on the amount of alimony or a division of marital property.

(D) No, because the wife was indigent and the attorney should have advanced her the filing fees.

GO ON TO THE NEXT PAGE

Question 10

A local attorney has recently defended a client in a civil action tried before a jury. The client lost the case, and the plaintiff was awarded a substantial amount of damages. The attorney receives an anonymous, handwritten letter stating that one of the jurors in the plaintiff's case was bribed to influence other members of the jury to side with the plaintiff and to award a large sum in damages. The lawyer hires a local private investigator to investigate the juror to determine if the anonymous charges are true, and instructs the investigator to take care to do nothing that would involve coercion or harassment.

Is it proper for the attorney to hire the private investigator?

(A) No, because the investigator did not notify the juror in question of his investigation and did not obtain her consent.

(B) No, because such an investigation is likely to affect the willingness of the jurors to serve on juries in the future.

(C) Yes, because the investigation may disclose evidence sufficient for the granting of a new trial.

(D) Yes, because the investigation is to be conducted in such a manner as not to harass the jurors.

Question 11

An attorney and his law partner each represent a criminal defendant in seemingly unrelated cases. During the attorney's interview with his client, the client tells the attorney that he was involved in the crime with which the other criminal defendant is charged and that he is willing to testify against him if he can be granted immunity from prosecution on that charge and plea bargain the crime with which he is presently charged down to a lesser offense.

Which of the following courses of action is proper for the attorney?

(A) Inform his law partner of what his client has told him and continue to represent his client.

(B) Inform his law partner of what his client has told him and withdraw from representing his client.

(C) Not inform his law partner and continue representation.

(D) Not inform his law partner and withdraw from representation.

Question 12

An attorney is embittered because he has recently had to expend a great deal of time and money defending himself against a frivolous malpractice suit brought by a disgruntled former client. To forestall such suits in the future, the attorney decides to take extra precautions.

Which of the following arrangements could the attorney enter into with clients without being subject to discipline?

(A) With the client's knowledge, taping a closing interview, during the course of which the attorney explains to the client each aspect of his handling of the case and asks the client if she understands fully the explanation, or if she has any further questions about the case.

(B) Agreeing to represent a client for no fee or for a low fee if the client promises not to sue him for malpractice.

(C) Refusing to return a client's papers until the client signs a release of liability for malpractice.

(D) Reserving the right to withdraw from representing a client at any time during the representation, whenever he gets a feeling that the client might mean trouble for him.

GO ON TO THE NEXT PAGE

Question 13

An attorney has an arrangement whereby a local radio station broadcasts four times each day a prerecorded tape advertising her services. The attorney pays the station its standard rate for "spot advertising." The advertisement states that the attorney will handle bankruptcies for $150 and uncontested divorces where there are no custody or property issues for $250 plus the filing fee. The ad also states that she will take personal injury cases on a contingency fee basis, and that her fee is 30% of the amount recovered after deduction for costs. The ad concludes by inviting prospective clients to make an appointment for a free consultation regarding their case.

Is the attorney's advertising proper?

(A) No, because a lawyer may not advertise contingent fees.

(B) No, because the attorney does not appear to be a certified specialist in personal injury law.

(C) No, because the attorney advertises free consultations.

(D) Yes; there is nothing wrong with the attorney's advertising.

Question 14

A law firm represents a successful businessman who has given the firm almost all of his substantial legal business. The businessman is presently involved in complex civil litigation in which he stands to receive a large damages award if the suit is successful. The attorney for the defendant in the case has filed a motion that, if granted, would result in dismissal of the suit. The named partners of the law firm have studied the motion and feel that there is some merit in the motion, and at least a 50% chance that the judge who is trying the case will rule in favor of the defendant. During the course of explaining the defendant's motion to the businessman, the two named partners call in a recently hired associate. The associate is the judge's former law clerk, and he wrote several speeches for her when she was running in a contested reelection campaign. The partners tell the businessman that it would be to his advantage for the associate to argue against the motion. The associate, during the course of the meeting with the businessman, tells him that the judge owes him a favor.

Is the associate subject to discipline?

(A) Yes, because his statement implies that the judge will give him preferential treatment due to their past association.

(B) Yes, because he plans to use his knowledge of the judge's character to his advantage.

(C) No, because he did not expressly state that the judge would rule in his favor.

(D) No, because he does not plan to use improper influence on the judge.

GO ON TO THE NEXT PAGE

Question 15

In April, a plaintiff sued a defendant in United States District Court for infringement of its copyright on a computer software program that protects computer data from being destroyed by so-called computer viruses. The plaintiff alleges in its complaint that the defendant infringed the copyright by copying its anti-virus program in January. In August, the plaintiff filed a document discovery request that asked the defendant to hand over a copy of the "source code" of its own anti-virus program as it existed in January. The source code is the precise material written in computer language by the programmer. Only by comparing source codes could a person be sure whether one software program had been copied from another program. Source codes are therefore vital evidence in software copyright infringement cases, and all competent lawyers who work in the field know that fact.

As is customary in the computer industry, the defendant periodically creates improved versions of the computer software it sells. Whenever the defendant creates an improved version, it routinely destroys the source code of the former version, keeping only the source code of the improved version. This routine destruction is the customary practice in the computer industry. In June, and again in September, the defendant created improved versions of its anti-virus program. On both occasions, the defendant asked its lawyer whether it would be all right to destroy the former source code. Without giving the matter much thought, the lawyer responded on both occasions: "Sure you may. It's the routine practice in the industry, and I see no problem with it." In due course, the plaintiff moved for a court order to enforce its document discovery request for the January source code. In response, defense counsel turned over the then-current version of the source code and explained why the January version was no longer available.

After a detailed factual hearing, the judge concluded that the defendant's two acts of destruction made it impossible for the plaintiff to prove that the defendant had copied its copyrighted material in January. As a sanction for destroying evidence, the judge entered a partial summary judgment in favor of the plaintiff on the copying issue. The judge also sanctioned defense counsel by ordering him to pay all of the expenses and attorneys' fees that the plaintiff had incurred due to the defendant's two acts of destruction.

Was the judge correct in holding defense counsel subject to litigation sanction?

(A) Yes, as respects the destruction in September (after the plaintiff's document request), but no, as respects the June destruction because the plaintiff did not request the source code until August.

(B) Yes, because in both June and September, defense counsel either knew or ought to have known that the January source code was vital evidence.

(C) No, because there is no evidence that defense counsel intended to commit a fraud on the court by allowing his client to destroy the January source code.

(D) No, because defense counsel did not actively encourage his client to destroy the January source code.

GO ON TO THE NEXT PAGE

Question 16

An attorney worked for two years for the Veteran's Administration ("VA"). While there, his main function was to investigate claims filed by veterans. During the course of his employment, he was responsible for investigating a claim filed by a veteran whose claim was denied by the VA after the attorney left his job there. He was not privy to confidential information regarding the veteran. The veteran comes to the lawyer, who is now engaged in private practice, and asks him to represent him in a suit against the VA for the benefits to which the veteran believes he is entitled.

Is the attorney subject to discipline if he accepts the veteran's case?

(A) No, because the attorney has left the VA.

(B) No, because the attorney was not privy to confidential information regarding the veteran, arising from his employment at the VA.

(C) Yes, because the attorney had at least some knowledge of the veteran's claim when he was employed by a government agency.

(D) Yes, because the attorney had substantial and personal responsibility for the veteran's VA claim.

Question 17

A woman visits an attorney whom she hires to bring a breach of contract action on her behalf. The client tells the attorney that she originally retained another lawyer about a year ago, but that as far as she knew he had not even filed the papers. According to the client, the other lawyer never returned her calls, and when she went to his office to find out the status of her case, he was drunk and verbally abusive. The client told her friends and family about the other lawyer's treatment

of her, and when her brother fared no better in getting information from him, he suggested that she contact another attorney. The client advises the attorney that because the other lawyer did not return her calls, she had sent a certified letter to him notifying him that he was discharged. The attorney knew that there was only a one-year statute of limitations on this type of action, so she quickly checked the dates and discovered that she had only a few days to file the action. The attorney called the other lawyer to get the information from the client's file. The other lawyer did not recall the letter of discharge and was surprised to get the attorney's call. He was, however, very cooperative and agreed to send a messenger to the attorney's office with the client's file. The other lawyer tells the attorney that he feels terrible about the situation, that his wife has been seriously ill, and that as a result he has not been himself. He asks the attorney to apologize to the client on his behalf, but asks the attorney to please keep this conversation "between the two of us." He says that with his wife's illness, he cannot afford to lose any other clients.

The attorney filed the papers in her client's suit on time, and did not report the other lawyer to the disciplinary authorities.

Were the attorney's actions proper?

(A) Yes, because she is an attorney, and the other lawyer asked her to keep the matter confidential.

(B) Yes, because it is the client's decision whether to report the other lawyer to the disciplinary authorities.

(C) No, because the other lawyer's actions indicate that he is not currently fit to practice law.

(D) No, because she did not urge her client to report the other lawyer to the appropriate authorities.

GO ON TO THE NEXT PAGE

Question 18

A law school graduate who is not a licensed member of the bar felt called to the ministry after he graduated from law school. He received a degree in divinity, and was formally ordained as a minister of his faith. He is now the pastor of a local church, where an attorney is a member of the congregation. As pastor, he has been very disturbed about the high rates of divorce and the breakdown in American family life. Therefore, he holds frequent "family counseling sessions" where, among other things, he explains to the parishioners who attend these sessions many of the legal ramifications of divorce, alimony, child support, and child custody. These sessions are usually followed by question-and-answer periods, during which the pastor gives legal advice to parishioners who cannot afford a lawyer. The pastor knows that the legislature has passed a new marriage dissolution law that changes the law substantially from what he was taught in law school. The pastor asks the attorney who is a member of the congregation if he will prepare an outline and a memorandum fully explaining the new law so that he will be better informed for the sessions with his parishioners.

If the attorney agrees to do this, is he subject to discipline?

(A) Yes, because the pastor may bring the attorney before the State Bar Disciplinary Committee if the attorney makes any mistake of law in the memorandum.

(B) Yes, because the attorney is assisting in the unauthorized practice of law.

(C) No, because the attorney has a duty to help educate the public regarding the law.

(D) No, because marriage counseling is an important part of the pastor's duties as pastor.

Question 19

A long-term named partner in a law firm was approached by officials of his political party about running for governor of the state, and after some deliberation, decided to run. The law partner won both the primary and the general election and was recently sworn in as the state's new governor. Although the law partner has made it clear to his other law partners and the public that he will not practice law during his tenure as governor, he still has fees coming due from prior cases and the senior partner of his firm has decided to leave the law partner's name on the firm's stationery and on the door of the firm's plush offices.

Is the senior partner's decision proper?

(A) Yes, because the now-governor would still have fees coming due from prior cases.

(B) Yes, because the now-governor had been a member of the firm for a period of at least five years prior to his election as governor.

(C) No, because the now-governor is not actually practicing with the firm.

(D) No, because it may create the appearance that the firm has special influence with the state government.

GO ON TO THE NEXT PAGE

Question 20

A local assistant district attorney ("ADA") has just finished prosecuting a case against a defendant who was accused of committing a serious felony. The ADA believed he had a strong case, but a judge trying the case ruled to acquit the defendant. The judge is running for reelection in a contested campaign. The judicial election will occur in two months. Immediately after the defendant's trial is over, the ADA holds a press conference, at which he says that the defendant was acquitted due to the erroneous rulings of the judge. The ADA also says that in every case he has had before that judge, the judge has made clearly erroneous rulings in favor of the defendant. Accordingly, the ADA says he intends to work hard for the judge's opponent in the forth-coming judicial election.

The ADA has personally tried four cases in front of the judge.

Is the ADA's statement during the press conference proper?

(A)   No, because the ADA is a public official and he should not have criticized another public official.

(B)   No, because the ADA has brought the administration of justice into disrepute.

(C)   Yes, because the ADA spoke out after the verdict had been rendered.

(D)   Yes, because the public needs to be informed about incompetent judges.

Question 21

A client brings an extremely complicated case to his attorney. This case is so complex that it will require the undivided attention of a qualified attorney for three months to do the necessary research, draw up the proper papers, and take the case to trial. The client, realizing the complexity of the case, makes the following offer to the attorney: The client promises to pay the attorney $30,000 in advance for three months if the attorney agrees not to work on other cases during that period of time, it being determined that the attorney's usual income from fees for a three-month period was $30,000. The attorney agreed to this arrangement and proceeded to work on the client's case only. During the first month that he was preparing the client's case, the attorney was approached by more than the usual number of prospective clients. Had he accepted employment from those who asked him to represent them during this period, he would have received $30,000 in fees from them. The attorney, however, in compliance with his agreement with the client, refused to take on any of these prospective clients. At the end of the first month, the attorney and the client had a conference to discuss the case. A number of points of disagreement arose between them; the client became angry, and summarily fired the attorney as his counsel. The client demands the return of the $30,000 fee advance.

Which of the following best describes proper conduct for the attorney?

(A)   Retain nothing because the work was not completed to the client's satisfaction.

(B)   Retain an amount that represents fair compensation for work actually performed on the case.

(C)   Retain the entire $30,000 because the attorney turned away business worth $30,000 to devote his full attention to the client's case.

(D)   Retain the entire $30,000 because the client, not the attorney, breached the agreement.

GO ON TO THE NEXT PAGE

Question 22

A judge who was considered a great personal injury litigator when he was in private practice is trying a very complicated commercial law case. He has carefully listened to the opposing attorneys' arguments and has read the briefs several times. He has found neither the oral arguments nor the briefs to be very enlightening. A former law partner of the judge is considered to be one of the leading experts on commercial law in the state, and the judge wishes to lend the briefs to her, and have her write an advisory memorandum on the issues of the case. The judge sincerely feels that this will enable him to render a proper judgment in a difficult case, so he approaches his former law partner and obtains her help.

Was it proper for the judge to seek such help from his former law partner?

(A) Yes, because the judge sincerely believed such advice was needed.

(B) Yes, because a judge may seek outside advice on any case.

(C) No, because he did not give notice to the parties and allow them time to respond to the former law partner's memorandum.

(D) No, because he did not obtain written permission from the parties prior to the consultation.

Question 23

An attorney and her client agree that the attorney will represent the client for a contingent fee of 25% of any eventual settlement or judgment in the client's personal injury action. The case comes to trial, and the judgment awarded is $20,000. The day after the trial, the client calls the attorney and tells her that her brother-in-law's cousin, who is a file clerk for an insurance company, told her that her claim was worth at least $40,000. The client says that the attorney did a poor job of representing her, and does not deserve any fee for obtaining an award of only $20,000. That afternoon, a check for $20,000, payable to the attorney from the defendant, arrives in the attorney's office.

It would be proper for the attorney to:

(A) Deposit the entire $20,000 in her client trust account until the matter is resolved.

(B) Send $15,000 to the client and deposit $5,000 in her client trust account.

(C) Send $15,000 to the client and deposit $5,000 in her personal account.

(D) Compromise by sending $17,500 to the client and depositing $2,500 in her personal account.

GO ON TO THE NEXT PAGE

Question 24

An attorney has been retained by a wealthy and socially prominent resident of the town where the attorney maintains his offices. This client has held a number of local political offices and is presently engaged in a hotly contested primary election contest for the seat in the United States Congress representing the town and surrounding environs. The client tells his attorney that he is being blackmailed by a young woman who is threatening him with a paternity suit. The client admits to a brief dalliance with the woman, but denies being the father of her child. The client tells his attorney that he is willing to settle with the woman for $10,000 to prevent the bad publicity that would result from the filing of a paternity suit against him and which would probably ruin his chances for election to Congress.

The attorney approaches the woman and tells her that he is willing to negotiate a settlement with her on his client's behalf. He strongly urges the woman to retain counsel, as there will be legal documents to be signed should the negotiations succeed, and she should be fully informed of her rights. The woman tells the attorney that she is presently unemployed and lacks the funds to employ a lawyer. She further tells him that she thinks she can adequately represent her interests herself.

The woman meets with the attorney in a private area of his law offices. During the course of their discussions, the attorney tells the woman that although blood tests will establish that the client is not the child's father, they are willing to offer $10,000 in settlement to avoid unfavorable publicity.

The next day, the woman calls the attorney and tells him that she will agree to the settlement. The attorney tells her to be in his office at 3 p.m. to sign the settlement papers and receive a $10,000 settlement check. The attorney shows the woman the settlement papers and explains them to her. The woman signs the papers and receives a $10,000 check from the attorney.

Is the attorney subject to discipline for negotiating with the woman?

(A) Yes, because she is a potential adverse party.

(B) Yes, because she is too poor to afford a lawyer.

(C) No, because he advised her to retain counsel.

(D) No, because this is not a criminal matter.

GO ON TO THE NEXT PAGE

Question 25

An attorney placed an advertisement in a newspaper of general circulation published daily in the community in which she practiced. The ad was to run every Tuesday and Thursday for a six-month period. The ad listed the attorney's office address and office telephone number and properly identified her as a lawyer. The ad also included the statement "after 5 p.m., call 555-4585," which was the attorney's home telephone number. The ad further included the attorney's fax number, which was identified as such.

Was the attorney's ad proper?

(A) Yes, because all restrictions on lawyer advertising are unconstitutional.

(B) Yes, because the information supplied will make it easier to contact her and make her services more accessible to more people.

(C) No, because it lists her home telephone number.

(D) No, because it is inappropriate to include a fax number in an ad.

Question 26

A recent law school graduate who has just been admitted to her state's bar returns to her hometown, a town of 20,000 in population in the center of the state. An attorney who has practiced out of a one-person office in the novice attorney's hometown for many years and is the only attorney in that town who regularly handles bankruptcy cases asks the novice attorney to associate with him. He produces an employment contract that he asks her to sign. The employment contract provides that the novice agrees to a salary of $40,000 plus medical benefits, and also agrees, for a period of one year after leaving the attorney's employ, not to accept any bankruptcy cases, not to accept business from clients who had been represented by the attorney's law firm during the period that the novice was employed there, and, in fact, not to practice law within a 50-mile radius of the town in which the attorney is located. The novice attorney agrees and signs the employment contract.

Which provision within the employment contract is proper?

(A) The prohibition against practicing law within a 50-mile radius of the town in which her former employer is located.

(B) The prohibition against accepting any cases dealing with bankruptcy.

(C) The prohibition against accepting business from clients who had been represented by the attorney's law firm during the period of the novice attorney's employment.

(D) The provision regarding salary and benefits.

GO ON TO THE NEXT PAGE

Question 27

Shortly after the county grand jury handed down an indictment for armed robbery against a fugitive, the district attorney met with the working press outside the door to the grand jury room. He tells the reporters that he is limited as to what he can say about pending cases and will make only three statements. Any other questions will be answered with "no comment."

Which of the following statements would not be proper to make to the press?

(A) "The fugitive has been indicted by the grand jury for armed robbery, but like all other American citizens he should be considered innocent until proven guilty."

(B) "He was indicted after grand jury testimony by two credible witnesses."

(C) "The public should be warned that this man is a fugitive and is considered to be armed and dangerous."

(D) "No comment."

Question 28

A partner in a law firm has represented a local manufacturing company for many years. The company gives the bulk of its legal business to the partner. The partner also does some collection work for the company. A number of the company's customers have not paid their bills, and the partner is in the process of obtaining judgments against them. These particular judgments are all default judgments, as none of the customers have filed answers to the complaints within the time limit stated. Thus, the judgments will be handled in a routine manner by the court with virtually automatic rulings in favor of the company. In the meantime, an associate in the partner's law firm who has never done any work for the company has been retained by a telecommunications company to draw up a number of contracts.

The partner files the papers for default judgments against the manufacturing company's delinquent customers. Among these customers is an unincorporated division of the telecommunications company, a fact that is not discovered by the partner until after he has filed the papers. The partner tells the associate who, in turn, tells the appropriate officer of the telecommunications company that he will have to withdraw from representing his company because of a conflict of interest. After explaining the problem fully to the telecommunications company's officer, they part on very cordial terms with the associate being given permission to withdraw. The partner proceeds with his cases against the manufacturing company's delinquent customers.

Is the law partner subject to discipline?

(A) Yes, because his firm has a conflict of interest.

(B) Yes, because he did not obtain informed consent, confirmed in writing, from the manufacturing company.

(C) No, because the default judgments are routine and uncontested.

(D) No, because the associate no longer represents the telecommunications company.

GO ON TO THE NEXT PAGE

Question 29

An attorney has done legal work for a waste management company for many years and is on very friendly terms with its officers and directors. The attorney is also chair of a state bar association committee. A bill has been introduced into the state legislature that would allow corporate boards of directors to vote by telephone, thus eliminating the necessity for the directors to be physically present at meetings. The state bar association committee that the attorney chairs has been studying the bill and is about to have a meeting where a vote will be taken on whether to recommend to the legislature that the bill be passed. The committee's recommendation will probably carry a great deal of weight with the legislators, and in fact may well be determinative of whether the bill is enacted into law. The attorney believes the bill is in the public's interest.

The attorney meets the president and the treasurer of the waste management company after work for cocktails at a private club to which the attorney and the officers of the company belong. Although the occasion is primarily social, the company's president tells the attorney that he is very interested in the work of the state bar association committee. The president tells the attorney that he and the other officers of his company strongly favor the bill pending in the legislature, as telephone voting would be much more efficient for the company and would save all the time and trouble of gathering the directors together for meetings. He urges the attorney to argue in favor of the bill in the committee meeting and to vote in favor of recommending that the bill pass. At the committee meeting, the attorney disclosed that one of his clients would benefit from the bill's passage, but then went ahead and voted for the bill.

Was it proper for the attorney to support the corporate voting bill in the state bar association committee?

(A) Yes, because he was acting to further the interests of a client.

(B) Yes, because he believed that the bill was in the public interest and he disclosed to the committee that one of his corporate clients would benefit if the bill passed.

(C) No, because he had a conflict of interest.

(D) No, because his vote potentially could be decisive in determining the state bar committee's recommendation.

GO ON TO THE NEXT PAGE

Question 30

A widow is greatly distraught because her late husband provided only a $1,000 bequest for her in his will. Under the terms of his will, the rest of his substantial estate (over $1 million) will go to a fraternal lodge of which the husband was a lifelong member. The widow consults an attorney who studies the will and determines that there has been an important flaw in its execution. The attorney success-fully challenges the will's validity, and the probate court rules that the husband's estate will descend by the laws of intestate succes-sion, which means, in this jurisdiction, that the widow will take all of the husband's estate. The attorney charges the widow a reasonable fee, which the widow pays promptly. The widow, however, is so pleased with the attorney's work that she wants to give the attorney a gift as a token of her gratitude. The widow goes to an antique shop and purchases a $500 vase. She smilingly presents the vase to the attorney.

Will the attorney be subject to discipline if she accepts the vase?

(A)   No, because there is nothing wrong with a lawyer accepting a gift from a client.

(B)   Yes, because the widow did not first discuss the gift with independent counsel.

(C)   Yes, because the attorney has been adequately compensated for her work on the widow's case and acceptance of the gift constitutes an excessive fee.

(D)   Yes, because the attorney would be overreaching if she accepted the gift.

Question 31

A journalist regularly wrote a column that appeared twice each week in a newspaper of general circulation in the town in which he lives. The journalist approached an attorney with offices in that town and told the attorney that her name would appear frequently in the column in a favorable light if the attorney would supply the journalist with "behind the scenes" items about local judges, lawyers, and important or otherwise interesting cases. The attorney readily agreed to the journalist's proposal, and she began supplying informa-tion to the journalist. The attorney's name did appear often in the journalist's column, and always in a very favorable light.

Is the attorney subject to discipline?

(A)   Yes, because she has given consideration for favorable publicity.

(B)   Yes, because it is unethical to spy on fellow lawyers and judges.

(C)   No, because she received nothing of pecuniary value from the journalist.

(D)   No, because her activities are protected by the First Amendment to the United States Constitution.

GO ON TO THE NEXT PAGE

Question 32

A man walked into the law offices of an attorney who, because she was not busy at the time, agreed to talk to the man right away. The man told the attorney that he was concerned that he might be indicted soon. He explained the details of his predicament at length to the attorney, but after he finished, the attorney explained that she only handled civil matters and urged the man to consult with a friend who was a criminal lawyer. The man went on to retain the friend. A few days after her interview with the man, the attorney read a news item announcing the man's indictment. It quoted the district attorney at some length. After reading the article, the attorney became convinced that something the man had told her during their interview would probably exonerate him or, at the very least, lead to a reduction in the charges against him if the district attorney became aware of the information in her possession.

May the attorney reveal the information to the district attorney?

(A) Yes, because the man did not retain the attorney as his counsel.

(B) Yes, because the information will help the man.

(C) No, because the attorney learned the information during the course of an attorney-client relationship.

(D) No, unless the man consents to the disclosure.

GO ON TO THE NEXT PAGE

Question 33

Several months ago, the president of a large company noticed that there were some discrepancies in the company's books, and that some funds seemed to be missing. He began checking the work of the company's accountant, after hours and unbeknownst to the accountant, and became convinced that the accountant has been embezzling funds from the company. The president, on behalf of the company, retains the services of an attorney to determine if the company has a case against the accountant. The attorney agrees with the company president that there is a strong indication that the accountant has been embezzling funds. In fact, the attorney has already determined that tomorrow he will file a civil suit against the accountant to recover the company's money and go to the prosecutor's office to sign an embezzlement complaint against the accountant. The attorney, however, tells the company president that the more evidence they can obtain against the accountant, the stronger their case will be. The company president suggests that the attorney interview the accountant before he presses charges, as the accountant may make some remarks that would implicate him in the embezzlement. The attorney readily agrees to this. The company president tells the accountant that the attorney is investigating some problems in account recordkeeping to make sure that the company's procedures comply with all applicable laws and regulations. He asks the accountant to explain how his operation works. The attorney and the accountant go to a private office, where the attorney interrogates the accountant for approximately two hours. During the course of the interrogation, the accountant becomes suspicious of the line of questioning and asks if he is in any trouble. The attorney tells him not to worry, as the amount of money involved is so small that the action may not be worth pursuing.

Is the attorney subject to discipline for questioning the accountant?

(A) Yes, because of his statements urging the accountant not to worry.

(B) Yes, because all communications with parties who are not represented by counsel are prohibited.

(C) No, because the attorney was trying in good faith to further the interests of his client.

(D) No, because the attorney has not yet filed suit on behalf of his client.

GO ON TO THE NEXT PAGE

Question 34

A buyer of materials employed by a midsize company that did some business with the state and local government was questioned by an attorney hired by the company president to look into suspected wrongdoing within the purchasing department. Initially, the buyer was told by the company president that the attorney was studying the buying process to make sure that the company's procedures comply with all applicable laws and regulations. During the questioning, the buyer broke down and admitted to taking bribes to fix bids. He also described company-wide practices that could subject the company to civil and criminal liability. In an effort to avoid publicity and liability, the company fired the buyer but agreed not to turn the matter over to the police. Additionally, the company hired a new buyer whose reputation for integrity was beyond reproach to take over the buying of materials for the company. Some time later, the company was sued by a customer for wrongdoing that arose out of one of the company-wide practices reported by the former buyer to the attorney. During the trial, the plaintiff calls the company's attorney to the stand to testify about his conversation with the former buyer. The attorney objects, claiming attorney-client privilege.

The objection should be:

(A)   Sustained, because the buyer talked to the company's attorney at the company president's request and his statements concern the buying of materials only.

(B)   Sustained, because the company can claim the privilege on behalf of the buyer, its employee.

(C)   Overruled, because the buyer was not seeking legal services from the company's attorney.

(D)   Overruled, because the buyer is no longer an employee of the company.

Question 35

An attorney represents a defendant who is being prosecuted in a jury trial for an armed robbery and attempted murder that occurred on June 15. The accused has pleaded not guilty to the charges, but the attorney knows that the accused is the perpetrator and that the crime occurred at approximately 10 p.m. The victim testifies that she is certain that the crime occurred at midnight. The accused has an airtight alibi for midnight. At 11:40 p.m. he was arrested on a drunk driving charge, and he was in police custody until 6 a.m. on June 16. On cross-examination, the attorney does nothing to challenge the victim's recollection of the time of the attack. Also, as the trial unfolds, the attorney does not introduce any evidence at her disposal that would help establish the time of the attack as 10 p.m. The attorney calls as a witness a police officer who testifies that the accused was in fact in custody at midnight on the night in question. The accused does not testify and is acquitted.

Are the attorney's actions proper?

(A)   Yes, because her client is a criminal defendant and constitutional protections take precedence over ethical rules.

(B)   Yes, because she did not present false evidence.

(C)   No, because she knew that the victim's testimony was wrong and would mislead the jury as to a crucial component of the case.

(D)   No, unless she notified the judge of the true facts outside the presence of the jury, and he instructed her to proceed.

GO ON TO THE NEXT PAGE

Question 36

The trustee of a trust for the care and support of the trustee's deceased sister's minor children wishes to sell some of the trust property to pay for the schooling of one of the children who has special needs. The trustee hires an attorney to file the appropriate papers to obtain court approval for the sale. In the course of the conversations between the attorney and the trustee, the trustee discloses that he has committed several breaches of trust in the past, including borrowing trust funds to pay for his home improvements and gambling trust funds at the race track. Most of the money has been repaid with reasonable interest, and the trustee tells the attorney that he has learned a few things about being a trustee, and will be much more careful about his handling of trust funds in the future. The attorney urges the trustee to tell the court of his wrongdoing and resign as trustee, but the trustee refuses. The attorney proceeds to represent the trustee in the proceeding seeking court approval for the sale of trust assets. The attorney fills out all of the court papers truthfully and does not in any way state anything false or misleading to the court. The court does not inquire about the management of the trust or any dissipation of trust assets, and neither the attorney nor the trustee volunteers the information.

Is the attorney subject to discipline?

(A) Yes, because he could have prevented future fraud by the trustee.

(B) Yes, because he owes a duty of candor to the tribunal.

(C) No, because the information was confidential.

(D) No, because it is the court's duty to supervise a trustee.

GO ON TO THE NEXT PAGE

Question 37

A lawyer represented a corporation in some business negotiations with a construction company. Only four persons were present during the negotiations: (1) the corporation's president; (2) the corporation's business lawyer; (3) the construction company's chief executive officer ("CEO"); and (4) the construction company's attorney. During the negotiations, the corporation's president and its business lawyer clearly heard the construction company's CEO make a certain representation that was vital to the success of the negotiation. Based on this representation, the parties reached an oral, handshake agreement to pursue a certain business opportunity as a joint venture. Six months later, after the corporation had invested $11 million in the joint venture, the corporation discovered that the representation made by the construction company's CEO was false and that he undoubtedly knew it was false when he made it. Due to the false representation, the joint venture failed, and the corporation lost its $11 million. The corporation sued the construction company and its CEO in federal court for intentional misrepresentation. The corporation selected one of its lawyer's law partners as its trial counsel. The defendants denied making the representation. The corporation's final pretrial statement listed the corporation's president and the lawyer as witnesses for the corporation, stating that they would testify that they heard the construction company's CEO make the representation. Counsel for the defendants then moved to disqualify the lawyer's law partner as trial counsel due to the lawyer's acting as a witness for the corporation.

Is the law partner subject to disqualification?

(A) Yes, because the lawyer is a necessary witness for the corporation; he is the only nonadversary witness who can corroborate the corporation president's testimony about the representation that the construction company's CEO made at the meeting.

(B) Yes, because the lawyer's testimony does not relate to a minor, uncontested matter or to the nature and value of the legal services rendered in the case; nor is this a situation in which disqualification of the law partner would work a substantial hardship on the corporation.

(C) No, because there is no conflict of interest presented by the lawyer's role as a witness for the corporation, and because a lawyer is ordinarily allowed to serve as trial counsel in a case where his law partner will testify on behalf of his client.

(D) No, because the lawyer's testimony will be merely corroborative; he will simply confirm the corporation president's testimony that the construction company's CEO made the representation at the meeting.

GO ON TO THE NEXT PAGE

Question 38

An attorney happened upon an accident scene and stopped his car to see if there was anything he could do to help. Several police officers were on the scene, and the attorney told one of them that he was a lawyer and asked if he could do anything to assist the accident victims. The police officer told the attorney that one of the victims was a physician who was convinced that he was going to die from his injuries and wanted a will. The attorney went over to talk to the physician, who lay on a stretcher. The physician begged the attorney to write a will for him on the spot. The attorney at first demurred, explaining to the physician that he had only been sworn into the state bar two weeks before, he had never written a will for a client, and he had received a "D" in his only law school class covering the subject. After listening to five minutes more of the physician's pleading, the attorney agreed to write the will for the physician. He wrote the will on the blank backside of an accident report. The physician signed the will and two police officers witnessed it. The physician died two hours later.

Was the attorney's conduct proper?

(A) Yes, because he acted in a humane manner appropriate to an emergency situation.

(B) Yes, because he was a licensed attorney when he wrote the will.

(C) No, because he lacked sufficient knowledge of the law of wills.

(D) No, because the physician should have agreed to limit the attorney's malpractice liability due to the emergency situation.

Question 39

Two attorneys represent two corporations who oppose each other in a civil suit. One of the attorneys has filed a petition with the court, seeking to have the other attorney removed as opposing counsel. She claims he has a conflict of interest because he once did certain work for her present client. He calls her and tells her that he thinks the conflict of interest matter can be resolved if she listens to his explanation. The attorneys meet and begin to negotiate the conflict of interest issue, and during the same meeting discuss a settlement of the lawsuit. They agree to meet again and continue their discussions. Immediately after the first meeting, the attorney who raised the issue of conflict of interest goes to her office and dictates a letter to the judge who is trying the case, telling the judge that she and the opposing counsel are attempting to resolve their differences on the conflict of interest matter and are also negotiating a settlement of the underlying lawsuit. She mails the letter to the judge that afternoon.

Is the attorney subject to discipline?

(A) No, because it is courteous to inform the judge that a settlement is being negotiated.

(B) No, if there were no false or prejudicial statements in the letter.

(C) Yes, because she did not send opposing counsel a copy of the letter.

(D) Yes, because she failed to inform the opposing counsel before she sent the letter.

GO ON TO THE NEXT PAGE

Question 40

An attorney defended a corporation in a state civil case brought by three named plaintiffs suing on behalf of a class of similarly situated people. The plaintiffs allege that the corporation owns nearly 100 apartment houses throughout the state and that it refuses to rent apartments to persons of color, in violation of the state's discrimination law. The civil discovery rules of the state do not require voluntary document production—i.e., a litigant does not have to produce a document until the adversary asks for it in a timely, specific document request. Immediately after the complaint was filed, and before any discovery had started, the attorney made a quick but careful investigation of the types of records that the corporation keeps concerning tenants and prospective tenants. She found that, starting more than 20 years ago, the manager of each of the corporation's apartment houses filled out a paper "application form" for each person who wanted to rent an apartment. The application form called for information about the person's age, sex, marital status, race, religion, current and past employment, and approximate yearly income.

About eight years ago, the corporation started entering information from the application forms into a computer system, but the computer version omits information about the person's race and religion. The computer system makes it unnecessary to keep and store the paper application forms. Nonetheless, through inertia and corporate ineptitude, the corporation has carefully preserved all of the paper application forms for the past eight years. The attorney advised her client to get rid of the old paper application forms. The corporation did as its attorney suggested.

Is the attorney subject to criminal liability for suggesting the destruction of the paper application forms?

(A) Yes, because the attorney knew that the paper application forms were relevant and would probably be requested by the plaintiffs.

(B) Yes, because a litigant's destruction of any documents whatsoever while a civil case is pending can be punished as a fraud on the court.

(C) No, because the class action is a civil case, and there is no criminal liability for discovery misconduct in a civil case.

(D) No, because the plaintiffs had not yet requested the production of documents.

GO ON TO THE NEXT PAGE

Question 41

A partner in a law firm has just been elected a judge of the circuit court. She has been assigned to the probate division. During her last week with the law firm, she filed a number of very routine, uncontested probate motions. At the time, she had no idea that she would be assigned to the probate division. These routine probate motions have been assigned to her courtroom by a lottery system of random assignment that the circuit court regularly employs to assign cases.

Is it proper for the judge to rule on these motions?

(A) Yes, because they are routine and uncontested.

(B) Yes, because reassignment would cause delay.

(C) No, because she has a conflict of interest.

(D) No, because judges may never rule on issues when their former law firm is involved.

Question 42

The owner of a parcel of real estate on the east side of town wants to trade his land for a parcel of land owned by a woman on the west side of town. The owner of the west side property retains an attorney and tells him that she wishes to complete the deal as cheaply as possible. She asks the attorney to draw up papers for the transfer of property and asks him to order a title search and survey of the other party's property. The attorney recommended to her that a similar search and survey be conducted for her own property as well, but she replied that she wished to save money and did not need a search and survey for her property. The two parties exchange warranty deeds, and each takes possession of the other's property as agreed.

A year later, the now-owner of the west side property—the property that did not have a title search and survey after the then-owner rejected the idea—contracts to sell the property. The prospective purchaser orders a title search and survey and discovers that there are defects that will substantially reduce the value of the property. The owner of this property eventually sells it at a price much lower than he could have commanded had the defects not been present. He sues the former owner for damages and receives an award of $10,000. The former owner, on the other hand, feels that her attorney is responsible for this, and she sues him to recover the $10,000.

Is the attorney subject to liability for malpractice?

(A) Yes, because a competent attorney would have insisted upon a title search and survey for the property.

(B) Yes, because his client was a foreseeable plaintiff in a malpractice case.

(C) No, because he was following his client's instructions.

(D) No, because the buyer did not insist on the seller's presenting a title search and survey.

GO ON TO THE NEXT PAGE

Question 43

An attorney represents a plaintiff in a sexual harassment case against her employer. The employer is represented by its regular corporate counsel. The plaintiff, who works on an assembly line, alleges that she was repeatedly harassed by the foreman on her work shift. Furthermore, she alleges that the plant manager was aware of this misconduct and did nothing to stop it. The plaintiff tells her attorney that two of her co-workers on the assembly line witnessed harassment incidents, but neither reported the incidents to supervisory personnel. One of the witnesses quit working for the employer at about the time the plaintiff filed her lawsuit.

The attorney wants to do some fact investigation before he starts discovery in the case, and wishes to interview the plant manager, the foreman, and the two co-worker witnesses.

Which of the following best states proper conduct for the attorney in interviewing these individuals?

(A) He may freely interview the plant manager and both witnesses because they are simply third-party witnesses, but he must obtain defense counsel's consent to interview the foreman.

(B) He may freely interview both witnesses, but he must obtain defense counsel's consent to interview the foreman and the plant manager.

(C) He may freely interview the witness who no longer works for the defendant, but he must obtain defense counsel's consent to interview the foreman, the plant manager, and the witness who still works for the defendant.

(D) It would be improper for him to interview any of these people without defense counsel's consent.

Question 44

An attorney who is engaged in private practice in the city in which he lives has many friends who belong to a fraternal and charitable society with chapters throughout the state. The attorney is not a member of the society, but knows a number of its officers socially and has performed legal work for them on matters unrelated to the society. The officers of the society are sometimes consulted by members who have legal problems. The officers, being very pleased with the quality of the attorney's work, often refer such members to him. The attorney has never asked the officers for such referrals, but is, of course, very pleased because he has earned substantial fees from these referrals.

The society is presently organized as an unincorporated association, but the leaders are interested in incorporating the society under the state's Nonprofit Corporation Act. One of the officers asks the attorney what his fee would be for incorporating the society. The attorney tells the officer that he is very grateful for the client referrals from the society and, as a token of his appreciation, he will not charge a fee for the incorporation work.

Is the attorney subject to discipline?

(A) Yes, because a lawyer must not give something of value in return for client referrals.

(B) Yes, because only clients unable to pay should be given free legal services.

(C) No, because a lawyer always has the option of waiving a fee.

(D) No, because the attorney did not solicit the referrals.

GO ON TO THE NEXT PAGE

Question 45

An attorney placed an advertisement that ran daily in the classified section of a newspaper of general circulation that is widely read in the area where the attorney practiced. Besides stating the attorney's office address and telephone number, and identifying the attorney as a licensed attorney, the advertisement included the following statement:

DIVORCES - LOW RATES!!!
Just $300, plus costs, for uncontested divorces

According to bar association surveys, the "low average" fee in the area for an uncontested divorce is $325, plus costs.

Is the attorney's advertising proper?

(A) Yes, because the legal profession imposes no substantive limitations on comparative advertising.

(B) Yes, because the attorney's rates really are low.

(C) No, because the attorney fails to state his range of fees for contested divorces.

(D) No, because the advertisement is in bad taste and constitutes a self-serving attempt to solicit business at the expense of fellow lawyers.

Question 46

An attorney who was popular in the legal community decided to run against an incumbent judge in the forthcoming election. The judge was widely regarded by members of the local bar as a "party hack," who had no business being on the bench. The opposition party was very pleased to be able to slate the attorney because she had a high reputation for intelligence, honesty, and overall competence as a lawyer. The attorney realizes that she will have to fight an uphill battle to unseat the judge because her political party is a minority party in the county and most voters know very little about judges and candidates for the judiciary and therefore, voters are likely to vote a straight ticket for judges of their own political party. The attorney wants the public to know that the judge has been a poor judge, but she also wishes to comply with all ethical rules governing judicial campaigns. The attorney's best friend and chief advisor, also a lawyer, suggests that the attorney should make some prepared statements during her campaign.

Assuming that all the facts cited in the statements are accurate, which statement would not be proper for the attorney to make during her judicial campaign?

(A) That her opponent has had the highest percentage of cases reversed on appeal of any judge in the state over the past two years.

(B) That 18 months ago, her opponent was publicly disciplined by the state's judicial conduct board.

(C) That a recent poll taken by the local bar association indicated that a majority of bar association members feel that her opponent lacks the proper judicial temperament.

(D) That a recent newspaper article comparing judges of the county stated that her opponent had handed out an average sentence of only two years to persons convicted of serious felonies, and that she would not be soft on crime.

GO ON TO THE NEXT PAGE

Question 47

A judge is known to grant continuances whenever requested by a lawyer, regardless of the substantiality of the lawyer's grounds. He has turned down a continuance request on occasion, but such occasions are so few and far between that local lawyers are shocked when they hear of them. When queried by a judicial colleague about his policy on continuances, the judge told her that granting continuances gives the parties that much more time to come to their senses and settle, which saves both the parties and the taxpayers the expense of a full-blown trial.

Is the judge's policy of granting continuances to promote settlements proper?

(A) Yes, because the granting of continuances is clearly within the bounds of judicial discretion.

(B) Yes, because the judge sincerely believes that his lenient continuance policy promotes settlements and that settlements promote a more rational and amicable system of justice.

(C) No, because judges have no duty to promote settlements.

(D) No, because judges have a duty to expedite litigation.

Question 48

A state legislature conducted open hearings concerning a bill pending before it that would make it much more difficult for corporations chartered in the state to be taken over by corporate raiders. By making unfriendly takeovers more difficult, the proponents of the bill hope to save jobs in the state and to encourage corporations not now chartered in the state to obtain state charters, which would bring added revenue to the state. An attorney who is a senior partner in a prestigious law firm asked to testify at the hearings. The attorney had been retained by a large corporation and was asked by its president to testify against the pending legislation at the legislative hearings. The corporation's president also told the attorney that under no circumstances was he to tell the legislature who hired him or mention the name of the corporation in his testimony. The attorney complied with the corporation's strictures and never mentioned that he was being retained to give testimony against the pending legislation. The attorney's testimony before the legislative committee was effective and hard-hitting. After his testimony, the attorney was asked a few questions by committee members, but he was never asked if he was appearing on some other party's behalf.

Was the attorney's conduct at the hearing proper?

(A) Yes, because his client specifically instructed him not to reveal the client's name.

(B) Yes, because no one asked him if he was appearing at the hearings on behalf of a client.

(C) No, because he did not disclose that he was appearing at the hearings in a representative capacity.

(D) No, because a lawyer may not practice deception upon a legislative body.

GO ON TO THE NEXT PAGE

Question 49

A wealthy landowner who is elderly and very infirm, although mentally very sharp, contacts his niece, a registered nurse who lives in another state. He urges his niece to live with him at his ranch and take care of him. He says that he understands she would be making a major sacrifice but if she will stay and care for him until his death, he will leave her one-third of his ranch in his will. The niece agrees to care for her uncle.

The niece arrives and is met at the train station by the landowner and his employee. On the way home, they stop at the office of his attorney to pick up some tax documents. The landowner tells his attorney, in the presence of both his niece and his employee, about his intention to have a new will drafted that would leave one-third of his ranch to his niece. However, the landowner falls into a coma before following through with his plan. The doctors have indicated that the landowner is near death and will never regain consciousness. Under the terms of his old will, everything he has is left to his son, who is his only child and a highly successful businessman in another state.

The son arrives to say goodbye to his father and to help get the affairs of his father in order. When he consults with his father's attorney, he mentions to the attorney that he thinks that it was very good of the niece to travel so far to care for his father, and that he is sure that his father would have wanted to reward her in some way, even though there is no mention of her in the will. The son says that he would like to do the "right thing," but has no idea what his father might have had in mind.

Which of the following states the *most* that the attorney may do in attempting to carry out his client's wishes?

(A) Remain silent.

(B) Suggest that the son might want to talk to his father's employee about his father's intentions.

(C) Tell the son about his father's statement about leaving one-third of the ranch to the niece, but offer no further advice.

(D) Tell the son about his father's statement and counsel the son to deed one-third of the ranch to the niece.

Question 50

An attorney who has been practicing law for two years is preparing a radio advertisement. He plans to state that: (1) he comes from a long line of lawyers, and that his father and grandfather are both judges; (2) he specializes in personal injury and divorce cases; (3) he has never lost a jury trial and 99% of his clients end up receiving some form of payment; and (4) he "succeeds where others fail."

Which of those statements is proper?

(A) That he comes from a long line of lawyers, and that his father and grandfather are both judges.

(B) That he specializes in personal injury and divorce cases.

(C) That he has never lost a jury trial, and 99% of his clients end up receiving some form of payment.

(D) That he "succeeds where others fail."

GO ON TO THE NEXT PAGE

Question 51

One state is right across the river from another state, and there is a constant flow of people and commerce between them. Many people work in one state and live in the other, and many people cross the river to shop, go to school, seek entertainment, attend religious services, and the like. An attorney who lives in the western state maintains his law office in the eastern state. He limits his practice to drunk driving defense. In 1967, the attorney became a member of the bar in both states, but a few years ago, he stopped paying his bar dues in the western state and stopped fulfilling that state's continuing legal education ("CLE") requirements. The western state placed him on its inactive list, which means that he cannot practice law there until he pays the balance in his dues account and completes the CLE requirements. Nevertheless, the attorney advertises his law office in the western state's Yellow Pages phone book and in various other media in the western state. He regularly represents drunk driving clients who live in the western state and who are charged with drunk driving in that state's courts. When a client who lives in the western state finds it inconvenient to travel to the attorney's law office in the eastern state, the attorney meets the client at the attorney's home in the western state. Recently, the attorney appeared on behalf of a drunk driving client before a young, newly appointed judge in the western state who asked him if he was admitted to practice in that state. The attorney responded cheerfully: "Your Honor, I was admitted to practice here back in 1967, long before Your Honor was born." The judge allowed him to proceed.

Is the attorney subject to discipline by the bar of the western state?

(A) No, because the attorney does not maintain a law office in the western state, and because his response to the young judge was the literal truth.

(B) No, because the western state has no jurisdiction to discipline a lawyer who is not actively engaged in law practice in the state.

(C) Yes, because he misled the judge by his half-true response to the judge's question.

(D) Yes, both because of his unauthorized law practice in the western state, and because he misled the judge by his half-true response to the judge's question.

GO ON TO THE NEXT PAGE

Question 52

A state has a so-called three strikes law that is designed to give life sentences to career felons. When a person is convicted of her third felony, the three strikes law forces the sentencing judge to give the person a life sentence, even if the third felony does not involve violence, and even if the maximum punishment for the third felony by itself would be as little as two years in state prison. Many judges in the state believe that the three strikes law is unconscionably harsh and should be repealed. The state's legislature, however, has refused to act. A citizen group was successful in qualifying a voter initiative to abolish the three strikes law. Many judges have spoken out publicly in favor of the voter initiative. An attorney who has both an accounting degree and a law degree earns most of her living by serving as a court-appointed master in complex cases where her dual skills are useful. The bulk of her service is in a court that is dominated by judges who favor the voter initiative. For the sole purpose of getting more court appointments from those judges, the attorney has contributed 200 hours of her time to the campaign in favor of the voter initiative.

Which of the following statements is true?

(A) The judges did not act properly in speaking out in public in favor of the voter initiative.

(B) The judges are subject to discipline for speaking out in public in favor of the voter initiative.

(C) The attorney acted properly in contributing her time to the campaign in favor of the voter initiative.

(D) The attorney is subject to discipline for contributing her time to the campaign for the purpose of getting more court appointments.

GO ON TO THE NEXT PAGE

Question 53

A law partner and her associate practice at a law firm located in a rural community in mid-America. Only three other law firms practice in that community. The partner volunteers her time every Saturday morning to sit in a room at the local public library where she provides quick answers to simple legal questions posed by community members who cannot afford to consult a lawyer in the ordinary manner. The program is sponsored by the County Bar Association, a nonprofit organization. The partner makes clear to each person that she will answer the person's question as best she can, without doing legal research, and that she will not represent the person in any long-term sense. One Saturday morning, the partner advised a farmer about how to represent himself, in propria persona, as plaintiff in a lawsuit against a local roofing company that put a defective roof on his barn. A few weeks later, the farmer filed the suit, and the roofing company hired the associate to defend it against the farmer's suit. That was the first time the roofing company consulted either the associate or the law firm where the associate and the partner work. When the associate agreed to defend the roofing company, he did not realize that the partner had previously advised the farmer on how to bring the suit; indeed, the partner purposely never tells her associate anything about her Saturday morning volunteer work.

Which of the following is correct?

(A) The associate may defend the roofing company, even though the partner had previously advised the farmer on the matter.

(B) The associate may defend the roofing company, but only if both the farmer and the roofing company give informed consent, confirmed in writing.

(C) The associate may defend the roofing company, but only if the partner is

screened off from the case and is apportioned no part of the fee in the case, and only if the farmer gives informed consent, confirmed in writing.

(D) The associate may defend the roofing company, but only if the partner promises in writing not to tell the associate anything that the farmer told her in confidence about the matter.

Question 54

A recent law school graduate who passed the bar set up his own solo practice law office. He hopes to develop a prosperous clientele of business clients, but meanwhile, he drives a taxi four nights a week. Sometimes when a taxi passenger appears to be a prosperous businessperson, the novice attorney mentions that he is looking for clients in his new business law practice; at that point, he usually hands the passenger one of his professional cards and says: "Please call me if you ever need a lawyer." When a taxi passenger is drunk, inexperienced, or not paying attention, the novice attorney sometimes does not start the taxi meter running. At the end of the ride, he charges the passenger as much as he thinks the passenger will pay without starting a fight. Because the ride is not recorded on the taxi meter, the novice attorney pockets the entire fare without having to divide it with the taxi company.

Is the novice attorney subject to discipline by the bar?

(A) Yes, because he must follow all of the legal ethics rules when he drives the taxi.

(B) Yes, because he sometimes cheats by failing to start the taxi meter.

(C) No, because he does not give his business card to persons known to need legal services in a particular matter.

(D) No, because he is not providing legal services to his taxi passengers.

Question 55

An attorney was in solo practice on the west coast. His wife got a new job on the east coast so he started looking for someone to buy his west coast practice. The attorney's labor and employment law practice consisted entirely of representing plaintiffs in ongoing litigation and administrative proceedings to redress employment discrimination, dangerous or hostile conditions in the workplace, sexual harassment, race discrimination in the workplace, and the like. All of the attorney's clients had signed contingent fee agreements in which they promised to pay the litigation or administrative expenses, and the attorney promised to represent them in return for 20% of their net pretax winnings. This arrangement is more favorable to the clients than any other arrangement they could get from other lawyers in the community for similar work. The attorney quickly found seven different interested buyers for his practice. Because he wanted to sell promptly, the attorney did not investigate the training, experience, or disciplinary records of the seven. Rather, he sold the practice to the one who offered the highest price. If he had investigated, he would have discovered that the purchaser had almost no experience in labor and employment law, and that the state bar had disciplined her twice for client neglect and client abandonment. The attorney gave the requisite notice of sale to his clients, and the purchaser took over the office, the case files, the books, the computers, the books of account, and the debts, duties, and assets of the attorney's practice. In due course, she worked her way through the case files, separating them into two piles—the likely winners and the likely losers. She then wrote letters to the likely losers, offering them a new contingent fee agreement that would give her 35% of their net pretax winnings. She explained that if they did not wish to sign the new agreement, she would seek permission from the tribunal to withdraw as their counsel.

Which of the following is correct?

(A) The attorney is subject to discipline for selling his practice to the highest bidder.

(B) The purchaser is subject to discipline for threatening to withdraw from representing clients who would not sign the new 35% contingent fee agreement.

(C) The purchaser's identification of likely winners and likely losers was proper, as was her offer of a new 35% contingent fee agreement to the likely losers.

(D) The attorney's decision not to investigate the backgrounds of the seven prospective buyers was proper, as was his decision to sell his law practice.

GO ON TO THE NEXT PAGE

Question 56

In the federal courts and the courts of some states, when a litigant claims that a document is protected by the attorney-client privilege, the trial judge can order the litigant to produce the document for in camera inspection (i.e., private, confidential inspection by the judge) so that the judge can decide whether the document really is privileged. The courts in one state follow the opposite rule: a trial judge must not force a litigant to produce a privileged document for in camera inspection; the trial judge must use the surrounding circumstances and whatever other evidence is available when deciding whether the privilege claim is valid. In a federal case where jurisdiction is based only on diversity of citizenship, the federal judge must apply the privilege law that would be applied by a state court in the state where the federal court sits. A federal district judge was presiding in a diversity case in the state. The defendant's attorney refused to produce a particular letter from defendant's outside patent counsel to defendant's president. The defendant's attorney asserted the attorney-client privilege on behalf of her client. The judge glowered down at the defendant's attorney and ordered her to produce the letter for in camera inspection so that he could see whether the letter was about a legal matter or some nonprivileged subject. The defendant's attorney would not allow the judge to see the letter, referring him to the clear law of the state in which the court sat. The judge growled and ordered her to hand him the letter.

Which of the following is the proper response for the defendant's attorney to make?

(A) To tell the judge not to push her around.

(B) To respectfully ask the court to stay the order to allow time to consult with the client and to seek an interlocutory appeal or extraordinary writ if necessary.

(C) To give the judge the letter but say she is doing so under protest and without waiving the attorney-client privilege.

(D) To tell the judge that he is out of line.

GO ON TO THE NEXT PAGE

Question 57

A multibillion-dollar company that makes and sells a range of vaccines, serums, and pharmaceuticals in the United States, Canada, Mexico, and several nations of the European Union ("EU") issues stock that is publicly traded in interstate commerce, placing the company within the jurisdiction of the Securities and Exchange Commission ("SEC"). The chief in-house legal officer of the company hired an outside attorney to supervise the preparation of the company's Form 10-K annual report to the SEC. When the outside attorney was eating lunch by himself in the company cafeteria one day, a low-echelon company employee passed him a note stating that she had heard from someone in a position to know that the company had sold 144 units of snake antitoxin in Germany without obtaining a proper EU sales clearance. Selling without a proper sales clearance violates EU law, for which the EU could theoretically fine the company 1% of the sales price, which in this case would be $26. Assume that a contingent liability of $26 is too low to require disclosure in the Form 10-K. When he asked around the company about the employee who had passed him the note, the outside attorney learned that she is a malicious gossip who passes along all kinds of stories, some true, some false.

Which of the following reasons would excuse the outside attorney from reporting the employee's information to the company's chief legal officer pursuant to the SEC's Sarbanes-Oxley regulations?

(A) The outside attorney was hired merely to supervise the preparation of the Form 10-K, not to appear before the SEC on behalf of the company.

(B) A reasonable lawyer would regard the employee's story as not credible.

(C) What the employee told the outside attorney is privileged, and he therefore must not reveal it to the company's chief legal officer.

(D) The outside attorney does not have actual knowledge of a material violation of the securities laws.

Question 58

An attorney has a regular client who is elderly and in failing health. The client has retained the attorney to draft his will. The attorney asked the client for a list of his assets to help her prepare the will. In a subsequent meeting, the attorney indicated her admiration for the client's classic car, which the client has maintained in mint condition. The client was pleased at the attorney's interest in the car, and directed the attorney to bequeath the car to herself in the will.

May the attorney include this bequest in the client's will?

(A) No, because this is a substantial gift, given in a context in which she potentially wielded undue influence.

(B) No, because a lawyer may never draft a will in which the lawyer is a beneficiary.

(C) Yes, because the attorney did not induce the client to make the gift.

(D) Yes, because the client may leave his property to whomever he chooses unless he is mentally incompetent.

GO ON TO THE NEXT PAGE

Question 59

Two attorneys represent opposing parties in a hard-fought civil case. Each attorney knows that the opposing attorney is diligent, forthright, and careful. One morning, the plaintiff's attorney received an e-mail from defense counsel's secretary, saying that defense counsel was ill and had asked the secretary to send along the four attachments appended to the e-mail message. The first three e-mail attachments were documents that defense counsel had agreed to produce in response to the plaintiff's attorney's discovery request. The fourth attachment was a letter to defense counsel from the in-house counsel of defense counsel's client. The plaintiff's attorney could tell from reading the first few lines that the letter was a confidential communication between attorney and client, and that defense counsel obviously did not intend for it to be sent to him.

Which of the following best states the proper course of action for the plaintiff's attorney to take?

(A) Continue reading the fourth attachment and preserve a hard copy for possible further use on behalf of his client.

(B) Delete the fourth attachment from his computer's memory and not tell anyone about the mistake.

(C) Stop reading the fourth attachment and notify the judge about the mistake.

(D) Stop reading the fourth attachment and notify defense counsel about the mistake.

GO ON TO THE NEXT PAGE

Question 60

A theater company owns the copyrights to a large repertoire of plays, and it licenses the copyrights throughout the United States. The company uses a large private law firm in the state in which its headquarters is located to do all of its legal work. The company licensed the movie rights from one of its copyrighted plays to a major motion picture studio located in another state. All of its law firm's lawyers are admitted to practice in the state in which the theater company has its headquarters, but not a single one of them is admitted to practice in the state in which the motion picture studio is located. The license agreement between the theater company and the motion picture studio was drafted by the latter's counsel, and it specifies that any dispute about the license will be resolved by arbitration in the state in which the motion picture studio is located. An attorney who is one of the copyright lawyers of the theater company's law firm represented the theater company in the license negotiations, which took place in the state in which the motion picture studio is located. When the studio finished making the movie, a dispute arose about how much royalty it owed the theater company under the license. Pursuant to the arbitration clause of the license, the parties arranged to arbitrate the dispute in the state in which the studio is located. The theater company asked one of its law firm's best litigators to represent it at the arbitration. The arbitration act in the state in which the arbitration is taking place says nothing about pro hac vice admission of out-of-state lawyers in arbitration proceedings.

Which of the following is correct?

(A) The copyright attorney who represented the theater company in the license negotiations is subject to discipline for negotiating the license in the state in which the negotiations took place, and the litigator who was hired by the theater company to represent the company at the arbitration will be subject to discipline if he represents the theater company in the arbitration in the state in which the arbitration is to take place.

(B) It was proper for the copyright attorney who represented the theater company in the license negotiations to negotiate the license in the state in which the negotiations took place, and the litigator who was hired by the theater company to represent the company at the arbitration may represent the theater company at the arbitration in the state in which the arbitration is to take place.

(C) The copyright attorney who represented the theater in the license negotiations is subject to discipline for negotiating the license in the state in which the negotiations took place, but the litigator who was hired by the theater company to represent it at the arbitration may represent the theater company at the arbitration in the state in which the arbitration is to take place.

(D) It was proper for the copyright attorney who represented the theater company in the license negotiations to negotiate the license in the state in which the negotiations took place, but the litigator who was hired by the theater company to represent the company at the arbitration will be subject to discipline if he represents the theater company in the arbitration in the state in which the arbitration is to take place.

ANSWER SHEET

1 (A) (B) (C) (D)		31 (A) (B) (C) (D)	
2 (A) (B) (C) (D)		32 (A) (B) (C) (D)	
3 (A) (B) (C) (D)		33 (A) (B) (C) (D)	
4 (A) (B) (C) (D)		34 (A) (B) (C) (D)	
5 (A) (B) (C) (D)		35 (A) (B) (C) (D)	
6 (A) (B) (C) (D)		36 (A) (B) (C) (D)	
7 (A) (B) (C) (D)		37 (A) (B) (C) (D)	
8 (A) (B) (C) (D)		38 (A) (B) (C) (D)	
9 (A) (B) (C) (D)		39 (A) (B) (C) (D)	
10 (A) (B) (C) (D)		40 (A) (B) (C) (D)	
11 (A) (B) (C) (D)		41 (A) (B) (C) (D)	
12 (A) (B) (C) (D)		42 (A) (B) (C) (D)	
13 (A) (B) (C) (D)		43 (A) (B) (C) (D)	
14 (A) (B) (C) (D)		44 (A) (B) (C) (D)	
15 (A) (B) (C) (D)		45 (A) (B) (C) (D)	
16 (A) (B) (C) (D)		46 (A) (B) (C) (D)	
17 (A) (B) (C) (D)		47 (A) (B) (C) (D)	
18 (A) (B) (C) (D)		48 (A) (B) (C) (D)	
19 (A) (B) (C) (D)		49 (A) (B) (C) (D)	
20 (A) (B) (C) (D)		50 (A) (B) (C) (D)	
21 (A) (B) (C) (D)		51 (A) (B) (C) (D)	
22 (A) (B) (C) (D)		52 (A) (B) (C) (D)	
23 (A) (B) (C) (D)		53 (A) (B) (C) (D)	
24 (A) (B) (C) (D)		54 (A) (B) (C) (D)	
25 (A) (B) (C) (D)		55 (A) (B) (C) (D)	
26 (A) (B) (C) (D)		56 (A) (B) (C) (D)	
27 (A) (B) (C) (D)		57 (A) (B) (C) (D)	
28 (A) (B) (C) (D)		58 (A) (B) (C) (D)	
29 (A) (B) (C) (D)		59 (A) (B) (C) (D)	
30 (A) (B) (C) (D)		60 (A) (B) (C) (D)	

Answer to Question 1

(C)   A lawyer at trial must not state her own personal opinion about the credibility of witnesses. [ABA Model Rule 3.4(e)] (C) reflects personal opinion on the credibility of a witness. (A), (B), and (D), on the other hand, contain comments that are acceptable. Thus, (C) is correct.

Answer to Question 2

(C)   ABA Model Rule 1.12(a) provides that a lawyer must not represent anyone in connection with a matter in which the lawyer participated personally and substantially as a judge, unless all parties to the proceedings give informed consent, confirmed in writing. Thus, (C) is correct, and (A) and (B) are incorrect. (D) is incorrect because a judge may subsequently engage in private practice, except she may not participate in cases where she was personally and substantially involved.

Answer to Question 3

(C)   Under ABA Model Rule 5.5(b), a lawyer must not aid a nonlawyer in the unauthorized practice of law. Although a lawyer may delegate certain tasks to laypersons, such delegation is professionally acceptable only if the lawyer: (1) supervises the delegated work, and (2) remains professionally responsible for the work product. [Comment 2 to ABA Model Rule 5.5] Reaching a settlement on behalf of a client clearly constitutes the practice of law, so the attorney is subject to discipline on the facts of (C). The drafting of forms by a law student is permissible if the lawyer complies with the conditions stated above, which the attorney here appears to have done from the facts. Thus, the facts in (A) do not subject the attorney to discipline. There is nothing impermissible about (B) and (D)—laypersons conducting interviews and obtaining the interviewees' signatures on written versions of the interviews or conducting legal research and drafting memoranda. Therefore, (C) is the only correct answer.

Answer to Question 4

(C)   If one lawyer within a firm has a conflict of interest and cannot take on a matter, no other lawyer in the firm may take on the matter either. [ABA Model Rule 1.10(a)] One situation that would create a concurrent conflict would be if there is a significant risk that the representation of a client will be materially limited by the lawyer's own interest or his responsibilities to another client, a former client, or a third person. [ABA Model Rule 1.7(a)(2)] The mayor would be prohibited from representing the development company in this matter because such representation would be materially limited by his responsibilities, as mayor, to the city. Thus, his law partner is also prohibited from such representation. Therefore, (A) and (B) are incorrect. (D) is also incorrect; it makes no difference whether the mayor has a direct role in the representation or shares any fees.

Answer to Question 5

(A)   In this case, the attorney has personally profited from her former client's confidential information; in essence, his information boosted the dollar value of the attorney's time. However, the attorney's use of the information did not harm her former client. Furthermore, the attorney used the information *in connection with her law practice.* Therefore, she does not have to account to her former client for the profits she earned from the information. [*See* Restatement §60(2)] A lawyer may use one client's confidential information for the benefit of another client, even if doing so might benefit the lawyer, if the original client would not be harmed. [ABA Model Rule 1.9(c)] (B) is incorrect because a lawyer's duty of confidentiality does not end when the lawyer-client relationship ends. (C) is incorrect because the attorney did not need her former client's consent to use his confidential information in her later practice of law. (D) is incorrect for the same reason—the attorney used her former client's confidential information in her later practice of law, not in some side venture.

Answer to Question 6

(C)   The defendant's attorney is not subject to discipline because he did not discuss the case with the plaintiff. It is permissible for a lawyer to talk to a represented party without his lawyer's consent if they do not discuss the subject of the representation. [ABA Model Rule 4.2 and comment 4] Because the attorney and the plaintiff discussed the charity, the weather, and sports, the attorney did not act improperly. Thus, (A) is wrong. (B) is wrong because this is not an ex parte communication. Ex parte means (roughly) "by one party only" and usually refers to contact with the trier of fact, and here both parties are present and neither is communicating with the trier of fact. The only limitation on opposing parties communicating with one another is the one stated above concerning a lawyer talking to a represented party. (D) is wrong because the attorney's knowledge of the seating assignment and his attempt to change it are not dispositive; the dispositive fact is

that the attorney and the plaintiff did not discuss the case.

Answer to Question 7

(B)   Under ABA Model Rule 1.15(d), a lawyer must promptly notify a client when a third party turns over money or property to the lawyer to hold on the client's behalf, and the lawyer must promptly pay or deliver to the client money or property that the client is entitled to receive. Because the attorney here failed to fulfill these obligations, he is subject to discipline. Thus, (B) is correct, and (D) is incorrect. (A) is incorrect because the attorney received the $2,000 settlement and thus was entitled to the agreed-upon fee. (C) is incorrect not because the attorney placed the funds in the trust account, but because he failed to notify his client of the settlement.

Answer to Question 8

(C)   The attorney is not subject to discipline because a lawyer may pay a witness's reasonable expenses, including travel expenses, hotel, and meals. [Comment 3 to ABA Model Rule 3.4; Restatement §117, comment b] (A) is wrong because the payment of expenses is not an improper inducement. It is simply the attorney's good fortune that the trial is in such a desirable tourist spot. (B) is wrong because it is not improper for lawyers to interview third-party witnesses without notifying the opposing side. (D) is wrong because there is no limitation on expenses other than reasonableness.

Answer to Question 9

(C)   ABA Model Rule 1.5(d)(1) subjects a lawyer to discipline if the fee in a domestic relations matter is contingent upon the securing of a divorce, the amount of alimony or support, or the amount of the property settlement. (A) is incorrect because the size of the fee is irrelevant because the ABA Model Rules forbid a contingency fee in this situation no matter what the amount of the fee. Although (B) states a rationale behind contingency fees, this rationale will not support a contingency fee in this case. (D) is incorrect because a lawyer may, but is not required to, pay or advance costs to an indigent client.

Answer to Question 10

(D)   ABA Model Rule 3.5 prohibits a lawyer from communicating with a discharged juror if the communication involves misrepresentation, coercion, duress, or harassment. [ABA Model Rule 3.5(c)(3)] Thus, the lawyer can hire a private investigator only if the investigation is not conducted in a harassing manner. (A) is incorrect because the investigator does not need to notify the juror of his investigation or obtain her consent. (B) is incorrect because if properly conducted, there is no reason to believe the investigation will affect future jury service. (C) is incorrect because new evidence will not justify the investigation if it is conducted in an improper manner.

Answer to Question 11

(D)   A lawyer must not represent a client whose interests are directly adverse to those of another client. [ABA Model Rule 1.7(a)] This conflict of interest is imputed to other lawyers in the lawyer's firm. [ABA Model Rule 1.10(a)] Because the attorney's law firm is now representing two clients whose interests are directly adverse, it would be proper for the attorney to withdraw from representa-

tion. Thus, (A) and (C) are wrong. Also, the attorney must maintain his client's confidence by not informing his law partner. [ABA Model Rule 1.6] Thus, (B) is wrong.

Answer to Question 12

(A)   Careful lawyers often preserve documents that will serve as evidence that they did not commit malpractice. For example, lawyers may keep copies of court papers and memoranda, or write their clients letters to record the fact that a particular decision was made by the client contrary to the lawyer's advice. It appears that the tape recording mentioned in (A) falls under the category of preserving evidence that the attorney did not commit malpractice, because it documents his handling of the case, as well as the client's understanding of the case. Thus, the attorney is not subject to discipline for the conduct in (A). On the other hand, lawyers are generally subject to discipline for attempting to exonerate themselves from or limit their liability to their clients for personal malpractice. ABA Model Rule 1.8(h)(1) prohibits a lawyer from making an agreement to limit such liability unless the client is independently represented in making the agreement. Clearly, these rules encompass the situations presented in (B) and (C). (D) is incorrect because under ABA Model Rule 1.16(b)(1), a lawyer may withdraw from representing a client only if the withdrawal can be accomplished without material adverse effect on the interests of the client or in certain other specific circumstances that do not apply here. On its own, a "feeling that the client might mean trouble" is not a permissible ground for withdrawal. This is especially true because the attorney wants to be able to withdraw "at any time," even during critical points in the litigation. Therefore, (A) is correct, and (B), (C), and (D) are incorrect.

Answer to Question 13

(D) The attorney's advertising complies with ABA Model Rules 7.1 and 7.2. As long as her ad is not false or misleading, she may properly advertise fee arrangements, fields of practice such as personal injury, and free consultations. Thus, (D) is correct, and (A), (B), and (C) are incorrect.

Answer to Question 14

(A) A lawyer must not state or imply that he is able to influence improperly or upon irrelevant grounds any tribunal. [ABA Model Rule 8.4(e)] (B), (C), and (D) are incorrect because regardless of the associate's lack of an express prediction or his plans to use improper influence on the judge, the statement itself subjects him to discipline.

Answer to Question 15

(B) The plaintiff filed its complaint in April. The defendant had 20 days after the filing date to study the complaint and respond to it by answer or otherwise. Starting with day 20, the defendant had a duty not to destroy evidence that it either knew or should have known would be relevant to the case. [See Computer Associates International, Inc. v. American Fundware, Inc., 133 F.R.D. 166 (D. Colo. 1990); Wm. T. Thompson Co. v. General Nutrition Corp., 593 F. Supp. 1443 (C.D. Cal. 1984)] The defendant was alert enough to ask its attorney whether it would be all right to follow the usual custom of destroying the former source codes when creating improved versions of the anti-virus program. The question states

that competent lawyers in the field know about the importance of source codes in copyright cases involving software. Defense counsel's nonchalant approval of the defendant's two acts of destruction made it impossible for the plaintiff to prove the defendant's copying of its software. The judge was correct in sanctioning the defendant by entering partial summary judgment for the plaintiff on the copying issue, even though that is a drastic sanction. The judge was likewise correct in sanctioning defense counsel; if he had been doing his job, the destruction would never have occurred. (A) is incorrect because the duty not to destroy relevant evidence does not depend on the adversary's formal request for the evidence. The duty arises when the litigant either knows or should know that the evidence is relevant to the case. (C) and (D) are incorrect because both of them state overly lenient legal standards for imposing sanctions on a lawyer who approves the client's destruction of relevant evidence.

Answer to Question 16

(D) ABA Model Rule 1.11(a)(2) states that a lawyer must not represent a private client in connection with a matter in which the lawyer participated personally and substantially as a public employee, unless the appropriate government agency gives informed consent, confirmed in writing. Thus, (A) is incorrect. (B) is incorrect because even if the attorney did not have confidential information, he substantially participated in the investigation of the veteran's claim. (C) is incorrect because the disciplinary rule requires responsibility in the matter and not mere public employment in an agency where the case is pending or casual contact with the case.

Answer to Question 17

(C) The attorney's actions were improper because a lawyer is subject to discipline for failing to report a disciplinary violation committed by another lawyer that raises a substantial question as to the other lawyer's honesty, trustworthiness, or fitness as a lawyer. [ABA Model Rule 8.3(a)] Here, the other lawyer committed numerous disciplinary violations, including neglecting a matter and failing to communicate with a client. His drunk and abusive behavior also indicates an unfitness to practice. (A) is incorrect because the other lawyer was not seeking legal services from the attorney and thus is not protected by the duty of confidentiality. (B) is incorrect because a lawyer has a duty to report a disciplinary violation by another lawyer. It is not up to the client, unless the lawyer's only knowledge of the violation is through a confidential client communication and the client refuses to allow disclosure. (D) is incorrect because the attorney's duty is not to encourage the client to report the other lawyer, but for the attorney to report the other lawyer herself.

Answer to Question 18

(B) Under ABA Model Rule 5.5(b), a lawyer must not aid a nonlawyer in the unauthorized practice of law. Under these facts, the attorney would improperly be assisting the pastor, who has not in fact been authorized to practice law despite his law school degree. (A) makes no sense; the pastor's potential remedy for the attorney's mistakes does not subject the attorney to discipline. (C) is incorrect because any duty a lawyer may have to educate the public does not justify a lawyer's assisting in the unauthorized practice of law. (D) is irrelevant.

Answer to Question 19

(C) A private law firm must not use the name of a lawyer who holds public office during any substantial period in which the lawyer is not regularly and actively practicing with the firm. [*See* comment 8 to ABA Model Rule 7.1] It logically follows that (A) and (B) are incorrect. (D) is incorrect because it states but one underlying justification for the general rule.

Answer to Question 20

(B) Under ABA Model Rule 8.2(a), a lawyer must not make a statement that the lawyer knows to be false or with reckless disregard as to its truth or falsity concerning the qualifications or integrity of a judge. The ADA's sweeping statement to the news media regarding the judge appears to be just such an unrestrained and intemperate action as to lessen public confidence in the legal system. Also, it appears to have been made with reckless disregard as to its truth or falsity. Thus, (B) is correct, and (D) is incorrect. (A) is incorrect because the ADA's status as a public official is not the key here; it is his status as a lawyer that brings the ethics rules into play. (C) is incorrect because the timing of the statement does not make it proper.

Answer to Question 21

(B) When an attorney-client relationship is prematurely terminated (either by the attorney or by the client), the attorney must return to the client any advanced fees that have not yet been earned. [ABA Model Rule 1.16(d)] The fee here was an advance, not a "true retainer." Thus, (B) is correct, and (D) is incorrect. (A) is incorrect; under the ABA Model

Rules, the attorney may keep the fees he earned. (C) is incorrect; the attorney is limited to the portion of the $30,000 he earned no matter how much money he could otherwise have made.

Answer to Question 22

(C) It is not improper for a judge to seek an outside expert's advice on legal issues if the judge informs the parties in advance of the person to be consulted and the subject matter of the advice to be solicited, and affords a reasonable opportunity to object and respond to the notice and advice. [CJC Rule 2.9(A)(2)] (A) is incorrect because to seek such help, more is needed than just the judge's sincere belief that such help would be beneficial or even necessary; the judge must meet the above requirements. (B) is incorrect because it does not take into account these requirements for such help. (D) is incorrect because written permission alone is insufficient.

Answer to Question 23

(B) If a client disputes the amount that is due to the lawyer, then the disputed portion must be kept in a client trust account until the dispute is resolved. [ABA Model Rule 1.15(e)] Choice (B) describes precisely what the lawyer should do. Thus, (B) is correct, and (A), (C), and (D) are incorrect.

Answer to Question 24

(C) During the course of a lawyer's representation of a client, the lawyer should not give advice to an unrepresented person, other than the advice to obtain counsel, if the client's interests conflict with those of the unrepresented person. [ABA Model Rule 4.3] In this case, the attorney urged the woman to retain counsel. He gave her no other advice. Thus, he is not prohibited from negotiating with her. (A) and (B) are irrelevant. (D) is incorrect as, even if this were a criminal matter, the attorney is a private lawyer—not one employed as a prosecutor.

Answer to Question 25

(B) This is correct because it presents a sound reason for the inclusion of a home telephone number and a fax number in the ad. (A) is incorrect because some limitations on lawyer advertising (e.g., the ban on false or misleading ads) are constitutional. (C) and (D) are incorrect because nothing in the ABA Model Rules can constitutionally bar use of a home telephone number or a fax number in lawyer advertising.

Answer to Question 26

(D) A lawyer must not be a party to, or participate in, a partnership or employment agreement with another lawyer that restricts the right of a lawyer to practice law after the termination of a relationship created by the agreement, except as a condition to the payment of retirement benefits. [ABA Model Rule 5.6(a)] (A), (B), and (C) restrict in some way the novice attorney's right to practice law after terminating the relationship with the attorney, but (D) does not. Thus, (D) is correct.

Answer to Question 27

(B) (B) is not proper because it includes an extrajudicial statement regarding the credibility of witnesses. [ABA Model Rule 3.6(a) and comment 5] Furthermore, a prosecutor in a criminal case must refrain from making extrajudicial statements that have a substantial likelihood of heightening public condemnation of the accused unless the statements are necessary to inform the public and serve a legitimate law enforcement purpose. [ABA Model Rule 3.8(f)] (A) is proper because a lawyer may announce that a party has been charged with a crime, provided there is an accompanying statement that the charge is only an accusation and the party is deemed innocent until proven guilty. [ABA Model Rule 3.6(b) and comment 5] (C) is proper because the public may be warned about the behavior of a person likely to result in harm to the public. [ABA Model Rule 3.6(b)(6)] (D) is proper because a prosecutor is not required to answer questions by the press.

Answer to Question 28

(B)   Here, there is a potential conflict because the partner's actions against the unincorporated division of the telecommunications company could be affected by the firm's past and possibly future representation of the telecommunications company. It would be proper that disclosure of the conflict of interest be made to the manufacturing company. [ABA Model Rule 1.7(b)] Thus, (B) is correct and (D) is incorrect. (A) is incorrect because disclosure to and consent by the manufacturing company will allow the partner to continue to represent the manufacturing company without being subject to discipline. (C) is incorrect because the partner must obtain the manufacturing company's consent even if the matters are routine.

Answer to Question 29

(B)   When a lawyer seeks to influence legislation and is purporting to act in the public interest (rather than as an advocate for a client), the lawyer should espouse only those positions he believes to be in the public interest. ABA Model Rule 6.4 imposes an additional requirement: "When the lawyer knows that the interests of a client may be materially benefited by a [law reform] decision in which the lawyer participates, the lawyer shall disclose that fact but need not identify the client." Thus, (B) is correct, and (C) is incorrect. (A) is incorrect because the lawyer in this situation also has a duty to the public. (D) is incorrect because if he complies with the ethical obligations above, he may properly vote on the matter.

Answer to Question 30

(A)   If a client voluntarily offers to make a gift to his lawyer, the lawyer may accept the gift without being subject to discipline. [Comment 6 to ABA Model Rule 1.8] (B) is incorrect because ABA Model Rule 1.8 does not require a client to discuss a gift such as the one in this case with an outside party. (C) is incorrect because the vase is not a payment of a fee—it is a gift; an unexpected, unrequested gratuity. (D) is incorrect because, as stated above, a lawyer may accept a gift.

Answer to Question 31

(A)   This is the best answer here because ABA Model Rule 7.2(b) prohibits a lawyer from giving anything of value in return for a recommendation of the lawyer's services. Therefore, (A) is correct, and (C) is incorrect because "value" does not necessarily mean that cash has changed hands. (B) is incorrect because there is no such restriction in the ABA Model Rules. (D) is incorrect because Supreme Court decisions broadening the range of advertising and solicitation have not extended into the

area of referral fees, and in fact allow the bar to ban misleading advertising.

Answer to Question 32

(D) A lawyer may reveal or use confidential information if the client gives informed consent. [*See* ABA Model Rules 1.6, 1.18] (C) is incorrect because it does not take into account exceptions to the general rule of confidentiality. (A) is incorrect because the man consulted the attorney in her capacity as a lawyer, and it is irrelevant that he did not retain her. (B) is incorrect because the attorney may not reveal information, even if it will help the client, unless the client consents or the information falls into recognized exceptions to the confidentiality rule, which are not present here.

Answer to Question 33

(A) When dealing on behalf of a client with an unrepresented person, a lawyer must not give advice to the unrepresented person, other than the advice to obtain counsel, if the interests of the client conflict with those of the unrepresented person. [ABA Model Rule 4.3] Because the attorney was representing the company, and the company's interests conflict with those of the accountant, the attorney should not have given the accountant advice (told him not to worry), other than to secure counsel. (B) is incorrect because it is too broad. (C) is incorrect because furthering a client's interest does not excuse violation of the ethics rules. (D) is incorrect because the ethics rules apply regardless of whether a lawsuit has been filed.

Answer to Question 34

(A) The objection should be sustained because the communication falls under

the attorney-client privilege. [*See generally* comment 3 to ABA Model Rule 1.6] When the client is a corporation, the privilege covers communications between the lawyer and an employee of the corporation if: (1) the employee communicates with the lawyer at the direction of his superior; (2) the employee knows the purpose of the communication is to obtain legal advice for the corporation; and (3) the communication concerns a subject within the scope of the employee's duties. Here, the buyer was directed to speak with the company attorney about buying practices, and he believed the reason was to procure advice for the company. (B) is wrong because the company is the client and is claiming the privilege on its own behalf, not the buyer's. (C) is wrong because the company, the client, was seeking the attorney's legal services, and the company is claiming the privilege. Likewise, (D) is wrong because the privilege is not abrogated by the buyer's dismissal.

Answer to Question 35

(B) The attorney's actions were proper because she did not offer false evidence, and she is under no duty to volunteer harmful facts. [*See* ABA Model Rule 3.3; comment 14 to ABA Model Rule 3.3] In fact, to do so would probably be a breach of ethics. (A) is incorrect because her actions were proper regardless of the constitutional protections afforded criminal defendants. (C) is incorrect because a lawyer is under no obligation to volunteer harmful facts in an adversarial proceeding even if the jury will be misled by the testimony of a witness. It is up to the state to establish the time of the crime; if it cannot do so, it has not met its burden of proof. (D) is incorrect because the attorney should not disclose the facts to anyone, not even the judge. These facts are information related to the case and cannot be disclosed or used to the client's disadvantage absent some recognized exception to the duty of confidentiality. None applies here. Had the attorney presented a witness (other than the accused) who testified that the time was midnight when the attorney knew it was 10 p.m., the attorney would have had to rectify the false testimony. Here, however, the testimony came from the opponent, and the attorney is under no obligation to rectify it.

Answer to Question 36

(C)   The attorney is not subject to discipline because the information concerning the misuse of trust funds was confidential and not subject to any exception. The ABA Model Rules contain an exception to the duty of confidentiality when the lawyer reasonably believes it necessary to prevent an act that is reasonably certain to cause death or substantial bodily harm. [ABA Model Rule 1.6(b)(1)] Here, the information concerned past, not future, acts and did not concern any future action that could lead to death or substantial bodily harm. The ABA Model Rules also contain an exception to the duty of confidentiality when the client intends on committing a crime or fraud that is reasonably certain to cause substantial financial harm to someone, if the client is using or has used the lawyer's services in the matter. [ABA Model Rule 1.6(b)(2)] Here, the trustee has not expressed an intent to commit a future crime or fraud that would result in substantial financial injury to his deceased sister's children. Thus, (A) is incorrect. (B) is incorrect because the duty of candor to the tribunal does not entail revealing confidential information unless necessary to prevent a fraud on the tribunal. Here, the attorney did not offer false evidence of any kind or make or allow anyone to make any misleading statements. (D) is incorrect because had the information not been confidential, the attorney would have a duty to bring it to the court's attention, regardless of whose duty it is to supervise a trustee.

Answer to Question 37

(C)   The rule that conflicts of interest are imputed to all lawyers who work in the same office does not ordinarily apply to the advocate-witness rule. [*See* ABA Model Rule 3.7(b)] Thus, (A) and (B) are incorrect; the advocate-witness rule would prevent the lawyer himself from serving as the corporation's trial counsel, but it does not prevent his law partner from serving as such. The imputation rule does apply, however, if there is some other kind of conflict of interest caused by a lawyer's role as witness. [*Id.*] Suppose, for example, that the lawyer's testimony would contradict the corporation president's testimony rather than corroborate it. If that were true, it would create a conflict under ABA Model Rule 1.7(a) between the lawyer's own interest (telling the truth) and the corporation's interest (proving the representation was made). That conflict could well be so serious that even the corporation's informed consent could not overcome it. No such situation is presented here, and the law partner may therefore serve as the corporation's trial counsel. (C) is better than (D) because (C) correctly invokes the principles of ABA Model Rule 3.7(b), while (D) invents a bogus "merely corroborative" exception to the advocate-witness rule.

Answer to Question 38

(A) In an emergency, a lawyer may assist a client, even if the lawyer does not have the skill ordinarily required in the field in question. However, the assistance should not exceed what is reasonably necessary to meet the emergency. [*See* comment 3 to ABA Model Rule 1.1] (B) is incorrect because ordinarily a lawyer should be competent to handle a particular issue before accepting a case. [ABA Model Rule 1.1] (C) is incorrect because an emergency is involved. (D) is incorrect because an attempt to limit malpractice liability makes a lawyer subject to discipline.

Answer to Question 39

(C) ABA Model Rule 3.5(b) prohibits ex parte communications by a lawyer with a judge except as permitted by law. Lawyers may generally communicate with a judge in writing if the lawyer sends a copy to the adversary. [Restatement §113, comment c] Thus the attorney's letter could be proper only if a copy was sent to the opposing counsel. Thus, (C) is correct, and (A) and (B) are incorrect. (D) is incorrect; the attorney need not inform opposing counsel *before* writing to the judge.

Answer to Question 40

(A) When a civil case is pending, a litigant must not destroy or conceal documents that the litigant knows are either relevant or likely to be requested by the adversary. [*See* United States v. Lundwall, 1 F. Supp. 2d 249 (S.D.N.Y. 1998)] The attorney would, of course, be subject to litigation sanctions in the civil case itself, and she could also be disciplined by the bar, but criminal liability for obstruction of justice is also appropriate in a blatant case such as this. [*Id.*] (C)

is wrong for the reason just stated. (B) is wrong because it is too broad; when a civil case is pending, a litigant may destroy documents that the litigant does not believe are either relevant or likely to be requested by the adversary. (D) is wrong because it is not necessary that the documents have already been requested by the adversary.

Answer to Question 41

(C) A judge should disqualify herself in a proceeding in which her impartiality might reasonably be questioned, including but not limited to instances where she served as lawyer in the matter in controversy. [CJC Rule 2.11(A)(6)(a)] The fact that these matters are routine or uncontested does not excuse her from this rule; thus (A) is incorrect. (B) is incorrect because avoiding delay does not allow a judge to ignore CJC Rule 2.11(A)(6)(a). (D) is incorrect because it is too broad.

Answer to Question 42

(C) The attorney suggested a title search for the property. Upon learning that his client did not want to spend money for it, he was not required to order the search and pay for it himself, or to try to force her to pay for it. All he can do is give advice. If his client unwisely decides to accept only part of that advice, and suffers because of it, the client cannot successfully sue him for malpractice. The client's injury cannot be said to have been proximately caused by any negligence on the part of the lawyer. Thus, (C) is correct, and (A) and (B) are incorrect. (D) is irrelevant.

Answer to Question 43

(B) It would be proper for the attorney to interview both witnesses, but for the others, he must first obtain defense counsel's consent. A lawyer must obtain the consent of an organization's counsel before communicating with: (1) a person who supervises, directs, or consults with the organization's lawyers about the matter (here, the foreman and the plant manager); (2) a person whose conduct may be imputed to the organization for purposes of criminal or civil liability (the foreman and the plant manager again); or (3) a person whose statements may constitute an admission by the organization (again, the foreman and the plant manager). [Comment 7 to ABA Model Rule 4.2] Consent is not needed, however, before talking with a former employee. Thus, the attorney can speak to the witness who no longer works for the defendant without defense counsel's consent. Likewise, consent of defense counsel is not necessary to interview an employee who is merely a witness to the incident in question and is neither a management employee nor involved in the incident. Thus, the attorney may interview the witness who still works for the defendant without defense counsel's consent.

Answer to Question 44

(A) A lawyer must not give anything of value to a person (or organization) for recommending his services. [ABA Model Rule 7.2(b)] Thus, (A) is correct, and (D) is incorrect. While a lawyer has the option of waiving a fee, under these facts, the attorney is in fact rewarding the society for past referrals, and so (C) is incorrect. (B) is incorrect; a lawyer may give free legal services to wealthy people if he chooses and if he does not violate the ethics rules.

Answer to Question 45

(B) (A) is incorrect because unsubstantiated statements of comparison are improper.

[*See* comment 3 to ABA Model Rule 7.1] Conversely, (D) is incorrect because the federal Constitution protects many ads that are in bad taste, self-serving, and designed to attract business. The difficult choice is between (B) and (C). Although statements that fail to state material information are considered misleading and therefore improper [ABA Model Rule 7.1], the attorney has clearly stated that the low rate applies only to uncontested divorces and does not imply in any way that contested divorces can be obtained for the same rate. Therefore, (B) is a better answer than (C).

Answer to Question 46

(D) ABA Model Rule 8.2(a) bars lawyers from making false statements about candidates for the judiciary. Furthermore, CJC Rule 4.1(A)(11) prohibits a judicial candidate from knowingly, or with reckless disregard for the truth, making a false or misleading statement. The question states that all the facts in the statements are accurate. Thus, (A), (B), and (C) are proper. However, in (D), the assertion that she will not be soft on crime violates CJC Rule 4.1(A)(13), which prohibits a judicial candidate from making pledges, promises, or commitments, with respect to cases, controversies, or issues that are likely to come before the court, that are inconsistent with the impartial performance of the adjudicative duties of the office.

Answer to Question 47

(D) CJC Rule 2.5 requires a judge to perform his duties competently and diligently. Comment 3 to that rule explains that a judge should ensure that court officials, litigants, and their lawyers cooperate with the judge in disposing of matters promptly. Thus,

(D) is correct, and (A), (B), and (C) are incorrect. A judge may choose to promote settlements only if such policy does not conflict with other requirements for proper judicial conduct.

Answer to Question 48

(C) ABA Model Rule 3.9 requires that a lawyer reveal the fact that he is appearing before a legislative body in a representative capacity. (A) is incorrect because a client's specific instructions do not vitiate the ethical rules. (B) is incorrect because a lawyer must volunteer the fact that he is appearing in a representative capacity. (D) is incorrect because it is an overbroad statement that does not deal with the specific ethical issue at hand with the exactitude of (C).

Answer to Question 49

(C) When a lawyer reasonably believes that his client has diminished capacity, is at risk of substantial physical, financial, or other harm unless action is taken and cannot adequately act in the client's own interest, the lawyer may take reasonably necessary protective action. Protective action may include consulting with individuals who have the ability to take action to protect the client. When taking protective action, the lawyer is impliedly authorized under Rule 1.6(a) to reveal information about the client to the extent reasonably necessary to protect the client's interests. [ABA Model Rule 1.14] Here, the landowner has diminished capacity because he is in a coma and cannot vocalize his wishes. Thus, the lawyer is authorized to take protective action to protect the landowner's interests. Under the circumstances, appropriate protective action would include communicating the landowner's wishes to the son, who will be in a position to distribute part of his father's estate to the niece. (C) is the best answer because the attorney is acting in a manner consistent with the best interests of his client, and because his client is unable to make any decisions or express his wishes, the attorney is advancing the interests of his client as stated by the client prior to his coma. Thus, (C) is correct, and (A) and (B) are incorrect. (D) is incorrect because the son should exercise complete discretion without outside influence in deciding whether to carry out his father's wishes.

Answer to Question 50

(B) A lawyer may state his area of concentration. [Comment 9 to ABA Model Rule 7.2] Note that the attorney must not state or imply that he has been certified as a specialist unless he satisfies ABA Model Rule 7.2(c). Choice (A) is improper because it implies that the attorney can obtain results by improper means; i.e., it implies that he receives favorable treatment because his father and grandfather are judges. [ABA Model Rule 8.4(e)] Choice (C) is improper because it creates unjustified expectations. Lawyers are generally not permitted to advertise their track record. [Comment 3 to ABA Model Rule 7.1] In two years, the attorney may have only tried one or two jury cases, and the people who received some form of payment may have received very small settlements. Choice (D) is improper because it makes an unverifiable comparison between the attorney and other lawyers. [*Id.*]

Answer to Question 51

(D) The attorney advertises his practice in the western state, he meets with clients in his home in that state, and he regularly represents drunk driving clients in that state's courts. Thus, he maintains a "systematic and continuous presence" for the practice of law in the western state. [*See* ABA Model Rule 5.5(b) and comment 4] That makes him subject to discipline for the unauthorized practice of law, and it gives the western state jurisdiction to discipline him. [*See* ABA Model Rule 8.5(a)] Furthermore, the attorney's response to the judge's question, though literally true, was artfully misleading and that makes him subject to discipline. [*See* ABA Model Rule 3.3(a)(1) and comment 2; ABA Model Rule 8.4(c)] (A) is wrong because the attorney maintains a systematic and continuous presence for the practice of law in the western state, and because his response to the judge was misleading. (B) is wrong because ABA Model Rule 8.5(a) permits the western state to discipline the attorney for unauthorized practice in the western state. Although (C) is correct in part, (D) is the better answer because it additionally acknowledges that the western state's bar can discipline the attorney for the unauthorized practice of law in the western state.

Answer to Question 52

(C) Lawyers are permitted to participate in the political process, except when the law or a legal ethics rule prohibits it. The legal ethics rule nearest to the point is ABA Model Rule 7.6, which prohibits a lawyer from making a political contribution for the purpose of securing judicially appointed legal work. That rule does not apply here for two reasons. First, the rule does not apply to voter initiatives and referendums, and second, the rule does not apply to contributions of uncompensated services. [Comment 2 to ABA Model Rule 7.6] Choice (A) is not true. CJC Rule 3.1 allows judges

to engage in extrajudicial activities that are not otherwise prohibited. Comment 1 to CJC Rule 3.1 *encourages* judges to speak out publicly on issues concerning the law, reasoning that judges are uniquely qualified to engage in activities that concern the law, the legal system, and the administration of justice. Choices (B) and (D) are not true for the same reason.

Answer to Question 53

(A) ABA Model Rule 6.5 loosens the ordinary conflict of interest rules for legal service programs that are sponsored by a nonprofit organization or a court and that provide quick, short-term legal advice without any expectation that the lawyer-advisor will continue to represent the client-advisee in the matter. When a lawyer dispenses advice in such a program, ABA Model Rule 6.5(b) modifies the ordinary rule of imputed disqualification, thus making it possible for someone else in the lawyer's firm to represent a client whose interests are adverse to the advisee. [*See* comment 4 to ABA Model Rule 6.5] (B) is wrong because ABA Model Rule 6.5 does not require consent of the affected clients. (C) is wrong because ABA Model Rule 6.5 does not require any of the three things listed in that answer choice. (D) is wrong because ABA Model Rule 6.5 does not require such a promise, nor would such a promise solve any other kind of conflict problem.

Answer to Question 54

(B) ABA Model Rule 8.4(c) makes a lawyer subject to discipline by the bar for engaging in "conduct involving dishonesty, fraud, deceit, or misrepresentation." The novice attorney's dishonesty toward passengers and the taxi company

makes him subject to discipline by the bar, even though the dishonesty did not occur in connection with his law practice. [*See* comment 2 to ABA Model Rule 8.4] (A) is wrong because the novice attorney's taxi driving is not a "law-related service" within the meaning of ABA Model Rule 5.7(b). Therefore, he need not follow all of the legal ethics rules when he drives the taxi. He must, however, refrain from conduct that violates ABA Model Rule 8.4, which applies to everything a lawyer does. [*See* comment 2 to ABA Model Rule 5.7] (C) is wrong. A solicitation is a communication initiated by a lawyer or firm that is directed to a specific person that the lawyer knows (or reasonably should know) needs legal services in a particular matter, and that offers to provide legal services for that matter. With certain exceptions, a lawyer is prohibited from using live person-to-person contact to solicit professional employment. [ABA Model Rule 7.3] Here, there is no indication that the novice lawyer gives his business card to passengers known to need legal services in any particular matter; he simply gives his card to passengers who appear to be prosperous businesspeople and advises them to contact him if they ever need a lawyer. Thus, the novice attorney's actions do not constitute solicitation. However, even though this answer choice recites a true statement, it is incorrect because the novice lawyer is still subject to discipline for his dishonesty relating to the taxi meter. (D) is wrong because the novice attorney's dishonesty toward passengers and the taxi company makes him subject to discipline by the bar even though the dishonesty did not occur in connection with his law practice.

Answer to Question 55

(B) A lawyer is expected to "carry through to conclusion all matters undertaken for a client" [Comment 4 to ABA Model Rule 1.3], unless the client fires the lawyer or the lawyer terminates the relationship by a mandatory or permissive withdrawal in accordance with ABA Model Rule 1.16. Furthermore, in the sale of a law practice, "existing agreements between the seller and the client as to fees and the scope of the work must be honored by the purchaser." [Comment 10 to ABA Model Rule 1.17] When a lawyer buys a law practice, she is "required to undertake all client matters in the practice . . . subject to client consent," except when she cannot do so because of a conflict of interest. [Comment 6 to ABA Model Rule 1.17] The reason ABA Model Rule 1.17 requires the sale of an entire practice, or area of practice, is to protect "those clients whose matters are less lucrative and who might find it difficult to secure other counsel if a sale could be limited to substantial fee-generating matters." [Comment 6 to ABA Model Rule 1.17] In short, ABA Model Rule 1.17 seeks to protect the very clients that the purchaser put into her "likely loser" pile. She should be disciplined for her empty, but coercive, threat to withdraw if the "likely loser" will not agree to a higher fee because ABA Model Rule 1.16 would not permit her to withdraw in these circumstances. (C) is wrong for the same reasons discussed above. (A) is wrong because there is no disciplinary rule against selling a law practice to the highest bidder. Note, however, that Comment 11 to ABA Model Rule 1.17 imposes an ethical obligation on the seller "to exercise competence in identifying a purchaser qualified to . . . undertake the representation competently." (D) is wrong because the attorney did not fulfill the ethical obligation just quoted; if he had done so, he would have discovered that the purchaser was inexperienced in the field and had twice been disciplined for client neglect and client abandonment.

Answer to Question 56

(B) Comment 15 to ABA Model Rule 1.6 explains what a lawyer should do when push comes to shove with a judge about a privilege issue: "A lawyer may be ordered to reveal information relating to the representation of a client by a court or another tribunal or government entity claiming authority pursuant to other law to compel disclosure. Absent informed consent of the client to do otherwise, the lawyer should assert on behalf of the client all nonfrivolous claims that the order is not authorized by other law or that the information sought is protected against disclosure by the attorney-client privilege or other applicable law. In the event of an adverse ruling, the lawyer must consult with the client about the possibility of appeal . . . . Unless review is sought, however . . . [the lawyer may] comply with the court's order." (A) is wrong. Here the judge spoke condescendingly to the defense attorney, in violation of CJC Rule 2.8(B), which requires a judge to be "patient, dignified, and courteous to litigants, jurors, witnesses, lawyers, court staff, court officials, and others with whom the judge deals in an official capacity." However, that does not license the defense attorney to be disrespectful in response. Comment 4 to ABA Model Rule 3.5 explains that "refraining from abusive or obstreperous conduct is a corollary of the advocate's right to

speak on behalf of litigants. A lawyer may stand firm against abuse by a judge but should avoid reciprocation; the judge's default is no justification for similar dereliction by an advocate." (D) is wrong for the same reason, although it is milder than (A). (C) is wrong because giving the judge a free and unauthorized look at the patent counsel's letter could seriously prejudice the defendant, especially if the judge will be presiding over further proceedings in the case. The attorney-client privilege belongs to the defendant, not to the defense attorney, and the defense attorney should not waive it without talking over the options with her client. [*See* comments 15 and 16 to ABA Model Rule 1.6]

Answer to Question 57

(B) The SEC regulations require a lawyer to report up the corporate ladder if the lawyer comes across "evidence of a material violation" of the securities laws or similar laws. The regulations use a tricky double negative to define "evidence." "Evidence" means "credible evidence, based upon which it would be unreasonable, under the circumstances, for a prudent and competent attorney not to conclude that it is reasonably likely that a material violation has occurred . . . ." [17 C.F.R. §205.2(e)] The SEC's comment on that definition says that a lawyer is "not required (or expected) to report 'gossip, hearsay, or innuendo.'" [*Id.*] If a reasonable lawyer would doubt the credibility of the employee's scrap of anonymous hearsay, that is more than enough to satisfy the double negative and thus to excuse the outside attorney from reporting the story to the company's chief legal officer. Thus, (B) is correct. (D) is incorrect because the "evidence of a material violation" standard does not require that the lawyer have actual knowledge of the violation. (A) is incorrect because the outside attorney must obey the SEC's Sarbanes-Oxley regulations because he is advising a securities issuer about a document that will be filed with the SEC. [*See* 17 C.F.R. §205.2(a)] (C) is incorrect for two reasons. First, the employee herself is not in a privileged relationship with the outside attorney, and her volunteered gossip probably would not be protected by the corporation's attorney-client privilege. [*See* Upjohn Co. v. United States, 449 U.S. 383 (1981); *but see* Restatement §73, comments d, f, and h] Second, even if her statement were protected by the corporation's attorney-client privilege, a disclosure by the outside attorney to the company's chief legal officer would not waive or destroy the privilege.

Answer to Question 58

(A)   ABA Model Rule 1.8(c) expressly governs this situation. According to this subsection, a lawyer may not "prepare on behalf of a client an instrument giving the lawyer . . . any substantial gift unless the lawyer . . . is related to the client." The clarity of this provision renders (A) the correct choice. (B) is incorrect because a lawyer may draft a will in which the lawyer is a beneficiary, but the prerequisite for doing so is that the client must be a relative. (C) is incorrect because inducement is not a prerequisite for the application of this portion of the rule. (D) is incorrect because although, assuming competency, the client may indeed leave his property to whomever he chooses, if he wishes to leave property to a lawyer to whom he is unrelated, he will have to retain a different lawyer to draft his will.

Answer to Question 59

(D)   ABA Model Rule 4.4(b) says that if a lawyer receives a document or electronically stored information relating to the lawyer's representation of a client, and if the lawyer "knows or reasonably should know that the document or electronically stored information was inadvertently sent, [the lawyer] shall promptly notify the sender." ABA Model Rule 4.4 does not touch on several related questions on which state law is presently split. These include whether the receiving lawyer must return the errant document to its sender or delete the electronically stored information, and whether a lawyer's transmission error can waive a privilege. (A) and (B) are wrong because they do not require the plaintiff's attorney to notify the sender about the mistake. (C) is wrong for two reasons. First, it does not require the plaintiff's attorney to notify the sender. Second, it needlessly shames defense counsel and involves the judge in a matter that does not need a judge's attention.

Answer to Question 60

(B)   The governing rule here is ABA Model Rule 5.5(c), which concerns temporary law practice in one state by a lawyer who is licensed in a different state only. The litigator who was hired by the theater company to represent the company at the arbitration may represent the theater company in the arbitration in the state in which the arbitration is to take place because the arbitration arises from the law firm's representation of the theater company in the theater company's home state. [*See* ABA Model Rule 5.5(c)(3)] Furthermore, it was proper for the copyright attorney who represented the theater company in the license negotiations to negotiate the copyright license in the state in which the negotiations took place because the negotiations are reasonably related to the law firm's representation of the theater company in the theater company's home state. [*See* ABA Model Rule 5.5(c)(4)] (A) is wrong with respect to both the copyright attorney and the litigator. (C) is wrong with respect to the copyright attorney. (D) is wrong with respect to the litigator.

CONVISER MINI REVIEW

PROFESSIONAL RESPONSIBILITY MINI REVIEW

I. REGULATION OF THE LEGAL PROFESSION

A. SOURCES OF REGULATION

1. **The State**

   States may regulate the practice of law in the exercise of their police powers. State courts, not state legislatures, have the ultimate power to regulate the legal profession.

   a. **Courts**

      The ultimate power of regulating the legal profession rests with the highest state court. Additionally, *case law*, *rules of court*, and *state statutes* are used in governing the practice of law.

      1) **Ethics Rules—ABA Model Rules and Judicial Code**

         Most states have adopted ethics rules patterned after models drafted by the American Bar Association ("ABA"). The majority of states have rules patterned after the Model Rules of Professional Conduct, while the remainder base their rules on the older Model Code of Professional Responsibility. Similarly, most states have enacted some version of the ABA Model Code of Judicial Conduct.

   b. **Bar Associations**

      Each state has a bar association. A majority of states have "integrated" bars, meaning that one must be a member of the bar association to practice law in the state. Administration of bar examinations, provision of continuing legal education programs, and assistance with discipline are functions of state bar associations.

   c. **Legislature**

      All state legislatures have enacted statutes governing some aspects of legal practice.

2. **The Federal System**

   Each federal court has its own bar, to which an attorney must belong in order to practice before that court. Federal practice is governed by federal statutes, case law, and court or agency rules. Federal government attorneys are subject to state ethics laws and rules in each state where the attorneys engage in their duties.

3. **Regulation by Multiple States**

   A lawyer is subject to regulation by each state in which she is admitted to practice.

B.   ADMISSION TO THE PRACTICE OF LAW

1.   **The Application**

a.   **False Statements**

In connection with an application to the bar or a bar disciplinary matter, an applicant or lawyer must not knowingly make a false statement of material fact.

b.   **Failure to Disclose Information**

In connection with an application to the bar or a bar disciplinary matter, an applicant or lawyer must not: (1) fail to disclose a fact that is necessary to correct a misapprehension known by the applicant or lawyer to have arisen in the matter, or (2) fail to respond to a lawful demand for information. These obligations do not apply to information protected by the ethical duty of confidentiality.

2.   **Character and Fitness—"Good Moral Character"**

Bar applicants are usually required to demonstrate that they are of good moral character. If a question arises as to an applicant's honesty and integrity, the applicant may be asked to appear at a hearing before the admissions committee, where the applicant will be afforded **procedural due process** rights.

a.   **Relevant Conduct**

All aspects of an applicant's past conduct are subject to review. An applicant's criminal conduct (conviction unnecessary) and other acts constituting **moral turpitude** (e.g., false statements or concealment of past conduct to admissions committee) are grounds for the denial of his application for admission to the bar. However, evidence of the applicant's **rehabilitation** will be considered. Note that an applicant's mere membership in an organization such as the Communist Party (without an indication that he advocated the violent overthrow of the government) is insufficient to show lack of moral character.

3.   **Citizenship and Residency—Not Valid Requirements**

A requirement that an applicant be a United States citizen or a citizen of a state is unconstitutional.

C.   REGULATION AFTER ADMISSION

1.   **What Constitutes Professional Misconduct**

A lawyer is subject to discipline not only for violating a disciplinary rule, but also for any of the following types of conduct:

a.   **Attempting to violate** a disciplinary rule;

b.   **Assisting or inducing another person** to violate a disciplinary rule;

c.   **Using the acts of another person** to violate a disciplinary rule;

d.   Engaging in **criminal conduct** that shows **dishonesty, untrustworthiness, or unfitness** to practice law;

e.   Engaging in **any conduct** involving **dishonesty, fraud, deceit, or misrepresentation**;

f.   Engaging in conduct that is **prejudicial to the administration of justice**;

g.   **Stating or implying an ability to improperly influence** a government agency or official or to achieve results by means that violate the law or legal ethics rules;

h.   **Knowingly assisting a judge in conduct that is illegal** or that violates the Code of Judicial Conduct; or

i.   Engaging in **discrimination or harassment in conduct related to the practice of law** on the basis of race, sex, religion, national origin, ethnicity, disability, age, sexual orientation, gender identity, marital status, or socioeconomic status. (Note that this rule does not limit a lawyer's ability to reject a case or provide legitimate advice or advocacy consistent with the RPC.)

2.   **Duty to Report Professional Misconduct**
A lawyer is subject to discipline for failing to report a disciplinary violation committed by another lawyer. The ABA Model Rules limit that duty to disciplinary violations that raise a **substantial** question as to the other lawyer's honesty, trustworthiness, or fitness as a lawyer. A lawyer's obligation to report disciplinary violations by judges is the same as that concerning violations by lawyers. The duty to report does not, of course, apply to information that is protected by the ethical duty of confidentiality or information gained by a lawyer or judge while serving as a member of an approved lawyers' assistance program designed to help lawyers and judges with substance abuse problems.

3.   **Disciplinary Process**
Disciplinary proceedings against a lawyer begin when a complaint is filed with the state disciplinary authority. If the complaint is not dismissed, the lawyer is requested to respond to the charges, and the grievance committee will investigate the charges and may hold a hearing on the matter. At the hearing, the accused lawyer is entitled to procedural due process. If discipline is imposed, the lawyer is entitled to review of the decision by the state's highest court.

4. Choice of Law in Disciplinary Proceedings

Generally, if a lawyer's alleged misconduct is related to a proceeding that is pending before a tribunal, the ethics rules of the jurisdiction in which the tribunal sits will be applied, unless the tribunal's rules provide otherwise. For any other conduct, the rules of the jurisdiction in which the conduct occurred will apply, but if the predominant effect of the conduct is in some other jurisdiction, that jurisdiction's rules will apply. Regarding conflicts of interest only, a lawyer and client may enter into an advance written agreement specifying the "predominant effect" jurisdiction. If the agreement is entered into with the client's informed consent, and the client later tries to disqualify the lawyer from another matter or files a disciplinary complaint, the court or disciplinary authority may consider the agreement in determining whether the lawyer reasonably believed the jurisdiction's rules would apply.

5. Effect of Sanctions in Other Jurisdictions

Under the majority view, sister **states** accept disciplinary action by one state as conclusive proof of a lawyer's misconduct, but are free to impose their own sanctions. However, each **federal court** makes an independent evaluation, accepting as competent evidence the lawyer's discipline by a state.

6. Disability Proceedings

Most jurisdictions have proceedings for incapacitated lawyers (e.g., those suffering from substance abuse), which result in the lawyers' suspension from the practice of law. Diversion into a rehabilitation program is a common procedure used for possible reinstatement.

D. UNAUTHORIZED PRACTICE AND MULTI-JURISDICTIONAL PRACTICE

1. Unauthorized Practice by Lawyer

A lawyer is subject to discipline for practicing in a jurisdiction without being licensed to do so.

2. Permissible Types of Temporary Multi-Jurisdictional Practice

If a lawyer is admitted to practice in one state, and is not disbarred or suspended from practice in any state, she may provide legal services in a second state on a **temporary basis** in the following situations:

a. Association with Local Lawyer

A lawyer may practice on a temporary basis in a state in which she is not admitted if she associates with a local lawyer who participates in the matter.

b. Special Permission to Practice in Local Tribunal

If a lawyer wants to handle a matter in a jurisdiction in which she is not admitted, she may request special permission from that tribunal to appear "pro hac vice" (i.e., for purposes of that matter only).

c. **Mediation or Arbitration Arising Out of Practice in Home State**
A lawyer may engage in alternative dispute resolution (e.g., mediation or arbitration) in a state in which she is not admitted to practice if her services arise out of her practice in the state in which she is admitted.

d. **Other Practice Arising Out of Practice in Home State**
A lawyer may temporarily practice in a state in which she is not admitted if her out-of-state practice is reasonably related to her home-state practice.

e. **Temporary Practice by Foreign Lawyers**
A lawyer who is licensed and in good standing in a foreign jurisdiction may engage in temporary practice in a United States jurisdiction under circumstances similar to those described in a. - d., above. Additionally, a foreign lawyer may provide legal services temporarily in the United States if the services are governed primarily by international law or the law of a foreign jurisdiction. However, foreign lawyers are subject to stricter standards than lawyers from different states (e.g., when seeking pro hac vice admission).

3. **Permissible Types of Permanent Multi-Jurisdictional Practice**
A lawyer who is admitted in one United States or foreign jurisdiction, and is not disbarred or suspended from practice in any jurisdiction, may open a law office and establish a practice in a different jurisdiction only in two limited situations:

a. **Lawyers Employed by Their Only Client**
A lawyer may practice on behalf of her only client (e.g., in-house corporate lawyers and government lawyers) in a state in which she is not admitted, but she must seek pro hac vice admission to litigate a matter in that state. A foreign lawyer practicing on this basis must consult with a local lawyer before advising her client on the law of a United States jurisdiction.

b. **Legal Services Authorized by Federal or Local Law**
Rarely, a lawyer is authorized by federal or local law to practice a restricted branch of law (e.g., patent prosecution) in a state in which she is otherwise not admitted to practice.

4. **Consequences of Multi-Jurisdictional Practice**
A lawyer who is admitted to practice in only one jurisdiction but practices in another jurisdiction as provided in 2. or 3., above, will be subject to the disciplinary rules of both jurisdictions.

5. **Unauthorized Practice by Nonlawyers**
A person not admitted to practice as a lawyer must not engage in the

unauthorized practice of law. A lawyer is subject to discipline for assisting a nonlawyer to engage in the unauthorized practice of law.

a. "Practice of Law"

"Practice of law" includes those activities: (1) involving legal knowledge and skill, (2) which constitute advice concerning binding legal rights, or (3) traditionally performed by lawyers (e.g., settlement negotiations, drafting legal documents). It is not unauthorized practice for a nonlawyer to appear before an agency that permits nonlawyer professionals (e.g., accountants) to do so, or for a nonlawyer to fill in the blanks on legal forms (e.g., real estate sales contracts). However, the giving of tax law advice by a nonlawyer would probably constitute the unauthorized practice of law.

b. Consequences of Unauthorized Practice

A nonlawyer engaged in the unauthorized practice of law may be subject to injunction, contempt, and criminal prosecution. A lawyer who assists a nonlawyer in the unauthorized practice of law is subject to discipline.

c. Delegating Work to Nonlawyer Assistants

A lawyer must supervise delegated work carefully and must be ultimately responsible for the results.

d. Training Nonlawyers for Law-Related Work

A lawyer may advise and instruct nonlawyers whose employment requires a knowledge of the law.

e. Helping Persons Appear Pro Se

A lawyer may advise persons who wish to appear on their own behalf in a legal matter.

f. Assisting a Suspended or Disbarred Lawyer

A lawyer who assists (e.g., hires) a suspended or disbarred lawyer to do work that constitutes the practice of law is subject to discipline.

E. RESPONSIBILITIES OF PARTNERS, MANAGERS, AND SUPERVISORY LAWYERS

1. Partners' Duty to Educate and Guide in Ethics Matters

The partners or managing lawyers of a firm, and other supervisory lawyers, must make reasonable efforts to assure that the other lawyers adhere to the Rules of Professional Conduct. A lawyer who directly supervises another lawyer's work must reasonably assure that the other lawyer adheres to the Rules of Professional Conduct.

2. How Duties Are Fulfilled

In a small private law firm, informal supervision may be sufficient. In a larger organization, more elaborate steps may be necessary.

3. **Ethical Responsibility for Another Lawyer's Misconduct**
A lawyer is subject to discipline for a disciplinary violation committed by a second lawyer if: (1) the first lawyer ordered it or knowingly ratified it, or (2) the first lawyer is a partner or manager or has direct supervisory responsibility over the second lawyer and learns of the misconduct at a time when it can be remedied but fails to take reasonable remedial action.

F. **RESPONSIBILITIES CONCERNING NONLAWYER ASSISTANCE**

1. **Duty to Educate and Guide in Ethics Matters**
A lawyer should instruct and guide her nonlawyer assistants (within or outside the firm) concerning legal ethics and should be ultimately responsible for their work.

2. **Duty of Partners and Direct Supervisors**
Law firm partners and managers and other direct supervisors must make reasonable efforts to assure that their **nonlawyer employees** act ethically.

3. **Ethical Responsibility for Nonlawyer's Misconduct**
A lawyer is subject to discipline when a nonlawyer does something that would violate a disciplinary rule if: (1) the lawyer ordered the conduct or knew about it and ratified it, or (2) the lawyer is a partner or manager or has direct supervisory responsibility over the nonlawyer and learns about the misconduct at a time when it can be remedied but fails to take reasonable remedial action.

G. **RESPONSIBILITIES OF A SUBORDINATE LAWYER**
If a supervisory lawyer orders a subordinate lawyer to commit a **clear** ethics violation, the subordinate lawyer will be subject to discipline if he carries out the order. A subordinate lawyer will not be subject to discipline, however, for following a supervisory lawyer's reasonable resolution of a **debatable** ethics question.

H. **PROFESSIONAL INDEPENDENCE OF A LAWYER**

1. **Fee Splitting with Nonlawyers**
Subject to the exceptions stated below, a lawyer must not share her legal fee with a nonlawyer.

a. **Death Benefits Permitted**
The lawyers in a firm may agree that when one of them dies, the others will pay a death benefit over a reasonable period of time to the dead lawyer's survivors.

b. **Compensation and Retirement Plans for Nonlawyer Employees**
The nonlawyer employees of a firm may be included in a compensation or retirement plan even though the plan is based on a profit-sharing arrangement.

   c. **Sale of a Law Practice**
One lawyer's practice can be sold to another lawyer (*see* J., *infra*). One who buys the practice of a dead, disabled, or disappeared lawyer may pay the purchase price to the estate or representatives of the lawyer.

   d. **Sharing Court-Awarded Fee with Nonprofit Organization**
When a court awards attorneys' fees to the winning lawyer in a case, the lawyer may share the fee with a nonprofit organization that hired or recommended him as counsel.

2. **Partnership with Nonlawyer to Practice Law Prohibited**
A lawyer must not form a partnership with a nonlawyer if *any* part of the partnership activities will constitute the practice of law.

3. **Nonlawyer Involvement in Incorporated Firm or Other Association**
A lawyer must not practice in an incorporated firm or association if a nonlawyer owns any interest in the firm or association, is a director or officer of the firm or association, or has the right to direct or control the professional judgment of a lawyer.

4. **Interference with Lawyer's Professional Judgment**
A lawyer must not allow a person who recommends, employs, or pays her for serving a client to direct or regulate the lawyer's professional judgment.

I. RESTRICTIONS ON RIGHT TO PRACTICE PROHIBITED

A lawyer's right to practice after termination of a partnership or employment relationship cannot be restricted except for an agreement concerning benefits upon retirement. Likewise, restrictions on the lawyer's right to practice as part of a settlement agreement are prohibited.

J. SALE OF A LAW PRACTICE

1. **When Sale Permitted**
A law practice or a field of law practice, including goodwill, may be sold if: (1) the seller ceases to engage in the private practice of law or the sold field of practice in the geographic area in which the practice has been conducted; (2) the entire practice or field of practice is sold to one or more lawyers or firms; and (3) written notice is given to the seller's clients. The seller must exercise competence in finding a qualified buyer.

2. **Protection of Seller's Clients After Sale**
The purchaser must undertake all client matters in the practice and not just those that generate substantial fees. Also, clients' fees cannot be increased because of the sale. The purchaser must honor existing fee agreements made by the seller.

K.   **LAW–RELATED (ANCILLARY) SERVICES**

Lawyers are permitted to provide law-related services (e.g., financial planning, accounting, lobbying, title insurance) to both clients and nonclients. Even though law-related services are not legal services, a lawyer who provides such services is subject to the Rules of Professional Conduct in two situations:

1.   **Nonlegal Services and Legal Services Provided Together**

    If a lawyer provides nonlegal services in circumstances that are not distinct from her provision of legal services to clients, then the Rules of Professional Conduct apply to both the legal and nonlegal services. Additionally, when a client-lawyer relationship exists between the lawyer and the individual receiving the law-related services, the lawyer must comply with Rule 1.8(a), which specifies the conditions a lawyer must satisfy when she enters into a business transaction with her own client. Specifically, the transaction must meet the following requirements: the terms of the transaction must be fair to the client; the terms must be fully disclosed to the client in writing, and such disclosure must cover the essential terms of the transaction and the lawyer's role in the transaction; the client must be advised in writing that he should seek advice from an independent lawyer regarding the arrangement; and the client must give informed consent in a writing signed by the client. (*See also* IV.C.2., *supra.*)

2.   **Nonlegal Services Provided by Entity that Is Controlled by the Lawyer**

    If a lawyer provides nonlegal services through an entity that is not her law office but that she controls, the lawyer must take reasonable steps to assure that people who receive the nonlegal services understand that those services are not legal services and that the Rules of Professional Conduct do not cover those services. If the lawyer does not take those reasonable steps, then the lawyer is subject to the Rules of Professional Conduct with respect to the nonlegal services.

II. THE CLIENT–LAWYER RELATIONSHIP

A.   **NATURE OF THE RELATIONSHIP**

The relationship between a lawyer and client is contractual, and the terms of such contract are derived from custom and mutual agreement. A lawyer is both the client's fiduciary and agent.

B.   **CREATING THE LAWYER–CLIENT RELATIONSHIP**

A lawyer-client relationship arises when a person indicates an intent that the lawyer provide legal services and the lawyer agrees or fails to clearly inform the person that he does not wish to represent her, resulting in implied assent, or when a tribunal appoints a lawyer to represent a client (see XI.B., *infra*).

1. **Implied Assent and Reasonable Reliance**
   A lawyer's assent is implied when he fails to clearly decline representation and the prospective client reasonably relies on the representation. Reasonableness is a question of fact.

2. **Duty to Reject Certain Cases**
   A lawyer must refuse employment when:

   a. The client's motive is to **embarrass, delay,** or **burden** a third person;

   b. The case presents a **factually or legally frivolous position** (but a good faith argument that the facts are as claimed or that the law should be changed is permissible);

   c. The lawyer is **incompetent** (or too busy) to handle the matter;

   d. The lawyer's strong **personal feelings** may impair his ability of effective representation; or

   e. The lawyer's **mental or physical condition** would materially impair the representation.

3. **Duties Owed to Prospective Client**
   If no lawyer-client relationship ensues from a consultation with a prospective client, the lawyer must: (1) protect the person's confidential information, including declining representation of others in the same or a related matter; (2) protect the prospective client's property; and (3) use reasonable care in giving the person any legal advice, e.g., whether the claim has merit.

4. **Ethical Obligation to Accept Unpopular Cases**
   A lawyer can fulfill his obligation to assist in the provision of legal services to those in need by accepting a fair share of unpopular matters or indigent or unpopular clients.

C. **ATTORNEYS' FEES**
   The nature and amount of an attorney's fee are subjects for contractual agreement between the attorney and the client (except when the fee is set by statute or court order).

   1. **When to Agree on Fee**
      The ABA Model Rules require a lawyer to reach a clear fee agreement with the client, preferably in writing, early in the relationship.

   2. **Discipline for Unreasonable Fee**
      A court will not enforce a contract for an unreasonably high fee or an unreasonably high amount for expenses, and the lawyer is subject to discipline for trying to exact such a fee or expenses.

a. Factors

Factors considered in determining reasonableness include: the time and labor required; the novelty and difficulty of the questions involved; the skill required; whether the lawyer is precluded from other work; what other lawyers in the community charge; the amount at stake and the results obtained; time limitations; the experience, reputation, and ability of the lawyer; and whether the fee is fixed or contingent.

b. Items that May and May Not Be Billed

The attorney must disclose the basis for charges and may not charge the client for ordinary overhead expenses. The attorney may charge the client the actual cost of special services (e.g., computer research, secretarial overtime). Alternatively, the attorney may charge a reasonable amount agreed to in advance.

3. Collecting and Financing Attorneys' Fees

a. Payment in Advance

A lawyer may require her fee to be paid in advance, but she must refund any unearned part of the advance if she is fired or withdraws. A lawyer need not return a true retainer fee (i.e., money paid solely to insure the lawyer's availability).

b. Property for Services

A lawyer may accept property in return for services, provided that this does not involve a proprietary interest in the cause of action or subject of litigation, but such an arrangement is subject to scrutiny to make sure the lawyer does not take advantage of the client.

c. Cutting Off Services

A lawyer must not make a fee agreement that could cut off services in the middle of the relationship and thus put the client at a disadvantage.

d. Credit Arrangements and Security

An attorney may permit the client to pay a fee by credit card, to finance fees through bank loans, or to pay by an interest-bearing promissory note. If local law permits, an attorney may use an attorney's lien to secure payment of a fee.

4. Contingent Fees

United States law tolerates contingent fees, in which the lawyer receives his fee only upon favorable resolution for his client. Often a contingent fee is a percentage of the client's recovery in the case.

a. Generally Prohibited in Criminal and Domestic Relations Cases

A lawyer is subject to discipline for using contingent fees in criminal cases and in domestic relations cases when the contingency is based

on the securing of a divorce, the amount of alimony or support, or the amount of a property settlement.

b. Contingent Fee Must Be Reasonable

A contingent fee must be reasonable in amount and must not be used if the facts of the case make it unreasonable to do so.

c. Written Fee Agreement Required

A contingent fee agreement is required to be in a writing signed by the client. The writing must spell out how the fee is to be calculated, what litigation and other expenses are to be deducted from the recovery, whether deductions for expenses will be made before or after the fee is calculated, and what expenses the client must pay.

5. Fee Disputes

A lawyer may not use illegal collection methods, improperly use confidential information, or harass a client to obtain compensation.

a. Remedies

In addition to filing suit to recover a fee, a lawyer can generally use a common law or statutory charging lien. Many states also permit the lawyer to exercise a retaining lien under which she can retain documents, funds, and property of the client until her fee is paid—but there is a strong minority view contra. Also, if the lawyer receives funds out of which his fee is to be paid, and the client disputes the fee, the lawyer must retain the disputed amount in a client trust account until resolution of the dispute. Moreover, many jurisdictions have arbitration or mediation services to resolve fee disputes.

6. Fee Splitting with Other Lawyers

Generally, a lawyer must not split fees with another lawyer, except as provided below.

a. Lawyers Within a Firm

A firm's partners and associates may pool and split legal fees. A law firm may also make payments under a **separation or retirement** agreement to a former partner or associate.

b. Certain Splits with Lawyers Outside Firm

A lawyer may split her fee with another lawyer who is not in her firm if:

1) The total fee is **reasonable**;

2) The split is **in proportion to the services performed by each lawyer**, or some different proportion if **each lawyer assumes joint responsibility** for the matter; and

3) The client agrees to the split **in writing**.

FEE SHARING

Is the person with whom a fee (or money comprised of legal fees) is to be shared *another lawyer*?

Yes → Is the lawyer the first lawyer's *partner or associate*?

No → Is the money a *death benefit* payable under an agreement between a deceased lawyer and his firm or the *purchase price* for the sale of a deceased, disabled, or disappeared lawyer's practice?

Is the lawyer the first lawyer's *partner or associate*?

Yes → **FEE MAY BE SHARED**

No → Is the lawyer a *former partner or associate* and the sharing pursuant to a *separation or retirement agreement*?

Yes → **FEE MAY BE SHARED**

No → Have the following conditions been met: (i) the share is *proportional* to the services performed by the lawyer, or in any other proportion if each lawyer assumes *joint responsibility,* (ii) *the client consents to the split in writing,* and (iii) *the total fee is reasonable?*

Yes → **FEE MAY BE SHARED**

No → **FEE MAY NOT BE SHARED**

Is the money a *death benefit* payable under an agreement between a deceased lawyer and his firm or the *purchase price* for the sale of a deceased, disabled, or disappeared lawyer's practice?

Yes → **FEE MAY BE SHARED**

No → Is the money being paid *into a retirement or compensation plan* for firm employees?

Yes → **FEE MAY BE SHARED**

No → Is the money being paid *to a nonprofit organization* that hired or recommended the lawyer?

Yes → **FEE MAY BE SHARED**

No → **FEE MAY NOT BE SHARED**

CMR Chart

7. True Referral Fees Are Unethical

When one lawyer simply refers a case to a second lawyer and the first lawyer neither works on the case nor assumes responsibility for the case, the second lawyer must not pay the first lawyer a forwarding or referral fee. A lawyer may, however, set up a *reciprocal referral arrangement* in which the lawyer agrees to refer clients to another lawyer or nonlawyer, provided the clients referred are informed of the arrangement.

D. SCOPE OF REPRESENTATION

1. May Limit Scope of Representation

A lawyer may limit the scope of the representation if: (1) the limitation is *reasonable* under the circumstances, and (2) the client gives *informed consent*.

2. Must Not Assist Client in Crime or Fraud

A lawyer must not advise or assist a client to commit a crime or fraud, but the lawyer may discuss the legal consequences of a proposed course of action with the client. A lawyer may also counsel or assist a client to make a good faith effort to determine the validity, scope, meaning, or application of the law (e.g., violating a statute to test its validity in an enforcement proceeding).

3. Decisions to Be Made by Client

A lawyer must abide by a client's decisions affecting the client's substantial legal rights, including:

a. Whether to accept a *settlement offer*;

b. What *plea* to enter in a criminal case;

c. Whether to *waive a jury trial* in a criminal case;

d. Whether the client will *testify* in a criminal case; and

e. Whether to *appeal*.

4. Lawyer's Authority to Bind Client

A lawyer is the client's agent, and the lawyer's actions on behalf of a client will legally bind the client if the lawyer acted with actual or apparent authority. *Actual authority* includes what the client has expressly told the lawyer to do, along with anything else impliedly authorized to carry out the representation. When dealing with the court and third parties, a lawyer has *apparent authority* when the court or third party reasonably assumes that the lawyer has authority to act based on some manifestation from the client that the lawyer had authority. Often the act of retaining the lawyer is enough to give the lawyer apparent authority, except with respect to settlement and other decisions that are always left to the client (*see* 3., above). Even if the lawyer acted without actual authority, the client is still bound if the lawyer had apparent authority. However, the client can sue the lawyer for damages.

a. When Lawyer's Authority Ends

A lawyer's actual authority ends when the matter is over, the lawyer is fired, the lawyer dies or is unable to continue the representation, or the client dies. The lawyer's apparent authority ends when the third party knows or should know that any of these events occurred. When a lawyer's actual authority ends, the lawyer must no longer purport to have authority and must notify third parties who are relying on the continued existence of the authority.

5. Client with Diminished Capacity

a. Lawyer's Duties

If a client is a minor or has diminished mental capacity, the lawyer has a duty, so far as reasonably possible, to maintain a normal lawyer-client relationship with the client. Even if the client has a guardian or other representative, the lawyer should, so far as possible, treat the client as a client, particularly in communicating with the client about significant developments.

b. Protective Action and Appointment of Guardian

When the client has diminished capacity and faces a risk of substantial physical, financial, or other harm, the lawyer may take reasonable actions to protect the client, including seeking the appointment of a guardian. Under these circumstances, the lawyer has implied authority to reveal the client's confidential information, to the extent necessary to protect the client.

6. Emergency Legal Assistance to Nonclient with Seriously Diminished Capacity

When a person with seriously diminished capacity facing ***imminent and irreparable harm*** to her health, safety, or financial interest consults a lawyer, that lawyer may take legal action on behalf of the person even if a lawyer-client relationship has not been established if the lawyer reasonably believes the person has no other representative. Any action taken should be limited to that necessary to maintain the status quo or to avoid the harm.

a. Lawyer's Duties

A lawyer has the same duties to an "emergency" nonclient as he would with respect to a client. Normally, the lawyer would not seek compensation for emergency actions taken on behalf of the nonclient.

xvi. PROFESSIONAL RESPONSIBILITY MINI REVIEW

E. COMMUNICATING WITH THE CLIENT

A lawyer must: (1) promptly inform the client of any decision that requires the client's informed consent, (2) keep the client reasonably informed about the status of the matter and the means to be used to accomplish the client's objectives, (3) respond promptly when a client makes a reasonable request for information, and (4) consult with the client if the client expects the lawyer to do something illegal or unethical.

1. Special Circumstances

The amount and kind of information the lawyer should give to the client depend on the client's situation; e.g., a client with diminished capacity may require extra explanation and assistance. If a lawyer regularly represents a client, the two may work out a convenient arrangement for occasional reporting of routine developments.

2. Withholding Information from Client

A lawyer may delay the transmission of information to a client if the client would be likely to react imprudently to an immediate communication. Moreover, if a court rule or order forbids a lawyer from sharing information with a client, the lawyer must comply.

F. CONTRACTS CONCERNING CLIENT-LAWYER RELATIONSHIP

Any contract concerning the client-lawyer relationship (e.g., as to fees, the nature of the services, etc.) is generally enforceable by either party if it is otherwise lawful. However, the client may avoid the contract (including a modification to an existing contract) in the following circumstances: (1) the contract was made some time **after the representation began**, unless the lawyer shows that the contract and circumstances of its formation were fair and reasonable to the client; or (2) the contract was made **after the lawyer's work was completed**, and the client was not informed of facts needed to evaluate the appropriateness of the lawyer's compensation or other benefits conferred on the lawyer by the contract.

G. TERMINATING THE LAWYER-CLIENT RELATIONSHIP

The lawyer-client relationship normally continues until the end of the matter, but it can terminate prematurely in three ways: (1) the client can **fire** the lawyer; (2) in some situations, the lawyer **must** withdraw; and (3) in some situations, the lawyer **may** withdraw.

1. Client Fires Attorney

The client can fire the attorney at any time, with or without cause. The client is then liable to the attorney in **quantum meruit** for the reasonable value of the work done. If the attorney and client had a contract for a flat fee or maximum fee, the attorney cannot recover more than the amount contracted for. If the attorney and client had a contingent fee agreement, the attorney's quantum meruit claim does not arise until the contingency comes to pass (typically until the client gets a favorable judgment or settlement).

2. **Court Permission to Substitute Attorneys**
   In a litigation matter, local court rules typically require court permission for a client to fire her attorney, and the court may deny permission if a substitution of attorneys would cause undue delay or disruption. For the same reasons, the court may deny an attorney's request to withdraw, even if there is good cause for withdrawal.

3. **Mandatory Withdrawal**
   An attorney **must** withdraw from representation in two situations: (1) the attorney's mental or physical condition would make it unreasonable for him to continue representing the client; or (2) continued representation would require the attorney to violate a law or disciplinary rule.

4. **Permissive Withdrawal**
   An attorney **may** withdraw from representation **for any reason** if withdrawal does not have a material adverse effect on the client's interest or the client consents. An attorney may withdraw despite an adverse impact when the circumstances are so severe as to justify harm to the client's interests and:

   a. The client persists in **criminal or fraudulent conduct** (if the conduct requires the attorney's assistance, the attorney **must** withdraw).

   b. The client has used the attorney's services to commit a **past crime or fraud**.

   c. The client's **objective is repugnant** or against the lawyer's beliefs.

   d. The client **breaks his promise** to the attorney.

   e. The representation imposes an **unreasonable financial burden** on the attorney.

   f. The client **will not cooperate** in the representation.

   g. Other **good cause** for withdrawal exists.

5. **Attorney's Duties Upon Termination of Representation**
   Before withdrawing, an attorney must give the client reasonable notice of his withdrawal and a chance to get another attorney. When an attorney withdraws or is fired, the attorney must refund any advance on fees not yet earned and expenses not yet spent, and must turn over all papers and property to which the client is entitled.

III. CLIENT CONFIDENTIALITY

As a general rule, a lawyer must not reveal any information relating to the representation of a client. A lawyer may, however, reveal such information if the client gives informed consent or any of the other exceptions discussed in C., *infra*, applies.

A. RELATIONSHIP BETWEEN ETHICAL DUTY AND ATTORNEY–CLIENT PRIVILEGE

1. **Compulsion vs. Gossip**

   The **attorney-client privilege** is an exclusionary rule of evidence law that prevents the **government from compelling** the revelation of privileged communications. In contrast, the **ethical duty** of confidentiality prevents the **attorney from voluntarily disclosing** or misusing confidential information, and it applies in every context where the attorney-client privilege does not apply. The ethical duty also requires the attorney to make reasonable efforts to protect a client's confidential information from inadvertent or unauthorized disclosure by the lawyer and those under the lawyer's supervision, and from unauthorized access by third parties.

2. **Kinds of Information Covered**

   The attorney-client privilege protects only confidential communications between an attorney and client or their respective agents. In contrast, the ethical duty covers communications that are protected by the privilege **plus any other information** the attorney obtains relating to the representation, no matter what the source.

3. **Disclosure vs. Use**

   The attorney-client privilege prevents the government from compelling the disclosure of privileged communications. In contrast, the ethical duty of confidentiality prohibits the lawyer from either disclosing confidential information without the client's informed consent or using confidential information to the disadvantage of a client, former client, or prospective client without the affected client's informed consent.

B. SUMMARY OF ATTORNEY–CLIENT PRIVILEGE

The attorney-client privilege prohibits a court or other governmental tribunal from compelling disclosure of confidential communications between an attorney and a client, or their respective agents, if the communication concerns the professional relationship.

1. **Client**

   A "client" is a person or entity that seeks legal services from an attorney. The privilege covers preliminary communications leading up to an attorney-client relationship, even if no such relationship ultimately develops.

a. **Corporate Clients**

When the client is a corporation, the privilege covers communications between the lawyer and a high-ranking corporate official. It also covers communications between the lawyer and another corporate employee if three conditions are met: (1) the employee communicates with the lawyer at the direction of the employee's supervisor; (2) the employee knows that the purpose of the communication is to obtain legal advice for the corporation; and (3) the communication concerns a subject within the scope of the employee's duties to act for the corporation.

2. **Attorney**

An "attorney" means a person who is authorized (or whom the client reasonably believes to be authorized) to practice law in any state or nation.

3. **Communication**

"Communication" means information transmitted orally or in writing in either direction between the attorney and the client or their respective agents.

a. **Mechanics of Relationship**

The privilege generally does not cover the client's identity or the fee arrangement between the client and attorney, unless disclosing those facts is tantamount to disclosing a privileged communication.

b. **Preexisting Documents and Things**

A preexisting document or thing does not become privileged simply by turning it over to an attorney; if it would be discoverable in the client's hands, it is equally discoverable in the attorney's hands. If an attorney comes into possession of the fruits of a crime, or an instrument used to commit a crime, the attorney may keep it long enough to obtain information needed to represent the client, but the attorney must then turn it over to the proper authorities.

4. **"Confidential" Defined**

To be a protected "confidential" communication, the communication must have been made by a means not intended to disclose the communicated information to outsiders. Confidentiality is not destroyed by the presence of a third party who is present to aid the attorney-client relationship, and an eavesdropper can be prevented from testifying about a privileged communication. However, the presence of a third party who is not present to further the attorney-client relationship destroys the privilege.

5. **Client Holds Privilege**

The client (not the attorney) is the one who can claim or waive the privilege. Waiver will occur when there is a failure to claim the privilege when there is a chance to do so or when there is an intentional revelation of a significant part of the privileged communication. A client may also waive the privilege

by putting the legal services at issue in the case. If the client has not waived the privilege, and if someone tries to obtain privileged information when the client is not present, the attorney must claim the privilege on the client's behalf.

6. **Duration of Privilege**
    The attorney-client privilege continues indefinitely, surviving termination of the relationship and even the death of the client.

7. **Exceptions to Privilege**
    The privilege does not apply in situations where:

    a. The client seeks the attorney's services to engage in or assist a *future crime or fraud*.

    b. The communication is relevant to an issue of *breach of the duties arising out of the attorney-client relationship*.

    c. Civil litigation arises between two persons who were *formerly joint clients* of the attorney.

    d. The attorney is asked for evidence about the *competency or intent of a client* who has attempted to dispose of property by will or inter vivos transfer.

8. **Related Doctrine of Work Product Immunity**
    Generally, material prepared by a lawyer for litigation or in anticipation thereof is immune from discovery or other disclosure unless the opposition shows a substantial need for, and an inability to gather, the material without undue hardship. A lawyer's mental impressions or opinions are always immune from discovery unless immunity is waived.

C. **ETHICAL DUTY OF CONFIDENTIALITY AND ITS EXCEPTIONS**
    The ethical duty of confidentiality applies in every context in which the attorney-client privilege does not apply, and the ethical duty covers a broader range of information. The **exceptions** to the ethical duty are as follows:

    1. **Client's Informed Consent and Implied Authority**
        The attorney may disclose or use confidential information if the client gives informed consent or the attorney has implied authority from the client.

    2. **Dispute Concerning Attorney's Conduct**
        The attorney may reveal confidential information to the extent necessary to protect herself against a claim of malpractice, disciplinary violation, complicity with the client in illegal acts, or the like.

INFORMATION RELATING TO REPRESENTATION: SCOPE OF PROTECTION

Information necessary to prevent reasonably certain death or substantial bodily harm

Information relevant to a dispute involving the attorney's conduct (e.g., fee dispute, malpractice case, misconduct charges)

Client communications revealing intent to commit future crime or fraud reasonably certain to result in substantial financial harm if lawyer's services used (or to prevent or mitigate financial harm if client has already acted)

DUTY OF CONFIDENTIALITY

All information relating to representation of client protected *from voluntary disclosure and from use harmful to client*

Communications between attorney and client with third party present

Communications made when client seeks attorney's services in future crime or fraud

ATTORNEY-CLIENT PRIVILEGE

Confidential comnications protected against *compelled testimony*

Conversations between attorney and client

Letters and other documents between attorney and client

Relevant preexisting documents and things

Information concerning past frauds involving attorney's services

Mechanical details of attorney-client relationship (e.g., fee arrangement, client identity)

Information for which disclosure expressly or impliedly authorized by client

Information required to be disclosed by law or court order

Information necessary to detect or resolve conflicts of interest

Information necessary for the lawyer to obtain legal ethics advice

CMR Chart

3. **Disclosure to Obtain Legal Ethics Advice**
A lawyer may disclose enough of the client's confidential information as is necessary to obtain legal ethics advice for the lawyer.

4. **Disclosure Required by Law or Court Order**
A lawyer may reveal her client's confidential information to the extent that she is required to do so by law or court order.

5. **Disclosure to Prevent Death or Substantial Bodily Harm**
A lawyer may reveal her client's confidential information to the extent that the lawyer reasonably believes necessary to prevent ***reasonably certain death or substantial bodily harm***.

6. **Disclosure to Prevent or Mitigate Substantial Financial Harm**
A lawyer may reveal the client's confidential information to the extent necessary to prevent the client from committing a crime or fraud that is reasonably certain to result in ***substantial financial harm*** to someone, if the client is using or has used the lawyer's services in the matter. The same is true if the client has already acted and the lawyer's disclosure can prevent or mitigate the consequent financial harm.

7. **Disclosure to Detect and Resolve Conflicts of Interest**
A lawyer may disclose limited client information (e.g., names, brief summary of issues involved in a matter) to detect or resolve conflicts of interest when the lawyer changes firms, when two law firms merge, or when a law practice is being purchased. However, the following conditions apply: (1) the disclosure may be made only after substantive discussions regarding the new relationship have occurred; (2) the disclosure must be limited to the minimum necessary to detect any conflicts of interest; (3) the disclosed information must not compromise the attorney-client privilege or otherwise prejudice the clients; and (4) the disclosed information may be used only to the extent necessary to detect and resolve any conflicts of interest.

Note: The above exceptions give the lawyer ***discretion*** to disclose the confidential information; they do ***not require*** disclosure.

IV. CONFLICTS OF INTEREST

A. **CONFLICTS OF INTEREST—THE GENERAL RULES**
A lawyer must not allow her personal interests, the interests of another client, or the interests of a third person to interfere with her loyalty to the client.

1. **Consequences of a Conflict of Interest**
If a conflict of interest is apparent ***before*** a lawyer takes on a client's matter, the lawyer must not take it on (unless the conflict can be solved with

consent). If a conflict becomes apparent **after** the lawyer has taken on the client's matter, the lawyer must withdraw (unless the conflict can be solved with consent). A lawyer's failure to handle a conflict properly can result in: (1) disqualification as counsel in a litigated matter, (2) professional discipline, and (3) civil liability for legal malpractice.

2.   **Imputed Conflicts of Interest**

Generally, lawyers who practice together in a "firm" are treated as a single unit for conflict of interest purposes—i.e., when one lawyer cannot handle a matter because of a conflict, the conflict is said to be "imputed" from the first lawyer to the other lawyers in the "firm." Whether a group of lawyers constitutes a "firm" depends on many factors, including whether: (1) they have a formal agreement, (2) they hold themselves out as if they practice as a firm, (3) they share their revenues and responsibilities, (4) they have physical access to each other's client files, (5) they routinely talk among themselves about the matters they are handling, and (6) the purpose of the particular conflict rule would be served by imputing one lawyer's conflict to other lawyers in the group.

   a.   **Exceptions to Imputed Disqualification**

   A conflict will generally **not** be imputed to other lawyers in the firm: (1) where the conflict is **personal to the disqualified lawyer** (e.g., a family or romantic relationship) and does not present a significant risk of materially limiting the representation of the client by the remaining lawyers in the firm; or (2) in certain situations where the conflict involves the disqualified lawyer's former employment or consultations, and the disqualified lawyer is **timely screened** from participation in the matter and is apportioned no part of the fee from the matter.

B.   **CONFLICTS OF INTEREST—CURRENT CLIENTS**

1.   **Concurrent Conflicts of Interest**

A lawyer must not represent a client if: (1) the representation of one client will be **directly adverse** to another client; or (2) there is a **significant risk** that the representation of one client will be **materially limited** by the lawyer's own interest or by the lawyer's responsibilities to another client, a former client, or a third person.

2.   **Informed Consent Can Solve Some Conflicts**

Despite a concurrent conflict of interest, a lawyer **may** represent a client if: (1) the lawyer reasonably believes that he can competently and diligently represent each affected client; (2) the representation is not prohibited by law; (3) the representation does not involve the assertion of a claim by one client against another client represented by the lawyer in the same litigation (or other proceeding before a tribunal); **and** (4) each affected client gives informed consent, confirmed in writing.

       a. **"Informed" Consent**

            "Informed" consent means that each affected client must understand how the conflict can harm him.

       b. **Revocation of Consent**

            The client can almost always revoke a previously given consent to a conflict of interest.

3. **Specific Conflict Situations Concerning "Direct Adversity"**

Examples of direct adversity include: (1) representing a client in a matter against another client that the lawyer represents in different matters; or (2) vigorously cross-examining a client in the course of representing another client.

       a. **Unnamed Members of a Class Do Not Count as Clients**

            In class action litigation, the unnamed members of a class ordinarily are *not* regarded as clients for purposes of this conflicts rule.

4. **Specific Conflict Situations Concerning "Material Limitation"**

As noted above, a lawyer must not represent a client if the representation of that client may be *materially limited* by the lawyer's own interests or by the lawyer's responsibilities to another client, a former client, or a third person, unless each affected client gives informed consent, confirmed in writing. The discussion in a. through e., below, provides specific illustrations of this rule.

       a. **Representing Multiple Parties in the Same Matter**

          1) **Representing Co-Parties in Criminal Litigation**

              Because the interests of criminal co-defendants are likely to diverge, a lawyer ordinarily should not try to defend two people in a criminal case.

          2) **Representing Multiple Parties in Civil Matters**

              In civil litigation, one lawyer *may* represent co-plaintiffs or co-defendants whose interests are potentially in conflict. A lawyer also may represent multiple parties in a nonlitigation matter. However, the conflict must be addressed in accordance with 3), below.

              a) **Confidentiality and Privilege Problems**

                 In litigation between two former joint clients of a single lawyer, neither client can claim the attorney-client privilege; therefore, before undertaking multiple representation, the lawyer should explain that whatever one client discloses will be shared with the other client.

LAWYER'S REPRESENTATION OF CURRENT CLIENTS WITH CONFLICTING INTERESTS

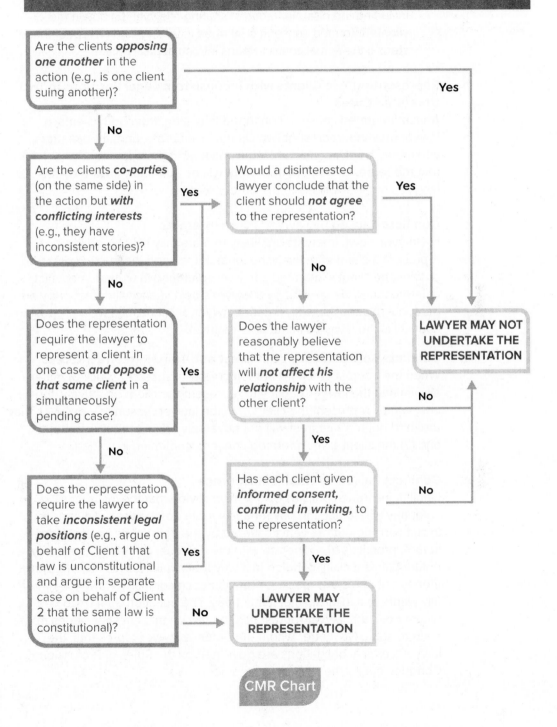

Are the clients **opposing one another** in the action (e.g., is one client suing another)?

No ↓   Yes →

Are the clients **co-parties** (on the same side) in the action but **with conflicting interests** (e.g., they have inconsistent stories)?

No ↓   Yes →

Does the representation require the lawyer to represent a client in one case **and oppose that same client** in a simultaneously pending case?

No ↓   Yes →

Does the representation require the lawyer to take **inconsistent legal positions** (e.g., argue on behalf of Client 1 that law is unconstitutional and argue in separate case on behalf of Client 2 that the same law is constitutional)?

No →   Yes →

Would a disinterested lawyer conclude that the client should **not agree** to the representation?

No ↓   Yes →

Does the lawyer reasonably believe that the representation will **not affect his relationship** with the other client?

Yes ↓   No →

Has each client given **informed consent, confirmed in writing,** to the representation?

Yes ↓   No →

LAWYER MAY NOT UNDERTAKE THE REPRESENTATION

LAWYER MAY UNDERTAKE THE REPRESENTATION

CMR Chart

3) Handling Multiple Representation Conflicts

In both litigation and nonlitigation matters, the lawyer should: (1) analyze the facts and determine whether she can effectively represent each client; (2) disclose the potential conflict to each client, including the disadvantages of sharing a lawyer; (3) obtain the clients' informed consent, confirmed in writing; and (4) repeat these steps if the actual conflict ripens into an actual conflict.

b. Representing Two Clients with Inconsistent Legal Positions in Two Unrelated Cases

Absent informed consent, confirmed in writing, from both clients, a lawyer must not represent two clients in separate, unrelated matters when they have inconsistent legal positions if there is a substantial risk that the representation of one client will be materially limited by the lawyer's responsibilities to the other client.

c. Conflicts Caused by Lawyer's Own Interests

If a lawyer's own interests are likely to materially limit his ability to represent a client effectively, he must not take on the matter unless he obtains the client's informed consent, confirmed in writing. A conflict of interest may be created by a lawyer's own financial interest or by his personal relationship with another lawyer or client (e.g., when opposing counsel is the lawyer's immediate relative).

d. Conflicts Between Client's Interest and Third Person's Interest

When the interest of a third person creates a substantial risk of materially limiting the lawyer's ability to represent the client effectively, the lawyer may represent the client if: (1) the lawyer reasonably believes that the third person's interest will not adversely affect the representation; and (2) the client gives informed consent, confirmed in writing.

e. Conflicts Raised by Liability Insurance

Liability insurance policies commonly provide that the insurance company will select and pay for a lawyer to defend the policyholder in suits arising out of events covered by the policy. The policyholder, in turn, promises to cooperate with the defense. Generally, the policyholder wants a claim handled in a way that minimizes his risk of paying money out of his own pocket. The insurance company, however, generally wants to minimize what it must pay. The question then becomes whom does the lawyer represent? The law on this question varies from state to state. No matter whom the defense lawyer represents, the lawyer's ethical obligations are governed by the Rules of Professional Conduct, not by the insurance contract.

C. CONFLICTS OF INTEREST—SPECIFIC RULES FOR CURRENT CLIENTS

1. **Misuse of Client's Confidential Information**
A lawyer must not use a client's confidential information to the client's disadvantage or to benefit the lawyer or someone else, unless the client gives informed consent or some other exception to the duty of confidentiality applies. The same rule applies to misuse of a former client's or a prospective client's confidential information. A lawyer who uses the confidential information for his own pecuniary gain (other than in the practice of law) may be subject to civil liability—i.e., he may have to account to the client, former client, or prospective client for his profits.

2. **Business Transactions with Client and Money or Property Interests Adverse to Client**
A lawyer must not enter into a business transaction with a client or knowingly acquire an ownership, possessory, security, or money interest that is adverse to a client unless all of the following conditions are satisfied:

   a. The terms of the business transaction (or the terms on which the interest is acquired) are **fair to the client**;

   b. The terms are **fully disclosed** to the client **in writing**, expressed in a manner that the client can reasonably understand;

   c. The client is advised **in writing** that he should get the **advice of an independent lawyer** about the arrangement before entering into it; and

   d. The client gives **informed consent, in a writing that the client signs**.

   This rule does not apply to an ordinary fee agreement between the lawyer and client or to standard commercial transactions in which the lawyer buys goods or services that the client routinely markets to the public.

3. **Proprietary Interest in Subject of Litigation**
A lawyer must not acquire a proprietary interest in the client's cause of action or the subject matter of the litigation. Contingent fees and attorney's liens are exceptions to this rule, even though each gives the lawyer a type of interest in the subject of the litigation.

4. **Gifts to Lawyer from Client Who Is Not a Relative**

   a. **Soliciting Substantial Gift**
   A lawyer is prohibited from **soliciting** a substantial gift from a client who is not the lawyer's relative. A lawyer may, however, accept a small gift from a client, such as a token of appreciation or an appropriate holiday gift. A lawyer also may accept a substantial gift from a client, although the gift may be voidable for undue influence.

b. Preparing Legal Instrument that Creates Substantial Gift

A lawyer must not prepare a legal instrument in which the client gives the lawyer or his relatives a substantial gift, except when the client is a relative.

c. Lucrative Appointments

A lawyer is not prohibited from seeking to have himself or his law partner or associate named as executor of an estate or counsel to the executor or to some other fee-paying position. However, the general conflict of interest principles do prohibit such efforts if the lawyer's advice is tainted by the lawyer's self-interest.

5. **Acquiring Literary or Media Rights Concerning a Client's Case**

A lawyer must not acquire literary or media rights to a story based in substantial part on the lawyer's representation of a client. However, a lawyer may acquire such rights *after* the client's legal matter is entirely completed, including appeals.

6. **Financial Assistance to Client in Litigation**

Except as permitted below, a lawyer must not give any financial help to a client in the context of pending or contemplated litigation.

a. Advancing Litigation Expenses

A lawyer may advance court costs and other litigation expenses on the client's behalf, and repayment may be contingent on the outcome of the case.

b. Paying Costs and Expenses for Indigent Client

A lawyer may pay the court costs and litigation expenses for an indigent client, without any provision for repayment.

c. Modest Gifts When Representing Indigent Client Pro Bono

A lawyer representing an indigent client pro bono may provide modest gifts to the client for food, rent, transportation, medicine, and other basic living expenses. However, the lawyer must not: (1) promise or imply the availability of such gifts prior to retention, or as an inducement to continue the client-lawyer relationship after retention; (2) seek or accept reimbursement from the client or anyone affiliated with the client; or (3) publicize or advertise a willingness to provide such gifts to prospective clients.

7. **Aggregate Settlement Agreements**

A lawyer who represents several co-parties in a matter must not participate in the making of an aggregate settlement agreement unless: (1) the *clients come to an agreement* about how the aggregate sum will be shared; (2) *the lawyer discloses to each client all terms of the sharing agreement* including the total amount that will be paid, the existence and nature of all claims, defenses, and pleas involved in the settlement, the details of every other client's participation in the settlement, and how and by whom the lawyer's fees will be paid; and (3) each client gives **informed consent in a signed writing**. Note that the extensive disclosures required by (2) above may require the lawyer to share one client's confidential information with the others. Thus, the lawyer should get informed consent to do so from each client at the outset of the matter.

a. **Class Action Settlements**

In a class action, the lawyer who represents the class ordinarily does not have a complete lawyer-client relationship with the unnamed members of the class. Even so, at settlement time, the class's lawyer must follow all of the class action rules concerning notice and other procedural requirements that protect the unnamed class members.

b. **Aggregate Settlement of Criminal Case**

The same rules that apply to an aggregate settlement in a civil case also apply to a joint plea bargain in a criminal case.

8. **Compensation from Third Person**

A lawyer must not accept compensation from a third person for representing a client unless: (1) the client gives informed consent, (2) the third person does not interfere with the lawyer's judgment in representing the client, and (3) the arrangement does not compromise the client's confidential information.

9. **Sexual Relationship Between Lawyer and Client**

A lawyer who has sexual relations with a client is subject to discipline, whether or not the client consents and whether or not the client is harmed— **unless** their consensual sexual relationship **predated** the lawyer-client relationship. When the client is an organization, this rule applies to any person who supervises, directs, or regularly consults with the lawyer concerning the organization's legal matters.

a. **No Imputation**

The other specific conflicts discussed in 1. - 8., above, are imputed to other lawyers in the disqualified lawyer's firm. However, a conflict created by a sexual relationship is **personal** in nature and is not imputed to the lawyer's colleagues.

b. **Pre-Existing Relationship May Still Cause Conflict**

Even where the sexual relationship predated the lawyer-client relation-ship, the sexual relationship might "materially limit" the lawyer-client relationship and implicate the general conflict of interest rule for current clients (see B., *supra*).

D. DUTIES TO FORMER CLIENTS

1. Continuing Duty of Confidentiality

An attorney has a continuing duty to preserve information gained in confidence during the representation, even after the representation ends.

2. Using Confidential Information to Former Client's Disadvantage

A lawyer must not use confidential information to a former client's disadvantage without informed consent, confirmed in writing, from the former client. This rule is inapplicable to generally known information or information the lawyer would be permitted to reveal under an exception to the duty of confidentiality.

3. Opposing Former Client in Substantially Related Matter

Absent informed consent, confirmed in writing, from the former client, a lawyer must not represent a client whose interests are materially adverse to those of the former client in a matter that is "substantially related" to a matter in which the lawyer represented the former client. Matters are substantially related if: (1) they involve the same transaction or legal dispute, or (2) there otherwise is a substantial risk that confidential factual information as would normally have been obtained in the prior representation would materially advance the new client's position.

4. Clients of Former Firm

A lawyer whose firm formerly represented a client in a matter and who acquired protected confidential information [Rule 1.6] or information pertaining to the representation [Rule 1.9(c)] may not thereafter represent another person in the same or a substantially related matter if that person's interests are materially adverse to those of the former client, unless the former client gives informed consent, confirmed in writing.

5. Disqualification of Lawyer's New Firm

If a lawyer is disqualified from representing a client under the rules set out in 3. - 4., above, and the lawyer joins a new firm, the new firm may be disqualified as well unless (1) the lawyer is properly screened (i.e., does not work on the case, discuss it with those who do, or have access to case files) and does not share fees from the matter, and (2) the former client is given notice.

6. Disqualification of Lawyer's Former Firm

A lawyer's former firm is prohibited from representing a person with interests materially adverse to those of a client of the formerly associated lawyer if: (1) the matter is the same or substantially related to that in which the formerly associated lawyer represented the client; and (2) any lawyer remaining in the firm has information protected by Rules 1.6 or 1.9(c).

E. CONFLICTS INVOLVING PROSPECTIVE CLIENTS

1. **Lawyer's Duty Concerning Confidential Information**
    The attorney-client privilege protects confidential communications between a lawyer and a prospective client. The ethical duty of confidentiality also applies to consultations between a lawyer and prospective client. Thus, the lawyer must not reveal or use information learned during those consultations, unless an exception to the duty of confidentiality applies.

2. **Lawyer's Duty Concerning Conflict of Interest**
    A lawyer who obtains confidential information during a consultation with a prospective client must not later represent a different person in the same or a substantially related matter if the confidential information could significantly harm the prospective client. This conflict is imputed to others in the lawyer's firm.

3. **How to Overcome a Prospective Client Conflict**
    One way to overcome a prospective client conflict is to obtain informed consent, confirmed in writing, from the affected client and the prospective client. A second way to overcome the conflict is to satisfy all of the following conditions:

    a. Demonstrate that the lawyer took care to *avoid exposure to any more confidential information than was necessary* to determine whether to represent the prospective client;

    b. Demonstrate that the disqualified lawyer is *timely screened from any participation in the matter* and will not share the fee; and

    c. Give *written notice* to the prospective client.

F. CONFLICT RULES FOR CURRENT AND FORMER GOVERNMENT OFFICERS AND EMPLOYEES

The government has a right to expect that its confidential information will not be abused by a lawyer who switches from government to private practice. On the other hand, the government needs good lawyers, and a rigid rule of disqualification would discourage some lawyers from entering government service. Thus, the ABA adopted disqualification rules (see below) that are narrow and flexible.

1. **Federal and State Conflict of Interest Laws**
    Lawyers who move between government and private jobs must comply not only with the legal ethics rules, but also with various state and federal conflict of interest statutes and regulations.

2. **Private Work Following Government Work on Same Matter**
    A lawyer who leaves government service and enters private practice must

not represent a private client in a *matter* in which the lawyer participated *personally and substantially* while in government service, unless the government agency gives informed consent, confirmed in writing. "*Matter*" means a specific dispute involving specific facts and parties. "*Personally and substantially*" means that the lawyer worked on the matter herself and that her work was more than trifling.

a. **Imputed Disqualification**
   If a lawyer is disqualified by the above rule, the other lawyers in her firm are also disqualified unless:

   1) The former government lawyer is *timely screened off* from the case;

   2) The former government lawyer is *not apportioned a part of the fee* earned in the case; *and*

   3) *Written notice* is given to the government agency to enable it to make sure that the above conditions are met.

3. **Subsequent Use of Information Gained During Government Service**
   A government lawyer who receives confidential government information about a person must not later represent a private client whose interests are adverse to that person, when the information could be used to harm that person.

   a. **Imputed Disqualification**
      If a former government lawyer is disqualified by this rule, then the other lawyers in her firm are also disqualified unless the former government lawyer is timely screened off from the case and is not apportioned any part of the fee earned in the case.

4. **Current Government Service After Private Practice**

   a. **Ordinary Conflict Rules Apply**
      The ordinary conflict rules regarding current and former clients apply to a lawyer who enters government service after private practice (or other nongovernmental work). (*See* IV.B., D., *supra*.)

   b. **"Personal and Substantial" Rule Also Applies**
      If a lawyer worked "personally and substantially" on a "matter" in private practice (or other nongovernmental employment), the lawyer must not work on that same matter when she later enters government service, whether or not the later work would be adverse to a former client. However, informed consent, confirmed in writing, can solve the conflict.

c. Negotiating for Private Employment

When a person in government service is currently working personally and substantially on a matter, she must not negotiate for private employment with any party or lawyer who is involved in that matter. There is an exception to this rule for law clerks (*see* G.3., below).

G. CONFLICTS INVOLVING FORMER JUDGES, ARBITRATORS, AND THE LIKE

1. Switching from Judicial Service to Private Law Practice

The conflict issues and the ethics rules about switching from judicial service to private practice are similar to those described above. The general rule is that a lawyer must not represent a private client in a matter in which the lawyer previously participated personally and substantially while serving as a judge or other adjudicative officer (or as a law clerk to such person) or as an arbitrator, mediator, or other third-party neutral, unless all parties to the proceeding give informed consent, confirmed in writing.

2. Screening Can Avoid Imputed Disqualification

If a lawyer is disqualified under this rule, the other lawyers in her firm are also disqualified unless the following conditions are met: (1) the lawyer is timely screened off from the matter; (2) the lawyer is not apportioned any part of the fee earned in the matter; and (3) written notice is given to the parties and the appropriate tribunal so that they can ensure that the above conditions are met.

3. Law Clerks Negotiating for Private Employment

A law clerk to a judicial officer must notify the officer before negotiating for private employment with a party (or the attorney for a party) in a matter in which the law clerk is participating personally and substantially.

4. Other Adjudicative Officers Negotiating for Private Employment

The lenient rule that applies to law clerks does not apply to judges, arbitrators, mediators, third-party neutrals, or other adjudicative officers. They are forbidden to negotiate for private employment with a party (or attorney for a party) in a matter in which they are participating personally and substantially.

V. COMPETENCE, MALPRACTICE, AND OTHER CIVIL LIABILITY

A. COMPETENCE

In representing a client, a lawyer must act competently and with the legal knowledge, skill, thoroughness, and preparation that are reasonably necessary for the representation.

1. Legal Knowledge and Skill

In determining whether a lawyer has the necessary skill to handle a matter, factors to be considered include the complexity and specialized nature of

the matter; the lawyer's general experience and his training and experience in the field in question; the amount of preparation and study the lawyer will give to the matter; and whether it is possible for the lawyer to refer the matter to, or consult with, another competent lawyer.

a. Becoming Competent Through Preparation
A lawyer may accept representation if the requisite competence can be achieved by reasonable preparation.

b. Emergency Situations
A lawyer who is not competent in the field may assist a client in an emergency, but the assistance should not exceed what is reasonably necessary to meet the emergency.

2. Thoroughness and Preparation
A lawyer must inquire into and analyze the facts and legal elements in order to adequately prepare a matter.

3. Retaining Other Lawyers to Assist in the Matter
Sometimes a lawyer may gain competence in a matter by consulting with other lawyers. Before a lawyer retains or contracts with lawyers outside her firm to assist in the provision of legal services to the client, the lawyer: (1) must reasonably believe that the services of the outside lawyers will contribute to the competent and ethical representation of the client, and (2) "should ordinarily" obtain the client's informed consent.

4. Maintaining Competence—Technology and Continuing Legal Education
Lawyers should keep abreast of changes in the law or its practice, including the benefits and risks associated with relevant technology. Moreover, a lawyer must comply with all applicable continuing legal education requirements.

B. DILIGENCE
Once a lawyer takes on a client's matter, the lawyer must:

1. Act on the client's behalf with *reasonable diligence and promptness*;

2. Act with dedication and *zeal*, taking whatever lawful and ethical steps are available to vindicate the client's cause;

3. Pursue the matter to *completion* (unless the lawyer is fired, or is required or permitted to withdraw); and

4. Either terminate the relationship or act with the required diligence if there is any doubt as to whether a *lawyer-client relationship exists*.

In addition to the above, a solo practitioner has a duty to plan for his untimely death or disability by designating another competent lawyer to review the clients' files and determine whether protective action is required.

C. **SINGLE VIOLATION SUFFICIENT TO IMPOSE DISCIPLINE**
A single incident of misconduct subjects a lawyer to professional discipline. Special circumstances are considered regarding sanctions, but not as to whether there is a violation. To avoid discipline, a lawyer must act reasonably to put his cases on temporary hold if necessary due to personal circumstances.

D. **MALPRACTICE AND OTHER CIVIL LIABILITY**

1. **Relationship Between Disciplinary Matters and Malpractice Actions**
A malpractice action differs from a disciplinary matter in three ways: (1) the forum in a malpractice action is a civil court, not a disciplinary tribunal; (2) in a malpractice action, the lawyer's adversary is an injured plaintiff, not the state bar; and (3) the purpose of a malpractice action is to compensate the injured plaintiff, not to punish the lawyer or to protect the public from future wrongs.

2. **Ethics Violation as Evidence of Malpractice**
The violation of an ethics rule does not automatically mean that the lawyer has committed malpractice, nor does it create a presumption of malpractice, but courts do treat it as *relevant evidence* of malpractice.

3. **Theories of Malpractice Liability**
The plaintiff in a legal malpractice action has a choice of legal theories, including: (1) *intentional tort* (such as fraud, misrepresentation, malicious prosecution, abuse of process, or misuse of funds); (2) *breach of fiduciary duties* (these duties include loyalty, confidentiality, and honest dealing); (3) *breach of contract* (either an express contract or an implied promise by the lawyer to use ordinary skill and care); and (4) simple *negligence*, the most common theory in legal malpractice actions.

   a. **Elements of Negligence**
   Simple negligence requires the plaintiff to prove four elements: a duty of due care, a breach of that duty, legal causation, and damages.

      1) **Duty of Due Care**
      An attorney owes a duty of due care not only to her *client*, but also to *any third party* where: (1) the third party was intended to benefit by the attorney's rendition of legal services, or (2) the attorney invited the third person to rely on her opinion or legal services. The standard of care for an attorney is the competence and diligence normally exercised by attorneys in similar circumstances. If an attorney represents to a client that she has greater competence or will exercise greater diligence than that normally demonstrated by attorneys undertaking similar matters, she is held to that higher standard.

2) Breach of Duty of Due Care

An attorney is not liable for "mere errors of judgment" as long as the judgment was well-informed and reasonably made. An attorney is expected to do reasonably competent legal research; if the answer to a legal question could have been found by using standard research techniques, the attorney's failure to find it is a breach of the duty of due care. Furthermore, if a reasonably prudent attorney would have referred a difficult matter to a legal specialist, a general practitioner's failure to do so can be a breach of the duty of due care.

3) Legal Causation

A malpractice plaintiff must prove that the injury would not have happened **but for** the defendant's negligence, and that it is fair under the circumstances to hold the defendant liable for unexpected injuries or for expected injuries that happen in unexpected ways.

4) Damages

A malpractice plaintiff must prove damages. The plaintiff can recover for direct losses and indirect but foreseeable losses.

4. Civil Liability Other than Malpractice

A lawyer also may be liable to a client on other grounds, such as breach of contract (e.g., by failing to comply with the fee agreement) or breach of warranty (but note that general predictions of success in the case will not result in liability).

5. Liability for Negligence of Others

An attorney can be held liable for injuries caused by a negligent legal secretary, law clerk, or other person acting within the scope of his employment (**respondeat superior**). In a general partnership, each law firm partner is jointly and severally liable for the negligence of other partners committed in the ordinary course of partnership business. (However, if the firm is set up as a limited liability entity, the partners may be shielded from personal liability for the misconduct of others.)

6. Malpractice Insurance

The ABA Model Rules and the vast majority of states do not require lawyers to carry malpractice insurance, but prudent lawyers carry ample coverage.

7. Settling Malpractice Claims

A lawyer must not settle a pending or potential malpractice claim with an unrepresented client or former client without first **advising that person, in writing, to seek independent advice** about the settlement and giving that person time to seek that advice.

> **CMR Exam Tip** A lawyer who has breached a duty to his client cannot escape discipline by reimbursing the client for any loss.

8. **Contracting with Client to Limit Malpractice Liability**

A lawyer is prohibited from contracting with a client to prospectively limit her malpractice liability, **unless the client is independently represented** in making the contract. (However, a lawyer may agree prospectively with a client to arbitrate all legal malpractice claims, provided that such an agreement is proper under local law and the client understands the scope and effect of the agreement.)

VI. LITIGATION AND OTHER FORMS OF ADVOCACY

A. MERITORIOUS CLAIMS AND CONTENTIONS ONLY

A lawyer is subject to discipline for bringing a frivolous proceeding or taking a frivolous position on an issue in a proceeding. A "frivolous" position is one that cannot be supported by a good faith argument under existing law and cannot be supported by a good faith argument for changing the law. This rule does not prohibit a lawyer for a **criminal defendant** from conducting the defense so that the prosecutor must prove every necessary element of the crime.

B. DUTY TO EXPEDITE LITIGATION

A lawyer has an affirmative duty to expedite litigation. The duty to expedite does not require the lawyer to take actions that would harm the client's interests, but realizing financial or other gain from delay is **not** a legitimate interest.

C. DUTY OF CANDOR TO THE TRIBUNAL

1. **Candor About Applicable Law**

An attorney is subject to discipline for **knowingly** making a false statement of law to the court or failing to correct a previously made false statement of material law. Furthermore, an attorney must disclose a legal authority in the **controlling jurisdiction** that is **directly adverse** to his client's position and that has not been disclosed by the adversary.

2. **Candor About Facts of Case**

An attorney is subject to discipline for **knowingly** making a false statement of fact to the court or failing to correct a previously made false statement of material fact. An attorney's **failure to speak** out is, in some contexts, the equivalent of an affirmative misrepresentation.

3. **No Obligation to Volunteer Harmful Facts**

An attorney generally has no duty to volunteer a fact that is harmful to his client's case, except that a lawyer in an **ex parte** proceeding must inform the tribunal of **all material facts** known to the lawyer that will help the tribunal make an informed decision.

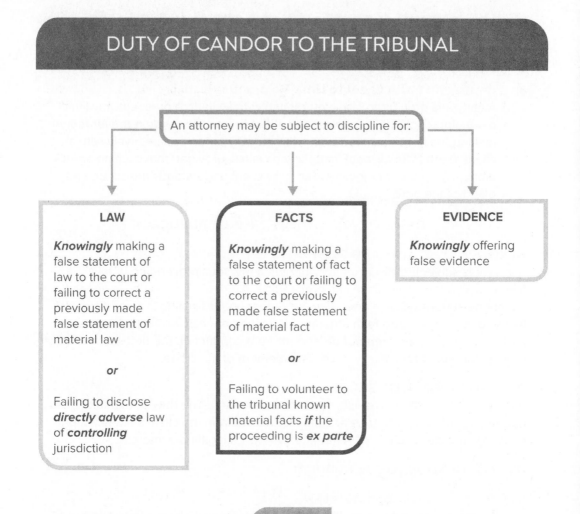

DUTY OF CANDOR TO THE TRIBUNAL

An attorney may be subject to discipline for:

LAW

Knowingly making a false statement of law to the court or failing to correct a previously made false statement of material law

or

Failing to disclose ***directly adverse*** law of ***controlling*** jurisdiction

FACTS

Knowingly making a false statement of fact to the court or failing to correct a previously made false statement of material fact

or

Failing to volunteer to the tribunal known material facts ***if*** the proceeding is ***ex parte***

EVIDENCE

Knowingly offering false evidence

CMR Chart

4. **Using False Evidence**

A lawyer is subject to discipline for offering evidence that the lawyer ***knows*** is false and may refuse to offer evidence that she ***reasonably believes*** is false, except for a criminal defendant's testimony on his own behalf. If a lawyer has offered a piece of evidence and later discovers that it is false, she must:

(i)   Talk to the client confidentially and ***try to persuade*** him to rectify the situation;

(ii) If that fails, seek to ***withdraw***; and

(iii) If withdrawal is not permitted or will not remedy the situation, the lawyer must make ***disclosure*** to the court.

Note that this obligation ceases at the conclusion of the proceedings, which include appeals.

> **CMR** Exam Tip
>
> Beware of an exam question in which the client prevails in a proceeding, the opposing party does not file an appeal, and the client *then* tells the lawyer in confidence that he lied. Remember that the lawyer is under no obligation to reveal the perjury to anyone because the proceeding is over.

a. False Testimony by Criminal Defendant

Under the ABA Model Rules and the Restatement, when the client insists on testifying to something that the lawyer knows is false, the criminal defense lawyer should follow the three steps stated above.

5. Other Corruption of an Adjudicative Proceeding

A lawyer who represents a client in an adjudicative proceeding must take appropriate measures to prevent any person from committing criminal or fraudulent conduct that will corrupt the proceedings. Examples of such conduct are: (1) hiding or destroying evidence, (2) bribing a witness, (3) intimidating a juror, (4) buying a judge, and (5) failing to obey a law or court order to disclose information.

D. DUTY OF FAIRNESS TO OPPOSING PARTY AND COUNSEL

1. Opponent's Access to Evidence

A lawyer must not suppress or tamper with evidence.

2. Falsifying Evidence and Assisting in Perjury

A lawyer must neither falsify evidence nor counsel or assist a witness to testify falsely.

3. Abusing Discovery Procedures

A lawyer must not make frivolous discovery requests or fail to make reasonable efforts to comply with a legally proper discovery request made by an adversary.

4. Paying Witnesses

A lawyer must not offer an inducement to a witness that is prohibited by law. Except when local law prohibits, the following payments to witnesses are proper:

a. Travel, meals, and lodging expenses;

b. Compensation for time lost from the witness's job; and

c. Reasonable fees to expert witnesses, but these may not be contingent on the outcome of the case or the content of the expert's testimony.

5. **Securing Absence or Noncooperation of Witness**
A lawyer must not advise or cause a person to secrete himself or to flee the jurisdiction for the purpose of making him unavailable as a witness. However, a lawyer may advise a person not to voluntarily give information to an opponent or other party if: (1) the person is a client or relative, employee, or agent of a client; and (2) the lawyer reasonably believes that the person's interests will not be harmed by not volunteering the information.

6. **Violating Court Rules and Orders**
A lawyer must not knowingly violate a rule of procedure, a rule of evidence, a rule of court, or an order made by the court, but a lawyer may refuse to obey such a rule or order in making a good faith challenge to its validity.

7. **Chicanery at Trial**
A lawyer is subject to discipline for chicanery at trial, including:

   a.   Referring to inadmissible material;

   b.   Asserting personal knowledge of contested facts; and

   c.   Asserting personal opinions about the justness of a cause, credibility of a witness, culpability of a civil litigant, or guilt or innocence of an accused.

8. **Using Threats to Gain Advantage in Civil Case**
A lawyer may bring, or threaten to bring, criminal charges against her adversary in order to gain an advantage for her client in a civil case if the criminal and civil matters are closely related and the civil case and criminal charges are warranted. However, a lawyer must not threaten to report adversary counsel for a disciplinary violation to gain such an advantage. Disciplinary violations cannot be used as bargaining chips.

E.   DUTY TO PRESERVE IMPARTIALITY AND DECORUM OF TRIBUNAL

1. **Improper Influence**
A lawyer must not seek to influence a judge, court official, juror, or prospective juror by improper means.

2. **Improper Ex Parte Communication**
While a proceeding is pending in a tribunal, a lawyer must not have an ex parte communication with a judge, court official, juror, or prospective juror except when authorized by law or court order.

   a.   **Judges and Court Officials**
   A *written* communication to a judicial officer is not ex parte if a copy of the communication is timely sent to the opposing parties. A lawyer,

however, must not communicate *orally* on the *merits* of a matter with a judicial officer without giving adequate notice to her adversary.

b. **Jurors and Prospective Jurors**

In general, before and during the trial of a case, a lawyer connected with the case must not communicate on *any subject* with a juror or prospective juror. She may, however, discreetly investigate members of a jury panel for limited reasons, e.g., background, grounds for challenge, etc. Although reviewing a juror's or prospective juror's public Internet presence is generally permissible, sending an "access request" to the person's social media account is prohibited. After the trial is over and the jury is discharged, a lawyer must not communicate with a former jury member if: (1) local law or a court order prohibits such communication; (2) the juror has told the lawyer that he does not want to communicate; or (3) the communication involves misrepresentation, coercion, or harassment. Also, even a lawyer who is *not* connected with the case must not communicate with a juror *about the case* during trial.

3. **Disruptive Conduct**

A lawyer must not engage in conduct intended to disrupt a tribunal.

F. **TRIAL PUBLICITY**

The litigants' right to a fair trial must be balanced against the rights of the press and the public to disseminate and to receive information. ABA Model Rule 3.6 prohibits a lawyer connected with the case from making out-of-court public statements that the lawyer reasonably should know will have a substantial likelihood of materially prejudicing the case.

1. **Right of Reply**

Despite the above rule, a lawyer may make a public statement that a reasonable lawyer would believe is required to protect a client from the substantial undue prejudicial effect of recent publicity not initiated by the lawyer or the lawyer's client.

2. **Additional Constraint on Criminal Prosecutors**

A prosecutor must not make extrajudicial comments that have a substantial likelihood of heightening public condemnation of the accused.

3. **Dry Facts About Case Permitted**

Despite the general rule against prejudicial statements, a lawyer connected with the case may publicly state certain "dry facts" about the case, including: (1) any information already in the public record, (2) what claim and defense are involved, (3) the names of the people involved, (4) the scheduling or result of any step in litigation, (5) the fact that an investigation is ongoing, (6) a warning of danger if appropriate, and (7) routine booking information about a criminal defendant (name, address, arresting officers, etc.).

4. **Rules Apply to Associated Lawyers**
   The rules on trial publicity apply equally to other lawyers who are associated in a law firm or agency with the lawyers participating in the case.

G. TRIAL COUNSEL AS WITNESS

1. **Reasons to Avoid Dual Role**
   Several problems arise when a trial lawyer also testifies as a witness: conflict of interest, confusion of advocacy with evidence, and unfairness to the adversary.

2. **Ethical Limitations Imposed**
   For the above reasons, a lawyer must not act as an advocate at a trial in which she is likely to be a *necessary* witness.

   a. **Exceptions**
      A lawyer-witness may continue as trial counsel if:

      1) Her testimony will concern only an *uncontested matter* or a *mere formality*;

      2) Her testimony will concern only the nature and value of the *legal services* rendered in the case;

      3) Her withdrawal as trial counsel would cause a *substantial hardship* on her client; or

      4) Another lawyer in her firm is likely to be called as a witness (unless to continue would constitute a conflict of interest).

3. **Conflict of Interest Rules Also Apply**
   In addition to complying with the above rule, a lawyer who is both an advocate and a witness must also comply with the general conflict of interest principles regarding current and former clients. (*See* IV.B., D., *supra*.)

VII. TRANSACTIONS AND COMMUNICATIONS WITH PERSONS OTHER THAN THE CLIENT

A. TRUTHFULNESS IN STATEMENTS TO THIRD PERSONS

1. **Must Not Make False Statements of Material Fact or Law**
   When dealing on behalf of a client with a third person, a lawyer must not make false statements of law or fact. Conventional puffery, however, is permitted.

2. **Must Disclose Material Fact to Avoid Client's Crime or Fraud**
   A lawyer must disclose material facts to a third person when necessary to avoid assisting the client in a crime or fraud—*unless* the lawyer is forbidden to do so by the *ethical duty of confidentiality*, in which case the ABA Model Rules require the lawyer to withdraw.

B. COMMUNICATION WITH PERSONS REPRESENTED BY COUNSEL

1. **When Communication Forbidden**

   A lawyer must not communicate about a matter with a person the lawyer knows is represented by counsel in that matter, unless that person's counsel consents, or unless the law or a court order authorizes the communication. This is true even if the represented person initiates or consents to the communication.

2. **Application to Organizations**

   Corporations and other organizations are "persons" for the purpose of this rule. Such entities are comprised of individuals referred to as constituents—i.e., officers, directors, employees, and shareholders of a corporation (or individuals in analogous positions in noncorporate organizations). Thus, a lawyer must get the consent of the organization's counsel before communicating with a *present* organization constituent: (1) who *supervises, directs, or regularly consults with the organization's lawyer* about the matter; (2) whose conduct may be *imputed* to the organization under civil or criminal law; or (3) who has *authority to obligate the organization* concerning the matter. However, if the constituent is represented in the matter by her own counsel, then consent by that counsel (rather than the organization's counsel) is sufficient. Consent is *not* needed before talking to a *former* constituent of the organization. However, when talking with either a present or former constituent, a lawyer must take care not to violate the organization's legal rights, such as the attorney-client privilege.

3. **Communications Allowed by Rule**

   A lawyer may communicate with a represented person when authorized by law or court order or when the communication does not concern the subject of the representation. Also, represented parties are not prohibited from communicating directly with each other. Furthermore, a lawyer is not prohibited from interviewing the intended unrepresented witnesses of the opposing party.

   a. **Exception—Lawyers Acting Pro Se**

      When a lawyer is representing themself (acting pro se), they are considered to be representing a client and therefore prohibited from communicating with a represented person.

C. DEALING WITH UNREPRESENTED PERSONS

When dealing with an unrepresented person, a lawyer must not state or imply that he is disinterested and must make reasonable efforts to correct any misunderstanding by the unrepresented person as to his role in the matter. Likewise, if the lawyer knows that his client's interests are likely to be in conflict with those of the unrepresented person, he must not give legal advice to that person (other than to get a lawyer).

ATTORNEY COMMUNICATIONS WITH THIRD PARTIES

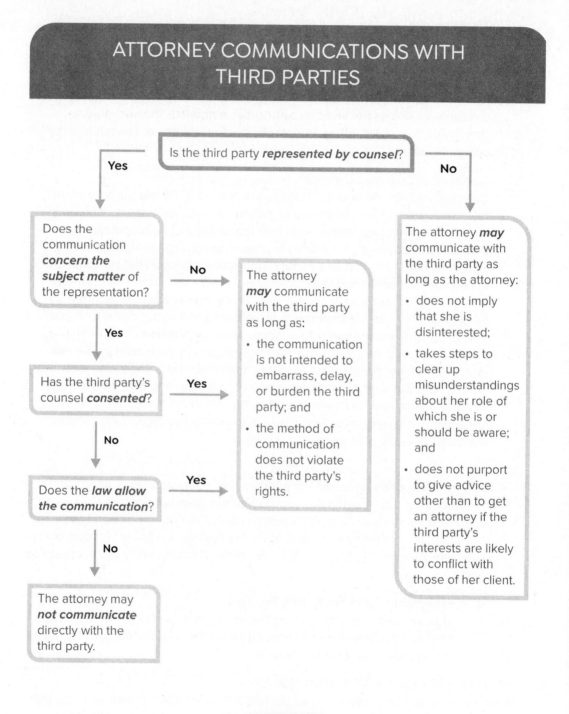

Is the third party *represented by counsel*?

Yes

No

Does the communication *concern the subject matter* of the representation?

No →

The attorney *may* communicate with the third party as long as:

- the communication is not intended to embarrass, delay, or burden the third party; and

- the method of communication does not violate the third party's rights.

Yes

Has the third party's counsel *consented*?

Yes →

No

Does the *law allow the communication*?

Yes →

No

The attorney may *not communicate* directly with the third party.

The attorney *may* communicate with the third party as long as the attorney:

- does not imply that she is disinterested;

- takes steps to clear up misunderstandings about her role of which she is or should be aware; and

- does not purport to give advice other than to get an attorney if the third party's interests are likely to conflict with those of her client.

CMR Chart

D. RESPECT FOR RIGHTS OF THIRD PERSONS

In representing a client, a lawyer must not use means that have no substantial purpose other than to embarrass, delay, or burden a third person. A lawyer must not use methods of obtaining evidence that violate the legal rights of a third person.

1. Documents Sent to Lawyer By Mistake

When a lawyer obtains a document or electronically stored information by mistake, and knows that it was sent by mistake, she must promptly notify the sender so that the sender can take protective measures.

VIII. DIFFERENT ROLES OF THE LAWYER

A. LAWYER AS ADVISOR TO THE CLIENT

1. Duty to Render Candid Advice

A lawyer must exercise independent judgment and render candid advice to the client.

2. Giving Advice Beyond the Law

A lawyer may give a client not only legal advice, but also moral, economic, social, or political advice when relevant to the client's situation.

3. Volunteering Advice

When appropriate, a lawyer may volunteer advice without being asked.

B. EVALUATION FOR USE BY THIRD PERSONS

A lawyer may evaluate a client's affairs for the use of a third person if the lawyer reasonably believes that making the evaluation is compatible with the lawyer's other responsibilities to the client. If the lawyer knows that the evaluation will materially harm the client, the lawyer must obtain the client's informed consent before making the evaluation.

1. Confidentiality

Except as disclosure is authorized in connection with a report of an evaluation, the ordinary rules of confidentiality apply to information gained during the evaluation.

2. Liability to Third Person

A lawyer may be liable to a third person for a negligent evaluation of a client's affairs.

C. LAWYER AS NEGOTIATOR

During negotiations, a lawyer must not make a false statement of **material fact**. However, a lawyer need not volunteer facts that would be detrimental to the client's position or correct an opponent's misapprehension regarding the strength

of his client's case. The key factor in determining whether a statement contains a material fact is whether the opponent would be reasonable in relying on the statement; e.g., ***estimates of price or value*** and ***what a party would accept as a settlement*** are ***not*** statements of material fact.

D. LAWYER AS THIRD-PARTY NEUTRAL

A lawyer serves as a third-party neutral when she assists two or more nonclients in resolving a dispute between them (e.g., arbitrator, mediator). When a lawyer serves as a third-party neutral, she is subject not only to the ordinary rules of legal ethics, but also to various codes of conduct devised by groups such as the American Arbitration Association.

1. Warning to Unrepresented Parties

A lawyer who serves as a third-party neutral does not represent any of the parties. Because a party may erroneously believe that the lawyer is protecting his interests, the lawyer must explain the situation to the unrepresented party. The lawyer should explain that the attorney-client privilege does not apply to communications between them.

2. Conflicts of Interest

A lawyer who serves as a third-party neutral in a matter must not thereafter become the lawyer for anyone involved in the matter, unless all of the parties give their informed consent, confirmed in writing. Such a conflict is also imputed to lawyers in the disqualified lawyer's firm, but may be cured by screening the disqualified lawyer and notifying the parties in writing about the screening arrangement. No conflict arises when a lawyer who served as a partisan arbitrator for a party is later asked to become that party's lawyer.

E. SPECIAL RESPONSIBILITIES OF A PROSECUTOR

A prosecutor must assure that a defendant is tried by fair procedures and that guilt is decided on proper and sufficient evidence.

1. Must Have Probable Cause

A prosecutor must not proceed with a charge that she knows is not supported by probable cause.

2. Protecting Accused's Right to Counsel

A prosecutor must make reasonable efforts to assure that the accused is advised of the right to counsel, advised of the procedure for obtaining counsel, and given a reasonable opportunity to obtain counsel.

3. Securing Waiver of Pretrial Rights

A prosecutor must not seek to obtain from an unrepresented accused a waiver of important pretrial rights.

4. Disclosing Evidence that May Help Defense

A prosecutor must timely disclose to the defense all evidence and information known to the prosecutor that tends to negate the guilt of the accused or mitigate the degree of the offense.

5.   **Disclosing Information that May Mitigate Punishment**
When a convicted person is to be sentenced, the prosecutor must disclose to the defense and the court all unprivileged mitigating information known to the prosecutor.

6.   **Disclosing Evidence to Remedy Conviction**
A prosecutor must promptly disclose new, credible, and material evidence that creates a reasonable likelihood that a defendant was wrongly convicted. Further, the prosecutor must seek to remedy the conviction of a defendant in his jurisdiction if he knows of clear and convincing evidence that the defendant was innocent.

7.   **Public Statements About Pending Matters**
Except for statements necessary to inform the public of the nature and extent of the prosecutor's action and that serve a legitimate law enforcement purpose, a prosecutor must not make extrajudicial statements that have a substantial likelihood of heightening public condemnation of the accused. The prosecutor must take reasonable care to prevent investigators, police, employees, and other subordinates from making such statements.

8.   **Subpoenaing Other Lawyers**
A prosecutor must not subpoena a lawyer to give evidence about a client unless the information is not privileged, is essential, and cannot be obtained in any other way.

9.   **Other Government Lawyers**
Many of the above duties also apply to all government lawyers. A government lawyer with discretionary power regarding civil litigation should not institute or continue unfair actions. A government lawyer has a responsibility to develop a full record and must not use her position or power to harass parties or to force unjust settlements or results.

F.   **ADVOCATE IN LEGISLATIVE AND ADMINISTRATIVE PROCEEDINGS**

1.   **Appearances in a Representative Capacity**
When a lawyer appears on behalf of a client before a legislative body or administrative agency, the lawyer must disclose that he is acting in a representative capacity.

2.   **Duties of Candor and Respect**
In such appearances, the lawyer must generally follow the same rules of conduct as though in court.

3. **Limits of These Rules**
   These rules do ***not*** apply: (1) when a lawyer represents a client in bilateral negotiations with the government, (2) in an application for a license or other privilege, (3) when the government is investigating the client's affairs, or (4) when the government is examining the client's compliance with a regular reporting requirement (such as the filing of tax returns).

G. ORGANIZATION AS CLIENT

1. **Duty of Loyalty to Organization**
   A lawyer owes a duty of loyalty to the organization, not to the people (stockholders, officers, directors, etc.) who are its constituents.

2. **Conflicts Between Organization and Its Constituents**
   When the interests of the organization and one of its constituents are in conflict, the lawyer for the organization should caution the person in question that she represents the organization, not the person.

3. **Protecting Organization's Interests**
   When a person associated with the organization advocates an action that may cause it substantial injury, a lawyer must protect the interests of the organization. The lawyer ordinarily must report the action to a higher authority in the organization, and if necessary to the highest authority. If the highest authority fails to take timely, appropriate action, the lawyer ***may report*** the relevant information to appropriate persons ***outside*** of the organization (even if the information is protected by the duty of confidentiality). The lawyer is only authorized to do so to the extent the lawyer reasonably believes is necessary to ***prevent substantial injury*** to the organization. However, when a lawyer is hired by the organization to investigate an alleged violation of law or defend the organization or its constituents against an alleged violation of law, the lawyer may not report any information outside of the organization.

4. **Representing Both Organization and an Associated Person**
   The lawyer for an organization may represent both the organization and one of its constituents if the ordinary conflict of interest rules are satisfied.

5. **Serving as Both Director and Lawyer**
   A lawyer may serve as both a director and as a lawyer for an organization, but the dual role can create conflicts of interest. For example, when a lawyer participates in a meeting as a director, the attorney-client privilege will not apply to communications at the meeting, but some of the other directors may not realize that. If there is a substantial risk that the dual role will compromise the lawyer's professional judgment, the lawyer should either resign as director or not act as the organization's lawyer.

6.   **Securities Lawyer's Duties Under Sarbanes-Oxley Act**
Congress passed the Sarbanes-Oxley Act, which instructs the Securities and Exchange Commission ("SEC") to make rules for securities lawyers who discover that their clients are violating federal or state securities laws. The following discussion includes highlights of the rules adopted by the SEC.

a.   **Application to "Securities Lawyers"**
The rules apply to lawyers who represent an issuer of securities and who practice before the SEC ("securities lawyers"). This includes lawyers who give advice about a document that will be filed with the SEC or advice about whether information must be filed with the SEC.

b.   **Reporting Requirement**
If a securities lawyer becomes aware of credible evidence that her client is materially violating a federal or state securities law, she **must** report the evidence to her client's chief legal officer ("CLO"). The same reporting duty applies to credible evidence that one of her client's personnel has breached a fiduciary duty under federal or state law, or has committed a "similar material violation" of federal or state law.

c.   **Investigation by CLO**
The CLO must investigate the situation to determine whether a violation occurred.

d.   **If Violation Found—"Appropriate Response" Required**
If the CLO concludes that a violation occurred, the CLO must take all reasonable steps to get the client to make an "appropriate response." That means that the client must stop or remedy the violation and make sure it does not happen again. The CLO must report those results to the securities lawyer.

e.   **When Appropriate Response Not Taken**
If the securities lawyer believes that the CLO did not achieve an appropriate response from the client, the securities lawyer **must** report the evidence to either the client's board of directors, the audit committee of the board, or a committee made up of outside directors. Note that the Sarbanes-Oxley reporting rule is **mandatory**, unlike ABA Model Rule 1.13(b), which gives the lawyer some discretion about how to proceed (*see* 3., *supra*).

f.   **Revealing Confidential Information**
A securities lawyer **may** reveal to the SEC any confidential information that is reasonably necessary to: (1) stop the client from committing a violation that will cause substantial financial injury to the client or its investors; (2) rectify such a financial injury if the lawyer's services were used to further the violation; or (3) prevent the client from committing or

suborning perjury in an SEC matter or lying in any matter within the jurisdiction of any branch of the federal government.

g. **Compliance with Rules**
A securities lawyer who complies with the Sarbanes-Oxley rules cannot be held civilly liable for doing so and cannot be disciplined under any inconsistent state rule.

h. **Action When Securities Lawyer Is Fired**
If a securities lawyer is fired for complying with the Sarbanes-Oxley rules, she may report the firing to the client's board of directors (thus setting up the client for an expensive wrongful termination suit).

IX. SAFEKEEPING FUNDS AND OTHER PROPERTY

A lawyer is subject to discipline for misappropriating or borrowing a client's money or property or for commingling it with her own money or property. The following rules apply to funds or other property held by a lawyer in connection with a representation.

A. SAFEGUARDING PROPERTY
A lawyer must identify a client's property as belonging to the client and must put it in a safe place. Lawyers are required to hold the property of others **with the care required of a professional fiduciary**. Accordingly, a lawyer cannot use the client's property for her own purposes, and must promptly take reasonable steps necessary to safeguard the client's property.

B. CLIENT TRUST FUND ACCOUNT
All money that a lawyer receives in connection with a representation must promptly be placed in a client trust fund account, separate from the lawyer's own personal and business accounts.

1. **Type of Account**
The client trust fund account must be located in the state where the lawyer practices (or elsewhere with the client's consent). Ordinarily, a lawyer must not put her own money into the client trust account, but she may do so for the sole purpose of paying bank service charges.

a. **Large Sum Held for Long Period**
If the lawyer is entrusted with a large sum for a long period, it should go into a separate interest-bearing account, and the interest belongs to the client for whom it is held.

b. **Small Sums**
If the lawyer is entrusted with a small sum to hold for a short period, the lawyer should put it into a pooled client trust account, which is typically

a checking account that holds money entrusted by numerous clients. Under Interest On Lawyer Trust Account ("IOLTA") programs, if a client entrusts a lawyer with a sum that is too small to earn any net interest, the lawyer must put it into a pooled checking account that earns interest. After the bank deducts its service charges from the interest, the bank sends the remaining interest to the state bar or to a legal foundation, which uses the interest to fund charitable legal programs. The United States Supreme Court has upheld the constitutionality of IOLTA programs.

2. **Funds that Must Be Placed in Account**

   a. **Advances**

   Advances for costs and expenses and legal fees not yet earned must be put into a trust account. The lawyer may make withdrawals as fees are earned if there is no dispute concerning the lawyer's right to do so.

   b. **Disputed Funds**

   If there is a dispute over funds (between the lawyer and the client, or between the client and some third person), the lawyer must keep the disputed portion in the client trust account until the dispute is resolved. This is further discussed in D., *infra*.

C. **DUTY TO NOTIFY, KEEP RECORDS, RENDER ACCOUNTINGS, AND PAY OVER PROMPTLY**

A lawyer must keep complete, accurate, and up-to-date records of money or property received on behalf of a client, must render periodic accountings to the client, must notify the client promptly when money or property has been received on the client's behalf, and must promptly pay over money or deliver property when it is due to the client or a third party.

D. **DISPUTED PROPERTY**

When a lawyer is in possession of property in which two or more persons (one of whom may be the lawyer) claim interests, the ***disputed portion of the property must be kept separate*** by the lawyer until the dispute is resolved. The lawyer must promptly distribute all portions of the property as to which the interests are not in dispute.

1. **Funds in Which Both Client and Lawyer Have Interest**

   When a lawyer receives funds that are to be used, in part, to pay the lawyer's fee, they must be put into a trust account until there is an accounting and severance of the respective amounts due the lawyer and the client. If the client disputes the amount that is due to the lawyer, then the disputed portion must be kept in the client trust account until the dispute is resolved.

 CMR Exam Tip   A common exam fact pattern asks whether an attorney who receives a settlement check or other payment to the client from which his fee is to be paid can properly forward the entire sum to the client. For exam purposes, the answer is yes, it is ethically proper. (As a practical matter, however, most attorneys would prefer to control the purse until the fee is paid; i.e., most attorneys would retain the *fee amount in the client trust fund account* pending an accounting.)

2. **Funds in Which a Third Party Has an Interest**
Sometimes a third party (e.g., client's creditor) has an interest in funds that come into the lawyer's possession on behalf of a client. Statute, common law, or contract may require the lawyer to protect the third party's interest against interference by the client; accordingly, when the third party's claim is not frivolous, the lawyer must refuse to surrender the funds to the client until the claim is resolved.

X. COMMUNICATIONS ABOUT LEGAL SERVICES

A. **CONTENT-BASED RULES FOR ADVERTISING AND OTHER COMMUNICATIONS**

1. **Basic Rule—Communications Must Be True and Not Misleading**
A lawyer is subject to discipline for any type of communication about the lawyer or the lawyer's services that is false or misleading. A statement can be false or misleading if it omits material information, would lead a reasonable person to an unfounded conclusion, creates unjustified expectations, or makes unsubstantiated comparisons. In some circumstances, including a disclaimer can cure the problem.

2. **Identification of Advertiser**
Every advertisement or other communication about the lawyer's or firm's services must include the name and contact information (website address, telephone number, e-mail address, or physical office location) of at least one lawyer or law firm that is responsible for its content.

3. **Firm Names, Letterheads, and Other Professional Designations**

a. **Using Names of Deceased or Retired Partners**
A private law partnership may be designated by the names of one or more of its current members. When partners die or retire, their names may be carried over to successor partnerships. However, a law firm name is misleading if it includes the name of a deceased lawyer who was not a former member of the firm, the name of any lawyer who is not associated with the firm or predecessor firm, or the name of a nonlawyer.

b. Using Names of Lawyers Who Have Entered Public Service

A private law firm must not use the name of a lawyer who holds public office (either as part of the firm name or in communications on the firm's behalf) during any **substantial** period in which the lawyer is not regularly and actively practicing with the firm.

c. Must Not Imply Connection with Public or Charitable Organization

Trade names (e.g., "The Bulldog Law Firm") are permitted, provided the name is not misleading and does not imply a connection with a governmental agency or with a public or charitable legal services organization. If the trade name is a geographical name (e.g., Greater Chicago Legal Clinic), a disclaimer explaining that it is not a public legal aid organization may be required.

d. False Indications of Partnership

Lawyers must not imply that they are partners or are practicing together as one law firm unless they really are.

e. Multistate Firms

A law firm that has offices in more than one jurisdiction may use the same name, Internet address, or other professional designation in each jurisdiction.

4. Identifying Fields of Practice

A lawyer may communicate that she does or does not practice in particular fields of law, and may claim to "specialize" or "concentrate" in a field if not false or misleading. However, a lawyer must not state or imply that she is **certified as a specialist** in a particular field of law, unless: (1) the lawyer has in fact been certified as a specialist by an organization that has been approved by the ABA or by an appropriate state authority; and (2) the name of the certifying organization is clearly identified in the communication.

a. Patent and Admiralty Lawyers

Lawyers who practice admiralty law may call themselves "Proctors in Admiralty," or something similar, and lawyers who have been admitted to practice before the United States Patent and Trademark Office may call themselves "Patent Attorneys," or something similar. A lawyer's communications about these practice areas are not prohibited by the rule above.

B. RECOMMENDATIONS

Subject to the exceptions below, a lawyer **must not compensate, give anything of value, or promise** to give anything of value to a person for recommending the lawyer's services.

> **CMR** Exam Tip
> Promising or giving something "of value" does not always mean giving money or property. It can also mean providing services for free, sending clients someone's way, etc.

1. **Paying for Advertising and Other Services**
   A lawyer may pay the **reasonable costs of permitted advertisements**. Additionally, a lawyer may pay the **usual charges of a legal service plan**, a not-for-profit lawyer referral service, or a qualified lawyer referral service.

2. **Purchase of a Law Practice**
   A lawyer may purchase a law practice, even though the seller is, in a sense, recommending the purchasing lawyer to her clients.

3. **Reciprocal Referral Arrangements**
   A lawyer may set up a reciprocal referral arrangement with another lawyer or with a nonlawyer professional. A reciprocal arrangement **must not be exclusive**, the referred client must be **told** about the arrangement, and the arrangement must not interfere with the lawyer's professional judgment as to making referrals or providing substantive legal services. Reciprocal referral arrangements should not be of indefinite duration and should be reviewed periodically to make sure that they comply with the ABA Model Rules.

> **CMR** Exam Tip
> Don't confuse reciprocal referral agreements with referral **fees** (which are generally prohibited, with certain exceptions). In a reciprocal referral agreement, no money is exchanged—the parties are simply referring clients or customers to each other.

4. **Nominal Gifts or Gratuities**
   A lawyer may give a nominal gift or gratuity as an expression of appreciation to a person who recommended the lawyer or the lawyer's firm, provided the gift or gratuity was not intended or reasonably expected to be a form of compensation for recommending the lawyer's services.

C. **SOLICITATION**
   A solicitation is a communication *initiated by a lawyer or firm* that is directed to a specific person the lawyer knows or reasonably should know needs legal services in a particular matter, and that offers to provide, or can reasonably be understood as offering to provide, legal services for that matter.

   1. **Live Person-to-Person Solicitation Generally Prohibited**
      A lawyer or firm must not, by live person-to-person contact, solicit professional employment when a significant motive for doing so is the lawyer's or firm's pecuniary gain (offers to represent a person for free are permitted). "Live person-to-person contact" means in-person, face-to-face, live

telephone, or other real-time visual or auditory person-to-person communications (e.g., Skype or FaceTime) where the targeted person is subject to a direct personal encounter without time for reflection.

    a. Exceptions to Prohibition—Certain Targets Are Considered Less Vulnerable

        A lawyer or firm is generally not prohibited from initiating live person-to-person contact with (1) other lawyers; (2) persons with whom the lawyer or firm has a familial, close personal, or prior professional or business relationship (including current and former clients); or (3) routine business users of the type of legal services offered by the lawyer or firm.

2. Written, Recorded, or Electronic Solicitation Generally Permitted

Generally, a lawyer is not prohibited from sending truthful, nondeceptive written communications (via mail, e-mail, text message, chat room message, etc.) to persons known to face a specific legal problem.

3. Circumstances Rendering All Contacts Impermissible

A lawyer is prohibited from soliciting professional employment, regardless of what method is used or who the target is, if the solicitation involves *coercion, duress, or harassment*, or if the person has indicated he does not wish to be solicited.

4. Use of Others to Solicit

A lawyer must not use agents or other third parties to solicit in a manner the lawyer may not, and supervising lawyers must make reasonable efforts to ensure all employees are trained on solicitation rules. Note that, generally, recommendations and referrals from former clients, friends, or family do not fall within the solicitation rules.

D. GROUP AND PREPAID LEGAL SERVICE PLANS

A lawyer may personally contact a group that proposes to adopt a prepaid or group legal service plan. Furthermore, the plan may itself make personal contact with prospective subscribers who are not known to need specific legal services. However, the lawyer must not participate in the plan if she owns or directs the operating organization.

E. GOVERNMENT REGULATION OF COMMUNICATIONS ABOUT LEGAL SERVICES

The Supreme Court has recognized lawyer advertising as commercial speech protected by the First and Fourteenth Amendments. States may thus adopt reasonable regulations to ensure that the advertising is not false or misleading, but they may not completely prohibit all lawyer advertising.

1. False and Misleading Ads and In-Person Solicitation May Be Banned

A state may prohibit all lawyer advertising that is false or misleading and may forbid in-person solicitation for profit. To prevent misleading commercial speech, the government may require commercial advertisers to make certain disclosures if such a requirement is not unduly burdensome and is reasonably related to the state's interest in preventing deception.

2. **Regulation of Truthful, Nondeceptive Advertising**
Regulation of commercial speech is subject to intermediate constitutional scrutiny, which means that it may be regulated only if: (1) the government asserts a *substantial interest*, (2) the government demonstrates that the restriction *directly and materially advances the interest*, and (3) the regulation is *narrowly drawn*.

XI. LAWYERS' DUTIES TO THE PUBLIC AND THE LEGAL SYSTEM

A. PRO BONO PUBLICO SERVICE
Every lawyer has a professional responsibility to provide legal service to people who cannot afford it. ABA Model Rule 6.1 *recommends* (but does not require) a minimum of 50 hours per year of uncompensated legal work for poor people or organizations that serve the needs of poor people.

B. COURT APPOINTMENTS
Lawyers have an ethical obligation to help make legal service available to all who need it by accepting a fair share of unpopular matters and unpopular or indigent clients. A lawyer must not seek to avoid court appointments to represent clients except for good cause. Examples of good cause are: (1) to represent the client would require the lawyer to violate a law or disciplinary rule, (2) representing the client would impose an unreasonable financial burden on the lawyer, or (3) the lawyer's personal feelings would prevent her from representing the client effectively.

C. LIMITED LEGAL SERVICES PROGRAMS
A lawyer may participate in a quick-advice program (also called a "limited legal services" program) sponsored by a court or nonprofit organization, such as a legal-advice hotline, advice-only clinic, or program that shows people how to represent themselves in small claims court. A lawyer-client relationship exists between the lawyer and person who obtains the quick advice, but neither the lawyer nor person expects the relationship to continue past the quick-advice stage.

1. **Client Consents to Short-Term, Limited Legal Service**
The lawyer must obtain the client's informed consent to the limited scope of the relationship. If the lawyer's quick advice is not enough to set the client on the right track, the lawyer must advise the client to get further legal help.

2. **Conflict of Interest Rules Are Relaxed**
The conflict of interest rules are relaxed somewhat in a quick-advice situation, but the remainder of the Rules of Professional Conduct fully apply. Because a lawyer who participates in a quick-advice program ordinarily has no time

to do an ordinary conflict of interest check, the conflicts principles regarding current and former clients do not apply unless the lawyer *actually knows* that giving the quick advice creates a conflict of interest. (*See* IV.B., D., *supra*, for a discussion of conflict of interest rules.)

3. **Imputed Conflict Rule Is Also Relaxed**
   The rule of imputed conflicts of interest is also relaxed in a quick-advice situation. A lawyer may dispense advice in a quick-advice program unless the lawyer *actually knows* that he is disqualified from doing so because of a conflict imputed from another lawyer in his firm. Conversely, a conflict created by advice a lawyer dispenses in a quick-advice program will not be imputed to others in the lawyer's firm.

4. **Conflicts Rules Apply Fully If Quick Advice Leads to Regular Representation**
   If a person who has received quick advice from a lawyer then wants to hire that lawyer to render further service in the matter, the ordinary conflict of interest rules apply to that further service.

D. **MEMBERSHIP IN LEGAL SERVICES ORGANIZATIONS**
   Lawyers are encouraged to support and work for legal services organizations that provide legal assistance to poor people. But conflicts of interest may arise between people thus served and a lawyer's regular, paying clients.

   1. **General Rule—May Serve as Director, Officer, or Member**
      A lawyer may serve as a director, officer, or member of a legal services organization, even though the organization serves persons whose interests are adverse to those of the lawyer's regular clients.

   2. **Limitations on Rule**
      A lawyer must not knowingly participate in a decision or action of the organization if doing so: (1) would be incompatible with the lawyer's obligations to a client under the general conflict of interest rules, or (2) would adversely affect the representation of one of the organization's clients.

E. **LAW REFORM ACTIVITIES AFFECTING CLIENT INTERESTS**

   1. **Activities that May Harm Client**
      A lawyer may serve as a director, officer, or member of a law reform group, even though a reform advocated by the group may harm one of the lawyer's clients.

   2. **Activities that May Benefit Client**
      When a lawyer is working on a law reform project and is asked to participate in a decision that could materially benefit one of the lawyer's clients, the lawyer must disclose that fact—but the lawyer need not identify the client.

F. ASSISTING IN JUDICIAL MISCONDUCT

A lawyer is subject to discipline for **knowingly** assisting a judge or judicial officer in conduct that violates the Code of Judicial Conduct or other law.

G. STATEMENTS ABOUT JUDICIAL AND PUBLIC LEGAL OFFICIALS

A lawyer must not make a statement that the lawyer knows is false (or with reckless disregard as to its truth or falsity) about the qualifications or integrity of a judge, hearing officer, or public legal official, or about a candidate for judicial or other legal office.

H. LAWYER RUNNING FOR JUDICIAL OFFICE

A lawyer who is running for judicial office must comply with the applicable provisions of the Code of Judicial Conduct.

I. ABILITY TO INFLUENCE GOVERNMENT OFFICIALS

A lawyer must never state or imply that he has the ability to improperly influence a government agency or official or to achieve results by means that violate the law or legal ethics rules.

J. POLITICAL CONTRIBUTIONS TO OBTAIN GOVERNMENT EMPLOYMENT

A lawyer or firm must not accept government legal employment or a judicial appointment if the lawyer or firm makes a political contribution **for the purpose of obtaining such employment or appointment**. *Exceptions:* This rule does not apply to employment or appointments: (1) for uncompensated services, (2) made on the basis of a lawyer's experience and following a process that is free from influence based on political contributions, or (3) made on a rotating basis from a list compiled without regard to political contributions.

XII. JUDICIAL ETHICS

A. SELECTION, TENURE, AND DISCIPLINE OF JUDGES

1. **Federal Judges**

   Federal judges are appointed by the President with the advice and consent of the Senate. They hold office for life during good behavior. A federal judge can be removed from office by impeachment.

2. **State Judges**

   In some states, judges are appointed by the governor or the state legislature, while in others they are elected by the voters. In still others, judges are initially appointed and later retained or rejected by the voters.

3. **Code of Judicial Conduct**

   The ABA's Code of Judicial Conduct ("CJC") serves as a model for state and federal judiciaries in formulating their own standards of judicial conduct. The CJC is binding on the judges and all persons who perform judicial functions in a jurisdiction where the CJC has been adopted by the appropriate authority.

B. **PROMOTION OF JUDICIAL INTEGRITY AND AVOIDANCE OF APPEARANCE OF IMPROPRIETY**

The CJC requires a judge to uphold and promote the independence, integrity, and impartiality of the judiciary and avoid actual impropriety as well as the appearance of impropriety.

1. **Compliance with Law and Promotion of Public Confidence in the Judiciary**

   A judge must comply with the law (including the CJC). ***At all times*** a judge must act so as to promote public confidence in the independence, integrity, and impartiality of the judiciary.

2. **Test for Appearance of Impropriety**

   An "appearance of impropriety" arises when a judge's conduct would create a reasonable perception that she has violated the CJC or acted in some other manner that reflects adversely on her honesty, impartiality, temperament, or fitness as a judge.

3. **Community Outreach**

   To promote public understanding of and confidence in the administration of justice, a judge should initiate and participate in community outreach activities.

4. **Abuse of Judicial Prestige**

   A judge must not abuse, or permit others to abuse, the prestige of her office to advance her personal or economic interests or those of others.

   a. **References and Recommendations**

   Based on personal knowledge, a judge may act as a reference or provide a recommendation for someone.

C. **IMPARTIAL, COMPETENT, AND DILIGENT PERFORMANCE OF JUDICIAL DUTIES**

The CJC requires a judge to perform the duties of judicial office impartially, competently, and diligently.

1. **Judicial Duties**

   Judicial duties take precedence over all of the judge's other activities.

2. **Hearing and Deciding Assigned Matters**

   A judge must hear and decide all matters assigned to her unless disqualification is required.

3. **Impartiality and Fairness**

   A judge must uphold and apply the law, and must perform her duties fairly and impartially.

4. **External Influences on Judicial Conduct**
   Family, social, political, or financial interests must not influence a judge's conduct or judgment.

5. **Competence, Diligence, and Cooperation**
   A judge must perform her judicial and administrative duties competently and diligently. Also, a judge must cooperate with other judges and court officials in the administration of court business.

6. **Ensuring Right to Be Heard**
   A judge must allow every person with a legal interest in a proceeding the right to be heard according to law. Although a judge may encourage settlements, he must not act so as to coerce a settlement.

7. **Avoidance of Bias, Prejudice, and Harassment**
   A judge must avoid bias, prejudice, and harassment, including that which is based on race, sex, gender, religion, national origin, ethnicity, disability, age, sexual orientation, marital status, socioeconomic status, or political affiliation.

8. **Ex Parte Communications**
   A judge must not initiate, permit, or consider communications between the judge and a representative for one side of a matter when no representative from the other side is present, except: (1) when expressly authorized by law; (2) with the consent of the parties in an attempt to settle or mediate a pending matter; or (3) as circumstances require in emergency or administrative matters, provided no party will gain an advantage and the other party is properly notified. Inadvertent receipt of an unauthorized ex parte communication relating to substantive matters requires prompt notification to the parties and an opportunity to respond.

9. **Communications from Others**
   Except in the following circumstances, a judge must not initiate, permit, or consider communications to the judge outside the presence of the parties concerning a pending or impending matter.

   a. **Court Personnel**
      A judge may consult other judges and court personnel whose function is to aid the judge in carrying out her responsibilities provided that the judge: (1) makes reasonable efforts to avoid receiving factual information that is not part of the record; and (2) does not abrogate her responsibility to decide the matter.

   b. **Disinterested Legal Experts**
      A judge may obtain the written advice of a disinterested legal expert, provided the parties' lawyers are notified of the expert's identity and the subject matter and given a chance to object and respond.

10. **Independent Investigation of the Facts**
    A judge cannot independently investigate the facts of a case and must consider only the evidence presented.

11. **Public Comments on Cases**
    When a case is pending in *any* court, a judge must not make any public comment that might reasonably be expected to affect its outcome or impair its fairness, or make any nonpublic comment that might substantially interfere with a fair trial. The judge must require like abstention from court personnel. This duty does not apply to a judge who is a litigant in a personal capacity.

12. **Promises with Respect to Cases Likely to Come Before Court**
    With respect to cases or issues that are likely to come before the court, a judge must not make pledges, promises, or commitments that are inconsistent with the impartial performance of her adjudicative duties.

13. **Decorum, Demeanor, and Communication with Jurors**
    A judge must require order and decorum in court proceedings, and must be patient, dignified, and courteous to persons with whom she deals in an official capacity. A judge must not commend or criticize jurors for their verdict other than in a court order or opinion.

14. **Administrative Appointments**
    Administrative appointments (e.g., appointments of assigned counsel, referees, special masters, guardians, and court personnel) must be made impartially on the basis of merit.

    a. **Appointments of Lawyers Contributing to Judge's Election Campaign**
       A judge must not appoint a lawyer if the judge knows (or learns through a timely motion) that the lawyer, or the lawyer's spouse or domestic partner, has contributed to the judge's election campaign more than the jurisdiction's specified dollar amount within a designated number of years prior to the judge's campaign. However, this prohibition does not apply if: (1) the position is substantially uncompensated; (2) selection occurs as part of a rotation of qualified lawyers; or (3) no other lawyer is willing, competent, and capable.

15. **Responding to Judicial and Lawyer Misconduct**
    If a judge has *knowledge* that another judge has violated the CJC in a manner that raises a substantial question as to the other judge's honesty, trustworthiness, or fitness as a judge, the judge must inform the appropriate authority. Similarly, a judge who receives information indicating a *substantial likelihood* that another judge has violated the CJC (or a lawyer has violated the RPC) must take appropriate action (e.g., communicate with the alleged violator; report the alleged violator).

16. **Disability and Impairment of Other Judges or Lawyers**
A judge having a reasonable belief that a lawyer or another judge is impaired by drugs, alcohol, or a mental, physical, or emotional condition must take appropriate action, e.g., making a confidential referral to a judicial or lawyer assistance program.

17. **Cooperation with Disciplinary Authorities**
A judge must cooperate and be honest with judicial and lawyer disciplinary agencies. Retaliation against persons for their cooperation with investigations is not permitted.

18. **Disqualification**

a. **General Rule—Whenever Impartiality Might Be Questioned**
A judge must disqualify himself in a proceeding in which the judge's impartiality might reasonably be questioned.

1) **Disclosure by Judge**
A judge should disclose any information the judge believes the parties might consider relevant to the question of disqualification.

2) **Rule of Necessity**
In emergency situations, case law has created a rule of necessity that overrides the rules of disqualification and allows a judge to hear a matter even though he would otherwise be disqualified from doing so but for the necessity.

b. **Bias or Personal Knowledge**
A judge must disqualify himself if there is reasonable ground to believe that the judge has: (1) a personal bias concerning a party or lawyer, or (2) personal knowledge of relevant evidentiary facts.

c. **Prior Involvement**
A judge must disqualify himself if he: (1) served as a lawyer or material witness in a matter; (2) was associated in law practice with a person who participated substantially as a lawyer in the matter while they practiced together; (3) presided as a judge over the matter in another court; or (4) worked for the government, and in such capacity participated personally and substantially as a lawyer or public official concerning the proceeding, or publicly expressed in such capacity an opinion concerning the merits of the matter in controversy.

d. **Economic Interest**
A judge must disqualify himself if he knows that he has an economic interest in the matter or in one of the parties. Disqualification is also required if the interest is held by the judge's spouse, domestic partner,

parent, or child (wherever residing) or by any other member of the judge's family who resides in the judge's household. A person has an "economic interest" if she owns more than a de minimis legal or equitable interest. There are certain exceptions to the definition of "economic interest" (e.g., ownership of an interest in a mutual fund).

e. **Involvement in the Proceeding**
A judge must disqualify himself if he knows that he, his spouse or domestic partner, a person within the third degree of relationship to either of them, or the spouse or domestic partner of such a person, is involved (as a party, lawyer, material witness, or interested third party) in the case. Anyone related closer than cousin is within the third degree of relationship.

f. **Persons Making Contributions to Judge's Election Campaign**
A judge who is subject to public election must disqualify himself when he knows or learns that a party, a party's lawyer, or the law firm of a party's lawyer has, within a certain number of years, made contributions to his election campaign that exceed a specified amount.

g. **Public Statements of Judicial Commitment**
A judge must disqualify himself if, while a judge or judicial candidate, he has made a public statement other than in a court proceeding, judicial decision, or opinion that commits or appears to commit the judge to reach a particular result or to rule in a particular way in the proceeding or controversy.

h. **Remittal of Disqualification**
The parties and their lawyers can remit (waive) all of the foregoing grounds for disqualification, except personal bias concerning a party or a party's lawyer.

D. **EXTRAJUDICIAL ACTIVITIES**
A judge must conduct extrajudicial activities to minimize the risk of conflict with the obligations of judicial office.

1. **In General**
When engaging in extrajudicial activities, a judge must not: (1) participate in activities that will interfere with the judge's duties, lead to frequent disqualification, or reasonably appear to undermine the judge's independence, integrity, or impartiality; (2) engage in conduct that would reasonably appear to be coercive; or (3) use court resources, except incidentally, for activities that concern the law, the legal system, or the administration of justice, unless such additional use is legally permitted.

2. **Governmental Hearings and Consultations**
A judge must not appear voluntarily at a public hearing before, or otherwise

consult with, an executive or legislative body or official except on matters concerning the law, legal system, or administration of justice.

3. **Testifying as Character Witness**
   A judge must not testify as a character witness, except when duly summoned to do so, i.e., by subpoena. Ordinarily, a judge should discourage parties from requiring his testimony as a character witness.

4. **Governmental Committees and Commissions**
   A judge must not accept an appointment to a governmental committee or commission or other governmental position that does not relate to the law, legal system, or administration of justice.

JUDGE'S EXTRAJUDICIAL ACTIVITIES INVOLVING THE GOVERNMENT

Activity	Allowable Only If:		
Appearance at hearing before or consultation with executive or legislative official(s)	**Relates to the law, legal system, or administration of justice**	Or	Pro se to protect judge's own interests
Appointment to governmental committee or commission	**Relates to the law, legal system, or administration of justice**	Or	Representing governmental unit on purely ceremonial grounds or for a historical, educational, or cultural activity

5. **Participation in Educational, Religious, Charitable, or Civic Organizations and Activities**
   Subject to the general restrictions on extrajudicial activities, a judge may take part in activities sponsored by organizations or governmental entities concerned with the law, the legal system, or the administration of justice, and those sponsored by or on behalf of nonprofit educational, religious, charitable, fraternal, or civic organizations.

6. **Affiliation with Discriminatory Organizations**
   A judge must not hold membership in an organization that practices invidious

discrimination based on race, sex, gender, religion, national origin, ethnicity, or sexual orientation. Moreover, even if the judge is not a member, she must not use the organization's benefits or facilities if she knows or should know that it practices one of the prohibited forms of discrimination.

JUDGE'S USE OF AND MEMBERSHIP IN DISCRIMINATORY ORGANIZATIONS

Permissible	Impermissible
Monday night men-only bridge club consisting of judge and his college chums	Men-only social club with 6,000 members and dining and health club facilities
Women's support group for breastfeeding mothers	Women's bar association that refuses to admit male members
Alumni association of historically Black college with no non-Black graduates	Community booster group limiting membership to African-Americans
The Bulgarian League, which limits membership to persons of Bulgarian descent and whose purpose is the preservation of Bulgarian traditions	The Irish Business Association, which admits only persons of Irish descent and whose purpose is to promote businesses in the community owned by persons of Irish descent
Talmudic study group that limits membership to members of the judge's temple	Country club that excludes members on the basis of race or religion

CMR Chart

7. **Use of Nonpublic Information**
   A judge must not intentionally disclose or use nonpublic information acquired in his judicial capacity for any purpose unrelated to his judicial duties.

8. **Financial, Business, or Remunerative Activities**
   Generally, a judge may not serve as an officer, director, manager, general partner, advisor, or employee of a business. However, a judge **may** hold and manage her own investments and those of her family and may manage or participate in a business closely held by the judge or a family member, or in a business primarily engaged in investing the financial resources of the judge or her family, unless such activity will interfere with performance of the

judge's duties, will lead to frequent disqualification, or will involve the judge in frequent or continuing relationships with persons likely to come before the court on which the judge serves.

9. **Acceptance and Reporting of Gifts, Loans, Bequests, Benefits, or Other Things of Value**
   A judge must not accept gifts, loans, bequests, benefits, or other things of value if acceptance thereof is prohibited by law or would reasonably appear to undermine the judge's independence, integrity, or impartiality. Some gifts may be accepted without being publicly reported (e.g., items of little intrinsic value, ordinary social hospitality, books supplied on a complimentary basis for official use). Other gifts must be publicly reported (e.g., gifts incident to a public testimonial, gifts from a person who is likely to come before the judge).

10. **Fiduciary Activities**
    Generally, a judge must not serve as a fiduciary (e.g., executor or trustee), unless she does so for a family member. Such service must not interfere with the judge's duties or involve her in proceedings that would ordinarily come before her or that take place in her court or one under its appellate jurisdiction. The judge should resign as fiduciary if there is a conflict between her duties as a fiduciary and her duties under the CJC.

11. **Service as Arbitrator or Mediator**
    A full-time judge must not act as an arbitrator, mediator, or private judge unless expressly authorized by law to do so.

12. **Practice of Law**
    A full-time judge must not practice law. She may, without compensation, give legal advice to or draft documents for a family member, but she may not act as a family member's lawyer in any forum.

13. **Compensation for Extrajudicial Activities**
    Reasonable compensation for a judge's extrajudicial activities (e.g., speaking, teaching, or writing) is permitted unless acceptance thereof would reasonably appear to undermine the judge's independence, integrity, or impartiality.

14. **Reimbursement of Expenses and Waiver of Fees or Charges**
    Unless otherwise prohibited by the CJC, a judge may accept reimbursements of necessary and reasonable expenses for travel, food, lodging, or other incidentals, or a waiver of tuition or registration expenses, from sources other than the judge's employer, if such expenses are associated with the judge's participation in extrajudicial activities permitted by the CJC.

15. **Reporting Requirements**
    A judge must publicly report the amount or value of: compensation received for permitted extrajudicial activities (*see* 13., *supra*); gifts and other things of

value (*see* 9., *supra*) that exceed a designated dollar amount; and reimbursement of expenses and waiver of charges (*see* 14., *supra*) that exceed a designated dollar amount.

E. **JUDGES' POLITICAL AND CAMPAIGN ACTIVITIES**
A judge or candidate for judicial office must not engage in political or campaign activity that is inconsistent with the independence, integrity, or impartiality of the judiciary. A "candidate" is a person who publicly announces her candidacy, declares with the election or appointment authority, authorizes solicitation or acceptance of contributions or support, or is nominated.

1. **Political and Campaign Activities of Judges and Judicial Candidates in General**
Generally, a judge or judicial candidate is prohibited from engaging in certain campaign activities, including: (1) campaigning for, soliciting funds for, contributing to, or endorsing a political organization or candidate (*note:* there are exceptions to these rules for certain activities of judicial candidates engaged in within a time period specified by other state law; *see* 2.a., *infra*); (2) personally soliciting or accepting campaign contributions other than through an authorized campaign committee; (3) using court resources in her campaign; (4) making a false or misleading statement; (5) making a statement that would reasonably be expected to affect the outcome or the fairness of a matter pending in court; or (6) in connection with cases, controversies, or issues that are likely to come before the court, making pledges, promises, or commitments that are inconsistent with the impartial performance of the adjudicative duties of judicial office. Note, however, that a statement of personal views on legal, political, or other issues is not prohibited.

2. **Political and Campaign Activities of Judicial Candidates in Public Elections**
A judicial candidate must act: (1) in a manner consistent with the independence, integrity, and impartiality of the judiciary; (2) comply with applicable election laws; (3) review and approve campaign materials prior to their dissemination; and (4) take reasonable measures to ensure that other persons do not undertake on her behalf activities that she would be prohibited from doing.

a. **Certain Activities Permitted**
Unless prohibited by law, a judicial candidate may, no earlier than a minimum amount of time (to be determined by other state law) prior to the first applicable election, do the following: (1) **establish a campaign committee**; (2) **speak on behalf of her candidacy** through any medium; (3) publicly endorse or oppose candidates **for the same judicial office** for which she is running; (4) **attend or purchase tickets for dinners or other events** sponsored by a political organization or a candidate for public office; (5) seek, accept, or use endorsements from any person or organization **other than a partisan political organization**; and (6) **contribute**

to a political organization or candidate, but not more than a maximum dollar amount to be determined by each jurisdiction to any one recipient.

3. **Activities of Candidates for Appointive Judicial Office**
   A candidate for appointment to judicial office may communicate with the appointing or confirming authority and may seek the endorsement of a person or organization (other than a partisan political organization).

POLITICAL AND CAMPAIGN ACTIVITIES OF JUDGES AND JUDICIAL CANDIDATES

Activity	Noncandidate Judge	Candidate Judge
Lead or hold office in political organization	Impermissible	Impermissible
Publicly endorse or oppose a candidate for *other public office*	Impermissible	Impermissible
Publicly endorse or oppose a candidate for *same judicial office*	Impermissible	Permissible (within allowable time period)
Contribute to a political organization or candidate	Impermissible	Permissible (within allowable time period and amount set by other state law)
Speak on behalf of political organization	Impermissible	Permissible to speak on behalf of judge's *own candidacy* (within allowable time period set by other state law)
Purchase tickets for or attend political gatherings	Impermissible	Permissible (within allowable time period set by other state law)
Solicit funds for a political organization	Impermissible	Impermissible

CMR Chart

4. **Campaign Committees**

A judicial candidate running in a public election may establish a campaign committee to manage and conduct her campaign. The candidate must direct the committee not to solicit or accept contributions more than a certain amount of time (designated by other state law) prior to the applicable election, nor more than a designated number of days after the last election in which the candidate participated. The candidate must also direct the committee to comply with campaign contribution limits and disclosure requirements.

5. **Activities of Judges Who Become Candidates for Nonjudicial Office**

When a judge becomes a candidate for a nonjudicial *elective* office, she must resign her judgeship unless applicable law permits the retention of her judicial office. If the judge becomes a candidate for a nonjudicial *appointive* office, she need not resign her judgeship, provided that she complies with all other provisions of the CJC.

F. **APPLICATION OF THE CODE OF JUDICIAL CONDUCT**

In jurisdictions that adopt the CJC, it applies to all persons who perform judicial functions, including magistrates, court commissioners, and referees. Part-time and retired judges are exempt from many, but not all, of the provisions that restrict outside activities and political activities.